··········· THE ···········
BLACKWELL PHILOSOPHER DICTIONARIES

A Kant Dictionary

Howard Caygill

First published 1995

Blackwell Publishers Ltd.
108 Cowley Road
Oxford   OX4 1JF
UK

Blackwell Publishers Inc.
238 Main Street
Cambridge, Massachusetts 02142
USA

British Library Cataloguing in Publication Data

A CIP catalogue record for this book is available from the British Library.

Library of Congress Cataloging-in-Publication Data

A CIP catalogue record for this book is available from the Library of Congress.

ISBN 0–631–17534–2 (hbk); 0–631–17535–0 (pbk)

Typeset in 10 on 12pt Baskerville
by Graphicraft Typesetters Ltd., Hong Kong
Printed in Great Britain by T.J. Press (Padstow) Ltd., Padstow, Cornwall

This book is printed on acid-free paper.

For everyone at 12 Willow Lane

A dictionary begins when it no longer gives the meaning of words, but their tasks.

Georges Bataille

Contents

Preface and acknowledgements

My first experience of reading Kant was not an altogether happy one. I was bewildered by his use of language and alienated by what seemed to be a manic desire to classify and establish endless fine distinctions. Fortunately, this initial disorientation soon settled into an abiding fascination – not that Kant has ever lost his ability to surprise. My book tries to stay true to this experience by offering an aid to orientation in Kant's philosophy which does not lose sight of what remains *disturbing* about it. I have not sought to embalm Kant by producing a philologically correct aid for 'professional' Kant scholars, a task I suspect to be beyond the powers of any finite individual – and certainly this one – and which would demand more than one volume. Instead I have written for readers and potential readers of Kant interested not only in philosophy but also in the humanities and social sciences which are heirs to the critical philosophy.

It is a pleasure to acknowledge the support and good humour given me by my family, friends and colleagues while writing this book. I am particularly indebted to my sister Caroline for her unfailing levity, to Greg Bright who deserves a martyr's palm for reading from A to Z, to Onora O'Neill for her perceptive critical comments at an early stage of composition, and to Jay Bernstein, Judith Mehta and Gillian Rose for sustaining my confidence in the project. I have benefited greatly from conversations on matters Kantian and non-Kantian with Richard Beardsworth, Sara Beardsworth, Monika Fludernik, David Owen and Alan Scott. Thanks are also due to Blackwell Publishers for their patience, to the British Academy for their support of a research trip to Berlin in 1990, and to the University of East Anglia for granting me study leave in the summer of 1992. Finally, I wish to acknowledge the assistance from beyond the grave of past generations of Kant lexicographers – above all Mellin, Schmid and Eisler – without whom I could not have begun.

Norwich, England
12 April 1994

Introduction: Kant and the language of philosophy

The influence of Kant's philosophy has been, and continues to be, so profound and so widespread as to have become imperceptible. Philosophical inquiry within both the 'analytic' and the 'continental' traditions is unthinkable without the lexical and conceptual resources bequeathed by Kant. Even outside philosophy, in the humanities, social sciences and natural sciences, Kantian concepts and structures of argument are ubiquitous. Anyone practicing literary or social *criticism* is contributing to the Kantian tradition; anyone reflecting on the epistemological implications of their work will find themselves doing so within parameters established by Kant. Indeed, many contemporary debates, whether in aesthetics, literary or political theory, show a peculiar tendency to mutate into disputes in Kant exegesis. All in all, in the less than 200 years since the death of its author, Kantian philosophy has established itself as an indispensable point of intellectual orientation.

While few would quarrel with the fact of Kant's influence, opinions differ widely regarding its significance and desirability, and nowhere more than in his innovations with respect to the language of philosophy. It is widely recognized that Kant transformed philosophical language, but there is little agreement as to whether this was a good thing; Isaiah Berlin for one considers him to have 'ruined' it. Whatever the final verdict, the main problem facing the lexicographer is more technical, and concerns the way in which Kant achieved this transformation and, to a lesser extent, his motives for doing so. For Kant did not only extend Christian Wolff's translation of Latin philosophical terminology into the vernacular, but he also confronted it with areas of experience previously excluded from philosophy. He reinvented philosophical language by introducing new terms and concepts from outside philosophy, as well as self-consciously re-defining many of its traditional ones. The matrix for this linguistic and conceptual transformation lies in the lectures which he delivered for over four decades in a wide range of subjects. In these he explicated the traditional philosophical concepts of the officially prescribed textbooks by

1

means of material drawn from contemporary natural science, newspapers, novels and poetry, as well as from medical and travel books.

The first generation of Kant's lexicographers, notably Mellin (1797) and Schmid (1798), prized Kant for improving the accuracy of philosophical language as well as for extending its limits. Both stressed the enhanced philosophical precision afforded by Kant's linguistic innovations. Yet throughout their lexicons there is a discernible tension between the accuracy arising from Kant's *improvements* to the language and the unsettling effects of his *enrichment* of it. A century later, however, this tension had all but disappeared: Eisler's monumental *Kant Lexicon* (1930) enshrined an academic orthodoxy which stressed Kant's accuracy and fidelity to tradition over his innovation. The sensitivity to the radical character of Kant's reinvention of philosophical language evident in the early lexicons had almost completely vanished. For Eisler, unlike Mellin and Schmid, Kant's philosophy is no longer contentious; its text is considered a self-sufficient whole and is approached by means of a lexicographic strategy which indiscriminately lists the uses to which a particular term was put at various points in the *oeuvre*. Eisler's lexicon was born of the same monumental desire which presided over the formulation of the editorial policy pursued by the editors of the Berlin Academy's canonical edition of Kant's writings.

Kant would probably have been dismayed by the imposing edifice created in his name by later editors and lexicographers. He himself took a problematic and a relational view of philosophizing and philosophical language, and allowed this approach to inform his linguistic innovations. In Kant's own terms, philosophical concepts were *acroamatic* and not *axiomatic*, by which he meant that they were the discursive outcome of an open-ended process of reflection upon philosophical problems. Unlike geometrical axioms, philosophical concepts are for Kant less the indisputable products of definition than the equivocal outcomes of a process of indirect presentation resting ultimately on analogy. Kant discussed this process of analogical definition in *Critique of Judgement* (§59) where he applied it to such philosophical concepts as 'substance' and 'ground' which transfer a particular relation between one set of terms to another. Not only are such concepts discovered in the course of reflection upon a problem or difficulty, but their 'definition' is accomplished by means of relating them to other terms. Substance, for example, is defined in complementary opposition to accident, as is concept to intuition, matter to form, and so on. Not only are many terms defined disjunctively, but they also participate in a network of related terms which further enrich and complicate their meanings. They bear with them traces of defunct problems, of which they may be purified, as Kant shows in the case of the term 'abstraction', or which are still active in ways which must be respected, as in the case of 'absolute'.

2

This dictionary attempts to map the problematic and relational aspects of Kant's philosophical vocabulary. Instead of presenting a concept as a fixed, axiomatic element of Kant's *philosophy* in the manner of Eisler, the entries stress the problematic, exploratory character of his *philosophizing*. To this end, an entry will review the history of the problem to which the term is a response, and show the ways in which Kant set about defining its meaning in the course of reflection. Furthermore, each entry will be preceded by a list of related terms which form the network within which it gains its full range of meaning. Finally, entries will also, where appropriate, consider the fate of concepts following Kant, thus underlining the pivotal position his work occupies between philosophical tradition and modernity. I hope this strategy will give the reader a sense of the power and range of Kant's philosophizing, and through this some insight into the reason for its enormous and seemingly inexhaustible influence upon modern culture.

System of citations and abbreviations

Citations of works by Kant

Most of the works by Kant referred to in the text are cited by abbreviations. To find the full title of any work, the reader should look first at the 'List of abbreviations' below. For each abbreviation, the 'List' gives the year of publication and a short title. To find the full titles in both German and English, the reader should then refer to the bibliography entitled 'Kant's published writings' (pp. 418–27).

Other works by Kant are cited in the text by means of a short title and year of publication. To find full titles, the reader should refer directly to the year of publication in the bibliography of 'Kant's published writings'.

Citations of particular sections of text by Kant usually specify the unit referred to (whether by page or by section, §). There is one important exception: references to the *Critique of Pure Reason*. Kant produced two editions of this work: the first edition (published in 1781) is cited as CPR A, the second, revised edition (published in 1787) as CPR B. Following convention, citations refer to one or both editions by page, but omit 'p.' (e.g., CPR A 324/B 380).

Where an abbreviation is followed by two page numbers (e.g., GMM p. 425, p. 33), the first refers to the German 'Academy Edition', the second to an English translation – both as listed in the bibliography of 'Kant's published writings'.

Citations of works by other authors

Works by other authors are cited by reference to author or editor and year of publication. To find full details, the reader should look under the author's name in the bibliography entitled 'Works referred to in the text' (pp. 428–35).

The reader's attention is drawn to the citation of works by Plato, Aristotle and Aquinas. Citations from Plato are taken from the 1961 collected translation and follow the standard system of reference according to the pagination and page subdivisions of particular dialogues in Henri Estienne's edition of 1578 (as in Plato, 1961, Rep. 2.378a). Citations from Aristotle are taken from the 1941 collected translation and follow the system of reference according to page, column (a/b) and line of Immanuel Bekker's edition of 1831–70 (as in Aristotle, 1941, 431b, 18). Citations from Aquinas's *Summa Theologica* refer to the 1952 translation, and are organized in terms of part, question and article (as in Aquinas, 1952, I, 85, 1).

List of abbreviations of Kant's published writings

A	1798b	*Anthropology from a Pragmatic Point of View*
CBH	1786b	*Conjectures on the Beginning of Human History*
CF	1798a	*The Conflict of the Faculties*
CJ	1790a	*Critique of Judgement*
CPR A	1781	*Critique of Pure Reason*; 1st edition
CPR B	1787	*Critique of Pure Reason*; 2nd edition
CPrR	1788b	*Critique of Practical Reason*
DRS	1768	*Concerning the ultimate Ground of the Differentiation of Regions in Space*
DS	1766	*Dreams of a Spirit-Seer elucidated by Dreams of Metaphysics*
FI	1790b	*First Introduction to the Critique of Judgement*
FPT	1791a	'On the Failure of all Philosophical Attempts at Theodicy'
FS	1762	*The False Subtlety of the Four Syllogistic Figures*
GMM	1785e	*Grounding for the Metaphysics of Morals*
ID	1770	'Inaugural Dissertation', *On the Form and Principles of the Sensible and the Intelligible World*
IUH	1784a	'Idea for a Universal History with a Cosmopolitan Purpose'
L	1800a	*Logic*
LE	1924	*Lectures on Ethics*
LF	1747	*Thoughts on the True Estimation of Living Forces*
LPT	1817	*Lectures on Philosophical Theology*
MF	1786a	*Metaphysical Foundations of Natural Science*
MM	1797a	*The Metaphysics of Morals*
ND	1755c	*Nova dilucidatio, A New Elucidation of the First Principles of Metaphysical Cognition*
NM	1763b	*Attempt to Introduce the Concept of Negative Magnitudes into Philosophy*
NT	1758	*A New Theory [or Conception] of Motion and Rest*

5

OBS	1764a	*Observations on the Feeling of the Beautiful and the Sublime*
OD	1790c	*On a Discovery according to which any New Critique of Pure Reason has been made Superfluous by an Earlier One*
OP	1936	*Opus postumum*
OPA	1763a	*The Only Possible Argument in Support of a Demonstration of the Existence of God*
P	1783a	*Prolegomena to Any Future Metaphysics that will be able to come forward as Science*
PC	1967	*Philosophical Correspondence*
PE	1764c	*'Prize Essay', Inquiry Concerning the Distinctness of the Principles of Natural Theology and Morality*
PM	1756d	*The Employment in Natural Philosophy of Metaphysics combined with Geometry, of which Sample I contains the Physical Monadology*
PP	1795	*Perpetual Peace*
R	1925–34	*Reflections*
RL	1793a	*Religion within the Limits of Reason Alone*
TP	1793b	'On the Common Saying: "This may be true in theory, but it does not apply in practice"'
UNH	1755a	*Universal Natural History and Theory of the Heavens*
WE	1784b	'An Answer to the Question: "What is Enlightenment?"'
WO	1786c	'What is Orientation in Thinking?'
WP	1791b	*What Real Progress has Metaphysics made in Germany since the Time of Leibniz and Wolff?*

Kant and the 'age of criticism'

de nobis ipsis silemus – of ourselves we are silent
(epigraph from Francis Bacon to the *Critique of Pure Reason*)

Kant's biography has been taken to exemplify the complete submersion of a philosopher's life in their work.[1] Described by Elias Canetti as a 'head without a world', it would seem as if, outside his writings, Kant did not lead much of a life: he lectured for several hours a week, he dined with friends and took regular, afternoon walks famed for their neurotic punctuality. In the memoirs of his contemporaries the incidentals of Kant's daily life have a quality of 'noises off', with the main action taking place in his study, or wherever it was that he read and wrote. The opposition between Kant's quiet life and explosive thought, between his provincial surroundings in the East Prussian city of Königsberg and the world-historic significance of his writings, have become the stuff of philosophical legend. Yet it must be said that such a view of Kant is severely distorted, and obstructs an appreciation of both his life and his work.

Suppose we respect Kant's reticence, and look only to his work, even then the sheer internal diversity of his *oeuvre* would urge caution. This diversity is apparent in spite of the best efforts of the editors of the monumental Berlin Academy of Sciences edition of Kant's writings (*Akademie Ausgabe*, now in its 29th volume) and the narrow focus of much Kant scholarship.[2] The uniformly bound volumes of the Academy Edition give the impression of a monolithic corpus, a body of writings severed from the circumstances of their original publication and inhabiting a philosophical Valhalla. Given the consistency of editorial treatment, it is not surprising that the Academy Edition has encouraged the proliferation of developmental narratives which bind together the various 'phases' of Kant's authorship. All of Kant's texts appear to be of the same status, with differences between them marked in terms of chronology and the regulation AK references; the edition gives an impression of the smooth unfolding of an intellectual project independent of circumstances – a work without a world.

7

But if we step behind the monument and reconsider its constituent parts, the sheer heterogeneity of Kant's writings is striking. And if we look beyond the philosophical letter to the publication details of the individual texts – who they were published by, and for whom – we begin to gain a complex appreciation of the internal diversity of Kant's work, one moreover which allows us to situate his authorship within the changing structures of intellectual life that characterised the German Enlightenment.

Recent work in the social history of the German Enlightenment has prepared the ground for a reconsideration of Kant's life and work within its emergent structures. Such a biography – when written – would contribute to the interpretation of Kant's thought by breaking down the monolithic kantian Text into diverse Kantian texts. Instead of simply relating Kant's texts to each other in some more or less sophisticated teleological narrative of his 'development', it would read these against other texts, events and processes of institutional change. To use Kant's own distinction, his thought would then be read less as a definitive body of philosophy than as an open-ended process of philosophizing, one in which the philosophical tradition was re-invented in the face of changes in the structures of University, Church and State, as well as in the publishing industry and the reading public. In such a biography, Kant's writings would be viewed as responses from within the philosophical tradition to the complex set of structural changes and cultural developments that typify modernity. Unfortunately, such a biography has yet to be written, although a few preliminary indications of the close relationship between Kant's writing and his world are possible on the basis of existing material.

A good place to begin is with Kant's definition of his own epoch. In the Preface to the first edition of the *Critique of Pure Reason* (1781) he writes:

> Our age is, in especial degree, the age of criticism, and to criticism everything must submit. Religion through its sanctity, and law giving through its majesty, may seek to exempt themselves from it. But they then awaken just suspicion, and cannot claim the sincere respect which reason accords only to that which has been able to sustain the test of free and open examination. (CPR A xi)

The age of criticism requires a critical philosophy, one which presumes, indeed demands the freedom to examine and criticize the institutions of Church and State. Kant presented what he saw as the preconditions for such a philosophy three years later in his essay 'An Answer to the Question: "What is Enlightenment?"'. Here the fundamental 'condition of the possibility' for the age of criticism is described as the 'freedom to make *public use* of one's reason in all matters' which for Kant means 'that use which anyone may make of it *as an intellectual* [*Gelehrter*] addressing the entire *reading public* (WE p. 37, p. 55). This freedom in turn requires not only the suspension of state and ecclesiastical censorship, but also the existence of a publishing industry capable of serving the needs of authors and the reading public. Thus in order to understand Kant's contribution to enlightenment, we cannot be content with looking only at *what* he said to his public; we must also pay attention to *how* he said it, and to the extent to which the said was determined by the saying. In more concrete terms, it is necessary to attend to the relationship between the content of reason and the forms through which it was addressed to the reading public, notably the media Kant used to exercise the public use of his reason, and in particular the channels of publication open to him and the reading public(s) they enabled him to reach. Moreover, Kant himself must be considered not only in his guise as a writer, but also as a reader, or as a member of the reading public addressed by other authors.

The relationship between Kant's public use of reason and the modes of addressing the reading public available to him is complicated by Kant's distinction between the private and public uses of reason. He somewhat counter-intuitively described the *private* use of reason as 'that which a person may make of it in a particular *civil* post or office with which he is entrusted' (WE p. 37, p. 55) as opposed to the public use of reason in addressing the reading public. The writer inhabits two worlds, one in which they act passively 'as part of the machine' and the other in which they freely address through their writings 'a public in the truest sense of the word' (WE p. 37, p. 56).[3] Writers occupy that ambiguous and vulnerable space permitted them by 'a ruler who is himself enlightened and has no fear of phantoms, yet who likewise has at hand a well-disciplined and numerous army to guarantee public security' and who can 'dare to say: *Argue as much as you like and about whatever you like, but obey!*' (WE p. 41, p. 59). Kant's wager is that the habit of thinking freely will gradually translate into the habit of acting freely, and thus eventually overcome the division between public and private uses of reason. But in 'the age of enlightenment, the century of *Frederick*' (WE p. 40, p. 59) the freedom to argue but obey is the lesser evil: while not as desirable as freedom in thought and deed, it is better than obedience in both.

Kant's examples of the private use of reason include the soldier who must obey orders while on duty, the citizen who must pay taxes and the clergyman who must instruct his congregation in the doctrine of the church. While each is obliged to obey while performing their office, they are also free as writers to address the reading public with their thoughts on military strategy, taxation and religion. It is striking that when discussing this distinction Kant does not refer to the example closest to home – his own profession of university teacher. In what sense does the distinction between the private and public use of reason apply to these employees of the state? There is clearly a tension between their capacities as state-employed intellectuals and those they exercise as free intellectuals addressing a reading public. This tension is evident throughout Kant's writings, and requires us to locate the public use of reason embodied in his writings not only with respect to the reading public, but also with respect to the private use of reason in his academic career.

The delicate balance between Kant's private and public use of reason was exposed after the death of Frederick the Great in 1786. Frederick's successor, Frederick William II, initiated a counter-Enlightenment which sought, by means of censorship, to curb the freedom of the press and to extend obedience to precisely those arguments concerning Church and State permitted by his predecessor. Following the publication of *Religion within the Limits of Reason Alone* (RL) in 1793, Kant received a Cabinet Order from Frederick William II which reprimanded him for his 'misuse of philosophy' to 'distort and disparage many of the cardinal and basic teachings of the Holy Scripture and Christianity'. It ordered him to give a 'conscientious account' of himself and to apply his authority and talents 'to the progressive realisation of our paternal purpose. Failing this, you must expect unpleasant measures for your continuing obstinacy'.[4] In reply, Kant maintained that in the private use of reason as a professor and 'teacher of youth' he never mixed 'any evaluation of the Holy Scriptures and of Christianity into my lectures' and merely followed the texts of Baumgarten 'which are the basis of my lectures'.[5] Furthermore, with respect to the public use of reason 'as a teacher of the people' he did 'no harm to the public *religion of the land*' since 'the book in question is not at all suitable for the public: to them it is an unintelligible, closed book, only a debate among scholars of the faculty, of which the people take no notice'.[6] The faculty, in their turn, Kant says, are sanctioned by the crown to debate religious matters and publicly to judge all contributions. Kant's defence of the public use of his reason hinges upon a distinction between a scholarly public authorized by the state to make judgements, and a wider reading public for whom such works are unsuitable. In other words, his public use of reason is defended – self-destructively – as the private use of reason by a publicly authorized 'scholar of the faculty'.

Kant ended his reply to the Monarch by undertaking 'hereafter [to] refrain altogether from discoursing publicly, in lectures or writings, on religion, whether natural or revealed'.[7] By making this undertaking he implicitly acknowledged the collapse of the distinction between public and private uses of reason on which he had founded his authorship. This was recognized by J.E. Biester, the beleaguered editor of the pro-enlightenment *Berlinische Monatsschrift*, when he read Kant's reply. He gently

observed in a letter to Kant dated 17 December 1794 that with his undertaking Kant prepared 'a great triumph for the enemies of enlightenment,
and the good cause suffers a great loss'. He believed that Kant did not
have to silence his criticism for the sake of obedience in this way, and
regarded him as having withdrawn from the struggle for enlightenment,
leaving it to others to 'continue to work on the great philosophical and
theological enlightenment that you have so happily begun'.[8] Although
Kant considered himself released from his promise with the death of
Frederick William II in 1797[9] Biester was correct in his assessment: Kant
was unable to go beyond the tension between obedience and criticism
which characterized both the Fredrician 'Age of Enlightenment' and the
Kantian 'Age of Criticism'.

The episode of the Cabinet Order reveals many of the institutional
forces and tensions which traversed Kant's texts. These include organs of
publication (book and journal) and the audiences for which they were
intended, the university as a place of teaching and research, and the role
of academic, ecclesiastic and public censorship. It points without ambiguity to the tension between being a 'teacher of youth' and a 'teacher of the
people'. Indeed, the tension between the private and the public use of
reason was especially marked in the case of a university teacher, since the
lines of demarcation between privately reasoning as a teacher and publicly
reasoning as an author were not strongly drawn. There were many points
of intersection between the two uses of reason, with some texts, such as
RL, attempting to serve both masters.

Nevertheless, it is possible, with reservations, to distinguish within Kant's
oeuvre texts which represent the private, semi-private, and public uses of
his reason. The texts of Kant's private use of reason include those intended to satisfy the formal requirements of entering and progressing
through an academic career and those concerned in some direct or indirect way with the 'teaching of youth'. Such texts, as we shall see, form a
large proportion of Kant's publishing output. With them is a further group
of semi-private texts which were produced in response to specific circumstances (such as the public questions set by the Berlin Academy) and in
which Kant appears as a university teacher addressing an intellectual public
beyond the university. Finally, of course, there are the books which make
up Kant's public use of reason as an author. These include books not
directly intended for a university audience, as well as articles written for
newspapers and journals, whether for local, regional or national audiences.

These distinctions within the Kantian text are best analysed in terms of
the development of Kant's career as an author and a teacher. He was born
in the East Prussian city of Königsberg (now Kaliningrad) at 5 a.m. on 22
April 1724, and remained, unlike Descartes, an habitual early riser. He was

the fourth of nine children (only five survived) born to Anna Regina and Johann Georg Kant, a harness-maker. He spent his childhood in an artisanal suburb of the city, growing up in an intensely pietist milieu. In many respects the time and circumstances of Kant's birth were extremely propitious for his subsequent upward social and professional mobility. The city of Königsberg had only been officially founded out of the amalgam of three large towns clustered around the mouth of the River Pregel in the year of Kant's birth. Its recent foundation was one reason, but not the most important, why it did not possess the closed and impervious urban elite characteristic of most German cities of the period. It was the second largest city in Prussia, and certainly one of the most economically and culturally dynamic in Germany. The city experienced a boom in trade throughout the eighteenth century, exporting agricultural produce from its rural hinterland to the markets of England and Scandinavia, and importing from them metal, manufactured goods and 'colonial products'. Its population of 40,000 inhabitants in 1724 had expanded to 50,000 in 1770, among whom were a number of expatriate English merchants, two of whom, Joseph Green and Robert Motherby, became Kant's closest friends and introduced him to English philosophy and literature.[10] Apart from its maritime links with the rest of Europe and the world, the city also acted as a regional capital, hosting a university – the Albertina – founded by Prince Albrecht in 1544, and a lively provincial culture of newspapers, journals and bookshops well abreast with the latest developments from the Leipzig and Frankfurt book fairs.[11]

Although Königsberg certainly possessed the relatively liberal climate and social openness characteristic of most major port cities, it was not this alone that permitted Kant to pursue his chosen career. Other, more specific factors also contributed, prime among which was the relative weakness of the local, patrician elites in comparison to those which dominated other German cities.[12] This was due not so much to the recent foundation of the city, nor to the influence of trade – the patrician elite maintained control in Hamburg until the end of the nineteenth century[13] – but more to the struggle for control of the city waged since the mid-seventeenth century between urban patricians, local rural aristocracy and the Prussian state. By Kant's time, the modernizing Prussian state was largely victorious over the other forces, and served as a counterweight to the particularism of local elites. A further factor was the decline in the fortunes of the German universities since the late seventeenth century, which continued into the eighteenth century with falling enrolments and the consequently diminished prestige and income of the professoriat.[14] This made the profession less attractive to patrician and aristocratic entrants, and more open to talent from Kant's social background. A fourth major factor was pietism, which at the time of Kant's birth was undergoing the transition from private, apolitical devotion to becoming an important feature of the institutional structure of the Prussian state. To these structural factors may be added the impact of the Russian administration of the city from January 1758 until August 1762. This was a period of levity and relaxation of manners, which did a great deal to soften and undermine any of the remaining rigid social distinctions and disciplines of Königsberg society.[15]

The development of pietist educational institutions in the early eighteenth century provides the setting for Kant's austere education in the Collegium Fridericianum between 1732 and 1740. The school owed its origin to a private, pietist foundation of 1698 which received the royal privilege in 1701. Recommended and aided by the Kant family pastor, Franz Albert Schutz, who was also principal of the school, Immanuel followed a rigorous and austere schooling in grammar and philology accompanied by a regime of inflexible piety. While Kant cherished the memory of the domestic pietism of his parents, he had nothing but scorn for the official version he encountered at school.[16] Kant's one inspiring school teacher, the Latin master Heydenreich, introduced him to a lifelong love of classical Latin literature; unfortunately, not one of his colleagues, Kant later reminisced with fellow sufferer Johannes Cunde, was capable of 'inflaming the sparks within us for the study of philosophy or mathematics' although they 'could certainly blow them out'.[17] Nevertheless, by the age of 16 Kant was more than capable of fulfilling the state-imposed matriculation requirement of the local university.[18]

The University of Königsberg was organized in terms of the four traditional faculties, the three 'higher faculties' of theology, law and medicine, and the fourth or 'lower faculty' of philosophy. Since Frederick William I saw the main function of the universities to consist in training civil servants – above all clergy, lawyers and medical practitioners – he ordained that students must enrol in one of the three higher faculties. It is not known which faculty Kant enrolled in; whether, as is conventionally assumed, in the faculty of theology, or in medicine.[19] Whichever it was, and in spite of great poverty, Kant did not pursue the qualification for a bureaucratic post in the Prussian administration, but dedicated himself to the 'lower faculty' of philosophy. For much of the eighteenth century the lower faculty of philosophy was the most dynamic and innovative in the university. Because its curriculum was not adapted to the demands of a profession, it was possible to extend the range of subjects covered by philosophy to include not only subjects such as physics and geography which were ignored by the higher faculties, but even those of religion, jurisprudence and medicine which were their protected domains.

It was the comprehensive character of the education provided in the philosophical faculty which attracted Kant to it as a student, and which led him to commit his life to defending and extending the claims of the discipline, even as late as 1798 in *The Conflict of the Faculties* (CF). However, the most important single factor in his enthusiasm for philosophy was the influence of his teacher, Professor Martin Knutzen.[20] Knutzen was born in Königsberg in 1714, and became Extraordinary Professor of Logic and Metaphysics,[21] a post he pursued with self-destructive diligence until his early death at the age of 37. A representative of the generation of pietist Wolffians of the late 1730s, Knutzen combined in his teaching and writing interests in philosophy, religion, mathematics and natural science. Through his daily six hours of lectures, and additional seminars and private sessions, Kant was introduced to a wide range of material, including Newton's *Mathematical Principles of Natural Philosophy.*

Kant technically remained a student or 'candidate' at the university until 1755, when he gained in quick succession his master's degree (*Magister*) and his *venia legendi* or licence to teach as a *Magister legens* or *Privatdozent.* This meant that his income as a teacher was dependent upon the fees of his students; he was not to receive the public salary of a full professor until 15 years later in 1770. The reason for the long period of study (1740–55) was largely economic; accounts of Kant during his early student years show him to be poor, if not wholly destitute.[22] In 1747 he left Königsberg to work in the surrounding countryside as a domestic tutor or *Hauslehrer.* His departure coincided with the long-drawn-out passage of his first book through the press, while his return in 1754 was marked by a minor explosion of journalism, academic theses and a book – *Universal Natural History and Theory of the Heavens* (UNH) – on which he had occupied himself during his period of rural exile.

Kant summed up his early career in a petition to the Russian Empress Elisabeth dated 14 December 1758 in support of his application for a vacant chair in logic and metaphysics. After describing how logic and metaphysics 'have always been the special fields of my study' he continued:

> Since becoming a lecturer at said university, I have taught logic and metaphysics every semester. I have publicly defended two dissertations in these subjects; in addition, I have published four treatises in the learned journal of Königsberg, three *Programmata* and three other philosophical tracts which give some sense of my research.[23]

The petition shows how the private and the public uses of reason were inextricably entangled in the case of a university teacher. Most obviously, Kant is using the products of his public use of reason to justify his case for an official position. What is more significant, however, is the way in which

14

he classifies his 12 publications. Five of them are directly concerned with fulfilling the requirements of an academic career, namely the two dissertations and the three *Programmata* or announcements of lectures essential to making a living as a *Privatdozent*. The remaining texts were divided into contributions to a local journal, addressing topics of local interest, and three extremely diverse books intended for specific audiences.

Kant prepared three dissertations in the mid-1750s, but only two were published: all three were written in Latin. The first, unpublished dissertation – *Concise Outline of some Reflections on Fire* – was submitted as Kant's master's thesis to the philosophy faculty on 17 April 1755 (see 1755b in 'Kant's published writings'). It comprised 12 handwritten pages, and was intended for a small academic audience.[24] The thesis was examined on 13 May and on 12 June Kant was admitted to the degree of Master of Philosophy at a formal ceremony. Three months later Kant submitted a second thesis for the purposes of obtaining the *venia legendi*, one which had to be defended in public. This was the remarkable 'A New Elucidation of the First Principles of Metaphysical Cognition' (ND) published by J.H. Hartung, the 'royally appointed Court and Academic Book Printer', in Königsberg in 1755.[25] The thesis was defended in the auditorium of the faculty of philosophy by means of a formal disputation. Kant was admitted to the faculty and received the *venia legendi*, which permitted him to give lectures in the university and to charge students a fee.

In the following April Kant applied for the extraordinary chair in philosophy left vacant since Knutzen's death. According to a regulation issued by Frederick II a *Privatdozent* could only be promoted to an extraordinary chair after three public disputations. In fulfillment of this requirement, Kant had already submitted in March a further thesis in Latin, the *Physical Monadology* (PM), again published by Hartung, which was disputed sometime in April with Kant's later biographer Borowski opposing. The petition for the chair came to nothing since the post was abolished, but left to posterity an invaluable statement of Kant's early thoughts on the relationship between physics and metaphysics.

Kant's *oeuvre* contains two other significant works intended exclusively for an academic audience, and which together with the above dissertations and a reply to a dissertation (1777) comprise the extent of his Latin authorship. The first was the dissertation he defended for the purposes of promotion to the chair in Logic and Metaphysics in 1770: *On the Form and Principles of the Sensible and the Intelligible World* (ID). In 1763 Kant had been offered the chair of poetry at Königsberg, but refused it, as he did the more financially attractive offers from the Universities of Erlangen (late 1769) and Jena (early 1770). These offers testified to the growing fame of the *Privatdozent*, and pointed to the need to promote him to a full chair.

An opening occurred with the death of Langhansen, the Professor of Mathematics. Kant marked the passing of his colleague with an elegy and a letter to Berlin proposing that either of his two colleagues, the Professor of Logic and Metaphysics F. Joh. Buck (who was preferred over Kant on grounds of seniority by the Academic Senate in 1758) or the Professor of Moral Philosophy, Christiani, be shifted sidewards to make room for Kant in the chair of Logic and Metaphysics. A fortnight later, Kant was appointed to the chair by Royal Order and granted an annual salary of 166 talers and 60 groschen.

In order to qualify for the chair, Kant was required to present another dissertation for public dispute, which he wrote over the summer vacation and defended on 21 August 1770. The 'Inaugural Dissertation' is a pivotal work, the most important of all Kant's writings before the three critiques, and one which sums up the achievements of the 1750s and 1760s while preparing the ground for the critical philosophy of the 1780s. It was published (or at least distributed) by Kant's main publisher of the 1760s, Johann Jacob Kanter (see below), but occupies a peculiar position in the publishing history of his works, being neither simply an academic thesis nor a work specifically intended for the reading public. Unlike Kant's other major writings, but like most academic dissertations intended for dispute at the University of Königsberg, the Inaugural Dissertation was hastily printed with a small print run in the city itself. It was not announced in the all important commercial catalogue of the Leipzig book fair, and seems to have been distributed outside Königsberg after a delay and almost as an afterthought.

Kant sent copies of the 'Inaugural Dissertation' to J.H. Lambert and M. Mendelssohn in Berlin via his erstwhile student and respondent in the debate Marcus Herz.[26] In his accompanying letter to Lambert he mentioned a plan to revise the work by adding a few pages 'before the publisher presents it at the coming bookfair', but this intended revision expanded into an entirely new work. This is first explicitly mentioned two years later in a letter to Herz (21 February 1772), where Kant muses it 'might perhaps have the title, "The Limits of Sense and Reason"'.[27] This comment is usually taken to mark the beginning to the compositional history of the *Critique of Pure Reason*.

Kant's remaining academic production in Latin is a minor, but nonetheless interesting address given in 1786 at the end of one of his periods as Rektor of the University: *On the Philosophers' Medicine of the Body*. This work closes an important phase of Kant's private use of reason in the university. Although the form and the occasions for composing the Latin writings were prescribed by official university requirements, the format of the academic dissertation and address provided an opportunity to Kant for exploratory reflection and the establishment of research agendas. However, the Latin dissertations did not exhaust that part of Kant's publications which was directed almost exclusively to the specific academic audience of the University of Königsberg. The 1758 petition to Empress Elisabeth also refers to three *Programmata*. These were the writings through which *Privatdozenten*, dependent on the fees of students attending their lectures, announced their forthcoming lecture programmes and gave students a taste of their work in the guise of a short reflection on a particular academic topic.[28] The *Programmata* were basically adverts for students, and were scrutinized by the academic censor; they were usually printed at the *Privatdozent's* own expense in small runs by a local print shop.

On receiving the licence to teach in 1755 Kant was obliged to make his presence felt with a number of *Programmata*. The petition of 1758 mentions three dating from 1756, 1757 and 1758; these were followed after the petition by a further four *Programmata* from 1759, 1762, 1765 and 1775. Together the seven *Programmata* form a significant if underestimated part of Kant's authorship. The first appeared on 25 April 1756 with an announcement of Kant's proposed lectures for the summer semester: *M[agister] Kant's New Notes Towards a Discussion of the Theory of Winds, which contains at the same time an Invitation to his Lectures*. It gives a sample of Kant's thought in the shape of a theory that relates wind to the rotation of the earth upon its axis. The inscription 'Printed in Driest's Königsberg Royally Privileged Book Press' shows that this publication was not supported by a publisher, but was privately printed and intended for a local student audience.[29] This accounts for the minimal impact of the work outside of Königsberg; it was written to impress local students and not the meteorologists in the wider reading public. Kant published the following three *Programmata* in the same way, with *M. Kant's Outline and Announcement of a Course of Lectures on Physical Geography together with an Appendix of an Inquiry into the Question of Whether the West Winds in our Regions are Humid because they have traversed a Great Sea* announcing the lectures for the summer semester of 1757, *M. Immanuel Kant's New Theory of Motion and Rest and its Consequences for the Primary Grounds of Natural Science, through which at the same time his Lectures for this Half Year are Announced* those for summer semester 1758, and *An Attempt at some Reflections on Optimism by M. Immanuel Kant also containing an Announcement of his Lectures for the coming Semester* for the winter semester 1759–60.

The two following *Programmata* from 1762 and 1765–6 differ from the previous four in that they were no longer privately printed by Driest, but published by Johann Jacob Kanter, and announced to a wider public in the Leipzig book fair catalogue. The first accordingly plays down its character as an announcement of lectures, and is entitled simply *The False Subtlety of the Four Syllogistic Figures demonstrated by M. Immanuel Kant*, although in it Kant presents the direction he intends to take in his 'course on logic' for the winter semester. This was available for sale throughout Germany, and thus straddles the genres of an independent published work and an internal university announcement.[30] The second *Programma* was also published by Kanter, and this time its title makes no attempt to conceal its pedagogic function: *M. Immanuel Kant's Announcement of the Programme of his Lectures for the Winter Semester 1765–1766.* However, it is in fact a deep meditation on the public significance of philosophy from a teacher fully aware of the exemplary character of his vocation, and should be read as a contribution to a redefinition of philosophy's place in the German university.[31] It also represents Kant's elevation of the genre of the *Programma* from its function as part of the private use of reason within the university to a way of practicing the public use of reason for the benefit of a wider reading public. In it Kant makes a case for the teaching of philosophy to both youth and the people as being the prime example of the public use of reason.

The last of Kant's *Programmata* is the text *On the Different Human Races, by way of Announcing the Lectures on Physical Geography for the Summer Semester 1775* from 1775. When he published this text with G.L. Hartung, the official academic publisher and the son of J.H. Hartung with whom Kant published his dissertations in the 1750s, Kant was already an ordinary professor in receipt of a salary, and thus not obliged to pursue students in the manner of a *Privatdozent.* His reasons for producing this text are not entirely clear; perhaps he found the genre congenial for the short, speculative exploration of a particular topic? This explanation is supported by Kant's reworking the text for re-publication two years later without the accompanying references to his lectures. Indeed, Kant's own editorial practice in this case was followed by many of his subsequent editors. With few exceptions, the texts Kant wrote in this genre are often published and read without any reference to their basic function as advertisments, and it has become accepted editorial practice to delete all references to lecture courses from their titles.[32] This practice serves tacitly to convert these contributions to the private use of reason in the teaching activities of the university into public uses of reason for a wider public. The 1775 *Programma* was the last of the genre for Kant; thereafter he developed other channels for publishing short, speculative essays which were dedicated unequivocally to the wider 'reading public' but which drew on the experience he had gained in presenting ideas in a concise and accessible way through the composition of *Programmata.*

Unlike the dissertations which were directed towards the faculty and the senate of the university and meant to ensure his passage through the academic bureaucracy, the *Programmata* were directed to students and were inseparable from the particular relationship between *Privatdozent* and paying students. The *Programmata* then point to another important link between Kant's private use of reason as a university teacher and his public use of reason as an author. However, they do not exhaust the direct and indirect ways in which Kant's teaching and publishing activities were deeply enmeshed with each other. However, in order fully to understand this relationship it is necessary to look more closely at Kant's activity as a teacher, and at the enormous demands it made upon his time and energy.

In a letter to J.G. Lindner of 1759, four years into his career as a *Privatdozent*, Kant paints a melancholy picture of himself at work:

> I sit daily at the anvil of my lectern and guide the heavy hammer of my repetitious lectures, always beating out the same rhythm . . . In this town where I find myself and with the modest prosperity for which I allow myself to hope, I make do finally with the applause I receive and the benefits I derive from that, dreaming my life away. (PC p. 4)

His first lecture in 1755 was a great occasion, and was given in the lecture room in Professor Kypke's house where he lodged at this time.[33] The room was full to overflowing as the student population and members of Königsberg society packed in to hear the diffident first of the many thousand lectures which Kant was to give over the next 41 years. Giving lectures was the main activity of a university teacher at this time, supplemented by the regulation *Disputatoria*[34] or seminars accompanying lectures which Kant regularly offered on Wednesdays and Fridays between 8 and 9 a.m. He offered in addition free sessions for repetitions of points and the solution of difficulties which may have arisen for students during the lectures, as well as private classes and tutorial sessions. Later, when he was promoted to his chair, the demands on his time from lecturing were augmented by his having to conduct matriculation examinations as well as other university duties.[35]

It is not surprising that Kant was depressed by the grind of lecturing, given the amount he had to do in order to survive as a *Privatdozent*.[36] He lectured regularly in the morning, with a minimum weekly average of 16 hours at the lectern. The subjects in which he lectured were extremely diverse. In his first winter semester of 1755 he offered lecture courses in logic, metaphysics and mathematics; he added in the following summer an innovative course in physical geography. In the following winter he added ethics, and in 1759–60 offered pure mathematics and mechanical sciences, and in 1767 offered a course in the then fashionable subject of natural law (*Naturrecht*). Then in 1772 he offered an introductory course in the encyclopaedia and history of philosophy, and in the same year divided his course on physical geography into separate courses on physical geography and anthropology; two years later he began lectures in natural theology and thereafter, in 1776–7, in pedagogy.[37] Throughout his career Kant gave 268 lecture courses: 54 on logic, 49 on metaphysics, 46 on physical geography, 28 on ethics, 24 on anthropology, 20 on physics, 16 on mathematics, 12 on jurisprudence, 11 on the encyclopaedia and history of philosophy, 4 on pedagogy, 2 on mechanics, and one each on mineralogy and theology. The attendance was greatest at the required lecture courses on logic and metaphysics: the crowd at the lectures on logic ranged between 45 (1775) and Kant's personal record of 100 in 1780, while attendance at the lectures on metaphysics ranged between 20 and 30 at the beginning of his career, rising to 70 at its end. Attendance at non-required but popular courses such as physical geography and anthropology ranged between 24 and 81 and 28 and 55 respectively.

According to government regulations a lecture course in a Prussian university was to consist of the lecturer explicating an authorized text or *compendium*. This rule was affirmed by the enlightened Prussian Minister of Church and Educational Affairs von Zedlitz, with the express exception of 'Professor Kant and his course on physical geography, for which as is known there is not a completely suitable teaching text'.[38] Thus in the *Programma* for his lectures of the winter semester 1765–6 Kant announces that his lectures on metaphysics will follow A.G. Baumgarten's *Metaphysics* (1739), those on logic, G.F. Meier's *Extract from the Theory of Reason* (1752), those on ethics, Baumgarten's *Fundamental Principles of Elementary Practical Philosophy* (1760). Kant's technique when lecturing on these and other handbooks in his other courses was to cover his texts with marginalia and to interleave pages covered with additional notes, remarks and marginalia to the marginalia. In this way his lectures transformed the text, often leaving little trace of the original. These commentaries now fill several volumes of the Academy Edition of his works, and, when added to the remainder of Kant's reflections, make up what Gulyga has nicely described as a 'scientific diary'.[39]

Kant's teaching activities had a significant direct and indirect impact upon his authorship. The most obvious direct impact, apart of course from the *Programmata*, consisted in the publication of his lectures. During his lifetime there was a considerable demand for the transcripts of Kant's lectures, some of which now offer invaluable information on the development of his thought.[40] Kant attempted to satisfy this demand at the end of his career by producing authorized versions of the lectures, especially the two most original series on anthropology and physical geography. He only completed the anthropology lectures, which were published in 1798 as *Anthropology from a Pragmatic Point of View* (A), but expressed doubts whether anybody else would be in a position to read his notes in order to prepare a text for physical geography. However, during his lifetime versions appeared of his lectures in logic (1800) edited by G.B. Jäsche, physical geography (1802) edited by F.T. von Rink, and pedagogy, again edited by Rink. After his death followed texts on philosophical theology (1817) edited by K.H.L. Pölitz, and metaphysics (1821), again by Pölitz.[41] This of course is not to mention the publishing programme of the twentieth-century Academy Edition.

The demand for transcripts and the publication of Kant's lectures shows that they were considered an integral part of his *oeuvre* even during his lifetime. However, his lectures also fed indirectly into his published texts. Tracing this influence is an extremely subtle branch of Kant scholarship which it would be inappropriate to pursue too closely at this point, although the following issues may be briefly addressed. First of all, the texts Kant lectured on often supplied the broad structure of his later works. This is notably the case with the *Critique of Pure Reason* which transforms the subject matter and organisation of Wolffian general and special metaphysics presented in Baumgarten's *Metaphysica*. Secondly, the marginalia Kant brought to his texts emerged from his wider reading and thinking, and point to the way in which he transformed and extended the philosophical tradition. He was famous for bringing to his lectures interesting examples drawn from a wide range of diverse sources. In this respect, the lectures reveal the process by which Kant was able, while working within the philosophical tradition, to adapt the tradition to the new concerns of modernity, whether those of natural science, politics, art and literature, or medicine. His lectures fused the traditional concerns and language of the philosophical *compendia* with new material drawn from the newspapers, journals and books satisfying the demands of a new reading public.

This conjunction of the private use of reason in the lecture theatre and the public use of reason on the printed page brings us to the two other basic categories of Kantian text, his journal publications and his books. Both categories are internally diverse. Kant wrote several sorts of journal articles and books meant for distinct geographically and socially determined audiences. Returning to the petition to the Empress Elisabeth from 1758, Kant claimed that he had published 'four treatises in the learned journal of Königsberg'. These mark the debut of a distinguished career in popular journalism which Kant pursued until the end of his life. He participated in the emergence of a new form of publication intended for a broad, and enlightened, reading public.[42]

The first four journalistic writings which Kant mentions were published after his return to Königsberg in 1754 in a local journal called the

Wochentliche Königsbergische Frag- und Anzeigungs-Nachrichten. The first essay was a reply to a question set by the Berlin Academy in 1752, 'Inquiry into the Question whether the Earth in its Rotation around its Axis, by which it produces the Change of Day and Night, has undergone any Alterations since the Time of its Origin'. This was published in two weekly instalments, and does not seem to have been entered into the Academy's competition. It marks the first of an important sub-genre of Kant's writings, namely the competition essay. His next try for an Academy medal, in 1764, was submitted and, although it did not win the competition, was judged worthy for publication by the Berlin Academy. This was the *Inquiry Concerning the Distinctness of the Principles of Natural Theology and Morality. In Answer to the Question which the Berlin Academy of Sciences set for the Year 1763.* It was this essay more than any which brought Kant to the attention of the enlightened public beyond Königsberg.[43]

The next three essays published in the *Wochentliche Königsbergische Frag- und Anzeigungs-Nachrichten* were 'The Question whether the Earth is aging, considered from a physicalist Point of View', serialized over four issues during the summer of 1754, and two essays on the Lisbon Earthquake published in January and April 1756. Between the latter, in March, Kant published a successful book on the earthquake with Hartung, thus co-ordinating his journal and book publications. He published one further article in this journal, the important essay 'Concerning the ultimate Ground of the Differentiation of Regions in Space' 12 years later in 1768. Following the four essays from the mid-1750s Kant did not publish any more short works in this form until 1764, when he commenced anonymous publication in the *Königsbergsche Gelehrte und Politische Zeitungen.* This journal, founded in 1764 by Johann Jacob Kanter, Kant's publisher of the 1760s, was edited by Hamann on the model of the literary and political journals he had read during his stay in England. It is a fine example of the new generation of journals which emerged all over Germany during the 1750s and 1760s. Although still intended for local circulation, such journals responded to, and to some degree led, a shift in public interest from scientific to literary and political topics. In the *Königsbergsche Gelehrte und Politische Zeitungen* Kant anonymously published the 'Essay on the Maladies of the Mind' (1764) as well as reviews of books by Silberschlag and Moscati in 1764 and 1771, the essays 'On the Dessau Philanthropin Academy' in 1776 and 1777, and the 'Report to Physicians' in 1782.

After 1771 Kant no longer published his short essays and reviews in the local journals. After a long period of silence he returned with a review in the *Raisonierendes Verzeichnis neuer Bücher* in 1783, followed in 1784 by 'Idea for a Universal History with a Cosmopolitan Purpose' in the *Berlinische Monatsschrift.* This was the first of a long and distinguished series of essays for this journal; indeed, with the exception of some short reviews for the *Allgemeine Literatur Zeitung* and the essay 'On the Use of Teleological Principles in Philosophy' for *Der Teutsche Merkur* in 1788, all Kant's shorter writings of the last two decades of his life were published in the *Berlinische Monatsschrift*.[44] Thus almost all the texts on the philosophy of history and the contributions to contemporary political, religious and scientific controversies described by Jean-François Lyotard as Kant's 'fourth critique' appeared in this one journal (see 'Kant's published writings' for full details).

The *Berlinische Monatsschrift* is remarkable not only for having published many of Kant's finest and most influential writings, but also for being the public face of an Enlightenment secret society in Berlin, the *Mittwochgesellschaft*, a group of intellectuals and senior bureaucrats who met secretly to discuss themes relevant to philosophy and contemporary Prussian society.[45] The secretary of this society who arranged the circulation of papers between its members was Johann Erich Biester, the secretary to Minister von Zedlitz and the editor of the *Berlinische Monatsschrift*. The first edition of 1783 presented itself as a 'Moral Weekly' but the journal quickly assumed a more explicitly pro-Enlightenment social, political and cultural agenda.[46] Through Biester the journal was closely associated with Zedlitz and reform circles in Berlin and dedicated to disseminating the cause of enlightenment throughout Prussia. Kant's publishing in this journal was a clear statement of position, as Biester underlined in his offer to Kant in a letter of 5 June 1785 to 'use our mouth to bring your speech to the public'. The *Berlinische Monatsschrift* was one of the main means by which Kant conducted the public use of reason which he recommended in his essay 'An Answer to the Question: "What is Enlightenment?"' published in its pages in 1784. He also continued to support Biester's journal with contributions after the change in political climate with the accession of Frederick William II in 1786, as well as after the episode with the censor which successfully halted the serialization of *Religion within the Limits of Reason Alone* in 1792.[47]

The final means by which Kant addressed the reading public was through his books, but even here his access to the media of publication changed during his career, and is reflected in the kinds of books he wrote. In the petition to Empress Elisabeth Kant mentions 'three other philosophical tracts which give some sense of my research'. The first of these, *Thoughts on the True Estimation of Living Forces*, was published over several years (1747–9) at Kant's own expense with the support of a relative, a shoemaker called Richter: it accordingly bears only the name of the printer – Martin Eberhard Dorn – and not that of a publisher. Kant himself observed that the circumstances of publication meant that his book did not enter the book trade and consequently was barely circulated making hardly any impact on the public.[48] His second venture into publishing was equally unsatisfactory, namely the anonymously published *Universal Natural History and Theory of the Heavens* of 1755 which was written during Kant's career as a domestic tutor. The book was published by Johann Friedrich Petersen of Königsberg and Leipzig who promptly went bankrupt. The stock was impounded with only a few copies escaping. Thus, although announced in the all-important catalogue of the Frankfurt and Leipzig book fairs, it did not gain wide circulation, though it did receive a review in the Hamburg journal *Freyen Urtheilen und Nachrichten*. It re-appeared for sale a year later in an advert in the *Wochentlichen Königsbergischen Frag- und Anzeigungs- Nachrichten* under the heading of 'things which can be bought in Königsberg' under Kant's name and available at 'the bookprinters Herr Joh. Driest' – presumably bankrupt stock accepted in lieu of payment by the printer from Petersen.[49] Kant's third philosophical tract was a quite different matter. Published by the official and academic bookseller Hartung in March 1756, the *History and Natural Description of the Most Remarkable Occurrences associated with the Earthquake which at the End of 1755 Shook a Large Part of the World* responded to local interest aroused by an article on the earthquake which Kant had published in January. This text is said to be unique in Kant's *oeuvre* for being printed as fast as it was written, although this also seems to have been the case with the *Observations on the Feeling of the Beautiful and the Sublime* and the *Critique of Judgement*. It was a local success in Königsberg, but does not seem to have been more widely distributed.

Following these inauspicious debuts, Kant's relations with his publishers settled into a more established pattern which may be presented chronologically. From 1762 until 1770 Kant published with Johann Jacob Kanter of Königsberg, and then, after an interval of 11 years (the 'silent decade') he resumed publishing activities in 1781 with Johann Friedrich Hartknoch of Riga with whom he stayed until 1788. In 1790 he published the *Critique of Judgement* with Lagarde and Friederich of Berlin and Libau, and from then until his death his books were published by Friedrich Nicolovius of Königsberg. In each case, with the exception of Lagarde and Friederich, Kant's relationship with his publisher was far more than economic. He relied on publishers not only to publish and distribute his books, but also to keep him supplied with the publications of others: they were his link to the public exercise of reason both as an author and as a reader. This was largely due to the structure of the eighteenth-century book trade in which a bookseller also served as a publisher in order to gain their stock by exchanging the books they produced with those of other publishers, above all at the Leipzig book fair. Kant's publishers, we shall see, were expected to keep him informed of recent publications, and to lend them to him when they came into the shop. While Kant did not demand a large cash honorarium from his publishers,[50] he certainly expected to be rewarded in kind.

The close relationship between author and publisher is immediately evident in the case of Kant's publisher during the 1760s, Johann Jacob Kanter (1738–86). Kanter published the *False Subtlety of the Four Syllogistic Figures* (FS) in 1762, *The Only Possible Argument in Support of a Demonstration of the Existence of God* (OPA) and the *Attempt to Introduce the Concept of Negative Magnitudes into Philosophy* (NM) in 1763, the *Observations on the Feeling of the Beautiful and the Sublime* (OBS) in 1764, the *Programmata* of 1765, the *Dreams of a Spirit-Seer Elucidated by Dreams of Metaphysics* (DS) in 1766, and finally (although this is not entirely certain) the 'Inaugural Dissertation' (ID) in 1770. Kanter combined the talents of an energetic and gifted entrepreneur with a commitment to disseminating Enlightenment ideas. The twenty-two-year old entered the bookselling business in Königsberg in 1760 with premises in Langgasse in the old town, and with success moved to the old town hall at Löbnicht. Kanter developed his business in several directions, pursuing a strategy of vertical integration by expanding from bookselling to book publishing, to publishing the *Königsbergsche Gelehrte und Politische Zeitungen* in 1764, and eventually to founding a paper factory; he also diversified into the lucrative sphere of gambling by becoming the organizer of a lottery.

Kanter was not only an ambitious businessman, he was also interested in providing a service to the intellectual community of Königsberg. He ran his bookshop as a form of meeting place for Königsberg intellectuals and students – it was described by a contemporary as the '*Börse für die Gelehrtenwelt der Stadt*'[51] or the 'Exchange for the intellectual world of the city'. Kant among many others included a visit to Kanter's as part of his daily routine in the early 1760s, and would there read the newspapers, borrow the latest books and discuss ideas with the other *habitués* as well as his own publishing plans with Kanter. In 1766 Kant moved to the second floor of the bookshop, where he lived and taught until 1769 (when he was driven out by the incessant crowing of a neighbour's cock). Thus Kant lived and even taught on the premises of his publisher,[52] and was given full access to the stock of books. He also enjoyed information on intellectual developments outside Königsberg brought to him by the peripatetic Kanter. The bookshop exemplified the notion of the reading public which Kant evokes in 'An Answer to the Question: "What is Enlightenment?"', where readers and authors meet and reason with one another regardless of their official capacities.

A fascinating insight into the relationship of author and publisher is afforded by Kant's correspondence with Lambert from the mid 1760s.

Lambert wrote to Kant from Berlin on 13 November 1765 bemoaning the difficulties of finding a publisher for his *Architectonic* – if it were a novel 'I think it would already have found numerous publishers . . .'. Lambert notes that Kanter is 'a man who will also publish philosophy and larger works' and encloses a sheet for Kanter to consider for publication. He makes three incidental observations that are of interest in connection with the development of philosophy publishing during this period. The first is his concern that the book should be printed in Leipzig, which would be better for various reasons, but above all because of the 'difference in prices and the freight charges'. It was increasingly the case that books published in a city such as Königsberg would be printed elsewhere, usually Leipzig, in order to benefit from economies of scale in the printing industry there, but also because of the pivotal role of its book fair in distribution and the consequent savings in transport costs. Lambert then mentions that Kanter might wish to publish the book in time for the Easter book fair, which was one of the main events in the publisher's diary. If a book was intended for more than a local market, then it had to be announced in the catalogue of the Leipzig fair and be available there for sale or exchange with books from other publishers/booksellers from all parts of Germany. Finally Lambert mentions a possible honorarium of around two hundred talers, which he considers moderate 'because the work will necessarily create a stir'.[53] This indicates that authors were paid by a system of down-payment or honorarium upon delivery of their manuscripts, and not by royalties on sales. Kant informed Kanter of Lambert's proposal, and forwarded a letter from Kanter proposing a meeting in Berlin.

Other details of Kanter's publishing enterprise also emerge from a closer consideration of Kant's publishing history. It seems as if most of Kant's writings for Kanter were printed in Königsberg, which suggests a small print run. Evidence for this is Hamann's claim in a letter to Nicolai on 21 December 1762 that Kant's OPA had just left the printers in Königsberg, as well as the episode surrounding the censorship of Kant's *Dreams of a Spirit-Seer*. Kanter was fined 10 talers by the senate of the University of Königsberg for publishing this book without the approval of the academic censor. In an appeal Kanter observed that Kant's manuscript was almost unreadable, and was sent to the printer in stages. This meant that the author corrected and revised it as he went along, and that there was accordingly no single copy which could have been submitted for censorship prior to the final printed version. Kanter thus printed in Königsberg, but announced his publications in the catalogues of the Leipzig book fair, to which he took samples of his product. The overall impression is that his business was first and foremost a local bookshop, which was supported by means of a specialized, but small-scale local publishing enterprise.

Hints of dissatisfaction with Kanter are discernible in Kant's reply to Lambert on 31 December 1765, which also contains the first mention of his future publisher, Johann Friedrich Hartknoch (1740–89). When referring to Kanter's being 'overwhelmed with other commitments' (the lottery perhaps?) he observes that 'He has gone into partnership with his former employee, Mr Hartknoch, who managed his affairs in Riga till now . . .'.[54] A near contemporary of Kanter, Hartknoch managed the expansion of Kanter's bookshop first into Mitau (1763) and then into Riga (1764), moving a year later into partnership with, and then independence from Kanter. Hartknoch studied theology at Königsberg University and was one of Kant's students. His enterprise was more efficiently organized, better focused and more ambitious than Kanter's, as is evident not only from the range and quality of authors he published (Hamann and Herder as well as Kant)[55] but also from his mastery of the international production and distribution of books.

The publication of the *Critique of Pure Reason* is a case in point. Informed by Hamann in September 1780 that Kant had almost completed this work, Hartknoch wrote offering his services; he would produce Kant's book with speed and taste, and could undertake that it would be widely distributed. The book was printed in Halle by the printing firm of Grunert, under the supervision of Spener's book company in Berlin. Printing began at the end of 1780, with Kant receiving the first 29 proof sheets in April 1781. The book appeared in the Easter book fair of the same year, with Riga as the place of publication.

Similar arrangements were followed with Kant's subsequent books published by Hartknoch, namely the *Prolegomena to Any Future Metaphysic that will be able to come forward as Science* (P) of 1783, the *Grounding for the Metaphysics of Morals* (GMM) of 1785, the *Metaphysical Foundations of Natural Science* (MF) of 1786 and the *Critique of Practical Reason* (CPrR) of 1788. All of these texts were printed by Grunert in Halle, to whom Kant directly sent his manuscripts (informing Hartknoch when he had done so), and were distributed at the bookfair. With respect to the *Prolegomena*, Hamann's correspondence with Hartknoch mentions that Kant is at work on a popular version of the first critique as early as summer 1781, and both publisher and his informer clearly regarded this work as a form of compensation for the unsuccessful tome which was 'too abstract and expensive for the crowd'. By publishing with Hartknoch, Kant's works were reliably available to a large audience throughout Germany even though their place of publication was on the eastern periphery of German culture. His audience was no longer primarily local, as was still the case when he published with Kanter. However, Kant's relationship with his publisher was again not exclusively economic: Hartknoch is known to have personally delivered to Kant the first copies of the *Grounding* in April 1785,[56] and to have sent him caviar from Riga.

On Hartknoch's death in 1789 Kant ceased to publish with the firm, even though he had given Hartknoch's son a vague undertaking to publish the third critique (CJ) with him. Kant seems to have considered his relationship with Hartknoch's firm to have ended with the death of the father, and to have doubted the capacity of the son to carry out the speedy and efficient distribution of the third critique. The latter considerations were foremost when he turned, through his former student J.G. Kiesewetter, to the Berlin book dealer and publisher de la Garde late in 1789. With the despatch of the first part of the manuscript on 21 January 1790 Kant stated that the 'first and most important condition' was that the work be published in time for the Leipzig Easter book fair. The rest of the manuscript followed in early March, quickly followed by the Preface and Introduction which, with minimal correction, were published on time. However, following this episode with de la Garde, Kant returned to his more accustomed relationship with a publisher, this time with the Königsberg publisher Friedrich Nicolovius (1768–1836), with whom he remained for the rest of his life.

Nicolovius, like Hartknoch, was one of Kant's students who opened a bookshop and publishing business in Königsberg, in 1790. In the same year he published Kant's polemic *On a Discovery according to which any New Critique of Pure Reason has been made Superfluous by an Earlier One* (OD), which appeared at the same Leipzig Easter book fair as the third critique. Following this successful trial run, Kant entrusted his remaining books to Nicolovius, namely *Religion within the Limits of Reason Alone* (RL) of 1793, *The Metaphysics of Morals* (MM) of 1797, *The Conflict of the Faculties* (CF) of 1798, the *Anthropology from a Pragmatic Point of View* (A) of 1798, and finally the authorized editions of the *Logic* (L) and *Education* edited by Rink. Nicolovius printed the books in Leipzig in large editions intended for a national audience,[57] and yet he also continued to serve Kant in much the same way as Kanter had done in the 1760s. Thus Jachmann reports in his biography that Nicolovius would send Kant his catalogue and that Kant would send back Lampe to borrow the interesting titles.[58]

Kant's relationships with his publishers underline the diverse character of his texts, and the different audiences for which they were intended. More work on Kant's publishing enterprise would clarify the nature and internal diversity of his address to the reading public, and introduce some important discriminations between his works. It would also serve to reveal the various rhetorics which he employed when addressing distinct publics. Yet even a brief consideration of his relations with his publishers shows that his relationship as author to the reading public was by no means straightforward. It also shows the extent to which Kant's participation in the reading public both as author and as reader was mediated through his publishers. They not only disseminated his works, but also provided him with a means of access to contemporary intellectual developments. This explains why, although a voracious reader, Kant did not possess a large private library. According to an inventory taken after his death, Kant owned 450 unbound volumes, most of them the gifts of publishers and not held in particular esteem by their owner.[59]

The history of Kant's publishing enterprise shows a steady development from his addressing first a local, then a national and ultimately an international audience. By the 1780s he possessed a reputation outside of Prussia in both Protestant and Catholic German principalities. His philosophy was known and taught in the universities and, as his correspondence testifies, was familiar to and esteemed by those excluded from the university such as women. In the 1790s his work was known and debated in England, France and Russia. However, upon his death, Kant's work was being severely criticized by a younger generation of German philosophers including Fichte, Hegel and Schelling who were impatient with its equivocations. Informing their considerable philosophical differences was a refusal to accept that the 'age of criticism' could be contained within the parameters of the 'age of enlightenment' and the 'century of Frederick'.

For the post-Kantians, criticism was revolutionary, and should not be restricted to oppositions such as those of theory and practice or the public and private uses of reason. For these philosophers, the vocation of the philosopher was to address both 'youth' and 'the people', while that of philosophy was to unite theoretical and practical criticism in order, in the words of one of the most radical of Kantians, not only to interpret, but also to change the world. These developments for good or ill would not have been possible without Kant's work, which, paradoxically, they both exceeded and fell short of: by seeking to realize philosophy, whether through the nation, the proletariat or the overman, the post-Kantians transformed Kant's philosophizing into philosophy. However, far from superseding Kant, it seems as if, after two revolutionary centuries, the 'lesser evil' of Kant's accommodation with the 'century of Frederick' and the studied equivocations and sensitivity to aporia which characterize his philosophizing still offer a future to which it might be worth returning.

Notes

1. Thus Gulyga writes in the preface to his excellent biography of Kant (1985, p. xi) that 'Kant has no biography other than the history of his thought.'
2. For a history of the Academy Edition see Lehmann's essay 'Zur Geschichte der Kantausgabe 1896–1955' in Lehmann, 1969.
3. The distinction between passive and active aspects of the author is analogous to other distinctions at work throughout Kant's philosophy, such as that between human beings as occupants of the realms of both intelligible freedom and natural causality.
4. This was subsequently published with Kant's reply in the Preface to *The Conflict of the Faculties* (CF), 1798, p. 6, p. 11.
5. Ibid., p. 7, p. 13.
6. Ibid., p. 8, p. 15. This defence was disingenuous, since RL was originally intended to be serialized in the journal *Berlinische Monatsschrift*, the extent of whose readership far exceeded that of the university. Indeed, the first part was published there, the rest of the text falling victim to the Berlin censorship.
7. Ibid., p. 10, p. 19.
8. PC p. 220.
9. His somewhat Jesuitical justification of this pledge troubled some of Kant's friends and admirers, notably Borowski who tried to justify his conduct in his biography; see Borowski et al., 1912, p. 67.
10. Kant's knowledge of English and Scottish philosophers such as Locke, Hume, Hutcheson, Kames, Burke and Smith is widely appreciated; less well known is his taste for English literature, especially Samuel Butler's *Hudibras* and Henry Fielding's *Tom Jones*; see Malter, 1990, p. 73.
11. See Stavenhagen, 1949, pp. 8–10. The often underestimated dynamic and cosmopolitan character of Königsberg was beautifully expressed by Kant himself in a footnote to the Introduction to A: 'A large city like Königsberg on the river Pregel, the capital of a state, where the representative National Assembly of the government resides, a city with a university (for the cultivation of the sciences), a city also favoured by its location for maritime commerce, and which, by way of rivers, has the advantages of commerce with the interior of the country as well as with neighbouring countries of different languages and customs, can well be taken as an appropriate place for enlarging one's knowledge of people as well as of the world at large, where such knowledge can be acquired even without travel' (p. 120, pp. 4–5).
12. See Walker, 1971.
13. See Evans, 1987.
14. See McClelland, 1980.
15. This period of the city's history is perhaps best captured in Kant's OBS, his most lighthearted and consistently popular text.
16. For the good memories of the everyday pietism of his parents, see Vorländer, 1911, pp. 4–5; for the bad memories of the pietism of the school, ibid., pp. 10–11.
17. Ibid., p. 11.
18. The matriculation requirement was ordained by the spartan King Frederick William I on 25 October 1735, and included familiarity with classical languages (Latin, New Testament Greek, Hebrew), elementary syllogistics, and

the basics of history, geography and letter-writing. For the full text of the regulation, see Vorländer, 1911, p. 15.

19. As suggested in Gulyga, 1985, p. 11.

20. Erdmann's 1876 book on Knutzen, despite its age, is still useful for its description of the conditions at the University at Königsberg during the first half of the eighteenth century.

21. There is some confusion surrounding the title of Knutzen's chair. According to Vorländer, 1911, it was in Logic and Metaphysics while the editors of the Academy Edition describe it being in Mathematics and Philosophy; Gulyga discreetly ignores the inconsistency.

22. Vorländer, 1911, pp. 26–7.

23. Cited in full by Gulyga, 1985, pp. 34–5.

24. It was kept in the records of the philosophy faculty and handed over to the university library after Kant's death. The text was first published in Rosenkranz and Schubert's edition of 1839.

25. The publisher Johann Heinrich Hartung was also a bookseller whose son (who took over the business) was the brother-in-law of Kant's biographer Borowski. Kant mainly published works intended for an academic public with the Hartungs, publishing the two early dissertations and the last of the *Programmata, On the Different Human Races*, in 1775. The sole exception was his scientific pot-boiler of 1756 on the Lisbon earthquake. However, he seems to have been in fairly constant contact with the firm through Borowski, later using his relation-ship with Borowski to secure Hartung's interest in publishing Fichte's *Critique of all Revelation* in 1791 (see Borowski, 1912, p. 70). We also know from an anecdote concerning Kant's obtuse servant Lampe that Hartung also pub-lished a newspaper of which Kant was a regular reader for over 38 years. For these four decades, and to Kant's intense annoyance, Lampe called the *Hartungsche Zeitung* the *Hartmannsche Zeitung*, apparently not to confuse it with the *Hamburger Zeitung*. Lampe's job was to fetch the paper from Hartung's shop and then return it when Kant had finished, an incidental detail which suggests the existence of a fairly formal circulation arrangement for journals and newspapers.

26. See PC pp. 58–70.

27. Ibid., p. 71.

28. 'It was customary for a *Privatdozent* at that time to print programmatic or short essays to attract prospective students giving an example of the sort of topics that might be dealt with in class and the manner in which they would be treated', Polonoff, 1973, p. 67.

29. Driest also printed another private commission for Kant, this time the small (eight sides) pamphlet of 1760, *Thoughts on the Premature Demise of Herr Johann Friedrich von Funk.*

30. It was thus announced for sale in the Berlin journal *Berlinische Nachrichten von Staats- und Gelehrten Sachen* on 7 October 1762 prior to receiving the approval of the academic censor in Königsberg on the 11th.

31. The Universities of Göttingen and Königsberg pioneered the change in the status of the philosophy faculty from being an 'ante-chamber to the higher faculties' to offering a broad curriculum which 'in addition to the traditional introductory course of logic, metaphysic, and ethics ... offered lectures in "empirical psychology", the law of nature, politics, physics, natural history, pure and applied mathematics (including surveying, military and civilian

architecture), history and its "auxiliary" sciences such as geography, diplomatics, science, art, and ancient and modern language' (McClelland, 1980, pp. 42–3). The main forces for change in the University of Königsberg were Kant and his close colleague, the Göttingen-trained disciple of Adam Smith, Christian Jakob Kraus (1753–1807).

32. The editor of the re-publication of *M. Kant's Outline and Announcement of a Course of Lectures on Physical Geography, together with an Appendix of an Inquiry into the Question of Whether the West Winds in our Regions are Humid because they have traversed a Great Sea* in 1807 removed all references to the origins of the text, and re-titled it as simply *On the Question of Whether the West Winds are Humid because they have traversed a Great Sea.*

33. Borowski, 1912, pp. 94–5 gives an invaluable eye-witness account of this event in his biography.

34. See Vorländer, 1911, pp. 41–2.

35. In the winter semester of 1777 Kant lectured for 28 hours a week. Kant scholars have often puzzled over the reasons for Kant's 'silent decade' of the 1770s – they should take a look at his workload of teaching and administration during this period.

36. Although Kant's income was sufficient to take on a servant in 1751 – the surly Lampe – most of his period as a *Privatdozent* was passed in relative poverty. His income from teaching was not high, and even so he would often excuse poorer students their fees, while the income from his publications was inconsiderable. In the difficult 1760s circumstances forced Kant to undertake additional duties such as that of Sub-Librarian at the Royal Library in the Castle (1766–72) and as custodian of a private natural history collection. The former post brought the 41-year-old Kant his first regular annual salary of 62 talers and various payments in kind such as corn, beer and firewood. (Kant incidentally, like Nietzsche, preferred wine to beer, considering beer the surest recipe for a short life; like Hegel, however, he was addicted to caffeine.) He also supplemented his income during this period by taking in lodgers, and in the mid-1760s even sold his books in order to make ends meet. He could not afford to buy a house until 1784, three years after publishing the *Critique of Pure Reason,* and at the age of 60.

37. Since Emil Arnold's 1894 work *Kritische Excurse im Gebiet der Kantforschung* it has become convention to divide Kant's lecture courses into four groups: (a) the required courses on logic, metaphysics and ethics, along with physical geography and anthropology; (b) those on philosophical encyclopaedia, natural law and pedagogy; (c) natural science and mathematics; (d) private lectures on military architecture and fortification given to Russian officers during the Russian administration. See also Lehmann, 1969, p. 75.

38. Vorländer, 1911, p. 43. See also 'Einführung in Kants Vorlesungen' in Lehmann, 1969. Zedlitz was the most powerful advocate of the Enlightenment in the Prussian Government, and was in his post from 1771 until replaced by the anti-Enlightenment Wöllner in 1788, two years after the death of Frederick I. He took a personal interest in Kant's work and career, attending the lectures on his philosophy in Berlin by Markus Herz, requesting transcripts of Kant's lectures, and encouraging Kant to move to a more influential and better placed post in Halle. Kant acknowledged his support by dedicating to him the *Critique of Pure Reason.* Zedlitz's secretary Biester subsequently played an

important part in disseminating Kant's ideas by opening to him the pages of the *Berlinische Monatsschrift.*

39. Gulyga, 1985, p. 59.
40. In the case of logic, for example, we possess transcripts of Kant's lecture series from three decades: from the early 1770s (the 'Blomberg Logic', named after an earlier owner of the transcript, and the 'Philippi Logic'); from the 1780s ('Vienna', 'Heschel' and 'Pölitz' Logics); and from 1792 (the 'Dohna-Wundlacken Logic').
41. The complex editorial procedures followed by these editors is still imperfectly understood. For some idea of the challenge they faced, see J.M. Young's introduction to his 1992 translation of Kant's *Lectures on Logic,* esp. pp. xvii–xviii.
42. For an analysis of the rapid expansion of journal publication and its place in the German Enlightenment, see Hans Erich Bödeker's 'Journals and Public Opinion: The Politicisation of the German Enlightenment in the second half of the Eighteenth Century', in Hellmuth, 1990, pp. 423–45.
43. The francophone Berlin Academy was distinct from both the universities and the 'enlightenment societies' which met in the capital to discuss philosophical and reform issues (see Horst Möller, 'Enlightened Societies in the Metropolis: The Case of Berlin' in Hellmuth, 1990, pp. 219–33). However, it provided a forum for the discussion and dissemination of enlightenment ideas to a national and international audience. As Kant's fame spread during the 1780s he was elected a full member of the Berlin Academy in 1786. Kant's posthumously published treatise *What Real Progress has Metaphysics made in Germany since the Time of Leibniz and Wolff?* is the third example in Kant's *oeuvre* of an answer to a question set by the Academy, this time in 1788.
44. The essay 'On a Presumed Right to Lie from Love of Mankind' was published in the *Berlinische Blätter,* the magazine that succeeded the *Berlinische Monatsschrift,* also edited by Johann Erich Biester (1749–1816).
45. The history of secret societies and discussion groups in the German Enlightenment is considered by Im Hof, 1982, and Kosselek, 1959, while the history of the *Mittwochgesellschaft* is covered by Möller in Hellmuth, 1990.
46. For the moral weeklies in general see Martens, 1968; for the specific history of the *Berlinische Monatsschrift* see Weber, 1985.
47. It appears as if Kant and the *Berlinische Monatsschrift* served as tests of strength for the censorship following Wöllner's counter-enlightenment religious and censorship edicts of 1788. Between them the two edicts represented an attempt to close down the space for the public exercise of reason. The first affirmed 'freedom of conscience' but ordered subjects to 'keep their opinions to themselves' while the second sought to rein in the 'excesses of the so-called enlighteners' and to end the freedom of the press (see Gulyga, 1985, p. 201 and Weber, 1985, pp. 283–4). These edicts were not enforced until 1791, and were then stringently applied in the case of Kant; for if he and the *Berlinische Monatsschrift* could be silenced, that would send a clear message to lesser writers and journals. It was for this reason that Biester was so dismayed that Kant eventually agreed to be muzzled with regard to publishing on religious subjects.
48. Borowski, 1912, pp. 31–2.
49. Borowski, 1912, p. 34, mentions this episode and describes the unhappy fate of UNH not gaining the attention of either the 'greater public' or of Frederick

the Great to whom it was dedicated. Its translator Jaki (1981, p. 27) regards it, uncharitably but not wholly implausibly, as a failed attempt at 'a rapid rise on the academic ladder'.

50. According to Borowski, 1912, Kant did not receive an honorarium for his early writings, and even with his later works received comparatively little (p. 73). His honorarium for the *Critique of Pure Reason* for example was 4 talers per sheet for 55 sheets (220 talers) plus 10–12 free copies, one on fine paper and bound for presentation to Zedlitz. All the same, the poor sales of the book in the years immediately following publication apparently led Hartknoch to consider selling it off as bulk paper.

51. Cited in Stavenhagen, 1949, p. 46. Kanter's office was graced with portraits of eminent Prussians, to which he added a portrait of Kant by J.G. Becker in 1768.

52. Kanter also performed a service for the student community by permitting them twice a week to read the stock free of charge.

53. All citations from Lambert in PC, p. 45.

54. PC p. 47. A further critical note regarding Kanter also enters this letter, with Kant observing that 'Mr Kanter, in true bookseller's fashion, did not hesitate to announce the title in the Leipzig catalogue when he heard from me that I might have a work with that title ['on the proper method of metaphysics'] ready for the next easter fair' (p. 48). This is one of the earliest references to what became the *Critique of Pure Reason*.

55. Stavenhagen, 1949, p. 31, notes that Hartknoch also published Russian authors, commenting that 'In the best style, Hartknoch understood his publishing vocation to consist in acting as an intermediary between the West and the intellectually emergent East'.

56. Letter from Hamann to Herder, 14 April 1785, *Immanuel Kant's gesammelte Schriften*, Vol. IV, p. 628.

57. His firm still had 1,100 copies of *The Conflict of the Faculties* in stock in 1832. This book generated litigation on account of parts of it being published elsewhere, and signalled the beginnings of the disputes around the lucrative publishing rights to Kant's works which also afflicted the publication of his lectures on physical geography.

58. Jachmann, in Borowski, 1912, p. 147.

59. See Borowski and Wasianski's observations in Borowski, 1912, pp. 79 and 277. For details of the inventory of Kant's library left after his death to Prof. Gensichen, see Warda, 1922.

A

a priori/a posteriori *see also* CONCEPT, DEDUCTION, EXPOSITION, INTUITION, JUDGEMENT, KNOWLEDGE, LOGIC, METAPHYSICS, ONTOLOGY, PURE, SYNTHESIS

The distinction between a priori and posteriori in the century before Kant was used to distinguish between modes of logical demonstration: 'When the mind reasons from causes to effects, the demonstration is called a priori; when from effects to causes, the demonstration is called a posteriori' (Arnauld, 1662, p. 301). It was still broadly used in this sense by Wolff and Baumgarten in the mid-eighteenth century, and it was this usage which Hume criticized in the *Treatise* (1739). Kant extended the distinction considerably in CPR, where the notion of a priori plays a pivotal role. While the two terms referred traditionally to forms of demonstration, and additionally in the Wolffian school to the kinds of knowledge gained in those demonstrations, Kant extended their range beyond kinds of knowledge first to judgements and then, more significantly, to the very elements of knowledge (intuitions and concepts).

For Kant, a posteriori knowledge and judgements did not pose any particular problem for philosophy: 'The possibility of synthetic a posteriori judgements, of those which are gathered from experience, [like analytic judgements] also requires no special explanation; for experience is nothing but a continual joining together (synthesis) of perceptions' (P §5). Such knowledge and its elements are derived from experience, their synthesis resting on 'custom' or 'association'. Kant is prepared to concede Hume's objections to the validity of this form of knowledge, but defends the validity of a priori knowledge and its constituent judgements and elements. Therefore most of Kant's analysis of the distinction between a posteriori and a priori focuses on the character of the a priori. The choice of this focus was motivated by the desire to defend the synthetic a priori character of the judgements which make up metaphysics.

The traditional criterion for distinguishing between the two forms of demonstration according to whether they moved from cause to effect or vice versa is clearly no longer valid for Kant. He thus develops new criteria for a priori knowledge: it is (a) pure and (b) universal and necessary. The criteria are employed separately, but more often together, with, on occasions, one criterion being assumed in order illegitimately to support an argument for the other.

The argument for the purity of a priori knowledge, judgements and elements holds that they are 'clear and certain' modes of knowledge independent of experience. They have 'arisen completely a priori, independently of experience' as opposed to those a posteriori modes of knowledge which are 'borrowed solely from experience' (CPR A 2). They are independent of experience in that they do not contain any 'admixture' of sensibility, and in that they may not be derived from it. Kant argues further that they are not only splendidly independent of experience – 'knowledge absolutely independent of all experience' (CPR B 3) – but are even the condition of experience.

The purity of the elements of a priori knowledge is proven by a process of abstraction. The 'pure forms of sensible intuition in general' – space and time – are discovered by abstracting from experience 'everything which the understanding thinks through its concepts' thus 'isolating' sensibility and then 'separating' off 'everything which belongs to sensation, so that nothing may remain save pure intuition and the mere form of appearances, which is all that sensibility can supply *a priori*' (CPR A 22/B 36). The same holds for the a priori concepts or 'categories' which are 'the *a priori* conditions upon which the possibility of experience rests, and which remain as its underlying grounds when everything empirical is abstracted from appearances' (A 96). However, establishing the purity of a priori principles itself requires a criterion, for how otherwise can it be known that the process of abstraction has reached its terminus in the a priori?

The criteria of universality and necessity are used to register the arrival at an a priori judgement or element. If this intuition or concept necessarily holds for every experience then it is said to a priori. Kant uses this argument on several occasions in CPR, moving between universal and necessary knowledge, judgements, concepts and intuitions, all described as a priori. On one occasion in the 'Second Introduction' he moves from a priori knowledge, to judgements, to concepts, and ends with a 'faculty of a priori knowledge'. He begins: 'Necessity and strict universality are thus sure criteria of *a priori* knowledge, and are inseparable from one another' (CPR B 4). Then he claims: 'it is easy to show that there actually are in human knowledge judgements which are necessary and in the strictest sense universal, and which are therefore pure *a priori* judgements' (CPR B 4), and cites the example of mathematical propositions.

From the analysis of a priori knowledge and judgements Kant moves quickly into the proofs for the existence of *a priori* principles. The first proof appeals to their necessary role in experience: 'it is possible to show that pure *a priori* principles are indispensable for the possibility of experience, and so prove their existence *a priori*. For whence could experience derive its certainty, if all the rules, according to which it proceeds, were always themselves empirical, and therefore contingent?' (CPR B 5). Here the purity of the a priori is used to support its universality and necessity. The second proof proceeds by way of abstraction. The proof of an a priori form of intuition abstracts from an empirical body all its qualities until it arrives at space as its ineluctable residuum or a priori form of intuition. The proof of an a priori concept abstracts from an object 'all properties which experience has taught us' in order to arrive at the concept or a priori category of, in this case, substance (B 5–6).

The proof of the purity or universality and necessity of an a priori form of intuition is called an exposition while that of an a priori concept of the understanding or category is called a deduction. If a priori principles or elements can be established through exposition and deduction, then Kant can claim not only to have established the existence of a priori principles, but also to have determined their extent. However, his arguments in the 'Transcendental Doctrine of Elements' provoked an enormous debate which shows no sign of abating. At stake is an account of justified knowledge which is neither empiricist nor idealist. Much of the debate has involved the source of a priori principles and their universality and necessity. The source does not lie in sensibility or experience (Locke), nor does it lie in God (Descartes and Malebranche), nor even in 'innate' or 'inborn' ideas (Leibniz and Wolff).

One of the main reasons for the longevity of the debate is the ambiguous and often cryptic account of the source of a priori universality which Kant offers in his published writings. However, these may be clarified by reference to his unpublished notes and reflections. In CPR Kant obliquely relates the source of a priori universality and necessity to the spontaneous activity of the subject, but his unpublished notes are less inhibited: 'All our and other beings' actions are necessitated, only the understanding (and the will insofar as it can be determined by the understanding) is free and a pure self-activity that is determined through nothing else but itself. Without this originary and unchangeable spontaneity we would know nothing a priori . . .' (R §5441). Here the theoretical problem of the a priori is unequivocally linked to spontaneity and freedom, and through them to practical philosophy. Thus the issue of the a priori threatens to dissolve the distinction between theoretical and practical philosophy, a step which was taken by Kant's immediate idealist heirs.

Fichte located the a priori in the simultaneously theoretical and practical activity of the subject. His argument had a great impact on mid- to late-nineteenth-century neo-Kantianism which largely set the agenda for the emphasis of twentieth-century Kant studies on the problems of the exposition and the deduction. Hermann Cohen's influential *Kants Theorie der Erfahrung* (1871) pursued a typical agenda of proving 'Kant's theory of a priority anew'. This was part of a general tendency to seek new a priori sources of universality and necessity, whether in psychology, physiology or sociology. One influential development was initiated by Frege, who shifted the emphasis away from the source of a priori universality and necessity to the justification of a priori judgements. In doing so he unconsciously returned to Kant's original problem of establishing criteria for a priori judgements, a return sealed by Wittgenstein's pre-Kantian definition of an a priori truth as being 'one whose possibility guaranteed its truth' (1922, 3.04).

absolute [*absolutus, Absolut*] *see also* ANTINOMY, COSMOLOGY, FREEDOM, GOD
'Absolute' is the past participle of *absolvere* 'to absolve, to acquit, to free from debt'. The term can be used adjectivally or substantively: it either qualifies something as free from any relation, condition or limitation, or designates that which is thus free. The philosophical use of the term is modern, appearing first in Spinoza where it echoes political discussions of 'absolute sovereignty' and theological discussions of God as absolute. Spinoza's use of the term is adjectival, as in 'absolute certainty', 'absolute motion', the 'absolute dominion of the mind over the affects' (see Deleuze, 1988, p. 44). Even God is only adjectivally qualified as absolute, and is defined in *Ethics* I def. 6 (1677) as 'a being absolutely infinite' (Spinoza, 1985, p. 409; see also pp. 237, 264, 595).

Kant too uses the term adjectivally, and usually in opposition to 'relative' and 'comparative'. His earliest recorded use appears in the distinction between absolute and relative position in OPA. In CPR he devotes over two pages to clarifying 'an expression with which we cannot dispense, and which yet, owing to an ambiguity that attaches to it through long-standing misuse, we also cannot with safety employ.' (A 324/B 380). The ambiguity involves two adjectival senses of absolute. The first refers to internal possibility – 'that which is in itself possible', i.e., the bare possibility or 'the least that can be said of an object'; the second indicates 'that something is valid in all respects, without limitation, e.g., absolute despotism, and in this sense the *absolutely possible* would mean what is *in every relation* (in all respects) *possible* – which is the *most* which can be said of the possibility of a thing.' (A 324/B 381). Kant opts for the second, broader sense of absolute, but warns that it must be used circumspectly.

Throughout the critical philosophy Kant criticizes pure reason's illegitimate claims to know the absolute. The cosmological ideas may claim to represent 'absolute completeness' in the composition, division, origination and dependence of appearances (A 415/B 443), but are shown upon critical scrutiny to yield the antinomies. Kant on the whole refrains from giving the absolute any substantive content; he does not use the term to qualify either the thing-in-itself or the categorical imperative. However, he does refer in passing to 'absolute self-activity (freedom)' (A 418/B 446), parenthetically suggesting a substantive identification of the absolute with freedom.

The thought suggested by this parenthesis was taken up by Fichte and Schelling, who developed philosophies of the substantive absolute based on the 'I' of the knowing and acting subject and the 'it' of nature and history (see Fichte, 1794, especially Part 1, §1; Schelling, 1856, especially 'Die Naturphilosophie'). Hegel's philosophy of absolute spirit, on the contrary, breaks with the opposition of adjectival and substantive absolute and rethinks the absolute as processional. (Hegel, 1807, especially 'Preface' and 'Introduction'; 1812, especially 'Actuality' and 'The Absolute Idea'). However, this departure was reduced to the terms of the substantive absolute by contemporary critics such as Schopenhauer (see 1813, pp. 59–62), and in this guise dominated nineteenth-century European and American idealism. Heidegger's attempts to deconstruct the opposition of adjectival and substantive absolutes in his readings of Hegel and Schelling during the 1930s (Heidegger, 1930, 1936) have contributed to a contemporary re-assessment of the absolute in philosophy, theology and social theory (see Derrida, 1974; Rose, 1981; Milbank, 1990).

abstraction [*aphairesis, abstrahere, Abstraktion*] *see also* CONCEPT, EMPIRICAL, INTUITION, REFLECTION

Kant refers on three occasions (ID §6; OD p. 199, p. 117; L pp. 592–3) to an 'extreme ambiguity' in the concept of abstraction which 'must preferably be wiped clean away beforehand lest it mar our investigation into things intellectual' (ID §6). He distinguishes between 'abstracting something from' (*abstrahere aliquid*) and 'abstracting from something' (*abstrahere ab aliquo*) (L p. 592). He maintains that 'an intellectual concept abstracts from everything sensitive, but is *not abstracted* from things which are sensitive, and perhaps it would more rightly be called *abstracting* rather than *abstract*' (ID §6). A chemist abstracts in the former sense when isolating a liquid from matter whereas the philosopher 'abstracts from that which he, in a certain use of the concept, does not wish to take into consideration' (OD p. 199, p. 117). Kant illustrates philosophical abstraction with the example of colour: 'With a scarlet cloth, for example, if I think only of the red colour, then I abstract from the cloth' (L p. 592); he does not abstract a quality 'red' from the cloth, but considers it in abstraction from the cloth.

Although the issue of abstraction was at first peripheral to critical philosophy, it became a major issue in its defence against empiricist objections. Kant uses it to distinguish his account of the origin of concepts from inductive arguments such as those of Eberhardt (see OD). Kant distinguishes between two senses of abstraction: (i) as an inductive account of the genesis of concepts from experience; (ii) as a specification of the use of concepts. In making this distinction Kant recognizes his debt to medieval philosophy: 'The neglect of this scholastic distinction often falsifies the judgement concerning the object' (OD p. 199, p. 117), although his proximate source seems to have been the debate between Locke and Leibniz.

The ambiguity Kant mentions first appears in Aristotle's two contrasting discussions of abstraction in the *Posterior Analytics* and *On the Soul*. Both are critiques of Plato's separation of ideas from matter, but with quite different points of emphasis. The first is an inductive account of the origins of ideas in sense perception (Aristotle, 1941, 81b, 1–9) while the second relies on the imaginative work of the active intellect (431b, 13–21) in separating the ideas from their material instantiation.

Aquinas, in commenting upon Aristotle's passage, anticipates Kant's distinction between the abstraction from particulars in search of a genus (genus from species) and the inductive abstraction of a genus from individual things (Aquinas, 1951, p. 451; see also Aquinas, 1952, I 85, 1). However, he notes that Aristotle's elliptical characterization of the first sense of abstraction in terms of 'the mind which is actively thinking is the objects which it thinks' (Aristotle, 1941, 431b, 18) ultimately raises a metaphysical aporia respecting the status of these neither ideal nor material abstractions. For the species or qualities present to the mind and from which it abstracts are themselves already the product of a primary abstraction.

The subsequent history of the concept of abstraction is characterized by various attempts to clarify the ambiguity between its transcendental and inductive senses, reaching its high point in Suarez's influential *Metaphysical Disputations* of 1597 (Suarez, 1976). However, in the seventeenth century, first with Hobbes and subsequently Locke, the inductive account of the genesis of concepts prevailed. Locke defines abstraction as the process 'whereby ideas taken from particular beings become general representatives of all of the same kind' (1690, p. 74). Leibniz criticized this view in the *New Essays on Human Understanding*, pursuing the transcendental sense of abstraction as involving 'an ascent from species to genera rather than from individuals to species' (Leibniz, 1765, p. 289).

Kant follows Leibniz in refusing to see abstraction as providing an account of the inductive origins of concepts or intuitions. Space and time are certainly abstracted from experience, but not in the sense of being derived from it; they are considered as far as possible in abstraction, or

40

apart from, experience (CPR A 78). Similarly, while formal logic abstracts from all content of knowledge, it is not itself abstracted from it (A 131/ B 170). Kant illustrates this use of abstraction with the example of the concept of body. Qualities such as size, colour, hardness and liquidity are not abstracted from bodies, although the concept of body may be considered in abstraction from them (L p. 593). With respect to concept formation, abstraction is only the 'negative condition', performing the regulative function of establishing the limits of a concept prior to the work of the constitutive 'positive conditions' of comparison and reflection (L p. 592).

In NM and A Kant further describes abstraction as the negation of attention, or the considered separation of one sense impression from all the others, which he illustrates by the example of 'shutting our eyes to the shortcomings of others' (A §3). This sense is crucial in the CJ where aesthetic judgement must abstract from both the concept and the matter of an aesthetic object. This is not to suggest that such objects are, or should be, without conceptual and material content, but that such content must be disregarded, or abstracted from, when making an aesthetic judgement.

Empiricist critiques of Kant have largely resorted to restatements of an inductive account of abstraction, regarding it as a source of concept formation. Kant's immediate successors responded to these criticisms by emphasizing the transcendental character of abstraction. This led to the further confusion of abstraction and analysis, one still evident in Paton's commentary (1936, p. 250). Yet Kant is careful to distinguish between abstraction and analysis: abstraction separates a single quality from a composite whole, whereas analysis distinguishes between all present qualities. While analysis is crucial to Kant's account of concept formation, abstraction plays a minor role.

In Fichte's development of the critical philosophy during the 1790s, abstraction is elevated to 'an absolute power' even 'reason itself': 'the same power which Kant made the object of his investigation in the *Critique of Pure Reason*' (Fichte, 1794, p. 216). It is abstraction which eliminates all objects of consciousness leaving only the *Ich* – which determines and is determined by itself – and the *Nicht Ich*. Here abstraction becomes the 'firm point of distinction between object and subject' and the locus for the derivation of the concepts of the theoretical and practical science of knowledge.

Hegel criticized Fichte's elevation of abstraction to the centre of philosophy on two grounds. Abstraction is the work of natural consciousness, as opposed to the concrete thought of philosophical consciousness. Ordinary abstract representations such as 'man, house, animal' 'retain out of all the functions of the notion only that of universality, they leave particularity and individuality out of account' (Hegel, 1830, p. 295; see also p. 180).

Fichte's account of abstraction mirrors this unphilosophical vanquishing of particularity and individuality in favour of abstract universals. Hegel describes the political consequences of such abstraction in the discussion of revolutionary terror in the *Phenomenology of Spirit* where the 'ultimate abstraction' can only negate the concrete in the 'fury of destruction' (Hegel, 1807, pp. 359–62). Abstraction for Hegel is but the negative moment of thinking and cannot be allowed to dominate the formation of concepts.

Kant's sensitivity to the received 'ambiguity' of abstraction was largely lost upon his successors, who used the concept as a means of combining inductive and transcendental arguments. An interesting exception is Marx, who rigorously distinguishes the two senses of abstraction. In the *Contribution to the Critique of Political Economy* he criticizes political economy for converting inductive abstractions such as 'production in general', 'population' and 'labour' into transcendental and thus transhistorical categories. Following Kant and the scholastic tradition, Marx restricts the use of abstractions to revealing specific differences through comparison with 'common specific qualities', in his case those between different social formations and the specific qualities they appear to have in common (Marx, 1859, pp. 190–1, 206–10).

The part played by abstraction in late-nineteenth and early-twentieth century inductive and psychologistic accounts of concept formation has led to its being discredited. Husserl consistently associates abstraction with induction, and distinguishes it from the 'phenomenological reduction' (Husserl, 1913, pp. 81, 141–2; 1948, p. 345), even though the reduction closely approximates Kant's non-inductive definition of abstraction.

accident [*symbebekos, accidens, Akzidens*] *see also* ANALOGIES OF EXPERIENCE, ESSENCE, HYPOTYPOSIS, 'I THINK', SCHEMATISM, SUBJECT

Accident is classically defined in opposition to substance, and features in late scholastic and Cartesian logic as one of five 'universal ideas' alongside genus, species, difference and property. Since Aristotle the term has combined logical and ontological senses: an accident is both that which may be predicated of a subject and which cannot exist without a subject. It is the inverse of substance or that which 'is neither predicable of a subject nor present in a subject' (Aristotle, 1941, 2a, 12). Following Aristotle, Aquinas defines an accident as that which has its 'being in another' (Aquinas, 1975, I, 63, 3), adding that 'a substance does not depend on an accident, although an accident depends on a substance' (ibid., I, 23, 7). Accidents can happen to a substance, although they are not necessary for its definition or existence. Descartes refines this point, using the example of a triangle to distinguish between the five 'universal ideas': a figure bounded by three lines forms the genus of triangle; some are differentiated from

42

others by possession of a right angle, which distinguishes them as a species; these right angles possess the property that the sum of the squares of the sides is equal to the square of the hypotenuse. Finally, some triangles are moved and others remain still; movement, however, is an accident and in no way essential to the definition of triangle (Descartes, 1644, p. 26; see also Arnauld, 1662, p. 58).

Leibniz largely followed Descartes but clarified the temporal character of substance and accident: 'An entity is either in itself [*per se*] or accidental [*per accidens*]; or, a term is either necessary or mutable. Thus, "man" is an entity in itself, but "learned man" or "king" are accidental entities. For that which is called "a man" cannot cease to be a man except by annihilation; but someone can begin or cease to be a king, or learned, though he himself remains the same' (Leibniz, 1966, p. 47). Substance is thus re-defined as that which can endure over time, while accidents are those qualities which can change over time without annihilating substance.

Hobbes, Locke and Hume tended to downplay the distinction of substance and accident. Locke notes: 'They who first ran into the notion of *accidents*, as a sort of real beings that needed something to inhere in, were forced to find out the word *substance* to support them' (Locke, 1690, p. 86). Hume is even less charitable: 'the same habit, which makes us infer a connexion betwixt cause and effect, makes us here infer a dependance of every quality on the unknown substance' (Hume, 1739, p. 222). But just as Kant sought to rescue the category of causality from Hume's scepticism, so too does he defend the relational category of substance and accident, but in its Leibnizian form as a mode of temporality.

Kant's discussion of substance and accidents has several interesting features: *substantia et accidens* comprises the first of the categories of relation (CPR A 80/B 106), but is 'assigned a place among the categories of relation . . . rather as the condition of relations than as itself containing a relation' (A 187/B 230). As Mellin observed, this makes the category 'the ground of all the others' (Mellin, 1797, Vol. 1, p. 49). Kant also observes that the distinction of accidents and substance has, 'in all ages', been recognized by 'not only philosophers, but even the common understanding' as 'lying at the basis of experience', and that 'while the need of it is felt', 'it has never itself been proved' (CPR, A 184–5/B 227–8).

Kant does not conclude from the absence of a proof that he should follow Hume and jettison accidents and substance, but that the form of proof itself should be reconsidered (P §46). Kant's insight into the futility of seeking the ground of relation in another relation leads him to challenge the equivocation between the logical and ontological aspects of accidents and substance. Substance cannot be considered as if it were the subject of a judgement or proposition, nor accidents as if they were simply

43

predicates. It is impossible to attain the ultimate subject – i.e., substance – by discursive means, since discursive thought tends to an infinite regress in which each subject is revealed as but the predicate of another subject. Kant concludes: 'we must not hold anything at which we can arrive to be an ultimate subject, and that substance itself never can be thought by our understanding, however deep we may penetrate, even if all nature were unveiled to us' (P §46). Least of all – and this is the lesson of the paralogisms – may we follow the Cartesians and consider the thinking subject, or the I of the *cogito*, as an absolute subject or substance.

Yet there is a need for a proof of accidents/substance, one which may only be satisfied by an analogical argument to the principle of permanence/alteration. Instead of considering substance as subject, as a 'thing in itself' to which accidents may be predicated, it is necessary to prove that the analogous principle of permanence and alteration forms a necessary condition for experience. This proof is presented in the first analogy of experience in the CPR.

With the argument by analogy Kant both preserves the traditional relation of accident and substance while translating it into the modern principle of permanence and alteration. In the translation, accident and substance are freed from their dependence on logical predication and considered in ontological terms of existence and time. Kant argues that alteration – the co-existence and succession of appearances – is dependent on permanence in a manner analogous to the dependence of accidents on substance. That is, alteration cannot be experienced, measured or represented without permanence.

Kant is not saying, as some analytical commentators maintain, that permanence in time itself becomes substance; rather that it stands in an analogous relation to alteration as substance to accidents. It is the 'abiding correlate' of alteration; it may be thought without alterable things, but they cannot be thought without it. The relation of permanence and alteration is analogous to that of substance and accidents: '*substance* remains . . . only the *accidents* change' (CPR A 184/B 227); 'an accident [is] simply the way in which the existence of a substance is positively determined' (A 187/B 230). It is what Kant called in the *Critique of Judgement* (1790) 'hypotyposis' or 'indirect presentation' (CJ §59). There he directly cites Locke and the example of substance and accident in order to illustrate the distinction of symbol and schema and the uses of analogical reasoning (§59). In this case accident and substance offer a symbol of a relation, while permanence and alteration provide its schema.

Since the understanding can only think substance and accidents under the category of relation, it artificially separates them from each other rather than seeing them as inextricable and mutually dependent. Analogously, the understanding separates permanence and alteration, seeing existents as undergoing alteration in time, rather than discerning the inextricability of permanence and alteration. Yet precisely this dependence is the ground for logical relation and thus for all categorical synthesis, and offers 'the criterion, consequently, of the substantiality of appearances' (CPR A 189/ B 232).

Kant's use of analogical reasoning was not fully recognized by his successors: most critics and commentators have either taken his account of substance and accidents literally, or ignored it altogether. In the *Science of Knowledge* Fichte criticizes Kant for not explaining the relation between substance and its accidents (Fichte, 1794, p. 23), and proceeds to do so by converting substance into the subject or 'positing I' (ibid., p. 185). Schopenhauer claims a specious Kantian legitimation for his identification of substance with matter, and accidents with modes of action or matter in motion (Schopenhauer, 1813, p. 119). Nietzsche, later in the nineteenth century, criticizes Kant for colluding in the traditional elision of the logical subject with ontological substance and thus converting appearances into mere manifestations of an unknowable substance (see Nietzsche, 1901, §§484–5). Recent work has led to a renewed understanding of analogical forms of argument (see Derrida, 1987, pp. 75–6) and has opened the way for a more subtle appreciation of Kant's strategic use of such classical terms as accident and substance.

acquisition [*Erwerbung*] *see also* DEDUCTION, INNATE IDEAS, QUAESTIO QUID JURIS, PROPERTY, RIGHT

This term, translated from Roman private law, undergoes a peculiar metamorphosis in Kant's philosophy. He translates the juridical discussion of the ways in which rights in things and over persons may be acquired – discussed in the section of MM on 'Private Right' (especially §10) – into a framework for analysing the acquisition and justification of theoretical and practical concepts. The critical philosophy is cast as a critical 'tribunal which will assure to reason its lawful claims, and dismiss all groundless pretensions' (CPR A xii), one which will establish an '*inventory* of all our possessions through *pure* reason' (A xx).

In ID Kant distinguishes his view of the acquisition of concepts from that of the empiricist tradition, stating that '*each of the concepts has,* without any doubt, *been acquired,* not, indeed, by abstraction from the sensing of objects (for sensation gives the matter and not the form of human cognition), but from the very action of the mind, which coordinates what is sensed by it, doing so in accordance with permanent laws' (ID §15). This passage focuses equally upon the *origins* of concepts through the coordinating activity of the mind and the *justification* of their possession according to 'permanent laws'. In the 'Transcendental Deduction' of CPR, on the whole, it is the latter approach – justifying the possession of concepts – which predominates in the guise of the deduction of the pure concepts of the understanding.

In CPR Kant refers to the juridical distinction between the question of right (*quid juris*) and the question of fact (*quid facti*). The statement of the 'legal claim' to the possession of a concept – its deduction – is complicated by critical philosophy's injunction against any appeal either to experience or to reason. There can be no appeal to the origins of a concept; in other words, to its original mode – legitimate or otherwise – of acquisition. However, in the face of criticisms concerning the origin of concepts, Kant in the 1790s admits consideration of the acquisition of concepts into the deduction or their justification.

This is most clearly apparent in OD where Kant denies innate or divinely implanted ideas in favour of regarding all representations as acquired. These include the forms of intuition and the pure categories of the understanding which are acquired in an act of 'original acquisition (as the teachers of natural right formulate it) . . . of that which previously did not exist, and therefore did not pertain to anything before the act' (OD p. 221, p. 135). This act of original acquisition, which distinguishes Kant's view of the origins of concepts from empiricist and rationalist accounts, bases the act of acquisition upon 'a ground in the subject which makes it possible for these representations to originate in this and no other manner'. He specifies this ground by distinguishing between forms of acquisition: intuitions are original acquisitions, whose ground is receptivity; while the concepts of the understanding are original acquisitions whose ground is 'the spontaneity of thought (in accordance with the unity of apperception)' (OD p. 223, p. 136). Particular concepts however are 'derived acquisitions' and presuppose the two former original acquisitions.

Kant deliberately exploits the 'analogy between the juridical relation of human actions and the mechanical relation of moving forces' (P §58), and uses, in Schopenhauer's words, 'Latin legal expressions . . . for interpreting the most secret stirrings of the human heart.' (1841, p. 105). For Nietzsche this represented an anthropomorphic projection of human legal relations onto nature. More radically, Rose has argued that Kant's framing of nature and human action in terms of Roman law marks the 'fusion of Roman dominium, absolute property, with modern subjective rights' in a usurpatory notion of freedom (Rose, 1984, chapter 1).

acroamata/ic (something heard) *see also* CONSTRUCTION, PRINCIPLE
Although Kant only explicitly distinguishes between acroams and axioms in L, the distinction is implied throughout his theoretical philosophy.

Both are basic principles (*Grundsätze*), but axioms are exhibited in intuition while acroams are presented discursively (L p. 606). The reason for the distinction between the two sorts of basic principle is to be found in Kant's polemics against Wolff's extension of mathematical forms of proof to philosophy. In PE Kant distinguishes between the 'unanalysable principles' of mathematics and philosophy, regarding the former (axioms) as figural, the latter (acroams) as discursive. As opposed to mathematical axioms, philosophical principles 'are never anything other than words' (PE Part I, §2).

In CPR the distinction between axioms and discursive principles is no longer immediately linguistic, but hangs on the condition of the temporal determination of experience. The acroams are the 12 principles of pure understanding (axioms of intuition, anticipations of perception, analogies of experience, postulates of empirical thought). These principles are not axiomatic, but discursive; they receive their authority through a discursive process of legitimation or proof. This proof is performed through the re-working of traditional philosophical terms, such as, in the case of the first analogy, those of 'substance and accident'. The acroams are open to constant discursive challenge, and are legitimated through language and the analysis of language. Kant's insight into the linguistic character of philosophical principles was largely lost until the twentieth century and the emergence of interpretations informed by hermeneutic and analytical philosophies of language (see, e.g., Bennett, 1966, 1974; Gadamer, 1960; Heidegger, 1929; Strawson, 1966).

action [*ergon/poiesis/praxis, opere/factio/actio, Handlung*] *see also* ACTUALITY, AUTONOMY, CAUSALITY, FREEDOM, LEGISLATION, SPONTANEITY, WILL
Kant's account of *Handlung* was heir to a tradition of discussion in the theory of action that originated in Aristotle and was shaped by the introduction of Christian moral perspectives. His work was informed by the equivocations of this tradition, especially with regard to the distinction between the various kinds of action, the problem of intention and the distinction between moral and political action.

For Aristotle the generic term for action was *ergon* (activity) from which he derived *energeia* (Aristotle, 1941, 1050a). When the latter was disclosed in 'things made' (*poieton*), its mode was poetic (*poiesis*); when disclosed in 'actions done' (*prakton*), its mode was practical (*praxis*). Aristotle rigorously distinguishes between *poiesis* and *praxis*: the former directs itself to the world according to rules of art (*techne*), while the latter directs itself to the life of the *polis* according to *phronesis* (Aristotle, 1941, 1140a; see Riedel, 1975, pp. 99–101). The former is technical, producing according to rules; the latter is deliberative and discursive. *Praxis* furthermore directs itself to the good of both individual and the *polis*; there is little trace in Aristotle of the later distinction between moral and political action.

The Christian reception of Aristotle in the thirteenth century considerably reworked his account of action, introducing new distinctions while blurring others. *Praxis* or *actio* no longer balances the good of the individual and the *polis* through *phronesis*; instead the relation between moral, legal and political goods becomes undefined and the subject of uneasy debate. Equally significant is the collapse of the distinction between *poiesis* and *praxis*, evident in Aquinas's translation of *praxis* as *factio*. 'Actions done' are increasingly thought of in terms of 'things made' or the movement through which a thing is produced. In the words of Aquinas's technical definition, 'action implies nothing more than order of origin, in so far as action proceeds from some cause or principle to what is from that principle' (Aquinas, 1952, I, 41, 1).

Action is thought of in terms of *techne*, as originating in a cause or a principle, rather than in a process of deliberation (*phronesis*). The consequences of this shift become evident in the problems Aquinas encounters with the temporality of action: instead of the coexistence of cause, action and effect in the moment of deliberation, action must now take place after the presence of the cause, but before the presence of the effect (Aquinas, 1952, I, 42, 2). This introduces two hiatuses into the account of action (between cause and action and action and effect), which in turn underpin the scholastic distinction between internal and external action. The theory of action is subsequently dominated by a three-stage account which moves from (i) the source of an act in an agent's motivation or intention, to (ii) its production or manifestation, and arrives at (iii) its effects or consequences.

This tradition proved extremely resilient. It survived Machiavelli's scission of political and ethical motivation, which merely drew the anti-Christian consequences of the Christian separation of ethics and politics. It also survived Luther's equally threatening separation of intention from manifestation in his rejection of justification by works, let alone his use of the distinction between motivation and external actions to support justification by faith. However, as is evident from the tortuous dialectic of Luther's *Freedom of a Christian* (1520), the pressures exerted by and upon this model of action led to extraordinary feats of imaginative practical reasoning, not only at the casuistic level of everyday conduct (Weber, 1904–5), but also in the more elevated reaches of philosophy and theology.

Kant's theory of action is the most enduring monument to the effort to maintain the Christian/Aristotelian synthesis in the face of the pressures released by protestant modernity. In conformity with the received elision of *poiesis* and *praxis*, action for Kant is fundamental to both theoretical and practical reason (O'Neill, 1989). Actions are produced according to rules which are themselves governed by higher laws of indeterminate origin. The understanding in theoretical reason acts through judgements which apply rules whose ultimate necessity rests in inscrutable higher laws. In practical reason, actions are produced by the will operating according to a subjective maxim which is in its turn policed by a higher law.

The core of Kant's theory of action is to be found not so much in his accounts of practical reasoning (CPrR, GMM) as in the 'Second Analogy' of the CPR. This concerns 'the coming into being or passing away of substance' (B 233) or, as in the title of the 1781 edition (CPR A), the 'principle of production'. Here Kant seeks a solution to the temporal hiatuses attendant upon the differentiation between cause, action and effect. He maintains first of all that cause and effect are ordered temporally – effect follows cause – even if there is no lapse of time between them (A 203/B 248). In this way order or relation defines action: 'Action signifies the relation of the subject of causality to its effect' (A 205/B 250). But in addition to this relation which exists between the subject of causality and its effect, action is also described as the 'self-revelation of substance' through 'activity and force' (*Tätigkeit und Kraft*) (A 204/B 249). In this view of action as the 'first ground of all change of appearances' (A 205/ B 250), the source of action in the self-revelation of substance is not itself ordered according to cause and effect.

The question then shifts to the character of the substance which reveals itself through action. The cause of action cannot itself be subject to action, but must freely and unconditionally initiate it. It is outside the relation of cause, action and effect, outside the succession and co-existence of appearances through which it reveals itself. Kant thus juxtaposes two accounts of action: one relates the 'subject of causality to its effect' while the other, the self-revelation of substance, acts spontaneously to produce the order of cause–action–effect. The separation of what may be described as the executive and the legislative aspects of human action is a consequence of thinking action in terms of the production of effects from causal principles. It contrasts with the inseparability of these aspects in the moment of *phronesis* which combines legislative and executive aspects of action.

The distinction between spontaneous, legislative action – autonomy – and action subjected to causality – heteronomy – is ubiquitous in Kant's practical philosophy. Here action is seen as determined either directly through the will's [*Willkür*] heteronomous inclination towards objects (sensible impulses) as articulated in its maxims, or indirectly by the reason's scrutiny (through the will – [*Wille*]) of such maxims for their conformity to the form of the supreme law – the fitness of the maxim to be a universal law. Because the maxims governing human action are prone to 'external' influence, reason's scrutiny can only be experienced as a command or prohibition. The will 'acts' legislatively when it commands or prohibits the choice of a particular maxim, while *Willkür* produces action according to maxims which combine the causality of the will and causality of objects. This dual aspect theory of action informs the further distinction of legal and moral action. In the former the action itself agrees with the law, whereas in the latter not only the action but also the agent's maxim is in agreement.

With this account Kant sought to avoid the implications of both the 'rationalist' accounts of action associated with the school of Christian Wolff and the 'empiricist' accounts of Shaftesbury, Hutcheson and Hume. The former considered the perception of a rational perfection to be a sufficient motivation for action, while the latter emphasized sensible motives for action. Kant's theory combines both forms of motivation while giving them a Rousseauesque accent in the distinction between an inscrutable legislative will and the acts of concrete particular wills.

Kant's theory of action set the agenda for subsequent developments in this branch of philosophy. Many philosophers, such as the late-nineteenth-century neo-Kantians and contemporary philosophers such as John Rawls, have continued to work within a Kantian framework. Others have chosen to emphasize one aspect of his account: Fichte, for example, stressed the absolute autonomy of human action, while the positivist sociology developed by Auguste Comte underlined its heteronomy by emphasizing the element of 'social determination'. Some theorists of action have looked elsewhere in Kant for an alternative theory of action, notably two of Heidegger's students, Arendt (1958, 1989) and Gadamer (1960), who read his account of common sense and reflective judgement in CJ as a modern restatement of classical *phronesis*.

Other theorists of action have fundamentally challenged the Kantian account of action while remaining indebted to it as a critical point of departure. The first was Hegel, who challenged Kant's oppositions between autonomy–heteronomy, morality–legality with a phenomenological attempt to 'think the absolute' as *Sittlichkeit* or 'ethical life'. Some idea of the fecundity of Hegel's work on action and the diverse responses it has provoked may be gained by a comparison of contemporary writers such as Derrida (1974), Rose (1981) and Taylor (1975).

Another influential critic of Kant's theory of action was Nietzsche, who exposed its anthropocentric character and its presumption that the acting subject must be in possession of a fixed 'human' identity. This critique has inspired anti-humanist theories of action which detach the theory of action from the problems of the acting subject and its motivation. In this tradition action is not seen as issuing from a unified subject, nor is it motivated by desire articulated in maxims and dedicated to the production of actions. Philosophers working within this extremely diverse tradition (often inaccurately described as 'post-structuralist' or 'postmodern'), which draws upon Marx, Freud and Heidegger, include Deleuze and Guattari (1972), Levinas (1961) and Lyotard (1983).

actuality [*energeia, actus, Wirklichkeit*] *see also* ACTION, BEING, EXISTENCE, POS-SIBILITY, POSTULATES OF EMPIRICAL THOUGHT, PRINCIPLES

Kant's use of the term actuality in the second postulate of empirical thought may be clarified by means of a comparison with the Aristotelian term *energeia*, which meant both action and actuality. The latter term usually referred to *energeia* in conjunction with *dynamis*, a term equivocally translated as either possibility or potentiality. *Energeia* meant the putting into action of *dynamis*, but without the requirement that *dynamis* be thought either ontologically or epistemologically prior to *energeia*. To make such a claim would entail subordinating both terms to the categorical determinations of being. This is unacceptable because *energeia* and *dynamis* are pre-categorical; indeed, for Aristotle they even give rise to the categories of quantity, quality, condition and location (Aristotle, 1941, 201a, 10). For this reason the relation between them cannot be stated categorically, but only analogically (see Aristotle, 1941, 1048a and 1065b).

Even though Kant situates the principle of actuality categorically, in terms of the second modal category of existence/non-existence, it still bears many of the features of Aristotle's initial statement, but as overdetermined by the Christian tradition. Aristotle's argument for the eternity of matter and the world posed obvious difficulties for the Christian doctrine of creation *ex nihilo* (see 'The Condemnation of 1277' in Hyman and Walsh, 1984). A solution favoured by the scholastics was to subordinate the cosmological exposition of actuality (which had its origins in Aristotle's attempts to explain change – *kinesis* – in the *Physics*) to an onto-theological one. God, in Aquinas, is thus self-actualizing and without potential, while the world receives both its potentiality and actuality from God as its creator (Aquinas, 1975, Book 1, chapter 16). In this way actuality becomes imbricated with the problem of the existence of God and the world; existence, or the making actual of a possible world, is treated as a predicate. For Kant this tradition of thought was exemplified by the philosophy of Christian Wolff, who included existence within the rational definition of a possible being.

Kant consistently opposed this position throughout his career; it stimulated the development of many of his characteristic positions, such as the doctrine of intuition. In OPA he made the celebrated claim against Wolff that 'existence cannot itself be a predicate' (p. 74, p. 120) and argued that the actual and the possible were generically distinguished. To add the predicate 'existence' as a complement to a possible being does not suffice to make it actual. At this stage in his argument Kant develops a subtle distinction between the existence posited 'in' a possible being and that posited 'through' it (p. 75, p. 121). However, in CPR's 'Postulates of Empirical Thought' Kant fundamentally recasts the traditional opposition of possibility and actuality in terms of what is logically possible and what actually conforms to the forms of intuition.

The postulates lay down the conditions for the empirical use of the modal concepts of possibility, actuality and necessity. The second postulate defines the actual as 'bound up with the material conditions of experience, that is, with sensation' (CPR A 218/B 265). However, actuality is not secured by mere, unarticulated sensation, but through a 'sensation of which we are conscious' or perception. Perception itself though is governed by the analogies of experience, so actuality involves conformity with the rules governing a possible experience. But as in Aristotle, actuality does not simply supplement a possibility with existence, but may precede it. It may actualize a possible concept, but it can also be manifest in a perception for which a concept is lacking. Thus while Kant introduces actuality as the principle of a discrete category, it quickly becomes apparent that it also underlies all forms of categorical judgement; for such judgements actualize concepts by determining them according to the conditions of existence in time.

Two features of Kant's discussion of actuality were important for subsequent philosophers. First, it did not simply mean 'reality' or sensation, but perception in accord with the analogies of permanence, succession and co-existence. Second, it was both a categorical principle and the condition for categorical synthesis. Thus in Fichte, there are two actualities: one is the original productive activity of the 'I' while the other is the result of the understanding distinguishing between it and possibility (Fichte, 1794, pp. 206–8). Hegel overcomes this distinction by describing actuality as both the absolute and its formally separated moments. In the *Logic* he presents a phenomenological analysis of the journey of actuality from its beginnings in being as activity through its reflections in the categories of essence and appearance (actuality opposed to possibility as outside to inside) to the 'absolute relation' of the absolute and its reflection. (Hegel, 1812, pp. 529–71; 1830, pp. 257–67).

During the nineteenth century actuality was increasingly confused with 'reality'; Hegel's dictum that the 'rational is actual, and the actual rational' (1821, p. 20) was an early casualty. Marx in his critique of Hegel reduces rational to ideal and actual to real, thus erasing the dynamic character of actuality. Kant's two senses of actuality were recovered in the twentieth century by Husserl, who distinguished between dormant and focal actualities: dormant actualities are perceived as present in the field of intuition, but are not 'singled out'; they form a zone for the emergence of focal actualities (Husserl, 1913, 105–7). In terms of his later thought, they form a life world, actual but unthematized, out of which may be drawn focal objects and relations.

The implication in Kant and Husserl that actuality was marked by 'presence' – by the bringing to presence or being present of things – was criticized by Heidegger in *Being and Time*. He contrasts actuality as the bringing to presence of possibility with the actualization of the possibility of death. The former 'annihilates the possibility of the possible by making it available to us' (Heidegger, 1927, p. 305); while the latter is actualized in a possibility 'as far as possible from anything actual' which is the 'possibility of authentic existence' (ibid., p. 307). With these comments Heidegger begins a re-description of the relation between actuality and action which originally informed Aristotle's conception of *energeia*.

aesthetic *see also* ART, BEAUTY, CULTURE, INTUITION, REFLECTIVE JUDGEMENT, SPACE, TASTE, TIME

Kant, consistent with eighteenth-century German usage, gives the term 'aesthetic' two distinct meanings. It refers to both the 'science of a priori sensibility' and the 'critique of taste' or philosophy of art. The first usage prevails in the 'Transcendental Aesthetic' of CPR, the second in the 'Critique of Aesthetic Judgement' – the first part of CJ.

As Kant himself notes in a footnote (CPR A 21/B 35), the two distinct meanings of the term were established by the Wolffian philosopher A.G. Baumgarten. In his *Reflections on Poetry* (1735) and later in his *Aesthetica* (1750–8), Baumgarten revived the Greek term '*aisthesis*' in order to remedy problems in the areas of sensibility and art which had become apparent with Wolff's system. Wolff's rationalism had reduced sensibility to the 'confused perception of a rational perfection' and had left no place for the philosophical treatment of art. Baumgarten tried to solve both problems at once by claiming that sensible or aesthetic knowledge had its own dignity and contributed to rational knowledge, and that art exemplified this knowledge by offering a sensible image of perfection.

Although Baumgarten revived the Greek term, his equation of art and sensible knowledge had no classical precedent. Some aspects of Kant's CJ are anticipated by Plato in the *Timaeus* when he relates *aisthesis* to pleasure and pain, but this was no part of Baumgarten or Kant's concern. Indeed, in the first edition of CPR Kant tries to reserve aesthetic for the 'doctrine of sensibility', excluding the philosophy of art (A 21/B 36). It forms the first part of the 'Transcendental Doctrine of Elements' which considers the ways in which objects are 'given' immediately to the human mind in intuitions. Much of the 'doctrine of sensibility', however, is concerned with the 'pure forms' of sensibility considered in abstraction from both concepts and the matter of sensation. Kant argues that there are two such 'pure forms of sensible intuition' which determine what can be intuited and limit the application of concepts in judgement: these are space, or the form of 'outer' sense, and time, the form of 'inner' sense.

In the 'Transcendental Aesthetic' Kant distinguishes his view of sensibility from the views of Leibniz and Wolff. The relation between the sensible and the rational is far more complex than the view that the former is merely a confused version of the latter (CPR A 44/B 61). Time and space are neither confused perceptions of an objective rational order, nor abstractions from empirical experience. For sensible perception in space and time has its own 'origin and content': it is not derived from either empirical sensation or understanding. Its relation to the conceptual framework of the understanding involves principles of judgement which mutually adapt spatio/temporal experience to abstract concepts. For these reasons the aesthetic is a crucial element in any account of knowledge.

In the second edition of CPR (B, 1787) Kant subtly extends the text of his limitation of the domain of aesthetic to include the critique of taste. Three years later he published the CJ, in whose first part 'aesthetic' now unequivocally means the 'critique of taste'. Aesthetic is no longer part of an account of determinant theoretical judgement, but is taken to exemplify another form of judgement – 'reflective judgement'. Determinant judgement possesses its concept and faces the difficulty of applying it properly to the multiplicity of spatio-temporal appearances, while reflective judgement is in search of its concept through this multiplicity. It obeys a peculiar principle – related to the feeling of pleasure and displeasure – which enables it to act as a bridge between the theoretical judgements of the 'faculty of knowing' analyzed in the first and the practical judgements of the 'faculty of desire' analyzed in the second critique.

The 'Critique of Aesthetic Judgement' in CJ is divided into an 'analytic' and a 'dialectic', with the analytic considering judgements of the beautiful and the sublime. In the 'Analytic of the Beautiful' Kant analyzes the various forms of the 'aesthetic judgement of taste' and the conditions which make valid the judgement 'this is beautiful'. The exposition of these judgements follows the analytic structure of the first critique by first classifying them according to their quantity, quality, relation and modality and then justifying their validity with a deduction.

The 'Analytic' proceeds by contrasting the account of aesthetic judgements proposed by the German aesthetic philosophy of art with that offered in the theory of taste developed by the British philosophers Shaftesbury,

Hutcheson, Hume and Burke. The quality of a judgement of taste concerns neither the interest in the agreeable (taste) nor that in reason (aesthetic); it is a judgement that pleases 'apart from any interest' (CJ §5). With respect to quantity, the judgement is universally valid; it pleases universally, but with reference neither to the sum of individual feelings (taste) nor to an objective good (aesthetic). In a judgement that something is beautiful, the subject is neither charmed by the object (taste) nor instructed by its perfection; the relation of such a judgement involves 'the form of finality in an object . . . apart from the representation of an end' (§17). Finally, the modality of a judgement of taste holds that something beautiful is necessarily so; it is an object of necessary delight, but not because it is 'in possession of a definite objective principle' (§20) nor because it rests on an individual sense of necessity.

In the 'Analytic' the positive characteristics of aesthetic are left relatively open, as is also the case in the 'Analytic of the Sublime' and the 'Dialectic of Aesthetic Judgement'. The 'Analytic of the Sublime', apart from distinguishing between the pleasures of exceeding judgement in the dynamic and mathematical sublimes, also offers a deduction of aesthetic judgement, an analysis of genius and a typology of the arts. The 'Dialectic' reviews the neither/nor structure of the 'Analytic of the Beautiful' through the 'antinomy of taste' in which it appears that aesthetic judgements are both based and not based on concepts. Kant's aesthetic ends with extremely suggestive comments on symbolization (hypotyposis) and cultural politics.

The impact of the third critique rests as much on its extraordinary ambition to bridge the realms of theoretical necessity and practical freedom as on the open character of its achievement. The principle of reflective judgement remains undetermined, although it clearly involves pleasure, the enhancement of life, communication through common sense and tradition, and hints of a supersensible harmony. These elements recur throughout the text in varying combinations; they are evident in the analytic of aesthetic judgement, in the various deductions and in the account of genius. The import of these themes, their location in what was widely perceived as the 'crowning phase' of the critical philosophy, and their indeterminacy, made Kant's aesthetic philosophy of art extremely fertile.

Kant's critics from Schiller (1793) and Hegel (1835) to Derrida (1978) and Lyotard (1988) are agreed that his use of the the table of judgements to describe aesthetic experience was ill-advised. Aesthetic experience cannot be contained within a logical framework borrowed from theoretical philosophy. This dissatisfaction was almost immediately apparent in the emergence of new forms of philosophical and para-philosophical writing in the field of aesthetics. These ranged from Schiller's edifying letters on aesthetic education, to Novalis and Friedrich Schlegel's fragments, to Kleist's

55

short stories, Jean Paul's ironic manual for beginners in aesthetics, and to Schelling and Hegel's historical narratives. Kant's aesthetics placed the problem of presentation high on the philosophical agenda, where it has remained, at least in the European tradition of philosophy.

Kant's vision of a reconciliation of freedom and necessity in the third critique motivated some of the most powerful and influential writings of German Idealism. Schiller and Schelling's philosophies of art drew aesthetic solutions to the split between nature and human freedom, which were mobilized in the cultural policies of modernizing restoration monarchies such as Prussia. Art and beauty were considered to be the highest sources of meaning, reconciling humanity with themselves and with nature. Withdrawing from similar early enthusiasms, Hegel extended reflective judgement into a speculative logic which eventually exceeded aesthetics with its proclamation of the death of art. For him the configurations of art were inadequate for the presentation of the absolute (see Hegel, 1835).

The implications of Hegel's reservations about art and aesthetics were not realized until the twentieth century, least of all by the eternal Schillerian Marx. Almost half a century after Hegel, the young Nietzsche came out of his studies of the third critique with a programme for cultural renewal in which 'we have our highest dignity in our significance as works of art' (1872, p. 52). He later inverted the significance of this phrase, moving from the Schillerian view of art as the highest source of meaning to regarding art as the highest source of meaninglessness.

Readings of Kant's aesthetic in the twentieth century have been largely dystopic, emphasizing the open character of his text and the ways in which it fails to deliver the promised reconciliation of freedom and necessity. Theodor Adorno pointed to the ecological and political implications of confining the reconciliation of freedom and necessity to art (Adorno, 1970) while Hannah Arendt stressed the communicative aspect of aesthetic reflective judgement in drawing pragmatic political consequences far removed from a programme of reconciling freedom and necessity (Arendt, 1989) . A similar return to Kant's CJ in search of an account of indeterminate judgement amid the ruins of the failed synthetic ambition has also characterized recent work by Lyotard (1991) and Derrida (1978) on CJ, while Caygill (1989) and Welsch (1987, 1990) have begun to re-explore the relationship between the two senses of aesthetic as a philosophy of sensibility and as a philosophy of art.

affect [*pathos, affectus, Affekt*] *see also* APPEARANCE, ENTHUSIASM, GEMÜT, IMAGINATION, PASSION, PSYCHOLOGY
The confusion surrounding this term is compounded by Kant's translators who have variously rendered it as 'passion', 'emotion' and 'affection'.

Following Strachey's translation of Freud's term *Affekt* as 'affect' helps to clarify Kant's usage, although the term is intrinsically ambiguous. Its ambiguity was already noted by Augustine in the fifth century. He observed in the *City of God* (426) that 'these agitations of the soul, which the Greeks call *pathê* [are described by] some of our Latin authors, Cicero for example ... as disturbances [*peturbationes*], others as affections [*affectiones*] or affects [*affectus*], or again as passions [*passiones*]' (Augustine, 1972, Book 10, chapter 4). Moreover, Augustine's contrast between the Platonic view that the passions are restrained by reason and the Stoic doctrine of *ataraxia* (freedom from passion) still underestimates the many meanings given to *pathos* in classical Greek philosophy.

Aristotle uses the term *pathos* in at least three complementary but distinct senses. First, it denotes a quality whose cause is not constitutive of the definition of its subject (see Aristotle, 1941, 9b, 28); thus change in quality or 'alteration' is defined in the *Metaphysics* as 'change in respect of an affection [*pathos*]' (Aristotle, 1941, 1069b, 12). A second sense emerges in the *Nicomachean Ethics* where *pathê* are 'the feelings that are accompanied by pleasure and pain' (Aristotle, 1941, 1105b, 23) and are distinguished from faculties and virtues. Third, in *De anima*, pathos is presented as a certain 'mode or movement of the body' (Aristotle, 1941, 403a).

The narrowing of the meaning of *pathos* from quality in general to the specific quality of the soul noted by Augustine persisted until Descartes and Spinoza. Descartes distinguished between *affectio*, which for him is synonymous with Aristotle's first sense of *pathos* as a quality, and *affectus* meaning feeling, emotion or 'passion of the soul'. Spinoza reworks this distinction in the *Ethics*, moving from affection as quality or mode of substance (as in Spinoza, 1985, Part I, proposition 4) to affect as synonymous with emotion (*commotionem, seu affectum*; in Part V, proposition 2). The transition is made in the crucial Part III, entitled 'The Origin and Nature of the Affects', where Spinoza naturalizes emotional affects by converting them into affections or qualities of nature (see Wolfson, 1962, Vol. 2, pp. 193–5).

Spinoza's reasoned overcoming of the Cartesian distinction between affect and affection is followed by Kant, who relates the two terms through the power of imagination, a solution by no means free of ambiguity. He presents affect as a concept of empirical psychology, but assumes throughout that it is the result of a human subject being affected by objects and ideas. Similarly, the epistemological discussion of affection in CPR assumes it to involve not only quality in general, as in Aristotle's first sense, but also a movement of the *Gemüt*; in other words, an emotional affect.

Kant discusses the empirical psychology of affect most extensively in A §§73–8; CF Part II, §6; MM §XVII; CJ §29. In each case affect is allied with passion (*Leidenschaft*) in so far as both 'exclude the sovereignty of reason' (A §73) and 'belong to sensibility' (MM p. 407, p. 208) as 'motions' of the *Gemüt*. Affect differs from passion in being unreflective; it is an 'intoxicant' while passion is reflective and brooding, an 'illness' (A §73). Affect is 'blind' to choice, whether of ends or means, and is an impulsive movement which makes 'free deliberation' and 'self determination' impossible. (CJ §29).

This characterization of affect recalls Aristotle's third sense of pathos as a movement of the body, but Kant extends it to include the second sense as well. For affect is not simply movement as such, but a movement which overcomes an obstacle 'like water that breaks through a dam' (A §74). This allies it with the feeling of pleasure and pain, and leads Kant to make a crucial distinction between two kinds of affect. In A the distinction is couched in terms borrowed from *Elementa medicina* (1780) by the Scottish physician John Brown (1735–88). Affects are either 'sthenic' – 'exciting and frequently exhausting' – or 'asthenic' – sedative and relaxing. Both are pleasurable in that they 'liberate from whatever curbs vitality' (A §76), but this pleasure may take different forms. This is apparent in CJ where Kant distinguishes between 'strenuous' and 'languid affects'; the former are characterized as sublime, and excite the 'consciousness of overcoming every resistance', while the latter are beautiful in that they neutralize the feeling of resistance (CJ §29).

The condemnation of affect is qualified in Kant's discussion of 'enthusiasm' – the 'affective participation in the good' (CF Part II, §6). This affect can be constitutive, as in the case of the revolution of the French people, yet it cannot wholly be esteemed since 'affects as such deserve censure'. Nevertheless, Kant develops a positive valuation of affect through his distinction between the beautiful and the sublime. If enthusiasm were a beautiful affect, then it would be condemned as 'a momentary glittering appearance which leaves one languid' (MM p. 409, p. 209). If it is regarded as a sublime affect, then it becomes formative, a movement of the *Gemüt* which 'leaves behind [it] a temper of mind [*Gemütsstimmung*] which, though it be only indirect, has an influence upon its consciousness of it own strength and resolution'. The affect of enthusiasm is consequential, but may be endangered by lapsing into either beautiful langour or fanatical passion.

Kant's characterization of affect as a motion of the soul (*Gemütsbewegung*) which combines sensuous and ideal aspects while evoking pleasure and pain identifies it as the expression of the power of imagination (*Einbildungskraft*). It is through this power that Kant relates affect to affection, or the mode or qualification of imagination central to CPR.

The discussion of affection in the 'Transcendental Aesthetic' and 'Deduction' of CPR has features which Kant himself describes as paradoxical.

Affection is the mode in which an appearance affects the *Gemüt*, a proposition which escapes tautology only if it is admitted that the forms of intuition which constitute appearances are 'the mode in which the mind [*Gemüt*] is affected through its own activity . . . and so is affected by itself' (CPR B 67). By so relating affection as a quality to the affects of the *Gemüt*, Kant raises 'problems' and 'difficulties' which he tackles in the second deduction in the course of what has become known as the problem of 'double-affection'.

The problem involves the relation between the empirical psychology of affect and the affection of apperception, or how the *Gemüt* can come to affect itself. Self-affection seems contradictory since 'we should then have to be in a passive relation [of active affection] to ourselves' (CPR B 153). One answer lies in double-affection, wherein the apperceptive I that thinks is distinguished from the psychological I that intuits. This argument rests on an implied distinction between the affection of the apperceptive I, which qualifies appearances according to the table of categories, and the intuiting I, which is affected both by categories and objects of perception. It is thus a Cartesian reading of this problem which insists on the separation of affection and affect.

Kant's text, with its stress on the role of the power of imagination, seems however to incline toward a non-Cartesian fusion of affect and affection. Imagination disposes itself actively and passively; it produces (CPR B 154) the categories and sensations which affect it. In terms of CJ, imagination is formative, leaving traces of its affects which in turn affect it or become affections or modes of appearing. This interpretation points to a controversial link between the first and third critiques which has been explored in recent French philosophy inspired by the psychoanalytic account of affect. It informs, for example, Lyotard's turn from a Freudian 'libidinal economy' (1974) to a Kantianism which stresses the role of enthusiasm and common sense (1988, 1991).

After Kant the discussions of affect and affection branched into psychology and epistemology. Psychologists largely accepted Kant's alignment of affect with non-conscious activity, although late-nineteenth-century naturalists did not accept his postulate of the soul. Probably the most influential employment of the term in twentieth-century thought was that of Freud, who gave it an important place in his metapsychological account of repression. In post-Kantian epistemology the discussion of affection was largely subordinated to wider problems of the relation of knowing subject and known object, and rehearsed the double-affection problem with philosophers defending one side against the other. However, Kant himself seems to have chosen not to solve the problem, but rather to leave it open as an ineluctable but fertile philosophical difficulty or 'aporia'.

affection *see* AFFECT

affinity [*Affinität, Verwandtschaft*] *see also* APPERCEPTION, ASSOCIATION, DEDUCTION, HETEROGENEITY, IMAGINATION, SYNTHESIS, UNITY

Affinity is an enigmatic concept used by Kant in various contexts to relate otherwise heterogeneous elements. In CPR it serves to relate both sensibility to understanding and understanding to reason. It is central to the 'first deduction' where it forms the 'objective ground of all association of appearances'. From it are derived not only the 'association of appearances' as 'data of the senses', but also their 'reproduction according to laws' and even 'experience itself' (CPR A 123). In the 'Appendix to the Transcendental Dialectic' it appears as a regulative idea or law prescribed by reason to the understanding. Here affinity combines the laws of 'generic homogeneity' and 'specific heterogeneity' in prescribing the continuity between genera and species (CPR A 658–9/B 686–7).

In the 'first deduction', affinity not only relates sensibility and understanding but also appears to possess both objective and subjective characteristics. It is the 'transcendental ground of unity' which secures the objective validity of associations between phenomena such as cause and effect. But while affinity thus establishes 'the possibility of the association of the manifold, so far as it lies in the object' (CPR A 113) it is itself 'nowhere to be found save in the principle of the unity of apperception' (A 122) and is 'only possible' by means of the 'transcendental function of imagination' (A 123). The latter is the work of 'productive imagination' securing the 'necessary unity in the synthesis of what is manifold in appearance' (A 123). With affinity the unity of the manifold created by productive imagination is thus treated as if it lay in the object.

Kant's argument in the 'first deduction' is clarified by some casual comments in A (§31c), which show him working with two senses of affinity, one genealogical, the other productive. In the first, Kant defines affinity as 'the union established by the derivation of the manifold from a single foundation'; in the second – resorting to a chemical analogy – he defines it as an interaction 'which links two elements specifically distinct from each other, but intimately affecting each other, whereby the combination creates a third entity that has properties which can only be brought about by the union of two heterogeneous elements' (§31c). In a suggestive footnote the scope of the analogy is extended from chemical synthesis to sexual reproduction, for both inorganic and organic nature, as much as body and soul, are 'based on separating and uniting the dissimilar'.

With regard to the deduction, affinity may be read genealogically as the 'transcendental ground' for the association of appearances, and productively as the work of imagination in producing experience out of the heterogeneous materials of sensibility and understanding. This reading is explicitly supported by the comment in A that 'Despite their dissimilarity, understanding and sensibility by themselves form a close union for bringing about our cognition, as though one were begotten by the other, or as though both had a common origin' (§31c). Kant admits that the union of genealogical and productive affinities is difficult to analyze, a point echoed throughout the CPR. These admissions have been used in the twentieth century to support 'anti-foundationalist' readings of Kant which emphasize the ongoing work of productive imagination against static views of there being fixed 'transcendental grounds' which serve as foundations for knowledge and action (Deleuze and Guattari, 1984; Heidegger, 1929).

affirmation *see* BEING, NEGATION, NOTHING, REALITY, TRANSCENDENTAL

agreeable [*Angenehm*] *see also* AESTHETIC, AFFECT, BEAUTY, DELIGHT, FEELING, PLEASURE, TASTE
One of a cluster of terms in Kant's aesthetic and practical philosophy, 'agreeable' is used to describe the feeling of pleasure. It appears as a term in an historical opposition which Kant rehearses in order to define his own position. He associates it with the writings of the British 'moral sense' school which he contrasts with the German rational–perfectionist school of Christian Wolff and his followers. In GMM the feeling of the agreeable subjectively 'influences the will only by means of sensation' (GMM p. 413, p. 24) and is opposed to the pure rational determination of the will proposed by the Wolffians. Kant situates himself between the two arguments by developing the concept of an imperative, which has both subjective and objective characteristics.

An analogous form of argument is pursued in CJ §§3–7, where the contrast between the agreeable (i.e., British theory of 'taste') and the good (i.e., German theory of 'aesthetic') is used to highlight Kant's own, third position. The agreeable, the good and the beautiful are all species of the genus 'delight'; each is a 'modification of the feeling of pleasure and displeasure' as well as a relation of a representation to its object (CJ §3). But the delight in the agreeable consists in what the 'senses find pleasing in sensation' (§3) or in the feeling of pleasure evoked by the presence of an object of sensation. Conversely, the good involves the presence of a concept of the understanding. Kant's view of the nature of the delight in the beautiful is defined negatively against this opposition as neither sensible nor rational, requiring the presence of neither object nor concept.

In order fully to exploit the contrast between agreeable and good, Kant exaggerates the unfortunate characteristics of the former. It dispenses

61

with judgement and gratifies desire, and as mere enjoyment it offers a delight 'pathologically conditioned (by stimuli)' (§5). Even worse, it is a significant factor 'even with irrational animals', a 'private feeling', essentially asocial. This form of argument has been taken as an example of the deleterious effects upon philosophical analysis of thinking in terms of dichotomies. Indeed some writers see Kant's procedure as complicit with a series of inherited dichotomous formulations which characterize Western philosophy, dichotomies which, among others, privilege reason over the body, male over female, European over non-European (see Irigaray, 1974 and 1984). However, Kant's procedure may be defended as the discovery of alternative philosophical formulations through the rehearsal of culturally received oppositions (see Caygill, 1989).

agreement/opposition *see* CONCEPTS OF REFLECTION

amphiboly *see also* CONCEPTS OF REFLECTION, SENSIBILITY, UNDERSTANDING
A term drawn from classical rhetoric, amphiboly denotes the ambiguity arising from the equivocal arrangement in a phrase of otherwise unequivocal terms. In Aristotle's *On Sophistical Refutations* it is one of six forms of philosophical fallacy arising from the sophistical misuse of language (Aristotle, 1941, 165b). For Kant the 'amphiboly of the concepts of reflection' occurs when either the empirical use of the understanding is confused with the transcendental, or when a concept of reflection properly applicable to either sensibility or the understanding is improperly applied to the other or to both terms (CPR A 260/B 316ff).

Most of Kant's argument in CPR is directed against the amphibolous use of concepts of reflection such as identity/difference, agreement/opposition, inner/outer, determinable/determination (matter/form) (CPR A 261/B 317). These are the orientational concepts which are employed prior to 'constructing any objective judgement' (A 262/B 317). Kant argues that they themselves must be properly oriented through transcendental reflection: this assigns each use of a concept of reflection to its proper faculty of knowledge. For example, when speaking of identity and difference it is necessary to distinguish between their distinct conceptual and intuitive applications, since the 'conditions of sensible intuition . . . carry with them their own differences' (A 270/B 326). The failure thus to distinguish between the sensible and intelligible fields of application results in a transcendental amphiboly which confounds 'an object of pure understanding with appearance' and generates illegitimate synthetic principles of knowledge.

Kant claims that the philosophies of both Leibniz and Locke were amphibolous. Leibniz applied to sensibility concepts of reflection proper to the understanding, and thus '*intellectualised* appearances' while Locke, in his account of conceptual abstraction, '*sensualised* all concepts of the understanding' (A 271/B 327). Kant steers a difficult course between these two positions, maintaining that concepts proper to sensibility and understanding must be distinguished while seeing knowledge as arising from their legitimate conjunction in properly justified a priori synthetic principles. The entire critical philosophy wagers that such principles exist, are not amphibolous, and respect the differences proper to concept and intuition while yet bringing them into conjunction.

Kant's analysis of amphiboly has received a new currency with respect to late-twentieth-century 'philosophies of difference' elaborated by among others Deleuze (1968), Derrida (1967, 1972) and Irigaray (1984). Critics of this philosophical movement such as Rose (1984) see it as resting upon an amphibolous use of 'difference' which effaces historically founded distinctions between concept and intuition.

analogies of experience *see also* ACCIDENT, ANALOGY, APPEARANCE, CATEGORY, CAUSALITY, PRINCIPLES, RELATION, TIME
The analogies of experience are the group of three principles which serve as rules for the objective employment of the categories of relation. Each group of categories has its corresponding group of principles: those of quantity, the 'axioms of intuition'; quality, the 'anticipations of perception'; and those of modality, the 'postulates of empirical thought'. The general function of the principles is to determine how things must appear to finite beings in time. In the case of the analogies, they must determine how things appear to be *related* in time. Our experience of the ways in which things are related to each other is not directly categorical – we do not experience the relations between things directly in terms of the categories of substance and accident, causality and dependence, and community – but then neither do we experience their relations as simply random coincidences. Appearances in time are related in terms of the three analogies which look both to intuition and to the categories: they 'precede' the empirical cognition of relation and are a 'rule for the objective employment' of the relational categories.

Kant's main discussion of the analogies is in CPR (A 176–218/B 218–65), supplemented by his further thoughts in P. They and the other principles were the outcome of the work of the 'silent decade' of the 1770s, in which Kant tried to reform the scholastic heritage by transforming the categories of ontology received via the Wolffian tradition into those of the transcendental analytic. In place of such eternally valid ontological relations as substance and accident, cause and effect, and community he proposed temporally specific principles of relation. They take the form of temporal analogies to the ontological predicates, analogies which are appropriate to the experience of a finite being who can know only appearances in space and time.

The general principle informing the analogies holds that experience is only possible 'through the representation of a necessary connection of perceptions' (CPR B 218). This requires that the perception of objects in time can be shown to be necessarily related to each other, and indeed that these relations are 'prior to all experience, and indeed make it possible' (A 177/B 219). This is achieved by showing that the relations between appearances are governed by the three 'modes' of time – duration, succession and co-existence. Each mode of time yields a particular rule for relating appearances; together they form the analogies of experience.

The first analogy is the 'principle of the permanence of substance'. The details of Kant's proof are internally inconsistent and vary between the 1781 and 1787 editions, but the general intent is clear. He argues that in order to experience change or co-existence in time it is necessary to postulate a permanence underlying things in time: 'Without the permanent, there is no time relation' (CPR A 183/B 226). However, he argues against the philosophical tradition's claim that the permanent is substance. It is unnecessary to hypostasize permanence as substance; it suffices to point to the principle of permanence as 'the mode in which we represent to ourselves the existence of things in [the field] of appearance' (A 186/B 229). The 'permanance of substance' does not refer to an ontological predicate, but to duration itself, or the way in which 'we' as finite beings represent appearances 'to ourselves' as in time.

The second analogy governs the relation of appearances in time thought under the mode of succession – the principle that 'All alterations take place in conformity with the law of the connection of cause and effect' (B 232). With this principle Kant tackles Hume's objections to the principle of causality by showing the necessity for causal relations. There is no such thing as 'causality' or 'sufficient reason', but there is a particular experience of time – its irreversibility – which requires us to order our experiences in time according to the analogy of cause and effect. Kant's proof for this principle argues that appearances are related to each other as successive, and that this succession is necessary; i.e., that the order of appearances in time cannot be reversed. Kant relates this property of time to the irreversibility of the causal chain, a necessary mode of alteration of appearances in time.

The third analogy governs the co-existence of appearances according to the 'law of reciprocity or community' (A 211/B 256) and corresponds to the temporal mode of co-existence. The relation of appearances in time is here thought in terms of simultaneity: everything that co-exists does so at the same time. Without this principle, Kant argues, experience would not be possible, since we would be unable to relate to each other with certainty the things which appear to occupy the same space and time. This co-existence is not an ontological predicate, existing outside its relata, nor is it a property of appearances; it is rather a condition for experiencing the relation of appearances which are manifest as simultaneous.

In common with the other principles, the analogies are among the most difficult and perplexing features of Kant's philosophy. They are both highly specific to his theoretical philosophy and crucial to his entire critical undertaking. For this reason, while they have not had a wide general philosophical impact they have been the subject of some of the most interesting if opaque works of Kant exegesis. For two contrasting accounts of the analogies see Heidegger, 1935, Guyer, 1987.

analogy [*analogon, proportio, ratio*] *see also* ANALOGIES OF EXPERIENCE, AS—IF, HYPOTYPOSIS, PRESENTATION, REASON, REGULATIVE IDEA, SCHEMATISM
A foundational term of philosophy, 'analogy' has a continuous if underestimated history since Pythagoras. A general theory of analogy was first developed by Eudoxus (?406–?355 BC) in response to the crisis of incommensurable ratios (*logoii*) encountered by the Pythagoreans. The overcoming of this early crisis of Greek reason (*logos*) is codified in the definitions of *logos* and *analogos* in book five of Euclid's *Elements*. These situate analogy in terms of the similarity between the ratios of different magnitudes, as in Definition 6: 'Let magnitudes which have the same ratio be called analogical' (Euclid, Vol. II, p. 114). Euclid makes a clear distinction between an analogy of terms and one of ratios, focusing his attention upon the latter. As a result, his account of analogy stresses the similarity in the relation between the antecedent and consequent terms of at least three ratios, and not any similarity between the terms themselves.

The philosophical implications of analogical similarity were first realized by Aristotle, who shows in the *Topics* how it might be used to relate 'things belonging to different genera, the formulae being "A:B = C:D" (e.g., as knowledge stands to the object of knowledge, so is sensation related to the object of sensation)' (Aristotle, 1941, 108a, 7–8). He proceeds to extend this form of reasoning to metaphysics (1017a), ethics (1096b) and politics (1296b).

The origins of analogy as a supplement to reason also characterized its subsequent development. It was, for example, crucial to Aquinas's philosophical theology, where it redeems the inability of human reason to understand God. While God's participation in creation cannot be grasped by human logos, it may be understood analogically in terms of the relation between human and divine knowledge and action. Kant's writings on the subject of analogy nearly all involve similar theological questions, and may be regarded as philosophical determinations of the forms of reasoning appropriate for thinking about the supersensible.

While Kant does not deny the value of analogical reasoning, he is concerned to confine its use within properly defined limits. Analogical similarity is an important supplement to logical identity, but must not surreptitiously be employed as a substitute for it. In P (§§57–8) and CJ (§59) he contrasts the symbolic/analogical with the schematic/logical judgement. Logical judgements involve the direct presentation of a concept to an object of intuition, while analogical judgements apply 'the mere rule of reflection upon that intuition to quite another object' (CJ §59). This is a classical restriction of the scope of analogy to the relation between terms, and not the terms themselves: for Kant, cognition by analogy 'does not signify (as is commonly understood) an imperfect similarity of two things, but a perfect similarity of relations between two quite dissimilar things' (P §58).

Analogy may be used legitimately to gain 'relational knowledge' but not objective knowledge, and the main object of such relational knowledge is God. It is only legitimate to reason analogically of God in such a way 'as the promotion of the welfare of children (=a) is to the love of parents (=b), so the welfare of the human species (=c) is to that unknown in God (=x), which we call love' if we admit that this argument holds only 'for us, though we have left out everything that could determine it absolutely and in itself' (P §58). In such reasoning we do speak of the object itself, but only of a way in which it might be made comprehensible to us.

Kant develops this thought in RL by dropping the distinction between symbolic and schematic procedures of judgement and regarding both objective and analogical determinations as forms of schematism. While it is permitted in the passage from the sensible to the supersensible 'to *schematize* (that is to render a concept intelligible by the help of an analogy to something sensible), it is on no account permitted us to *infer*' (RL p. 65, p. 59). We cannot infer from the analogy that makes a concept such as God intelligible to us the conclusion that 'this schema must necessarily belong to the object itself as its predicate' (RL p. 65, p. 59). It is legitimate to employ analogy to speak of the supersensible, but not to use it as if it gave us objective knowledge; its use is permitted as an aid to human self-understanding, but not as a source of objective knowledge of such objects as God, the World and the Soul.

Kant also discussed analogy in L, distinguishing between inductive and analogical conclusions to judgements, although his discussion here is largely derivative of Baumgarten. After Kant analogical reasoning seems to have been confined to theology, with a consequent loss of sensitivity on the part of Kant exegesis to the role of argument by analogy in the critical philosophy. There are, however, signs of a renewed sensitivity to the issue in the writings and Kant commentaries of Derrida (1978) and Lyotard (1983). It would appear that a greater appreciation of the role of analogical reasoning in Kant would not only clarify some of the problems of Kant exegesis – notably the 'transcendental object = x' – but would also deepen our understanding of the structure of the 'Kantian argument'.

analysis [*analusis*] *see also* ANALYTIC, MATHEMATICS, METHOD, SYNTHESIS
Kant combines two senses of analysis in his work, one derived from Greek geometry, the other from modern physics and chemistry. Both remain close to the original Greek sense of analysis as a 'loosening up' or 'releasing', but each proceeds in different ways. The former proceeds 'lemmatically' by assuming a proposition to be true and searching for another known truth from which the proposition may be deduced. The latter proceeds by resolving complex wholes into their elements.

Diogenes Laertius mentions that Plato was 'the first to explain to Leodamus of Thasos the method of solving problems by analysis' (1925, Vol. I, p. 299). That this does not refer to the general platonic method of division is stressed by Proclus in his *Commentary on the First Book of Euclid's Elements*, where analysis is presented as a method of investigation by means of lemmas (Proclus, 1970, p. 165). This method of geometrical analysis is most clearly presented by Arnauld in *The Art of Thinking*: geometers faced with a problem to solve grant the truth of the proposition and examine the consequences of this assumption. They conclude that what is assumed is in fact true if during the course of their examination they arrive at some clear truth from which the assumption can be inferred as a necessary consequence (Arnauld, 1662, p. 308). Following the discovery of the 'clear truth', the proof of the proposition may then be reconstructed synthetically.

The specific, geometrical method of analysis ascribed to Plato was paralleled by a more general account originating in Aristotelian physics. In *On Generation and Corruption* Aristotle describes an 'analysis' (which he also ascribes to Plato) which moves from complexes to elements: 'he carries his analysis of the "elements" – solids though they are – back to "planes"' (Aristotle, 1941, 329a, 24). The Aristotelian tradition emphasized this mode of analysis, using it to justify the passage from physics to metaphysics. Aquinas, for example, described 'the ultimate end of analysis' as the 'attainment of the highest and most simple causes, which are the separate substances' or, in other words, 'the consideration of being and the properties of being as being' (Aquinas, 1986, p. 72). Here too, analysis is contrasted with synthesis, analysis proceeding from 'effects to causes', synthesis from 'causes to effects'.

Descartes seems to suggest a combination of the geometrical and the reductive senses of analysis in the 'Reply to the Second Objection'. He wrote: 'Analysis shows the true way by which a thing was methodically discovered [geometric analysis] and derived, as it were effect from cause [physical analysis]' (Descartes, 1968, Vol. II, p. 48). He also suggested that the ancients concealed their method of analysis behind their synthetic presentation in terms of axioms, postulates and definitions. Unlike Aquinas and the scholastic heritage, Descartes saw no smooth transition between analysis of physics and metaphysics. The 'primary notions' of the latter are 'contradicted' by the senses, and so can only be analyzed and not given a synthetic presentation. Descartes comments: 'This is why my writing took the form of Meditations rather than that of Philosophical Disputations or the theorems and problems of a geometer', although he was to prove inconsistent on this point.

Following Descartes the combination of geometrical and physical analysis was taken for granted, although there were further developments. Spinoza in a letter to Heinrich Oldenburg mentions Boyle's chemical analysis of nitre, an experiment destined not only to undermine scholastic doctrines of substance, but also to introduce the metaphor of chemical analysis into philosophy. Newton and Leibniz also broadened the meaning of analysis to include their development of calculus. In the *Mathematical Principles* Newton concealed his analytical 'method of fluxions' behind a synthetic, geometrical presentation while Leibniz attempted openly to extend 'analysis' to include *analysis situs*, a precursor of topology (1976, pp. 254-9).

While all of these changes in the meaning of analysis fed into Kant's use of the term, this was mainly governed by an elision not only of geometrical and physical analysis but also of the methods of discovery and presentation. In the PE Kant distinguishes between mathematics and philosophy in terms of their methods of achieving certainty; mathematics employs a synthetic method, philosophy an analytic method (PE p. 276, p. 248). Philosophy analyzes 'confused or insufficiently determined' concepts, and proceeds through the two stages of, first, clarifying their qualities and then, second, determining the relation of these qualities to each other.

At this stage Kant restricts philosophy to analysis, criticising Wolff's use of the geometrical form of synthetic presentation. While refraining from geometrical presentation, philosophical analysis as a method of discovery follows the lemmatic procedures of geometrical analysis. Kant illustrates the method of analysis with the example of time: 'The idea of time has to be examined in all kinds of relation if its characteristic marks are to be discovered by means of analysis [clarification]: different characteristic marks which have been abstracted have to be combined together to see whether they yield an adequate concept [determination]' (PE p. 277, p. 249). By working through hypothetical examples, qualities and combinations, Kant seeks – like the geometers – to discover the essential elements. To use any other procedure is to rely on the 'fortunate accident' that the given qualities and determinations prove to be the right ones.

Kant clarifies the distinction between geometrical and physical analysis in the ID, aligning philosophical with reductive analysis. Philosophical analysis does not proceed solely from effects to causes, but instead explores the possible parts of a given concept through hypothesis: 'analysis, taken in its first sense, is a regression from *that which is grounded to the ground*, whereas, in its second sense, it is a regression from a *whole to its possible or mediate parts*' (ID §1). Philosophical analysis does not proceed in search of a causal or principial hierarchy, but seeks through experiment and hypothesis to determine elementary qualities and their possible combinations.

The geometrical form of analysis deeply informs the CPR, although its presence has been obscured by Kant's distinction in P between synthetic and analytic forms of presentation. There he describes the CPR as 'executed in the synthetical style' and the P as 'sketched out after an analytical method'. The two modes of presentation indeed move in different directions: one moves from 'principles to consequents, or from the simple to the composite' while the other 'begins with the conditioned and with what is grounded and goes on to principles' (L p. 639). Analysis as 'the method of discovery' follows a different procedure: just as the Greek geometers discovered their proofs by means of analysis but presented them synthetically (OD p. 191, p. 111), so too Kant makes his discoveries through analysis, but presents them in synthetic form.

Consequently, analysis is presented in the CPR as a lemmatic procedure, assuming the forms of judgement and then determining the elements and combinations that make them possible. In the 'Introduction' analysis is accordingly distinguished from 'doctrine' (which would be a form of presentation) and described as a 'transcendental critique', 'a touchstone of the value, or lack of value, of all *a priori* knowledge' (CPR A 12/B 26). The analysis proceeds by hypothesizing possible qualities and combinations in order to see how they correspond to each other.

This analytical procedure is illustrated by the 'B' deduction, which begins with the discovery that 'combination' or the quality of combining concept and intuition is fundamental. Kant then analyzes combination and discovers in it the 'act of a subject' and an extra-categorical unity. Following the discovery of these qualities it becomes necessary to hypothesize determinations, or relations between them, for which Kant follows the 'clue' of the table of judgements. He adds a further, characteristic twist by maintaining that if analysis analyzed itself it would find itself constituted by combination 'since only as having been combined *by the understanding* can anything that allows of analysis be given to the faculty of representation' (CPR B 130).

The term analysis has been widely employed in the twentieth century and often illegitimately projected back upon Kant. Most contemporary usage, to quote Wittgenstein, 'oscillates between natural science and grammar' (Wittgenstein, 1953, §392) and largely overlooks the geometrical method of analysis employed by Kant. But there are similarities between Kant's and modern forms of analysis. Freud, for example, while analogically relating his use of 'analysis' to chemistry is like Kant in pursuit of clarified 'qualities' and their 'determinate relations': 'we point out to the patient these instinctual motives, which are present in his symptoms and of which he has hitherto been unaware – just as a chemist isolates the fundamental substance, the chemical 'element' out of the salt in which it had been combined with other elements' (Laplanche and Pontalis, 1973, p. 368). Wittgenstein's influential programme of 'grammatical investigation' analyzes forms of expression through a process 'like one of taking a thing apart' (Wittgenstein, 1953, §90) although unlike Kant and Freud he is not in search of 'qualities' or analogical 'salts' but is content to state determinate relations. Mathematical analysis, however (i.e., the study of the properties of continuous functions), has little to do with Kant and traces its genealogy to Descartes' geometry and the development of calculus.

analytic *see also* ANALYSIS, DIALECTIC, ONTOLOGY, PRINCIPLES, REASON
Aristotle's work on demonstrative reasoning was known under the titles *Prior* and *Posterior Analytics*, the former analyzing the syllogism, the latter the conditions of demonstrative knowledge. They formed, along with the *Categories, On Interpretation, Topics* and *Sophistical Refutations*, the influential collection of logical treatises known to the tradition as the 'Organon'. They were the subject of intense commentary by Boethius in the sixth century AD and were rediscovered in Northern Europe during the thirteenth century. Their influence was challenged first by the Renaissance humanists, then by Ramus in the sixteenth century. Ramus sought to break the hegemony of the Organon by re-organizing logic on the basis of the rhetorical distinction between the 'invention' of arguments and their 'disposition'.

Ramus's distinction was maintained even during the German Aristotelian revival of the seventeenth and eighteenth centuries. 'Invention' was rephrased in Aristotelian terms as the 'analytic', and 'disposition' as the 'dialectic'; the former was deemed to 'discover' the basic elements of judgement, while the latter presents their use in persuasive but not necessarily valid syllogisms. The extent of the elision of Ramus and Aristotle is evident in Kant's ascription of the distinction between analytic and dialectic

70

to Aristotle himself (L p. 534). Kant went on to adopt this framework as the structure for the contents of the three critiques. The task of critical analytics is to 'discover through analysis all the actions of reason that we perform in thinking' (L p. 531). They uncover in the first critique the 'concepts and principles' of theoretical reason, in the second critique the principles of 'pure practical reason' and, in the third the principles of aesthetic and teleological powers of judgement.

The 'Transcendental Analytic' of the CPR forms the first division of the 'Transcendental Logic'. It resolves 'understanding and reason into its elements' and is a 'canon of judgement' or 'negative touchstone of truth' (CPR A 60/B 85). It precedes the second division of the 'Transcendental Logic' or 'Transcendental Dialectic' which is a 'logic of illusion' or scrutiny of the illegitimate extension of judgement beyond its legitimate objects. The analytic is described as the 'part of transcendental logic which deals with the elements of pure knowledge yielded by the understanding, and the principles without which no object can be thought' (A 62/B 87) and is accordingly divided into an 'analytic of concepts' and an 'analytic of principles'. The former discovers the concepts which compose the totality of pure understanding by means of a deduction, while the latter presents the conditions or 'principles' under which concepts may legitimately be related to 'sensibility in general'. As the presentation of the 'rules for the exposition of appearances', transcendental analytic takes the place of an 'Ontology that presumptuously claims to supply in systematic doctrinal form, synthetic *a priori* knowledge of things in general' (A 247/B 303).

The 'Analytic of Pure Practical Reason' in CPrR also offers an 'analytic' or 'rule of truth' for practical judgements, but here the logical framework sits uncomfortably with the content of moral philosophy. Similarly, the 'analytics' of aesthetic and teleological judgement in CJ contain material which patently exceeds the framework of analytic and dialectic. The insights of Kant's philosophical modernity, in other words, could no longer be contained within the traditional framework of presentation. His successors were uniformly critical of his use of this framework and rejected it; in its place they developed the diversity of presentations characteristic of post-Kantian philosophy. Indeed, the historically specific form of presentation in terms of analytic and dialectic died with Kant, and survives in a philological limbo as something that has to be mastered only in order to understand the three critiques.

analytical judgement *see also* ANALYSIS, JUDGEMENT, RATIONALISM, SYNTHETIC A PRIORI JUDGEMENT

The distinction between analytic and synthetic a priori judgements is central to Kant's theoretical philosophy and developed out of his early critique of

71

the 'rationalist' philosophy of the Wolffian school. In the course of his exposure of this philosophy's shortcomings, Kant elaborated a distinction between analytic and synthetic judgements. The Wolffian philosophers treated all judgements as if they were analytical, whereas, Kant claimed, they were only a specific class of judgement which he contrasted with the distinct class of synthetic judgements. He noted later in P that 'whatever be their origin or their logical form, there is a distinction in judgements, as to their content, according to which they are merely *explicative*, adding nothing to the content of the cognition, or *ampliative*, increasing the given cognition: the former may be called *analytic*, the latter *synthetic*, judgement' (P §2).

The main distinguishing feature of analytic judgements is that their predicates 'belong to the subject . . . as something which is (covertly) contained in this concept' (CPR A 6/B 10). The subjects of analytical judgements 'contain' their predicates, although covertly or 'confusedly'. It follows from this basic characteristic that the act of making an analytic judgement adds 'nothing through the predicate to the concept of the subject, but merely break[s] it up into those constituent concepts that have all along been thought in it, although confusedly' (A 7/B 11). Such a judgement serves 'merely more clearly to represent and assert what is already thought and contained in the given concept' (OD p. 228, p. 141). Through all this work of 'breaking up', 'representing' and 'asserting' the virtual content of a given concept, the analytic judgement is governed by the principle of contradiction: 'For the predicate of an affirmative analytic judgement is already thought in the concept of the subject, of which it cannot be denied without contradiction' (P §2).

Kant's account of the distinction between analytic and synthetic judgements rests on the difference between their content. The predicate of the synthetic judgement adds something to the subject, while the predicate of the analytical judgement simply draws out what is already present in the subject. During the nineteenth century, various candidates emerged as the source for synthetic judgements, including psychological, physiological and sociological factors as well as the abstract considerations of value and validity beloved of the neo-Kantians. Frege in *The Foundations of Arithmetic* revolutionized the question of judgement and undermined Kant's distinction by turning away from the problem of content to that of the 'justification of assertions' (Frege, 1950, §3). This development shifted attention away from the content of judgements, and led to the rejection of Kant's transcendental logic.

This radical move against Kant's distinction between analytic and synthetic judgements was anticipated by Kant's earliest critics, beginning with Eberhard and Maimon, who assumed that the critical philosophy stood or fell with the distinction. However, this distinction emerged from, and was but a formula for, the critique of the Wolffian philosophy; it was a result of the critical philosophy and not its fundamental assumption.

Anthropology from a Pragmatic Point of View Published in 1798, Kant's manuscript was derived from notes for a series of lectures on anthropology he had given since the autumn semester of 1772–3. These in their turn had developed out of the series of lectures on physical geography which Kant had delivered since 1756. In a note to his introduction, Kant refers to his having lectured twice a year 'for some thirty years' to an audience comprised of students and the general public on 'knowledge of the world', namely anthropology and physical geography. Although Kant states that his manuscript for the physical geography lectures was illegible to anyone but himself, a text edited by Friedrich Theodor Rink was published in 1802, and may profitably be read alongside A. The text of A published according to Kant's manuscript in 1798 is known as the 'A edition' while the version published in 1800 and incorporating minor revisions and stylistic changes is known as the 'B edition'. Most modern editions and translations tend to follow the 'B edition', sometimes incorporating material drawn from the 'A edition'.

In his introduction Kant defines anthropology as a 'systematic doctrine containing our knowledge of man' and suggests this knowledge may be given a physiological or a pragmatic perspective. The former involves knowledge of the things of the world, or man as an object of and in nature; the latter is knowledge of man as a 'freely acting being' or 'as a citizen of the world'. Kant's anthropology pursues the pragmatic perspective, and divides its material according to 'Anthropological Didactic' and 'Anthropological Characterisation'. The former is described as the 'art of knowing the interior as well as the exterior of man' and is subdivided into three books: (i) 'On the Cognitive Faculty'; (ii) 'On the Feeling of Pleasure and Displeasure'; (iii) 'On the Faculty of Desire'. These books, which shadow the organization of the three critiques, offer several distinctive perspectives on cognition, pleasure and morality which both augment and occasionally undermine the critical accounts of the same phenomena. By contrast, 'Anthropological Characterisation' is dedicated to knowing 'a man's interior from his exterior' and consists in the anecdotal reflections on such salient characteristics of the human species as personality, sex, nationality and race.

Kant's anthropology has been the subject of increasing attention, especially in the anti-foundationalist readings of his work (see Heidegger, 1929). Anti-foundationalist readings stress the historical and political features of Kant's work over the strictly logical ones, which were the focus of earlier

73

interpretations. The homology between the 'Anthropological Didactic' and the three critiques has led some scholars to explicate the latter by means of the former. A notable example is provided by Heidegger, whose account of the work of imagination in CPR is supported by reference to A. For him, the lectures on anthropology, predating CPR by at least a decade, 'provide us with information concerning the already-laid ground for metaphysics' (Heidegger, 1929, p. 88) which may be used to interpret later, critical doctrines.

anticipations of perception [*Antizipationen der Wahrnehmung*] *see also* ANALOGIES OF EXPERIENCE, AXIOMS OF INTUITION, POSTULATES OF EMPIRICAL THOUGHT, PRINCIPLES, REALITY

Anticipations of perception are the principles corresponding to the categories of quality. Along with the axioms of intuition, corresponding to the categories of quantity, they form the two sets of 'mathematical principles' which are complemented by the 'dynamic principles' of the analogies of experience (corresponding to the categories of relation) and the postulates of empirical thought (corresponding to the categories of modality). Overall the principles determine how appearances will manifest themselves to the sensible intuition of a finite being without the capacity for direct categorical intuition. The anticipations of perception specifically determine the quality of appearances for such a being, namely their reality, negation and limitation in space and time.

Kant claims that the quality of appearances requires that they possess an 'intensive magnitude': 'In all appearances, the real that is an object of sensation has intensive magnitude, that is, a degree' (CPR B 207). In the A edition of CPR Kant specifies this principle as 'anticipating all perceptions' and describes the 'real' as that which corresponds to sensation in the object. Both editions agree that the real that corresponds to the object of sensation possesses an intensive magnitude: it is impossible for us to perceive appearances unless they possess this intensive magnitude.

Kant uses the term 'anticipation' to translate Epicurus's term *prolepsis*, which designates a preconception that allows perception to take place. Kant regards the understanding as 'ascribing a degree to all that is real in appearances' (CPR A 175/B 217), distinguishing between the accidental qualities of an empirical act of sensation – 'colour, taste, etc.' – and the anticipation that every sensation will possess a degree of reality. This is the only quality which may be assumed a priori, and is the basis for the subsequent assignment of any empirical qualities. Kant illustrates the point with the examples of the empirical qualities of colour, heat and gravity (A 169/B 211). It is a condition for perceiving each of these qualities that it should possess a degree of reality, however infinitesimally small this may become. In the case of colour, when red approaches the point of zero reality it remains red; but when it attains to degree zero reality it ceases to be the quality red, since this quality has no meaning unless it can be anticipated to possess some degree of reality.

Sensation then possesses a degree of reality, and as such has magnitude. But this is not the extensive magnitude of the axioms of intuition which is born of the 'successive synthesis' of the imagination in space and time, but an instantaneous synthesis 'generated in the act of apprehension' (CPR A167/B 209). It *anticipates* sensation and its intuitive, spatio-temporal synthesis.

Without this anticipation, the possibility might be entertained of perceiving objects which were not real, perceptions which Kant considered to be unavailable to a finite being. Indeed, for Kant, perceiving the absence of reality by means of sensible intuition was a contradiction in terms. An object of sensible intuition must possess a degree of reality, for without such it cannot be an object of sensible intuition. In other words, and in conformity with the 'general principle' of the four groups of principles, a condition of experience is also a condition for an object of experience.

The anticipations can be interpreted as the most fundamental of the principles. They chart the 'givenness' of the real prior even to the forms of intuition, for in the words of P, under the anticipations 'sensation is not an intuition that *contains* either space or time, though it posits [*setzt*] the object corresponding to sensation in both space and time' (P §24). Kant himself found the idea of a pre-intuitive positing perplexing: it 'must always appear somewhat strange to anyone trained in transcendental reflection' (CPR A 175/B 217). However, the analysis of this positing was pursued systematically by Fichte, who proceeded to establish the science of knowledge on a primal act of positing. It was also considered by the phenomenological school, who through the eidetic reduction sought to describe the givenness of phenomena (see Husserl, 1913, and the phenomenological exegesis of the anticipations in Heidegger, 1935, pp. 206–24).

antinomy of pure reason *see also* CAUSALITY, COSMOLOGY, DIALECTIC, FREEDOM, IDEAL, INFERENCE, NATURE, PARALOGISMS, UNCONDITIONED
Antinomy is a rhetorical form of presentation cited by Quintilian (35–100) in his *Institutio oratoria* of 92–5 (Book VIII, chapter 7) in which opposed arguments are presented side-by-side with each other. The form was widely used in seventeenth-century jurisprudence (as in Eckolt's *De Antinomiis* of 1660) to point to differences between laws arising from clashes between legal jurisdictions. Kant uses the form in the 'dialectic' of each of the three critiques as a key part of his analysis of 'dialectical assertions'. The form is well suited to this purpose since it can show reason making

opposed and yet equally justifiable inferences. Kant claims that such inferences point to an illegitimate extension of finite human reason beyond its proper jurisdiction.

Kant considered the antinomy as a 'decisive experiment, which must necessarily expose any error lying hidden in the assumptions of reason' (P §52b). He regarded the discovery of the theoretical antinomy of the cosmological ideas to be, along with Hume's scepticism, one of the shocks that awoke him from the dogmatic slumbers of speculative philosophy (P §50). In the CPR the form of antinomy is used in the second of the three major divisions of the 'Transcendental Dialectic'. Here Kant shows how the three disciplines and objects of traditional metaphysics, exemplified by Wolff (1719), rest on dialectical inferences. 'The Paralogisms of Pure Reason' show this to be the case for the science of psychology and its object the human soul; 'The Antinomy of Pure Reason' for cosmology and its object the world; 'The Ideal of Pure Reason' for theology and God.

The 'Antinomy of Pure Reason' forms one of the largest single sections of the CPR. In it Kant presents four sets of dialectical inferences about the nature of the world which correspond to the four groups of categories. The mathematical categories of quantity and quality and the dynamic categories of relation and modality yield the mathematical and dynamic antinomies. Each antinomy formally presents opposed arguments on the nature of the world taken from the history of philosophy; Kant even goes on to refer to them in juridical terms as opposed 'parties'. The presentation of the antinomy consists of two supposedly opposed and yet equally convincing arguments placed side-by-side on opposite pages (not on the same page as in the Kemp Smith translation of 1929) as proofs of thesis and antithesis.

The first, or quantitative antinomy, is concerned with the limits of the world. It opposes to the thesis that the 'world has a beginning in time, and is also limited as regards space' (CPR A 426/B 454) the antithetical claim that the world 'has no beginning, and no limits in space; it is infinite as regards both time and space' (A 427/B 455). The second, or qualitative, antinomy presents opposed claims respecting the constitution or quality of the world. The thesis argues that 'nothing anywhere exists save the simple or what is composed of the simple' (A 434/B 462) while the antithesis claims 'there nowhere exists in the world anything simple' (A 435/B 463). The third or relational antinomy considers the nature of the causal relation in the world, with the thesis that causality is in accordance with both the laws of nature and freedom opposed by the antithesis that 'There is no freedom; everything in the world takes place solely in accordance with laws of nature' (A 445/B 473). Finally, the modal antinomy opposes to the thesis that 'There belongs to the world, either as its part or as its cause, a being that is absolutely necessary' (A 452/B 480) the antithesis that 'An absolutely necessary being nowhere exists in the world, nor does it exist outside the world as its cause' (A 453/B 481).

Kant does not present the opposed arguments in order to prove one superior over the other, but rather to show that both are dialectical. Proceeding from spatio-temporal experience they claim to offer insight into 'absolute completeness' of the composition and division 'of the given whole of all appearances' as well as absolute completeness in 'the origination of an appearance' as well as '*Dependence* of *Existence* of the alterable in appearance' (CPR A 415/B 443). It is the search for 'absolute completeness' on the basis of spatially and temporally limited experience that leads reason into the antinomies. Kant considers it 'unavoidable' and 'natural' for reason to do so, but by presenting the antinomy hopes both to shake reason from 'the slumber of *fictitious* conviction' while not casting it into 'sceptical despair' – the '*euthanasia* of pure reason' – or leading it to the 'death of sound philosophy' in the dogmatic attachment to a single position (A 407/B 434). The 'solutions' to the antinomies, developed at great length and subtlety, consist in showing how they arise from reason's failure to comprehend its own limits; that is, its mistaking appearances for things in themselves. The solutions are thus carried out on the basis of the results of the analytic, which limited legitimate knowledge to the bounds of human experience.

Kant also uses the antinomic form in the 'Dialectics' of the second and third critiques to present opposed positions drawn from the history of ethics and aesthetics. The practical antinomy consists in the opposed claims that 'the desire for happiness must be the motive to maxims of virtue' and 'the maxim of virtue must be the efficient cause of happiness' (CPrR p. 115, p. 119). Both claims are then shown to be insupportable. For the solution to this antinomy, Kant refers back to the third theoretical antinomy of freedom and natural causation, and distinguishes between freedom in the noumenal and natural causality in the sensible world.

In the third critique the antinomy of aesthetic judgement opposes the claim that the 'judgement of taste is not based on concepts' to its antithesis that 'the judgement of taste is based on concepts'. The antinomy follows from the opposition between the British theory of taste and German perfectionist aesthetics which informs the entire critique of aesthetic judgement. Kant's solution broadly suggests that both claims assume a narrow definition of the 'concept', and that they may be compatible if the 'concept' in question is defined as an indeterminate one. The solution is then taken controversially to point to a 'supersensible ground' informing both subject and object, a suggestion which was to prove significant for the development of German idealism.

In the second part of CJ on teleological judgement, Kant describes an antinomy of reflective judgement. Here the antinomy consists in the opposed maxims of reflection: the thesis reads 'All production of material things and their forms must be estimated as possible on mere mechanical laws'; the antithesis is that 'Some products of material nature cannot be estimated as possible on mere mechanical laws' (§70). Kant converts these maxims of reflective judgement into constitutive principles of determinant judgement in order to show that it is only in the latter case that they form a true antinomy. For reflective judgement, the solution to the 'antinomy' is that the opposed maxims 'do not contain any contradiction at all'; they are complementary maxims for the exercise of reflective judgement.

The antinomies after Kant were reincarnated in the bizarre form of the schematic 'Marxist' dialectic of thesis–antithesis–synthesis. This schema arose from a misunderstanding of Hegel's claim in the *Encyclopaedia Logic* that 'the antinomies are not confined to the four special objects taken from Cosmology: they appear in all objects of every kind, in all conceptions, notions and Ideas' (Hegel, 1830, §48). Hegel wished to extend the anti-dogmatic import of Kant's statement of the antinomies from cosmology to all areas of thought; however, it ironically became a new schematic dogmatism. The anti-dogmatic character of antinomy was revived in Lukács's analysis of German idealism in *History and Class Consciousness* (1922). In the section entitled 'The Antinomies of Bourgeois Thought' he points to the 'reified structure of consciousness' which concentrates on the products of human activity to the exclusion of that activity itself. Following Lukács, the antinomic form of argument was further developed by 'Western Marxist' philosophers, notably T.W. Adorno.

apodeictic judgements or propositions *see also* ACTUALITY, CATEGORIES, CERTAINTY, CONSCIOUSNESS, HOLDING-TO-BE-TRUE, JUDGEMENT, KNOWLEDGE, NECESSITY Apodeictic judgements and propositions are those 'which are bound up with the consciousness of their necessity' (CPR B 41). They are contrasted with problematic and assertoric judgements, all three of which correspond to the modal categories of possibility (problematic), actuality (assertoric) and necessity (apodeictic). Each is characterized by a distinctive mode of subjective assent to, or 'consciousness of', the truth claim or 'holding-to-be-true' (*Fürwahrhalten*) of a judgement. This consciousness is either necessary, assertoric or problematic: the first assents to the certainty of a judgement, the second to its uncertain but subjectively sufficient status, the third to its uncertain and objectively insufficient status. Certainty is the holding-to-be-true characteristic of universal and objective knowledge; it yields apodeictically certain knowledge. Subjectively sufficient uncertainty is believed to be true, and yields assertoric belief, while insufficient uncertainty is problematically held to be true, and yields only opinion.

appearance [*Erscheinung*] *see also* ACTUALITY, EXPERIENCE, FORM, IDEAL, ILLUSION, MATTER, NOUMENON, PHENOMENON, SENSIBILITY, TRUTH

In CPR and P Kant refines the traditional philosophical account of appearance by distinguishing between appearance, phenomenon and illusion. He insists on these distinctions in order to redeem appearance from the obloquy it suffered at the hands of the philosophical tradition: it is not simply illusion – the deceptive semblance of sensible perception – but rather experience within the limits of human intuitions of space and time. However, Kant did maintain a qualified version of the ancient distinction between appearance and truth – between phenomena and noumena – along with its correlates of becoming and being, the sensible and the ideal, matter and form. For this compromise Kant was subsequently criticized, most vehemently by Nietzsche, for being inconsistent and retreating from his insights into the ineluctability of appearances.

In ID Kant is still working within a traditional opposition of appearance and reality. Appearance is an object of sensible knowledge and is opposed to the intellectual or rational knowledge of the intellect. The objects of each branch of knowledge, Kant comments neutrally, were called 'in the schools of the ancients' (ID §3) phenomenon and noumenon. Furthermore, appearance (here indistinguishable from phenomena) is unequivocally opposed to truth, and identified with the matter of sensation as opposed to the form of the intelligence: 'things which are thought sensitively are representations of things *as they appear*, while things which are intellectual are representations of things *as they are*' (ID §4). In spite of such unequivocal statements, even in this text Kant is already undermining this opposition, and by the CPR he has gone a considerable distance towards rejecting it.

In CPR appearance is itself divided into matter and form: its matter is what in it 'corresponds to sensation', while its form is that 'which so determines the manifold of appearance that it allows of being ordered in certain relations' (CPR A 20/B 34). The form which orders sensation, Kant claims, cannot itself be sensation, from which he infers that it is an a priori form of intuition. He discovers two such a priori forms of appearance in space and time. He will show that we cannot have legitimate knowledge outside these forms of intuition, and consequently that we can only properly know appearances in space and time. Appearances then are not potentially deceptive sensible impressions, but possess their own order and organization. However, this order by itself may be further articulated by a priori concepts of the understanding or 'categories'. Appearances

79

which are thus 'synthesized' become phenomena: 'Appearances, so far as they are thought as objects according to the unity of the categories, are called *phaenomena*' (CPR A 249). Thus phenomena are appearances which have been organized within the unifying framework of the categories.

The transition from appearances to phenomena is the occasion for some of the most involved and intricate argument in CPR. The complexity is largely due to Kant's reluctance to fall back into the traditional opposition of truth and appearance which still characterized his position in ID. While we can only have knowledge of appearances, our knowledge is not exclusively drawn from appearances. The understanding organizes appearances in space and time according to a priori concepts whose origin does not lie in the realm of appearances but which have no meaning if they are applied outside it: 'since that which is not appearance cannot be an object of experience, the understanding can never transcend those limits of sensibility within which alone objects can be given to us. Its principles are merely rules for the exposition of appearances . . .' (CPR A 246/B 303).

Appearances then are not arbitrary sense impressions indistinguishable from illusion (*Schein*). Quite the contrary, for illusion consists in taking appearances as if they were objects in themselves: 'in the relation of the given object to the subject, such properties depend upon the mode of intuition of the subject, this object as *appearance* is to be distinguished from itself as object *in itself*' (CPR B 69). For appearance, Kant specifies in a footnote, is 'That which, while inseparable from the representation of the object, is not to be met with in the object in itself, but always in relation to the subject' (B 70). A judgement made without limiting itself to this relation to the subject gives rise to illusion.

Kant's distinction between appearance and illusion in terms of the relation to the subject carries with it the further implication of a relation to the 'object in itself'. This implication has led to much controversy, since by admitting it Kant seems to restore a distinction between appearance and truth. Many critics, from Nietzsche to Strawson, can follow Kant to the bounds of sense, but quail at his tendency to point beyond them to an object or thing in itself. How indeed can he accept a relation to the object in itself since he consistently insists that such objects cannot be known: 'What objects may be in themselves, and apart from all this receptivity of our sensibility, remains completely unknown to us' (CPR A 42/B 59). If it is unknown, indeed unknowable, why does Kant insist upon deriving appearances not only from their relation to a subject, but also to an object?

Kant emphasizes one or the other of the particular relations to subject or object according to the position he is criticizing. When distinguishing his account of appearance and sensible intuition from Leibniz and Wolff he strenuously underplays the relation of appearance to the object in itself: 'It is not that by our sensibility we cannot know the nature of things in themselves in any save a confused fashion; we do not apprehend them in any fashion whatsoever' (CPR A 44/B 62). Conversely, when he is arguing against empiricism or scepticism, he stresses the case for appearances being grounded in a 'transcendental object' even if this is unknowable: 'Neither the *transcendental object* which underlies outer appearances nor that which underlies inner intuition, is in itself either matter or a thinking being, but a ground (to us unknown) of the appearances which supply to us the empirical concept of the former as well as of the latter mode of existence' (CPR A 380).

Kant seems to adopt an undogmatic and experimental approach to the issue of appearances. While insisting that they are neither simply illusory nor true, he nevertheless refuses to commit himself to an exclusively subjective or objective account of them. He uses his understanding of appearance to criticize the one-sided and opposed positions on the issue bequeathed to him by the philosophical tradition. Unfortunately many of his successors returned to an insistence on the exclusive character of one position over the other, even reading these back into Kant as his 'true' position. Thus Fichte insisted on the exclusive relation of appearances to the subject, while Schelling insisted on their relation to the object: both claimed justification for their positions from Kant. Following them, Hegel (1807, 1812) chose to thematize the opposition and make the subjective and objective relations moments of a dialectic.

apperception *see also* COMBINATION, CONSCIOUSNESS, DEDUCTION, IDENTITY, 'I THINK', KNOWLEDGE, PARALOGISM, PSYCHOLOGY, SPONTANEITY, SUBJECT, SYNTHESIS, TRANSCENDENTAL

Apperception is a term coined by Leibniz in the *New Essays* (1765) from the French *s'apercevoir de* – to be aware of – which had been used by Locke's translator Pierre Coste to translate 'perceive' (Leibniz, 1976, p. 553). He used it in the *Monadology* (written 1714, published 1720) to criticize the Cartesian *cogito* for taking no account of unconscious perceptions, or 'perceptions that are not apperceived' (1720, §14). He defines perception as 'The transitory state which enfolds and represents a multiplicity in a unity' (§14) or, from the 1714 text of *The Principles of Nature and Grace*, as 'the inner state of the monad representing external things' (1976, p. 637). Apperception 'is consciousness or reflective knowledge of this inner state itself and which is not given to all souls or to any souls all of the time' (p. 637). The concept played a central role in Kant's theoretical philosophy, and is one of the reasons why he was able to describe the CPR as 'the genuine apology for Leibniz' against 'his partisans' (OD p. 250, p. 160).

Kant adopted Leibniz's distinction between perception and apperception, roughly mapping it onto that between intuition and the understanding. But he considerably extended the function of apperception, in many
respects adapting it to the Cartesian *cogito* to which it was originally a
critical response. Leibnizian apperception proper features in CPR as 'empirical apperception' or the 'inner sense' which is 'Consciousness of self
according to the determinations of our state in inner perception' (CPR A
107). Empirical apperception, as with the Leibnizian version, is episodic
and 'in itself diverse and without relation to the identity of the subject'
(CPR B 133). As such it forms a minor part of psychology, while its partner
'transcendental apperception' is one of the cornerstones of the critical
philosophy, of particular significance for the deduction of the a priori
universality and necessity of the categories.

As early as 1762 Kant referred to the 'mysterious power' which 'makes
judging possible' as 'nothing other than the faculty of inner sense, that is
to say, the faculty of making one's own representations the objects of
one's thought' (FS p. 60, p. 104). In CPR the 'mysterious power' is revealed as 'transcendental apperception'. The combination of concept and
intuition in knowledge requires a unity which is not conceptual, 'which
precedes a priori all concepts of combination' (CPR B 130). The unity
which enables judgements to be made has to be sought 'yet higher' 'in
that which itself contains the ground of the unity of diverse concepts in
judgement, and therefore of the possibility of the understanding, even as
regards its logical employment' (B 131). It is found in transcendental
apperception or 'the highest principle in the whole sphere of human
knowledge' (B 135).

Kant approached transcendental apperception from two directions: (i)
by distinguishing it from intuition; (ii) by showing that it is disposed
according to the categories of the understanding. Intuition is the 'representation which can be given prior to all thought' but is meaningless
without 'a necessary relation to the "I think" in the same subject in which
[its] manifold is found' (CPR B 132). For this intuition to be my intuition,
it must be related to an apperceptive 'I think'. The 'I think' itself however
'is an act of spontaneity' which does not originate in or belong to sensibility. It is the product of a 'pure' or 'originary' apperception, namely
'that self-consciousness which, while generating the representation '*I
think*' . . . cannot itself be accompanied by any further representation'
(B 132). The 'I think' of transcendental apperception allows intuitions to
be considered as proper objects of knowledge; it is also the condition for
their synthesis by the understanding.

The 'I think' of transcendental apperception permits intuitions to
belong to a subject and to be bought before it for combination through

judgement. Thus it makes, in the words of FS, 'one's own representations into objects of one's thoughts' (FS p. 60, p. 104), but can only do so according to the categories or functions of judgement. These themselves originate in transcendental apperception, indeed the understanding 'can produce *a priori* unity of apperception solely by means of the categories, and only by such and so many' (CPR B 145). Transcendental apperception permits intuitions to belong to a subject, and is distributed according to the categories; it is also the ground for the unity of concepts and intuitions in judgement.

The account of apperception proved crucial for the development of German idealism. The emphasis on self-consciousness was transformed into Fichte's subjective idealism in which subjective self-consciousness was the basis for the derivation of the intuitions, concepts and ideas in the *Science of Knowledge* (1794). However, in Kant, apperception served only as the ground for combination in judgement: it allowed intuitions to belong to the subject and was the source of the a priori concepts of the understanding while also providing the ground for their combination in judgement. It could not itself be further determined, although Kant was extremely careful to distinguish it from any form of intellectual intuition.

apprehension *see* SYNTHESIS

archetype (*archetypon, Urbild*) *see also* FAITH, IDEA, IDEAL, IMITATION
The archetype for Kant is to the ectype as original is to copy, or as the possible holistic understanding of an *intellectus archetypus* to a 'discursive understanding that has need of images (*intellectus ectypus*)' (CJ §77). Underlying these distinctions is a critical engagement with Platonism. In CPR Kant criticized Plato's 'mystical deduction' of the 'ideas' which hypostatized them by making them into the 'archetypes of the things themselves' (CPR A 313/B 370). Kant claims that Plato's 'flight from the ectypal mode of reflecting upon the physical world-order to the architectonic ordering of it according to ends, that is, according to ideas' (CPR A 318/B 375) makes 'regulative principles' for the systematic completion of knowledge into constitutive principles of the origin of things. Kant's critique of Plato's practical philosophy follows similar lines, by arguing for an idea of the good which would serve as a regulative principle for 'any judgement as to moral worth' but which would not itself be an archetype. Yet this principle can serve as an archetype when it serves as an ideal for imitation. In CPR Kant describes the wise man of the stoics as just such an archetype which serves 'for the complete determination of the copy; and we have no other standard for our actions than the conduct of this divine man within us, with which we compare and judge ourselves, and so reform ourselves,

although we can never attain to the perfection thereby prescribed' (CPR A 569/B 597). In RL the stoic archetype has been replaced by Christ as the 'archetype of humanity well-pleasing to God' (p. 119, p. 109) which it is our duty to imitate. This understanding of the archetype as an ideal for imitation also appears in Kant's aesthetics in CJ. There he uses the opposition of arche- and ectype as a means of distinguishing between sculpture and painting: the 'fundamental basis' of both is the aesthetic idea as 'archetype' and its mode of expression or ectype, whether in the 'bodily extension' of sculpture or in its 'appearance when projected on a flat surface' characteristic of painting (CJ § 51).

architectonic *see also* IDEA, PHILOSOPHY, SYSTEM, TECHNIC
Architectonic refers to both the art of constructing a system of science on the basis of an 'idea of the whole' of the science, and to that idea itself, its 'general delineation or outline' (L p. 590). Kant thus combines Baumgarten's definition of architectonic in §4 of his *Metaphysica* (1739), where it designates the structure of metaphysical knowledge, with Lambert's more methodological approach in his *Architectonik* (written 1764, published 1771) which sees it as the art of establishing such a structure.

Kant specifically explores the subject of architectonic in the third chapter of the CPR's 'Transcendental Doctrine of Method' entitled 'The Architectonic of Pure Reason'. There he sees it as 'the doctrine of the scientific in our knowledge' or the art of making 'a system out of a mere aggregate of knowledge' (CPR A 832/B 860). The system is characterized by an 'organised unity' which is the end to which the parts of the science relate, and in which they relate to each other. The architectonic end is distinguished from a 'technical' one by not being derived from empirical criteria arising from scientific discoveries; rather, it anticipates them.

Earlier in CPR Kant defined human reason as 'architectonic' by nature, and saw all knowledge as belonging to a possible system. The possible system or 'architectonic' of human reason is unveiled in 'The Architectonic of Pure Reason' as philosophy. Not philosophy as it exists, but philosophy as a 'general delineation or outline' of the system of human reason. The ideal philosopher practising this architectonic would not simply reflect on the products of human reason – which would be 'technical' and thus the work of an artificer – but would act as 'the lawgiver of human reason' (CPR A 839/B 867). Kant goes on to outline the architectonic of human reason: it would have two objects, nature and freedom, underwriting the division between the philosophy of nature which 'deals with all *that is*, [and] the philosophy of morals with that which *ought to be*' (CPR A 840/B 868).

With this concern for the philosophical system Kant inherited the Wolffian project of encyclopaedic philosophy or *philosophia generalis*. This project was the form in which German philosophy defended its claims against the discrete sciences (and faculties) of law, theology and medicine as well as the emergent natural sciences. The view of philosophy as an architectonic system flourished after Kant in the systems of Fichte (1794), Schelling (1800) and Hegel (1830), but was abandoned by the middle of the nineteenth century.

art [*techne, ars, Kunst*] *see also* ACTION, AESTHETIC, BEAUTY, TECHNIC

Kant follows Aristotle's definition of art as a skill or disposition for producing things. In this definition a 'work of art' is anything produced by the practice of an art. In the *Nicomachean Ethics* (Aristotle, 1941, 1140a) and *Posterior Analytics* (100a, 3–9) Aristotle gathered Plato's various uses of the term into a rigorous and consequential distinction between the art (*techne*) of producing things (*poiesis*), the episteme of theoretical knowledge (*theoria*), and the deliberation (*phronesis*) of action (*praxis*). Art consists in rules generalized from experience and applied to the realization of an intention.

This distinction had an extraordinarily long-lived and widespread influence. Aquinas defines art as 'nothing else but the right reason about certain works to be made' (Aquinas, 1952, II, 57, 3) but distinguished between the servile arts 'ordered to works done by the body' and those of the soul or 'liberal arts'. The latter formed the basis of the early medieval curriculum of the seven liberal arts divided into the trivium (grammar, dialectic, rhetoric) and quadrivium (arithmetic, geometry, astronomy, music). By the eighteenth century, although the sense of art as a skill remained, it was frequently illustrated by reference to the art of producing poetry or painting. Meissner's Wolffian *Philosophisches Lexicon* (1737) defines *Kunst* as the 'ability' or 'skill' of a human being 'to bring into existence a thing outside of itself', as for example when 'the skill of a poet brings a poem into existence'.

Kant's main discussion of art is to be found in sections 43–53 of CJ. He defines it as 'human skill, distinguished from science (as *ability* from *knowledge*), as a practical from a theoretical faculty, as technic from theory (as the art of surveying from geometry)' (CJ §43). He reserves particular attention for the fine arts, distinguishing these activities from handicrafts, which produce without an intention, and the mechanical arts, which perfectly realize their intention. The practice of fine arts produces works which paradoxically 'must be clothed with the aspect of nature, although we recognise it to be art' (CJ §45). The consideration of this kind of productive art led Kant into his theory of genius, regarded as the ability or disposition to produce correct works of art which yet show no sign 'of the artist having always had a rule present to them'.

Kant classifies the fine arts by an analogy with the three ways in which human beings communicate with each other: through speech, gesture and tone. The arts of speech are rhetoric and poetry, those of gesture (or the 'formative arts') include the plastic arts of architecture and sculpture and the art of painting, while the tonal arts include those of music and colour. He also admits of mixed arts. The key to understanding these divisions is to remember that they refer to skills or practices and not primarily to objects. The same may be said of his reference in CPR to schematism as 'an art concealed in the depths of the human soul' (A 141, B 181) – it is a skill or an activity which produces schemas, and not itself an object.

Kant's philosophy of art is often confused with his account of aesthetics, or his anatomy of aesthetic judgement. This allowed many of his successors, including Schiller and Hegel, to criticize him for producing an aesthetic which excluded the production of works of art. In fact his account combines aspects of the traditional Aristotelian account of art as a skill with the new emphasis on the fine arts. This combination has been of considerable importance in recent debates in aesthetics, which have sought to restore the element of skill into accounts of the production and reception of art.

as-if [*als ob*] *see also* ACTION, ANALOGY, IDEA, REGULATIVE PRINCIPLE
A form of analogical argument, as-if is often used by Kant in his theoretical, practical and aesthetic philosophies. It appears in theoretical philosophy as a maxim of regulative judgement, and is ubiquitous in the conclusion to CPR's 'Transcendental Dialectic'. Having proved that God, the world and the soul are not appropriate objects for a limited human judgement, Kant proceeds to re-admit them as regulative principles. Thus in theology, although we can never know whether God is the cause of the world, we can nevertheless view 'all objects *as if* they drew their origin from such an archetype' (CPR A 673/B 701). Similarly in cosmology, we can never know whether the world has a beginning or an end, although we are able to conduct an inquiry '*as if* it had an absolute beginning, through an intelligible cause' (CPR A 685/B 713). Finally, in psychology, although we can never know the nature of the soul, we can 'connect all the appearances, all the actions and receptivity of our mind, *as if* the mind were a simple substance which persists with personal identity' (CPR A 672/B 700).

Apart from serving as the form of the regulative principles of theoretical judgement, the as-if is also crucial to the maxims of practical judgement. The most significant, but often ignored, use of the as-if form is in conjunction with the 'kingdom of ends' and the formulae of the categorical imperative. In GMM Kant states that 'every rational being must so act as if he were through his maxim always a legislating member in the universal

86

kingdom of ends' or, stated more formally, 'So act as if your maxims were to serve at the same time as a universal law' (GMM p. 438, p. 43). The as-if also discreetly features at crucial junctures of the CJ: the finality of form of a work of art, for example, 'must appear just as free from the constraint of arbitrary rules as if it were a product of mere nature' (CJ §45). Thus analogical reasoning in the ubiquitous, but often overlooked form of the as-if is central to all areas of Kant's philosophy. Its ubiquity, but not its relation to Kant's use of analogical reasoning in general, was recognized by Vaihinger in his *Philosophy of As If* (1911), which led to the formation of a fan club called 'The Society of Friends of the Philosophy of As If'!

assertoric *see* APODEICTIC, JUDGEMENT, NECESSITY

association *see also* AFFINITY, IMAGINATION, PSYCHOLOGY, SYNTHESIS
The psychological phenomenon of joining together different objects of consciousness, association was mentioned by Plato and Aristotle in connection with mnemonics, but came to play an important part in empiricist epistemology. Locke distinguished between natural (simultaneous) and acquired (successive) associations of ideas, the latter being due to chance or custom. Hume too devoted considerable attention to association, concentrating on the relations according to which ideas were associated with each other.

Association did not play a major part in Kant's epistemology, largely because of his interest in justifying synthetic a priori judgements. Association is a psychological or empirical phenomenon which does not have a prominent place in the transcendental justification of these judgements. Indeed, in CPR Kant criticized Locke and Hume for their pre-occupation with association, especially the place given by the latter to custom 'which arises from repeated association in experience' (CPR A 94/B 127). Kant is happy to grant association a place in synthesis as 'the subjective and empirical ground of reproduction according to rule' in empirical reproductive imagination. Yet even this empirical rule of association is for him not self-sufficient, and always subject to the transcendental question of 'How is this association itself possible?' (CPR A 113). The answer is that it too has a ground in the 'transcendental affinity, of which the empirical is a mere consequence' (CPR A 114). Thus association is a relatively peripheral issue for Kant, although it has been the subject of considerable interpretation from critics working within the empiricist tradition.

atom *see* CONTINUITY, DIVISIBILITY, MATTER, MONAD

attraction *see* FORCE, IMPENETRABILITY, REPULSION

autonomy [*Autonomie*] *see also* CATEGORICAL IMPERATIVE, COMMAND, FREEDOM, SPONTANEITY, WILL

The early modern ideology of political autonomy developed by Machiavelli in the *Discourses* (1531) combined two senses of autonomy: the first was freedom from dependence, the second the power to self-legislate. The political aspects of autonomy thus developed in the context of the early modern city-state were given their complement in the spiritual life by Luther in his *Freedom of A Christian* (1520). For him, autonomy as freedom from dependence was translated into the 'spiritual, new, and inner, man's' freedom from the body and its inclinations as well as freedom to obey God's law' (Luther, 1961, p. 53). Kant's account of autonomy in his practical philosophy in its turn marks a philosophical transposition and critique of Luther's religious autonomy into moral autonomy.

Kant's practical philosophy combines the two aspects of autonomy within an account of the determination of the will. His position emerged from the critique of a number of then prevailing perspectives. These included his pre-critical opposition to the accounts of moral action proposed by the dominant rational, perfectionist account of the Wolffian school and the contemporary British theory of the moral sense, his critique of pietist theological appeals to the will of God, and finally Montaigne's view of the importance of custom in human action. He later identified all of these accounts as based on 'heteronomous principles' and sought to develop a moral philosophy based on an 'autonomous principle' of self-legislation.

The opposition between heteronomous and autonomous principles persists throughout Kant's moral philosophy. In GMM an autonomous will gives itself its law, and is distinguished from a heteronomous will whose law is given by the object 'because of its relation to the will' (GMM p. 441, p. 45). In the latter case the maxims of the will depend on heteronomous principles, which Kant identifies in terms of the contemporary accounts of moral action cited above. The former are 'drawn from the principle of happiness, and are based upon either physical or moral feeling' while the latter are 'drawn from the principle of perfection, [and] are based upon either the rational concept of perfection as a possible effect of our will or else upon the concept of an independent perfection (the will of God) as a determining cause of our will' (GMM p. 442, p. 46). The heteronomous principles yield only hypothetical imperatives – 'I ought to do something because I will something else' – rather than the categorical imperatives of the autonomous principle which abstracts from every object of the will.

The autonomous principle of the categorical imperative commands nothing other than its own autonomy. The principle of autonomy is stated as 'Always choose in such a way that in the same volition the maxims of the choice are at the same time present as a universal law' (GMM p. 440,

p. 44). Such a principle is only possible 'on the pre-supposition of freedom of the will' (GMM p. 461, p. 60) which establishes the 'will's autonomy as the formal condition under which alone the will can be determined' (p. 461, p. 60). This means that the will must will its own autonomy and that its freedom lies in thus being a law to itself. This freedom is 'intelligible', that is to say, 'independent of any determination by alien causes' and formal/universal in that it does not stand in any relation to an object.

Kant's purification of the will from the influence of any heteronomous principle or object has been consistently criticized since Hegel, most notably by Nietzsche (1887) and Scheler (1973). Such an autonomy has been seen as at best empty, formalistic and irrelevant, or at worst tyrannical. It is seen to subjugate sensibility to reason and, in Hegel's eyes, to do violence to both (Hegel, 1807). Kant's account of autonomy has however recently been re-appraised and defended by O'Neill (1989) as providing an adequate methodological basis for both theoretical and practical reasoning.

axiom *see* ACROAMATA, AXIOMS OF INTUITION, PRINCIPLES

axioms of intuition *see also* ANALOGIES OF EXPERIENCE, ANTICIPATIONS OF PERCEPTION, CATEGORIES, JUDGEMENT, PRINCIPLES, QUANTITY, UNITY
These axioms are a group of principles which serve as rules for the objective employment of the categories of quantity. Each group of categories has its corresponding principles which serve to determine how things must appear in time: those corresponding to the categories of quality are the 'anticipations of perception', those of relation the 'analogies of experience' and those of modality the 'postulates of empirical thought'. Since our experience of the world cannot be directly categorical, we are unable to organize our quantitative experience in terms of the categories 'unity', 'plurality' and 'totality'; we thus require principles to make them conform to the conditions of finite intuition.

The 'axioms' and the 'anticipations' form the 'mathematical principles' in contrast to the 'dynamic principles' of the 'analogies' and the 'postulates'. The mathematical principles translate the categories into principles adequate to the intuition of objects in space and time – those of extensive and intensive magnitude. The leading principle of the axioms, which is all Kant gives us in the CPR, is in the A edition (p. 162) 'All appearances are, in their intuition, extensive magnitudes' and in B (p. 202) 'All intuitions are extensive magnitudes'. This means that it is impossible for an appearance to become an object of intuition unless it possesses an extensive magnitude: the latter is a condition both of experience and of all objects of experience. Kant describes magnitude in terms of the process of moving from unity or a 'representation of a part' through plurality over a period of time, to the achievement of totality or a whole at the end of the period of time. He gives the example of the construction of geometrical line, which proceeds over time from a point, to a plurality of points, to a line (CPR A 162/B 203).

In common with all Kant's principles, the axioms convert formal predicates of being into temporally and spatially defined principles of appearances. Thus the 'mathematics of space (geometry)' is founded on the 'successive synthesis of the productive imagination' (CPR A 162/B 203) which proceeds from unity at an instant of time, to plurality in the course of time, to totality at the end of a period of time. Even the maintenance of unity through time requires a successive synthesis, without which the unity would suffer an inadmissible change of quality – it would instantaneously pass out of existence and become something else. The objects of geometry are the product of this construction over time, as are the numbers and the arithmetical operation of addition. Operations involving the persistence or change of magnitude are accomplished by a synthesis of the imagination over time.

Kant concludes with the claim that 'The synthesis of spaces and times' – the generation of extensive magnitude through the move from unity to plurality and totality – 'is what makes possible the apprehension of appearance, and consequently every outer experience and all knowledge of the objects of experience' (CPR A 165/B 206). This makes the axioms conform with the 'general principle' of all four groups of principles, namely that the conditions for experience are the conditions for objects of experience.

B

beauty *see also* AESTHETIC, ART, GOOD, TRANSCENDENTAL, TRUTH, UNITY

In *Hippias Major* Socrates summed up his dialogue on beauty with the Greek proverb 'all beauty is difficult'. The main philosophical difficulty involved reconciling beauty as an objective idea with the subjective pleasure taken in beautiful things. In Plato's *Symposium* the reconciliation is accomplished by means of eros, with the emphasis falling on the experience of, and pleasure taken in, beauty. The Platonic alignment of beauty and eros was countered by Aristotle's more objectively inclined definition in the *Metaphysics* which held that 'The chief forms of beauty are order and symmetry, and definiteness' (Aristotle, 1941, 1078b, 1). The two differences in emphasis already evident in Greek philosophies of beauty persisted until and beyond Kant in the distinction between subjective and objective accounts of beauty.

The objective account of beauty prevailed in medieval philosophy, wherein beauty was classified as one of the transcendentals, or those attributes including the One, the Good and the True which accord with every genus. Aquinas famously describes the three 'conditions' of beauty as '*Integritas* or perfection . . . due proportion or harmony [*consonatia*]; and lastly, brightness or clarity [*claritas*] . . .' (Aquinas, 1952, I, 39, 8). These conditions allow beauty to be 'convertible' with the other transcendentals: *Integritas* with the One, *consonatia* with the good and *claritas* with the true.

The transcendental view of beauty was subsequently combined by Leibniz with the experience of pleasure; an objective perfection perceived obscurely was held to evoke subjective pleasure. An analogous view was also held by Shaftesbury in his *Characteristics* (1711). However, the successors of Leibniz and Shaftesbury tended to exaggerate either one of the objective and subjective aspects of beauty. For Wolff and his school, most notably his disciple Baumgarten, beauty consisted in 'perfection' or the unity of a manifold. For followers of Shaftesbury such as Hutcheson, beauty was based on an inner, subjective 'sense' of beauty without any obvious objective correlates beyond those provided by providence.

Kant was well acquainted with both accounts of beauty as early as the

91

1760s. On the whole his pre-critical reflections and the account of aesthetic developed in L emphasize the objective side of beauty. In L (pp. 547–9) he sides with the Wolffians in identifying perfection as the ground of beauty, and seeing the experience of pleasure in the beautiful as arising from the subjective, sensible perception of such perfection. Perfection in its turn comprises the 'harmonious union' of 'manifoldness and unity' (L p. 547).

In the critical account of beauty elaborated in CJ, Kant abandons the perfectionist position inherited from the Wolffians. His analysis of the judgements of the beautiful in the 'Analytic of the Beautiful' shows that they conform to neither the subjective nor the objective accounts of beauty. Judgements of the beautiful are defined negatively in the CJ according to the table of the categories as: (quality) that which 'pleases apart from any interest' (§5); (quantity) that which 'pleases universally' without a concept (§9); (relation) the 'form of finality in an object . . . perceived in it apart from the representation of an end'; and (modality) the object of a 'necessary delight' 'apart from a concept' (§22). In each case Kant distinguishes the beautiful from the prevailing accounts of beauty which rested on the basis of perfection or a sense. He presents the nature of beauty either in terms of the negations of sensibility and the concept, or in terms of paradoxical formulations such as finality without an end (*Zweckmässigkeit ohne Zweck*).

This approach led Kant into some fresh difficulties with beauty. By distinguishing beauty from any content, whether rational or sensible, he severely limited its scope. If sensible content were to play any part, then the object would not be beautiful but only agreeable; if a concept were involved, then the beautiful would be too easily convertible with the rational. If they could exist, such beauties would be 'dependent' and contrasted with the 'free' beauties which 'represent nothing' and cannot strictly speaking even be artifacts. Consequently, Kant appeared to many critics as unduly privileging the beauty of nature over the beauty of art, even on those occasions when he attempts to rescue the beauty of art by insisting that it appear as if it were natural. He also, on one celebrated occasion (CJ §59), claimed beauty to be a 'symbol of morality' precisely because of its paradoxical properties. Here the beautiful allows judgement to find 'a reference in itself to something in the subject itself and outside it, and which is not nature, nor yet freedom, but still is connected with the ground of the latter, i.e., the supersensible . . .' (CJ §59).

The influence of Kant's account of beauty has been enormous, partly because of its ability to mean everything to everyone. To the German idealists it marked the attempt to bridge the realms of nature and freedom, and features prominently in Schiller, Schelling and Hegel. In the late nineteenth and early twentieth centuries, the third critique's focus upon the purity of the judgement of the beautiful endeared it to neo-Kantians, and after the Second World War it was used by critic Clement Greenberg among others as a theoretical justification for abstract art. As a result, Kant's account of beauty continues to serve as a starting point for a great deal of philosophical reflection on beauty, and perhaps less in spite of its inconsistencies and shortcomings than because of them.

being [*to on, ens, Sein*] *see also* ACTUALITY, ESSENCE, EXISTENCE, NOTHING, ONTOLOGY, SYNTHESIS

Kant's account of being is heir to a long and complex philosophical development of the theme, one whose significance remains the subject of intense debate. For Aristotle in the *Metaphysics*, the question of being – 'what is being?' – 'was raised of old and is raised now and always, and is always the subject of doubt' (Aristotle, 1941, 1028b, 2). Kant's most significant innovation was the translation of traditional themes and distinctions into modern terminology, restating the traditional problem of the relation between being and *logos* in terms of judgement. It was on the basis of both received distinctions and the re-statement that Kant developed his consequential distinctions between being, actuality and existence.

The traditional starting point for the question of being in Western philosophy are the fragments of Parmenides (sixth century BC). There being is distinguished from non-being in terms of the distinction between the way of truth and the way of opinion. There can be no transition from non-being to being, no change or motion; being is all that can be known, and is one (Barnes, 1987, pp. 129–42). The problems posed by Parmenides and their accentuation in Zeno's paradoxes were tackled by the following generation of Greek philosophers, above all Plato and Aristotle. Plato paradoxically both softened and intensified Parmenides' distinction between being and non-being. The latter is no longer the absolute opposite to being, but participates in being to varying degrees; being at once informs the ideas as well as forming a higher idea in itself. Aristotle in the *Metaphysics* however emphasizes the participation of discrete beings in Being in general, establishing a repertoire of ways in which Being may be spoken of beings (see Aristotle, 1941, 1012a). He makes a crucial distinction between *energeia* and *dynamis*, which later evolved first into that of *esse* and *essentia* and then into that of existence and actuality.

In their reception of the extremely diverse heritage of the Greek thought of Being, the medieval Islamic and Christian commentators systematized some of its more salient features. The basic problematic of describing the various ways in which Being may be spoken of beings persisted, as did the insight into the aporetic character of this relation (Booth, 1983). And as in Plato and Aristotle, being continues to be understood as a 'transcendental' term which cannot be predicated categorically. For the Thomist tradition being could only be predicated analogically – the being of God and the being of the world are only analogically the same. For the Scotist tradition, being may be predicated univocally, with the same sense of being meant when it is predicated of the world or of God. The scholastics agreed in distinguishing between being as existence, being as actuality and being as such: being as existence, or *esse* designated the existence of an essence, as in the 'being' of mankind; being as *essentia* designated the individual here and now actuality of, say, this woman or man; while being as such, that being whose essence is existence and actuality, can only be said of God.

The terms and distinctions of the scholastic discussions of being continued to inform the Cartesian inauguration of philosophical modernity (see Gilson, 1949). Although for Descartes and Leibniz (but not Spinoza) the focus for the question of the being of God, the world and the soul shifted from God to the soul and its certainty of its own existence, the basic structure of the problem persisted. For the moderns, Being remains extra-categorical, and is not something that can simply be predicated in a judgement like any other predicate. For them, *esse* now designates possibility, or that which is without contradiction, while *essentia* are those phenomena which are perceived to exist, while being as such is now taken to refer to the privileged being in itself, whether this is described in terms of God or *causa sui*, the subject, or the being-in-itself of the new, post-Cartesian science of ontology.

Kant's discussion of being follows precedent in claiming that being can be spoken of in many ways, but for him what is common to them all is the notion of synthesis. In OPA he defines the concept of being (*Sein*) in terms of a 'positing or setting' (p. 73, p. 119) which underlies the relations of logical judgement, describing it as 'the positing of this relation [which] is nothing other than the copula in a judgement' (p. 73, p. 119). Here being denotes a purely logical synthesis, one operating at the level of *esse*, a synthesis that conforms to the law of contradiction. When however both the relation and the related are posited, then being becomes existence, and is spoken of as *essentia*; that is, in terms of both logical and actual relations.

In CPR Kant largely repeats this earlier distinction, but goes on to use it to refute the ontological proof for the existence of God. Being is not a predicate, it adds nothing to the subject of a judgement, but designates 'merely what is possible, by my thinking its object' (CPR A 599/B 627). The statement that 'there is a God' may be without contradiction. It is a way of speaking of being at the level of *esse*, but it says nothing about the existence of its object. If we wish to speak of being in terms of existence, then we must pay heed to the conditions of synthetic knowledge, for 'Our consciousness of all existence . . . belongs exclusively to the unity of experience' (CPR A 601/B 629). This critical perspective enabled Kant narrowly to specify the ways in which being may be spoken by referring to actuality, or the principle corresponding to the second modal category of existence/non-existence.

With such comments it would seem as if Kant was severely qualifying the traditional significance of being. This certainly seemed to be the case to Hegel, who attempted to restore the question of being by giving it a new exposition in the *Science of Logic* (1812). It also seemed the case to Nietzsche, who saw himself as radicalizing Kant's insight into the illusory character of being by describing it as a 'mere vapour'. For an extremely influential current of interpretation, Kant marks the move in the history of philosophy from ontology to epistemology. However, in the twentieth century, ontological readings of Kant by Heidegger (1929) and Heimsoeth (1956) have taken seriously his claim to have replaced ontology with an 'analytic of the understanding'. Heidegger in particular has pointed to the ontological significance of synthesis in Kant, and the crucial role played in it by imagination (1929). Such readings have proven extremely influential in recovering the structures of traditional ontology which continued to inform the critical philosophy.

belief *see* FAITH

binding [*Verbindung*] *see* OBLIGATION, SYNTHESIS

body [*soma, Körper*] *see also* ACCIDENT, HETERONOMY, LIFE, MATTER, MOTION, PLEASURE, SPIRIT
In CPR Kant considered the meaning of the concept of body to be so immediately obvious that he used it to illustrate the distinction between synthetic and analytical judgements: 'All bodies are extended' is analytical judgement because the concept of body contains the predicate of extension, along with 'impenetrability, figure etc'; 'All bodies are heavy' is a synthetic judgement because the concept of weight is not intrinsic to the concept of body (A 7–9/B 11–13). Unfortunately Kant could not have chosen a less straightforward example, since even in his own work the nature of body was far from obvious and was a matter of considerable debate and even disquiet.

Kant's discussions of body may be divided, somewhat artificially, according to whether they emphasize the physical or the phenomenological aspect of the concept. The first concentrates on the natural scientific notion of body as comprising material objects, while the second focuses on the human body. Even the first view of body is far from straightforward in Kant; it is by no means simply the rule for the unity of the manifold serving our knowledge of external appearances which is blandly presented at one point in CPR (A 106). Kant's first published work, LF (1747), is a sustained scrutiny of the nature of physical bodies. In it he disputes both the Cartesian view that body is defined by extension, and the Aristotelian view that it possesses an entelechy or principle of motion. He defends the Leibnizian thesis that body contains an essential force 'prior to its extension' (LF §1), and goes so far as to claim that the three dimensions of spatial extension may be derived from the working of this force. He thus distinguishes between the constitution of the mathematical body in terms of extension and the constitution of natural bodies in terms of an inherently expansive force. These discussions are dedicated, among other things, to showing that the concept of body must be distinguished from that of substance.

Although Kant did not sustain all the details of this early position throughout his career, it is by no means the case that he simply accepted the Cartesian view of body which seems to underlie the discussions in CPR. The relationship between body and space continued to puzzle him: do bodies occupy or constitute space, or do they merely denote a rule for the synthesis of intuitions? These questions continue to inform the critical definitions of body ventured in MF, where body features as 'matter between determinate boundaries' (MF p. 525, p. 80). Yet Kant is aware that even the mechanical definition of body which sees it only as a 'mass of determinate shape' itself assumes the prior qualitative occupation of a discrete space. These analyses of the quantitative and qualitative aspects of body continued into OP and were left unresolved by him on his death; they may without exaggeration be described as one of the most important single, continuous pre-occupations of his authorship.

Alongside his discussion of the physical body of natural science, Kant also developed an analysis of the human body. In the 'Paralogisms' of CPR he touches on the Cartesian mind–body problem, but his interest in the significance of the experience of the human body for philosophy was far more wide-reaching. In the pre-critical DRS (1768) he derived the spatial ordering of above–below, left–right, front–back so crucial for his account of intuition from the spatial experience of the human body (DRS pp. 378–9, pp. 366–7). Analogously, in FS he derived the phenomenon of impenetrability from an object's resistance to the body's touch. Thus the analysis of the experience of the human body is implied throughout the more technical theoretical analyses of CPR.

The experience of the body is also central to Kant's practical and aesthetic philosophies. The 'Doctrine of Virtue' in MM is largely concerned with bodily management, an approach to the physical regimen that Kant also developed in terms of medicine in his essay on 'Philosophers' Medicine of the Body' (1786). The issue of bodily pleasure and pain features prominently in A, as well as in the CJ, where it forms part of an increasingly evident Epicurean agenda. Thus in the latter, Kant analyzes the different experiences of bodily pleasure ranging from the agreeable to the aesthetic, and relates them to the promotion of life to the hindrance and furtherance of the pleasures of the body. He also in CJ discusses the ideal body and its artistic representation. Regarding differences between bodies, Kant was predictably insensitive to the significance of sexual difference, and in the A and some shorter works he contributes to a debate among his contemporaries regarding racial distinctions between human bodies.

Kant's broad and wide-ranging analysis of the human body far exceeded the limits of the Cartesian mind–body debate, so far indeed as to remain neglected until the twentieth century. Many of his insights were recovered by the phenomenological movement in the course of its deconstruction of Cartesian dualism. In *Being and Time* (1927) Heidegger engages directly with Kant's text DRS, and its influence is also evident in Merleau-Ponty's (1962) phenomenology of the body. Foucault's influential work on the body was not only inspired by Kant's work (he translated the A), but also contributed to making the body a proper object of study and led to a reconsideration of some of Kant's previously overlooked texts and arguments (see Foucault, 1976, 1980, 1984, 1988).

boundary *see* LIMIT

C

canon *see also* ANALYTIC, DISCIPLINE, JUDGEMENT, LOGIC, METAPHYSICS, RULE

The historical basis of Kant's contrast between canon and organon is the critique of the Aristotelian organon by Epicurus (341–271 BC). In place of Aristotle's *Organon*, which presented rules for achieving demonstrative knowledge, Epicurus proposed a *Canon* of the rules for making correct judgements. The title of his text on the subject was entitled *The Canon*, and comprised various rules and criteria for discriminating between true and false judgements (Diogenes Laertius, 1925, Vol. II, pp. 559–61). Epicurus distinguished canonics from dialectics, seeing it as concerned with the correctness of judgement rather than with the extension of knowledge.

Kant formalizes this historical distinction in CPR, although he alludes to its origins in L, where he refers to logic as the 'universal art of reason (*canonica Epicuri*)' (L p. 529). His own formal distinction between canon and organon remains very close to its historical precedent. The transcendental analytic, for example, was conceived in the spirit of Epicurus's canon as a means of distinguishing between true and false judgements, 'for passing judgement on the empirical employment of the understanding' (CPR A 63/B 88). It does not, like the Aristotelian organon, profess to give rules for the extension of the understanding; indeed, for Kant 'it is misapplied if appealed to as an organon of its general and unlimited application' (A 63/B 88).

In the section of CPR on 'The Transcendental Doctrine of Method' – Chapter II 'The Canon of Pure Reason' – Kant identifies the 'sole use of a philosophy of pure reason' to be a canon which serves 'not as an organon for the extension but as a discipline for the limitation of pure reason' (A 795/B 823). He describes the analytic part of general logic as 'a canon for the understanding and reason in general' and the transcendental analytic as a 'canon of the pure *understanding*; for understanding alone is capable of true synthetic modes of knowledge *a priori*' (A 796/B 825). He goes on to consider the canon of pure reason, which can be applied only in the context of reason's practical employment. The canon of pure reason deals with two questions relating to the practical interest, namely 'Is there a God? and, Is there a future life?' (A 803/B 831). These questions are translated into the two criteria of the canon of pure reason: 'what ought I to do?' and 'What may I hope?' (A 805/B 835) which yield the postulates of the existence of God and a future life.

The notion of the canon received from Epicurus can be extended to characterize the entire critical enterprise. Critical philosophy may be said to offer the rules or criteria for distinguishing between true and false judgements while not immediately proposing a systematic account of correct judgements and the means of extending them. In this sense Epicurus's discipline of canonics may be said to have been revived by the critical philosophy and continued in the critical disciplines inspired by it.

categorical imperative *see also* AS-IF, AUTONOMY, FREEDOM, HETERONOMY, IMPERATIVE, LAW, MAXIM, PRACTICAL PHILOSOPHY, WILL

The categorical imperative is without doubt one of the best known and most disputed aspects of Kant's practical philosophy. It has been variously interpreted as the principle of an empty formalist moral philosophy, a glorification of the Prussian virtue of disinterested obedience to the call of duty, and the founding principle of an objectivist, rational account of moral action. For Kant himself the categorical imperative seems to combine two possibly inconsistent philosophical ambitions. The first, more modest ambition, was to establish the categorical imperative as a canonical principle for discriminating between maxims of action, while the second saw it as a means of justifying a metaphysically grounded account of freedom as the autonomy of the will. Subsequent debate has consisted in assessing the coherence of Kant's account of the categorical imperative, and in particular whether it is sustainable without the entailment of a metaphysics of freedom.

Before looking at Kant's statements of the categorical imperative in GMM and CPrR it may be helpful to define what is meant by the terms 'categorical' and 'imperative'. Kant defines an imperative as every 'proposition that expresses a possible free action, whereby a certain end is to be made real' (L p. 587). Such statements are grounded in a 'kind of necessity' which is distinct from that of theoretical statements; rather than stating what *is*, they state what *ought* to be the case. And just as there are various ways of stating the 'is' in a proposition, so are there various ways of stating the 'ought'. These are the various forms of imperative, of which the categorical is but a special and privileged case.

The form of necessity expressed by the 'ought' common to all imperatives expresses for Kant 'the relation of an objective law of reason to a will that is not necessarily determined by this law because of its subjective constitution' (GMM p. 413, p. 24). The imperative can be either hypothetical or categorical, with the distinction depending on whether or not the relation of law to will is directed toward the achievement of an end. In the case of hypothetical imperatives, this relation is directed toward achieving an end, while in the case of the categorical imperative it is not. Kant further subdivides hypothetical imperatives according to whether they are assertoric or problematic; that is, whether they are directed toward an actual or a possible end. The principles of a hypothetical actual imperative are described as 'rules of skill' or 'technical imperatives' while those of a hypothetical possible imperative are 'counsels of prudence' or pragmatic imperatives.

It is clear from both GMM and CPrR that Kant regards the received tradition of moral philosophy as having only explored the forms of hypothetical imperative (see for example the historical table of the grounds of moral principles in CPrR p. 40, p. 41). They all offer statements of the form 'act so as to realize the end X' (X = happiness, beatitude, pleasure, welfare, perfection, the glory of God). The categorical imperative, by contrast, declares an action to be necessary 'without reference to any purpose' and is concerned only with 'the form of the action and the principle from which it follows' (GMM p. 416, p. 26). In this case the necessity which relates the objective law to the will 'holds as an apodeictic practical principle' (p. 415, p. 25).

Kant offers several conditions to account for why this imperative of the law holds categorically for a subjective will. The first is that it is formal. This follows from its not being concerned to realize any particular end; the categorical imperative 'is not concerned with the matter of the action and its intended result, but rather with the form of the action and the principle from which it follows' (p. 416, p. 26). Another condition entails that the categorical imperative must be known immediately, which leads to the most important condition, which is that the categorical imperative states the universality of the law. This informs the statement of what Kant describes as the one and only categorical imperative, which is 'Act only according to that maxim whereby you can at the same time will that it should become a universal law' (p. 421, p. 30).

Kant employs this statement of the categorical imperative as 'the canon for morally estimating any of our actions' (p. 424, p. 32). He uses it to clarify actions accomplished within the terms of the imperative of duty. Such imperatives are categorical when they obey the form 'Act as if the maxim of your action were to become through your will a universal law of nature' (p. 421, p. 30). Yet Kant was not content with the considerable results which could be achieved by this canonical use of the categorical imperative. The categorical imperative had itself to be justified: it was necessary 'to prove a priori that there actually is an imperative of this kind'. But not only this, the categorical imperative was also called upon to show 'that there is a practical law which of itself commands absolutely and without any incentives, and that following this law is duty' (p. 425, p. 33). As a result he drove a wedge between the practical law and the 'special characteristics of human nature' analogous to that between the noumenal and phenomenal realms in his theoretical philosophy.

The need to prove the existence of the imperative led first to the search for the law which commanded absolutely, and then to the 'something which as an end in itself could be a ground of determinate laws' (p. 428, p. 35). This would form the ground of both the practical law and the categorical imperative. Kant diverts the search for an end in itself into that for beings with 'absolute value' who were ends in themselves. He very quickly identifies these beings with 'persons' and proceeds to derive the universality of the categorical imperative 'from the conception of what is necessarily an end for everyone because this end is an end in itself'. The formula of this imperative now reads: 'Act in such a way that you treat humanity, whether in your own person or in the person of another, always at the same time as an end, and never as a means' (p. 429, p. 36). This imperative is then used canonically in order to judge the maxims informing concrete cases.

Kant admits that the move to a 'metaphysics of morals' which is necessary to buttress the categorical imperative puts practical philosophy into a precarious position. This risk was motivated by the importance Kant attached to the concept of freedom. It is freedom which permits the transition from a 'metaphysics of morals' to a 'critique of practical reason', but freedom is held both to justify and be justified by the categorical imperative. This follows from the two senses which Kant gives to the concept of freedom. He distinguishes between negative freedom, which consists in freedom from 'determination by alien causes' (heteronomy), and freedom as autonomy, which consists in a subject giving itself its own law. The latter consists in the will being a law to itself, which is nothing other than acting according to a maxim which can 'at the same time have itself as a universal law for its object' (p. 447, p. 49). The idea of freedom as autonomy is thus uncovered as the ground for the categorical imperative, the necessary presupposition accorded by us to ourselves and other rational beings in so far as they possess a will or 'consciousness of [their] causality as regards actions' (p. 449, p. 51). Yet we are only secured in the possession of such freedom in so far as we make categorical imperatives.

The direction of the critique of the categorical imperative by Kant's successors is best summed up in Nietzsche's phrase 'the categorical imperative smells of cruelty' (Nietzsche, 1887, p. 65). Kant's attempt to ground the categorical imperative in a positive notion of freedom as autonomy failed, since freedom and the categorical imperative could only be defined in reactive terms as the suppression or exclusion of heteronomy, of human feelings and inclinations. This critique was but an extreme statement of a direction of criticism inaugurated by Hegel and Schopenhauer's critiques of the categorical imperative. Hegel, while regarding favourably Kant's definition of freedom as autonomy of the will, nevertheless saw its moral formulation in the categorical imperative as formal and abstract, resting on the exclusion of 'all content and specification'. Schopenhauer considered himself to have 'put to death' the categorical imperative and the moral law, and with it the entire attempt to ground practical philosophy on the freedom of the will. Recent work in Kantian ethics has largely accepted these doubts concerning the metaphysical basis of the categorical imperative, and has focused on its use as a canonical formula for testing maxims of action for their consistency and universalizability (see O'Neill, 1989).

categories [*Kategorien*] *see also* ANALYTIC, DEDUCTION, JUDGEMENT, LOGIC, PRINCIPLES, SYNTHESIS, TABLE OF JUDGEMENTS/CATEGORIES
Categories are the forms according to which objects of experience are structured and ordered. The classical Greek term *kategorein* meant 'to accuse', 'to say of' or 'to judge', and was adopted by Aristotle to describe the ways in which it was possible to speak of being. In the *Categories* he proposed a list of ten such 'categories': substance, quantity, quality, relation, place, time, position, state, action, affection. Even in the classical period this list was criticized for containing repetitions, and attempts were made to reduce the number of categories, in many cases to a single opposition such as 'substance and accident', 'matter and form' or, as in the case of Plotinus, 'motion and stability' (Plotinus, 1971, p. 253). These reductions were to a certain extent supported by passages drawn from some of Aristotle's other works.

Through Boethius's translation of Aristotle's *Categories* the schema of the ten categories exercised an enormous influence upon the development of early medieval European philosophy. Yet with the expansion of the Aristotelian corpus available in Latin during the thirteenth century, a tension was discerned between Aristotle's account of being in terms of the categories and his other, more economical descriptions of being in terms such as 'substance and accident'. The authority of Aristotle obliged philosophers such as Aquinas and Duns Scotus to reconcile the categories with other aspects of Aristotelian ontology, with complex and often baffling results. The increasingly baroque character of the doctrine of the categories was an important factor in the rejection of scholasticism by early modern philosophers such as Hobbes and Descartes. Their reasons for rejecting the Aristotelian categories were summed up in the mid-seventeenth century by Arnauld, who claimed that the categories 'of which so much mystery has been made' 'help but slightly in the formation of judgement, the true end of logic.' What is more, they are 'entirely arbitrary and founded on the imagination of a man who had no authority to prescribe a law to others' (Arnauld, 1662, p. 43), and encourage philosophers to speak with authority about 'arbitrary classifications' rather than about the things themselves.

The categories were rescued from the general opprobrium by their resuscitation in CPR, a remarkable episode in what Tonelli (1964) has described as the 'revival of German-Aristotelian vocabulary'. In order to rescue the categories from the prevailing disrepute into which they had fallen, Kant had to answer the kind of objections made by Arnauld, and not only distinguish his table of categories from the Aristotelian 'rhapsody' but also show that they were authoritative and contributed to the 'formation of judgement'. This task required him to attend to (a) the derivation of the categories – they could no longer rest on Aristotle or any other philosopher's personal authority; (b) their systematic presentation in a 'table of categories'; (c) their justification or 'deduction'; and (d) their application in making judgements.

In a letter to Marcus Herz of 21 February 1772, and later in P §39 ('Of the System of the Categories'), Kant accounted for his discovery of the categories in terms of a revision of the Aristotelian 'rhapsody'. He claims that Aristotle's categories were derived from 'ordinary knowledge' and laid out largely 'as he found them', a method Kant compares with collecting elements of grammar from the observation of usage. He, by contrast, seeks to give a reason for why knowledge, like a language, 'has just this and no other formal constitution' and why it has 'exactly so many, neither more nor less, of such formal determinations' (P §39). 'After long reflection on the pure elements of human knowledge (those which contain nothing empirical)' Kant claimed that he was able to distinguish space and time as 'pure elementary concepts of sensibility' allowing him to exclude the '7th, 8th, and 9th categories from the old list' (P §39).

The exclusion of the spatio-temporal categories corresponds largely with the stage reached by Kant in the ID. But the problem remained of how to derive the remaining categories. In the letter to Herz, Kant confesses that in respect of the 'intellectual representations' the outcome of the ID was negative – they were *not* 'produced by the object'. But this left the problem of 'how is the understanding to construct for itself entirely a priori concepts of things, with which the things are necessarily in agreement?'; that is, principles which both agree with and are yet independent of experience. In the 'silent decade' of the 1770s Kant sought a solution to this problem: 'I looked about for an act of the understanding which comprises all the rest and is differentiated only by various modifications or moments, in bringing the manifold of representation under the unity of thinking in general' (P §3). He 'found this act of the understanding to consist in judging' which he described in terms of the bringing into agreement of the representations of things and the a priori concepts of the understanding.

The act of judgement thus became the source from which to derive the basic concepts that together form the grammar of thinking. Since judgement for Kant is the unification of a manifold, the basic concepts refer to the various ways in which manifolds may be unified. Kant drew on the anatomy of judgement given by logicians in order to map the various 'modifications' of the act of judgement, and thus to 'exhibit a complete table of the pure functions of the understanding'. These were modes of judgement which were pure constructions of the understanding 'undetermined in regard to any object'. These modes were then extended to apply to 'objects in general'; that is, not to discrete judgements but to the conditions that made such judgements not only possible but also objectively valid: these conditions or 'pure concepts of the understanding' were given 'their old name of categories' (P §39).

The derivation of the categories from the various modes of the act of judgement is the core of CPR's 'Analytic of Concepts'. The basic argument of this extremely involved and much discussed part of CPR is relatively straightforward. All acts of the understanding are judgements, and the understanding is the faculty of judgement. The 'functions of unity in judgement' can be divided into four sets, each of which contains three members: collectively they comprise the table of judgements (see table 1).

The quantity of a judgement is determined by whether a predicate includes all, some or one of its subjects; the quality refers to the ways in which a predicate may be predicated of a subject; the relation involves the manner in which predicates may be related to a subject, while modality specifies the relation of the judgement to the conditions of thought in general.

Kant then proceeds to relate judgement to synthesis, describing as categories those concepts which give unity to pure synthesis, and thus provide the conditions for objectivity in general. These concepts correspond to the basic acts of judgement listed above, and in their turn yield a table of categories (see table 2).

These fundamental concepts, which Kant also calls 'original and primitive', are embedded in every act of judgement, and have their own peculiar properties. The categories of quantity and quality share the property of referring judgement to objects of intuition and are entitled 'mathematical',

Table 1 Table of judgements

I
Quantity of Judgements
Universal
Particular
Singular

II	**III**
Quality	**Relation**
Affirmative	Categorical
Negative	Hypothetical
Infinite	Disjunctive

IV
Modality
Problematic
Assertoric
Apodeictic

Source: CPR A 70/B 95

Table 2 Table of categories

I
Categories of Quantity
Unity
Plurality
Totality

II	**III**
Of Quality	**Of Relation**
Reality	Of Inherence and Subsistence
Negation	(*substantia et accidens*)
Limitation	Of Causality and Dependence
	(cause and effect)
	Of Community
	(reciprocity between agent and patient)

IV
Modality
Possibility–Impossibility
Existence–Nonexistence
Necessity–Contingency

Source: CPR A 80/B 106

while the categories of relation and modality are labelled 'dynamical' and refer judgement to a relation either between the objects of intuition themselves, or these objects and the understanding. Within each group, Kant observes, the first pair of categories in each set forms a dichotomy, with the third arising from their combination.

The derivation of the categories also serves in part as their justification. The 'metaphysical deduction' consists in showing their agreement with the 'logical functions of judgement', while the 'transcendental deduction' shows that the categories form the conditions for objectively valid judgements of experience. With this the categories can become, in Arnauld's words, 'formative for judgement' (1662, p. 43), since they can now determine empirical judgements. By themselves they are merely 'logical functions', but when they are brought into conformity with the conditions of sensuous intuition through schematism and the principles, then they make possible 'judgements of experience in general'. Although produced autonomously by the understanding in the act of judgement, the categories nevertheless agree, through the principles, with the manifold of intuition or, in the language of the letter to Herz, with 'the things' themselves (PC p. 72).

Kant's revival of the categories has been the source of incessant philosophical controversy, both within and outside the framework of the critical philosophy. Fichte claimed that Kant's deduction was a failure: 'he by no means proved the categories he set up to be conditions of self-consciousness, but merely said that they were so' (Fichte, 1794, p. 51). He attempted to remedy the alleged shortcomings of the Kantian deduction by re-orienting Kant's view of judgement within an account of 'positing' as the I's basic mode of action. Hegel saw Fichte's insistence upon a fresh deduction of the categories as justified, but criticized him for not questioning sufficiently the implied opposition between unity and plurality. This opposition itself is an abstraction, worthy of an abstract notion of the I or subject. Schopenhauer too rejected the 'complicated clockwork' of Kant's categories in favour of immediate, intuitive knowledge.

The early critiques of Kant's categories all shared the critical project of deriving the grammar of knowledge from a fundamental principle or act. The neo-Kantians later in the nineteenth century were more pragmatic, borrowing their categories in an act of second order reflection upon the natural and human sciences. The ethos of twentieth-century philosophy has been largely unsympathetic toward systems of categories. Wittgenstein's work in particular, investigating judgements without any attempt to uncover their basic structure, seems akin to the 'study of the actual use of words' as opposed to that of the 'formal constitution' of a language which Kant had earlier considered, but rejected, as a model for philosophical reflection.

causality [*Kausalität*] *see also* ANALOGIES OF EXPERIENCE, ANALYTIC, CATEGORIES, FORCE, FREEDOM, NATURE, PRINCIPLES, SUCCESSION

Causality is a theme central to both Kant's theoretical and practical philosophy. His theoretical discussion of causality is couched entirely in terms of a modern conception of causality which rejected the Aristotelian order of material, formal, efficient and final causes and confined causality to local motion. Although this conception may be traced back to Galileo, he himself did not explain motion in terms of causality; he destroyed the old notion of causality and left the justification of the new to the philosophers.

Kant's response to the problem of justifying theoretical causality underwent several changes in the course of his career. In ND he followed the Wolffian school's identification of causality with the rational principle of ground and consequence. This ontological justification of causality was abandoned in DS and other works of the 1760s where the relation of cause and effect is described as a 'fundamental relation' which cannot be further determined: 'It is impossible for reason ever to understand how something can be a cause, or have a force; such relations can only be derived from experience' (DS p. 370, p. 356). Already Kant is uneasy in his dogmatic slumbers, but was finally woken up by what he saw as Hume's demonstration that causality rested upon custom rather than any a priori necessity (see CPR A 760/B 788).

Hume's doubts regarding the principle of causality were taken by Kant as a challenge to a priori knowledge and thus to metaphysics (P p. 259, p. 4). In response, Kant sought a critical position in which causality is based neither on a custom derived from repeated experiences nor on the a priori ontological order of ground and consequence governed only by the laws of contradiction and sufficient reason. The results of this search were presented in the 'Transcendental Analytic' of CPR where causality takes its place within the broader architectonic of categories and principles. For in course of seeking to justify causality, Kant discovered a number of other concepts 'by which the understanding thinks the connection of things a priori' (P p. 260, p. 6). These were not derived from experience, but from the acts of judgement performed by the pure understanding. A particular judgement that A caused B was shown by Kant to be synthetic; that is, one which combined an intuition with an a priori concept.

Within the 'Transcendental Analytic', causality – more properly 'causality and dependence (cause and effect)' – features as the second of the categories of relation. These are derived from the pure judgements of relation, the second of which concerns the logical relation of ground to consequence. Causality, along with the other categories, is justified in the deduction as a form of 'connection and unity' which 'precedes all experience' and without which experience would not be possible. However, along with

107

the other categories, causality by itself cannot be applied directly to intuitions; it has to be schematized; that is, adapted to intuitions, in the course of which it becomes 'the succession of the manifold, in so far as that succession is subject to a rule' (A 144/B 183).

This is also achieved in 'Analytic of Principles' which aligns the categories – justified in terms of 'transcendental judgement' with reference to 'universal conditions' – with the actual conditions of the 'relation to sensibility in general' (CPR A 148/B 187). To the categories of relation correspond the principles of the analogies of experience which determine how appearances are ordered temporally. As the second category of relation, causality yields the second analogy which states that all experience obeys the law of succession according to cause and effect. This analogy is then justified by aligning the irreversibility of causal succession with the irreversibility of time.

With such arguments Kant attempted to prove that causality was a condition of experience and could not be derived from it. His argument has subsequently been criticized from all directions, with Hegel (1817) regarding causality as the relation posited between substance and accident, and Nietzsche (1901) reducing it to a necessary fiction. Although interpretations and critiques of Kant's understanding of causality continue, his working within the framework of Galilean science has now made his work on causality largely of historical interest. Even in orthodox Kantian terms the discovery of the Uncertainty Principle which suspends causal laws at a quantum level refutes the claim that the category of causality and its principle are indispensable preconditions of experience.

Kant also distinguished between the causality of nature and the causality of freedom. The 'law' of causality prescribed by the understanding for nature is not the same as that prescribed by reason for freedom. The opposition between the two forms of causality forms the conflict of the 'third antinomy' in CPR. This opposes the spontaneity of a free cause to the utter determination of the laws of nature. For Kant it is essential for both theoretical and practical philosophy that the two causalities be not confused. This is not to deny that for human beings who inhabit both intelligible and sensible realms 'the causality of freedom . . . is the causality of a natural cause subordinated to freedom' (CJ, §IX), but rather to insist that the causality of freedom, or the ground of intelligible determination, while qualified by the causality of nature is not reduced to it. By the same principle the laws of natural causality are restricted to appearances, and may not be extended to supersensible objects.

censorship of reason *see also* CRITICAL PHILOSOPHY, FACT, METHOD, REASON, TRUTH
The censorship of reason is described in CPR as the second, sceptical

stage in the development of pure reason. The first stage is the dogmatic, identified with the Wolffian school, which proposes transcendent principles without properly justifying them; the second is the sceptical censorship of these principles, identified with Hume; while the third stage is the critical scrutiny of the limits of reason accomplished by Kant himself. In the third stage, Kant claims, the sceptical censorship of the facts of reason or its present bounds is succeeded by criticism of its limits (CPR A 760/ B 788).

certainty [*certitudo, Gewissheit*] *see also* FAITH, HOLDING-TO-BE-TRUE, KNOWLEDGE
The problem of certainty was peripheral to medieval philosophy – Aquinas defines certitude as knowledge which does not depart from that which is found in the thing. Certitude was assured ontologically through a 'cause' of knowledge in the thing producing an effect in the mind, with the order of things and the mind objectively proportioned to each other. Early modern philosophers were not so certain about certainty, as is evident from Descartes' attempt in the *Discourse on Method* (1637) to establish the certitude of perceptions and judgement in the face of doubt. With this text Descartes inaugurated the peculiarly modern pre-occupation with epistemology; for him, as for subsequent philosophers as diverse as Malebranche and Spinoza, truth itself is defined as certainty, or, in Spinoza's words, as 'that which removes all doubt' (Spinoza, 1985, p. 313).

The theme of certainty plays a specific role in Kant's philosophy; it is not part of a general problematic of doubt which extends from the evidence of the senses to that of reason, but specifically concerns the subjective validity of judgements. The beginnings of this position are evident in the third reflection of PE – 'Of the nature of philosophical certainty' – where Kant distinguishes between philosophical and mathematical certainty. Both disciplines make judgements which are governed by 'laws of identity and contradiction', but for Kant these laws are negative conditions of certainty. They are the necessary but not sufficient conditions of certainty, for while a concept or judgement that does not conform to them definitely lacks certainty, they cannot in themselves serve as sufficient sources of it. In order to be certain, mathematical concepts, while conforming to the laws of identity and contradiction, must in addition possess intuitive certainty, and philosophical concepts must possess discursive certainty. With this claim Kant detached himself from rationalist accounts of certainty, and then began to search for criteria of certainty beyond mere absence of doubt.

In the critical philosophy the problem of certainty is restricted to the 'subjective validity of a judgement' or our subjectively 'holding it to be true' (*Fürwahrhalten*) (CPR A 822/B 850; see also L pp. 570ff). For this reason the critical discussion of certainty is largely confined to the section of CPR on 'The Transcendental Doctrine of Method'. Judgements are held to be subjectively and/or objectively sufficient: 'subjective sufficiency is termed *conviction* (for myself), the objective sufficiency is termed *certainty* (for everyone)' (A 822/B 850). A judgement of opinion is neither subjectively nor objectively sufficient; one which is believed to be true is subjectively sufficient; while one which is known to be true is both subjectively and objectively sufficient.

In the critical philosophy, certainty is important in establishing the limits of what can be known; it consists in reason coming 'to a decision either in regard of the objects of its enquiries or in regard to the capacity or incapacity of reason to pass any judgement upon them' (CPR B 22). However, certainty does not serve as a criterion for truth, but only as a mark of the subjective experience of the truth of a judgement. The sources of truth themselves lie elsewhere than in subjective certainty. In restricting the importance of certainty in this way, Kant deviates considerably from the Cartesian epistemological tradition. Nevertheless, this has not prevented many commentators from attempting to return him to this tradition, and to interpret the Transcendental Analytic of CPR as a search for truth through certainty.

children *see* MARRIAGE, SEX, WOMAN

Christ *see* ARCHETYPE, CHURCH, GOD

church [*Kirche*] *see also* GOD, STATE, THEODICY, THEOLOGY
Kant's understanding of the church may be situated within the broad context of Protestant ecclesiology. This was concerned above all with the problems of the relation of the church to its believers and to the state. His treatment of the two problems in RL and MM evince an often unstable combination of themes drawn from the Calvinist and Pietist traditions then prevailing in Prussia.

The most obvious inheritance from Calvinism is Kant's distinction between the invisible and visible church. The former is the 'idea of the union of all the righteous under direct and moral divine world government' (RL p. 101, p. 92). The invisible church would be the realization of the ethical commonwealth, but this may also be pursued through the visible church which is the 'actual union of men into a whole which harmonises with that ideal'. Kant describes the characteristics of the true visible church in terms of the categorical schema of quantity, quality, relation and modality: it would be quantitatively universal and unified, qualitatively pure, its internal and external relations would be governed by the principle of freedom, and it would be modally unchangeable.

With respect to the constitution of the visible church Kant refuses to accept either the Catholic or Orthodox reliance on monarchic and aristocratic forms of ecclesiastical organization; he also rejects the representative democratic forms of organization pursued by the Calvinists. Instead, surprisingly, he prefers the Pietist, patriarchal form of church organization modelled on an analogy with the holy family. He writes: 'its constitution is neither *monarchical* (under a pope or patriarch), nor *aristocratic* (under bishops and prelates), nor *democratic*... It could best of all be likened to that of a household (family) under a common, though invisible, moral Father...' (RL p. 102, p. 93) The son makes the father's will known to the family, in which spirit they 'enter with one another into a voluntary, universal, and enduring union of hearts' (ibid.).

When Kant turns to the relation of church and state he abandons the quietistic apolitical stance of Pietism in favour of a more Calvinist approach. The state cannot legitimately interfere with the church since its sphere of influence does not extend thus far. It cannot impose a religion upon a people, nor require conformity, nor dispossess the church of its property or ministers (MM p. 368, p. 173). However, this is not to say that a church enjoys its autonomy in perpetuity. For Kant, now in a strong Calvinist vein, the organization of a church and the rights and privileges of its clergy are the result of a contract with its members. If they withdraw from this contract, then the church and its clergy may legitimately be dispossessed 'since the reason for their possession hitherto lay only in the *people's opinion* and also had to hold as long as that lasted. But as soon as this opinion lapses, and even lapses only in the judgement of those who by their merit have the strongest claim to guide judgement, the supposed property has to cease, as if by an appeal of the people to the state' (MM p. 325, p. 135).

Perhaps because of its eclectic character, Kant's ecclesiology has had relatively little impact upon modern theology. Nor has it played a central role in interpretations of his philosophical or religious thought. It has, however, been the object of renewed scrutiny as part of the growing interest in Kant's account of social and political organization.

citizenship *see* STATE, WOMAN

civilization *see* CULTURE, HISTORY

clarity [*Klarheit*] *see also* CONSCIOUSNESS, ENLIGHTENMENT, HOLDING-TO-BE-TRUE, KNOWLEDGE, TRUTH
In the *Meditations on Knowledge, Truth, and Ideas* (1684; see Leibñiz, 1976, pp. 291–5) Leibniz distinguished between grades of knowledge in terms of

111

the contraries clear–obscure, confused–distinct, adequate–inadequate and symbolic–intuitive. The first pair of contraries proved enormously influential, and were pivotal in the development of German Enlightenment philosophy, especially that of Christian Wolff. For Leibniz, a clear concept is one which suffices to recognize a representation; it is distinct when the 'marks' which enable it to be recognized can be described and enumerated. For Leibniz's Enlightenment successors, clarity and distinctness became characteristics marking stages in the perfection of knowledge. The move from obscurity to clarity and distinctness was considered in terms of the move from knowledge of the senses to that of the understanding, or from prejudice to enlightenment.

This progressive schema was first challenged by the Pietist opponents of the Wolffian enlightenment who argued that there were limits to the perfection of knowledge. This view was adopted and developed by Kant in PE where he argued for the existence of basic, unanalyzable concepts (p. 279, p. 252). This early critique of the Enlightenment model of the progressive perfection of knowledge towards greater clarity and distinctness was largely sustained by Kant, although the terms clarity and distinctness do not feature prominently in any of the Critiques. The model does appear in some of the Reflections and published lecture transcripts, notably in A and L.

In L Kant reproduces Leibniz' and Wolff's distinction between the perfection of cognition according to the quality of clarity, and distinctness as the 'clarity of marks'. Indeed, in A he couches the distinction in orthodox Leibnizian terms, defining clarity as 'the consciousness of one's representations sufficient for distinguishing one object from another' and distinctness as 'consciousness which makes the composition of representations clear' (§6). He also follows Baumgarten in distinguishing between the subjective clarity and distinctness of aesthetic cognition and the objective variants of rational cognition. He develops an intriguing attempt to adapt the Wolffian schema to his own critical insights by distinguishing between analytic and synthetic distinctness: analytic clarity and distinctness apply to concepts and simply break them down into their parts, while their synthetic counterparts apply to objects and expand the concept. This distinction was later carried over into that between formal and transcendental logic proposed in CPR (A 150/B 190) but without the schema of clarity and distinctness. Although there was an attempt to revive the schema by neo-Leibnizian critics of Kant such as Eberhard (see OD) and Maimon (1790), it remained largely dormant until the return to the analysis of concepts inaugurated by Frege at the end of the nineteenth century.

co-existence *see* ANALOGIES OF EXPERIENCE, SUCCESSION

cognition [*Erkenntnis*] *see also* CONCEPT, FACULTY, HOLDING-TO-BE-TRUE, INTUI-
TION, KNOWLEDGE, PERCEPTION, REPRESENTATION, THINKING
Kant's distinctions between cognition (*Erkenntnis*), knowledge (*Wissen*) and
thinking (*Denken*) have not been consistently respected by his translators
– nor were they on occasion by Kant himself. Even Kemp Smith in his
influential translation of CPR systematically elides the distinction between
knowledge and cognition by translating *Erkenntnis* as 'knowledge'. In his
typology of representations in CPR A 320/B 377, Kant defines cognition
as 'objective perception' or objective 'representation with consciousness'.
There are two sorts of cognition, namely intuitions and concepts, which
correspond to the two sources of cognition in sensibility and understanding (A 294/B 351). Cognition is with occasional exceptions (such as CPR
A 69/B 94) distinguished from both knowledge and thinking. Knowledge
signifies the subjective and objective sufficiency of a judgement, and is
thus a qualification of thinking. Thinking, in turn, consists in the unification
of representations in a consciousness, or judgement. While the categories
of thinking 'are not limited by the conditions of our sensible intuition',
the cognition 'of that which we think, the determining of the object,
requires intuition' (CPR B p. 166). For as Kant reflected, 'to cognise an
object I must be able to prove its possibility, either from its actuality as
attested by experience, or *a priori* by means of reason. But I can think
whatever I please, provided only that I do not contradict myself . . .' (CPR
B xxvi). Cognition of that which we think requires not only that cognitions
in the shape of concepts and intuitions be present, but also that the
judgement which unifies them satisfies the principle of contradiction: such
conditions are met in the case of synthetic a priori judgements.

combination [*Verbindung*] *see also* ACTION, APPERCEPTION, CONSCIOUSNESS, MANI-
FOLD, SUBJECT, SYNTHESIS, UNITY
Of all the representations, combination 'cannot be given through objects'
but is 'an act of the self-activity of the subject' (CPR B 130). It contains
not only the 'concept of the manifold and of its synthesis' but also the
concept of the *unity* of the manifold. The latter is not an object of possible
experience, but is nevertheless its essential condition. The concept of the
unity of the manifold represents the 'synthetic unity of a manifold' and is
the condition for combination. This unity is then related by Kant to the
identity of consciousness guaranteed by the 'synthetic unity of apperception'.

command [*Gebot*] *see also* CATEGORICAL IMPERATIVE, INCLINATION, LAW, SYLLOGISM,
WILL
The concept of command is central to Kant's moral philosophy, express-
ing the relationship between objective law and the will. In GMM Kant

113

defines it as the 'representation of an objective principle insofar as it necessitates the will' (p. 414, p. 24) distinguishing it from the law which it represents, and the imperative through which it is formulated. Because of the 'subjective constitution' of the human will – the fact that it is 'not thoroughly good' – the command is expressed as an ought, as the law's outweighing of the will's inclinations. For this reason Kant often casts the command as ensuring 'submission to law' as in CPrR where it is said to 'constrain the sensuously affected subject' (p. 81, p. 83). Kant rigorously distinguishes this 'command (law) of morality' associated with the categorical imperative from the 'rules of skill' and 'councils of prudence' derived from hypothetical imperatives (GMM p. 416, p. 26).

The complex structure underlying Kant's use of the term is most apparent in MM. There the command is described as that which is proper to the executive arm of the state, situated between the legislator and the judiciary, and responsible for ensuring conformity to law. It also appears immediately afterwards as the middle term of a practical syllogism: 'the major premise, which contains the *law* of that will; the minor premise which contains the *command* to behave in accordance with the law, i.e., the principle of subsumption under the law; and the conclusion, which contains the *verdict* (sentence) . . .' (MM p. 313, p. 125). There is thus an analogy at work between the practical syllogism, the organization of the state and the articulation of moral judgement in terms of the distinction between law, command and imperative.

common sense [*sensus communis, Gemeinsinn*] *see also* COMMUNICABILITY, FEELING, GEMÜT, PUBLICITY, REFLECTION, REFLECTIVE JUDGEMENT, SENSE, TASTE
Common sense has two distinct meanings in Kant which are elided in the English translation of the term. The first appears in the Preface to P and refers to colloquial 'plain common sense' (*gemeinen Menschenverstand*) and the appeal to it by so-called 'common sense' philosophers such as T. Reid (1710–96) and J. Priestly (1733–1804). For Kant, the way in which these writers 'missed the point of [Hume's] problem was positively painful' (p. 258, p. 4): 'To appeal to common sense when insight and science fail, and no sooner – this is one of the subtle discoveries of modern times, by means of which the most superficial ranter can safely enter the lists with the most thorough thinker and hold his own' (p. 259, p. 5). In this context, common sense 'is but an appeal to the opinion of the multitude' in which 'the popular charlatan glories' (p. 259, p. 5).

In CJ however, Kant develops a positive account of 'common sense' (*sensus communis*) which is central to his discussion of reflective judgement. It appears in §40 entitled 'Taste as a kind of *sensus communis*' where it is distinguished from the 'vulgar' common sense of the *gemeinen*

114

Menschenverstand. Sensus communis is a 'public sense', a 'critical faculty which in its reflective act takes account of the mode of representation of everyone else, in order, as it were, to weigh its judgement with the collective reason of mankind'. With this view of common sense Kant revives the Renaissance humanist understanding of *sensus communis* as a form of republican virtue, and goes even further in this direction when he aligns this reflective form of judgement with taste. Thus Kant concludes: 'that the aesthetic, rather than the intellectual, judgement can bear the name of a public sense, i.e., taking it that we are prepared to use the word "sense" of an effect that mere reflection has upon the mind; for then by sense we mean the feeling of pleasure' (CJ § 40). This definition of an 'enlightened', 'critical', and yet also public 'common sense' is set against prejudice of the 'vulgar' commonsense of the British philosophers.

By describing the act of reflection as a 'sense' Kant also retrieves the original Aristotelian connotations of *sensus communis*. For Aristotle it is not a 'special sense' or a faculty, but rather a 'general sensibility' which informs the five discrete senses. This sensibility is neither 'of the flesh' (Aristotle, 1941, 426b, 15) nor is it intelligible, but is an 'awareness' of, and sensitivity to, differences (see Welsch, 1987). For Kant too, *sensus communis* is reflective without being an intuition or a concept – he describes it as 'internal feeling of a final state of the *Gemüt*' occasioned when 'the imagination in its freedom stirs the understanding, and the understanding apart from concepts puts the imagination into regular play'. It points to a pleasurable mode of communication dominated by neither concept nor law, one for which the aesthetic judgement of taste is paradigmatic.

The importance of 'common sense' for Kant's notions of 'critique', 'enlightenment' and 'judgement', as well as its broader implications for theoretical, practical and aesthetic philosophy were not fully appreciated until the twentieth century. Then it became crucial not only for the interpretation of Kant, but also in the fields of political philosophy and aesthetics. Kant's notion of *sensus communis* is central to Arendt's attempts to develop a post-totalitarian account of political judgement (see Arendt, 1989) as well as Lyotard's elaboration of new models of reflective judgement appropriate to the scientific, political and aesthetic experience of postmodernity (see Lyotard, 1983, 1988, 1991).

communicability [*Mitteilung*] *see also* AESTHETICS, COMMON SENSE, COMMUNITY, HISTORY, PLEASURE, PUBLICATION, TASTE

Communicability is central to Kant's anthropology and philosophy of history, as well as to his account of the aesthetic judgement of taste. In CBH he describes the 'urge to communicate' of the first man, expressed in sounds intended 'to announce their existence to living creatures outside themselves' (p. 110, p. 222). In CJ §41 he describes the end of history in terms of the refinement of this capacity: 'Eventually, when civilization has reached its height it makes this work of communication almost the main business of refined inclination, and the entire value of sensations is placed in the degree to which they permit of universal communication.' This state of pure communication is anticipated in the reflective activity of the *sensus communis* or 'public sense' which abstracts from the content of a judgement, attending only to its formal communicability. This is grounded upon, but also grounds, the relation of imagination and understanding 'without the mediation of a concept' (§40) which is peculiar to the aesthetic judgement of taste. Kant also suggests that the interest in communicability may explain why judgements of taste are felt to involve 'a sort of duty' which is not, however, based on the moral law.

Kant's comments on communicability have become increasingly important for twentieth-century philosophy. They have informed Arendt and Lyotard's attempts to apply Kant's model of reflective judgement to politics and art, as well as Habermas's attempts to establish a communicative ethics on the basis of a communicative theory of action (Habermas, 1981). In terms of Kant exegesis, they point to a dimension of intersubjectivity which underpins the more austere accounts of theoretical and practical judgement essayed in the first two critiques.

community [*Gemeinschaft*] *see also* ANALOGIES OF EXPERIENCE, CATEGORIES, CHURCH, COMMUNICABILITY, COSMOPOLITANISM, STATE
Community is strictly speaking the third category of relation, and like all categories is derived from a form of judgement, in this case the disjunctive. It yields a schema and a principle in the third analogy. A disjunctive judgement is one which includes propositions which are mutually exclusive but which between them add up to a totality of knowledge. Kant represents totality as 'a whole divided into parts (the subordinate concepts), and that since no one of them can be contained under any other, they are thought as co-ordinated with, not subordinated to, each other, and so determining each other, not in one direction only, as in a series, but reciprocally, as in an aggregate' (CPR B 112). By analogy he extends this logical relationship of concepts to 'a whole which is made up of things', claiming that in the latter 'a similar combination is being thought'. This is because, in contrast to the category of causality, 'one thing is not subordinated, as effect, to another, as cause of its existence, but, simultaneously and reciprocally, is co-ordinated with it, as cause of the determination of the other' (CPR B 112). This co-ordination is characterized by parts existing independently of each other and 'yet combined together in one whole' (CPR B 113).

As with all the categories, Kant derives from community a schema and a principle. The schema adapts the abstract category to the conditions of a finite intuition; for community this results in the 'schema of community or reciprocity' that 'the reciprocal causality of substances in respect of their accidents, is the co-existence, according to a universal rule, of the determinations of the one substance with those of the other' (CPR A 144/ B 183). The principle, as expressed in the third analogy of experience, holds that substances perceived to co-exist in space 'stand in thorough-going community, that is, in mutual interaction' (CPR A 211) or 'are in thoroughgoing reciprocity' (CPR B 256). This is a principle which cannot be derived empirically from the mere existence of several objects – their co-existence must be assumed a priori and cannot 'be an object of a possible perception' (CPR A 212/B 258).

In the discussion of the third analogy Kant identifies an 'ambiguity' in the word *Gemeinschaft* which he settles by making a distinction in Latin between *communio* and *commercium*. He defines the category of community in terms of the latter, 'as signifying a dynamical community, without which even local community (*communio spatii*) could never be empirically known' (CPR A 213/B 260). Without the dynamic reciprocal influence of substances in *commercium* there could be no empirical relation of co-existence or *communio*.

The latter distinction is of interest with respect to Kant's views on social and political community. Kant's understanding of political community is primarily oriented towards *commercium* rather than *communio*. The latter term, deriving from the Latin word for a fortification, sees community in terms of an exclusive sharing of space protected from the outside, while the former derives from the processes of exchange and communication. Thus when Kant describes social or political community, it is usually in terms of free exchange and respect between individuals rather than in terms of shared characteristics or space. He markedly prefers the term *Gesellschaft* (society) or *Reich* (kingdom) over *Gemeinschaft* (community) – indeed he uses the latter very rarely, although on occasion he uses the term *Gemeinwesen* (commonwealth). Nevertheless, Kant's view of social and political community is close in spirit to the category of community, stressing co-ordination and co-existence of mutually exclusive interests which although opposed to each other nevertheless add up to a whole. This model is extended from the relations between individuals, to those between social groups, and eventually to those between states (see RL Book III, Division 1; CJ §83; PP p. 367, p. 113).

comparison *see* REFLECTION

comprehension *see* SYNTHESIS

concept [*Begriff*] *see also* CATEGORY, EPISTEMOLOGY, IMAGINATION, METAPHYSICS, REPRESENTATION, SYNTHESIS, UNDERSTANDING, UNITY

The German word for concept – *Begriff* – translates the past participle of the Latin verb *concipere*: 'to take to oneself, to take and hold'. As a substantive it does not appear in the philosophical vocabulary before the late seventeenth century; prior to this it meant a 'provisional sketch' of a legal document or agreement, or even a poetic conceit. It was first used in a logical and epistemological context by Leibniz, most probably in his influential *Meditations on Knowledge, Truth, and Ideas* (1784; see Leibniz, 1976, pp. 291–5). This names the product of conception as the 'concept', a deliberate neologism directed against the Cartesian reliance on terms such as 'idea' and 'notion' (although Leibniz also uses these). The neologism was accepted by Wolff in his *Logic* and through this became part of the German philosophical language. Meissner's *Philosophisches Lexicon* (1737) gives *notio* and *idea* as synonyms of *Begriff,* but they are clearly in the process of being distinguished from each other. Concepts are broadly defined by Leibniz and his followers as 'any representation of a thing' and are classified according to their degrees of clarity, distinctness, completion and adequacy. This is the context in which Kant began to use the term in his pre-critical writings, and certain ambiguities inherent in this usage are carried over by him into the critical philosophy, notably with respect to the relationship between the logical and epistemological senses of the term.

The Cartesian account of conception to which Leibniz objected was itself an intervention within an extremely ancient philosophical debate on the nature of knowledge and its sources. Aristotle set the terms for this debate in his review of early Greek philosophy in the *Metaphysics.* He criticized his predecessors for 'supposing knowledge to be sensation' and for seeking the origins of knowledge in 'physical alteration' (Aristotle, 1941, 1009b). He introduced a distinction between two operations of the mind – *noiesis* and *aisthesis* – 'perceiving' and 'thinking'. While this distinction solved some problems, it also raised others which were destined to have a long and perplexed future. Basically, if *noiesis* and *aisthesis* were really radically distinct operations of the mind, how then could they be related to each other in order to generate knowledge? One option was to derive the *noeta* from the *aistheta*, privileging sensation; another would be to derive *aistheta* from *noeta*, privileging thought. The first option was pursued by Atomists such as Democritus (but not, we shall see, by Epicurus), while the second was pursued by the Platonists and later neo-Platonists. Aristotle's own position was a complex combination of both positions which regarded both *aistheta* and *noeta* as abstracted sensible and intelligible forms. The Epicurean school developed a further compromise which was crucial for Kant: in this the senses are held to produce sensible images which are apprehended proleptically by the mind. The *noeta*, in other words, anticipate the shape of the *aistheta*, but possess no meaning apart from them.

Medieval Aristotelianism developed an extremely sophisticated version of Aristotle's account of the abstraction of sensible and intelligible forms. However, by the seventeenth century this account had become narrowed by the focus upon the problem of conception, or the abstraction of ideas and notions from sensible experience. The human subject was divided into faculties of sensibility and intellect, and the problem of how to bring together sense data and intellectual ideas was solved either rationalistically, by deriving sensibility from ideas, or empirically, by deriving ideas from sensibility. In order to avoid this impasse Leibniz placed sense data and ideas on a continuum of representation and gave them the generic name 'concepts'. However, his follower Christian Wolff gave the new term a further rationalist twist which provoked renewed empiricist objections. These in turn led, in the 1730s, to the attempt by the Wolffian philosopher A.G. Baumgarten to clarify matters by restating the ancient distinction between *aisthesis* and *noiesis*.

It was in this context of terminological inconsistency that Kant developed his account of the concept. His version is complicated not only by the inherent equivocality of the term, but also by the close relationship between the epistemological problem of conception involving the validity of a concept's relation to the world, and the logical problem of judgement, or the use of concepts in making valid judgements. Kant combined the two problems in the transcendental logic of the first critique, but he had already prepared for this move in the pre-critical writings. In these he avoided both extremes of the empiricist–rationalist opposition by refusing to derive concepts from either abstraction from sensible perception or from the rational principle of non-contradiction; he looked instead to the process of imaginative reflection on the form and content of experience. He refers in FS to the 'fundamental capacity' of the human mind to make 'one's own representations into objects of one's own thoughts' (p. 60, p. 104) and derives concepts from this capacity. Thus the concept of a solid body is derived not from the experience of such a body, nor from its rational necessity, but by the philosopher representing to himself what is known of such a body, and reflecting upon this representation. Reflection takes 'what is known immediately of a thing as its attribute' and if it finds the thing unthinkable without the attribute, it converts it into the concept of the thing. In the case of a body, the attribute 'impenetrability' is first abstracted, and then reflected upon; when it is recognized to be indispensable to the thought of body it may be accepted as a concept (p. 58, p. 102).

119

In the course of this analysis of the process of conception Kant discovered two classes of concept. The first includes derived or complex concepts, which are open to analysis; the second includes concepts described in NM as 'simple and unanalysable' and in other places as 'basic' or 'elementary'. Kant also describes the basic concepts as 'undemonstrable fundamental judgements' which are means of 'producing' knowledge. At this stage Kant is by no means certain about the properties of such basic concepts, except that they are 'unanalysable'. His exploration of their properties was to prove one of the main sources of the later critical philosophy.

After reflecting on the sources and extent of the basic concepts for over a decade Kant made them, in the guise of 'categories', into the prime object of metaphysical investigation. He discovered that they had several important properties which distinguished them from other products of conception. Both basic and derived concepts were generically distinct from intuitions; all were cognitions, but intuitions were singular while concepts were general or reflected presentations. Derived or 'empirical' concepts are drawn from experience by means of comparison, reflection and abstraction while basic or 'pure' concepts 'are not abstracted from experience' (L p. 590) and are 'investigated by metaphysics'. Having made this distinction, Kant is faced with the problem of how pure concepts may be related to intuitions. If they are used without an object, they become ideas – concepts without any possible object of experience – but what prevents all such pure concepts becoming ideas?

Kant's solution in CPR is to see the pure, a priori concepts of the understanding as fundamental to experience. Beginning with the various functions of judgement carried out by the understanding, Kant proceeds to describe the concepts as a parallel order of 'concepts of intuitions in general' which adapt intuitions to judgements. Judgements unify a manifold, and the basic unities through which this is accomplished are the categories. Thus the pure concepts of the understanding or categories are derived from the table of judgements (forming four groups of three under the titles quantity, quality, relation and modality). These concepts adapt themselves to the conditions of appearances in space and time, a process Kant describes as schematism, or they adapt intuitions to themselves by anticipating intuitions in the shape of the system of principles. In CPR Kant concentrates on the latter, developing the Epicurean position that *noeta* (concepts) anticipate the shape in which *aestheta* (intuitions) are presented to the understanding.

The ambition of the 'transcendental logic' of CPR is to reform metaphysics on the basis of a fusion of the logical and epistemological aspects of the concept. The one account views the concept as a function of the unity of judgement, while the other sees it as a *noeta* related to an *aestheta*.

In the latter the concept takes its place within the general Kantian problem of synthesis, with its connotations of freedom, spontaneity and finitude. This aspect was developed in the systematic logics of the German idealists – Fichte, Schelling and above all Hegel. In the *Science of Logic* (1812) Hegel draws out the ambiguities of the Kantian account of the concept, showing that its attempt to reconcile logic and epistemology is informed by an ontology, and that its equivocal relationship between concept and intuition may be analyzed in terms of the relationship between universality, particularity and individuality.

The programme of transcendental logic was severely challenged in the century following Kant, with criticism focusing on the nature of the concept. For Frege concepts are objective and subject only to the laws of logic; they must not be confused with epistemological 'ideas'. In direct criticism of Kant he maintained that 'The concept has a power of collecting together far superior to the unifying power of synthetic apperception' (Frege, 1950, §47). An analogous dislocation of the transcendental logic was carried out by Wittgenstein when he treated the concept not in terms of its relation to the world through perception, but in its syntactical relation to other concepts. A different route was taken by neo-Kantian critiques of psychological and empiricist accounts of the origin of concepts. Their discussion of 'concept formation' regarded it as neither an introspective, psychological process nor a process of abstracting from empirically given data, but paid homage to Kant by regarding it as a form of transcendental reflection. An important version of the latter was developed by Husserl, who sought the process of concept formation in the work of the imagination, distinguishing the 'lived experience of the imagination' from both psychological and abstractive processes.

concepts of reason *see* REASON

concepts of reflection *see also* AMPHIBOLY, CATEGORIES, CONCEPTS, FORM, IDENTITY, INNER/OUTER, JUDGEMENT, MATTER, ORIENTATION, REFLECTION
The concepts of reflection are employed in an act of judgement to compare given concepts with each other and with intuitions, and thus unlike concepts of the understanding have no reference to an object. Kant lists them as identity and difference, agreement and opposition, inner and outer, and matter and form (CPR A 260–80/B 316–36). They are orientational concepts applied by the judgement to both concepts and intuitions, and for this reason are prone to amphiboly, that is, being used illegitimately to elide the distinction between understanding and intuition. For Kant the concepts of reflection point to an operation of the faculty of judgement prior to the act of judgement which synthesizes concept and intuition.

121

This prior work of judgement reflects on the character of a representation (whether it is a concept or an intuition) through transcendental reflection, and then assigns it a place according to a transcendental topic.

The transcendental topic, Kant claims, 'contains no more than the above-mentioned four headings of all comparison and distinction. They are distinguished from categories by the fact that they do not present the object according to what constitutes its concept (quantity, reality), but only serve to describe in all its manifoldness the comparison of the representations which is prior to the concept of things. But this comparison requires in the first place a reflection; that is, a determination of the location to which the representations of the things that are being compared belong, namely whether they are thought by the pure understanding or given in appearance by sensibility' (CPR A 269/B 326). On the basis of this account of the concepts of reflection, Kant accused Leibniz and Locke of making an amphibolous use of these concepts, with the former using them to 'intellectualise appearances' and the latter to 'sensualise the concepts of the understanding' (CPR A 271/B 327). The danger of the amphibolous use of concepts of reflection such as identity and difference is that it permits them to 'intrude into ontology' and to appear as if they were properties of things rather than a means for orienting judgement.

concepts of the understanding *see* CATEGORIES, CONCEPTS, UNDERSTANDING
The pure concepts of the understanding are another name for the categories (see CPR A 79/B 105).

condition [*Bedingung*] *see also* ABSOLUTE, ACCIDENT, APPEARANCE, CAUSALITY, DIALECTIC, EXPERIENCE, INTUITION, SPACE, SUCCESSION, TIME
Appearances are conditioned by space and time, while judgements are conditioned by 'the unification of given representations in a consciousness'. Together they form the conditions for objects of possible experience, and the knowledge of such objects. Reason, however, strives for the unconditioned in knowledge and experience, and when it infers an unconditioned or absolute on the basis of an extended series of conditions it exceeds the bounds of possible objects and legitimate knowledge of experience. Kant calls such illegitimate inferences of the unconditioned from the conditioned 'dialectical', and gives an analysis of them in the 'Transcendental Dialectic' of CPR.

Conflict of the Faculties First published by Nicolovius in autumn 1798, CF comprises, in Kant's words, 'three essays that I wrote for different purposes at different times' with a preface and an introduction. The three essays – 'The Conflict of the Philosophy Faculty with the Theology Faculty', 'The Conflict of the Philosophy Faculty with the Faculty of Law' and 'The

Conflict of the Philosophy Faculty with the Faculty of Medicine' – address the general problem of the relationship between knowledge and power and the specific problem of the relationship between the university and the state by means of a discussion of the relationship of the 'lower faculty' of philosophy to the three 'higher faculties' of theology, law and medicine. The broad background to CF was the increasing tension throughout the second half of the eighteenth century between the claims of higher faculties largely dedicated to vocational training of priests, lawyers and doctors and those of the lower, philosophical faculty to speak philosophically upon theological, legal and medical issues. The immediate context of Kant's text, however, was the tightening of the censorship following the accession of Frederick William in 1786 with the intention to reverse the process of enlightenment encouraged by Frederick II.

The first essay concerns the conflict of philosophy with the theology faculty. It arose directly from Kant's difficulties with the religious censor over the publication of RL. This was to have been published in four parts by the Berlin enlightenment journal *Berlinische Monatsschrift* in 1792. The first instalment was approved by the philosophy censor for publication, and appeared in April 1792. The remaining three parts were submitted to the religious censor, who withheld approval. The editor of the *Berlinische Monatsschrift* then appealed unsuccessfully to both the Censorship Commission and the King. Kant's response was to submit the manuscript first to the Königsberg theology faculty in order to establish it as a work of philosophy, and thus under the jurisdiction of the philosophy censor, and then for censorship to the philosophy faculty of the University of Jena. The text as a whole received the imprimatur, and was published in Königsberg in 1793.

Following the events surrounding the publication of RL, Kant was invited on 14 June 1794 by Carl Friedrich Stäudlin, the editor of the Göttingen theological journal, to contribute an article. Kant replied on December 4th of the same year declining the invitation, for the reason that, although he had written the article, he had since received a Cabinet Order dated October 1st which accused him of misusing his philosophy to 'distort and disparage many of the cardinal and basic teachings of the Holy Scriptures and Christianity' and of leading youth astray. The Order threatened 'unpleasant measures' in the case of 'continuing obstinacy'. Kant replied defending himself against the charges, but undertaking 'hereafter [to] refrain altogether from discoursing publicly, in lectures or writings, on religion, whether natural or revealed'. The text he had written for Stäudlin was the first casualty of this vow, and was withheld until after the death of Frederick William in 1797, when it formed the first of the three parts of CF. The Cabinet Order and Kant's reply were also published as the preface to CF along with some barbed comments on 'any new invasions of obscurantism'.

The second essay on the conflict between the philosophy and the law faculties was also written for the *Berlinische Monatsschrift* and also refused the imprimatur by the censor. The article, 'An Old Question Raised Again: Is the Human Race Constantly Progressing?' was written in 1795, and was published again following the death of Frederick William II. The third essay concerning the conflict with the medical faculty was the exception in not falling foul of the censor. It takes the form of a letter to C.W. Hufeland and was written in response to a copy of Hufeland's *Macrobiotics, or the Art of Prolonging Human Life* which the author sent to Kant late in 1796. Kant's philosophical account of the body and health was first published by Hufeland in 1798 in the *Journal of Practical Pharmacology and Surgery* before its appearance in CF.

The three essays are brought loosely together by an introduction which reflects on the mission of the University, the tension between the demands of scholarship and those of the state, and a call for the academic freedom of the lower faculty. The characteristics and the purposes of the teachings of the three higher faculties are described and distinguished from those of philosophy. The higher faculties are concerned with policing the interpretation of religious and legal texts and the training of doctors, while the lower faculty is concerned above all with public criticism. Kant proceeds to explore these, more or less tangentially, with great insight and wry humour. In spite of the book's contrived character, Kant makes several insightful points concerning the relationship of power and knowledge which eventually cohere into a consistent case for academic freedom as well as a still timely assessment of the forces within and without the university which threaten it.

conscience [*syneidesis, conscientia, Gewissen*] *see also* CONSCIOUSNESS, FEAR, FREEDOM, GOD, JUDGEMENT, POSTULATE, PUNISHMENT
Conscience is originally a Greek ethical term meaning 'joint knowledge'. It was systematically developed as a part of Christian doctrine by Paul in the New Testament (e.g., Acts 24:16). It is a sense or conviction that a thought or course of action is correct, one which is held to originate in the voice of God. Kant's use of the concept is more indebted to Calvin and Calvinism than to Luther and the Pietists. The latter regarded conscience as being in a state of torment which was healed by God's grace. Pietists such as Arndt considered the state of grace to consist in the passive renunciation of the world (Arndt, 1605, p. 122) and saw the joy of conscience as arising from an inner piety. Calvin, on the contrary, saw conscience as an important aspect of Christian liberty. He distinguished between the

'external forum' of the world and the 'forum of conscience' not in order to justify a retreat from the world but in order to live a just life in the world. He defines conscience as 'knowledge or science' to which 'a sense of the divine justice [is] added as witness'; it stands as it were between God and man, not suffering man to suppress what he knows in himself' (Calvin, 1962, Vol. II, p. 141).

Kant's discussions of conscience in RL, LE and MM all follow Calvin in considering conscience to be an inner forum or court. In the first text Kant defines conscience as 'a state of consciousness which in itself is duty' (RL p. 185, p. 173), and by this he means that it is 'the moral faculty of judgement passing judgement on itself'. It does not judge actions as if they were cases falling under a law, but is reason judging itself 'as to whether it has really undertaken that appraisal of actions (as to whether they are right or wrong) with all diligence, and it calls the man himself to witness *for* or *against* himself whether this diligent appraisal did or did not take place' (RL p. 186, p. 174). In LE this self-judgement is described as the passing of a sentence: conscience 'pronounces a judicial verdict, and, like a judge who can only punish or acquit but cannot reward, so also our conscience either acquits or declares us guilty and deserving of punishment' (LE p. 130). In fairly orthodox fashion, Kant considers conscience to be 'the representative within us of the divine judgement seat: it weighs our dispositions and actions in the scales of a law which is holy and pure; we cannot deceive it, and, lastly, we cannot escape it because, like the divine omnipresence, it is always with us' (LE p. 133).

The workings of the inner court of conscience are described most fully in MM. It is the 'inner judge' by which everyone 'finds themselves observed, threatened, and in general, kept in awe' (MM p. 438, p. 233). Before an action is undertaken, conscience issues a warning, but after the deed has been done 'the prosecutor comes forward in conscience' accompanied by a defence council. The dispute cannot be settled amicably, and the judge of conscience has to pass sentence, acquitting or condemning. An acquittal does not bring reward or joy (as the Pietists thought) but only a relief from anxiety. In an interesting reflection on his own judicial analogy, Kant suggests that the existence of conscience may be used to support the postulate of the existence of God as an 'omnipotent moral being' (MM p. 439, p. 234).

consciousness [*Bewusstsein*] *see also* APPERCEPTION, COGNITION, I, 'I THINK', IDENTITY, PARALOGISMS, PERCEPTION, PSYCHOLOGY, REPRESENTATION, SPONTANEITY, SUBJECT, SYNTHESIS, UNITY

Kant defines consciousness in L as the 'representation that another representation is in me' which forms the 'universal condition of all cognition in general' (L p. 544). It is held to 'accompany' all cognitions, determining their form or the 'how' (as opposed to the matter or 'what' of cognition). With the notion of a 'condition' which is also an 'accompaniment' to cognition, Kant shows himself to be heir to a deeply perplexed tradition of thought concerning the precise status of consciousness.

In *De Anima* Aristotle rehearsed many of the problems which subsequently informed the attempt to define consciousness. He asks whether the awareness of seeing is given us by sight 'or some sense other than sight', and, if the latter, whether 'we must either fall into an infinite regress, or we must somewhere assume a sense which is aware of itself' (Aristotle, 1941, 425b, 17). Aristotle prefers the latter option, but the problem of the status of the 'awareness' or 'consciousness', with regard to what it is conscious of, remains a cause of concern. The same problem arises with the mind which 'is itself thinkable in exactly the same way as its objects are' (Aristotle, 1941, 430a, 2). Were it not, we would then be required to seek a form of consciousness capable of containing both the mind and its objects, and then how could we become conscious of this? In other words, the consciousness which accompanies a perception always points beyond itself to a more inclusive form of consciousness.

Prior to the seventeenth century there was no specific term corresponding to 'consciousness'; it was not considered to be a property of the mind or senses but one of their actions. Descartes describes acts of becoming conscious, not acts of a consciousness, while Spinoza describes the act of the soul becoming aware of itself as 'sensibility'. The term consciousness is first used consistently by Locke (1690), and following him Leibniz (1765, where he uses the term *consciosite*). Locke defines consciousness as 'the perception of what passes in a man's own mind' (1690, p. 42) and derives it from acts of consciousness. His main concern, however, is to argue from the fact of consciousness to that of personal identity, making consciousness the basis of a subject: 'For, it being the same consciousness that makes a man be himself to himself, *personal identity* depends on that only ...' (p. 163). Consciousness, from being the action of the mind or senses, becomes an act of self-consciousness which serves as a condition for all other acts of consciousness. With this the Aristotelian fear of an infinite regress is allayed. Kant develops the thought that consciousness is one with self-consciousness, but refuses to regard the latter as the property of an empirical subject.

The Wolffian school of philosophy regarded consciousness as the act of being conscious (*Bewust seyn, conscium esse*), or as Meissner (1737) defined it, 'a characteristic by which we know that we are thinking'. It is a purely formal characteristic without any implications for the issues of self-consciousness and personal identity. Kant subscribed to this view of

126

consciousness, maintaining in the third paralogism that the 'identity of the consciousness of myself at different times is therefore only a formal condition of my thoughts and their coherence, and in no way proves the numerical identity of my subject' (CPR A p. 363). This formal condition is the product of an 'act of spontaneity' which cannot be invested in any empirical subject; it is 'that self-consciousness which, while generating the representation "*I think*" (a representation which must be capable of accompanying all other representations, and which in all consciousness is one and the same), cannot itself be accompanied by any further representation' (CPR B p. 132). This act, identical with pure apperception, produces the '*transcendental* unity of self-consciousness' which is both the condition and accompaniment of experience while not being itself a possible object of experience. It provides an a priori horizon for the judgements of experience which are none other than 'the uniting of representations in a consciousness' (P §22). As such it must be radically distinguished from the consciousness of ourselves as empirical, finite beings, which is the concern of 'psychological (applied) consciousness' (A §7).

The immediate post-Kantian generation of philosophers made self-consciousness the 'highest principle' of their philosophical systems. Schelling, for example, claimed that 'primary knowledge is for us without doubt the knowledge of ourselves, or self-knowledge' (1800, p. 23). Hegel, however, attempted to work through and beyond the philosophy of consciousness. He distinguished between consciousness, which involved a relation to an object, and self-consciousness which involved the relation between a subject and another self-consciousness. He criticized Kant and Fichte for eliding consciousness and self-consciousness, arguing that this led to the positing of an unknowable and yet sovereign self-consciousness which treated other self-consciousnesses as if they were things. In the *Phenomenology of Spirit* he gave an exposition of the emergence of consciousness and self-consciousness in terms of a struggle for recognition in which self-consciousness was discovered through the recognition of another self-consciousness. This development away from the theoretical alignment of self-consciousness and the unitary subject anticipated many twentieth-century developments in the philosophy of consciousness, especially those in the field of psychoanalysis, where the unconscious is considered to be a source of meaning situated beyond the individual subject (see Freud, 1915). The theme of consciousness took on political significance in Marxist theory and its account of class consciousness (see Lenin, 1902; Lukács, 1922).

constitution [*Verfassung*] *see also* COSMOPOLITANISM, GOD, HISTORY, LAW, STATE, SYSTEM, THEODICY, WORLD

The term 'constitution' is first used by Kant in UNH to describe the 'systematic constitution of the universe' or the order of the stars and planets (UNH p. vi, p. 100). The bodies making up a constituted system relate both to a 'common centre' such as the sun, and to each other by sharing a common plane or ecliptic. The constitution of the universe is dynamic and progressive, manifesting a process of eternal creation which relates the parts of the universe to each other, and all to the original creative act of God. The course of creation will 'enliven all spaces of the presence of God and will gradually place them into the regularity which is appropriate to the magnificence of his plan' (UNH p. 114, p. 154). In DS this view of constitution is extended to the moral world where it refers to the '*moral unity* [of] a systematic constitution, drawn up in a accordance with purely spiritual laws' (p. 335, p. 322). Once again, this constitution is an aspect of a theodicy in which 'A secret power forces us to direct our will towards the well-being of others or regulate it in accordance with the will of another, although this often happens contrary to our will and in strong opposition to our selfish inclination' (p. 334, p. 322).

That Kant discerned a relationship between the physical and the moral and political aspects of constitution is evident in texts from the critical period such as IUH and CJ – even CPR. In defence of the thesis that the 'history of mankind' is the 'realisation of a hidden plan of nature to bring about a perfect political constitution', Kant appeals to evidence that the universe 'is constituted as a system' (IUH p. 27, p. 50). From this he argues further that nature is working slowly through 'reformative revolutions', towards universal government. Similarly, in CJ the formal condition for attaining 'The Ultimate End of Nature as a Teleological System' is 'a constitution so regulating the mutual relations of men that the abuse of freedom by individuals striving one against another is opposed by a lawful authority centred in a whole, called civil society' (§83). Such a constitution is necessary for 'the greatest development of natural tendencies' but must be supplemented by a 'cosmopolitan constitution' or a 'system of all states that are in danger of acting injuriously to one another'. In CPR the same constitution is described as one which allows '*the greatest possible human freedom* in accordance with laws by which *the freedom of each is made to be consistent with that of all the others*' (CPR A 316/B 373).

Kant's discussions of the constitutional forms of state and international relations in PP and MM, as well as those of the church in RL, are set within the context of progressive history. This allowed him to abjure the right to revolution, and to prefer a reformist course of historical development. The idea of a civil constitution, he says in MM, is 'an absolute command [of] practical reason' (MM p. 372, p. 176) but it may not be acted upon by any subordinate authority in the state, even if the organization of the state is faulty. The authoritarian implications of this idea are hinted at in a footnote on the French Revolution in CJ in which, while every member is called at to be an end and not a means, they should nevertheless, because of their contribution to 'the possibility of the entire body', 'have their position and function defined by the idea of the whole' (CJ §65). This emerges in PP as the defence of a republican, but not democratic, constitution founded upon the three principles of '*freedom* for all members of society', *dependence* of everyone upon a single common legislation (as subjects) and 'legal *equality* for everyone (as citizens)' (p. 350, p. 99). This idea of a republican constitution offers a canon for judging existing monarchic, aristocratic and democratic constitutions, as well the idea for a future constitution which combines the greatest freedom for individual persons and individual states to relate to each other with their mutual dependence upon a lawful authority or 'common centre'.

constitutive principles *see also* IDEAS, PRINCIPLES, RULES
Constitutive principles 'seek to bring the *existence* of appearances under rules *a priori*' (CPR A 179/B 221) and are distinguished in CPR from regulative principles which offer rules 'according to which a unity of experience may arise from perception' (CPR A 180/B 223). Kant uses the distinction in his discussions of the 'principles of pure reason' and the 'transcendental ideas'. Of the four principles only the axioms of intuition and the anticipations of perception are constitutive, in so far as they describe the ways in which 'perception or empirical intuition in general itself comes about'. The analogies of experience and the postulates of empirical thought offer rules according to which experience may be organized; unlike the former they do not involve the constitution of appearances, but only the ways in which they may be regulated. Similarly, the cosmological ideas concerning the beginning of the universe and its divisibility are not constitutive but regulative, 'not indeed as the *axiom* that we think the totality as actually in the object, but as a problem for the understanding' (CPR A 508/B 536). The principle of reason which regresses from the conditioned to the unconditioned is not constitutive, 'enabling us to extend our concept of the sensible world beyond all possible experience', but is a rule 'postulating what we ought to do in the regress, but not anticipating what is present in the object as it is in itself, prior to all regress' (CPR A 509/B 537).

The entire 'Transcendental Dialectic' in CPR may be considered as an analysis of what happens when regulative ideas are applied constitutively. When ideas of reason such as God, the world and the soul are used constitutively 'as supplying concepts of certain objects, they are but pseudo rational, merely dialectical concepts' (CPR A 644/B 672) and are liable to come into conflict with themselves (see also A 666/B 694). When used constitutively, the ideas are given an illusory existence; however, when they are restricted to their proper, regulative use, they serve only to direct 'the understanding towards a certain goal upon which the routes marked out by all its rules converge, as upon their point of intersection. This point is indeed a mere idea, a *focus imaginarius*, from which, since it lies quite outside the bounds of possible experience, the concepts of the understanding do not in reality proceed' (CPR A 644/B 672). The regulative principles and ideas, in other words, contribute to the orientation of the understanding without claiming to constitute an object, nor to contribute directly to knowledge.

construction *see also* HYPOTYPOSIS, MATHEMATICS, SCHEMATISM
In his *Commentary on the First Book of Euclid's Elements* Proclus lists construction along with enunciation, exposition, specification, proof and conclusion as the constituent parts of a Euclidean geometrical theorem. It 'adds what is lacking in the given for finding what is sought' (Proclus, 1970, p. 159). Kant maintained this geometrical sense of the word, but broadened its scope to include a general account of presentation or *hypotyposis*. His account of construction is crucial for both his specific philosophy of mathematics and his more general account of knowledge and cognition.

Kant answers the question posed in P, 'how is pure mathematics possible?', by stating its 'first and highest condition of possibility', which is that 'some pure intuition must form its basis, in which all its concepts may be presented or constructed, *in concreto* and yet *a priori*' (P §7). Construction combines the a priori and the concrete, and does so by means of 'presenting its concepts in intuition'. When the concept of the understanding or 'ground of the unity of construction' is presented in intuition, it accordingly 'determines space to assume the form of a circle, or the figures of a cone and a sphere' (P §38). Kant described the insight into the nature of construction as the 'intellectual revolution' which gave rise to mathematics, one which consisted in the mathematician bringing out 'what was necessarily implied in the concepts that he had himself formed *a priori*, and had put into the figures in the construction by which he presented it to himself' (CPR B xii).

Kant extends his account of construction in two not entirely consistent directions. In the methodology of CPR he uses it to distinguish between geometrical and philosophical method. This was the continuation of his quarrel with the Wolffian style of geometrical presentation commenced in PE. Mathematical knowledge is *axiomatic* and considers 'the universal in the particular, or even in the single instance' while philosophical knowledge is *acroamatic* or discursive, and 'considers the particular only in the universal'

(CPR A 714/B 742). However, Kant also made the notion of construction pivotal in his account of the origins of experience in the combination of concept and intuition. In OD, construction is defined as 'all presentation of a concept through the (spontaneous) production of a corresponding intuition' (OD p. 192, p. 111). Such construction is pure 'if it occurs through the mere imagination in accordance with an a priori concept' and empirical 'if it is practised on some kind of material' (ibid.). The first kind of construction is *schematic* and is carried over into the schematism chapter of CPR, while the latter is *technical* and is discussed in CJ, notably in the 'First Introduction'. In both cases, the significance of construction is extended beyond the original geometrical context into a general account of the presentation of concepts in intuition.

Kant's extension of geometrical construction into an account of presentation in general has been important for radical developments in twentieth-century phenomenology, notably Husserl's *Origins of Geometry* (1954) and the commentary upon it by Derrida (1962), as well as in Lyotard's work on 'presentation' since (1971), above all in *The Differend* (1983). It offers a point of departure for an inquiry into the presentation of the concept or law which nevertheless respects concrete singularity.

content *see* FORM

contingency *see* NECESSITY

continuity *see also* ANALOGIES OF EXPERIENCE, ANTICIPATIONS OF PERCEPTION, CAUSALITY, CONTRACT, HOMOGENEITY, MAGNITUDE

For Kant continuity is a fundamental property which informs intuition, the understanding and reason. It is defined in CPR as 'the property of magnitudes by which no part of them is the smallest possible; that is, by which no part is simple' (A 169/B 212). It underlies the claim made in the anticipations of perception that the real of appearances possesses intensive magnitude or degree, and is the only quality which may be known a priori of magnitudes (CPR A 176/B 218). The forms of intuition – space and time – are described as continuous quantities (*quanta continua*) because they have no smallest part; points and instants are described as 'limit positions' which 'presuppose the intuitions which they limit or are intended to limit' (CPR A 169/B 211). The categories too obey the 'law of the continuity of all alteration', as may be illustrated by the discussion of the category of causality in the second analogy of experience. The action of causality is continuous; a change of state occurs continuously over time since 'neither time nor appearance in time consists of parts which are the smallest' (CPR A 209/B 254). Reason too 'prepares the field

131

for the understanding' (A 657/B 685), by the regulative principle of continuity. It is introduced as the 'union' of the principles of generic homogeneity and specific variety or heterogeneity which allows us 'even amidst the utmost manifoldness [to] observe homogeneity in the gradual transition from one species to another . . .' (A 660/B 688). Although Kant concedes that the 'logical law of the *continuum specierum* (*formarum logicarum*) presupposes a transcendental law (*lex continui in natura*)' (A 660/B 688) he carefully specifies that such transcendental continuity cannot be an object of experience, nor as a principle may it be given a deduction, but may only be used regulatively as a 'heuristic principle' for the 'guidance of the empirical employment of reason' and the 'elaboration of experience' (A 663/B 691).

Continuity also plays a considerable role in Kant's philosophy of right. In his discussion of possession in MM, he claims that transfer by contract 'takes place in accordance with the law of continuity (*lex continui*)' (MM p. 274, p. 93). This is necessary to prevent ownership of the object lapsing even for an instant in the course of its transfer. Kant justifies this use of continuity by recourse to the notion of 'united will' through which, at the moment of transfer, both parties to a contract form a third, 'united will' which ensures continuity of possession.

contract *see also* CONTINUITY, JUSTICE, LAW, MARRIAGE, OBLIGATION, PROPERTY, RIGHT, STATE, WILL

Contract has become the dominant form of social relationship in modern society, giving shape to our conceptions of volition, consent and obligation. Originally limited in Justinian's *Digest* of Roman law to private law obligations between citizens, the scope of contract was extended in the early modern period to include not only the formation of the state (as in Rousseau's *Social Contract* of 1762) but also moral and ethical relationships. This extension of the scope of contract is evident in, and promoted by, Kant's practical philosophy, especially MM. This was indebted to the systematization of Roman legal concepts carried to an extreme by Wolffian philosophers of law in the period immediately prior to Kant.

Kant defines a contract in terms of 'two acts that establish a right: a promise and its acceptance' (MM p. 284, p. 102). Since he wishes to develop a transcendental account of contract he abstracts from the matter of contracts – their objects – and concentrates upon the form of obligation. He accordingly emphasizes the personal over the real aspects of contract, not regarding delivery and acquisition as constitutive parts of a contract, but only as its effects. To ensure the desired result, Kant postulates three parties to a contract: a promisor, an acceptor and a guarantor. This leads to a duplication of contracts, that between the promisor and acceptor being supplemented by that between the promisor and guarantor. Kant proceeds to divide contracts according to three types. The first grants 'unilateral acquisition' and is a 'gratuitous contract' such as trust, loan and gift. The second form of contract – 'onerous contract' – grants acquisition to both parties, and includes barter, sale, loan and agency. The third group comprises contracts of guarantee which provide security through pledge and assumption of liability. With this Kant develops a typology of contracts which emphasizes the personal form of liability and obligation over the real objects of contract.

The emphasis on the personal aspects of the contract follows from Kant's voluntaristic characterization of the contractual act. The 'preparative' and the 'constitutive' elements of a contract are dedicated to achieving a unity of will between the parties. In the preparatory stage of 'negotiating' a contract, an offer is made and assented to; this is followed in the constitutive or concluding stage by a promise and an acceptance. What is acquired initially is not a real right to an external thing, but a right '*against a person* . . . a right to act upon his causality (his choice) to *perform* something for me . . .' (MM p. 274, p. 93). A right to a thing only follows after performance, but this transfer of ownership raises considerable problems for Kant's account of contract. If all rights are fundamentally personal, then a hiatus in ownership arises in the course of transferring an object from one party to another. Kant attempts to solve this difficulty by appealing to a third united will comprised of that of the two parties which provides continuity of ownership even while the object is transferred from one party to the other.

Kant extended the scope of contract from basically commercial transactions between individuals to ethical and political relations. A notorious example is his definition of marriage as the contract which ensures 'the union of two persons of different sexes for lifelong possession of each other's sexual attributes' (MM p. 277, p. 96 – a complex example which threatens the distinction between real and personal possession). He also discusses the founding of a state in terms of the idea of an original contract, as 'the act by which a people forms itself into a state' (MM p. 315, p. 127). In this contract, everyone exchanges their 'external freedom' for 'civil freedom'. Three distinct contracts are in fact undertaken in the formation of the state: the first is between future citizens in which 'each complements the others to complete the constitution of a state' (MM p. 315, p. 127); the second is between the people and a superior, the contract of 'subordination'; and the third is between the superior and the people through which 'each subject is apportioned his rights' (MM p. 316, p. 127). The idea of this original contract provides a regulative idea by which 'to think of the legitimacy of a state' (MM p. 315, p. 127) and thus 'involves an obligation on the part of the constituting authority to make the *kind of government* suited to the idea of the original contract' (MM p. 340, p. 148). Kant extends this original contract within a state to that between states, proposing a 'league of nations' based on an association of sovereign authorities.

The indirect influence of Kant's account of contract is incalculable, since his contractual accounts of property, government and international relations have given rise to an enormous polemical literature which now bears little relation to his original texts and their intentions.

contradiction [*Widerspruch*] *see also* CERTAINTY, CONCEPT, EXISTENCE, FORCE, MOTION, TIME, TRUTH

The law or principle of contradiction is described by Aristotle in the *Metaphysics* as the most 'certain' and 'indisputable' of principles. However, his definition – 'that the same attribute cannot at the same time belong and not belong to the same subject and in the same respect' (Aristotle, 1941, 1005b, 18–20) – contains a crucial, and extremely consequential temporal qualification. This is spelt out in his work *On Interpretation*, where the principle is said to hold only on the assumption of temporal simultaneity: 'since these same affirmations and denials are possible with reference to those times which lie outside the present' (Aristotle, 1941, 17a, 30). This significance of this proviso had been lost by the early eighteenth century, with Christian Wolff establishing a rationalist philosophical system based on the primacy of the principle of contradiction. According to Wolff's reading of the principle, being follows non-contradiction: 'something cannot simultaneously be and not-be' (1719, §10) is interpreted to mean that anything which is not contradictory can *ipso facto* exist. Kant's early critiques of Wolff's reliance on this principle formed one of his major steps towards the position of the critical philosophy, and broadly consisted in a reconsideration of the significance of the Aristotelian temporal qualifier.

The ND of 1755 is dedicated to a critical investigation of 'the things which are asserted, usually with more confidence than truth, concerning the supreme statements – usually put forward with more confidence than accuracy – about the supreme and undoubted primacy of the principle of contradiction over all truths' (p. 387, p. 5). In this text Kant sought to uncover additional principles of truth, but in subsequent writings he focused increasingly on the limitations of logical affirmation and negation. In NM he distinguished between logical and real opposition, the former consisting in 'simultaneously asserting and denying something of the same thing' while in the latter 'two predicates of a thing are opposed to each other, but not through the law of contradiction' (p. 171, p. 211). He illustrates his point with the example of motion and rest (previously discussed in NT). According to the principle of contradiction a body cannot both be and not-be in motion, yet Kant observes 'The motive force of a body in one direction and an equal tendency of the same body in the opposite direction do not contradict each other; as predicates they are simultaneously possible in the same body. The consequence of such an opposition is rest' (p. 171, p. 211). Kant then develops his point further by insisting on the importance of the temporal horizon: what may be contradictory at one time is not necessarily so at another.

The points made in the early writings against the principle of contradiction are developed systematically in the critical philosophy. The principle of contradiction is a 'negative criterion of truth' and restricted to serving as the '*principle of all analytic knowledge*' (CPR A 151/B 191). It is a purely formal principle, for in the words of L, 'a cognition that contradicts itself is of course false, but if it does not contradict itself it is not always true' (p. 559). Kant maintains that while it is a 'necessary logical condition that a concept of the possible must not contain any contradiction . . . this is not by any means sufficient to determine the objective reality of the concept, that is, the possibility of such an object as it is thought through the concept' (CPR A 220/B 268). For the latter kind of synthetic a priori knowledge it is necessary to supplement the principle of contradiction with a series of additional principles which respect the spatial and temporal conditions of finite human cognition.

Copernican revolution The 'revolution' was described by Nicolaus Copernicus in the Introduction to his book *On the Revolutions of the Heavenly Spheres* (1543) as the 'hypothesis' 'which sets the earth in motion and puts an immovable sun at the centre of the universe'. It attempted to explain the appearances of planetary motion by replacing a geocentric, Ptolemaic explanatory framework with a heliocentric one while maintaining the Ptolemaic machinery of epicycles and circular celestial motion. In the Preface to the Second Edition of CPR, Kant described his critical philosophy as proceeding along the lines of 'Copernicus's primary hypothesis'. While previously metaphysics assumed that 'our knowledge must conform to objects', now 'we must make trial' and 'suppose that objects must conform to our knowledge' (CPR B xvi). Thus Copernicus, 'Failing of satisfactory progress in explaining the movements of the heavenly bodies on the supposition that they all revolved around the spectator, tried whether he might not have better success if he made the spectator to revolve and the stars to remain at rest'. Yet while Copernicus's revolution was based on an hypothesis only subsequently confirmed by Kepler, 'who found an unexpected means of reducing the eccentric orbits of the planets to definite laws', and Newton 'who explained these laws in terms of a universal natural cause' (IUH p. 18, p. 42) Kant maintains that his CPR will go further than Copernicus by *proving* 'apodeictically not hypothetically, from the nature of our representations of space and time and from the elementary concepts of the understanding' (CPR B xxiii) that objects conform to knowledge, not knowledge to objects.

cosmotheological proof (of the existence of God) *see* THEOLOGY

cosmology *see also* ABSOLUTE, ANTINOMY, CAUSALITY, DIALECTIC, NATURE, ONTOLOGY, PSYCHOLOGY, THEOLOGY, WORLD

Cosmology is one of the three branches of 'Special Metaphysics' which with ontology comprise the influential system of metaphysics developed by Christian Wolff (1719). While ontology considered being-in-general, the branches of special metaphysics concentrated upon the being of particular objects: theology considered the being of God, psychology the being of the soul and cosmology the being of the world. Wolff's metaphysics was the 'pure reason' criticized by Kant, and the CPR closely follows its structure: ontology is replaced by transcendental analytic, and special metaphysics by the transcendental dialectic. In the critical revision of special metaphysics, the soul or 'idea of the absolute subject', the world or 'idea of the complete series of conditions', and God or 'idea of a complete complex of that which is possible' are revealed to be dialectical, and their sciences ridden with dialectical inferences – psychology with paralogism, cosmology with antinomy and theology with transcendent ideas.

Kant's early essay in cosmology, UNH, is a collection of speculative hypotheses concerning the constitution of the universe which idiosyncratically combines arguments drawn from physics, theology and anthropology. It is precisely the kind of enterprise which CPR would prove to be ill-founded and illegitimate, for the basic reason that it treated its hypothetical or 'regulative principles' as if they were apodeictic or 'constitutive'. The critical cosmology concerns itself with showing the dialectical consequences of over-extending categories properly applicable only to appearances. The results are presented in the four antinomies, which reveal what happens when the quantitative, qualitative, relational and modal categories are made absolute, or extended beyond their proper spatio-temporal limits in the world of appearances.

Kant begins with the dialectical employment of the categories of quantity. If we consider the magnitude of the world, whether it is finite or infinite, we discover that we cannot conclusively prove that it is either; we are left with the first antinomy which presents two opposed, but equally convincing cases for the finitude and infinitude of the world. A similar strategy of argument is pursued in the second, qualitative antinomy, which concerns the quality of the basic elements of the world. This too yields both the thesis that the world is composed of simple atoms or monads and the equally convincing antithesis that there are no simples and the world is constituted of complexes. In these 'mathematical' antinomies, the dialectical illusions arise out of the equivocation of appearances in time and space and things in themselves; we treat our conditions of knowledge as if they were the absolute conditions of things.

The second pair of 'dynamical' antinomies also yield dialectical inferences, but for the reason that we presume on the basis of our spatio-temporally limited experience to make contradictory what might from another standpoint be compatible. Our categorical understanding of causal relations when extended to an absolute object becomes dialectical: either everything is causally related and there is no independent cause, or there is independent causality through freedom. Similarly with the modal categories: when they are extended beyond appearances they produce the antinomy that either there is an absolutely necessary being or there is not.

Kant's critical cosmology is 'canonical' in his sense of providing criteria for establishing falsity. His cosmology is presented as a precautionary measure taken against the 'natural illusion' of human reason which seeks absolute knowledge of the world. It shows that when reason extends the concepts of the understanding beyond the world of appearances in space and time it falls into conflict with itself. With this Kant effectively abandoned the project of a philosophical cosmology, even though he left open the possibility for a regulative use of the cosmological ideas. After him Hegel and Schelling attempted to rescue the enterprise with the philosophy of nature, but this was largely a rearguard action in the face of the movement of cosmological concerns out of philosophy and into natural science.

cosmopolitanism *see also* FEDERALISM, HISTORY, JUSTICE, NATURAL RIGHT, PEACE, RIGHT, STATE, WAR

Cosmopolitanism is described in IUH as the 'matrix within which all the original capacities of the human race may develop' (p. 28, p. 51). It is a necessary step towards the solution of the 'greatest problem for the human species', which is that of 'attaining a civil society which can administer justice universally' (p. 22, p. 45). This end cannot be achieved within an individual state which participates in an antagonistic order of external relations. Consequently, in this text and in PP Kant focuses upon a 'cosmopolitan system of general political security' (p. 26, p. 49) between states, one which he describes as a 'federation of peoples in which every state, even the smallest, could expect to derive its security and rights not from its own power or its own legal judgement, but solely from this great federation (*foedus Amphictyonum*), from a united power and the law governed decisions of a united will' (p. 24, p. 47). By contrast, in the closing pages of A, cosmopolitanism is itself described as the goal of the development of the human species. It is not a constitutive but a regulative principle which demands that each individual, and not just each state, 'yield generously to the cosmopolitan society as the destiny of the human race' (A p. 331, p. 249). In accordance with the cosmopolitan regulative idea, each individual should direct their actions towards the 'progressive organisation of the citizens of the earth within and towards the species as a system which is united by cosmopolitan bonds' (A p. 333, p. 251.)

critical philosophy *see also* CANON, ENLIGHTENMENT, HISTORY OF PHILOSOPHY, JUDGEMENT, KNOWLEDGE, PEACE, PHILOSOPHY, PUBLICITY, WAR

Critical philosophy is the name given to the philosophical project executed by Kant in the three critiques, of Pure Reason, Practical Reason and Judgement. It was Kant's response to what he described as his epoch: 'Our epoch is, in especial degree, the epoch of criticism, and to criticism everything must submit' (CPR A xii). Not only 'Religion through its sanctity, and law-giving through its majesty' must submit to reason's 'test of free and open examination' but even reason itself. The 'matured judgement of the epoch' issues 'a call to reason to undertake anew the most difficult of all its tasks, that of self-knowledge' (CPR A xi) and to do this it must institute a 'tribunal which will assure to reason its lawful claims', one which will be 'at once strict and just' (CPR A 395). The use of the juridical metaphor for the self-examination of reason is not fortuitous, since for Kant, without this tribunal reason is in a 'state of nature, and can establish and secure its assertions and claims only through *war*' (CPR A 751/ B 779). While the warring parties of dogmatism and scepticism settle their disputes by each claiming victory and declaring a temporary armistice, the critique of reason conducts its affairs 'solely by the recognised methods of *legal action*'. It does so according to 'fundamental principles of its own institution, the authority of which no-one can question' (CPR A 751/B 779).

Critical philosophy gains its fundamental principles not through the 'critique of books and systems' but through that of 'the faculty of reason in general' (CPR A xii). Its procedure is to 'investigate the faculty of reason in respect of all its pure *a priori* knowledge' (A 841/B 870) and is the propadeutic or preparation for a future metaphysical system of principles. Kant phrases the preparatory nature of critical philosophy in several ways: it is a canonical investigation of reason prior to its organization into an organon; a negative clarification of the limits of reason prior to its positive exposition, and even the 'making room for faith' (CPR B xxx). It is distinguished from dogmatism and scepticism in that it does not 'lay claim to such insight into [its] object as is required to assert or deny something in regard to it' but 'confines itself to pointing out that in the making of the assertion something has been presupposed that is void and merely fictitious' (CPR A 389). In other words, critical philosophy 'does not consider the question objectively, but in relation to the foundation of the knowledge upon which the question is based' (CPR A 484/B 512).

Kant's claim that western society had entered a critical age in which nothing was exempt from criticism has been conclusively supported by the experience of the two centuries since the publication of his critiques. The objects of critique have ranged from religion, to political economy, to literature and have produced powerful institutions or 'tribunals' of criticism. Yet even Kant's contemporaries found his claims to be establishing a critical tribunal to be disingenuous, with Hamann (1967) and Herder (1953) pointing out in their 'metacritiques' that the 'purism' of reason overlooks its absolute reliance on an existing institution, namely language. The immediately succeeding generation of philosophers such as Hegel were unconvinced that reason was in a position adequately to criticize itself. Later philosophers such as Marx and Nietzsche were similarly sceptical of the 'critical tribunal', applauding the negative, critical moment of Kant's philosophy while deploring his attempts to be a philosopher-legislator. For them, and for many twentieth-century philosophers, critique must remain vigilant against any relapse into institutional and intellectual dogmatism. This *ethos* has even returned into recent Kant exegesis, which has downplayed the 'foundational' aspects of the critical philosophy in favour of its 'anti-foundationalist' methodology.

Critique of Judgement Published in 1790, the *Critique* forms the third work in the critical trilogy, the one with which Kant claimed to bring his 'entire critical undertaking to a close'. Quite what he meant by this claim is a subject of controversy. The third critique may be regarded as the text which brings together the otherwise opposed realms of nature and freedom discussed in the theoretical philosophy of the first critique and the practical philosophy of the second. Or it may be the text which rounds off the discussion of the faculty of the understanding in the first critique, and of reason in the second with a discussion of the faculty of judgement; or alternatively the faculty of pleasure and pain. It may even be that the third critique closes the critical undertaking simply by adding a critical discussion of the aesthetic judgement of taste to those of the theoretical and practical judgements ventured in the first two critiques. Characteristically, Kant's two introductions to CJ (the first, longer version initially discarded as being too long and later published separately) can be called upon to license all of these interpretations of the significance of the text in the critical trilogy. Yet they also point beyond them to a more inclusive interpretation, which includes all of the above themes, and more.

It must be remembered that CJ in fact comprises two critiques, each complete with its own analytic and dialectic: the first is a critique of the aesthetic judgement of taste, the second a critique of teleological judgement. Thus before any decision can be made on the place of the third critique in the critical trilogy, it is necessary to establish what is at stake in the text's internal organization. The clue to solving both problems is given in the title: this is a critique of the power of judgement (*Urteilskraft*), or a critique of our ability to make judgements. In this respect, the text addresses what was taken for granted in the previous two critiques. They assumed that it was possible to make theoretical and practical judgements, and set about justifying the conditions for this possibility. The third critique, however, inquires into the conditions of the possibility *not* of discrete theoretical or practical judgements but of judgement itself. It does so by means of an analysis of two particularly problematic forms of judgement, the aesthetic judgement of taste and the teleological judgement.

These forms of judgement are problematic in that they do not assume the givenness of a law or condition for the synthesis of a manifold. Thus they seem to point to an operation of the power of judgement distinct from, and perhaps prior to, that analyzed in the first two critiques. Kant states this distinction formally in terms of the difference between determinant and reflective judgement: the former subsumes a manifold of intuition under a concept or law given by the understanding; the latter discovers its law in the course of reflecting on the manifold which is presented to it. This process of reflection, Kant suggests, might be considered to lie at the origin of the categories themselves; that is, determinant judgement might be a species of a generic reflective judgement. What is more, this process of reflective judgement is inseparable from the experience of pleasure, which is evidently present in reflective judgement, and even, Kant hints, at one time accompanied determinant judgement which has now become habitual and unnoteworthy (CJ §VI).

The relationship hinted at here between judgement and pleasure contains several extraordinary and exciting implications. First of all, it suggests an expanded view of imagination, which no longer serves as an intermediary between intuition and understanding, merely facilitating synthesis as in the first critique, but lies at the root of both faculties. Second, the introduction of pleasure into the equation points to a new relationship between the knowing subject and the objects of its knowledge and judgements. This subject is no longer the abstract apperceptive 'I' but has become embodied, a living part of nature. Throughout the 'Critique of Aesthetic Judgement' Kant refers repeatedly to the 'feeling of life'

140

which is augmented by pleasure and diminished by pain, a feeling which is an integral part of human nature. The analysis of the pleasure and pain of embodiment in nature described in the 'Critique of Aesthetic Judgement' may be complemented by the analysis of nature itself, of which human beings form a part, undertaken in the 'Critique of Teleological Judgement'. The two parts of CJ may be read as offering access to the originary experience of judgement, one in which a live, embodied subject engages with its world. It is a finite, embodied subject which through imagination inhabits past, present and future, and which experiences the pleasure and pain of its judgements.

In CJ aesthetic no longer comprises simply the sensibility discussed in the aesthetic of CPR, nor is it restricted to the analysis of our experience of works of art, but instead explores the place of the body in nature and its resultant pleasures and pains. The 'Critique of Aesthetic Judgement' considers this relationship to nature by means of an analysis of judgements of taste which stresses the role of the 'subjective' experience of imagination and reflective judgement in pleasure, while the 'Critique of Teleological Judgement' considers the role of the 'objective' experience of imagination and reflective judgement in the finality (*Zweckmässigkeit*) which we impute to nature. Together, both present an account of nature and the place of human beings in it which far exceeds the oppositional framework informing some parts of the first and all of the second critique.

The 'Critique of Aesthetic Judgement' loosely follows the structure of the previous critiques with a doctrine of the elements and a methodology. The doctrine of the elements is similarly divided into an analytic and a dialectic. However, the exposition of the argument proceeds by means of a neither/nor opposition which opposes an argument drawn from the British theory of taste (Burke, Hutcheson, Hume and Kames) to one drawn from the German theory of aesthetic (Baumgarten). Following the schema of the table of the categories, Kant maintains that the quality of the judgement of taste is disinterested, unlike the arguments presented by the competing traditions. The quantity of the judgement is universal, which distinguishes it from the lack of universality in the theory of taste, and the rational universality proposed by the aesthetic tradition. The relation of a judgement of taste is, unlike in the theory of taste, 'final', but, now unlike in the theory of aesthetic, it is a finality without an end. Similarly, the modality of a judgement of taste is necessary, which distinguishes it from the theory of taste, but it is not the rational necessity of an obscurely perceived perfection as maintained by the theory of aesthetic.

The second part of the analytic moves to the consideration of the sublime, divided according to the mathematical and the dynamical sublime. While the beautiful evoked pleasure directly, in the case of the sublime pleasure arises from overcoming an initial experience of pain. This is followed by a deduction of the aesthetic judgement of taste, which summons various possible sources of justification of the peculiar universality and necessity of these judgements, notably the common sense (*sensus communis*), the 'universal voice', and a supersensible ground. The 'Dialectic of Aesthetic Judgement' comprises an examination of the antinomy of the principle of taste, with the thesis claiming that the judgement of taste is not based on concepts, the antithesis claiming that it is (§56). The antinomy is 'solved' on the basis of the results of the analytic, by claiming that the aesthetic judgement of taste rests upon an indeterminate concept. Finally, following some fascinating comments on beauty as a symbol for morality, Kant presents a few thoughts on the teaching of taste by way of a methodology.

On the evidence of most interpretations of CJ a reader would be justified in thinking that the book ended with the 'Critique of Aesthetic Judgement'; in fact this comprises only the first half, and is followed by the 'Critique of Teleological Judgement'. This text is unjustly neglected, since it is one of the most interesting, challenging and accomplished of Kant's later texts. The analytic makes the case for a teleological explanation of nature as opposed to the mechanical one, but specifies the rigorous conditions which it must satisfy. These come down to the fact that teleology may only be treated as a mode of judgement, and that finality in nature can only be considered *as if* it were objective. In this way Kant prepares for his solution to the antinomy discussed in the dialectic between the thesis of considering all material things as produced according to mechanical laws, and the antithesis of regarding some material things as requiring a different causality, namely final causality. The antinomy is 'solved' by regarding both thesis and antithesis as principles of reflection. The larger part of the 'Critique of Teleological Judgement' is devoted to the method, or the use of teleological judgement as a methodological device for extending our knowledge of nature. In the succeeding reflections on nature and judgement, Kant discusses the difference between the Epicurean and the Spinozist systems of nature, as well as analyzing history as the cultivation of nature. He ends the text with sustained reflections upon physico- and ethico-theology, and by repeating his earlier critiques of the ontological and cosmological proofs of the existence of God.

The first two critiques assumed a particular place for human beings in nature, either opposed to it as subject to object, or uneasily inhabiting both natural and intelligible realms. In CJ the place of human beings in nature is rendered far more complex with the introduction of the themes of pleasure, embodiment, imagination and judgement. The opposition informing the first two critiques between the sensible and intelligible is broken down and replaced by a complex account of our self-orientation in nature and in history. This aspect of Kant's thought has captured the imagination of many of his readers, from Goethe, to Nietzsche, to the contemporary focusing of critical attention upon the third critique. Quite in what sense it marks the closure of the critical undertaking still remains open to interpretation. It might even be argued that CPrR and CJ mark distinct and irreconcilable developments of tendencies present in CPR, and that CJ marks Kant's turning away from the dualistic tendency in critical philosophy taken to an unwholesome extreme in CPrR.

Critique of Practical Reason Published in 1788, this *Critique* is the second text in the critical trilogy and the second of Kant's three mature works in moral philosophy. It was preceded in 1785 by the *Grounding for the Metaphysics of Morals* and succeeded in 1797 by *The Metaphysics of Morals*. As with CPR, CPrR follows a synthetic method of exposition, proceeding from moral principles through the moral law to freedom. In its justification of the postulates of God, freedom and immortality it delivers the promise made in the second preface to CPR 'to deny *knowledge,* in order to make room for *faith*' (B xxx). The work follows the organization of the critical text established in CPR, with a 'Doctrine of the Elements of Pure Practical Reason' followed by a 'Methodology of Pure Practical Reason'. As in CPR, the 'Doctrine of Elements' is divided into an analytic and a dialectic. The former begins with the definition of a practical principle as a 'general determination of the will' distinguished as maxims, if subjectively valid, and laws if objectively valid.

The first chapter of CPrR opens with eight theorems which establish the nature of objective, practical principles by means of a polemic against the principles of moral judgement – i.e., happiness, moral feeling, perfection – as defended by moral philosophers prior to Kant. After establishing the basis of the moral law in freedom, and its relationship to autonomy and the categorical imperative, Kant proceeds to a deduction of the principles in terms of the moral law's causality 'in an intelligible world (causality through freedom)' (p. 49, p. 50). On this basis Kant presents a 'table of categories of freedom' which are organized according to the familiar schema of quantity, quality, relation and modality (CPrR p. 66, pp. 68–9). This is followed by an interesting section on the 'typic of pure practical judgement' which parallels the discussion of schematism in CPR, proceeding to the pivotal section on the 'Incentives of Pure Practical Reason'. Here Kant discusses the feeling of respect for the moral law as a mode of the will's self-determination, and makes the important distinction between acting according to, and from, duty, identifying the latter with acting with respect for the law.

The 'Dialectic of Pure Practical Reason' focuses upon the antinomic definitions of the highest good, presented in terms of the opposition between the Epicurean and Stoic schools. This is translated into the opposed positions on whether the desire for happiness is the motive for maxims of virtue, or maxims of virtue the efficient cause of happiness (CPrR p. 114, pp. 117–18). Kant argues away the opposition by claiming that both principles assume 'existence in this world to be the only mode of existence of a rational being', thus overlooking our 'existence as that of a noumenon in an intelligible world' (p. 114, p. 119). This then leads into the section 'On the Postulates of Pure Reason' which follow from the existence of the moral law: these are immortality (to supply the necessary duration for fulfilling the moral law), freedom (to satisfy the conditions of independence from sensibility and the intelligible determination of the will), and God (as the necessary condition of an intelligible world and the highest good) (p. 132, p. 137). The postulates are then held to satisfy practically the needs of reason whose speculative extension was severely limited by the 'Transcendental Dialectic' of CPR. The text is completed in the methodology by some comments on the extension of the influence of practical reason, or 'the way we can make objectively practical reason also subjectively practical' (p. 151, p. 155).

From the mass of criticism and commentary upon CPrR which has accumulated, I select a particularly suggestive, and entirely plausible, passage from Nietzsche's *The Gay Science*:

> And now don't cite the categorical imperative, my friend! This term tickles my ear and makes me laugh despite your serious presence. It makes me think of the old Kant who had obtained the 'thing in itself' *by stealth* – another very ridiculous thing! – and was punished for this when the 'categorical imperative' crept stealthily into his heart and led him *astray – back* to 'God,' 'soul,' 'freedom,' and 'immortality,' like a fox who loses his way and goes astray back into his cage. Yet it had been *his* strength and cleverness that had *broken open* the cage! (Nietzsche, 1882, §335)

Critique of Pure Reason The first of the critiques was published in 1781, with a considerably revised second edition following in 1787. The original edition is known as 'A', the second as 'B'. The *Critique* was over ten years in the writing, and was followed in 1788 by the *Critique of Practical Reason* and in 1790 by the *Critique of Judgement*. It presents among other things Kant's mature reflections on metaphysics, epistemology, cosmology, psychology and theology, and has become famed as the founding text of 'critical' and 'transcendental philosophy'. It is one of the most interpreted texts in the history of philosophy, and set the agenda for many subsequent developments. The barriers to entry posed by the text are, as Kant himself acknowledged, formidable, but should not be exaggerated. Since the main obstacle for contemporary readers lies in the unfamiliar organization of the contents, which often leads to sight of the wood being lost for the trees, this entry will concentrate on the overall ambition of the text, and on the ways in which its various parts fit together. More detailed information on the parts of CPR may be gathered from other entries (*see* especially CONCEPT, COSMOLOGY, INTUITION, METAPHYSICS, PRINCIPLE, PSYCHOLOGY, REASON, THEOLOGY, UNDERSTANDING).

CPR is in many respects a janus-faced text, one which looks back to the philosophical tradition and forward to new developments both in philosophy and natural science. This accounts not only for the mingling of traditional and modern terms and distinctions throughout the text – such as 'transcendental unity of apperception', which combines the scholastic 'transcendental' with the modern 'apperception' – but also for its themes and organization. CPR provides a traditional doctrine of the categories, but bases them on the modern *cogito* or thinking subject. It takes a traditional philosophical concept such as substance and reworks it to justify Newtonian physics. It proclaims a 'Copernican revolution' in philosophy, proposing that 'objects must conform to our knowledge', and then studiously presents the results in the guise of a traditional metaphysical treatise. An appreciation of these ironies, of which Kant himself was very much aware, can contribute considerably to the pleasure of the text; if they are not appreciated, the text can quickly become a burden.

In P Kant described the plan of CPR as 'executed in the synthetical style' (p. 263, p. 8), which meant that the 'structure of a peculiar cognitive faculty' was presented in its 'natural combination'. This is evident from the contents of CPR following the Prefaces and the Introduction, which are presented schematically in table 3.

The basic structural division is between the transcendental doctrines of 'elements' and 'method'. The meaning of the terms 'transcendental' and 'doctrine' is by no means fixed in Kant's writings, but here they mean that the teaching of the elements and the method are not derived from empirical experience. The distinction of elements and method itself originates in the parts of classical rhetoric, namely 'invention', or the discovery of the basic elements of a speech; 'disposition', their organization in a speech; and 'elocution', the delivery and presentation of the speech. Ramus used a variant of this schema in his reorganization of Aristotelian logic which brought together the parts of rhetoric as 'method', focusing upon invention and disposition (see Ong, 1983). In Kant, this schema is superimposed upon a more traditional Aristotelian organization. His doctrine of method concerns the disposition of the elements of pure reason discovered in the

145

Table 3 Schematic representation of contents of the *Critique of Pure Reason*

Critique of Pure Reason

Transcendental Doctrine of Elements — Transcendental Doctrine of Method

First Part: Transcendental Aesthetic — Second Part: Transcendental Logic

Space — Time

First Division: Transcendental Analytic — Second Division: Transcendental Dialectic

Book I: Analytic of Concepts — Book II: Analytic of Principles

Transcendental Illusion — Pure Reason as the Seat of Transcendental Illusion

Clue to the Discovery of all Pure Concepts of Understanding — Deduction of the Pure Concepts of Understanding

Schematism — System of all Principles — Phenomena and Noumena

Book I Concepts of Pure Reason — Book II Dialectical Inferences of Pure Reason

Paralogisms (psychology) — Antinomies (cosmology) — The Ideal (theology)

doctrine of the elements into a 'complete system of pure reason'. The doctrine of elements, which forms the bulk of CPR, concerns the invention of the basic elements of knowledge which can be systematically disposed and presented through the method.

The CPR stands or falls with the assessment of the doctrine of the elements which presents the basic, underiveable elements of experience. Yet it also presents several difficulties, not least of which is its polyphonic character: it contains several complex, often overlapping and conflicting internal articulations and thematic directions. The first part on 'Transcendental Aesthetic' and the two divisions of the second part 'Transcendental Logic' may be read as the analysis of the parts of a 'cognitive faculty', beginning with sensibility and its intuition of objects, moving to the understanding and its use of concepts in making judgements about intuited objects, and then to reason and its inferences from and beyond these judgements. The same sections can also be read in terms of the analysis of a peculiar form of judgement in which the predicate enlarges the meaning of its subject and does so in ways which can be shown to hold universally and necessarily. For such 'synthetic a priori judgements' to be possible, it is necessary that both the spatial and temporal conditions of experience, as well as its concepts, be shown to possess universal and necessary validity, one which Kant establishes on the basis of an idiosyncratic inflection of the Cartesian *cogito* or 'I think'.

These two readings of the doctrine of the elements by no means exhaust all the possibilities; the same sections may also be read as a deconstruction of traditional metaphysics, but in at least two ways. It may most plausibly be read as a systematic, critical analysis of the dominant metaphysical tradition as established by Christian Wolff (1719). On this reading, transcendental analytic takes the place of general metaphysics or ontology, with the three disciplines of special metaphysics – psychology, cosmology and theology – being subject to critical scrutiny in the transcendental dialectic. Finally, and perhaps less plausibly, the entire doctrine of the elements can be read as a modern reworking of Aristotle's *Organon* with the transcendental aesthetic replacing *The Categories* by providing the basic elements of knowledge; the transcendental analytic taking the place of *Of Interpretation* and perhaps the *Prior and Posterior Analytics* with its account of judgement; and the transcendental dialectic taking the place of the *Topics* and *Sophistical Refutations*.

Each of these readings has some truth, all of them together a great deal, but they do not exhaust the range of concerns explored in the 'Transcendental Doctrine of Elements'. They all, to varying degrees, exert an influence on the general and discrete arguments, and in this respect contribute to its perennial fascination for interpreters. These often show great (if not perverse) ingenuity in playing one thematic current off against another (the 'cognitive faculty' version being a favourite target). However, the subtlety of such manoeuvres and their attention to the fine grain of the argument often obscures the neo-classical simplicity of Kant's exposition.

The general line of Kant's argument can be discerned beneath the various thematic modulations. He follows Baumgarten in dividing the elements of experience into *aestheta* and *noeta*, things sensed and things known, which correspond to the 'Transcendental Aesthetic' and 'Transcendental Logic'. The former considers the ways in which objects are intuited, and proposes that this takes place by means of the forms of space and time. These are neither merely subjective nor the property of objects, but necessary conditions of our initial experience of the world. This is followed by the first division of the 'Transcendental Logic', namely the 'Transcendental Analytic'. This section presents the intelligible elements of our experience, and has two basic directions of argument. The first, comprising the 'Analytic of Concepts', is to derive the set of 'pure concepts of the understanding' from the various forms of logical judgement, and to justify their fundamental, a priori (that is, underived) character as elements by means of a deduction. The second direction, followed in the analytic of principles, seeks ways of adapting the categories to the spatio-temporal conditions of our intuition of objects, through the schematism and the set of principles corresponding to each category.

The basic lesson of the transcendental aesthetic and analytic is summed up in CPR A 158/B 197 as 'the conditions of the *possibility of experience* in general are likewise conditions of the *possibility of the objects of experience*'. This put simply means that we can experience the objects that we are able to experience, those which appear to us, and not the 'things in themselves' allegedly beyond our experience. It follows from this that objects beyond our ability to experience are not legitimate objects of knowledge, and yet they are nonetheless of great interest to human beings. In the second part of the 'Transcendental Logic', entitled 'Transcendental Dialectic', Kant shows how attempts to talk about such objects on the basis of our experience are internally inconsistent. Psychology's attempts to know the soul as if it were an object of experience lead to paralogisms; cosmology's attempt to know the spatial and temporal extent of the universe as if it were an object of experience leads to antinomies; while theology's attempts to prove the existence of God are shown to be illusory and dialectical. Thus in the 'Doctrine of Elements' Kant establishes the limits of experience, and criticizes those attempts to reason as if they did not exist. This leads the way to the 'Doctrine of Method' and its presentation of the means of reasoning and gaining knowledge within the critically established limits of our experience.

A confessional note which Kant jotted down while writing CPR reveals the motivation behind the work in progress. It is the same project of defending metaphysics as had already been announced in DS: human beings are impelled to ask metaphysical questions such as 'From whence am I? What is the origin of all that is?' (R p. 128). In order to make any judgement in response to these questions, it is necessary to be oriented in the realm of metaphysics. But this realm does not lie without, but within us, and so 'the critique of pure reason thrusts a torch into this gloom, but it illuminates the dark spaces of our own understanding, not the things unknown to us beyond the world of sense' (R p. 128). The image captures nicely the equivocal character of CPR: the torch illuminates our own dark spaces, but it also puts whatever is in them to the flame. God, the world and the soul are revealed as our own shadowy projections, products of our own lack of enlightenment or, in Kant's terms, our 'self-imposed tutelage'.

The impact of CPR has been commensurate with its ambition. The attempt to ground the conditions for the possibility of objects in the conditions of the possibility of experience led to the great systematic syntheses of German idealism. But this constructive aspect of the critique was rejected by thinkers who embraced its destructive potential, including Young Hegelians such as Bauer, Feuerbach and Marx, and perhaps above all Nietzsche. In Nietzsche's radical Kantianism, God, the world, the soul and even reason itself are criticized to death. Against this radical direction, other readings of CPR have stressed its philosophical justification of science (e.g., those of the late-nineteenth-century neo-Kantians such as Cohen and Rickert), its ontology (Heidegger and Heimsoeth), its analysis of the bounds of sense (Strawson) and more recently its work of orienting a finite understanding within the world and the events of history (Arendt and Lyotard).

culture *see also* COSMOPOLITANISM, DISCIPLINE, FEDERALISM, FINALITY, HISTORY, HUMANITY, NATURE, PEACE, SOCIABILITY, WAR

Culture is defined as the 'ultimate end which we have cause to attribute to nature in respect of the human race' (CJ §83) and consists in the 'aptitude and skill for all manner of ends for which [humanity] may employ nature both external and internal'. It is characterized by two, often antagonistic features. The first is the ability to choose ends, the second is the skill to realize them. The discrepancy between the two provides for both the progress and the ruination of culture. Kant discovers the origins of culture in the restriction of human freedom – 'all the culture and art which adorn mankind . . . are the fruits of their unsociability' (IUH p. 22, p. 46) – and describes culture as a discipline of the will and inclinations. However, the discipline of the will and inclinations in the choice of ends has no necessary relation to the ability to realize them. This results in a social conflict between those who, 'in a mechanical kind of way that calls for no special art, provide the necessary conveniences of life' and others who 'apply themselves to the less necessary branches of culture in science and art' (CJ §83). The former are kept in a state of imposed tutelage – 'in a state of oppression, with hard work and little enjoyment' – unable to develop the aptitude for choosing their own ends, while the latter, who do not have to labour to gain the skill necessary to realize their ends, become over-civilized and pursue luxury and superfluous ends. Kant sees this 'splendid misery' of culture as tending to catastrophe at the same time as developing the 'natural tendencies' of humanity towards a cosmopolitan civil society in which the aptitude for choosing ends and the skill to realize them will be in harmony.

Kant's theory of culture, while deeply indebted to Rousseau's *Emile, or On Education* (1762), nevertheless recognized the necessity of conflict. This aspect of his theory of culture was developed further by Hegel and Marx. His account of the conflict between the oppressed masses and the luxurious but superfluous masters anticipates the master–slave dialectic of Hegel's *Phenomenology of Spirit* and Marx's claim in the *Communist Manifesto* that the 'history of all hitherto existing societies has been the history of class struggle'. Kant's focus on material culture distinguishes his theory of culture from his contemporary linguistic and idealist theories such as that of Herder. However, it is not until very recently that these features of Kant's theory of culture have played any significant role in the exegesis of his philosophy.

D

death *see* FEAR, FINITUDE, IMMORTALITY, PUNISHMENT, TIME

deduction [*deductio, Deduktion*] *see also* APPERCEPTION, CATEGORIES, COMBINATION, CONCEPTS, FACT, IMAGINATION, INDUCTION, INTUITION, POSSESSION, SPACE, SYNTHESIS, TIME, UNDERSTANDING

In each of the analytics of the three critiques Kant offers a deduction: in CPR it involves the pure concepts of the understanding; in CPrR the principles of pure practical reason; and in CJ, the legitimacy of pure aesthetic judgements of taste. Unlike Descartes, Kant does not use deduction in the geometrical sense to mean 'everything which is necessarily concluded from certain other things which are known with certainty' (Descartes, 1968, p. 8). On the contrary, his usage is drawn from the practice of the Imperial jurists who 'when speaking of rights and claims, distinguish in a legal action the question of right (*quid juris*) from the question of fact (*quid facti*); and they demand that both be proved. Proof of the former, which has to state the right or the legal claim, they entitle the *deduction*' (CPR A 84/B 116). The philosophical deduction in each of the three critiques is required to justify the possession and/or employment of the theoretical pure concepts of the understanding, the practical principles of pure practical reason, and the aesthetic judgements of taste.

Kant consistently described the 'deduction of the categories' in CPR as a 'matter of extreme difficulty' and one which had been 'never before attempted' (CPR A 98). In it he undertook to justify 'how these concepts can relate to objects which they yet do not obtain from any experience' (A 85/B 117). He distinguished this form of *transcendental deduction* which sought to establish the legitimacy of such concepts from an *empirical deduction* which sought their origins in experience. In P and the second edition of CPR he attributed the former procedure to Locke and Hume (P p. 260, p. 6, CPR B 127) and contrasted it with his own transcendental deduction which, as if to stress the point, he once again described as 'the most difficult task undertaken in the service of metaphysics' (P p. 260, p. 6). Theirs was a 'physiological derivation', concerned not with the

151

legitimacy (*quid juris*) but with the fact (*quid facti*) of the possession of concepts.

Kant's procedure of transcendental deduction has several stages. The first stage establishes the legitimacy of the forms of intuition, space and time. Since objects may only appear to us 'by means of such pure forms of sensibility', space and time are legitimate 'pure intuitions which contain *a priori* the condition of the possibility of objects as appearances' (CPR A 89/B 121). From this Kant goes on to ask whether '*a priori* concepts do not also serve as antecedent conditions under which alone anything can be, if not intuited, then at least thought as object in general. In that case all empirical knowledge of objects would necessarily conform to such concepts, because only as thus presupposing them is anything possible as *object of experience*' (CPR A 93/B 126). The deduction of the categories will be accomplished if it can be proven that 'by their means alone an object can be thought' (CPR A 97). The number and character of the categories had already been established in a *metaphysical deduction* from the forms of judgement (see CPR A 70/B 95ff).

In P and the Preface to the second edition of CPR Kant expressed his dissatisfaction with the second chapter of the analytic on the transcendental deduction, and rewrote it for the 1787 edition. Consequently there are differences between the two versions which have led to them being described, with some exaggeration, as the 'subjective' and 'objective' deductions. The key to both deductions is that 'appearances in experience must stand under the conditions of the necessary unity of apperception, just as in mere intuition they must be subject to the formal conditions of space and time' (CPR A 110). The unity of apperception introduces 'order and regularity in the appearances' (A 125) achieving the 'synthetic unity of all appearances' according to the forms of the categories. In the 1781 deduction, the account of the unity of apperception is couched in terms of the synthetic activities (apprehension, reproduction, synthesis) of a finite subject all of whose representations are 'subject to time, the formal condition of inner sense' (A 99). This version emphasizes the work of the 'productive imagination' which in relation to the 'unity of apperception' constitutes the understanding, with its categories or 'pure *a priori* modes'.

The account of the transcendental deduction in the second edition differs in respect of the character ascribed to the unity of apperception: it is now 'entitled *objective*, and . . . distinguished from the *subjective* unity of consciousness, which is a *determination* of *inner sense*' (CPR B 139). This leads to a greater emphasis upon combination and the playing-down of subjective synthesis, but the overall conclusion remains unchanged: '*laws* of appearances in nature must agree with the understanding and its *a priori* form, that is, with its faculty of *combining* the manifold in general' (B 164).

Nevertheless, expressing a preference for one or other of the deductions has become a shibboleth in Kant studies, with Heidegger and the continental tradition preferring the first, and the more Cartesian Anglo-American tradition opting for the second version.

Kant's deductions in the second and third critiques are far less elaborate than the transcendental deduction of the first. In the second critique Kant claims that the 'objective reality of the moral law' cannot be proven through a deduction, but can itself serve ('unexpectedly') as a 'principle of the deduction of an inscrutable faculty which no experience can prove' (CPrR p. 47, p. 48). This is 'freedom as a causality of pure reason' and its deduction through the moral law supplies a lack in the cosmological ideas of the first critique, which Kant claimed were unamenable to 'objective deduction' (CPR A 336/B 393). The deduction in the third critique is also peculiar in that the object of deduction is a form of judgement. Here the deduction consists in legitimating the claims of the aesthetic judgement of taste to be universally and necessarily valid, even though it is a subjective judgement. Kant proposes a number of grounds for this validity, ranging from a postulated 'universal voice' to the 'mutual harmony of imagination and understanding' to a 'supersensible ground'.

definition [*definitio, Erklärung*] *see also* ANALYSIS, ESSENCE, METHOD, PHILOSOPHY, TRUTH
Kant describes definition in CPR as the presentation of 'the complete, original concept of a thing within the limits of its concept', with 'completeness' further defined as 'clearness and sufficiency of characteristics'; 'limit' is defined as the precise number of characteristics in a concept; and 'original' refers to the underived character of the limit (CPR A 728/B 756). Kant goes to some length to show that, strictly speaking, there can be no philosophical definitions. Empirical concepts cannot be defined because it is impossible to know their precise limits, nor is it possible to be certain that they are original. They may be *explicated* by making their contents explicit, but they do not fulfil the criteria of definition. Nor do a priori concepts, since it is impossible to be certain that analysis has been completely effected: 'the completeness of the analysis of my concept is always in doubt, and a multiplicity of suitable examples suffices only to make the completeness *probable*, never to make it *apodeictically* certain' (CPR A 729/B 757). Such concepts may be given an *exposition*, which is but a probabilistic 'approximation' (L p. 633) to a definition. The only concept which may be defined is one 'which I have invented' (CPR A 729/B 757) because then I am sure of its conforming to the requirements of 'limit' and 'originality'. Only mathematics possesses such concepts, so only it is in possession of definitions.

Kant immediately relaxes his austere strictures on the use of the word definition in philosophy on the grounds that 'The German language has for the [Latin] terms *exposition, explication, declaration,* and *definition* only one word, *Erklärung*' (CPR A 730/B 758). But he remains adamant that the philosophical use of the term be distinguished from the proper, mathematical one. This concern goes back to his earlier, anti-Wolffian, attempt in PE to distinguish the synthetic method of mathematics from the analytic method of philosophy. Mathematics produces its definitions synthetically, is apodeictically certain of them, and on the basis of this can confidently proceed to synthetic deductions. Philosophy, on the other hand, cannot begin with definitions, but has only confused concepts which it must subject to analysis. Kant disarmingly notes that 'Philosophy is full of faulty definitions' and would be in a 'pitiable plight' if it could make no use of a concept until it was adequately defined (CPR A 731/B 759). Its analytical expositions of concepts may not achieve the rigour required by definition proper, but its approximations may be close to truth and 'employed with great advantage' (ibid.).

In the account of definition in L §§105–8 Kant remains within the orbit of the Wolffian tradition, and provides a series of criteria for establishing philosophical definitions. Since his practice regarding definition in CPR often belies his preaching in that text, it may be helpful to present some of the most important distinctions. The first is the distinction between nominal and real definition, the former comprising the nominal meaning of a term, its 'logical essence' which distinguishes it from other terms, while the latter 'suffice[s] for cognition of the object according to its inner determinations' (L p. 634). Kant additionally presents the requirements of definition in terms of the table of categories: its quantity concerns the 'sphere of the definition', its quality its 'completeness' and 'precision', its relation, that it be not tautological, and its modality, which is that it be necessary (p. 635). Finally he offers some extremely Wolffian rules for testing whether definitions are true, distinct, complete and adequate to their objects (ibid.). Although these criteria and rules are never spelt out in CPR, the extent to which they inform its exposition is striking.

delight (satisfaction) [*Wohlgefallen*] *see also* AESTHETIC, AGREEABLE, BEAUTY, FEELING, GOOD, LIFE, PERFECTION, PLEASURE, SENSATION, SUBLIME
Delight is defined by Kant as the 'sensation [*Empfindung*] (of a pleasure) [*Lust*]' (CJ §3) which he further specifies as a 'determination of the feeling of pleasure or pain'. It is a modal term describing the ways in which this feeling is affected by different objects. As such it assumes a number of distinct forms: delight in a desired object is agreeable, delight in the good or perfection is 'pure and practical', while delight in the beautiful

has to satisfy the criteria outlined in the analytic of CJ. These follow the headings of the table of categories, and hold that delight in the beautiful must be without interest (quality), subjectively universal (quantity), final without an end (relation), and necessary but without a concept (modality). In addition Kant specifies that delight in the beautiful is positive, while that in the sublime is negative; this is because the former augments the feeling of pleasure and pain, while the latter diminishes it.

While the notion of delight is central to Kant's aesthetic, its precise character remains obscure. It is not only related to the 'feeling of pleasure and pain' but is also described as a sensation, one furthermore which is capable of possessing the properties of the understanding without formally being subsumed by it. Yet in CJ Kant neither fully justifies why delight should involve a 'sensation of pleasure' in addition to the feeling of pleasure and pain, nor how it can possess the properties of the understanding. At issue is the role of consciousness in the sensation of delight, but on the rare occasions when Kant directly addresses this problem, his arguments are impenetrably obscure (CJ §1; see Caygill, 1989, pp. 321–4). A hint is given in the methodology of CPrR, where delight is said to be 'produced' by a 'consciousness of the harmony of our powers of representation' which strengthens 'our entire cognitive faculty (understanding and imagination)' (p. 160, p. 164). Here it is the 'strengthening' of the 'cognitive faculty' which occasions delight; that is to say, less the harmony of imagination and understanding itself than the augmentation of power which it occasions.

dependent beauty *see* BEAUTY

desire *see* INCLINATION, INTEREST, NEED, PLEASURE, WILL

determinant judgement *see also* ANALYTIC, CATEGORIES, JUDGEMENT, REFLECTIVE JUDGEMENT, REFLECTION, SCHEMATISM, SUBSUMPTION

In CJ Kant contrasts determinant with reflective judgements in terms of two ways of 'thinking the particular as contained under the universal' (CJ §IV). In determinant judgement 'the universal (the rule, principle, or law) is given' (ibid.) and the judgement subsumes the particular under it. By contrast, in reflective judgement only the particular is given and the universal has to be found for it through a process of reflection. Determinant judgement is subsumptive, which means 'it has no need to devise a law for its own guidance to enable it to subordinate the particular in nature to the universal' (ibid.). It is neither autonomous nor 'independently nomothetic' 'for it *subsumes* merely under given laws, or concepts, as principles' (CJ §69). Such judgements are exemplified by the theoretical judgements of CPR in which the concepts of the understanding are the

155

given laws and concepts which subsume the particulars of the manifold of intuition through schematism and the principles.

determination [*Bestimmen*] *see also* ABSOLUTE, GROUND, LOGIC, PREDICATE, SUBJECT, THEOLOGY
Kant first discusses determination in the context of his critique of Wolff in ND. He defines it in terms of positing 'a predicate while excluding its opposite' (ND p. 391, p. 11). From this he goes on to define a ground or reason (*ratio*) 'as that which determines a subject in respect of any of its predicates', showing that determination is concerned with the logical relation between a subject and predicate. Some relations of subject and predicate determine *why* a particular subject is as it is, and these Kant entitles grounds/reasons which determine antecedently; others determine *that* a subject is as it is, and these are grounds/reasons which determine consequently. To give an example, gravity is the antecedently determining ground/reason for the orbits of the planets – it explains why they are thus; but the ground/reason that they are thus is determined consequently by the combined mass of the sun and planets. The point of this distinction is to criticize Wolff's definition of ground/reason as that by which to understand why something *is* rather than is not. Determination gives a ground/reason not only for why something is, but also why it is in this and not any other way.

Determination re-appears in CPR in the guise of the transcendental ideal. Here Kant supplements the Wolffian account of determination according to the principle of contradiction with one of 'complete determination'. According to the first or 'principle of determinability', 'of *every two* contradictorily opposed predicates only one can belong to a concept' (CPR A 571/B 599). According to the second principle of 'complete determination' which governs the possibility of things, 'if *all the possible* predicates of *things* be taken together with their contradictory opposites, then one of each pair of contradictory opposites must belong to it' (CPR A 572/B 600). This means that each thing is determined not only according to its relations to contradictory predicates (such that if a thing is coloured it cannot be not-coloured) but also to the 'sum-total of all predicates of things'. This latter is an a priori condition which serves as the background for the determination of particular things with particular predicates. Affirmation and negation of predicates are therefore not only governed by their contraries, but also by the sum of all other possible predicates. Kant finds such determination acceptable if the sum of possible predicates is recognized as the field of appearances constituted by the categories; that is, as 'the context of possible experience' (CPR A 582/B

610); however, it is unacceptable and 'dialectical' if it is hypostatized into an *ens realissimum*, 'being of all beings' (ibid.).

Kant's account of determination was further developed by Hegel, who used it to dissolve the fixity of specific determinations. Not only are predicates only thinkable in the context of their opposites, but this opposition itself is only thinkable in relation to the absolute (Hegel, 1812, 'Introduction'). A notion of determinate negation has also been developed in the twentieth century by Adorno in his *Negative Dialectics* (1966); his version, however, restricts itself to exploring the mutual determination of opposed predicates while relinquishing the possibility of situating them with regard to the absolute or sum of possible predicates.

dialectic *see also* ABSOLUTE, ANALYTIC, ANTINOMY, COSMOLOGY, GOD, IDEA, ILLUSION, PARALOGISM, PSYCHOLOGY, SUBJECT, THEOLOGY, TRANSCENDENT, UNITY, WORLD
The contents of transcendental logic in CPR are divided under the two headings of 'Analytic' and 'Dialectic'. The analytic resolves the formal procedures of the understanding and reason into their elements, and serves as a canon, or 'negative touchstone of truth', while dialectic consists in using these elements 'as if [they] were an *organon* for the actual production of at least the semblance of objective assertions' (CPR A 61/B 85). It is a '*logic of illusion*' which is countered in the critical philosophy by 'a *critique of dialectical illusion*' (CPR A 62/B 86). Dialectic as the critique of dialectical illusion thus finds its place following the analytic in each of the three critiques.

Kant justifies his use of dialectic with a reference to the 'various significations' 'in which the ancients used "dialectic" as the title for a science or art' (CPR A 61/B 86) but his own definition is resolutely Aristotelian. This was but one of the three influential definitions of the term transmitted from antiquity. The first was Plato's, which elevated dialectic 'above all other studies to be as it were the coping stone – and that no other study could rightly be placed above it' (Plato, 1961, Rep. 534e). It was no less than the method of scientific investigation itself, which sought definition through the dialectical procedures of collection and division (Plato, 1961, Phaed. 266b). Aristotle, by contrast, distinguished sharply in the *Topics* between 'demonstrative' (scientific) and dialectical reasoning, with the former reasoning from premises that are 'true and primary' and the latter reasoning 'from opinions that are generally accepted' (Aristotle, 1941, 100a, 28–30). In the *Posterior Analytics* dialectic is likened 'in principle' to rhetoric in that it uses syllogistic and inductive reasoning from premises accepted by a given audience to persuade and convince. For Aristotle it is indeed, in Kant's words, a logic of illusion.

Cicero further developed the rhetorical potential of dialectic in his attempt to elevate rhetoric above philosophy. He divided rhetoric or the science of argument into two parts: the first concerned with the invention of the materials of an argument he entitled 'Topics', the second, concerned with the method of making judgements, he entitled 'Dialectic' (Long and Sedley, 1987, p. 185).

Through Boethius the dominant tradition of dialectic bequeathed to Western European philosophy was Cicero's, with the entire science of argument now entitled 'Dialectic'. Following this, the tradition of dialectic moved between the Ciceronic and Aristotelian positions, with the final major attempt to reconcile them being Ramus's *Dialectical Institutions* (1543). This divides dialectic – 'the power of precise discoursing' – into invention and disposition (judgement) (see Ramus, 1549, pp. 12–14). This division was widely reproduced and became standard for the presentation of logical texts: Kant's own division of logic into analytic (invention) and dialectic (judgement) echoes this division, but also decisively undermines it. His dialectic no longer offers rules for executing convincing judgements, but teaches how to detect and uncover judgements which bear a semblance of truth but are in fact illusory. It is a 'critique of dialectical illusion' and not (as previously) 'an art of producing such illusion dogmatically (an art unfortunately very commonly practised by metaphysical jugglers)' (CPR A 63/B 88).

The illusions which Kant will criticize are not simply sophisms born of the desire to convince, but follow from the 'natural and inevitable illusion' of human reason. Such transcendental illusion arises from the 'fundamental rules and maxims for the employment of our reason' having 'the appearance of being objective principles' (CPR A 297/B 353). The basic source of illusion is human reason's pursuit of completeness and unity 'to advance towards completeness by an ascent to ever higher conditions and so to give our knowledge the greatest possible unity of reason' (CPR A 309/B 365). Reason seeks the absolute totality of conditions for a given conditioned thing, but instead of regarding this search as the pursuit of a regulative asymptotic principle, the reason, through 'transcendent and *dialectical inferences*' hypostatizes the goal of completeness into '*transcendent concepts* of pure reason' (CPR A 309/B 366). These are the object of criticism in the two books of the 'Dialectic'.

The first book of the 'Dialectic' criticizes the transcendent concepts of God, the world and the subject (soul), while the second criticizes the inferences of the sciences which pretend to knowledge of these objects. The science of God, theology, is shown to resort to ideals in its reasoning; that of the world, cosmology, falls into antinomies; while that of the soul, psychology, is paralogistic. In each case, the attempt to produce completeness and unity with regard to God, the world and the soul is exposed as dialectical, as resting on illusory premises and unjustifiable inferences.

Kant also organized the contents of the second and third critiques in terms of analytic and dialectic. The dialectic of practical reason arises from the attempt to define the 'highest good', which leads to the 'antinomy of practical reason' (CPrR p. 108, p. 112). Kant then offers a 'critical resolution' of this antinomy based on the results of the analytic of pure practical reason. Similarly in CJ, the dialectics of aesthetic and teleological judgement arise from the search for fundamental principles of judgement. The 'antinomy of taste' involves the thesis and antithesis that the judgement of taste is, and is not, based on concepts. Once again this is given a critical resolution which rescues the opposition by defining the concept involved as 'indeterminate'. The dialectic of teleological judgement presents an antinomy between the maxims of physical/mechanical and teleological explanations, which Kant critically resolves by exposing a confusion between principles of reflective and determinant judgement.

In the latter two critiques the dialectic has lost much of the focus it possessed in CPR. In the dialectic of aesthetic judgement it has become little more than a miscellaneous collection of thoughts and observations. Its main distinguishing feature is no longer the logic of illusion, but the antinomy of thesis and antithesis followed by a critical synthesis. What was once simply one form of dialectical inference (the antinomy) has now come to characterize the entire dialectic. Following Kant, only Hegel in the *Science of Logic* (1812) pursued dialectic as the logic of illusion with comparable rigour to that achieved in CPR. After Hegel, dialectic became almost exclusively identified with the narrow antinomic schema. In the Marxist tradition this view of dialectic reached extravagant heights in 'dialectical materialism' which, in the name of dialectic, extended the antinomic schema of thesis–antithesis–synthesis to the history of the world, nature and everything. In spite of Kant's efforts in CPR, dialectic was once more in the hands of the 'metaphysical jugglers'.

difference *see* CONCEPTS OF REFLECTION, IDENTITY

discipline *see also* CULTURE, HABITUS, HISTORY, INCLINATION, REASON, RULES
Discipline is defined in CPR as the 'compulsion, by which the constant tendency to disobey certain rules is restrained and finally extirpated' (CPR A 709/B 737). It is there distinguished from culture, 'which is intended solely to give a certain kind of skill, and not to cancel any habitual mode of action already present', although in CJ Kant does discuss 'culture by way of discipline' (§83). Discipline has two objects: in MM and *Education*

(1803) it is the inclinations that are restrained, while in CPR it is the extravagant tendency of the reason to overstep the bounds of legitimate knowledge. Kant's discussion of the discipline of the inclinations emphasizes that discipline should take second place to 'moral culture', the point being to cultivate the will to desire the good rather than disciplining the inclination to choose evil: 'the one prevents evil habits, the other trains the mind to think' (*Education*, 1803, §77). Excessive discipline of the inclinations brings about violent social and individual discontent; the former is discussed in CJ §83, the latter in MM, where it is described as 'opposed to man's duty to himself' (MM p. 452, p. 246).

In CPR the object of discipline is the tendency of reason 'towards extension beyond the narrow limits of possible experience' (A 711/B 739). Along with the canon, architectonic, and history of reason it is accorded a chapter in the 'Transcendental Doctrine of Method'. Because in the case of reason 'we come upon a whole system of illusions and fallacies, intimately bound together and united under common principles', Kant claims it is necessary to propose 'a quite special negative legislation' in the shape of 'a system of precautions and self-examination' in the face of which 'no pseudo-rational illusion will be able to stand' (CPR A 711/B 739). He does so by giving rules for exposing the dogmatic, polemical, hypothetical and demonstrative employments of pure reason. In the course of so doing Kant wrote some of the most exquisitely ironic passages of CPR, confirming his claim in MM that discipline 'can become meritorious and exemplary only through the cheerfulness that accompanies it' (MM p. 485, p. 274).

disjunctive judgement *see also* ANALOGIES, COMMUNITY, JUDGEMENT, RELATION, TABLE OF JUDGEMENTS/CATEGORIES
The disjunctive judgement is the third of the judgements of relation presented in CPR's 'Table of Judgements' (A 70/B 71) – see table 1 in CATEGORIES. It is defined as containing 'a relation of two or more propositions to each other, a relation not, however, of logical sequence, but of logical opposition, in so far as the sphere of the one excludes the sphere of the other, and yet at the same time of community, in so far as the propositions taken together occupy the whole sphere of knowledge' (CPR A 73/B 99). This form of judgement has the property of 'a certain community of the known constituents, such that they mutually exclude each other, and thereby determine in their totality the true knowledge' (A 74/B 99). An example of such a judgement is: 'The world exists either through blind chance, or through inner necessity, or through an external cause.' This judgement is disjunctive because all of these propositions add up to the totality of possible knowledge of the existence of the world, yet each mutually excludes the other.

Kant employs the table of judgements to derive the categories, from which he further derives the schemas and principles. The disjunctive judgement accordingly yields the third category of relation, namely community, the schema of 'reciprocity' and the principle of the third analogy of experience which states that co-existing substances are governed by the law of reciprocity or community.

disposition [*Gesinnung*] *see also* AFFECT, EVIL, INCLINATION, LAW, MAXIM, WILL, WILLKÜR
Disposition features in Kant's later moral philosophy as a subjective affect of the moral law and the source of the value of moral actions. It is the 'ultimate subjective ground of the adoption of maxims' (RL p. 25, p. 20) and is itself freely chosen, 'although the subjective ground or cause of this adoption cannot further be known' (ibid.). The disposition forms the bedrock of Kant's moral philosophy, for if we could know the conditions for choosing it we could incorporate this choice into a further maxim, the choice of which itself would then require explanation. It consequently plays an important role in his account of moral action. Disposition orients the *Willkür* positioned between will and inclination in one direction or the other. It influences whether *Willkür* is disposed to accept the maxims of the will or inclination, but plays little role in the concrete and specific choices which are made by *Willkür*.

dispute [*Streit*] *see also* ANTINOMY, WAR
Kant's first published text, LF, is a critical review of a dispute concerning the force possessed by bodies: it examines the positions of the Leibnizian and opposing parties and seeks to adjudicate between them. This mode of argument characterized a number of Kant's works, including the three critiques, in spite of the claim made in CPR that it was a critique of the faculty of reason in general – not a judgement of competing 'books and systems'. The second critique establishes the critical position by opposing accounts of the highest good with each other (Stoic and Epicurean for example) while the critique of judgement is structured around the dispute between the perfectionist account of beauty defended by Baumgarten and claims for a sense of taste defended by Hutcheson, Burke and others. However, Kant's rehearsal of disputes and polemics in the critical philosophy is quite distinct from that in LF. In the later texts the opposed positions are made the anonymous manifestation of the conflict of reason with itself. This served the purposes of the critical philosophy extremely well, since the 'critical tribunal' of CPR aspired to be a fresh start in metaphysics, and not just another moment in the metaphysical tradition. As a result, the positions criticized in the dialectic, especially in the antinomies, are presented as reason in dispute with itself rather than reasoners in dispute

161

with each other. The discipline of pure reason too, a strategic manual for settling the disputes of reason, presents itself as an objective instance rather than as a participant in a debate. This tendency to purify reason of its tradition had the effect of reducing philosophy to a soliloquy, a tendency criticized by Hamann (1967) and Herder (1953) in their 'metacritiques' and which was taken to an extreme by Fichte (1794). Nevertheless, when Kant did enter into dispute around the meaning of the critical philosophy, in OD, he dropped the mask of the impartial judge of the critical tribunal and clearly revealed himself and the critical philosophy to be interested parties in the dispute over the heritage and custody of metaphysics.

distinctness [*Deutlichkeit*] *see* CLARITY

divisibility [*Teilbarkeit*] *see also* CONTINUITY, MATTER, MONAD, SPACE, SUBSTANCE
Divisibility along with continuity was a constant preoccupation in Kant's thought. It was present in PM and still being explored in the second antinomy of CPR and in MF. It formed the key part in his argument that although matter in space was infinitely divisible, it was not as a consequence composed of an infinite number of simple parts. Kant presents this thought in the third proposition of PM as 'Space which bodies fill is divisible to infinity; space does not, therefore, consist of primitive and simple parts' (PM p. 149, p. 54). His reasoning at this stage was that since space is a relation, the infinite division of a relation will never arrive at simple parts or substances. In the critical version, in the second antinomy of CPR, the cases for and against the infinite divisibility of matter are both criticized for forgetting that it is *appearances* in space and time that are being divided. Since the 'composites' are appearances, so are any imagined parts, for 'the division reaches only as far as such experience reaches' and it is impossible through the division of appearances to reach 'an existence previous to experience' (P §52c). Kant thus maintains that the choice presented by the antinomy between a finite and an infinite number of simple parts is the result of a 'misunderstood problem' which does not recognize that the object of division is a spatio-temporally limited appearance. In MF he amplifies this point by arguing that since intuitive space is infinitely divisible mathematically, so is matter in space; thus the proposition 'Matter is divisible to infinity, and indeed into parts each of which is again matter' (MF p. 503, p. 49) underlines the point that divisibility is infinitely iterated without reaching ultimate, simple parts.

dogmatism *see also* CRITICAL PHILOSOPHY, HISTORY OF PHILOSOPHY, PHILOSOPHY, RATIONALISM, SCEPTICISM
In the preface to P Kant made the famous claim that 'my remembering David Hume was the very thing which many years ago first interrupted my

dogmatic slumber and gave my investigations in the field of speculative philosophy a quite new direction' (P p. 260, p. 5). Whatever its biographical interest, this passage brings together what Kant regarded as the three main possibilities for philosophy: dogmatism, scepticism and criticism. He presents them in the preface to the first edition of CPR by means of an analogy with forms of government: the government of reason 'under the administration of the *dogmatists*, was at first *despotic*', but through 'intestine wars gave way to complete anarchy; and the *sceptics*, a species of nomads, despising all settled modes of life, broke up from time to time all civil society' (CPR A ix). The 'critical tribunal' will, contrary to both, 'assure to reason its lawful claims, and dismiss all groundless pretensions, not by despotic decrees, but in accordance with its own eternal and unalterable laws' (A xi).

The 'sweet dogmatic dreams' (CPR A 758/B 786) of reason which incline it to despotism arise from the 'presumption that it is possible to make progress with pure knowledge, according to principles, from concepts alone' (CPR B xxv). For Kant, dogmatists believe that on the basis of pure reason it is possible to attain knowledge of the existence of God, of freedom in a world governed by necessity, and of the existence and even immortality of the soul. Dogmatic philosophers such as Plato (CPR A 5/B 8), Spinoza and Mendelssohn (WO p. 143, p. 246), but above all Wolff – 'the greatest of all the dogmatic philosophers' (CPR B xxxvi) – were in danger of 'philosophical zealotry' (WO p. 138, p. 242) or pretending to knowledge which they could not legitimately possess and defending their pretensions with whatever means available.

Kant claimed that the '*Critique* clips the wings of dogmatism completely as far as knowledge of supra-sensory objects is concerned' (WO p. 143, p. 246). In place of the dogmatists' enquiry 'into things', it proposes a '*critical* enquiry concerning the limits of my possible knowledge' (CPR A 758/B 786), an enquiry which reveals that our knowledge is limited to appearances constituted by human understanding. Yet this is not simply a retreat from dogmatism to scepticism, which is for Kant but a 'short cut'; it is necessary to combine the strengths of both dogmatism and scepticism in the critical method. He accordingly distinguishes between dogmatism and the 'dogmatic method' of 'orderly establishment of principles, clear determination of concepts, insistence upon strictness of proof, and avoidance of venturesome, non-consecutive steps in our inferences' (CPR B xxxvi). The latter method, exemplified by Wolff, is necessary for any scientific presentation, but must be supplemented by a critique of pure reason itself, for those 'who reject both the method of Wolff and the procedure of a critique of pure reason can have no other aim than to shake off the fetters of *science* altogether, and thus turn work into play, certainty into opinion, philosophy into philodoxy' (CPR B xxxvii).

double-affection *see* AFFECT

drive [*Trieb*] *see also* INCENTIVE, INCLINATION, PASSION
Drives are described by Kant in the 'Essay on the Maladies of the Mind' (1764) as constitutive of human nature and manifest in the various grades of the passions. They are also mentioned in OBS as being 'proportioned' when the inclinations are subordinated to a wider viewpoint. Although it was rarely mentioned by Kant himself, the notion of an economy of drives underlying the practical topology of reason and inclination has been repeatedly revived and developed, first by Fichte (1794) and Schopenhauer (1841), and more recently by psychoanalytically inspired writers such as Kristeva in *Revolution in Poetic Language* (1974) and Lyotard in *Libidinal Economy* (1974).

dualism *see* IDEALISM, THING-IN-ITSELF

duration *see* ANALOGIES OF EXPERIENCE, ANTINOMIES, CONTINUITY, DIVISIBILITY, EXISTENCE, FINITUDE, IMMORTALITY, INFINITY, MATTER, SUCCESSION, TIME

duty [*Pflicht*] *see also* CATEGORICAL IMPERATIVE, FREEDOM, IMPERATIVE, INCLINA-TION, LAW, MAXIM, NATURAL RIGHT, PERSON, RESPECT
A central concept in Kant's practical philosophy, the remote origins of duty lie in the Stoic critique of classical ethics. The Stoics replaced the classical 'highest good' as the main criterion for ethical action with that of the 'rightness of action' or action in accordance with 'right reason'. The 'rightness' of an act depended on the actor's disposition, not on the act's consequences. The proper disposition consisted in acting in accord with the duties imposed both by universal reason and particular circumstances (see Cicero, *On Duties*). Although Kant was well acquainted with the Stoics, references to whom appear throughout his writings, the more proximate source of his account of duty was the seventeenth-century Stoic revival in Holland which was particularly important in Prussia (see Oestreich, 1982). The reception of the Stoic texts was influenced by three factors: first, the Protestant emphasis on intention rather than works; second, natural rights theory with its emphasis on 'right reason'; and, third, the disciplinary practices of the early modern police state (see Caygill, 1989, chapter 3). From Pufendorf (1672) these elements fed into the practical philosophy of the Prussian Universities, first through Thomasius (see Bloch, 1968) and then, above all, through Christian Wolff (1720, 1721).

Wolff's practical philosophy – *Vernünftige Gedanken von der Menschen Thun und Lassen zu Beförderung ihrer Glückseligkeit* (1720) – consisted of an attempt to adapt the revised Stoic account of duty to an Aristotelian concept of the highest good. Part One, comprising three chapters on 'Human Action in General', discusses the highest good – which is to act according to natural law – and the obstacles to it presented by the senses, imagination and affections. The remaining three parts of the book, 15 chapters, are concerned exclusively with duty defined as 'actions which are in accord with the law' (§221). Part Two presents the 'Duties of Humans Toward Themselves'; Part Three, 'Human Duties toward God'; and Part Four, 'Human Duties towards Others'. This text gave rise to a Wolffian school of practical philosophy, whose literature included the two texts by Wolff's follower Baumgarten (*Ethica philosophica*, 1740, and *Initiae philosophiae practicae primae*, 1760) which Kant used as the basis of his lectures on ethics. Kant developed his practical philosophy in the course of commenting on these texts in his lectures, and thus his emphasis on duty is in some respects part of the tradition of Prussian practical philosophy. Yet in his critical philosophy he transformed this tradition, maintaining the form of its view of duty while radically reworking its content.

In Kant's *Lectures on Ethics* (LE), 'essential morality' is presented as synonymous with 'our proper duties towards everything in the world' (p. 117). This standpoint is maintained in the critical practical philosophy, where it is developed in terms of three thematic groups: (a) the definition of duty, its sources and function in an account of moral action; (b) the modalities of duty (perfect/imperfect, etc.); (c) the objects of duty (self, others, God, animals, nature). The definition underlines Kant's concern with the proper way of being in the world, a perspective which is often neglected in the more narrowly focused interpretations of his practical philosophy.

In the preface to GMM, the first statement of his mature practical philosophy, Kant distinguishes his critical project from the 'celebrated Wolff's moral philosophy' (p. 390, p. 3), in particular from its propaedeutic which Wolff 'calls universal practical philosophy'. Wolff is criticised for basing his practical philosophy on 'volition in general', and thus combining pure and empirical elements. Kant's critical propaedeutic to practical philosophy on the contrary (GMM, CPrR) will investigate 'the idea and principles of a possible pure will and not the actions and conditions of human volition as such' (GMM p. 390, p. 4). Kant's efforts to distinguish his practical philosophy from Wolffian orthodoxy leads him in GMM to argue for an extremely purified definition of duty as 'a practical, unconditioned necessity of action [which] must hold for all rational beings (to whom alone an imperative is at all applicable) and for this reason only can it also be a law for all human wills' (GMM p. 425, p. 33).

In CPrR Kant confirms that duty is peculiar to human beings, but without conceding that it is anthropologically determined. All rational beings are subject to universal law, but only human beings experience this subjection in the form of an imperative, one which because of its unconditioned source is categorical. This form of subjection is necessary because human beings are in possession not only of a 'pure will' but also of 'wants and sensuous motives' which conflict with it. The tension between pure will and sensuous motives which informs human volition requires that the relation of human will to law be 'one of dependence under the name of "obligation"' which 'implies a constraint to an action' (CPrR p. 32, p. 32). This constraint is 'called duty' and opposes pure objective to subjective grounds of motivation in a will which, although 'pathologically affected', is not pathologically determined.

Kant makes an important distinction between two functions of duty: in the first, duty 'requires of an action that it subjectively agree with the law', while in the second it 'demands' of the maxim of action 'subjective respect for the law as the sole mode of determining the will through itself' (CPrR p. 82, p. 84). The former consists in the 'consciousness of having acted *according to duty*' and is called 'legality', while the latter is consciousness of having acted '*from duty*, i.e., from respect for the law', and is morality proper. With this Kant bases his morality on intention, for while it is possible to act according to duty with maxims determined by inclination, moral action follows only from duty, that is, according to maxims conformable to the law. This distinction served as a propaedeutic to the later division of MM into doctrines of right and virtue.

In his celebrated, if not notorious apostrophe to duty – 'Thou sublime and mighty name . . .' – Kant inquires into the genealogy of duty, 'the root of thy noble descent which proudly rejects all kinship with the inclinations . . .' (CPrR p. 87, p. 89). It originates in a source which 'elevates man above himself as a part of the world of sense' and is no less than personality or 'the freedom and independence from the mechanism of nature', a being participating in the 'intelligible world' and subject only to 'pure practical laws given by its own reason' (ibid.). The source of duty is the self-legislation of human reason, possible because of the equivocal character of human beings, inhabiting both realms of nature and freedom. When we consider these laws under the aspect of divinity, then 'the moral law leads to religion' (CPrR p. 130, p. 134) wherein all duties are recognized as divine commands, but commands which cannot ever be fulfilled. Kant makes this move late in CPrR in order to prepare for the re-introduction of the 'highest good' into his practical philosophy. This is eventually accomplished in CJ (§83), but above all in RL, where human beings pursue duty for the sake of a highest good whose disposal is in the hands of God: here 'humans know concerning each duty nothing but what they must themselves do in order to be worthy of that supplement [the highest good] unknown, or at least incomprehensible to them' (RL, p. 139, p. 130).

In MM Kant presented the 'system of our proper duties to all the world' on the basis of the critically scrutinized concept of duty developed in GMM and CPrR. Duties are first subjected to a generic distinction of their modes and objects, and then to a further subdivision. With respect to the modes of duty, Kant distinguishes between juridical and ethical, positive and negative, and perfect and imperfect duties. The latter two distinctions, drawn by analogy from the theory of rights, concern the relative extent and direction of the obligations entailed by duties. Imperfect duties are of broad extent while imperfect duties are narrow; positive duties command, negative duties forbid. The distinction of juridical and ethical duties parallels the distinction between 'in accordance with' and 'from duty', although with some important distinctions. Here the ground of the distinction is whether legislation admits an incentive to action other than the idea of duty itself, or whether this idea alone suffices. The former gives rise to the legality of the law, the latter to its morality (MM pp 219–20, pp. 46–7). Finally Kant also distinguishes in MM between the objects of duty, which range across duties to God, to animals and to human beings, the last considered as both animal and rational. These considerations are explored through a fascinating yet extremely questionable casuistry.

Kant's account of duty has been the subject of almost two centuries of continuous criticism and mockery. In spite of their other differences, Hegel, Schopenhauer and Nietzsche were as one in abhorring its reliance upon a pseudo-Platonic and ultimately repressive distinction between the sensible and intelligible worlds, one which had been critically undermined in CPR. This response supported the widespread view that with his account of duty Kant merely justified one of the less attractive 'Prussian virtues'. Another widely held critical view regards Kant's practical philosophy as a deontological, a priori account of moral action. With these interpretations much of the background to and subtlety of Kant's texts have been lost; for in order to be fully appreciated his account of duty must be set in the context of the wider tradition of neo-Stoic writings on duty, and the specifically Prussian political and religious conditions of its reception.

dynamics *see also* ANTICIPATIONS OF PERCEPTION, CATEGORIES, MATTER, MECHANICS, MOTION, PHENOMENOLOGY

The chapter on dynamics is the largest of four chapters in Kant's treatment of natural science in MF. Following his definition of natural science as 'either a pure or an applied doctrine of motion', each of the four chapters considers motion according to the four headings of the table of categories. Phoronomy considers the quantitative aspects of motion; dynamics the qualitative; mechanics the relational; and phenomenology the modal. As the qualitative analysis of motion, dynamics focuses upon 'the quality of matter under the name of an original moving force' (MF p. 477, p. 14). Its 'universal principle' states that 'all that is real in the objects of our external senses and is not merely a determination of space (place, extension, and figure) must be regarded as moving force' (MF p. 523, p. 77). In accordance with the three categories of quality, the force is considered in terms of its affirmative reality, matter's occupation of space 'through repulsive force'; its negation, or 'attractive force by which as far as may be, all space would be penetrated'; and finally, the mutual limitation of attractive and repulsive force 'and the consequent perceptible determination of the degree of a filling of space' (MF p. 523, p. 76).

dynamical categories, principles and ideas *see also* ACROAMATIC, AXIOM, CATEGORIES, IDEAS, PRINCIPLES, REGULATIVE IDEA, SUBLIME
In the 'Transcendental Dialectic' in CPR Kant refers to an 'essential distinction that obtains among the objects, that is, among those concepts of understanding which reason endeavours to raise to ideas' (CPR A 529/B 557). This is the distinction between mathematical and dynamical categories and principles. The table of categories comprises 12 categories gathered under the four headings of quantity, quality, relation and modality. The first two groups are identified as the mathematical, the second as the dynamical categories. The mathematical categories of quantity and quality are 'concerned with objects of intuition, pure as well as empirical' while the dynamical categories of relation and modality are concerned with the 'existence of these objects, in their relation either to each other or to the understanding' (CPR B 110). In order to apply the categories to possible experience it is necessary to transform them into principles, and these too, discussed in the 'Analytic of Principles', are divided into mathematical and dynamical principles.

The mathematical principles comprise the axioms of intuition and the anticipations of perception, and are constitutive of intuition. Since experience is not possible without intuition, the principles form 'absolutely necessary conditions of any possible experience' and their employment 'is unconditionally necessary, that is, apodeictic' (CPR A 160/B 199). The dynamical principles of the analogies of experience and the postulates of empirical thought determine the 'existence of the objects of a possible empirical intuition' and are not apodeictic. They are, however, constitutive of empirical experience, and thus 'possess the character of *a priori* necessity' but this necessity can only be proven after the fact of experience, and so 'notwithstanding their undoubted certainty throughout experience, they will not contain that immediate evidence that is peculiar to the former' (CPR A 160/B 200). The mathematical principles present the conditions necessary for an object to appear in space and time, while the dynamical principles present the conditions necessary for an object to appear to us, especially with respect to its relations with other appearances (relation) and to our understanding (modality). Both sets of principles are nevertheless constitutive of experience, the mathematical in directly constituting intuition, the dynamical in rendering 'the *concepts*, without which there can be no experience, possible *a priori*' (CPR A 664/B 692).

With the discussion of the mathematical and dynamic ideas the distinction becomes crucial. If all four antinomies are treated as if they were mathematical, as if the condition was homogeneous with the conditioned, or 'a member of a series along with the conditioned' (CPR A 528/B 556), then the antinomies would appear irresolvable. For in the case of 'the mathematical connection of the series of appearances no other than a *sensible* condition is admissible', but if the connection of the series is thought dynamically, according to a 'synthesis of the *heterogeneous*' then 'a heterogeneous condition, not itself part of the series, but *purely intelligible*, and as such outside the series, can be allowed' (CPR A 530/B 558). With this view of the series it is possible to satisfy both the understanding and reason with respect to the antinomies first of freedom and causality, and then of contingency and a necessary being. In this case, reason cannot be employed constitutively, but only regulatively through maxims for the systematic unity of the employment of the understanding.

The distinction between mathematical and dynamical is also significant in the 'Analytic of the Sublime' in CJ, where the distinction of the 'mathematical' and 'dynamical' replaces the 'Table of Categories' used in 'Analytic of the Beautiful'. In the first case the sublime object is considered 'mathematically' in terms of its scale, as that which is 'absolutely' or 'beyond all comparison great' (CJ §25). In the second, the dynamical sublime is registered by its 'affection of the imagination' or the fear and terror aroused in the viewer by the sublime spectacle.

E

ectype *see* ARCHETYPE

education *see* CULTURE, HABITUS, HISTORY, METHOD

elements [*stoicheion*] The Greek term for elements referred originally to the letters of the alphabet, but this meaning was adapted by philosophers to mean basic, underived principles. These range from the four physical elements of early Greek cosmology to the elements of an intellectual discipline such as geometry. Thus in Proclus' commentary on Euclid, elements are defined as 'those theorems whose understanding leads to the knowledge of the rest and by which the difficulties in them are resolved' (Proclus, 1970, p. 59). He goes on to say that, like the letters of the alphabet, elements do not make sense outside of their use; their meaning is determined by the order (*taxis*) and position (*thesis*) in which they are placed with regard to each other. Although Kant discusses the physical elements in early texts such as UNH and PM, his main use of the term occurs in those sections of the first two critiques (CPR, CPrR) concerned with presenting the basic elements of theoretical and practical judgement. The critiques are accordingly divided between 'Transcendental Doctrines of the Elements' and 'Methodology'; in the former Kant seeks to establish the basic, underivable elements of judgement, whether the forms of intuition and the pure concepts of the understanding for theoretical, or the moral law for practical judgement. It should be added that Kant was well aware that these elements were meaningless in abstraction from their use in judgement, and that contrary to the opinion of many critics, he did not intend the doctrine of elements to provide the basis for a total, rationalistic theory of judgement.

empirical, empiricism, empiricists *see also* ABSTRACTION, CRITICAL PHILOSOPHY, DOGMATISM, HISTORY OF PHILOSOPHY, PURE, RATIONALISM
An empirical concept or intuition is one which 'contains sensation' and thereby 'presupposes the actual presence of the object' (CPR A 50/B 74).

170

It is contrasted with a pure intuition which 'contains only the form under which something is intuited' and a pure concept which contains 'only the form of the thought of an object in general' (A 51/B 75). An empirical intuition or concept is only possible *a posteriori*, while a pure intuition or concept is *a priori*. For this reason, transcendental objects which exceed the bounds of sense are said to be 'empirically unknown'. Informing this distinction between empirical and pure is a further distinction between empiricism and rationalism, often indeed between named empiricists and rationalists. In the antinomies, the antithesis represents the empiricist riposte to the rationalist thesis. Kant finds that a 'pure empiricism' undermines the practical interest of reason, but has advantages for the speculative interest (CPR A 468/B 496). As a control upon rationalism's excesses, empiricism is useful, but 'as frequently happens' 'empiricism itself becomes dogmatic in its attitudes towards ideas, and confidently denies whatever lies beyond the sphere of its intuitive knowledge' (A 471/B 499). Thus in theoretical philosophy and aesthetics Kant's strategy is to play empiricism and rationalism off against each other, while only in practical philosophy does he unequivocally privilege the rationalist over the empiricist position (CPrR p. 72, p. 74).

The contrast between empiricism and rationalism quickly reveals itself to be one between named empiricists and rationalists. In CPR the contrast is introduced as one between the 'empiricist' Epicurus and the 'rationalist' Plato (A 471/B 499); this is subsequently repeated in terms of the *object* of knowledge, with Epicurus cast as the sensualist and Plato the intellectualist, but supplemented by the contrast of Aristotle and Plato with respect to the empirical and ideal origins of knowledge, the former labelled an empiricist the latter a noologist. The latter distinction is transferred on to that between Locke and Leibniz (CPR A 854/B 882), and is developed in the 'Note to the Amphiboly of the Concepts of Reflection' (CPR A 269/B 325ff). In GMM and CPrR the named empiricists include Hutcheson and the British theorists of the 'moral sense' (GMM p. 442, p. 46) and Hume (CPrR p. 13, p. 13), all of whom are opposed to the rationalist Wolff. A similar cast is present in CJ, which opposes the empirical theory of taste (Burke, Hutcheson, Hume and Kames) to the perfectionist aesthetic of Wolff and Baumgarten. Whether Kant derived the opposition of empirical and rational from the named empiricists and rationalists or *vice versa* is an open question, but an important one for judging his claim to have provided a critique of the 'faculty of reason alone' rather than one of 'books and systems' (CPR A xii).

end [*telos, Zweck*] *see also* CAUSALITY, CULTURE, FINALITY, FREEDOM, HUMANITY, KINGDOM OF ENDS, LIMIT, TELEOLOGY

Kant's concept of an end is a version of the Aristotelian 'final cause'. In the *Physics* Aristotle presented four causes of physical change: the material cause, or 'that out of which a thing comes to be'; the formal cause, or the 'essence' which determines the shape of the matter; the efficient cause which is 'the primary source of the change or coming to rest'; and the final cause or 'the sense of end, or "that for the sake of which" a thing is done' (Aristotle, 1941, 195a, 23–35). The causes are ways of answering the question of 'why' a thing has come to be or passed away, and were extended by Aristotle from physical to metaphysical questions (see 983a, 24–30). Yet the final cause was special in applying not only to physical and metaphysical questions – answering 'Why?' with 'for the sake of this particular end' – but also in extending to questions of human action. Accordingly, the *Nicomachean Ethics* describes ethical and political action as directed above all to achieving the end of the good (see Aristotle, 1941, 1094a). Thus the notion of 'end' classically crosses over between theoretical and practical philosophy, a role it also plays in Kant's philosophy.

In the early modern period teleological explanations of physical change were increasingly discredited. Galileo rejected all aetiology in favour of the analysis of local motion, and while Descartes was reluctant to follow him this far (see Descartes, 1644, p. 104), he did conclusively reject the investigation of final in favour of efficient causes (ibid., p. 14). Kant's theoretical philosophy likewise refrains from using final causes as principles of explanation, although he does contrive a new role for the use of 'ends' in theoretical philosophy. Like Aristotle, his practical philosophy places the concept of an 'end' in the foreground, and in CJ it becomes the main means by which Kant establishes a transition between the natural necessity of theoretical and the freedom of practical philosophy.

Kant's most extended discussion of ends and purposes is in the second part of CJ, the 'Critique of Dialectical Judgement'. Here he distinguishes between physical and moral teleologies, or the explanation of physical nature and human action according to ends. In both cases he refers to a distinction between efficient and final causation – the 'mechanical' causality of the *nexus effectivus* (efficient cause) and the final causality of the *nexus finalis* (final cause) (CJ, 'Introduction', Part II; see also GMM p. 450, p. 52). The theoretical philosophy of the first critique is overwhelmingly concerned with the explication of efficient causes, but with a limited role for final causality according to an end as a regulative idea for securing the systematic completion of knowledge (CPR A 626/B 654). This scope and these parameters for a limited 'physical teleology' are further developed in CJ Part II. In the general introduction to CJ Kant distinguishes between an *end* as the 'concept of an object, so far as it contains at the same time the ground of the actuality of this object' and *finality*, which is the

172

'agreement of a thing with that constitution of things which is only possible according to ends' (CJ §IV). He uses this distinction to argue against deriving 'physical ends' from the appearance of finality presented by nature. We cannot know such an objective end nor can we make it a constitutive principle; we can, however, postulate such an end as a regulative principle for reflective judgement, and by so doing 'extend physical science according to another principle, that, namely, of final causes, yet without interfering with the principle of the mechanism of physical causality' (§67). The notion of an end as a 'subjective maxim' or principle of reflective judgement may be used to supplement and extend the determinant judgements of mechanical causality, but it is not permitted to encroach upon them, let alone replace them.

While Kant severely limits the extent and operation of physical teleology, the same restriction does not apply to moral teleology. In fact Kant's practical philosophy, like Aristotle's, is resolutely teleological, insisting as it does that action is end-directed. In GMM he defines the will 'as a faculty of determining itself to action in accordance with the representation of certain laws' and defines the 'end' as that which serves as 'the objective ground of its self-determination' (p. 427, p. 35). He further distinguishes these ends according to whether they are subjective or objective: the former are 'material' ends entitled 'incentives'; the latter are 'formal' ends which are abstracted from subjective ends and are able to serve as 'motives' valid for all rational beings. Rational beings are 'ends in themselves' whose existence possesses 'absolute worth', a derivation which leads Kant to the statement of the categorical imperative of acting so as to treat the other 'always at the same time as an end and never simply as a means' (p. 429, p. 36). Underlying these and the other formulas of the categorical imperative is the notion of a kingdom of ends in which each member is both legislator and legislated.

In all three critiques Kant alludes to the 'ultimate end' which unites the realms of theoretical and practical philosophy. In CPR the 'ultimate end' is 'no other than the whole vocation of humanity' and is described in terms of the unity of the two objects of 'the legislation of human reason (philosophy)' namely nature and freedom, which although at first are presented in 'two distinct systems' ultimately form 'one single philosophical system' (CPR A 840/B 868). The character of this 'ultimate end' and thus the 'vocation of humanity' is considered extensively in CJ §83, entitled 'The Ultimate End of Nature as a Teleological System'. Here human beings are described as the '*ultimate end* of nature, and the one in relation to whom all other natural things constitute a system of ends'. This follows from the human capacity, founded in freedom, 'of setting before themselves ends of their deliberate choice' and culturing nature in accord with them. At this point Kant makes a transition to a fascinating discussion of physical and ethical theology, in the course of which he presents grounds for the existence of God as the moral author of the world.

Kant's analysis of ends was carried over into the systematic philosophy of German idealism. This was based upon a Kantian view of human freedom as the ability to posit ends, and also to legislate systems of freedom and nature. However, much of the detail of Kant's discussion of physical and moral ends in CJ Part II has been comparatively neglected by Kant scholarship. This is unfortunate because the concept of an end provides an extremely useful way of reading Kant's philosophy as the integral and systematic whole that he desired it to be.

enlightenment [*Aufklärung*] *see also* COMMON SENSE, CRITICAL PHILOSOPHY, HISTORY OF PHILOSOPHY, PUBLICITY, REASON
The eighteenth-century European intellectual movement known as the Enlightenment went through three distinct phases in Germany. The first, rationalist phase was inaugurated at the beginning of the century at the University of Halle by Thomasius, and codified by Christian Wolff. Both abandoned academic Latin in favour of the vernacular, with Wolff aiming his works beyond the confines of the universities and professions. His system commenced with logic, and proceeded through metaphysics to ethics, politics and economics. Under political pressure from the Prussian monarch Frederick William I, Wolff was forced to leave Prussia in 1723. He went into exile, where he re-wrote his system, this time in Latin for an international audience of scholars. With his return to Prussia on the accession of Frederick II in 1740, Wolff already seemed like an intellectual fossil. The temper of the Enlightenment had changed, now emphasizing scepticism and common sense over the exercise of abstract reason. In the middle of the century very few philosophers wrote rational systems, the preference being for witty 'sceptical' essays modelled on those of Hume. Kant's pre-critical writings fall into this phase of the Enlightenment, which is exemplified by his *Observations on the Feeling of the Beautiful and the Sublime* (1764). However, in the 'silent decade' of the 1770s Kant returned to rigorous, systematic philosophy, taking sides with Wolff against those (including his younger self) who 'have no other aim than to shake off the fetters of *science* altogether' (CPR B xxxvii). With the publication of CPR in 1781 he launched the third phase of the Enlightenment, which sought to combine critical scepticism with systematic rigour.

In the preface to the first edition of CPR, Kant describes his epoch as one of *criticism*; criticism of religion, politics and even reason itself. Criticism involved putting religious, political and intellectual beliefs to 'the test of free and open examination' (CPR A xii) leaving the verdict to 'the agreement of free citizens, of whom each one must be permitted to express, without let or hindrance, his objections or even his veto' (CPR A 739/B 767). In the essay 'An Answer to the Question: "What is Enlightenment?"', (1784) he characterizes the 'age of enlightenment' in very similar terms. Enlightenment is defined famously as the 'emergence from self-incurred immaturity' or inability to judge without the guidance of another. This self-emergence can exceptionally be achieved by individuals, but is overwhelmingly the work of a public freely using its reason. The public must not submit to the guidance of religion, nor to that of the state, but only to that of its own reason. Frederick II's dictum 'Argue as much as you like and about whatever you like, but obey!' indicates for Kant that he lives, if not in an 'enlightened age', then in 'an age of enlightenment', one in which at least some of the obstacles to the free, public use of reason had been removed.

Many critics have regarded Kant's willingness to adapt his view of enlightenment to the Fredrician state as a powerful argument against his philosophy. However, in many respects his position is extremely consistent, especially since he believed that freedom to think created the ability to act freely, while the inverse did not necessarily hold. He also distinguished between the responsibility exercised when using one's reason publicly to that exercised when occupying a private 'office', such as that of clergyman or bureaucrat: the former for Kant always took precedence. In this way the public sphere of reason becomes the highest instance of criticism, even if judgements pronounced in it are religiously unorthodox, or 'entail forthright criticism of the current legislation' (WE p. 41, p. 59).

The arguments around the meaning of the Enlightenment provoked by Kant raised a substantial echo in the twentieth century, one largely inspired by Nietzsche's ruthless extension of enlightenment critique to reason itself. Kant's instrument of criticism, the basis of enlightenment, has itself been seen as a threat to enlightenment. This argument featured in Adorno and Horkheimer's critique of technical reason in *Dialectic of Enlightenment* (1944) as well as in the work of French philosophers such as Derrida (1967), Foucault (1984) and Lyotard (1983). In an influential polemic, Jürgen Habermas in *The Philosophical Discourse of Modernity* (1985) has accused these writers of being opposed to the Enlightenment. However, it seems more accurate to describe them as quintessentially enlightened, as publicly exploring, in a distinctly Kantian spirit, the consequences of extending the critical impulse of enlightenment to reason itself.

enthusiasm *see also* AFFECT, FEELING, HISTORY, IMAGINATION, SUBLIME
Enthusiasm is a feeling of the sublime arising from the combination of an idea with an affect. It is described in OBS as the 'inflammation' of the

175

mind by a principle, be it the 'maxims of patriotic virtue, or of friendship, or of religion' but is distinguished from fanaticism, which 'believes itself to feel an immediate and extraordinary communion with a higher nature' (OBS p. 108). Kant maintains this distinction in CJ where enthusiasm is described as the 'unbridling' and fanaticism the 'anomaly' of the imagination. As the affect of the idea of the good, enthusiasm gives the *Gemüt* 'an impetus of far stronger an enduring efficacy than the stimulus afforded by sensible representations' (CJ §29). It arises from the fusion of affect, idea and imagination, and can serve as a spur to action. The implications of enthusiasm for Kant's philosophy of history have been explored by Lyotard in *The Differend* (1983), where it is described as the paradoxical 'abstract presentation which presents nothingness'. As the irruption of the idea into affect and action, enthusiasm is capable of inspiring events which break the continuum of history; the main example of this for Kant was the contemporary French Revolution inspired by the idea of the republic, an event which was both the outcome of enthusiasm and the source of enthusiastic feelings in its spectators.

epistemology This term, meaning theory of knowledge, is derived from Greek *episteme*, knowledge, and *logos*, an account of; it was not used by Kant and only appeared later in the middle of the nineteenth century. The German term *Erkenntnistheorie* (theory of knowledge) often translated as epistemology, is also post-Kantian, and was coined by K.L. Reinhold as part of his attempt to transform the critical philosophy into a theory of representation in *Letters on the Kantian Philosophy* (1790–2). This translated a term used by Baumgarten – *gnoseology* – of which Kant was aware and to which he made allusion on some insignificant occasions. Paradoxically then, although Kant's philosophy has since come to epitomize the theory of knowledge, or epistemology, he did not himself use the word or any synonym for it. This suggests that reading the critical philosophy as an epistemological project is an anachronistic, *post hoc* interpretation, one based on the nineteenth-century pre-occupation of distinguishing between epistemology and ontology. Kant himself described the 'Transcendental Analytic' of CPR – his most apparently 'epistemological' text – as a reformulation of ontology (see CPR A 247/B 303). Once the anachronistic distinction between epistemology and ontology is suspended many of the puzzling features of CPR become less enigmatic, such as the claim that 'the conditions of the *possibility of experience* in general are likewise conditions of the *possibility of the objects of experience*' (CPR A 158/B 197). From the perspective of the nineteenth century this claim is inexplicable, appearing to confuse the ontological and the epistemological orders.

essence [*ousia, essentia, Wesen*] *see also* ACCIDENT, DEFINITION, EXISTENCE, FORM, MATTER, NATURE, SUBSTANCE, SYNTHESIS

Essence is classically that which constitutes the specific nature of a thing and which is given in its definition. The notion of essence was developed by Aristotle in the *Metaphysics* as part of an answer to the question of 'what is a thing?'. In the definition of a thing the essence is distinguished from accidents and substance: accidents are always predicated of a subject and serve only to qualify an essence (Aristotle, 1941, 1007b, 1–15), while substance denotes *that* and not *what* a thing is. Essence accordingly defines the 'species of a genus' or its specific character (1030a). Aquinas clarifies these points when he discusses essence as a function of the composition of matter and form. The definition of essence is not formal, not separated from matter, nor is it material and derived from 'individualizing matter'. Using the example of the essence of 'humanity', Aquinas says that it is neither the 'form' of humanity nor 'the flesh, the bones, and accidents designating this matter' but rather the 'formal constituent *in relation* to the individualizing matter' (Aquinas, 1952, I, 3, 3, my emphasis).

One of the effects of the Aristotelian definition of essence was the emergence of an equivocal relation between essence and existence. As a function of the relation of form and matter, essence was neither purely formal, distinct from existence, nor purely material, identified with existence. With Descartes, and following him Spinoza, this ambiguity was transformed into an opposition between what can be conceived and what exists. Thus in the 'Fifth Meditation' Descartes attributes essence to possible objects, even though they may not exist, a point which he stresses in the *Conversations with Burman* where he claims that the object of physics is 'something actually and physically existing' while that of mathematics 'considers its object merely as possible' (Descartes, 1976, p. 23). The transformation of essence into possibility was systematized by Wolff and his school, for whom essence became defined as simple possibility (for example – 'The essence of a thing is its possibility', Meissner, 1737, entry on *Wesen*). It is from this tradition that Kant received his notion of essence.

In MF Kant defines essence in Wolffian terms as 'the primal, internal principle of everything that belongs to the possibility of a thing' and distinguishes it from nature or 'the primal, internal principle of everything that belongs to the existence of a thing' (p. 467, p. 3). This distinction is informed by Kant's claim in L that it is impossible to define 'the *real* or *natural essence* of things' (pp. 566–7) and that our understanding is restricted to 'logical essence'. His reasoning is clarified in a letter to K.L. Reinhold of 12 May 1789 in which he criticizes Baumgarten and other Wolffians for giving metaphysical status to the 'discussion of *essence, attributes,* and so on' (PC p. 139). He, on the contrary, insists that the possibility is only of logical significance. Logical essence or the 'primary *constitutiva* of a given concept' can be determined 'by the analysis of my concepts into all that I think under them'; while the '*real* essence (the nature) of any object, that is, the primary *inner* ground of all that necessarily belongs to a given thing, this is impossible for man to discover' (PC p. 140). The concept of matter possesses the logical essence of extension and impenetrability which are 'all that is necessarily and primitively contained in my, and every man's concept of matter', but the real essence of matter, 'the primary, inner, sufficient ground of *all* that *necessarily belongs to* matter, this far exceeds the capacity of human powers' (ibid.). The reason for this is that there is a 'ground of synthesis' for essence which 'brings *us* at least to a standstill'. Thus it is precisely the classical status of essence as a function of the combination of form and matter (in Kant's term 'synthesis') which limits our knowledge of logical essence to the synthetic constitution of appearances and disqualifies us from any knowledge of real essence.

estimate [*Beurteilung*] *see also* CANON, JUDGEMENT, REFLECTIVE JUDGEMENT, SUBSUMPTION, TRUTH

Estimation and subsumption are the two modes of judgement recognized by Kant: the former distinguishes 'whether something does or does not stand under a given rule' while the latter is the 'faculty of subsuming under rules' (CPR A 132/B 171). Estimation is concerned with the canonical use of judgement in distinguishing between true and false judgements, while subsumption effects judgement, and is part of its organon. Kant discusses the estimative use of judgement in the context of theoretical, practical, aesthetic and teleological judgements, referring on occasions to the 'faculty' or 'power' of estimation (*Beurteilung*) (a term consistently mistranslated as faculty or power of *judgement*). In GMM Kant refers to a 'principle' which while not known 'abstractly in its universal form' serves as a 'standard' or 'compass' for distinguishing between good and evil actions (p. 404, p. 16), and which is yet not so effective in the case of theoretical judgements. Estimative judgements do not require the knowledge of a rule, but simply the ability to discriminate; this makes it particularly significant for aesthetic and teleological reflective judgements, which are defined by the absence of a definite rule. Accordingly, most of the judgements discussed in CJ are estimative: the aesthetic judgements of §9, to take only one example, are estimates of objects according to the subjective free play of imagination and understanding, while teleological judgements are estimates of nature according to an '*analogy* to the causality that looks to ends' (CJ Part II, Introduction).

The significance of Kant's distinction between estimative and subsumptive judgement has only recently been fully appreciated. This is largely the result of the recent emphasis in cultural and political philosophy upon difference and differential judgement. The interpretations of Kant's reflective judgement by Arendt (1989) and Lyotard (1983), for example, explore the implications of discriminative judgement for political action and the practice of art and literary criticism.

ethics *see* CATEGORICAL IMPERATIVE, COMMAND, EVIL, GOOD, IMPERATIVE, MAXIMS, RIGHT, WILL

ethical commonwealth *see* CHURCH

evidence [*Evidenz*] *see also* ACROAMATIC, AXIOMS, CERTAINTY
Evidence is the intuitive certainty restricted to the intuitive principles or axioms of mathematics (CPR A 733/B 761). It is not applicable to the discursive principles, or acroamata, of philosophy. Kant illustrates the contrast by comparing the evidence of mathematical axioms, such as 'three points lie in a plane', with the philosophical proposition that 'everything has a cause'. The former 'combines the predicates of the object both *a priori* and immediately' while the latter cannot be known 'directly and immediately from the concepts alone' but requires a deduction or proof which appeals to the 'condition of time determination in an experience' (CPR A 733/B 761).

evil [*kakon, malum, Böse, Übel*] *see also* DISPOSITION, FREEDOM, GOOD, MAXIM, WILL
Kant's discussion of evil was heir to a long and internally complex philosophical and religious tradition, outside of which many of his critical distinctions and emphases are almost incomprehensible. This tradition, which combined Judaic, Christian and Greek philosophical ideas, was concerned above all with (a) the place and (b) the origin or cause of evil. With regard to the former, evil was invariably placed in a dualistic opposition to the good, whether the good was conceived philosophically as virtue or excellence, or religiously as righteousness or God-fearing. The nature of the good in its turn was variously conceived, whether in terms of the idea of the good, as the will of God, or as the good or pleasant life. The definition of the good determined to a large extent the definition of evil. If the good was considered to be an idea, as it was by Plato, then did this entail considering evil also as an idea, or was it to be identified with the opposite of the idea, i.e., matter, or was it a principle in its own right, in conflict with the good? Plato argues in various places for each of these positions, as indeed did Kant later. Similarly, the conception of the divine

institution of the good also raised problems concerning the status of evil; did it, like the good, also originate in God, or in an adversary to God, or was it just an illusion caused by the lack of human insight into the ways of God? These problems were avoided in Aristotelian and Epicurean accounts of evil, the former regarding it as an extreme deviation from the mean, the latter as whatever caused pain, but these positions themselves bequeathed further problems to posterity.

The definition of evil was further complicated by differences concerning the proper focus of discussions of evil. Should evil be considered supernaturally, with reference to the theology of evil, or naturally with reference to evil events in the world, or even psychologically, with reference to human evil dispositions and actions? Most authors combined aspects of all three, notably Plato and the Stoics in philosophy, the author of the book of Job in the Jewish tradition, and the authors of the Christian canon. Christians increasingly emphasized the psychological dimension of evil – an emphasis derived from the theologically and naturally founded doctrine of original sin – and emphasized in turn the role of will over reason. This orientation reached its theological *apogee* in the writings of Augustine which served to focus subsequent Christian reflection upon the problem of the good and evil will (see Augustine, 1960, Book VII). Subsequent medieval Christian speculation upon evil may broadly be divided in terms of the natural/supernatural emphasis of Aquinas and the more supernatural/voluntaristic direction taken by Augustinians such as Bonaventura, and much later by Luther.

The specific focus of Kant's discussion varied at different stages of his career, although his concern with the connection between evil and the human will remained constant. In ND Proposition IX, for example, he moves from a theological discussion of the coexistence of good and evil in God's most perfect creation to an aetiology of evil, one which finds its origin not in God but in 'an inner principle of self-determination' proper to human beings. This principle, it subsequently becomes clear, is not as the rationalist Wolff had argued, based on our defective knowledge of the good, but is a radically evil principle inherent to the human will. In terms of the distinction offered in ND, human evil is a negative evil of defect (*malum defectus*) not of reason but of the will; it is not a positive evil of privation (*malum privationis*); the former involves a negation of the good, while the latter proposes positive grounds for superseding the good.

By the time of his mature writings, Kant has focused his account of evil almost exclusively on the problem of the human will. While he shows himself conversant with arguments for and against the compatibility of the existence of God with evil in the world, he states clearly in FPT that the question of evil posed in this way cannot be addressed by knowledge.

180

What can be addressed by knowledge, however, is the evil discernible in the human will, and this Kant considers in CPrR and RL.

In the context of a discussion of the objects of practical reason in CPrR, Kant develops a distinction between two forms of evil. The only possible objects of practical reason are good and evil, terms which Kant says are used to translate *bonum* and *malum*. He then points out that the 'German language has the good fortune to possess expressions' (CPrR p. 61, p. 59) which permit a distinction to be made between two forms of good and evil. Kant translates *bonum* as both *das Gute* or the good and *das Wohl* or well-being, corresponding to which he translates *malum* as *das Böse* or evil and *das Übel* or bad. The opposition of well-being and bad holds with respect to the 'sensibility and to the feeling of pleasure or displeasure which it produces' (CPrR p. 60, p. 62). It thus repeats the Epicurean alignment of good and evil with pleasure and pain, and is distinguished by Kant from good and evil proper. These do not refer to 'the sensory state of the person' but indicate 'a relation to the will' which is 'not a thing but only the manner of acting . . . only the maxim of the will . . ,' (CPrR p. 60, p. 62).

The locating of evil within the maxims of the will is explored further in RL, where Kant develops the thesis of radical evil. The source of evil lies not in an object determining the will, nor in an inclination or natural impulse, but only in 'a rule made by the will for the use of its freedom, that is, in a maxim' (RL p. 21, p. 17). The ground for choosing between a good or evil maxim cannot be found in experience; it is a free act based neither upon sensible inclinations nor upon a further maxim of the will. Human beings choose between maxims which determine the will according to incentives of either the moral law or their sensuous natures. The distinction between a good and an evil will depends upon 'which of the two incentives [is made] the condition of the other' (RL p. 36, p. 31). Kant continues by saying that this predicament of choice is ineluctable because of the radical character of evil, which is described as a 'natural propensity, *inextirpable* by human powers' (RL p. 37, p. 32). But while human nature is frail, it is not diabolic – it does not make evil itself into an incentive of the will; rather, human nature lacks the strength to follow principles and the discrimination to distinguish between incentives. Yet because of the same freedom which leads to the *malum defectus* of radical evil it is nevertheless possible for human beings to overcome, if not extirpate, the propensity to prefer the incentives of their sensuous natures over the moral law. So while the propensities to good and evil do battle to direct the maxims of the will, the 'seed of goodness [is prevented] from developing as it otherwise would', although this does not prevent the will from being cultured and possessing a history. This is not to suggest that there is a quasi-Aristotelian mean between good and evil – Kant expressly rules this out in a footnote on RL p. 39, p. 34 – but rather that good and evil are continually struggling for predominance (RL p. 82, p. 77).

Kant's notion of radical evil is an example of a *malum defectus* and not of a *malum privationis*: it negates the good or the moral law as an incentive for maxims of the will, but does not replace it with an incentive to prefer the evil maxim. This concept of evil allowed Kant to maintain the possibility of a progressive human history in which the good is achieved through the culturing of the will. The subtleties of this position were overlooked by many of his critics, who regarded his doctrine of radical evil as qualifying his defence of human freedom and thus, in the words of Goethe, 'besmirching his philosophical robe'. Nevertheless Kant's version of the relationship of freedom and evil inspired some of the great nineteenth-century philosophical meditations on evil, notably Hegel's *Philosophy of Right* (1821, §§139–40), Schelling's *Of Human Freedom* (1809), Kierkegaard's *Concept of Anxiety* (1844), and Nietzsche's *Genealogy of Morals* (1887). In the light of political events in the twentieth century, Kant's notion of radical evil as a *malum defectus* seems to many critics to be insufficient. The Jewish Holocaust in World War II has been regarded by some writers as a diabolic *malum privationis* involving the choice of an evil principle; others, notably Hannah Arendt (1964), have spoken in a more Kantian vein of the 'banality of evil' arising from a will informed not by diabolic or even sensuous incentives, but from an unreflective, bureaucratic obedience to 'duty'.

example/exemplarity [*Beispiel, exemplarisch*] *see also* CANON, ESTIMATE, EXHIBITION, GENIUS, IMITATION, JUDGEMENT

Examples are intuitions corresponding to empirical concepts, and serve as 'the go-cart [*Gängelwagen*] of judgement' (CPR A 134/B 173). Kant says that those without a natural talent for applying general rules to particular cases cannot dispense with the use of examples. They are a pragmatic means for avoiding the 'aporia of judgement' which arises with the search for rules for the application of rules. Examples for imitation are produced by genius, whose works are exemplary precisely because 'though not themselves derived from imitation, they must serve that purpose for others' (CJ §46). Such works do not provide a formula or a rule, but act as a standard by which the followers of genius may put their talent to the test. Thus examples provide a canon for estimative judgement, they do not provide a rule of judgement but simply a standard by which to distinguish between good and bad judgements.

exhibition [*exhibitio*] *see also* CONSTRUCTION, EXAMPLE, JUDGEMENT, PRESENTATION, SYNTHESIS

Exhibition is the function of judgement which presents to a given concept its corresponding intuition (see CJ § VIII). There are two forms of exhibition. The first, in which the corresponding intuition is added a priori to a concept, is entitled construction. The second, in which an intuition is presented to an empirical concept, is called an example. Kant claims that without the basic addition of concept to intuition through *exhibitio* there can be no knowledge, because the intuition would be blind and the concept empty (WP p. 325, p. 181).

existence [*Dasein, Existenz*] *see also* ACTUALITY, BEING, CATEGORIES, GOD, NE-CESSITY, ONTOLOGY, POSSIBILITY, POSTULATES OF EMPIRICAL THOUGHT, SOUL, SUBREPTION, THEOLOGY, WORLD

Kant followed Aristotle in distinguishing between being, actuality and existence, regarding each term as a distinct way in which to speak of being. The difficulty in defining the generic and specific differences between the terms follows from their place within, and beyond, the order of categorical judgement. Not only may none of these terms be used subreptively as a predicate, it is equally unacceptable to describe the relations between them in terms of categorical functions such as quantity, quality, relation or modality. Yet although each of these terms is extra-categorical – denoting the 'relation' through which categorial judgements take place – they nevertheless form the basis of categorial judgement and are thus crucial to it.

Kant describes the entire 'Analytic of Concepts' of CPR as covering the ground of ontology, or the doctrine of being. The two main sections of the analytic thus correspond to being thought of first as existence (in the order of the categories) and then as actuality (in the principles). With this distinction Kant implicitly follows Aristotle's distinction between *dynamis* and *energeia*, the one designating potentiality, the other actuality. Although the former is actualized by the latter this does not imply that the former has an ontological or even epistemological priority, they are inextricable. Thus the categories structure potential relations to objects which are actualized by the principles, without either necessarily having priority over the other.

The categorical order determines not only the contours of a possible experience, but also the object of such an experience. The determination is described as 'existence', which is not a predicate that may be applied in a discrete act of judgement, but the position of the understanding as a whole with respect to a possible object of experience. To qualify, this object must exist for the understanding. Indeed, 'existence' denotes the way in which an object of possible experience comes into being through the categorical structure of the understanding; it is distinguished from

183

actuality, which is the coming into being in space and time of the object of experience. The general relation between existence and actuality as 'modes' of being (although, strictly speaking, such recourse to the categories of modality is illegitimate when speaking extra-categorically) is underlined by the transformation of the second modal category of existence–nonexistence into the second postulate of empirical thought.

The limitation of the term existence to the categorial order of being holds also for its use in describing the being of such objects as God, the world and the soul. Kant maintains that the being of these objects cannot be spoken of in terms of existence, nor, of course, of actuality. In the case of each of these objects the condition through which they may (or may not) be thought is hypostatized, leading to subreptions in which existence is applied as if it were a predicate. The being of God cannot be spoken of in terms of existence because 'all existential propositions are synthetic' (CPR A 598/B 626) or presuppose the relation through which judgements of objects of possible experience may be made. God is by definition not such an object, however much human reason may 'persuade itself' (CPR A 586/B 614) to the contrary. Similarly with the world: we may persuade ourselves of the existence of the world dogmatically, and thus overlook the fact that all existence can tell us is the way in which 'objective reality' 'is capable of being given to us' (CPR A 217/B 264). Finally the soul – or 'the correlate of all existence' – cannot properly be said itself to exist unless it could think itself through itself, a procedure evidently unacceptable to Kant since 'I cannot know as an object that which I must presuppose in order to know any object' (CPR A 402).

Kant's subtle distinctions between being, existence and actuality were largely eroded in the reception of his philosophy. While his critique of hypostatizing existence into a predicate and seeking to apply it to all beings was well understood, his narrow distinction between existence and actuality was largely overlooked. The relevance of the distinction was recovered by Heidegger in *Being and Time* (1927), where he also further distinguished between *Dasein* and *Existenz*, terms which Kant invariably used synonymously.

experience [*empeiria, experientia, Erfahrung*] *see also* CONCEPT, CONSCIOUSNESS, INTUITION, KNOWLEDGE, ONTOLOGY, REFLECTION, SENSIBILITY, UNDERSTANDING
At the end of the *Posterior Analytics* Aristotle re-capitulates the essentials of his account of knowledge, which consists in the movement from sense perception of particulars to universals. Experience plays an important part in his argument, since it is both what emerges from the memory of repeated sense perceptions and the source of the 'universal now stabilised in its entirety within the soul, the one beside the many which is a single identity

within them all' (Aristotle, 1941, 100a, 7–8). As such it the source of the skill of the craftsman in the 'sphere of becoming' and the knowledge of the scientist in the 'sphere of being'. Experience thus mediates between the particulars of perception and the universal of knowledge, and was consistently considered in medieval philosophy as the class of knowledge associated with sense perception, and characterized by being received from an external source.

The emphasis upon the external sources of experience is maintained by Descartes, although he adds a significant qualification. In the *Rules for the Direction of the Mind* (1628) he describes experience as 'what we perceive by sense, what we hear from t'·e lips of others, and generally whatever reaches our understanding either from external sources or from that contemplation which our mind directs backwards on itself' (Descartes, 1968, pp. 43–4). Here, along with the external sources of experience, is added an internal source of the mind's reflection on itself. This could be construed in a routine Aristotelian fashion as 'memory', although that would underestimate the implications raised by Descartes' revision of the notion of experience. For the relationship between external and internal sources of experience could be construed in two directions. The first would be to regard external experience as the source of internal experience, to see internal experience as derived by means of reflection from outer experience. The second would be to regard both sources of experience as independent of each other, but nevertheless related, with the data of external experience being complemented by that which is produced by means of the mind's internal reflection on itself.

The first direction, which regarded external experience as primary and succeeded secondarily by internal reflection was followed in the work of Locke and Hume. Locke, for example, opens his *Essay Concerning Human Understanding* with the claim that it is from experience 'that all our knowledge is founded, and from that it ultimately derives itself' (1690, p. 33). By experience he intends, following Descartes, that derived from either '*external sensible objects*' or '*the internal operations of our minds perceived and reflected on by ourselves*', namely, sensation and reflection. Reflection for Locke was the reflection on sensation, a restriction which leads him to the sceptical doubt concerning whether '*our knowledge reaches* much further than our experience' (p. 285), an insight developed by Hume in his account of experience in the *Treatise of Human Nature* (see, for example, Hume, 1739, p. 87). Leibniz, however, in his critical commentary on Locke in the *New Essays on Human Understanding*, shifted the emphasis away from external to inner experience, seeing the 'innate truths' of inner experience as prior to, and conditions of, the data and truths of external experience (Leibniz, 1765, pp. 83–4). Kant, who at the end of his career described CPR as 'the genuine apology for Leibniz' (OD p. 251, p. 160), attempted to develop a concept of experience which combined both directions opened by Descartes, bringing into balance the aspects of inner and outer experience emphasized by Leibniz and by Locke.

Kant agreed with Locke's limitation of knowledge to the bounds of experience, even if his definition of experience was quite distinct. In fact, the concept of experience used in such early writings as DS (1766) is not far removed from Locke's. There, when he programmatically rejects the view of metaphysics as the 'search for hidden things' in favour of its redefinition as the 'science of the limits of human reason', he describes with relief his return to the 'humble ground of experience and common sense' (DS p. 368, p. 355). While never repudiating this definition of metaphysics and its consequent limitation of knowledge to the limits of experience, Kant considerably redefines his concept of experience, making it something far from humble and commonsensical. The first stages of this redefinition are evident in ID. Kant rejects Locke's view that ideas (in his case concepts and intuitions) may be derived from outer experience, and inclines to Leibniz's position that they are presupposed by experience. He defines experience as the 'reflective cognition, which arises when several appearances are compared by the understanding' but immediately qualifies this position (which would be compatible with Locke's) by saying that 'there is no way from appearance to experience except by reflection in accordance with the logical use of the understanding' (ID §5). Thus the reflection is itself pre-determined by the logical use of the understanding.

The elements of Kant's new concept of experience in ID are developed in the critical philosophy. He defines experience as 'the synthetic connection of appearances (perceptions) in consciousness, so far as this connection is necessary' (P §22). Experience is accordingly synthetic, described as 'this product of the senses and understanding' which may be analysed into elements. There are first of all 'intuition[s] of which I become conscious, i.e., perception (*perceptio*), which pertains merely to the senses' (P §20). These provide the element of external experience, but do not add up to a full experience. There is the synthesis in a judgement, but this synthesis has particular properties; it does not 'merely compare perceptions and connect them in a consciousness of my state' as was claimed by empiricist accounts of perception, but subsumes intuitions under a concept 'which determines the form of judging in general with regard to the intuition' (P §20). These are the a priori concepts of the understanding, such as cause, which are not derived from experience but which give it its character of necessity.

In the more subtle account of experience in CPR, the synthesis which constitutes experience is not the simple conceptual unification of an intuited manifold, but takes place on the basis of a mutual adaptation of concept and intuition. Kant maintains that all synthesis, 'even that which renders perception possible, is subject to the categories; and since experience is cognition by means of connected perceptions, the categories are the conditions of the possibility of experience, and therefore valid *a priori* for all objects of experience' (CPR B 161). Kant ultimately derives the categories from the spontaneity of the understanding, thus establishing the conditions of the possibility of experience in the mutual adaptation between outer experience (receptivity of sensibility) and inner experience (spontaneity of understanding). The a priori forms of intuition (space and time) as well as the pure concepts of the understanding or categories establish the conditions of possible experience which determine the limits of legitimate knowledge. As Kant noted with respect to the categories, 'everything which the understanding derives from itself is, though not borrowed from experience, at the disposal of the understanding solely for use in experience' (CPR A 236/B 295).

Kant's concept of experience has rightly been one of the main areas of critical contention in the interpretation of his philosophy. His attempt to maintain the virtues of both empiricist and idealist accounts of experience naturally provoked empiricist and idealist critiques of it. Similarly, the subversive potential of his limitation of knowledge to objects of possible experience provoked critiques from those who would defend the ideas of God, the world and the soul. A popular avenue of criticism claims, largely on the basis of P, that Kant in CPR worked with an impoverished concept of experience, namely one restricted to the objects of Euclidean geometry and Newtonian mechanics. Against this it was possible to point to CPrR and CJ for broader notions of moral and aesthetic experience. This position however, exaggerates the restrictions on the concept of experience employed in CPR, and underestimates the ways in which the three critiques complement each other in extending and refining aspects of the received notions of experience.

explication *see* DEFINITION

exposition *see* DEFINITION

extension [*Ausdehnung*] *see also* BODY, DYNAMICS, EXTENSION, FORCE, MATTER
Extension was defined by Descartes in the *Rules for the Direction of the Mind* (1628) as 'whatever has length, breadth, and depth' and which thus 'occupies space' while remaining distinct from body (Descartes, 1968, p. 57). His definition was motivated by the attempt to undercut metaphysical notions of substance by replacing them with extension. This was resisted

187

by Leibniz, who defended the view that extension was an attribute of substance. Kant largely adhered to the latter view, agreeing with Leibniz in LF that a force inheres in body 'prior to its extension' (LF §1). For Kant as for Leibniz, extended objects occupy space not because of their extension, but by virtue of the dynamic qualities of impenetrability and resistance. Kant thus claims in MF that ' "to fill a space" is therefore a closer determination of the concept "to occupy a space" ' (MF p. 497, p. 41). For these reasons he differed from the Cartesians in not regarding extension as a fundamental property of matter, and thus it plays a relatively insignificant part in his philosophy.

extra-terrestrial life This is discussed most fully in the third part of UNH. Although the treatment verges on irony at the expense of humanity, it is clearly meant seriously. There Kant argues from natural theology and the 'infinity of nature' to the existence of extra-terrestrial life. He maintains that most planets are inhabited, and that the inhabitants' bodily characteristics are determined by their environments (see the discussion of the characteristics of Venusians and Jovians, UNH pp. 185–7, pp. 188–9). He concludes with the thought of human migrations to other planets, adding that 'such uncertain pictures of the force of imagination' (UNH p. 199, p. 196) are insufficient for the 'hope of future life'. In CJ §91 he underlines the hypothetical nature of the claim for the existence of extra-terrestrial life by presenting it as an example of an empirical 'matter of opinion': 'for if we could get nearer to the planets, which is intrinsically possible, experience would decide whether such inhabitants are there or not, but as we shall never get so near to them, the matter remains one of opinion'.

F

fact [*factum, Faktum, Tatsache*] *see also* DEDUCTION, FREEDOM

Although Kant uses both the Latinate *Faktum* and the German *Tatsache* as equivalents for *factum*, the Latin past participle of *facere* (to do) meaning 'something done', he consistently distinguishes between the two terms. He uses the term *Faktum* in CPrR in order to signal that it is being used by analogy with *Tatsache*. However, the situation is complicated by his inconsistent use of *Tatsache* in CPR and CJ. *Faktum* in the CPrR's 'fact of reason' is used by analogy with the narrow sense of *Tatsache* in CPR, while in CJ *Tatsache* is given a broader significance which contains both theoretical and practical senses of the term.

In the deduction chapter of CPR, Kant translates *quid facti* or the question of fact ('What has been done?') as 'die Frage . . . die Tatsache angeht'. The question of fact addresses the employment and origin of a concept and not the legitimacy of using it (CPR A 84/B 116). Here fact refers to the sheer givenness of empirical concepts which allows us to use them – 'appropriating to them a meaning, an ascribed significance' (ibid.) – without the justification of a deduction. The immediacy of fact is used by analogy in CPrR to describe the consciousness of the moral law, but this usage is severely qualified by CJ §91 where Kant divides the genus of 'knowable things' into 'matters of opinion', 'matters of fact' (*Tatsachen*) and 'matters of faith'. Now, far from being immediately and unproblematically given, facts are objects which 'answer to concepts which can be proven' whether through experience or pure reason. These include the properties of geometrical magnitudes, things verifiable by experience and finally, and exceptionally, one idea of reason, the only one which may be proven through experience. This is freedom, the only factual idea whose 'reality as a particular kind of causality' is verified by the both the 'practical laws of pure reason' and the 'actions which take place in obedience to them'.

In the deduction of freedom as a fact Kant signals a change in strategy from that pursued with respect to the 'fact of reason' in CPrR. In CPrR *Faktum* is unverifiable; it describes the immediate consciousness of the fundamental law of pure reason which 'forces itself' upon us as a 'fact of reason' without presupposition, and which 'proclaims itself as originating law' (p. 31, p. 31). The moral law or 'fact of pure reason' is 'apodictically certain', not through any verifiable grounds but because we are 'a priori conscious' of it. It is like *Tatsache* of CPR in that it has not been called to answer any question of right or *quaestio quid juris*, but unlike it in so far as it can never be called to do so; it is 'firmly established of itself' (p. 47, p. 48). Thus Kant is using the term analogically, and clearly indicates this by saying that the moral law is given 'as it were' (*gleichsam*) through a fact. It is not that the moral law *is* a fact, but rather that its peculiar immediacy may be described in terms of an analogy with that of a fact. In CJ however, Kant abandons the argument by analogy, preferring to argue that freedom, like any other fact, may be verified by both freedom and experience.

faculty [*dynamis, facultas, Fakultät, Vermögen*] *see also* DRIVE, POSSIBILITY, POWER
The English word 'faculty' translates two distinct ideas: the first signifies a part of the structure of a university, the second a potential or power to realize some end. Kant's concern with the first sense arose from the anomalous place of philosophy in the curriculum and organization of the eighteenth-century university. Philosophy did not have a natural place in any of the three 'higher faculties' of law, medicine and theology, and usually served as a propaedeutic to study in one of these disciplines. Kant was a part of a cultural movement which sought to re-define the place of philosophy in the university, as well as to justify its encroachments upon the higher faculties in the areas of philosophical jurisprudence and theology. His main contribution to the debate between the 'lower' and the 'higher' faculties is CF (1798), a work which addressed the conflict between philosophy and theology, law and medicine.

The second sense of faculty translates the term *Vermögen* which in its turn is derived from Latin *facultas* and Greek *dynamis*. Although the latter was used by several pre-Socratic philosophers, notably Empedocles, its meaning was definitively fixed by Aristotle in the *Metaphysics*. He broadly attributed two senses to the term: the first referred to an ability or power to achieve an end, the other to a potential for change which would be actualized through *energeia*. This dual definition of faculty was enormously influential, and remained remarkably stable throughout its transmission in medieval Aristotelianism. It was especially prominent in the discussion of the nature of the soul, which was divided into various potentials or faculties of action. The two senses of faculty as potentiality and as a power of the mind persist in Descartes and even as late as Wolff: Meissner's Wolffian *Philosophisches Lexicon* (1737) gives *facultas* and *potentia* as synonyms for *Vermögen*, and defines it in Aristotelian terms as the possibility of either doing or suffering an action. He further specifies the faculties of desire as

190

sensible desire or appetite and the will, and the faculties of knowing as sensibility and reason.

The term faculty is ubiquitous in Kant's writings, and indeed underlies the architectonic of the critical philosophy. He reflects upon it most systematically in the Introduction to CJ, where he distinguishes between faculties of the soul and faculties of cognition. Faculties of the soul, variously described as *Seelenvermögen* or *gesamte Vermögen des Gemüts* or capacities (*Fähigkeiten*) (§III), comprise a fundamental, tripartite 'order of our powers of representation'; these are: (a) the faculty of knowledge; (b) the feeling of pleasure and displeasure; and (c) the faculty of desire. The architectonic of the critical trilogy corresponds to the three faculties, with the capacity for pleasure and displeasure forming a transition between the theoretical and the practical, even though none of them may be derived from a common principle.

Kant introduces the fundamental faculties of the soul by way of an analogy to a related or kindred family (*Verwandschaft mit der Familie*) of cognitive faculties (*Erkenntnisvermögen*) (CJ §III). These faculties form a distinct but related order of cognitive powers, divided between lower and higher; the former are the faculties of sensibility, the latter the faculties of reason, judgement and the understanding. Kant points to an analogy between the two 'orders' of faculties, aligning the cognitive faculty of understanding with the knowledge-faculty of the soul; reason with desire; and judgement with the feeling of pleasure and displeasure. He later (§IX) distributes them according to a systematic table, in which the two sets of faculties are supplied with a priori principles and objects of application: the faculties of knowledge/understanding are accorded the principle of 'conformity to law' and the object of application 'nature'; those of reason/desire are accorded 'final end' and 'freedom'; while the faculties judgement/pleasure and displeasure correspond to 'finality' and 'art'.

Thus it is clear that for Kant the faculties form internally articulated orders which are analogous to each other. However, in spite of the importance of the term faculty for the entire critical project, he never fully discusses or analyses it – unless, of course, the entire critical philosophy is viewed as such. The lack of precision around this central term has proven extremely fruitful, giving rise to psychologistic and other forms of Kantianism. Indeed, even anti-psychologistic Kantianism maintains the division of the cognitive faculties, to surrender which would probably be to leave the ambit of the Kantian tradition. The reliance on the notion of faculty by Kant and his followers was mocked by Nietzsche in §11 of *Beyond Good and Evil* as the 'honeymoon time of German philosophy' when 'the young theologians of the College of Tübingen [Hegel, Schelling and Hölderlin] went straightaway off into the bushes – all in search of

191

"faculties" '. He regarded the appeal to faculties as analogous to the appeal to a *virtus dormitiva* (a sleep-inducing faculty) to explain why opium induces sleep, and proposed replacing the question 'How are synthetic a priori judgements possible?' with 'Why are they necessary?' Such a question, of course, intentionally and shrewdly challenges the entire ethos of Kantianism at one of its most vulnerable points.

faith [*fides, Glaube*] *see also* BELIEF, HOPE, KNOWLEDGE, LOVE, OPINION, POSTULATES
The concept of faith played a relatively minor role in classical Greek philosophy; it was used by Plato to describe one of the grades of knowledge by opinion (Plato, 1961, Rep., 511e) and also to describe belief in the gods (ibid., Laws, 966d). For Aristotle, faith refers to a form of proof based upon induction or rhetorical persuasion. The philosophical concept of faith derives from the Christian tradition, and in particular its Pauline strand. This provenance led to a tension between faith and knowledge, or religious doctrine and philosophy. It stimulated various imaginative efforts at reconciliation, which continued up to and after Kant.

In the New Testament faith is an attitude of belief in Christ, whether in his words, his gift of healing or his works; it was codified by Paul, who uses the term over 200 times in his *Epistles*, as a means of distinguishing the Christian attitude towards the law from that of the Jews. He also initiated the extremely influential idea that faith was a gift of grace: 'For by grace you have been saved through faith; and this is not your own doing, it is the gift of God' (Ephesians 2:8). This idea was developed by Augustine in several works, and given its place within the medieval Aristotelian revival by Aquinas. In the *Summa contra gentiles* he distinguishes the ascent of natural knowledge to God from the descent of the knowledge of faith through grace from God, movements which he regards as complementary (Aquinas, 1975, p. 39). Another relationship between faith and philosophy (or knowledge) was explored by Anselm, in whose *Proslogion* faith serves as the condition of understanding, a thought which led to the view that faith has precedence over understanding, and then to the confession *credo quid absurdum* – 'I believe because it is absurd'. Following the Reformation, arguments for faith as a subjective gift of grace were used to criticize the doctrine of justification through works, and to support the case for ecclesiastical and secular toleration (see Luther, 1961, p. 385).

Kant's discussion of faith is heir to the arguments between faith and knowledge, and appears in several different contexts. In one he presents his discussion of faith within a framework analogous to Plato's three forms of knowledge (Plato, 1961, Rep. 511e); faith, knowledge and belief are modes of subjective assent or 'holding-to-be-true' (*Fürwahrhalten*). In CPR he presents such assent in terms of subjective and objective sufficiency:

opinion is neither subjectively nor objectively sufficient; knowledge is both subjectively and objectively sufficient; while faith is subjectively yet *consciously* not objectively sufficient (CPR A 822/B 850; see also WO). In CJ the distinction is framed in terms of the objects of opinion, knowledge and faith: an object of opinion is one whose existence is empirically possible but unprovable; while the existence of an object of knowledge may be attested to both factually and by means of pure reason. Objects of faith, however, while they are thought a priori are nevertheless 'transcendent for the theoretical use of reason' (CJ §91); they are ideas which have subjective conviction, but 'whose objective reality cannot be guaranteed theoretically'. Kant gives three examples of such objects: (a) 'the highest good in the world attainable through freedom'; (b) the existence of God; and (c) the immortality of the soul. Finally, in L Kant distinguishes between the three forms of holding-to-be-true in terms of the modality of their judgements: opinion is problematic, knowledge is apodeictic and faith is assertoric.

The three objects of faith listed in CJ echo the three 'postulates of pure practical reason' – freedom, immortality and the existence of God – which in CPrR are presented in terms of the objective reality given to the ideas of reason. They are not objects of theoretical knowledge, but possess their own practical dignity. The same three ideas serve in the preface to the second edition of CPR to disqualify 'all *practical extension* of pure reason' and thus, in Kant's famous phrase, 'to sublate [*aufheben*] *knowledge* in order to make room for *faith*' (CPR B xxx). Yet this is far from conceding *credo quid absurdum*, since for Kant the subjective certainty of faith is well founded and need neither appeal to nor negate knowledge. This is even the case for 'doctrinal faith' such as physico-theology which applies the subjective certainty of moral faith *analogously* (CPR A 825/B 853) to objects of nature. An example, analysed at length in CJ Part II, is the purposiveness of the world which follows from 'postulating' analogously a 'wise author of the world'. The claim cannot be theoretically justified, but the degree of subjective conviction associated with it far exceeds that of opinion.

Kant regards such doctrinal faith as inherently unstable, unlike the moral faith and the rational faith to which it gives rise. Moral faith bestows certainty on the existence of freedom, immortality and God, and this certainty is based upon the inability to disclaim these postulates without 'becoming abhorrent in my own eyes' (CPR A 828/B 856). The rational faith issuing from this moral certainty involves an insight into the conditions necessary to achieve 'the unity of ends under the moral law' (see also WO). And even if one were indifferent to moral laws, rational faith would give rise to a negative faith along the lines of Pascal's wager; since it is impossible to achieve 'any *certainty* that there is *no* such being and *no* such life' (CPR A 830/B 858) such faith would form an 'analogon' of good sentiments, namely a check on the outbreak of evil ones.

Kant's discussion of faith emphasizes what differentiates it from knowledge while aligning it with the practical ideas of reason. Although Kant seems to stress the existence of God and immortality, his concerns are not *primarily* religious ones. However, this does not mean that he excludes religious considerations, for these are discussed at considerable length in RL. There Kant uses the idea of faith as a gift conferring subjective certainty upon its recipient to justify the distinction between religion, of which there is only one, and faiths of which there are several (Jewish, Moslem, Hindu, Christian). Religion is 'hidden within and has to do with moral dispositions' (RL p. 108, p. 99) while 'ecclesiastical faiths' are external, empirical and several. Kant discerns (and recommends) a transition from partial ecclesiastical faiths to the universal church of religion; every individual 'possesses' a 'saving faith' or 'pure religious faith' – i.e., practical faith – even if they practice an ecclesiastical faith (RL p. 115, p. 106). The latter are developments of 'historical faiths' founded upon specific and attested acts of revelation, and stress outward acts of 'drudging and mercenary faith' which, unlike saving faith, may well be performed with an evil disposition.

Saving or 'pure religious faith' has two elements: the first is faith in an atonement or reparation for unjust actions, while the second is 'the faith that we can become well-pleasing to God through a good course of life in the future' (RL p. 115, p. 106). Both elements are derived from each other, but in certain circumstances one may take precedence over the other. Ecclesiastical/historical faith privileges atonement, conferring priority upon faith in a 'vicarious atonement' over leading a good life, while in religion the inverse holds, with the practical faith preferred over faith in revelation. Kant sees a possible fusion of the two positions in a form of Christology wherein Christ is an object of saving faith not because he once existed and was the son of God, but because he is an exemplary 'archetype lying in our reason . . . of a course of life well-pleasing to God' (RL p. 119, p. 110).

Kant's discussion of religious and ecclesiastical faith may be criticized for its crypto-Pauline elements, which prefer a 'Kingdom' founded upon an ahistorical saving faith over other religious orientations which are indifferent to matters of faith but which emphasize their historical character. This, however, was not the aspect of his account of faith which most intrigued his successors (with the exception of Hermann Cohen who aligned Judaism with the religion of pure reason which Kant described in terms of Christianity). Most were interested in Kant's version of the perennial problem of faith and knowledge, with F.H. Jacobi (1743–1819) at the end of the eighteenth century arguing for faith against knowledge in much the same way as Hamann had done in his metacritiques of Kant (see Jacobi, 1787, Hamann, 1967). Hegel in *Faith and Knowledge* (1802) attempted to sublate the distinction by showing how an abstract conception of knowledge gives rise to an opposition of faith and knowledge. Kierkegaard's anti-Hegelian discourse on faith in *Fear and Trembling* (1843) defends faith both as a presupposition of knowledge and as a leap without knowledge into the absurd. Nietzsche, on the contrary, inquires into the genealogy of faith, describing his 'basic problem' as 'whence this omnipotence of faith?' (Nietzsche, 1901, §259), whether in morality or truth. Although this inquiry is presented as a critique of Kant, it characteristically maintains several Kantian aspects, notably in the self-loathing and abhorrence of the 'ugliest man' following the collapse of faith and the death of God.

fear [*Furcht*] *see also* AFFECT, EVIL, FEELING, SUBLIME
Fear is defined as the emotional 'aversion to danger' and is of varying degrees, ranging across anguish, anxiety, horror and dread (A §77). Anxiety, for example, is defined as 'fear of an object that threatens an undetermined evil', while anguish is fear combined with reflection. The emotion that may be evoked by the terrors of the sublime is not actual fear, but is an astonishment which vertiginously exemplifies the superiority of the imagination over internal and external nature.

federalism *see also* AS-IF, COSMOPOLITANISM, CULTURE, HISTORY, IDEA, PEACE, RIGHT, STATE, WAR
The idea of federalism is discussed by Kant in the context of international law and the federation of states, and marks a stage in the realization of the idea of perpetual peace. The theme is discussed in MM in the context of 'Public Right', in TP in the context of cosmopolitanism, and in PP as the second of three 'definitive articles of a perpetual peace'. While these discussions differ significantly in detail, they share certain underlying characteristics. The first is an analogy Kant draws between the formation of a federation of states and 'that [process] by which a people becomes a state' (MM p. 350, p. 156). Just as individuals before the formation of a state are in a condition of war, so too are states before the constitution of a federation. As often happens in Kant's arguments from analogy, the similarity is accompanied by a difference, namely that states remain in the condition of war and retain their sovereignty, thus permitting them to leave or renew the federation of states. In PP and TP the analogy is extended to an historical genealogy of the federation. The distress occasioned by universal violence 'makes a people submit to the coercion which

reason itself prescribes' and to 'enter into a civil constitution' which will also lead them 'into a cosmopolitan constitution' (TP p. 310, p. 90).

The motivation for entering into a federation of states lies in the concern for mutual security arising from the perpetual state of war that prevails between states; neighbouring states, writes Kant in PP, 'are a standing offence to one another by the very fact that they are neighbours' (PP p. 354, p. 102). The character of such a federation, however, poses problems. It is here that the analogy with the constitution of the civil state breaks down. This 'league of nations' must 'involve no sovereign authority (as in a civil constitution) but only an *association* (federation)' (MM p. 344, p. 151) from which states may exit and whose terms they can renegotiate. Indeed Kant sees an 'international state' as 'contradictory' since it requires the subordination of individual states to an international state, an act which would found an empire and not a federation, and which would effectively dissolve the constituent states (PP p. 356, p. 103). Kant describes the league of nations as a 'pacific federation' which would not possess 'public laws and a coercive power' (PP p. 356, p. 104) but which, without power, would secure the freedom of each state. However, quite how it would achieve this end is unclear, and Kant himself is not sanguine about its chances. He refers in MM to a 'permanent congress of states' which is even weaker than a federation; it is a voluntary coalition 'that can be dissolved at any time, not a federation (like that of the American states) which is based on a constitution' (MM p. 351, p. 156). It would serve ultimately to provide a forum in which disputes between nations could be decided juridically, by analogy with civil disputes, but without the law and means of enforcement possessed by the civil state.

Kant's idea of a federation of states was influential in the discussions which surrounded the constitution of the League of Nations and later the United Nations. However, the difficulties faced by these institutions in constituting a juridically effective forum of states were anticipated by Kant. On his analysis it could be argued that the constitution of a federation of states is an asymptotic idea, one which cannot be realized in space and time and which will give rise to antinomies and contradictions. The most fundamental would be that of constituting an international legal order which would govern the behaviour of states without a coercive apparatus of enforcement: a legal order without such enforcement has little power over constituent states; but one with such power would threaten to become an imperial state, one with the potential to dissolve the independent existence of its constituents. Kant's characteristic solution is to argue in terms of analogy and the as-if: he says it is in the interest of member states to act *as if* they were participating in a legal order which did possess the means of enforcing its judgements.

196

feeling [*Gefühl*] *see also* AFFECT, COMMON SENSE, FACULTY, GEMÜT, INCLINATION, LIFE, PLEASURE, RESPECT, SENSIBILITY

Feeling is one of Kant's most ambiguous and therefore fascinating concepts. Much of his writing may be read as the attempt properly to situate 'feeling' with respect to theoretical and practical philosophy, with the concept shifting continuously between the margins and the centre of his philosophy. This movement is exemplified by the place of feeling with respect to the faculties of cognition and desire: Kant excludes feeling from the critical practical philosophy only for it to return in the shape of the feeling of respect for the law (e.g., CPrR p. 76, p. 79); it is similarly excluded from consideration in CPR as lying 'outside our whole faculty of knowledge' (A 802/B 830) only to return in the Introduction to CJ as a necessary condition 'of the most ordinary experience' (§VI). But not only does it appear unsettlingly in the contexts of theoretical and practical philosophy, it even features as the object of a special branch of philosophy concerned with feelings of pleasure and pain and their correlates beauty and the sublime (OBS, A, Book Two), which serves as a bridge between the two branches of philosophy and ultimately, in CJ, as their shared terrain.

Although it is described along with space and time in PE as a partially analyzable concept, Kant does consistently attribute certain characteristics to feeling. First of all, it expresses the subjective condition of a finite, sensible being 'constantly compelled to pass beyond the present state' (A p. 133) and whose experience is of an overwhelmingly sensuous character (CPrR p. 67, p. 79). This feature not only relates feeling to the themes of embodiment and life, but also accounts for its polar structure as the feeling of pleasure and pain (*Lust und Unlust*). In NM (p. 181, p. 220) and A (§60) pleasure and pain are described as 'counterparts' which determine each other; and since for Kant the life of a finite being consists in activity, the feeling of pleasure and pain serves both as an expression of and as an incentive to further activity. Such activity consists in mutually defined surges and checks on the 'vital power' which generate 'erratic sequences of pleasant feelings (constantly interspersed with pain)' (A §60). The oscillation between pleasure and pain provokes all the 'various feelings of enjoyment or displeasure' and rests 'not so much upon the nature of the external things that arouse them as upon each person's own disposition to be moved by these to pleasure and pain' (OBS p. 207, p. 45). This wavering informs the plethora of feelings 'which we experience in the highly complex circumstances of life' (NM p. 182, p. 220) including feelings such as sympathy/hostility, friendship/enmity, love/hatred, beauty/sublime.

In the pre-critical philosophy Kant established the pattern of examining the feelings of pleasure and pain both in their own terms and with respect to the opposition of theoretical and practical philosophy. In OBS he offers

197

an empirically oriented analysis of feeling through reflections on examples organized in terms of the beautiful and the sublime. The anthropological slant of this text is systematically extended in his lectures on Anthropology, and in particular in Book Two 'On the Feeling of Pleasure and Displeasure' which forms the transition from Book One on the 'cognitive faculty' to Book Three on the 'faculty of desire'. Alongside this characterization of feeling in terms of a transition between theoretical and practical philosophy Kant also tries to distinguish it from both. In the final pages of PE he distinguishes between the faculty of representing the true or cognition and that of representing the good or feeling, describing the latter as necessarily relative to 'a being endowed with sensibility' (p. 299, p. 273). This feeling of the good issues neither from cognition nor from a supposed moral sense, although Kant admits that, regarding first principles, in practical philosophy the precedence of feeling or cognition has yet to be determined (p. 300, p. 274).

A similar structure persists in the critical practical philosophy of GMM and CPrR, where Kant identifies feeling and rational principles as 'heteronomous principles of morality' (GMM p. 442, p. 46; CPrR p. 40, p. 41). There, however, sensuous feeling – 'the condition of all our inclinations' – is also a condition for the feeling of respect occasioned by the reverence for the law of 'pure practical reason'; it is this which removes 'in the judgement of reason, the counterweight to the moral law which bears on a will affected by the sensibility' (CPrR p. 76, p. 78). Although respect is a 'singular feeling' which cannot be compared with other feelings, it remains nevertheless a feeling. Yet it has two peculiarities which render it incomparable: the first is that its object, as distinct from the feeling of pleasure and pain, is always a person, never a thing (p. 77, p. 79); the second is that it does not arise from the oscillation of pleasure and pain which characterizes the life of a finite being, and gives neither pleasure nor pain (p. 78, p. 80). Yet in spite of the latter distinction, the feeling of respect does have distinct effects; it has a negative effect when it serves as a 'check' on the inclinations experienced as 'humiliation' and a positive one when it serves as an incentive for obedience to the law (p. 80, p. 82).

In CPrR Kant redefined feeling in order to establish a place for respect as a special kind of feeling. In CJ, his treatise on feeling and judgement, he pursues an altogether more audacious strategy. At first glance Kant seems to be following the approach of OBS and A in developing a special philosophy of the aesthetic feelings of the beautiful and sublime, one which inhabits the interstices between the theoretical and practical domains. However, this special philosophy soon assumes the role not only of facilitating a transition from one realm to the other, but also of providing the common ground between them. The feeling of pleasure and pain is held to offer a key to the 'riddle of judgement' (CJ Preface) which perplexed theoretical and practical philosophy. In CJ the alignment of feeling and judgement has several fascinating consequences: it makes feeling both subjective (in the free-play of the cognitive faculties) and objective (as a necessary and universal judgement); it also dissolves the distinction crucial to CPrR between the objects of the feeling of pleasure and displeasure and the feeling of respect, for it refers to both objects and persons; finally, feeling is no longer 'internal' and subjective but as a form of common sense becomes 'social' and intersubjective (for a short and dense statement of these points see, *inter alia*, CJ §12). These augmented properties of feeling are further extended to underlie both theoretical and practical philosophy: feeling provides the basis for the former in the intimation of an accord between the finality of nature and our understanding (Introduction §VI) and the latter as the *summum bonum* of a flourishing life (e.g., §87). In the CJ the domains of theoretical and practical judgement are shown to follow from a prior arrangement of feeling, nature, intersubjectivity and judgement.

The direction of the argument in CJ has given it a peculiar status in Kant's *oeuvre*, making it for some the crowning phase of, and for others an indiscreet coda to, the critical philosophy. At stake in these contrary judgements is not just a difference of opinion concerning the proper place of feeling in Kant's philosophy, but the far broader problem of the relationship of philosophical speculation to areas of human life and activity which do not obey limited or formal notions of rationality. The issue of feeling raises in acute form the question of the nature of philosophy and its relationship to 'non-philosophical' areas of experience. The working through of this issue is not confined to the reception of Kant's philosophy, but is clearly present throughout Kant's own texts.

finality [*Zweckmässigkeit*] *see also* CAUSALITY, END, NATURE, REFLECTIVE JUDGEMENT, TELEOLOGY
Finality is an extremely rich concept which Kant developed in CJ. In CPR the 'finality of nature' is referred to on a small number of occasions with the warning that it must 'be explained from natural grounds and according to natural laws' (A 773/B 801). In CJ, however, finality plays a central role in the accounts of both aesthetic and teleological judgement, as well as having been given retrospective significance with respect to the determinant judgements analysed in CPR.

In CJ Kant gives two definitions of finality, both of which relate it to the notion of an end. In the first definition an 'end' is 'the concept of an object, so far as it contains at the same time the ground of the actuality of this object' (CJ §IV), while in the second it is 'the object of a concept so far as this concept is regarded as the cause of the object' (§10). Both definitions of 'end' yield *formal finality* or, in the first case, the 'agreement of a thing with that constitution of things which is only possible according to ends' (§IV) and in the second 'the causality of a concept in respect of its object' (§10). The first describes subjective finality, the second objective finality. It is necessary to assume some form of finality in order for any judgement to take place; this is because finality describes an attunement between human judgement and the world, without which, in Kant's words, the 'understanding could not feel itself at home in nature' (§VII).

Kant's account of the aesthetic judgement of taste rests on the distinction between subjective and objective finality. Objective finality is causal: it realizes an end. Subjective finality is merely the power of judgement discerning the possibility of an end. Kant first criticizes views which ground beauty in external objective finality, in the utility or agreeableness of the object, and then goes on to criticize Baumgarten's account of aesthetic judgement in terms of internal objective finality for basing its estimate of an object's beauty upon its perfection, or the extent to which it realizes its end (§15). Kant, however, grounds aesthetic judgement in subjective finality, or 'finality without an end' (*Zweckmässigkeit ohne Zweck*), or the agreement of the form with the subjective harmony of the imagination and understanding. Furthermore, the consciousness of such finality is defined by Kant as 'pleasure itself' generated by the agreement of the imagination and understanding.

In the second part of CJ – 'Critique of Teleological Judgement' – Kant further develops the distinction between the forms of finality, but adds a further specification in his distinction between the 'idealism' and the 'realism' of the finality of nature: the former regards finality as accidental and without an author, while the latter sees it as inherent to matter (hylozoism) or derived from an original source (theism) (§72). He criticizes both for treating finality as a constitutive principle, and suggests its use be restricted to serving as a regulative principle of reflective judgement.

finitude *see also* FEELING, IMMORTALITY, IMPERATIVE, INTUITION, NEED, REASON, RECEPTIVITY, SENSIBILITY, SYNTHESIS, TIME, UNDERSTANDING
In the closing pages of CPrR Kant evokes the 'awe and admiration' evoked by 'the starry heavens above me and the moral law within me' (p. 162, p. 166). The reflection on the two objects creates a movement between the feelings of finitude and insignificance and those of immortality and infinite worth. The sense of the annihilation of 'my importance as an animal creature, which must give back to the planet (a mere speck in the universe) the matter from which it came, the matter which is for a little time

200

provided with vital force' co-exists with the revelation through the moral law 'of a life independent of all animality and even of the whole world of sense' (p. 162, p. 166). This movement informs the entire critical philosophy, and is manifest in the limitation of knowledge to the bounds of a finite intuition and understanding accompanied by the elevation through the moral law beyond those limits. Human finite intuition is distinguished from divine or 'intellectual' intuition by the temporal character of the synthesis which constitutes experience and knowledge. The various syntheses which unify concept and intuition are oriented with respect to past and future experience, and remain essentially incomplete. With respect to practical philosophy, the inclination towards discrete ends arise from human need, which for Kant follows from the finitude of the human condition. It is the tension between a 'finite practical reason' and the moral law which renders necessary the moral imperative and the 'endless task' of pursuing the model of a holy will (CPrR, p. 32, p. 32).

In CPR Kant insists upon the finitude of human experience, limiting its scope to appearances or the perceptions of a finite intuition. The only exception is moral experience which for Kant includes faith. Yet many critics, above all Nietzsche and later Heidegger, have questioned Kant's admission of non-finite dimensions of moral experience. There is a definite fault line in his philosophy between the rigorous accounts of experience in terms of human finitude that broadly informs the first and third critiques (i.e., CPR, CJ), accounts which may be described as Epicurean, and the more Platonic emphasis on the opposition between finite and infinite worlds presented in CPrR. Whether it is possible to maintain the former emphasis while rejecting the latter is an open question. A satisfactory answer to it would largely hinge on whether it was possible to conceive of moral experience in the absence of infinity (which Kant could not), and whether the crucial role played by freedom and spontaneity in all branches of the critical philosophy could be sustained within a rigorously finite framework.

force [*vis, Kraft*] *see also* ACTUALITY, BODY, MATTER, MOTION, POWER, REPULSION This concept arises from philosophical and scientific reflection upon the causes of the motion of material bodies. The currently prevailing definition is the natural scientific one, which regards force as an action that alters the state of rest or uniform motion of a body. In the seventeenth and eighteenth centuries, the concept of force was ill-defined scientifically and philosophically (insofar as the two approaches were separable), leading to considerable confusion in which Kant fully participated. One of the fundamental confusions arose from the distinction between inertial and active force. The former, in Descartes' terms, was the force by which a body remained at rest, the latter the force by which a body commenced and remained in motion (see Descartes, 1981, p. 79). By conceiving of inertial force as 'innate' and active force as externally caused, some philosophers, including Leibniz and Kant, went on to regard force in traditional, Aristotelian terms as a principle or cause of motion. This led to further confusion around the distinction between what became known as the two 'external forces' – body and surface forces. Body forces such as gravity act throughout material bodies, while surface forces are applied by one solid body to another. The illegitimate extension of the model of surface forces to the account of force as a whole underlies Kant's central distinction between attractive and repulsive force.

The philosophical reflection upon the concept of force remained a constant throughout Kant's career. His first work LF (1747) defines 'essential force' not as *vis motrix* but as *vis activa* – as active rather than motive force. Kant's conception of essential force, it is clear from §3, combines inertial and active force. The 'essential force' in question cannot be known mathematically (according to the 'Cartesian measure') since such knowledge is restricted to external appearances of motion. Its full appreciation requires metaphysical knowledge, which is not confined to external motion but also extends to the internal *vis activa* which is a property of both material and intelligible substance. The latter move permits Kant in §6 to extend the range of the concept of force from physics to psychology, using it to 'solve' the Cartesian difficulty of the relationship between body and soul.

Although there are many instances of this metaphysics of force in Kant's pre-critical writings, there is also a clear realization of its dangers. In DS Kant describes those fundamental forces not derived from experience as 'wholly arbitrary' and warns against inventing 'fundamental forces' in place of connecting 'the forces, which one already knows through experience, in a manner which is appropriate to the phenomena' (p. 371, p. 357). This view is sharpened in ID where Kant rails against the kind of metaphysics of force exemplified by his own LF: 'so many vain fabrications of I know not what *forces* are invented at pleasure . . . they burst forth in a horde from any architectonic mind, or if you prefer, any mind which inclines to chimaeras' (§28). This development corresponded to Kant's redefinition of metaphysics as 'a science of the *limits of human reason*' (DS p. 368, p. 354), and intimates his later critical account of force.

Yet in spite of this development, Kant's account of force does not entirely escape its initial limitations. Already in PM (1756), in the context of discussions of inertial force, Kant introduces a distinction between attractive and repulsive force (p. 484, p. 62). The distinction generalizes the action of surface force to internal 'active force' and was extended by Kant from the realm of physics to moral and political phenomena. The view of the mutual determination of attractive and repulsive forces offered a useful analogy by which to explain a wide variety of phenomena, ranging from the impenetrability of matter to the 'asocial sociability' of Kant's practical philosophy.

In CPR force, along with action, is described as a derived concept of causality, one which the understanding thinks in regard to body (A 20/B 35), particularly with respect to 'successive appearances, as motions, which indicate [the presence of] such forces' (A 207/B 252). The forces themselves, however, are for us 'inscrutable' and unavailable to observation (A 614/B 642). Kant maintains this position in MF, except that here he acknowledges the existence of the two 'fundamental forces' of attraction and repulsion. The fundamental forces lie at the root of the concept of matter, but cannot themselves be comprehended or constructed for presentation in a possible intuition. This means that they cannot be given a mathematical analysis (MF p. 524, p. 78). Later however, in the OP, Kant attempts to articulate the empirical forces which make up physics into a rational and systematic unity. As the 'Transition from the Metaphysical to the Physical Principles of Nature' this derives an a priori system of possible forces from the table of categories and the general properties of matter; the unification of force and matter is accomplished by the concept of ether.

Kant's reliance on ether in his final account of philosophical physics indicates the limitations of his concept of force. Yet the basic opposition of the fundamental forces of attraction and repulsion seems to have appealed to Kant for philosophical rather than scientific reasons, and was used for a similar reason in Schelling's (1813) and Schopenhauer's (1813) philosophies of nature. Hegel critically analyzed the oppositional structure of the concept of force (Hegel, 1812, pp. 518–23), but after him the philosophical and the natural scientific analyses of force diverged substantially.

form *see also* ARCHETYPE, BEAUTY, CATEGORIES, CONCEPTS OF REFLECTION, FORMALISM, FORMS OF INTUITION, IDEAS, MATTER, PURE
The analysis of 'the forms of thought' is described in 1796a as 'the ever proceeding labour and careful work' (p. 404, p. 70) of metaphysical philosophy. Kant justifies this claim by a historical account of the problem of form in Plato and Aristotle, and their influence upon the 'recently elevated tone in philosophy'. Kant criticizes Plato for seeking the origins of the forms in the 'divine understanding' or 'primal ground of all things' instead of in our own understanding. This leads in Kant's view to a doubling of the world into arche- and ectypal aspects which permits philosophical and religious enthusiasts to claim immediate intuitive knowledge of the 'true world' without going through the bother of philosophizing. Aristotle

too is indicted for the same offence in trying to extend the forms of knowledge from the physical to the metaphysical world. But it is Plato, above all, who for Kant is to blame for philosophical enthusiasm, even though Kant does not hold him personally responsible (p. 391, p. 54). The 'recently elevated tone' that Kant decries either mystically intuits form or rejects it as 'mere pedantry' or 'form-manufacturing' (p. 404, p. 70). Against both of these tendencies Kant proposes the critical treatment of form as a pure a priori feature of experience.

In ET Kant approvingly cites the scholastic formula *forma dat esse rei* ('form gives the essence of things') and gives it a critical inflection. If the things in question are 'objects of sense' then the forms of things are the 'forms of intuition' identified in CPR as space and time. Mathematics, he adds, is nothing but the doctrine of the forms of pure intuition. Metaphysics or 'pure philosophy', on the contrary, is based upon the 'forms of thought' under which every object or 'matter of knowledge' may be subsumed. These forms of the understanding are the conditions of the possibility of synthetic knowledge. In CPR, Kant also adds that the 'ideas of reason' are forms of reason, but in ET he insists (not inconsistently) on restricting the formal employment of reason to practical laws, in which it is not the material aspect of an action – its desired end – but only its form which is morally significant. This consists in the suitability of a maxim for being made into a universal law. To Kant's summary of the importance of form in theoretical and practical philosophy in ET may be added the role it plays in his aesthetic philosophy. In CJ the quality of a judgement of taste is abstracted from the matter of the art object, and consists only in its 'form of finality' (§17).

While form is a central concept in the critical philosophy, it is not free of ambiguity. This stems largely from Kant's maintaining a Platonic distinction between form and matter while also trying to overcome it: he at one moment shows form and matter to be inseparable while at the next denies that they are in any way implicated in each other. Thus on one occasion in CJ he can claim that the quality of a judgement of taste consists in its pure finality of form, while at another showing that this form can only be revealed by means of contrasting it with 'charm' or the matter of a judgement of taste (§14). More significantly, in the discussion of the concepts of reflection in CPR, matter and form are taken together to 'underlie all other reflection', with matter serving as 'the determinable in general [and form as] its determination' (A 266/B 322). Both are mutually implicated, since form as determination is meaningless without a matter to be determined. Furthermore, the opposition of form and matter is played out analogously in other oppositions scattered throughout Kant's texts, such as those between form as purity, matter as impurity; form as

204

universality, matter as particularity; form as identity, matter as difference; and even form as subject and matter as object.

If form means very little outside of its opposition to matter, then problems arise when the attempt is made to separate formal and material elements. These problems have been worked through in various guises by Kant and his subsequent followers and critics. They may rather crudely be reduced to two related classes of problem: the first concerns the subsumption of matter by form, the second the sources or origins of form. If form stood in no relation whatsoever to matter, if there were no relation between determining and determinable, then there would be no knowledge or moral action: for knowledge is knowledge of determinable appearances, and moral actions are those of a determinate finite being. In the face of this Kant develops some extremely subtle analogues for Platonic participation, such as schematism and the principles in CPR and the typic in CPrR. The analysis of pleasure in CJ also marks the attempt to relate formal and material aspects of aesthetic pleasure, although here, on occasions, it does seem as if Kant renounces the residual Platonic opposition of matter and form in favour of a broader notion of 'proportionality'.

The main difficulty that Kant engages with in these parts of his argument is one of keeping matter in its place, allowing it to relate to form without becoming too insubordinate. This problem is compounded in Kant's analysis of the accounts of the sources of form. Kant does not admit the empiricist argument that form may be derived by abstraction from the experience of matter; he maintains that form precedes 'the things themselves' (A 267/B 323) and does so by restricting the scope of the critical philosophy to the analysis of appearances in space and time. But he also wishes to avoid the contrary position, namely that form is of purely rational origin; this would expose him to the risk of regarding form in Leibnizian or Wolffian terms as an intuition of rational perfection, or in Malebranchian terms as a gift of God. He is also wary of any psychological genealogies of form, whether as an innate idea or as the issue of feeling. His own, notoriously complex position(s), derive form from the transcendental unity of apperception, as in CPR, or from the negotiation between subject and the world in CJ and later writings.

The problems surrounding the notion of form gave and continue to give rise to a great deal of critical commentary. As one of the fundamental problems of philosophy it will probably remain perennial, and not only within the confines of Kant criticism. What is undeniable is that Kant, in spite of remaining within a Platonic opposition, substantially redefined the terms of the problem, seeing it as one which spanned theoretical, practical and aesthetic philosophy and which has as its starting point not the supersensible realm, but the experience of finite human subjects.

formal logic *see* LOGIC

formalism A blanket criticism often directed against the critical philosophy, formalism has taken various guises. Versions range from those of Hamann and Hegel to those of Nietzsche and Husserl, with more recent contributions from phenomenology and critical theory. It basically maintains that Kant's preoccupation with the formal aspects of experience and action led him to suppress their material and affective sides. The alleged preoccupation with form is held by many to lead to a distorted and partial account of experience and action which cannot fully justify its own formal premises and represses other aspects of experience. The table of categories, the moral law and the aesthetic 'form of finality' are all cited as evidence of a formalistic orientation.

Many philosophers have attempted to trace the origins of Kant's alleged formalism. His earliest critic Hamann saw its source to lie in the purification of language (see Hamann, 1967); for Hegel it arose from an abstract, ahistorical account of experience (see Hegel, 1807); while for Nietzsche, the origins of the 'will to form' were traced to the need for ascetic philosophers to rule over the body and its affects (see Nietzsche, 1886). Critical theorists such as Adorno saw in Kant's formalism an example of the dialectic of enlightenment which reduced experience to a formal calculus the better to control it (see Adorno and Horkheimer, 1944). This genealogical critique is often, but not necessarily, accompanied by an attempt to develop a non-formalistic philosophy such as Max Scheler's non-formalist (i.e., anti-Kantian) ethics based on sympathy and other affects (Scheler, 1973), and Georges Bataille's anti-formal, anti-idealist materialism (Bataille, 1985).

forms of intuition *see also* AESTHETIC, FORM, INTUITION, SENSATION, SENSIBILITY, SPACE, TIME

In the first part of CPR on 'Transcendental Aesthetic', intuition is defined as the immediate relation of a mode of knowledge to its objects (A 19/B 33). The effect of the intuition of objects on the faculty of representation is sensation, which has material and formal aspects. The matter of intuition is 'the appearance which corresponds to sensation' and the form 'that which so determines the manifold of appearance that it allows of being ordered in certain relations' (A 20/B 34). Following a process of abstraction which first isolates sensibility from the understanding and then further removes everything belonging to sensation, Kant derives the 'two pure forms of sensible intuition, serving as principles of *a priori* knowledge' (A 22/B 36) which he identifies as space and time.

foundation *see* GROUND

freedom [*libertas, Freiheit*] *see also* ANTINOMY, AUTONOMY, CAUSALITY, LAW, REASON, SPONTANEITY, SYNTHESIS, WILL

Freedom is a pivotal concept in Kant's philosophy, informing both its theoretical and practical sections. It has two significant and related qualities, which were first described in the early modern conception of freedom developed by Machiavelli: freedom involves both independence from any form of dependency – freedom *from* – and the power for a subject to legislate for itself – freedom *to*. Achieving the correct balance of these two aspects of freedom is the implicit aim of the critical philosophy, as is evident in both the theoretical philosophy of CPR and the practical philosophy of CPrR, GMM and MM. In the former freedom features as spontaneity as opposed to receptivity, in the latter as autonomy as opposed to heteronomy.

In CPR Kant identifies spontaneity as the theoretical analogue of freedom; in the discussion of the third antinomy and the problem of natural and free causality he refers to the cosmological and practical senses of freedom. By the former he understands 'the power of beginning a state *spontaneously*' and describes it as reason creating 'for itself the idea of a spontaneity which can begin to act of itself, without requiring to be determined to action by an antecedent cause in accordance with the law of causality' (CPR A 533/B 561). This spontaneity is thus opposed to natural causes, and has the grounds for its determination within itself. In the analytic of CPR this spontaneity is described as one of the sources of knowledge along with receptivity. Kant consistently opposes the spontaneity of the imagination and understanding to the receptivity of the sensibility; spontaneity is the '*Gemüt*'s power of producing representations from itself' (A 51/B 75), but it is a power incapable of producing knowledge without the contribution of receptivity. For the spontaneous act of synthesis to take place there has to be something present in sensibility to be synthesized. Thus on the one hand freedom as spontaneity is absolute in giving itself laws of synthesis, but on the other it is intrinsically qualified by receptivity.

The problem of the pure spontaneity of the understanding being dependent upon receptivity in order to become effective is described by Kant in connection with practical freedom as 'the real source of the difficulty by which the question of the possibility of freedom has always been beset' (A 533/B 561). In the case of practical freedom it is the motivating grounds of the will which have to be autonomous. Instead of the heteronomous principles of the will, whether of rational provenance (perfection) or empirical provenance (pleasure, happiness), Kant insists on an intelligible freedom based upon the autonomy of the will. Yet this freedom finds extreme difficulty both in freeing itself from heteronomy, and once it has thus freed itself, in restraining its inherent anarchic and perhaps even self-destructive impulse, for 'it is in the power of freedom to pass beyond any and every specified limit' (A 317/B 374). Accordingly, in GMM freedom is defined negatively and positively. In the first case, 'The will is a kind of causality belonging to living beings insofar as they are rational; freedom would be the property of this causality that makes it effective independent of any determination by alien causes' (GMM p. 446, p. 49) or freedom from. In the second case, freedom consists in self-legislation, 'What else, then, can freedom of the will be but autonomy, i.e. the property that the will has of being a law unto itself?' (p. 447, p. 49).

The imperatives appropriate for such a conception of freedom can be neither hypothetical nor material; they are not rules of skill for attaining some determinate, material end, but are categorical and formal: they 'are not concerned with the matter of the action and its intended result, but rather with the form of the action and the principle from which it follows' (GMM p. 416, p. 26). Yet these actions have to be effective in a world of space and time beset by competing and incompatible material ends. If the imperative had no application in this world then it would be empty, like the pure spontaneity of the understanding. The outcome was a bifocal moral philosophy: at its most ambitious but ill-focused extreme, autonomy is the core of a metaphysically grounded account of freedom; but at the other extreme it is but the more modest basis of a canonical principle for testing maxims of action.

Kant's immediate successors pursued the ambitious programme of a metaphysically grounded account of freedom. Both Fichte (1794) and Schelling (1800) transformed spontaneity and autonomy into subjective and objective absolutes, a practice which Hegel was the first to criticize for positing absolutist and insatiable demands which remained empty and incapable of realization except through destructive terror, one which indeed passes 'beyond any and every specified limit'. While accepting that modern philosophy was one of freedom, he sought to qualify the absolute demands of freedom with respect to the categories and to ethical life. Hegel's discovery of a suppression of receptivity and heteronomy at the heart of freedom was developed by Nietzsche who famously claimed that 'the categorical imperative smells of cruelty' (Nietzsche, 1887, p. 65). Twentieth-century philosophers from Heidegger (1947) to Adorno and Horkheimer (1944) have defended the view of freedom as intrinsically qualified by its other against neo-Fichtean accounts such as that of Sartre. They claim that absolutist accounts of freedom based on absolutely autonomous and spontaneous subjects insensitive to the ways in which their freedom is qualified lead to terror and subjugation in the very name of freedom.

friendship [*philia, amica, Freundschaft*] *see also* AFFECT, LOVE, REPULSION, SOCIABILITY

Friendship was central to Greek and Roman theoretical and practical philosophy, where its meanings ranged from Empedocles' metaphysical contrast of friendship and strife to Aristotle's praise of friendship in the *Nicomachean Ethics*, and to the Roman Stoic conception of friendship for the human race. In Christian philosophy it is secondary to considerations of love, but with Kant assumes again an important place in ethics.

Kant regards friendship as an ideal defined as the 'union of two persons through equal mutual love and respect' (MM p. 469, p. 261). Friendship consists in achieving a balance between the attraction of love and the repulsion of respect. For this reason Kant regards it as extremely difficult both to attain and sustain. He distinguishes between moral and aesthetic/pragmatic friendship: the former emphasizes the element of respect and is defined as 'the complete confidence of two persons in revealing their secret judgements and feelings to each other, as far as such disclosures are consistent with mutual respect' (p. 471, p. 263), while the latter emphasizes love, and is based on feelings of benevolence.

function [*Funktion*] *see also* APPERCEPTION, COMBINATION, JUDGEMENT, REPRESEN-TATION, SYNTHESIS, TABLE OF JUDGEMENTS, UNITY

In CPR Kant defines function as 'the unity of the act of bringing together various representations under one common representation'. Such an act of the understanding is judgement, the 'mediate knowledge of an object' or 'the representation of a representation' (A 68/B 93). Kant claims that it is possible to discover all the functions of the understanding through the statement of the functions of unity in judgment. He organizes these under the four headings of the quantity, quality, relation and modality of judgements and derives from them the table of the categories. He traces the source of the unity of a function, also described as its ability to combine synthetically, to the transcendental unity of apperception or 'the original and necessary consciousness of the identity of the self' (CPR A 108). In the discussion of 'Phenomena and Noumena' Kant further maintains that such functions of unity are meaningless without a relation to an object, since they supply only the formal conditions of cognition which have to be supplemented by schemas and principles.

future *see* FINITUDE, HISTORY, HOPE, IMAGINATION, MEMORY, TIME

G

gap/interval *see* CONTINUITY

Gemüt [*animus*] *see also* AFFECT, BODY, FEELING, IDENTITY, LIFE, PLEASURE, REFLECTION, SOUL, SUBJECT

Gemüt is a key term in Kant's philosophy and is variously translated as 'mind', 'mental state' and 'soul', even though these translations fail to do justice to the term's significance. It does not mean 'mind' or 'soul' in the Cartesian sense of a thinking substance, but denotes instead a corporeal awareness of sensation and self-affection. Indeed, at one point in CPR he explicitly distinguishes *Gemüt* and *Seele* (A 22/B 37), a distinction expounded in *Zu Sömmering über das Organ der Seele* (*To Sömmering, Concerning the Organ of the Soul*, 1796) in terms of the 'capacity to effect the unity of empirical apperception (animus) but not its substance (anima)' (1796c, p. 256). *Gemüt* does not designate a substance (whether material or ideal) but is the position or place of the *Gemütskräfte* (the *Gemüt*'s powers) of sensibility, imagination, understanding and reason.

Kant's use of *Gemüt* remains close to the meaning the term possessed in medieval philosophy and mysticism, where it referred to the 'stable disposition of the soul which conditions the exercise of all its faculties' (Gilson, 1955, pp. 444, 758). This contrasts with Leibniz's restriction of the term to mean 'feeling' as opposed to understanding (Leibniz, 1976, p. 428). For Kant 'the *Gemüt* is all life (the life-principle itself), and its hindrance or furtherance has to be sought outside it, and yet in the man himself, consequently in connexion with his body' (CJ §29). With this view of the *Gemüt* Kant sought to bypass many of the problems of mind–body relations bequeathed by Cartesian dualism, a strategy explicitly stated again in *Zu Sömmering über das Organ der Seele*, but insufficiently appreciated by many of his later critics. This view of *Gemüt* also provides a linkage across the three theoretical, practical and aesthetic/teleological sections of the critical philosophy, once again explicitly stated by Kant, this time in a variant of A §7 where it is described as the 'essence [*Inbegriff*]' of all representations which in the same place occupy a sphere which includes the three basic

210

faculties of knowledge, the feeling of pleasure and displeasure, and the faculty of desire . . .'.

In CPR Kant locates the origin of knowledge in 'two basic sources of the *Gemüt*: the first source is that of 'receiving representations (the receptivity of impressions)', the second is that of 'knowing an object through these representations (spontaneity of concepts)' (A 50/B 74). The *Gemüt* may accordingly be disposed either passively or actively, in the former mode receiving representations, in the latter creating concepts. The mutual workings of passive and active aspects of *Gemüt* may be seen most clearly in Kant's discussion of intuition. In the opening paragraph of CPR it is said that objects can only be given to us 'insofar as the *Gemüt* is affected in a particular way' (A 19/B 33). The *Gemüt* here is in its receptive, sensible mode of 'external sense' through which we represent objects as outside of us and in space. Apart from being passively affected by means of external sense, the *Gemüt* however can also be actively affected by means of the inner sense. In this case the '*Gemüt* intuits itself or its inner condition' giving rise to the 'determinate form' of time (A 23/B 37).

The passive affection of the *Gemüt* by external objects and its active self affection is also crucial to the argument of CJ, where this property is described as the 'life principle' itself, and the source not only of the faculties of knowledge and volition, but also of pleasure and displeasure. In CJ §1 Kant distinguishes between perceiving a 'regular and appropriate building' and being conscious of this representation with a feeling of delight. Here the pleasure concerned emerges from both the receptive and spontaneous work of the *Gemüt*. The perception of the building is received and then 'tied wholly to the subject, indeed to its feeling of life'. The delight arises from the *Gemüt* becoming conscious, through this representation, of its condition, or 'whole capacity for representation'; in other words, it makes itself an object of reflection, and thus finds delight in its own powers. Kant describes this reflection in terms of a harmony between the *Gemütskräfte* of the understanding and imagination, one which he says occasions delight by 'quickening' or by the 'relieved play of the mutually harmonising enlivened powers [*Gemütskräfte*] (the imagination and understanding)' (CJ §10).

Although Kant's discussion of *Gemüt* is central to his understanding of mental topography, and clearly significant for his theories of knowledge, action and aesthetic, it has never been the object of sustained scholarly scrutiny. The significance of the concept was still appreciated by Mellin in his 1797 *Encyclopädisches Wörterbuch der kritischen Philosophie*, but thereafter disappeared from view. It has recently reappeared, however, in the work of Heidegger and Derrida in the context of reflections on the notions of spirit and soul. It features in *Being and Time* (Heidegger, 1927) as that which

211

has not been correctly understood in Cartesian subjective metaphysics; it is also scrutinized and given an historical genealogy as the topos of spirit by Derrida in *Of Spirit* (see Derrida, 1987, pp. 78, 127). But these fresh insights have yet to be systematically employed in the interpretation of Kant's use of the term.

genus [*genos, genus, Gattung*] *see also* CONTINUITY, DEFINITION, DETERMINATION, ESSENCE, HOMOGENEITY

A genus is a 'type' or 'kind' and is usually used in conjunction with the term species. Originally developed by the Greeks, the notion of genus had both ontological and logical significance. In Plato genus is often used synonymously with 'idea', and in *Sophist* the division of ideas according to genus is said to define 'dialectic' (Plato, 1961, Sophist 253b). In Aristotle, the ontological significance of genus is downplayed in favour of its logical properties of predication. Here genus is specified, or determined, into species by means of a specific difference, which internally articulates the genus. Within this predicational framework Aristotle presented the categories as those ultimate genera of being which could not themselves be derived from higher genera. The ontological possibilities of this view were developed by neo-Platonic metaphysicians such as Plotinus into an hierarchical, emanationalist view of the participation of the ideas and individual beings. This had an enormous influence upon medieval philosophy, which in broad terms equivocated between logical and ontological senses of genus. Aquinas, for example, identified four senses of genus: the first, as the sense of the principle which generates species; the second, as *arche* or first generator or cause; the third, as the underlying 'subject' of accidents belonging to different species; and the fourth, as that which is stated first in a definition and of which specific differences are qualities (i.e., genus = animal; specific difference = rational/non-rational; definition = 'rational animal', namely 'man').

Kant's explicit discussion of genus and species is fairly limited, being confined to L and CPR; however, the schema is assumed implicitly throughout his philosophy. In L Kant describes concepts in terms of genus and species, and points to the 'subordination of concepts' or their property of being both genus and species: 'A *conceptus communis* is called genus in regard to concepts that are contained under it, but *species* in regard to the concepts under which it is contained' (L p. 191). This approach to the articulation of concepts in terms of genus and species is developed further in Kant's reflections on the systematic completion of knowledge in CPR. It is a condition of the employment of reason that different individuals may be gathered under species, and the species under genera. This gives rise to the three regulative principles of reason: homogeneity, specification, continuity. The first is the generic principle, the second the specific and the third the principle which permits the passage from the homogeneity of the genus to the variety of the species (CPR A 658/B 686).

Throughout his work, Kant's accounts of theoretical, practical and aesthetic judgement are couched in terms of subsumption under universal genera – whether categories, laws or rules – and discrimination of specific differences in instances, examples and particular cases. Many of the most interesting problems arising in his work may be traced back to difficulties generated by the schema, difficulties which have a long philosophical pedigree. The schema also informs his discussion of the classification of animals – and, indeed, his classification of human beings into discrete races.

general logic *see* LOGIC

genius [*Genie*] *see also* AESTHETIC, ART, BEAUTY, EXAMPLE, IMAGINATION, IMITATION, ORIGINALITY

Kant's main discussions of genius are to be found in A and in CJ §§46–50. The essential characteristic of genius for Kant is originality, and a genius is accordingly one 'who makes use of originality and produces out of himself what must ordinarily be learned under the guidance of others' (A §6). Originality itself has two aspects: the first is 'non imitative production' (A §30); the second is 'discovering what cannot be taught or learned' (A p. 318, p. 234). In the former, genius imitates neither nature nor other artifacts; in the latter, genius features as an ability which cannot be taught or otherwise passed on. Such originality, although rare, is potentially 'fanatical' since it is by definition disciplined by neither an object nor a canon. Consequently, Kant attempts to limit it by proposing that 'originality of imagination is called genius when it harmonises with concepts' (§30), a thought which he expanded and developed further in CJ.

In CJ Kant brings together the various aspects of genius proposed in A. Genius is still defined in terms of originality, but this is now described as 'a talent for producing that for which no definite rule can be given' (CJ §46). This talent is limited by the requirement that its products be exemplary, that 'though not themselves derived from imitation, they must serve that purpose for others' (ibid.). In addition, a genius cannot give an account of the rule informing its product, which is prescribed to art by nature. Kant goes on to distinguish between imitating and following works of genius: the former is 'slavish' while the latter involves a follower putting 'their own talent to the test', and allowing the product of genius to provoke 'original ideas' in them. Consequently fine art, or the product of genius, presents 'aesthetic ideas' which are representations of the imagination –

213

a 'second nature [created] out of the material supplied to it by actual nature' – which excite 'a whole host of kindred representations' (CJ §49). The aesthetic idea is produced by, and provokes, a harmony of the faculties of imagination and understanding characteristic of genius.

Through Goethe and the early Romantics, Kant's views on genius were extremely influential in the early nineteenth century. They have also undergone fresh scrutiny since the 1980s. This is due to an increased sensitivity to the political implications of CJ, and in particular the intimations of non-hierarchical forms of political judgement implied in the accounts of reflective judgement and genius. The notions of originality and exemplarity discussed in the context of genius have been developed in the direction of a non-subsumptive form of legislation and political judgement by such writers as Castoriadis (1987) and Lyotard (1991).

geography *see also* ANTHROPOLOGY FROM A PRAGMATIC POINT OF VIEW, HISTORY
In his *Announcement of the Organisation of his Lectures in the Winter Semester 1765–1766* Kant describes how, early in his career, he tried to provide students with 'knowledge of historical matters which could make good their lack of *experience*'. He did so by means of a course on physical geography, one which reflected his interest during the 1750s in such questions as the reasons for changes in the earth's rotation, the age of the earth and the causes of earthquakes. In 1765 he divided the subject matter of his lectures according to physical, moral and political geography, with the first concerned with the 'natural relationship which holds between all the countries and seas in the world', the second with 'man' and the third with the interaction of the former in the 'condition of the states and nations throughout the world' (p. 312, p. 299). In the subsequent development of his teaching, the second part of the course was separated off to form the lectures on anthropology. This was subsequently published in 1798 as *Anthropologie in pragmatischer Hinsicht* (*Anthropology from a Pragmatic Point of View*), with the lectures on physical geography following in 1802 as *Physische Geographie* edited by F.T. von Rink.

In the introduction to the lectures on physical geography, Kant describes his subject as complementing anthropology as part of the knowledge of the world. He assigns to anthropology whatever is revealed to the inner sense or 'soul of man', while physical geography deals with the objects of outer sense or 'knowledge of nature . . . or description of the earth'. Kant also distinguishes geography from history, this time in terms of the description of time and space: history is concerned with events which occur successively in time, geography with 'appearances under the aspect of space which occur simultaneously'. Physical geography, however, is the foundation of history, as well as of all other forms of geography which

Kant lists as: 'mathematical geography', 'moral geography', 'political geography', 'commercial geography' and 'theological geography'. In addition to this explicit treatment of geography in his lectures, it is interesting to note Kant's reliance on geographical terms and metaphors in his more strictly defined philosophical work.

geometry *see* MATHEMATICS

go-cart [*Gängelwagen*] *see* EXAMPLE

God *see also* ANALOGY, CHURCH, FAITH, POSTULATE, THEODICY, THEOLOGY
Kant's philosophical understanding of God remained constant throughout his authorship. It is clearly stated in the final sentence of OPA, where he concluded a critical review of proofs for the existence of God with the disclaimer: 'It is absolutely necessary that one should convince oneself that God exists; that his existence should be demonstrated, is not so necessary' (p. 163, p. 201). This sentiment is echoed in the hostage to fortune Kant offered in the second Preface of CPR, where he admitted that in matters of God, freedom and immortality he 'found it necessary to sublate *knowledge*, in order to make room for *faith*' (CPR B xxx). His writings on the subject of God are all informed by the tension between faith in God and demonstrative knowledge of his existence, and may be divided into five distinct groups.

In the first group, which includes the theological writings OPA, 'The Ideal of Pure Reason' in CPR and LPT, Kant undermines the onto-, cosmo- and physico-theological proofs of the existence of God proposed by philosophical theology. In these texts he opposes the pretensions to speculative knowledge of God possessed by such 'dream castle builders' of reason (DS p. 324, p. 329) as Christian Wolff, the codifier of philosophical theology. In the second group, which contains DS, WO and RL, he corrects the balance by opposing the pretensions to direct intuitive experience of God maintained by such fanatics of faith as Swedenborg, Hamann and Jacobi. While philosophers believed that their demonstrative proofs yielded them knowledge of God, the fanatics believed that their crude anthropomorphic analogies gave them a mystical experience of divinity. From the standpoint of his critique of philosophical theology, Kant restricted knowledge of God to analogy and its use as a regulative idea; this restriction along with his critique of the mystical experience of God combined to establish the parameters of the third group of writings which include CPR, RL and above all CPrR. These locate the proper place of God to be in practical experience, and explore the moral meaning of God as a 'postulate of pure practical reason' (CPrR p. 133, p. 137ff) necessary for ensuring reverence

215

for the law. A fourth group of writings, consisting mainly of RL, analyzed the institution of the church, while a fifth and somewhat ambiguous group of texts including CJ, IUH, PP and FPT, focus on the role of God in history, with particular reference to theodicy and providence.

Of the five groups of writings, the most influential have been the first and the third. The relationship between the critique of theology and the argument for practical faith has intrigued generations of interpreters. Additionally, a large amount of work has been done on the detail of the critique of the three philosophical/theological proofs for the existence of God. The recent upsurge of interest in Kant's philosophy of history has led to increased sensitivity around the issue of providence, and the relation of this view of God with the critique of theology and moral faith. However, a comprehensive account of the entirety of Kant's view of God, one which would encompass all five groups of texts, is still awaited.

good [*Gut*] *see also* AGREEABLE, DUTY, EVIL, FORMALISM, GOOD WILL, HIGHEST GOOD, PRACTICAL PHILOSOPHY

In CJ §4 Kant defines the good as 'that which by means of reason commends itself by its mere concept' and distinguishes between 'good for something' and 'good in itself'. He further distinguishes between the agreeable and the good in terms of the presence or otherwise of an end: the agreeable concerns the relation between an object and sense, the good the relation implied in 'a concept of an end . . . as an object of will'. On another occasion, in TP, Kant develops these thoughts into a rigorous distinction between absolute and relative good; that is, between 'something absolutely good in itself, as opposed to that which is evil in itself' and something 'relatively good, as opposed to something more or less good than itself' (TP p. 278, p. 67). He distinguishes between absolute good or 'obedience to a categorically binding law of the free will (i.e., of duty) without reference to any ulterior end', which is 'good in itself', from the relative good of the pursuit of happiness in which 'no law is absolutely binding but always relative to the end adopted' (TP p. 278, p. 67). Absolute good disregards any particular or substantive ends and is purely formal. This means that the determinant of the good 'is not the content of the will (i.e., a particular basic object) but the pure form of universal lawfulness embodied in its maxim' (TP p. 27a, p. 68). This position has led to the criticism of Kant's account of the good, and indeed of his practical philosophy as a whole, for being formalistic.

good will *see also* EVIL, GOOD, HIGHEST GOOD, PRACTICAL PHILOSOPHY

In GMM Kant describes the only unqualified good as being a 'good will', and in so doing effected a new beginning in moral philosophy. He argued that the traditional virtues of moral philosophy such as courage and resolution, moderation and self-control, along with talents such as wit and judgement, gifts of fortune such as power and wealth can all, in certain circumstances, be put to bad use. The good will, however, is an unqualified good, 'good only through willing' and not 'because of what it effects or accomplishes' (GMM p. 393, p. 7). It is for Kant the basis of the good use of all the traditional characteristics of virtue, and may be discerned through the concept of duty. By analysing duty Kant is able to show that 'the pre-eminent good which is called moral can consist in nothing but the representation of the law in itself, and such a representation can admittedly be found only in a rational being insofar as this representation, and not some expected effect, is the determining ground of the will' (GMM p. 401, p. 13). This means that the good will is determined by the universal form of law as such, rather than by any end envisaged by the law. This requires that action be willed in accordance with the categorical imperative, or that the maxim of the will 'should become a universal law' (GMM p. 402, p. 14).

grace *see* FAITH

ground [*arche, aiton, ratio, Grund*] *see also* CAUSALITY, CONTRADICTION, LOGIC, ONTOLOGY, PRINCIPLE, REASON, TRANSCENDENTAL
Ground is an extremely rich and ambiguous concept which Kant uses in several senses, including 'formal ground', 'natural ground', 'moral ground', 'metaphysical ground' and 'teleological ground' to list but a few. It is often synonymous with ratio or reason as well as with cause and, on occasions, with principle. This polysemy has generated severe problems with translating the term, which has consequently rendered Kant's usage even more opaque. However, it is possible to identify three broad senses in which the term is used: (a) as a premise in an argument or motivating ground for a judgement; (b) the cause of an effect; (c) the reason or intention for an action. Although each of these senses shares an underlying pattern of thought with the others, an ambiguity which Kant often exploited, he was also concerned to distinguish and establish boundaries between them.

Kant's motive for both exploiting and clarifying the ambiguity surrounding ground may be traced to his critical opposition to what was known as the 'Leibniz–Wolff philosophy'. Wolff in particular founded his entire philosophical system upon the ambiguities of the term ground, using it to unite the fields of logic, metaphysics, ethics and politics into a rationalistic system. Kant consistently opposed this project throughout his career, from ND (1755) to OD (1790), and the focus of his criticism was precisely the ambiguous notion of ground.

In ND Kant defines ground as that 'which determines a subject in respect of any of its predicates' or which 'establishes a connection and a conjunction between the subject and some predicate or other' (ND p. 392, p. 11). He stresses that ground 'always requires' a subject and a predicate which can be joined to the subject. The relation of subject and predicate is the pattern of thought which underlies the logical, ontological and practical senses of ground. Kant then proceeds to distinguish between 'antecedently' and 'consequentially' determining grounds, the first being the ontological 'ground *why*, or the ground of being or becoming' while the second is the logical and epistemological 'ground *that*, or the ground of knowing' (ibid.). This distinction is used expressly by Kant to criticize 'the celebrated Wolff' for eliding ontological and logical ground with the implication that this elision compromises his entire rationalist system.

It would not be too much of an exaggeration to regard Kant's subsequent philosophical work as the attempt systematically to think through the implications of rejecting the unity of logical and ontological ground (crudely, knowing and being) while not abandoning science to mysticism in the manner of Crusius (see Caygill, 1989, pp. 207–11). In CPR Kant approves the *method* of Wolff while criticizing his dogmatic claim that the distinction between the sensible and the intelligible was merely logical and not transcendental (see CPR B xxxvii and A 44/B 61). In place of the elision of the grounds of knowing and being, Kant separates them in order to explore the parameters of their proper relationship. One result of this inquiry was the distinction between real and logical grounds (echoing that between antecedently and consequentially determining grounds), with the former further divided according to 'formal-real ground' or the intuition of an object, and 'material-real ground' or the existence of an object (see the letter to Reinhold of 12 May 1789 outlining the nature of Eberhard's misunderstanding of the critical philosophy, PC, p. 139). A further result was the distinction between both real and logical grounds and the practical ground. The grounds of action cannot be subordinated to either of the latter since this would qualify freedom of action (a critique repeatedly urged against Wolff in the eighteenth century). Accordingly, practical grounds are 'grounds of reason [which] give the rule universally to actions, according to principles, without influence of the circumstances of either time or place' (P §53).

The theoretical aspects of the critical account of ground are spelt out by Kant in his riposte to Eberhard's Leibnizian objections to the programme of CPR. Kant identifies in Eberhard an elision of the 'logical (formal) principle of knowledge' that '*every proposition must have a ground*' subordinated to the 'principle of contradiction' with the 'transcendental (material) principle' that '*everything must have its ground*' subordinate to the principle of sufficient reason (OD pp. 193–4, pp. 113–14). Kant then insists repeatedly on the separation of the two senses of ground, restricting the latter to 'objects of sensible intuition' (OD p. 194, p. 113). The order of knowledge and that of being are related, but in far more complex ways than are admitted by their simple elision. The CPR has shown experience to be impossible without 'the harmony between understanding and sensibility in so far as it makes possible an a priori knowledge of universal laws', but it does not provide any reason for why 'two otherwise completely heterogeneous sources of knowledge always agree so well as to permit empirical knowledge' (OD p. 250, p. 159) The two understandings of ground do agree, but the grounds for this agreement cannot themselves be easily identified, let alone assumed.

The discussion of ground continued after Kant, and provoked a splendid essay and historical review of the topic from Schopenhauer (1813). In it he showed that the problem of ground is a refraction of a fundamental philosophical problem concerning the relationship between being and logos. This position also informs Heidegger's reflections on the problem of ground in the *Metaphysical Foundations of Logic* (1928) which proposes an explanation for the relationship between logical, real and practical ground, or in his terms reason, cause and intention. For him this consists in the relationship between *logos* and *techne,* or our 'being engaged in the world in producing one being from another' (*techne*) and our being engaged in speech with each other (*logos*) (p. 118).

Grounding for the Metaphysics of Morals Published in 1785, GMM was the first of Kant's three critical texts in moral philosophy. It was followed in 1788 by the *Critique of Practical Reason* and in 1797 by the *Metaphysics of Morals.* It marks a first statement of the main themes of Kant's critical practical philosophy, including duty, the categorical imperative and the free will. It differs from CPrR above all in its method, which is analytical rather than synthetic. It begins with the 'common experience' of morality as something known and proceeds to its sources in the 'supreme principle of morality'. The analytical method employed accounts for the organization of the contents of the text, which does not follow the critical schema of 'Doctrine of Elements' and 'Methodology'. The contents are organized in three sections, the first two of which involve transitions from 'Ordinary Rational Knowledge of Morality to the Philosophical' and from 'Popular Moral Philosophy to a Metaphysics of Morals'. The third section makes the 'Final Step from a Metaphysics of Morals to a Critique of Pure Practical Reason'.

Each of the sections pursues the 'Supreme Principle of Morality' by means of criticizing previous accounts of it and establishing the conditions of an 'unqualified good'. The latter is described as a 'good will' which is nevertheless prone to 'subjective restrictions or hindrances' which are gathered together under the concept of duty. In the first section Kant explicates this principle by means of popular casuistry, in the second by an analysis of the forms of imperative 'ought' which accompany moral action. He distinguishes hypothetical and categorical imperatives, considering only the latter to qualify as moral. Through this distinction he is able to criticize previous philosophical accounts of the 'supreme principle of morality', both 'empirical' and 'rational', for relying upon forms of the hypothetical imperative. Only the categorical imperative is the autonomous form of willing able to test maxims for their universalizability. The third section reflects on freedom and autonomy in an attempt to answer the question 'How is the categorical imperative possible?' It concludes that human beings are members of both the sensible and the intelligible realms. This means that the freedom of the will, as a property of the intelligible world, is strictly speaking unintelligible in terms of our sensibly conditioned forms of knowledge. The text thus concludes, on an appropriately aporetic note, that 'even though we do not indeed grasp the practical unconditioned necessity of the moral imperative, we do nevertheless grasp its inconceivability'.

H

habitus *see also* ART, CULTURE, FEELING, MOTIVE, NATURE, SENSIBILITY
Kant introduces this term in his discussion of moral feeling in LE, using it to bring the impulses of the sensibility under the sway of the moral rules of the understanding. It is one of the means by which 'the understanding could move the sensibility to conformity and induce motives in it' (LE p. 46). Kant believes that since human beings are not naturally disposed to this desirable result it is advisable to 'produce a *habitus*, which is not natural, but takes the place of nature, and is produced by imitation and oft-repeated practice' (LE p. 46). Kant developed this thought in his later theory of culture in CJ, and in his writings on education. A suggestive affinity can also be detected between the *habitus* and the work of art, which too is a 'second nature [created] out of the material supplied to it by actual nature' (CJ §49). Common to both is a sense of cultivation – in the first case of nature within, in the second case of nature without oneself – through free but also disciplined activity.

happiness [*eudaimonia, felicitas, Glückseligkeit*] *see also* AUTONOMY, FREEDOM, GOOD, HIGHEST GOOD, HOPE, PLEASURE
In the *Nicomachean Ethics* Aristotle discovered that the 'chief good' or 'final end' of human action – 'something final and self-sufficient, and the end of action' (Aristotle, 1941, 1097b, 22) – is happiness. His account of happiness is admirably balanced: perfect happiness consists in leading the contemplative life, but not to the exclusion of other aspects of the good life such as bravery, liberality and pleasure (ibid., 1178a–1179b). However, Aristotle's balanced view of happiness was gradually transformed by the Platonic distinction between the happiness and self-sufficiency of the mind and soul and the pleasures of the body. In Aquinas's work this distinction takes the form of the objective experience of *beatitudo* (blessed happiness) and the less preferred and subjective experience of *eudaimonia*. This distinction was largely preserved by Descartes, for whom happiness (*heur*) 'depends only on outward things' as opposed to blessedness (*béatitude*) which consists in 'a perfect contentment of mind and inner satisfaction'

221

(letter to Elizabeth, 4 August 1645, Descartes, 1981, p. 164). With Kant the distinction is preserved in modified form, with objective happiness issuing from free and autonomous action, and subjective happiness from heteronomous feelings of pleasure and well-being.

Kant's discussion of happiness is thoroughly permeated by an opposition between freedom and happiness. The opposition is most apparent in the distinction in MM between '*eudaimonism* (the principle of happiness)' and '*eleutheronomy* (the principle of the freedom of internal law-giving)', with its accompanying claim that if the former is made the basic principle of action the result would be the '*euthanasia* (easy death) of all morals' (MM p. 378, p. 183). Kant tackles the eudaimonist objection to his account of duty, which claims that duty is pursued because of the pleasure resulting from doing duty, by replying that while pleasure may be involved in obedience to law it cannot precede it as a motivational ground. Pleasure preceding duty or observance of the law is 'sensibly dependent' and part of the natural order, while pleasure which follows duty is based on intelligible freedom and is part of the moral order. The distinction between the two accounts of obedience to law has several consequences which duly unfold throughout Kant's practical philosophy.

The opposition between *eudaimonia* and *eleutheronomy* is developed into a series of consistent corollaries. The first, already mentioned, is the distinction between the natural and the moral orders: the natural order is the realm of causality, inclination and heteronomy; the moral order the realm of freedom, self-determination and autonomy (MM p. 216, p. 44). Principles based on happiness and heteronomy are material, subjective and partial as opposed to those based on freedom and autonomy which are formal, objective and universal (GMM p. 442, p. 46). The idea of the good as happiness is, because of its many potential goods, indeterminate; while that of the good as freedom is focused and determinate (CJ §83). The pursuit of happiness determines the will only indirectly, the eudaimonist does their duty 'only by means of the happiness they anticipate' while duty commands the will directly and is not directed towards any end outside itself (MM p. 377, p. 183). As a consequence, the imperatives associated with the pursuit of happiness are hypothetical 'counsels of prudence' conditioned according to 'whether this or that man counts this or that as belonging to his happiness', while those of the law of freedom are categorical and unconditioned commands (GMM p. 416, p. 26). This form of oppositional argument leads to the repressive proposition in IUH that humanity 'should not partake of any other happiness or perfection than that which they have procured for themselves without instinct and by their own reason' (p. 19, p. 43).

Yet while Kant excludes happiness from any role in the determination of the will to action, he nevertheless regards it as a vital aspect of the highest human good. At one point in CPR he assumes that happiness will automatically follow freedom: 'I do not speak of the greatest happiness, for this will follow [the greatest possible freedom] of itself' (CPR B 373). Here the constitution which permits the greatest possible freedom is described as a necessary idea for human progress which will bring with it happiness; in CJ, however, happiness itself is the idea according to which human beings 'seek to make their actual state of being adequate' (§83). Kant has already potentially reconciled the terms of this opposition in his answers in CPR to the three questions of the interest of reason: '1. What can I know? 2. What ought I to do? 3. What may I hope?' (CPR A 804/ B 832). Happiness features in the answers to these questions, although not as an achieved state but as worthiness for being happy. The highest good consists in both worthiness to be happy or 'morality' and in actual happiness – one without the other is partial and incomplete. Characteristically for Kant, happiness is excluded from the determination of moral action only to return as its indispensable accompaniment in the highest good.

heautonomy *see also* AUTONOMY, HETERONOMY, JUDGEMENT, REFLECTIVE JUDGEMENT
Heautonomy is a principle of reflective judgement according to which the subject gives itself a law 'not to nature (as autonomy), but to itself (as heautonomy), to guide its reflection upon nature' (CJ Introduction §V). It may be described as 'the law of the specification of nature' and is not 'cognised a priori' and thus applied to nature in the way of a scientific law. Rather it is a rule used by the judgement in order to facilitate its investigations of nature – 'finding the universal for the particular presented to it by perception' – and to relate the universal laws of the understanding with the specific empirical laws of nature.

heterogeneity *see* HOMOGENEITY

heteronomy *see also* AUTONOMY, CAUSALITY, HAPPINESS, INCLINATION, LAW, LEGIS-LATION, PERFECTION, WILL
In GMM Kant contrasts the freedom of the will manifest in autonomy with the dependence of the will on external or heteronomous causes and interests. The moral law under heteronomy would only be valid because of an interest that we held in obeying it, which would amount to 'the dependence of practical reason on sensibility, viz., on an underlying feeling whereby reason could never be morally legislative' (GMM p. 461, p. 60). Kant deemed a great deal of previous moral philosophy to be based on heteronomous principles which act 'as an attracting stimulus or as a constraining force for obedience' (GMM p. 433, p. 39). He accordingly

contrasts his 'principle of the autonomy of the will' with 'every other principle, which I accordingly count under heteronomy' (ibid.). Such heteronomous principles may be either empirical or rational, the former 'drawn from the principle of happiness, are based upon either physical or moral feeling', while the latter, drawn from the principle of perfection, are 'based upon either the rational concept of perfection as a possible effect of our will or else upon the concept of an independent perfection (the will of God) as a determining cause of our will' (p. 442, p. 46).

highest good [*summum bonum, höchstes Gut*] *see also* ABSOLUTE, AUTONOMY, GOOD, GOOD WILL, HAPPINESS, HOPE, WILL

The highest good is described in CPR as the combination of happiness and worthiness to be happy. Kant's practical philosophy rigorously separated the heteronomy of happiness and its doctrine of *eudaimonia* from that of the autonomy of freedom and its doctrine of *eleutheronomy* (MM p. 378, p. 183). However, when considering the highest good in terms of the answers to the questions of the three interests of reason (What can I know? What ought I to do? What may I hope?), Kant claims that neither happiness nor moral freedom by itself is adequate to serve as the highest good. It must be a combination of both which brings together morality or 'worthiness to be happy' with the hope of actual happiness: 'Happiness, taken by itself, is, for our reason, far from being the complete good. Reason does not approve happiness (however inclination may desire it) except insofar as it is united with worthiness to be happy, that is, with moral conduct. Morality, taken by itself, and with it, the mere *worthiness* to be happy, is also far from being the complete good' (CPR A 813/B 841). The answer to the second question of the interest of reason – 'What ought I to do?' – is 'make yourself worthy of happiness', and to the third question – 'What may I hope?' – is 'hope you will participate in happiness'. Kant concludes that 'Happiness . . . in exact proportion with the morality of the rational beings who are thereby rendered worthy of it, alone constitutes the supreme good of [the] world' (CPR A 814/B 842) and sees the reality of this unity as based on the 'postulate' of an intelligible, 'supreme original good'.

history *see also* CULTURE, GEOGRAPHY, HUMANITY, KNOWLEDGE, TIME

Kant's view of history may be divided into two broad subspecies, the first indicating a form of knowledge, the second a pattern informing the events of natural and human history. With regard to the first, Kant adopts the Wolffian distinction between 'rational' and 'historical' knowledge. Using one of Wolff's examples, he distinguishes in P between the historical knowledge of the fact that the sun warms a stone and the rational knowledge of why it does so (P §20). In the words of CPR, 'Historical knowledge is *cognitio ex datis*; rational knowledge is *cognitio ex principiis*' (A 836/B 864). However, within this division of forms of knowledge Kant establishes further distinctions. In the introduction to his lectures on physical geography he defines history as an account of events which have succeeded each other over time, and geography as an account of events which take place simultaneously in space: the former account is a narrative, the latter a description. Kant himself offered several such narratives including the summary histories of Judaism and Christianity in RL (pp. 124–36, pp. 115–28), of logic in the 'Jäsche Logic' (L pp. 531–5), and of pure reason in CPR (A 852/B 880ff).

The second main division of Kant's concept of history involves the philosophy of history or the re-working of traditional theodicy. Kant's attitude towards the philosophy of history was distinctly ambiguous: he severely criticized Herder's *Ideas on the Philosophy of History of Mankind* (1785), and wrote an essay 'On the Failure of all Philosophical Attempts at Theodicy' (1791) while at the same time clearly acknowledging in IUH the virtues of a philosophy of history. There he describes history as giving an account of human actions in terms of 'the will's manifestations in the world of phenomena' in order, through the examination of 'the free exercise of the human will *on a large scale* . . . to discover a regular progression among freely willed actions' (IUH p. 17, p. 41). The point of such an account is to show 'that what strikes us in the actions of individuals as confused and fortuitous may be recognized in the history of the entire species, as a steadily advancing but slow development of humanity's original capacities'. Through this individuals would realize 'that they are unconsciously promoting an end which, even if they knew what it was, would scarcely arouse their interest' (ibid.).

This approach to the philosophy of history complements Kant's attempt to develop an account of culture, notably in the second part of CJ where it is set within the context of a discussion of the 'ultimate end of nature as a teleological system'. It should be added, however, that this teleological view of history is paralleled by another view of history which regards it as the result of breaks and innovations heralded by genius and enthusiasm. It is this latter, relatively underdeveloped view in Kant's own text, which has been increasingly important in contemporary philosophy of history.

history of philosophy *see also* AMPHIBOLY, CONCEPTS OF REFLECTION, CRITICAL PHILOSOPHY, DISPUTE, PHILOSOPHY, REASON

Although Kant claimed in the Preface to CPR to be criticizing 'the faculty of reason in general' and not 'books and systems', the history of philosophy nevertheless plays an important role in his philosophy. The 'books and systems' of the history of philosophy are omnipresent in CPR and are even explicitly addressed in its concluding pages on 'The History of Pure Reason'. Yet Kant consistently treats historical philosophers as if they were his own contemporaries, attributing them respect not by virtue of their being historical, but only insofar as they contribute to the critical philosophy. His interpretative principle, or 'key to the interpretation of all the products of pure reason' (stated at the close of his polemic with Eberhard), is the 'critique of reason itself'. While the 'historians of philosophy, with all their intended praise, only attribute mere nonsense' he, with the critical key, is able to recognize 'beyond what the philosophers actually said, what they really meant to say' (OD p. 251, p. 160).

Kant's most systematic account of the history of philosophy is to be found in the introductions to his lectures on logic. For the general outline of his history, Kant is indebted to J.H.S. Formey's *Histoire abrégée de la philosophie* (1760) and F. Gentzke's *Historia philosophia* (1724), although he was naturally acquainted with several original sources. His account is informed by the enlightenment prejudice that philosophy originated with the Greeks, and is barely to be discerned in ancient Chinese, Persian, Egyptian and Arabic thought. It also reflects the prejudice that philosophical innovation was largely confined to the classical and modern periods, with the medieval scholastics being traduced as 'slavish' imitators of Aristotle and proponents of 'pseudo-philosophizing' (L p. 543). Yet within the accounts of the history of classical and modern philosophy Kant expresses some surprising preferences, and makes some unexpected judgements.

Kant's discussion of the pre-Socratic philosophers is, with one exception, summary and unenthusiastic; the only philosopher who merits a more extended discussion is Pythagoras. He regards the 'most important epoch of Greek philosophy' as commencing with Socrates, and praises the 'new *practical* direction' opened by his work (L p. 542). When describing the philosophical succession to Socrates, Kant does not share the modern fascination with Plato and Aristotle, but gives equal if not more weight to the Hellenistic philosophical schools of the Stoics, Epicureans and Sceptics. With regard to these he evinces a nuanced and detailed knowledge, both of their doctrines and the differences between them. This preference is also evident in his critical work, where references to Epicurus exceed references to Plato. However, recent interpretations tend to focus on Platonic elements in Kant's thought, perhaps because these correspond to our assumptions about what is important in the history of philosophy. Yet the procedure of critique itself, the view of the canon and prolepsis in the CPR, as well as that of pleasure and *Gemüt* in CJ, are taken directly from Epicurus. References to Stoic and ancient sceptics also abound throughout his work, but have been overshadowed by the subsequent interpretative focus upon Plato and Aristotle.

The role Kant accords Plato in the history of philosophy is extremely ambiguous. In CPR he praises Plato's *Republic* and its model of the philosopher (A 316), but sees considerable danger in Plato's notion of the transcendent ideas. Kant's opposition to this aspect of Plato's thought was fired and fed by his opposition to the Platonic mysticism of some of his contemporaries. This is evident in his late texts on the history of philosophy, 'On a Newly Arisen Superior Tone in Philosophy' and 'Announcement of the Near Conclusion of a Treaty for Eternal Peace in Philosophy' (both 1796). In these texts Kant distinguishes between the philosophical and mystagogic tendencies in Platonism, seeing the latter as exemplified in ancient and modern Neo-Platonism (see 1796a p. 399, p. 64). Aristotle features primarily in Kant's writings as the inventor of logic, and while he shows awareness of other aspects of the Stagirite's thought, his enthusiasm is distinctly bounded.

When discussing modern philosophy Kant refers repeatedly to the Reformation, drawing a parallel between the reformation of the Church and that of philosophy. Bacon and Descartes are noted, the former for his emphasis on experiment and observation, the latter for his criterion of truth; but the 'greatest and most meritorious reformers of philosophy in our times' (L p. 543) were Leibniz and Locke. Kant opposes both Leibniz and Locke at several points, particularly in CPR. Indeed, many of his early writings engage with Leibniz and the dominant 'Leibnizian' school of philosophy led by Christian Wolff. The consistent object of Kant's criticism was the continuum Leibniz established between sensibility and reason, which regarded sensibility as a confused perception of reason; this was contrasted with the argument in Locke, which abstracted reason from sensibility through reflection. Although both positions seemed diametrically opposed, Kant saw them as sharing the confusion of sense and reason.

In CPR Kant brings together classical and modern philosophy in order to present a drama of pure reason. One example is the history of the decline, fall and revival of metaphysics discussed in the first Preface. Under the 'dogmatists' the government of metaphysics was despotic; this collapsed into anarchy under the onslaught of the nomadic sceptics; Locke's attempt to put an end to controversy did not succeed, and with the triumph of Newtonian science there arose an indifference to metaphysical issues. In the face of this indifference, CPR represents a call to order and the establishment of a metaphysical tribunal. This 'political history' of the government of philosophy given at the beginning of CPR contrasts with the 'revolutionary' history at its end. Here, in the 'History of Pure Reason', Kant makes the history of philosophy contemporary by identifying the three controversial issues of the 'object of knowledge', the 'origin of knowledge' and the 'method' of philosophy. With respect to the first issue, Kant distinguishes between 'sensualists' such as Epicurus and idealists such as Plato; with respect to the second, Kant distinguishes between the empiricist school of Aristotle and Locke and the 'noologists' Plato and Leibniz; and with respect to method Kant first distinguishes between the 'scientific' and the 'naturalistic' methods (regarding the latter as 'mere misology') and then distinguishes between the dogmatic scientific method represented by Wolff and the sceptical scientific method represented by Hume. Although he names individual philosophers, they are but representatives of a drama of reason in which other players may be left 'unnamed' (CPR A 856/B 884) and which culminates in the critical philosophy.

holding-to-be-true [*Fürwahrhalten*] *see also* CERTAINTY, FAITH, JUDGEMENT, KNOWLEDGE, OPINION
Holding-to-be-true concerns the validity of a judgement, which may be subjectively and/or objectively sufficient, and is distributed into three distinct classes. The first is opinion, which is consciously insufficient objectively and subjectively. The second is faith, which is consciously insufficient objectively but sufficient subjectively. The third is knowledge, which is both subjectively and objectively sufficient or 'certain' (CPR A 822/B 850). Each class has: (a) its own object – matters of opinion, faith and knowledge (CJ §91); (b) its own particular modality of judgement – opinion is hypothetical, faith is assertoric, knowledge is apodeictic (L p. 571).

homogeneity *see also* CONTINUITY, GENUS, REGULATIVE PRINCIPLE
Homogeneity, along with continuity and variety, comprise the three regulative principles of reason which 'prepare the field for the understanding' in its systematic elaboration of experience. It is one of the 'antecedent rule[s] of reason' without which the understanding could not function, since Kant argues 'it is only on the assumption of differences in nature, just as it is also only under the condition that its objects exhibit homogeneity, that we can have any faculty of understanding whatsoever' (A 657/B 685). While the principle of variety states that the manifold is differentiated according to 'lower species', the principle of homogeneity claims that the manifold is homogeneous according to 'higher genera'. The two principles are fused into a third, and apparently more fundamental principle of continuity. The principles also correspond to transcendental laws which are not objects of experience, nor open to deduction, but which nevertheless 'possess, as synthetic *a priori* propositions, objective but indeterminate validity, and serve as rules for possible experience' (A 663/B 691). The law of homogeneity 'keeps us from resting satisfied with an excessive number of different original genera, and bids us pay due regard to homogeneity', while that of variety 'in turn, imposes a check upon this

tendency towards unity, and insists that before we proceed to apply a universal concept to individuals we distinguish subspecies within it' (CPR A 660/B 688). Finally, the law of continuity combines the two former 'by prescribing that even amidst the utmost manifoldness we observe homogeneity in the gradual transition from one species to another' (ibid.).

hope [*elpis, spes, Hoffnung*] *see also* FAITH, LOVE
Hope along with faith and love forms the set of 'theological virtues' first elaborated by Paul in Corinthians 13:13 (see Aquinas, 1952, II, I, 62). They were contrasted with the four 'cardinal virtues' of temperance, justice, prudence and fortitude. The theological virtues were the ends for which the cardinal virtues were means. Largely absent from classical Greek philosophy, hope features prominently in the New Testament as an eschatological expectation of future salvation; the importance of hope is underlined by Paul's description of God as the 'God of hope' (Romans 15:13).

The concept of hope is central to Kant's thought, and yet he nowhere explicitly addresses it. In DS he introduces a 'bias of reason' into the scales by which we weigh arguments, claiming that the tray with the inscription 'future hopes' always outweighs that marked 'speculation'. This explains for Kant the fascination with tales of the after-life and of the spirits inhabiting it. Our hopes for a future outweigh our judgements of the present. This 'bias of reason' towards hope becomes in CPR one of the three 'interests of reason' expressed in the questions: '1. What can I know? 2. What ought I to do? 3. What may I hope?' (A 805/B 833). He emphasizes what is at stake in this question by claiming that 'all *hoping* is directed to happiness' and arrives 'at the conclusion that *something is* (which determines the ultimate possible end) *because something ought to happen*' (A 806/B 834).

The ecstatic structure of hope is evident throughout Kant's historical and political writings. In PP he sees the guarantee that perpetual peace is not an 'empty idea' to lie in the '*gegründete hoffnung*' or 'well grounded hope' that it can actually be achieved; this hope itself can serve to realize the idea, bringing it from the future into the present (PP p. 386, p. 130). It is also evident in the practical philosophy, where the hope of an eternal life shapes the courses of action taken in this one. Less obvious but equally significant is the role it plays in the theoretical philosophy, as is shown in Heidegger's interpretation of the projective and proleptic role of the imagination in the act of synthesis described in *Kant and the Problem of Metaphysics* (1929). While Kant himself did not seem to be fully aware of the philosophical implications of his own concept of hope, these have been expounded and further developed by twentieth-century philosophers such as Heidegger in his notion of ecstatic temporality, Benjamin with his notion of Messianic time (see Benjamin, 1973, pp. 255–66) and Bloch with his wide-ranging exploration of *The Principle of Hope* (1959).

humanity *see also* COMMUNICATION, CULTURE, HISTORY, IMPERATIVE, PERSON, SOCIABILITY

Humanity is defined in CJ §60 as 'on the one hand, the universal *feeling of sympathy*, and on the other, the faculty of being able to *communicate* universally one's inmost self – properties constituting in conjunction the befitting *social spirit* of mankind, in contradistinction to the narrow life of the lower animals'. In RL the distinction of humanity from animality is maintained, but supplemented by a further distinction between humanity and personality. Kant identifies three dispositions in mankind: the first is the 'predisposition to *animality* in man, taken as a *living* being', the second that to '*humanity* in man, taken as a living and at the same time as a rational being', with the third being that to '*personality* in man, taken as a rational and at the same time an *accountable* being' (RL p. 26, p. 21). Thus humanity occupies an intermediate position between animality and a purely rational, free and accountable personality.

The definition of humanity is filled out considerably in MM, while remaining within the basic distinction between humanity and animality. Human beings, unlike animals, possess the capacity to set themselves ends, and to cultivate this capacity (MM p. 392, p. 195). Animal impulses are aimed at self-preservation, preservation of the species, and the preservation of the capacity to enjoy life; against these the duty of an individual consists, according to Kant, in the consistency of the formal maxims of the will with the dignity of humanity (MM p. 420, p. 216). The latter is closely associated with the idea of humanity, with mankind as it ought to be – potential, free, rational beings – rather than with what it is. Indeed, Kant maintains that freedom or 'independence from being constrained by another's choice' is the 'only original right belonging to every man by virtue of his humanity' (MM p. 237, p. 63). This definition of humanity deeply informs Kant's moral philosophy, featuring prominently in one of the formulations of the categorical imperative: 'Act in such a way that you treat humanity, whether in your own person or in the person of another, always at the same time as an end, and never as a means' (GMM p. 429, p. 36).

hypothetical *see also* APODEICTIC, CATEGORICAL IMPERATIVE, DISJUNCTIVE, IMPERATIVE, JUDGEMENT, RELATION

Hypothetical judgements and imperatives play a considerable role in Kant's theoretical and practical philosophy. In CPR hypothetical judgements form the second group of the judgements of relation in the table of judgements, following categorical and preceding disjunctive judgements (A 70/B 95). Categorical judgements concern the relation of subject and predicate, disjunctive judgements the relationship between discrete judgements, while hypothetical judgements concern the relation of ground to consequence. The form of the hypothetical judgement relates two propositions, the first the hypothesis, the second the consequence, as in 'If there is a perfect justice, the obstinately wicked are punished' (CPR A 73/B 98), which relates a hypothetical first proposition with its consequence in the second proposition. The hypothetical imperative obeys a similar form. In GMM Kant describes all imperatives as commanding either categorically or hypothetically. Hypothetical imperatives 'represent the practical necessity of a possible action as a means of attaining something else that one wants (or may possibly want)' (GMM p. 414, p. 25). Kant divides the hypothetical imperatives into those of skill and prudence. Imperatives of skill point to a course of action which will attain a possible end and are 'technical (belonging to art)', while those of prudence point to the means for attaining a given end and are 'pragmatic (belonging to welfare)' (GMM p. 417, p. 27). Unlike categorical imperatives, hypothetical imperatives are concerned 'with the matter of the action and its intended result' and are thus determined heteronomously.

hypotyposis *see also* ACROAMATIC, ANALOGY, CONSTRUCTION, PRESENTATION, SCHEMATISM

Kant's formal discussion of hypotyposis occurs in CJ §59, but it appears throughout his philosophy in the guise of 'presentation' or the rendering of concepts and ideas 'in terms of sense'. Such presentation is two-fold, differing according to whether it is a concept or an idea that is being rendered. In the first case the rendering of a concept is *schematic*, 'where the intuition corresponding to a concept comprehended by the understanding is given *a priori*', while in the second it is *symbolic*, 'where the concept is one which only reason can think, and to which no sensible intuition can be adequate' (CJ §59). The first form of hypotyposis gives rise to schemata or 'direct' and 'demonstrative' presentations, the second generates symbols, which are indirect presentations governed by analogy. Kant analyzed schematic hypotyposis more fully in the 'Schematism' chapter of CPR, and thus concentrates in CJ upon its symbolic operation. The latter consists 'first in applying the concept to the object of a sensible intuition, and then, secondly, in applying the mere rule of its reflection upon that intuition to quite another object, of which the former is but the symbol' (CJ §59). His examples of symbolic hypotyposis include: the analogy between the properly constituted state and a living body; a despotic

state and a handmill; philosophical concepts such as ground, dependence, flow, substance 'and numberless others'; all knowledge of God; and
finally the analogy between beauty and the morally good. This passage has
become particularly important for those twentieth-century interpretations
of Kant which stress the role of indeterminacy in his accounts of judgement and method.

I

I [*Ich*] *see also* ABSTRACTION, APPERCEPTION, CONSCIOUSNESS, 'I THINK', IDENTITY, PARALOGISM, PSYCHOLOGY, SELF-CONSCIOUSNESS, SUBJECT

Kant distinguished between two senses of 'I', even though he varied the terms in which he framed the distinction, referring on occasion to the 'empirical' and the 'transcendental' I, the 'psychological' and the 'logical' I, and the 'I as object' and the 'I as subject'. The bifurcation of the I follows from the nature of self-consciousness: 'That I am conscious of myself is a thought that already contains a two-fold I' (WP p. 270, p. 73) – it requires that the I be thought both as an object of intuition and as that which thinks (see also CPR B 155). The first I is the 'psychological I' which underlies 'all perceptions and their connection, whose apprehension (*apprehensio*) is the way the subject is affected' (WP p. 270, p. 73). This I may be considered as an object of intuition, and its workings described through psychological or anthropological observations (see A §1).

The second I is more difficult to describe since it is not an object of intuition. Kant warns repeatedly against converting the transcendental I as a logical subject of knowledge, namely the I of 'I think' or 'that which remains after all the accidents (as predicates) are abstracted' (P §46) into a substance. This I cannot be an '*absolute subject*' or even a concept but 'only the reference of the internal phenomena to their unknown subject' (P §46). To make this I into a substance capable of acting as a 'ground of thought' is to commit a paralogism and to apply to something which is not an appearance the categories of substance and cause properly applicable only to appearances. Nevertheless, while very little can be said of the transcendental I of 'I think', it nevertheless remains central to Kant's account of experience. It serves as 'the one condition which accompanies all thought', not as an object of a possible experience, but as 'only the formal condition, namely, the logical unity of every thought, in which I abstract from all objects' (CPR A 398).

Kant describes the transcendental I as a 'mere prefix [designating] a thing of indeterminate signification' (MF p. 543, p. 103) and as a 'completely empty representation "I" . . . we cannot even say that this is a

233

concept, but only that it is a bare consciousness which accompanies all concepts' (CPR A 436/B 404). It is but the logical terminus of a process of abstracting from the predicates of knowledge to a postulated, ultimate subject which underlies them and which cannot be further specified. Kant is prepared to characterize it in terms of analogy: on one occasion he maintains that by 'this I, he or it (the thing) which thinks, nothing further is represented than a transcendental subject of the thoughts = X' (CPR A 346/B 404), while on another he describes it as 'the universal correlate of apperception and itself merely a thought' (MF p. 542, p. 103). He insists that I is an 'entirely empty expression' which designates nothing more than 'the thought of an absolute, but logical unity of the subject' (CPR A 356); it does not of itself exist as an ultimate substance or ground underlying knowledge and experience, but is simply a necessary logical function which accompanies it.

Far from making the I into the straightforward subject of thought and action, Kant insists that its character can never be known except by analogy. He describes the relationship between the empirical I of the individual person and the transcendental I as the subject of knowledge as extremely difficult – if not impossible – to specify. His immediate successors were less reluctant to convert the I into a transcendental subject whose character and workings were knowable in principle. Transcendental idealists, above all Fichte (1794) and Schelling (1800), made the transcendental I into a substantive ground for all knowledge and action. Hegel (1807) criticized Kant for positing a formal distinction within the I of self-consciousness, and Fichte and Schelling for dissolving all distinctions in the transcendental I. Instead, by means of a phenomenology, he traced the historical shapes assumed by the diremptions of the I, thought both as subject and as substance. Subsequently, 'Young Hegelians' such as Feuerbach (1830) and Marx (1843) sought to unify the transcendental and empirical I's into a human subject, a development which remained enormously influential and persuasive through to post-World War II existentialists such as Sartre (1960). However, in recent decades the identification of empirical and transcendental subjects in the human subject has been questioned by accounts stimulated above all by Nietzsche (1886) and Freud (1915). Such accounts once more separate the transcendental I (or 'unconscious') from the empirical I, and resist the temptation to assign an ultimate subject – human or otherwise – to thought and action.

'I think' [*cogito, Ich denke*] *see also* APPERCEPTION, CONSCIOUSNESS, I, IDENTITY, PARALOGISM, PSYCHOLOGY, SELF-CONSCIOUSNESS

Descartes regarded his proposition 'I think therefore I am' (widely known in its Latin form, *Cogito ergo sum*) in the *Discourse on Method* (1637) to be a truth 'so certain and assured' that it could serve as a touchstone for certainty. Descartes' discovery of the *cogito* by means of a process of sceptical abstraction, which discounted the claims of all knowledge reached by means of authority and experience, is widely recognized as the foundational moment of modern philosophy. However, the reception of Descartes' proposition by German philosophers before Kant was extremely cautious and sceptical. Leibniz generalized the problem of the *cogito* into one of consciousness and self-consciousness in general (see Leibniz, 1976, pp. 291–5), a development which was codified by Christian Wolff in his 'German Logic' (1719). The first proposition of this work maintained: 'We are conscious of ourselves and other things, and therefore it is clear that we exist' (§1). Kant's reception of the *cogito* was even more qualified: unlike Wolff he did not believe it was possible to prove existence by means of consciousness, but he was prepared to admit the *cogito* or 'I think' as the ultimate, but unknowable, result of a process of abstraction from the discrete contents of experience and as its necessary complement.

Kant points to the anomalous status of the 'concept' or, if the term is preferred, the judgement 'I think' when he describes it as one 'which was not included in the general list of transcendental concepts but which must yet be counted as belonging to that list, without, however, in the least altering it or declaring it defective' (CPR A 341/B 400). It is clearly not a category among categories, even though it belongs to the table of categories; it is, Kant specifies, 'the vehicle of all concepts' with no special designation 'because it serves only to introduce all our thought, as belonging to consciousness' (ibid.). The proposition 'I think' is not itself an experience, nor, unlike the categories, is it 'a condition of the possibility of a knowledge of objects'; it is the 'form of apperception, which belongs to and precedes every experience' (CPR A 354). It accompanies and precedes experience as the subject of experience, but only in a formal sense: the 'I' of 'I think' can be regarded as neither a subject nor an object of experience but only as its 'vehicle' and 'necessary accompaniment'.

Kant further claims that 'I think' is the *necessary* vehicle/form/accompaniment of experience: to have a representation it is necessary to accompany it with 'I think' or else the representation 'would not belong to the subject' (CPR B 132). With this claim he draws back from some of the extremely radical implications of his dissolution of the substantive character of the ultimate subject of experience, and implicitly commits the very paralogism of the subject which he himself exposed. The disquieting implications of his position were subsequently explored by Nietzsche, who pursued to its limit Kant's suggestion that the substantive 'I' in 'I think' be replaced by 'he or it (the thing) which thinks ... the transcendental subject of the thoughts = X' (CPR A 346/B 404). Nietzsche's (1886) destruction of the *cogito* along with Freud's (1915) excavation of the unconscious paved the way for twentieth-century critiques of the *cogito* by the tradition represented by philosophers such as Heidegger (1927), Foucault (1988), Deleuze and Guattari (1972), and Derrida (1967).

idea [*eidos, forma, Idee*] *see also* ARCHETYPES, CONSTITUTIVE PRINCIPLES, FORM, IDEAL, INNATE IDEAS, POSTULATES, REASON

Kant deliberately and self-consciously redefined the meaning of this ancient philosophical term. In the extraordinary Question XV of the *Summa theologica* – 'Of Ideas' – Aquinas provides a lapidary summing up of the classical debates around the definition of ideas: 'by ideas are understood the forms of things existing apart from the things themselves . . . [these are either] the type of that which is called the form, or the principle of the knowledge of that thing' (Aquinas, 1952, I, 15, 1). The former are the transcendent Platonic ideas which provide a pattern for the things themselves; the latter are the Aristotelian and later Stoic ideas which are abstracted from sensible perception and serve as concepts for knowing objects. Both positions, as Aquinas shows, relate to objects, whether as their paradigmatic form or as their abstracted principle of knowledge. This relationship between idea and object survived the philosophical controversies of the early modern period such as those between Descartes and Spinoza and between Leibniz and Locke, both of which focused on the origin of ideas. While the participants differed over whether ideas were 'innate' or abstracted from sensible perception, they did not radically question the basic relationship of idea and object. For Kant, however, 'The *idea* is a concept of reason whose object can be met with nowhere in experience' (L p. 590), or precisely that which does *not* stand in any relation to an object.

Kant's main discussion of ideas is in the 'Transcendental Dialectic' of CPR. This begins with a reflection on philosophical language and the situation which arises when a thinker finds themself 'at a loss for the expression which exactly fits their concept' (A 312/B 368). Rather than resort to the 'desperate expedient' of neologism, Kant looks for the term in a 'dead and learned language'. This excursus introduces his justification for using the term 'idea', which hinges on a contrast of Plato and Aristotle. For Kant, both philosophers captured important aspects of the term 'idea', but exaggerated some characteristics and neglected others. In Kant's reading, Plato used the term to mean 'something which not only can never be borrowed from the senses but far surpasses even the concepts of the understanding (with which Aristotle concerned himself)' (CPR A 313/B 370). For him, Plato hypostatized the ideas, making them into archetypes by means of a 'mystical deduction', while Aristotle confined their scope to empirical experience. With his use of the term, Kant sought to establish a middle position which both acknowledged the transcendence of the ideas and the rigorous distinction of idea and concept (P p. 329, p. 70).

Kant considered the distinction between transcendental ideas or 'pure concepts of reason' and the categories or 'pure concepts of the understanding' to be one of the main achievements of CPR. The categories of the understanding relate to possible objects of experience, while the ideas of reason refer to the 'absolute totality of all possible experience' which, Kant says, 'is itself not experience' (P §40). Having thus established the generic transcendence of the ideas, Kant proceeds to derive their specific character from the basic function of the reason, which is to make syllogistic inferences. In this he mirrors the procedure applied earlier to the deduction of the categories from the understanding's function of making judgements. For Kant the syllogism consists in relating a particular judgement to a universal condition, in his words 'in the conclusion of a syllogism we restrict a predicate to a certain object, after having first thought it in the major premise in its whole extension under a given condition' (CPR A 322/B 379). The idea corresponds to the unconditioned totality of conditions necessary for any given conditioned state.

Having established the general link between ideas and the form of the syllogism, Kant proceeds to derive discrete ideas from the three categorial forms of relation which connect the universal condition of the major premise with the particular judgement of the conclusion. They are the categorical relation of substance and accident, the hypothetical relation of cause and effect, and the disjunctive relation of community, each of which respectively permits the derivation of 'an *unconditioned* first, of the *categorial* synthesis in a *subject*... the *hypothetical* synthesis of the members of a *series* ... [and] the *disjunctive* synthesis of the parts in a *system*' (CPR A 323/ B 379). The first idea involves the relation to a thinking subject, the second the relation to the world as the sum of all appearances, and the third the relation to things in general, or the *ens realissimum.* These ideas form the 'objects' of the sciences of psychology, cosmology and theology, namely the three divisions of 'special metaphysics' in the Wolffian system. It is when these ideas are treated as if they were objects that these sciences lapse into errors of inference, treating the totality of experience in the major premise of the syllogism as if it were a possible object of experience. Such errors are anatomized by Kant in his scrutiny of the 'dialectical inferences' of the psychological paralogisms, the cosmological antinomies and 'impossible proofs' of theology in the 'Transcendental Dialectic' of CPR.

It might seem as if Kant has so painfully derived the ideas only to deny them any possible utility; yet this is not the case. He wishes to avoid the illegitimate use of the ideas as constitutive principles, as referring to objects of possible experience, but does not rule out their regulative employment as maxims for the orientation of the understanding with respect to the totality of knowledge. While this holds for the theoretical ideas, the case with the practical ideas is somewhat different; as the postulates of pure practical reason, the ideas of immortality, freedom and God are validated, not as objects of knowledge but as part of an a priori 'practical concept of the highest good as the object of our will' (CPrR p. 133, p. 138). Finally, in CJ, Kant makes a further distinction between the transcendental and aesthetic ideas. The former are 'referred to a concept according to an objective principle and are yet incapable of ever furnishing a cognition of the object', while the latter are 'referred to an intuition, in accordance with a merely subjective principle of the harmony of the cognitive faculties (imagination and understanding)' (CJ §57). While the transcendental ideas stimulate the extension of the understanding, and the practical ideas together constitute the concept of the highest good, the work of the aesthetic ideas is to stimulate the harmony of understanding and imagination through vividness and unity in variety, and thus contribute to the augmentation of pleasure.

Although Kant's redefinition of 'idea' has generated a great deal of exegesis and criticism, it has not been broadly influential until recently (see Lyotard, 1983). Since members of the generation of German idealists after Kant were dedicated to breaking down Kant's distinction between reason and understanding, his distinction between idea and category was an inevitable casualty, and with it the entire challenge to the traditional understanding of the term 'idea'. As a result many philosophers in the nineteenth and twentieth centuries, both within and without the ranks of the Kantians, revived the traditional opposition between the Platonic and Aristotelian understandings of the 'idea' thus overlooking Kant's innovation.

ideal *see also* ARCHETYPE, DETERMINATION, EXAMPLE, GOD, IDEA, IMITATION
The ideal is defined as the 'representation of an individual existence as adequate to an idea' (CJ §17). In CPR Kant specifies that the ideal is 'the idea, not merely *in concreto*, but *in individuo*, that is, as an individual thing, determinable or even determined by the idea alone' (CPR A 568/B 596). Although a self-determined individual being, the ideal stands as an archetype which completely determines its copies: Kant's examples in CPR are the stoic wise man, existing in 'complete conformity with the idea of wisdom' (A 569/B 597), and God or the transcendental ideal. Both serve as archetypes for imitation, but in different ways: the stoic sage as an exemplar, and God as a source of all being. God as the *ens realissimum* is

an individual being whose existence is adequate to the idea of the being of beings; for Kant God is the only true ideal, the only ideal which satisfies the condition of being 'completely determined in and through itself, and known as the representation of an individual' (CPR A 577/B 605). In the analysis of the 'Ideal of Reason' in the 'Transcendental Dialectic' Kant refutes all attempts to prove the existence of God as a transcendental ideal; it is not a knowable object, but must be thought in terms of reason's need for the unity of knowledge, or that being to which all beings may ultimately be referred. Later, in the 'Canon of Pure Reason', Kant also discusses the ideals of the 'supreme' and 'original' goods of practical reason, or the supreme reason which brings together happiness and morality. The two aspects of the ideal, as exemplar and source, play an important role in the discussion of the production of art in CJ (see §§17 and 60). The ideal of the beautiful consists in the exemplary products of genius; the products of genius do not follow rules, but are nevertheless exemplary, self-sufficient archetypes.

idealism *see also* HISTORY OF PHILOSOPHY, I, REALISM, SUBJECT, SUBJECTIVE
Kant described the 'dictum of all genuine idealists, from the Eleatic school to Bishop Berkeley' as ' "All cognition through the senses and experience is nothing but sheer illusion, and only in the ideas of the pure understanding and reason is there truth" ' (P p. 374, p. 113). He distinguishes three tendencies within modern idealism: the first is the 'dogmatic' and sometimes visionary idealism of Berkeley; the second is the 'sceptical' or 'problematic' idealism of Descartes. Both of these are in turn opposed as 'empirical' idealisms to the third, Kant's own 'transcendental', 'formal' or, as he later renamed it, 'critical' idealism. Initially in CPR Kant was happy to describe his work as 'transcendental idealism', but with the proviso that his idealism be accepted as a 'reversal' of empirical idealism. He underlined this position in P, following misunderstandings of CPR, where he simultaneously protests 'against all charges of idealism' while at the same time defining his philosophy as 'idealist'.

The idealism which Kant was concerned to reverse doubted the reality of external objects: in the case of Cartesian 'sceptical' idealism only inner experience was indubitable; the existence of eternal objects could not be established; while for Berkeley's visionary idealism, space and the things in it are 'merely imaginary entities' (CPR B 275; see also p. 293, p. 36 and p. 375, p. 114). Kant's reversal consisted in proposing a transcendental idealism which was also an empirical realism, one which proves that 'even our inner experience, which for Descartes is indubitable, is possible only on the assumption of outer experience' (CPR B 275). P gives a stronger version of this: 'All cognition of things merely from pure understanding or pure reason is nothing but sheer illusion, and only in experience is there truth' (p. 374, p. 113).

The terrain upon which Kant defended his 'transcendental' or 'critical' idealism consisted of the forms of intuition and the character of the 'I'. For transcendental idealism it is axiomatic that 'objects of experience . . . are *never* given *in themselves*, but only in experience, and have no existence outside it' (CPR A 492/B 521). The objects in the space of outer intuition and those in the time of inner intuition cannot be present without these forms of intuition. But, Kant adds, 'this space and this time, and with them all appearances, are not in themselves *things* [as a transcendental realist would claim]; they are nothing but representations, and cannot exist outside our mind' (CPR A 492/B 520). Similarly the pure concepts of the understanding generated by the spontaneity of the I are not themselves things, but are the conditions of the possibility of things. Both the forms of intuition and the concepts of the understanding originate in the subject, and may thus be described as 'idealist', but the way in which they organize experience is objectively valid. While it may be possible to postulate objective correlates as underlying the appearances of the subject and objects of experience in a 'transcendental subject' and a 'transcendental object', these are by no means necessary to secure the claims of transcendental or critical idealism.

Kant's transcendental idealism gave rise to a generation of idealist philosophers, whose leading representatives were Fichte and Schelling. Their idealism radicalized Kant's claims, placing more emphasis on the spontaneity of the I and demoting those aspects of empirical realism and sensibility which remained in Kant's account. Kant regarded this development as retrograde, a return to the forms of idealism which he had countered in CPR. His disquiet was reflected in an 'open letter' on Fichte's *Science of Knowledge* (1794) on 7 August 1799 in which he condemned the new idealism as 'mere logic' and berated its attempt 'to cull a real object out of logic' as a 'vain effort and therefore a thing that no one has ever done' (PC p. 253).

identity [*Identität*] *see also* APPERCEPTION, CONCEPTS OF REFLECTION, DIFFERENCE, I, PARALOGISM, PSYCHOLOGY, SUBJECT, UNITY

The notion of identity plays a variegated and complex role in Kant's philosophy. It features in the pre-critical writings as the logical 'supreme principle in the hierarchy of truths' and in the disputed Leibnizian ontological principle of the 'identity of indiscernibles'. In CPR it features in conjunction with difference as one of the concepts of reflection, and as the pre-categorical double of the category of unity. In the latter capacity it provides the guarantee for the extra-categorical 'logical' identity of the 'I' indispensable for experience.

In ND (1759) Kant moves from claiming that 'all reasoning amounts to uncovering the identity between predicate and subject' (p. 390, p. 9) to proposing as the supreme principle of truth the 'principle of identity' which states that 'whatever is, is, and whatever is not, is not' (p. 389, p. 7). His preference at this stage for the principle of identity arose out of his opposition to the Wolffian principle of contradiction, but already by the time of writing NM (1763) he is dissatisfied with both formal principles. He distinguishes there between the identity of logical ground and consequence and the identity of real cause and effect, claiming that 'the real ground is never a logical ground, and the rain is not posited by the wind by virtue of the rule of identity' (p. 203, p. 240). With this development Kant anticipated his later, critical distinction between formal and transcendental logic.

Another aspect of identity which Kant explores in the pre-critical writings is the Leibnizian law of the identity of indiscernibles. In §9 of his *Monadology* Leibniz argues that no two beings exist for which 'it would not be possible to find a difference that is internal or founded on an intrinsic denomination' (Leibniz, 1720, p. 62). Already in ND Kant disputes the 'metaphysical universality' (p. 410, p. 36) of the law, appealing to the difference of position between indiscernibles as sufficient to justify rejecting the law. This view of position, later developed into the spatial form of intuition of ID and CPR, marks another qualification of logical identity, here discussed in terms of 'internal denomination' by the real determination of spatial position.

Kant continues his critique of the law of indiscernibles in the section of CPR devoted to the concepts of reflection (A 260/B 316ff). Identity and difference are concepts of reflection which serve to orient judgement when it is presented with appearances. They denote characteristics of the spatial form of intuition, and not 'things in themselves'. Kant maintains that Leibniz regarded identity and difference as ontological characteristics of things rather than as products of the reflection upon the ways in which appearances are organized in terms of space, time and the categories. This for Kant resulted in the elision of the conditions of sensibility and the understanding, with the result that conceptual or logical identity and difference were confused with sensible or real identity and difference. This elision made possible the allegedly false claims of the law of indiscernibles, such as 'all things which are not distinguishable from one another in their concepts (in quality or quantity) are completely identical (*numero eadem*)' (A 281/B 337).

In CPR Kant rarely refers to the logical principle of identity, and indeed regards the principle of contradiction as the 'highest principle of analytical judgements'. Yet the logical application of the principle of identity maintains a crucial, if covert, position in the critical architecture. This becomes apparent when Kant discusses the identity of the transcendental subject or I. A number of interesting problems cluster around the transcendental subject: it is the subject which underlies and accompanies all acts of predication but which may not itself serve as a predicate, nor however can it be described as a substance. Kant insists that this is because substance is a category, and the I is prior to categorial determination; thus the I cannot be known in terms of the categories. The problem arises, however, of the numerical identity of the transcendental subject: it must be one to ensure the continuity of acts of predication, but it cannot be a unity since unity is a category of quantity, which cannot legitimately be applied to the transcendental subject.

Kant relies on the notion of identity as opposed to categorical unity in order to secure the transcendental subject. The self-conscious I of transcendental apperception must be 'fixed and abiding' and this 'numerical identity' must be one which 'precedes all experience, and which makes experience itself possible' (CPR A 107). Since it is the '*a priori* ground of all concepts' it cannot be properly determined by such concepts as unity and substance, and so in a difficult passage Kant derives the 'unity of consciousness' (how it appears to our category of unity) from the consciousness of 'the identity of function whereby it [unity] synthetically combines [the manifold] in one knowledge'. This is the 'original and necessary consciousness of the identity of the self' which informs the 'equally necessary unity of the synthesis of all appearances' (CPR A 108). Thus the identity of the transcendental subject secures the unity of its consciousness.

Kant is extremely careful not to attribute the categorial qualities of unity to identity. In the discussion of the third paralogism in the 1781 edition of CPR Kant refused to move from consciousness of numerical identity to the notion of a person. He insists that the 'identity of the consciousness of myself at different times is only a formal condition of my thoughts and their coherence, and in no way proves the numerical identity of my subject' (CPR A 363). Furthermore, the permanence of identity over time does not point to the I being a substance, but is itself the consequence of identity. In his 1787 restatement of the paralogisms in the second edition of CPR Kant underlines that the identity of the transcendental subject cannot be resolved into a 'simple substance' since this would require it to become an 'object of intuition' to which the categories of unity and substance would be applicable (CPR B 407–8). Were this to be admitted, the consequence would be the relegation of the identity of the transcendental subject which founds the categories into an object of the categories, thus converting the transcendental into an empirical subject, with catastrophic consequences for the critical project. Instead Kant chooses to restrict identity to the logical identity of a subject rather than to extend it to that of a thinking and unified substance.

illusion [*Schein*] *see also* AESTHETIC, APPEARANCE, BEAUTY, DIALECTIC, SUBREPTION, TRUTH

The analysis of the nature of illusion is one of the abiding themes of Kant's work, and the main motivation of his redefinition of metaphysics. As early as DS (1766) Kant programmatically declared metaphysics to be the 'science of the *limits of human reason*' which 'eliminate[s] the illusion and the vain knowledge which inflates the understanding' (DS p. 368, p. 354). He adopts a similar position in ID (1770), where metaphysics is called to purge itself of the illusory axioms and principles 'which deceive the understanding and which have disastrously permeated the whole of metaphysics' (ID §24). CPR, in accordance with this project, is divided into the analytic, which determines the limits of metaphysics, and a dialectic, or 'logic of illusion', which shows how these limits are transgressed by the reason in producing transcendent and thus illusory ideas.

Kant's understanding of the nature of illusion developed considerably between the pre-critical writings and CPR. In DS he focuses upon the illusions of the imagination which he understands by means of an analogy with optical illusion. He is here interested in the way in which 'spirit-seers' such as Emanuel Swedenborg 'transpose the illusion of their imagination and locate it outside themselves' (p. 343, p. 331). A similar view of illusion as a form of visual error also prevails in A (§13). Alongside this view of illusion as avoidable delusion in DS, Kant also hints at a more fundamental and unavoidable human tendency to illusion in his metaphor of the biased scale of human understanding, unavoidably weighted towards 'hope for the future' (DS p. 349, p. 337).

In ID Kant has considerably refined his account of illusion, concentrating upon 'illusions of the understanding' or 'subreptic axioms' 'which try to pass off what is sensitive as if it necessarily belonged to a concept of the understanding' (ID §24). He proposes to inquire into them further in order to discover a 'touchstone' by which to distinguish true from illusory judgements. To this end he presents three species of subreptic axioms or 'illusions of sensitive cognitions': the first is that the condition of the possibility of intuiting an object is taken for a condition of possibility for the object itself; the second that the sensitive conditions by which to compare what is given in order to form a concept are taken for conditions of the possibility of the object; and the third, that the sensitive conditions of

243

subsuming an object under a concept are taken to be conditions of the possibility of objects (ID §§26–9). In each case the illusion assayed consists in mistaking an appearance for the truth. In ID Kant still subscribes to Descartes' suspicions concerning the illusory nature of appearance *per se*, although he does begin to develop the distinction, crucial for the critical philosophy, between appearance and illusion. This distinction appears in *Concerning Sensory Illusion and Poetic Fiction* of 1777 (p. 203) and forms one of the central arguments of CPR.

In CPR Kant presents his mature analysis of illusion. He firmly distinguishes appearance from illusion in terms of judgement: the appearances given to the sensibility are not illusions but necessary appearances while 'truth and error . . . and consequently also illusion as leading to error, are only to be found in the judgement, *i.e.* only in the relation of the object to our understanding' (CPR A 293/B 350). Our understanding may, for example, falsely infer that things of appearance intuited through the forms of intuition (space and time) are not objects of appearance but things in themselves. In this case 'out of that which I ought to reckon as appearance, I [have] made mere illusion' (B 69). This development of the subreptic axioms of ID is crucial to the critical analysis of the limits of the understanding, but it is no longer the main focus of Kant's anatomy of illusion in CPR. This now lies in the 'transcendental illusion' of human reason which is surveyed in the 'Transcendental Dialectic' and its scrutiny of illusory inferences.

Kant opens the transcendental dialectic with an introduction entitled 'Transcendental Illusion' in which he distinguishes transcendental from the accidental and avoidable 'logical illusions' of fallacious judgements and the related 'empirical illusions' of subreption. Transcendental illusion is '*natural* and inevitable' (CPR A 298/B 354) and consists in the 'deceptive extension of [the concepts of] *pure understanding*' to their absolute conditions beyond the limits of possible experience. The transcendental dialectic is directed towards revealing the transcendent extension of the concepts of experience, and the necessary dialectic which it evokes, one which is 'inseparable from human reason, and which, even after its deceptiveness has been exposed, will not cease to play tricks with reason' (A 298/B 355). Kant describes three cases of the natural dialectic of transcendental illusion upon which are founded the 'pretend sciences' of psychology, cosmology and theology. In each case the properties of the 'subjective condition of thinking' are extended and regarded as 'knowledge of the object' (A 396), in these cases knowledge of objects such as the soul, the world as a whole and God. Kant goes on to show how in each case the sciences of these illusory objects succumb to a 'natural dialectic' and then gives an account, or a logic, of their illusions.

244

In CJ Kant develops a further account of illusion, in this case artistic illusion. The beautiful work of art must not appear as a product, but 'must be clothed *with the aspect* of nature, although we recognise it to be art' (CJ §45). This position was largely a consequence of the strict conditions which Kant established for a valid aesthetic judgement of taste in the 'Analytic of the Beautiful', which stripped such judgements of any reference to interest. The view that the work of art represents an illusory 'second nature' proved immensely significant for romantic aesthetics, and persisted long after the recognition of the limits of Kant's description of the aesthetic judgement of taste.

image [*Bild*] *see also* IMAGINATION, MANIFOLD, SCHEMATISM, SYNTHESIS
In Kant's critical architecture the image occupies the grey area between concept and intuition. As a form of mediation between the heterogeneous faculties of understanding and intuition it has a distinctly equivocal status. The image is understood both as a presentation of a concept to intuition, as with the concept of 'substance in *appearance*' which is presented as 'an abiding image of sensibility' (CPR A 525/B 553; see also OD p. 222, p. 136) and as something generated from the manifold of intuition and presented to the understanding. Most of Kant's discussion focuses on the latter, since the presentation of a concept to intuition is largely covered by the schema, which is a 'representation of a universal procedure of imagination in providing an image for a concept' (CPR A 140/B 179) rather than the concept itself. Schematism is the work of transcendental imagination which 'aims at no special intuition' while the discrete image is a product of empirical imagination. The generation of images by empirical imagination from the manifold of intuition is central to the account of synthesis in the 'deduction' of the first edition of CPR. Kant refers there to imagination as the 'active faculty for the synthesis of [the] manifold' (CPR A 120) and sees its work as the forming of an image through the syntheses of apprehension and reproduction. The image is then suited for presentation to the concepts of the understanding in order to be worked into knowledge.

The account of the generation of images from the manifold of intuition is both paralleled and extended in the account of the 'aesthetic normal idea' developed in CJ. Kant here tries to explain how the aesthetic normal idea may be normative without the subsumptive requirements of a concept. The problem is resolved into that of presenting an aesthetic idea '*in concreto* in a model image' (CJ §17), one whose solution can only be hinted at since 'who can wrest nature's whole secret from her?' (§17). The *Gemüt* superimposes several images of a particular object upon each other until arriving at a 'mean contour which serves as a common standard for all'. The latter phenomenon is illustrated by an analogy with the optical presentation of images where the mean contour is the 'place illuminated by the greatest concentration of colour' (§17). The 'mean contour' is neither a concept of the understanding nor simply a derivative of the manifold of intuition, but is 'a floating image for the whole genus, which nature has set as an archetype underlying those of her products that belong to the same species' (§17). With this account of the image, Kant seems both to supplement the account of the image under subsumptive, determinate judgement in CPR and to give substance to the workings of reflective judgement in CJ.

imagination [*phantasia, facultas imaginandi, Einbildungskraft*] *see also* AES-THETIC, GENIUS, ILLUSION, IMAGE, INTUITION, JUDGEMENT, REASON, SCHEMA(TISM), SYNTHESIS, UNDERSTANDING

In *De anima* Aristotle described imagination as 'different from either perceiving (*aisthesis*) or discursive thinking (*noesis*), though it is not found without sensation, or judgement without it' (Aristotle, 1941, 427b, 16). The peculiar, intermediate status of imagination, accepted by Aquinas as self-evident in his commentary on *De anima*, contributed to the considerable fascination of philosophers and artists with the concept. In the synthesis of Plato and Aristotle ventured by the Renaissance philosophers Ficino and Pico della Mirandola, imagination featured as the vehicle of participation between human sensation and the ideas, with the art of genius featuring prominently as the perfect expression of their unity (see Cassirer et al., 1948). Imagination maintained this elevated status in spite of the best efforts of Descartes to bring it down to earth 'by dissecting the heads of various animals' in search of it. Imagination posed considerable problems for rationalist philosophers such as Christian Wolff who saw its association with sensibility as detracting from the clarity and distinctness of rational thought. By the mid 1730s dissatisfaction with this position had led some Wolffians to call for a logic of the imagination and senses to complement that of the understanding. In the hands of the Wolffian lexicographer Heinrich Meissner this entailed subordinating imagination to empirical psychology, but for the philosopher A.G. Baumgarten and the critic Jacob Bodmer it led to the extension of philosophy to include aesthetics and poetics (see Caygill, 1989, chapter 3).

Kant's view of imagination was developed in this context, and displays several classical features, above all the intermediate status of imagination between sensibility and the understanding as well as its role in artistic production. However, he also gave it several characteristic inflections when situating it within the context of his broader philosophical concerns. With one signal exception Kant's discussion of imagination in the pre-critical writings is usually confined to berating its bad influence, as in the analysis of the illusions of imagination in DS (see p. 344, p. 331) and less directly ID (§27). Exceptionally in NM Kant offers a more sophisticated analysis which anticipates his later positions. He reflects on the ability to entertain and exclude a representation 'by virtue of the power of imagination' and sees its task as the bringing into existence and destruction of representation, rather than as a straightforward act of presentation and removal. He alludes to this activity as 'concealed within the depths of our minds which goes unnoticed even while it is being exercised' (p. 191, p. 229), terms which anticipate his latter description of the schematizing work of imagination as 'an art concealed within the depths of the human soul' (CPR A 141/B 181).

In the Blomberg Logic (L pp. 5–246) from the early 1770s imagination features as an obstacle to knowledge; there Kant maintains that 'From this mingling of the imagination with the understanding arise effects that do not agree perfectly with the rules of the understanding and of reason' (L p. 79). Yet by CPR , Kant's position on the imagination had undergone a near complete reversal. The extent of this change may be gathered from the comments on imagination in A, which to a large degree codify the assumptions about imagination which inform and underlie the three critiques (CPR, CPrR, CJ). These comments combine aspects of argument such as the place of imagination in logic and metaphysics (A §4) and in genius and taste (A §67) which were later separated and distributed between the first and third critiques.

Kant divides sensibility into sense (*Sinn*) and imagination, the former comprising the 'faculty of intuition in the presence of an object' and latter 'intuition without the presence of an object' (A §15). The non-presence of the object for imagination can be thought in two ways: either the object was present but is no longer, or its presence lies in the future. Considered from the standpoint of empirical imagination, this gives rise to the faculties of memory and prevision, which recollect and predict the presence of discrete objects. However, Kant also introduces another distinction within the concept of imagination which allows him to distinguish between (a) empirical or recollective imagination and (b) productive or poetic imagination. This is the distinction between imagination as 'a faculty of the original representation of the object (*exhibitio originaria*), which consequently precedes experience' and as 'a faculty of the derived representation (*exhibitio derivativa*), which recalls to mind a previous empirical perception' (A §28). It is the work of the productive imagination which most interests Kant, and which he puts to most use.

The reference to productive imagination producing an 'original representation of the object' prior to experience is a clear anticipation of Kant's critical idealism. He subsequently describes 'pure perceptions of space and time' as belonging to the productive faculty. What is crucial here is that the productive imagination produces *original* representations, i.e. they are not derived from experience but provide conditions of experience, and they are furthermore not wilful or accidental (this constitutes 'fantasy') but ordered. At this point the subsequently divided arguments of the first and third critiques overlap. Kant analyzes the 'three distinct varieties of the sensory productive faculty' of 'pictorial representation in space (*imaginatio plastica*), associative perception in time (*imaginatio associans*), and the sensory productive faculty of affinity' (A §31) in terms of artistic invention. The three forms of productive imagination testify to the 'common origin' or 'close union' of 'understanding and sensibility' (A §31), which also characterizes the original productions of genius (where 'imagination harmonises with concepts', §30) and the aesthetic judgement of taste with its 'judgement about the harmony or discord concerning the freedom of play between imagination and the law-abiding character of the imagination' (A §67). Yet the three modes of productive imagination also feature crucially as the 'three-fold synthesis' in the first critique's analysis of experience.

In both CPR and CJ imagination is situated both between sensibility and the understanding and beyond both them and itself. This paradoxical location may be clarified by the distinction between empirical and productive imagination, with the former situated between the other faculties and the latter encompassing them all. At several points in CPR, such as A 95, imagination attends to the synthesis of the manifold between the synopsis of sense and the unification of original apperception. Yet on other occasions synthesis in general is described as the 'result of the power of imagination, a blind but indispensable power of the soul, without which we should have no knowledge whatsoever, but of which we are scarcely ever conscious' (CPR A 78/B 103). The all-encompassing role given to imagination is consistently maintained in both A and B deductions. In the former the 'principle of the necessary unity of pure (productive) synthesis of imagination, prior to apperception, is the ground of the possibility of all knowledge, especially of experience' (CPR A 118) while in the latter imagination features as the spontaneous source of all synthesis (CPR B 152). It thus informs all the modes of the synthesis of the manifold of intuition – apprehension, reproduction and recognition – even while, as empirical imagination, serving as one of the discrete moments of synthesis, as well as featuring in the schematic synthesis of concept and intuition which generates knowledge and experience (see CPR A 140/B 179).

In CJ the discussion of imagination assumes even greater complexity. It appears in §VII of the 'First Introduction' in the context of the three-fold synthesis as a discrete faculty beside judgement and reason. But in the course of the work, the relationship between imagination and judgement, already adumbrated in CPR in terms of synthesis, is deepened. Imagination and judgement do not merely apply the laws of the understanding but in reflective judgement simultaneously invent and apply laws: that is, their function is not reproductive and imitative, but productive and original. Furthermore the 'unity' of imagination and judgement also evokes pleasure, as may be discerned most clearly in the aesthetic judgement of taste – with its 'conformity to law without a law, and [its] subjective harmonising of the imagination and the understanding without an objective one' (§22) – as well as in the productive activity of genius, whose primary quality is 'originality' or the 'talent for producing that for which no definite rule can be given' (§46).

The crucial role of imagination in Kant's philosophy was first urged by Heidegger (1929), and has since been widely accepted by Kant scholarship, although often without a full appreciation of its implications. These are not only textual in providing a bridge between the first and third critiques, but also substantive, transforming Kant from a normative philosopher concerned with rules and their correct application to one concerned with issues of production, originality and pleasure. It is, however, noteworthy that imagination does not feature prominently in Kant's practical philosophy, and where it is mentioned it is usually in a dismissive context, as in the discussion of the typic in CPrR (p. 69, p. 71). According to the reader's temperament, the absence of imagination from CPrR may be regarded as the saving grace of Kant's practical philosophy, or as good reason for seeking his practical philosophy in the pages of the first and third critiques.

imitation [*Nachahmung*] *see also* ENLIGHTENMENT, GENIUS, IDEA, IMAGINATION, ORIGINALITY

Kant was consistently critical of imitation, seeing the spirit of imitation as the worst of 'all the things that can only harm and be opposed to the philosophical spirit' (L p. 128). From his description of imitation as 'the cultivation of one's understanding, will, indeed, of choice, according to the example of others' it is clear that it is imitation which is castigated in WE as 'self-imposed tutelage' and which is given 'no place at all in moral matters' in GMM (p. 408, p. 21). On the question of artistic imitation in CJ, however, Kant's position is rather more nuanced. He distinguishes imitation as producing copies of the work of genius (*Nachmachung*) and imitation as an emulation or following (*Nachahmung*) which puts the follower's 'own talent to the test' of the comparison with the productivity of genius (CJ §47). In the latter case, the pupil's own talent and originality is stimulated by the example of genius, which thus 'arouses like ideas on the part of their pupil' (ibid.).

immanent *see* TRANSCENDENT

immortality *see also* I, FINITUDE, PARALOGISM, POSTULATE, PSYCHOLOGY, SOUL, SUBJECT

In CPR Kant claimed to have refuted speculative proofs of the immortality of the soul – such as those proposed by Moses Mendelssohn in *Phädon* (1767) – by exposing them as paralogistic (see CPR B 413ff). Such proofs depend on the assumption that the I as formal condition or logical subject of thought is also a substantial self which possesses the quality of permanence. While Kant conclusively destroyed the bases of such speculative proofs, this did not require him to abandon the conviction of immortality. It re-appears in CPrR along with freedom and God as a 'postulate of pure practical reason' which 'consigns to the subject the requisite duration' (p. 133, p. 138) that was denied it by the paralogisms which afflicted the speculative proof. The postulate of immortality, Kant observes, 'derives from the practically necessary condition of a duration adequate to the perfect fulfilment of the moral law' (p. 132, p. 137), a condition which is supported by its accompanying postulates of freedom and God. Subsequent writers, such as Heine (1965, p. 295) and Nietzsche (1882), rejected all three postulates either as Kant's attempts to placate his manservant Lampe or as lapses from the radical destruction of the speculative proofs accomplished in the transcendental dialectic of CPR. Both positions are probably unfair, although it is noteworthy that few contemporary defences of Kant's account of freedom and moral action refer to the other supposedly inseparable postulates of God and immortality.

impenetrability [*Undurchdringlichkeit*] *see also* EXTENSION, FORCE, MATTER

Impenetrability is defined as 'the fundamental property of matter whereby it first reveals itself as something real in the space of our external senses, [and] is nothing but matter's capacity of extension' (MF p. 508, p. 56). Although Kant seems to be working within the Cartesian view of matter as extension, this is quickly belied by the claim that the 'ground' of matter's impenetrability is its 'repulsive force'. For Descartes, impenetrability was part of the essence of extended substance, it was certainly not grounded in a repulsive force. In MF Kant criticizes this view as part of a 'mechanical mode of explication' which prevailed from Democritus to Descartes whose main assumption was 'the absolute impenetrability of the primitive matter' (MF p. 533, p. 91). His first published work, LF, which appeared fifty years before MF, had already attacked this view of matter with arguments for the presence of an active force in a body 'prior to extension' (§1). This position was quickly refined, and in PM and later NM Kant argued that the repulsive force evinced by impenetrability had to be countered by an opposed attractive force; if not, 'bodies would have no cohesive structure at all, for the particles would only repel each other' (PM ·p. 484, p. 61), an argument which also appears in MF. The 'force of impenetrability' thus 'prevents anything external from approaching more closely' (p. 484, p. 61) and is the property of a body which excludes another body in contact with it from the space which it occupies. Yet it is always limited by the force of attraction which does not operate through contact (Kant here has in mind the force of gravity). These forces not only constitute physical bodies, but also the elements of matter itself. Kant retained these positions in MF, adapting them only slightly to the new critical framework established by CPR.

imperative *see also* CATEGORICAL IMPERATIVE, COMMAND, HYPOTHETICAL
While the representation of an object which commands the will is a command, the formula of such a command is an imperative. Such formulas of command are always 'expressed by an *ought* and thereby indicate the relation of an objective law of reason to a will that is not necessarily determined by this law because of its subjective constitution (the relation of necessitation)' (GMM p. 413, p. 24). Imperatives thus recommend courses of action to refractory wills, necessitating them against their inclinations. Kant sees imperatives as taking several forms, but makes a fundamental division between hypothetical and categorical varieties. The former command hypothetically, by recommending a course of action appropriate to a particular end. If this end is a 'possible end' then the imperative is hypothetical and problematic or a 'rule of skill' of the form 'if you would achieve w and x, then do y and z'. If this end is 'presupposed as actual for all rational beings' (p. 415, p. 26), such as 'happiness', then the imperative is hypothetical and assertoric or a council of prudence of the form 'if you would be x (= happy) then do y'. By contrast, a categorical imperative 'declares an action to be of itself objectively necessary without any purpose' (p. 414, p. 25) and is thus an apodeictic law of morality expressed in the form 'Act only according to that maxim whereby you can at the same time will that it should become a universal law' (p. 421, p. 30).

impression [*Eindruck*] *see also* AFFECT, GEMÜT, RECEPTIVITY, REFLECTION, SENSIBILITY
Sense-impression was the main source of experience and knowledge for classical anti-Platonic sensualist and sceptical philosophies such as those of Democritus, Lucretius and Pyrrho. Diogenes Laertius reports that the Stoics regarded impressions and sense perception as prior to thought and the

source of the 'criterion which decides the truth of things'. They also divided impressions according to whether they were sensory or other than sensory, a distinction developed by their modern successors Locke and Hume in their distinction between sensible and reflected impressions. For Kant, the notion of an 'impression' became prominent in the pre-critical DS, the text where Kant is most anxious to secure the proper boundaries between 'real' and 'imaginary' experience. It maintains a somewhat underdeveloped but emphatic presence in Kant's account of the receptivity of sensibility, where it serves as the bottom line of perception, the matter of sense-perception. In ID, for example, the discovery that space and time are the formal elements of intuition is qualified by the claim that they, and other formal aspects of cognition, are not derived from sense impressions as 'reflected impressions' but are only excited into action by them; through them the mind 'joins together in a fixed manner the sense-impressions made by the presence of an object' (§15). Impressions have a similarly residual status in CPR, where the receptivity of the mind through which objects are given to us is defined as the 'receptivity for impressions' (A 50/B 74). It was necessary for Kant's 'critical idealism' to preserve the impressions in some form in order to avoid the Scylla of 'absolute idealism', but they had also to be marginalized in order to avoid the Charybdis of empiricism.

'Inaugural Dissertation' (On the Form and Principles of the Sensible and Intelligible World) *see* PRE-CRITICAL WRITINGS

incentive [*Triebfeder*] *see also* CATEGORICAL IMPERATIVE, DRIVE, IMPERATIVE, MOTIVE, PRACTICAL PHILOSOPHY, RESPECT, WILL
In GMM Kant distinguishes between the incentive as a 'subjective ground of desire' and the motive as the 'objective ground of volition' (p. 427, p. 35). Both supply ends for the determination of the will; the incentive supplies a subjective and the motive an objective end. Practical principles based on subjective ends and incentives are 'material' and relative to a particular subject, and can only supply grounds for hypothetical imperatives. By contrast, practical principles which abstract from subjective ends are formal, and potentially universalizable for all rational subjects and capable of serving as a categorical imperative.

Although Kant does not consider incentives as providing grounds for properly moral actions (they suffice only for rules of skill and counsels of prudence), he does explore the notion of a moral incentive in CPrR, chapter 3. There he defines incentive consistently with GMM as a 'subjective determining ground of a will whose reason does not by its nature necessarily conform to the objective law' (p. 72, p. 74), and acknowledges that this raises the 'insoluble problem for the human reason' of 'how a law in itself can be the direct determining ground of the will'. Instead of seeking an answer in terms of an incentive appropriate to the moral law, Kant asks instead what the moral law 'effects (or better, must effect) in the mind, so far as it is an incentive' (p. 72, p. 75). The answer is 'reverence for the law', not as the incentive to morality but as 'morality itself, regarded subjectively as an incentive', one which rejects the 'rival claims of self-love' and which as 'moral feeling' is 'an incentive to make this law itself a maxim' (p. 76, pp. 78–9).

inclination [*Neigung*] *see also* AFFECT, COMMAND, DUTY, FEELING, IMPERATIVE, INCENTIVE, INTEREST, PRACTICAL PHILOSOPHY, RESPECT, SENSIBLE WORLD, WILL
Kant's moral philosophy is structured around the opposition between duty and inclination. For him duty 'proudly rejects all kinship with the inclinations' (CPrR p. 87, p. 89); it is grounded in freedom from the world of sense in which inclination is firmly rooted. For this reason inclination is called in Kant's practical philosophy to represent the subjective, materially founded and partial aspects of human moral experience which are countered by the objective, formal and universal categorical imperative. Inclination is 'the dependence of the faculty of desire on sensations . . . which accordingly always indicates a need' (GMM p. 413, p. 24), and for Kant to possess a will determined exclusively by inclination is to be without spontaneity, merely reacting to stimuli, a condition Kant describes as 'animal choice (*arbitrium brutum*)' (MM p. 213, p. 42). Human choice can be affected but not determined by inclination, which for Kant serves only to undermine the freedom of the will. Inclination, then, is the source for the heteronomy of the will, namely its determination by objects outside of the will; in its case the will 'does not give itself the law, but the object does so because of its relation to the will' (GMM p. 441, p. 45). The objects of inclination have only a 'conditioned value'; that is, they are not desired 'for their own sake' but only for the sake of satisfying ends outside of them, namely the needs of inclination (GMM p. 427, p. 35). This for Kant makes them unworthy to serve as principles of moral judgement, for as they cannot be universalized they can only serve as the basis of hypothetical and not categorical imperatives.

incongruent counterparts [*inkongruentes Gegenstück*] *see also* INTUITION, ORIENTATION, SPACE
Kant's most extended discussion of incongruent counterparts is to be found in DRS (1768) where it forms the core of his proof in support of Newtonian absolute space against the view of his Leibnizian contemporaries that space 'consists in the external relation of the parts of matter

which exist alongside each other' (p. 383, p. 371). He argues that 'the complete determination of a corporeal form does not depend simply on the relation and position of its parts to each other; it also depends on the reference of that physical form to universal absolute space' (p. 381, p. 369). A counterpart of an object is one which is identical to it with respect to its definition and internal relations, as in Kant's example of the right and the left hand. He argues that even if the counterparts are formally identical, there remains an 'inner difference' which consists in the property that 'the surface enclosing the one cannot possibly enclose the other' (p. 383, p. 371). This inner difference relates 'exclusively to *absolute* and *original space*' since it would be inexplicable on the premises of Leibnizian relative space. Kant maintained an interest in topological arguments even after he had rejected the concept of absolute space; the notions of directionality and orientation implied in his discussion of incongruent counterparts are explored in his essay on orientation (WO) and are germane to his understanding of space and geometry.

individual *see* MONAD, PERSON

induction [*Induktion*] *see also* DEDUCTION, INFERENCE
Induction is defined in the 'Blomberg Logic' as an inference of the form 'what belongs to as many things as I have ever cognised must also belong to all things that are of this species and genus' (L p. 232). He describes this form of inference as a 'crutch' for the understanding, without which most of our cognition would be impossible, but one which is 'completely opposed to logical rule'. In the 'Hechsel Logic' he expands on the latter point by maintaining that the 'universality' of the inference is only empirical, as opposed to rational universality in which 'what I attribute to the concept universally actually does belong to all the things without exception' (p. 408). The ground of such rational universality is the principle of contradiction, which informs deductive inferences.

In CPR the logical point concerning induction is extended to the universality and necessity of the rules of synthesis proper to synthetic a priori judgements. While analytical judgements are justified according to the principle of contradiction, this does not suffice to justify synthetic a priori judgements. The categories possess a strict universality and necessity which can be justified by neither the principle of contradiction nor through induction. This is exemplified by the category of cause discussed in the second analogy. Kant criticizes the inductive derivation of the concept of cause from the 'perception and comparison of events repeatedly following in a uniform manner upon preceding appearances' for yielding only an 'empirical' and 'fictitious' universality and necessity (CPR A 196/B 241).

He maintains that only the transcendental turn will supply the desired criteria, and furthermore, that it underlies the very possibility of induction: 'We can extract clear concepts of [a priori representations] from experience, only because we have put them into experience, and because experience is thus itelf brought about only by their means' (A 196/B 241).

inference [*Aufschliessen*] *see also* ANTINOMIES, DIALECTIC, IDEAS, ILLUSION, LOGIC, PARALOGISMS

Kant distinguished the *immediate* knowledge that, say, in a figure bounded by three straight lines there are three angles from the *inferred* knowledge that the sum of these angles is equal to two right angles. The inference consists in the logical sequence which moves from the truth of a fundamental proposition or judgement to the conclusion that is drawn from it. A case in which the conclusion is directly drawn from the fundamental judgement is an immediate 'inference of the understanding'. Inferences of reason are those which require at least one further judgement in addition to the primary one in order to secure a conclusion. The classic example of a mediated inference is the syllogism, whose three parts – (a) major premise, (b) minor premise and (c) conclusion – are rephrased by Kant in terms of (a) understanding thinking of a rule, (b) judgement subsuming under a rule, (c) reason determining the predicate of the rule (CPR A 304/B 361). Kant believed that faulty inferences lay at the root of illusion and error. Fallacious inferences of the understanding 'treat as being immediately perceived what has really only been inferred' (A 303/B 359), while those of reason arise from drawing conclusions which exceed the limits of experience, converting the predicates of rules of the understanding employed in the major premises into unconditioned totalities. Kant analyzes three forms of dialectical inference: the first moves from the transcendental concept of the subject to the absolute unity of the subject and takes the form of a paralogism; the second moves from the series of conditions for an appearance to the absolute totality of these conditions and takes the form of antinomy, while the third moves from the totality of conditions of an object of experience to those of objects in general and generates 'the dialectical syllogism I shall entitle the *ideal* of pure reason' (A 340/B 398).

infinity [*Unendlichkeit*] *see also* ANTINOMIES, IMMORTALITY, MATHEMATICS, TIME, WORLD

The paradoxes generated by attempts to conceive of the infinite have proven a perennial problem for philosophers since the early Greek speculations of Anaximander, Parmenides and Zeno. A.W. Moore (1990) has helpfully distinguished between metaphysical and mathematical infinity, and shown how the paradoxes of infinitely big, infinitely small, and the one and the many arise from the application to space and time of the endless divisibility and iteration of a mathematical series. These paradoxes, classically stated by Zeno (Barnes, 1987, pp. 150–8) were criticized by Aristotle who sought to redefine the terms of thinking the infinite by means of the distinction between potential and actual. An actual infinite would have to exist in time, a potential infinite over time; yet the former would require traversing the infinite in time, which contradicted the original notion of the infinite (see Moore, 1990, p. 40).

Kant's response to the speculative problems of the infinitely large and infinitely small in the first two 'cosmological' antinomies of CPR pursues a similar strategy of argument. The infinitely large or small cannot be objects of experience, and are illusions produced by the dialectical inferences of the reason. In the first antinomy Kant opposes the thesis that the world has a beginning in time and is limited in space with the antithesis that it has no beginning and no limits in space and is infinite with regard to both (CPR A 426/B 454). The second antinomy concerns the infinite divisibility of the substance of the world, with the thesis maintaining that composite substances are composed of simple parts and that only they can exist, opposed by the antithesis that no composite thing is made up of simple parts, and that simples do not exist (A 434/B 462). Kant subscribes to neither position, but uses them to show the dialectical consequences provoked by reason's attempt to infer absolute, unconditioned consequences from premises conditioned by finite human understanding.

While theoretical philosophy has to recognize the dialectical character of applying the mathematical infinite to nature, Kant insists that metaphysical infinitude in the guise of immortality be granted as a postulate of pure practical reason. In the celebrated concluding apostrophe to CPrR, on 'the starry heavens above and the moral law within', Kant contrasts the infinity of the cosmos whose 'countless multitude of worlds annihilates . . . my importance as an animal creature' to the infinitude of personality revealed by the moral law from which may be inferred 'a vocation which is not restricted to the conditions and limits of this life, but reaches into the infinite' (p. 162, p. 166). Thus in a form of dialectical opposition, the inability of theoretical reason to comprehend the infinite is countered by the moral law's intimations of immortality.

Kant's reflections on the infinite were extremely critical for the development of transcendental idealism. Fichte, Schelling and above all Hegel sought ways of 'thinking the absolute' or returning the infinite to theoretical philosophy. For Hegel (1812, 1830), Kant had developed a 'bad infinity' in both his theoretical and practical investigation of the concept. The infinities criticized in CPR were 'bad infinities' of the endless mathematical series extending to the infinitely large and descending to the infinitely small. Similarly, the infinity postulated in the practical philosophy was one which made morality an 'endless task', something to be striven for across the whole of eternity. In place of these views of infinity, Hegel proposed an actual infinity similar to that of Aristotle, one in which the infinite was not simply viewed as negation of the finite but as actualized within it, and where ethical life (as opposed to Kantian 'morality') could be made actual within this life and did not require the endless task implied by the postulate of immortality.

innate ideas *see also* ABSTRACTION, ACQUISITION, CATEGORIES, IDEA
In the *New Essays on Human Understanding* Leibniz opposed Locke's account of the abstraction of ideas from sense impressions with one which stressed the role of innate ideas. Such ideas as '*being, possible* and *same* are so thoroughly innate that they enter into all our thoughts and reasoning' (Leibniz, 1765, p. 102); they are presupposed by perception, not abstracted from it. Kant shared with Leibniz the critique of empiricist accounts of concept formation, but in his early writings distinguished his position from that of Leibniz. Already in ID (1770) the concepts of metaphysics are 'not to be sought in the senses' but nor are they 'innate concepts'; for Kant such concepts are acquired by abstraction 'from 'the laws inherent in the mind' (ID §8). The difference between this and Leibniz's view is very subtle, and led to inevitable misunderstandings of the CPR which Kant clarified in his reply to Eberhard's Leibnizian critique in OD. There he insists that the forms of intuition and the categories are 'acquired and not innate' and presuppose 'nothing innate except the subjective conditions of the spontaneity ·of thought (in accordance with the unity of apperception)' (p. 223, p. 136).

inner/outer [*das Innere und Äussere*] *see also* CONCEPTS OF REFLECTION, IDENTITY, ILLUSION, OPPOSITION
This opposition, along with those of identity and difference, agreement and opposition, and matter and form comprise the concepts of reflection discussed in CPR. These are concepts employed by the judgement prior to synthesis, and serve to assign representations to the intuition or the understanding. If these concepts are applied directly to experience, they give rise to amphibolies such as those Kant identified in the work of Locke and Leibniz, who respectively 'intellectualised appearances' and 'sensualised all concepts of the understanding' (CPR A 271/B 327). In the case of inner and outer, the amphiboly consisted in relational concepts for the orientation of concept and intuition being taken for objective qualities; instead of marking a .relation between objects and our judgements they

257

are improperly considered to be objective relations between things. The illusions to which this amphiboly gives rise are a species of the illusions of the understanding first discussed in DS in terms of the confusion of inner and outer.

inner sense [*innere Sinn*] *see also* APPERCEPTION, INTUITION, JUDGEMENT, SENSE, SENSIBILITY, TIME

In FS Kant finds the 'mysterious power which makes judging possible' and so distinguishes humans as rational beings from animals to be 'nothing other than the faculty of inner sense, that is to say, the faculty of making one's own representations the objects of one's thoughts' (FS p. 60, p. 104). Kant does not follow Descartes and later Mendelssohn in seeing inner sense as the source for the certainty of the subject's existence in the *cogito* or 'I think', but distinguishes rigorously between inner sense and the pure apperception of the *cogito*. The perceptions of inner sense are psychologically founded and have no transcendental reference; the psychological subject that experiences inner sense is not to be confused with the transcendental subject of the 'I think'. The latter is the spontaneous source of synthesis, while the former, as a sense, is receptive. This distinction is taken as axiomatic in CPR, for without it there arises the paradox that the I must be both active/spontaneous and passive/receptive, thus requiring us 'to be in a passive relation [of active affection] to ourselves'. It is to avoid this contradiction, Kant continues, that he carefully distinguishes psychological inner sense 'from the faculty of apperception' (CPR B 153).

Kant further undermines the Cartesian primacy of the inner sense by adopting Wolff's view of the inseparability of the consciousness of self and of the world. Both inner and outer senses are 'necessarily bound up' with each other 'if experience is to be possible at all' (CPR B xli). With the outer sense 'we represent to ourselves objects as outside us, and all without exception in space' (CPR A 22/B 37): space is the pure form of its sensible intuition, through which external objects are determined or determinable in terms of 'shape, magnitude, and relation to one another'. By means of inner sense the 'mind' (*Gemüt*) 'intuits itself or its inner state' not as an object but as the 'determinate form in which alone the intuition of inner states is possible' (A 23/B 37). The form of inner sense is time, and determines the 'relation of representations in our inner state' and the 'immediate condition of inner appearances (of our souls), and thereby the mediate condition of outer appearances' (A 34/B 51). Kant indeed privileges the inner over the outer sense, although without denying the indispensability of each to the other. 'Time', he says, 'is an *a priori* condition of all appearance whatsoever' (ibid.) since all representations, whether their objects are internal or external, must be objects of the inner sense. At this point his strong distinction between psychological and transcendental subjectivity protects him from any reproach of idealism, since time as the form of inner sense is receptive and cannot be said to constitute appearances.

intelligible world [*mundus intelligibilis*] *see also* APPEARANCE, KINGDOM OF ENDS, NOUMENON, SENSIBILITY, TRANSCENDENT, TRANSCENDENTAL, TRANSCENDENTAL OBJECT, WORLD

In CPR Kant criticizes the use by 'modern philosophers' of the 'expressions *mundus sensibilis* and *intelligibilis*' for leading to an 'empty play on words' (A 257/B 312). The usage he criticizes regards the 'sensible world' as the 'sum of appearances, in so far as they are intuited' and the 'intelligible world' as the relations between appearances as they are 'thought in conformity with the laws of understanding'. As an example of this misplaced distinction he cites the 'sensible world' of observational astronomy and the intelligible world of theoretical astronomy according to Copernicus and Newton. He notes that this distinction illegitimately moves from sensible and intellectual ways of knowing to sensible and intellectual objects.

Kant's own distinction, first developed in ID (*On the Form and Principles of the Sensible and Intelligible World*), is stated in terms of the subjective form and principles of the sensible world, or the 'universal connection of all things, in so far as they are phenomena' and the objective principle or cause of the intelligible world 'in virtue of which there is a combining together of the things which exist in themselves' (ID §13). He does not regard the latter in terms of invisible forces such as gravity, and indeed says very little about it; most of his discussion concentrates upon space and time as the subjective principles of the sensible world. Even in section 4 of ID, entitled 'On the Principle of the Form of the Intelligible World', Kant is remarkably reticent about this principle which should combine the plurality of substances. His characterization closest to a definition is the negative one of the intelligible as 'devoid of all that is *given* in human intuition' (ID §10).

This reticence is justified in CPR, where Kant claims that 'intelligible objects' or 'those things thought through pure categories' without schemas of sensibility, cannot be objects of experience (CPR A 286/B 342). Yet he also considers it undeniable that such objects can be thought, and furthermore that they accompany sensible knowledge, as is suggested in his definition of the intelligible as 'whatever in an object of the senses is not itself appearance' (A 538/B 566). Nevertheless, there can be no knowledge of intelligible objects except as noumena or problematic objects whose existence can be neither proved nor disproved. And if intelligible objects are inadmissible as objects of positive knowledge, what of an intelligible world or totality of such objects (ID §§32 and 34)? Such a world, Kant notes in the observation appended to the first antinomy, 'is nothing but the general concept of a world in general, in which abstraction is made from all conditions of its intuition' (CPR A 433/B 462). The transcendent use of such a general concept would regard the intelligible world as lying outside the sensible world and serving as the transcendental ground or model of the latter. This broadly Platonic view of the intelligible world as an existent realm behind appearances is disallowed by Kant; what is permitted is the transcendental use of the concept in terms of an intelligible cause which 'signifies only the purely transcendental and to us unknown ground of the possibility of the sensible series in general' (CPR A 564/B 592).

From the standpoint of CPR the only permissible intelligible world is the 'moral world, in the concept of which we leave out of account all the hindrances to morality' (A 809/B 837). The main object of this world is freedom, which is in turn evinced in the 'intelligible character' of the subject 'free from all influence of sensibility' (A 541/B 569). It is freedom which signifies the 'intelligible cause' which grounds the intelligible character of causality. While the empirical character of causality connects appearances with appearances in the sensible world, the intelligible character grounds the series of efficient causes in a 'law of causality' which is not itself subject to efficient cause (A 539/B 567). The latter is transcendental, that is to say, a condition of the extension of thought which cannot itself ever be an object of thought. With this Kant aligns the sensible and intelligible worlds with the worlds of nature and freedom, which he says 'can exist together without any conflict, in the same actions, according as their actions are referred to their intelligible or to their sensible cause' (A 541/B 569). In GMM the intelligible world is identified with the 'world of rational beings (*mundus intelligibilis*) as a kingdom of ends' (p. 438, p. 43) which human beings partially inhabit; they are not, however, 'solely members of the intelligible world' since all their actions would then 'perfectly conform to the principle of the autonomy of a pure will' (GMM p. 54, p. 453).

intellectual intuition *see* INTUITION

interest *see also* AESTHETIC, AGREEABLE, CATEGORICAL IMPERATIVE, DRIVE, GOOD, INCLINATION, IMPERATIVE, INCENTIVE, PRACTICAL PHILOSOPHY, REASON, RESPECT
Interest is a term which features in each of the three critiques, but with slightly different meanings. In CPR the 'twofold interest' of reason manifests itself in the diverse ways of thinking of the 'students of nature'. Those whose interest makes them 'hostile to heterogeneity are always on the

watch for the unity of the genus', while those whose interest is more empirically directed 'are constantly endeavouring to differentiate nature' (A 655/B 683), with the former stressing the search for the genus, the latter the search for the species. In this theoretical context, interest signifies a pre-commitment to a mode of thought which is not itself rationally founded.

The use of interest in the practical philosophy is quite distinct from the use in CPR, and is also more precisely defined. In GMM Kant distinguishes between (a) pure and practical and (b) mediate and pathological forms of reason. Both signify the dependence of a 'contingently determinable will on principles of reason', but the interest of the former 'indicates only dependence of the will on principles of reason by itself' while the latter indicates dependence 'for the sake of inclination' (GMM p. 413, p. 24). The former interest is directed towards an action for its own sake, the latter towards an 'object of action (so far as this object is pleasant for me)'; that is, it regards the principles of reason as means to achieving the ends set by inclination. In the case of the immediate interest of reason, the 'universal validity of the maxim of action is a sufficient determining ground of the will', while in the pathologically mediated interest reason can only determine the will 'by means of another object of desire or under the presupposition of some special feeling in the subject' (GMM p. 460, p. 59). What is at stake in this distinction is the choice between the autonomy or the heteronomy of the moral law; whether we are interested in the moral law for heteronomous, pathologically mediated reasons, or whether 'the moral law interests us because it is valid for us as human beings' (p. 461, p. 60).

In CPR Kant combines the speculative and the practical interests of reason into the questions '1. What can I know? 2. What ought I to do? 3. What may I hope?' (A 805/B 833). The first is a speculative interest, which Kant deems satisfied by the answer supplied in CPR. The second interest is practical and can only be satisfied by a moral answer. The third interest is satisfied by the 'worthiness of being happy' (A 806/B 834). The 'interests' evoked by these questions are not discrete ends desired by reason, but rather denote its basic orientation in the world.

In CJ Kant defines the quality of the aesthetic judgement of taste as 'apart from any interest' (§5), whether pure or pathological. The pure interest in the good and the pathological interest in the agreeable link the subject's desire with 'the real existence of the object' (§5) which vitiates the contemplative character of the aesthetic judgement of taste. This should be concerned only with the pleasure and displeasure evoked by the object. Quite what this entails remains unclear in CJ, whose argument proceeds by negation of existing accounts of aesthetic judgement. The interest in the object evinced by the agreeable refers to the accounts of beauty given by the British theory of taste in the eighteenth century, that in the good to the Wolffian account of beauty as a confused perception of perfection. Both are informed by an interest in their respective objects, but one which Kant shows cannot serve as the basis for a judgement of the beautiful, even though in the case of natural beauty, the intellectual interest may contribute to the pleasure evoked by the object (CJ §42).

interest of reason *see* HAPPINESS, HOPE, INTEREST, KNOWLEDGE

international relations *see* FEDERATION OF STATES, GEOGRAPHY, HISTORY, PERPETUAL PEACE, POLITICS, WAR

interpretation [*Auslegung*]
In CF Kant distinguishes between the authentic and doctrinal interpretations of a biblical text. In the former 'exegesis must conform literally (philologically) with the author's meaning', while in the latter the interpreter is obliged 'to ascribe to the text (philosophically) the meaning it admits of for formally moral purposes (the pupil's edification); for faith in a merely historical proposition is, in itself, dead' (CF p. 66, p. 121). Kant applies this distinction between interpreting the letter and the spirit to the interpretation of his philosophical predecessors. In OD he describes CPR as 'the genuine apology for Leibniz' against his partisans who, like many historians of philosophy, 'cannot comprehend the purpose of these philosophers because they neglect the key to the interpretation of all products of pure reason from mere concepts, the critique of reason itself'. They remain confined to authentic and ignore the doctrinal interpretation of the philosophical text, and, in Kant's concluding words, are 'incapable of recognizing beyond what the philosophers actually said, what they really meant to say' (OD p. 251, p. 160).

intuition [*Anschauung*] *see also* A PRIORI, AESTHETIC, AXIOMS, FORM, INNER SENSE, MATHEMATICS, RECEPTIVITY, SENSE, SENSIBILITY, SPACE, TIME, TRANSCENDENTAL OBJECT
In the Aristotelian tradition there was considerable perplexity concerning the relationship between Aristotle's account of intuitive and demonstrative knowledge in the *Posterior Analytics* and the account of intelligible and sensible perception (*noesis* and *aisthesis*) in *De anima*. In the *Posterior Analytics* Aristotle claims that the 'primary premises' of scientific knowledge are apprehended intuitively, and that intuition is the 'originative source of scientific knowledge' (Aristotle, 1941, 100b). Intuitive apprehension is thus immediate as opposed to the mediated, discursive knowledge of scientific demonstration. According to *De anima*, knowledge arises out of the abstraction of *noeta* from *aistheta*, but with the proviso that the sensible

and intelligible elements thought separately do not exist separately, or in Aristotle's words, 'that the mind which is actively thinking is the objects which it thinks' (Aristotle, 1941, 431b, 18).

The perplexity facing the tradition was whether to unite these two accounts of knowledge, and if so, in what way. Apart from denying any relationship between them, there were basically three available options. One was to emphasize the Platonic elements in Aristotle, and to identify immediate intuitive knowledge with the *noeta*; another was to identify intuitive knowledge with sense perception or *aistheta*; while a third was to postulate a group of objects occupying an intermediate position between *noeta* and *aistheta* (see Wolfson, 1962, Vol. II, p. 156). In formal terms, Kant's doctrine of intuition adumbrated in ID and developed in CPR may be situated within the terms of the third option, but emphasizing the paradoxical character of such intermediate objects.

Prior to Kant, Descartes and Spinoza distinguished radically between intuitive and other forms of knowledge. Although Descartes makes great play in the *Rules for the Direction of the Mind* (1628) of 'paying no attention' to the 'way in which particular terms have of late been employed in the schools', his professedly 'new use of the term *intuition*' departs little from the Aristotelian tradition. He distinguishes it from the 'testimony of the senses' and defines it as an 'undoubting conception of an unclouded and attentive mind [which] springs from the light of reason alone' (Rule III). Unlike deductive knowledge it is immediate and simple, and is exemplified by the individual's 'intuition of the fact that they exist, and that they think'. Spinoza in *Ethics* (1677) followed Descartes in distinguishing between three forms of knowing: knowledge of opinion grounded in the senses and imagination (broadly Aristotle's *aistheta*), knowledge of reason grounded in common notions or concepts (*noeta*) and, finally, immediate, intuitive knowledge of the formal essence of the attributes of God and things in general (1985, pp. 475–8).

Both Descartes and Spinoza lean towards a Platonic view of intuitive knowledge which prefers the immediate knowledge of the intelligible realm to the mediated knowledge of the senses. Locke in *An Essay Concerning Human Understanding* agreed that intuitive knowledge was not only immediate, but also 'the clearest and most certain that human frailty is capable of' (Locke, 1690, p. 272). Yet for him this knowledge is not derived from the intelligible *noeta*, as it was with Descartes and Spinoza, but from the objects of external perception: 'there can be nothing more certain than that the *idea* we receive from an external object is in our minds: this is intuitive knowledge' (p. 277). This knowledge is immediate, but oriented more towards *aistheta* than to *noeta*. Leibniz, in his critique of Locke in the *New Essays on Human Understanding* (completed 1705 but published in 1765), attempted to reconcile Descartes and Locke by proposing intuitive truths of both fact and reason (Leibniz, 1765, pp. 361–7), but his follower and popularizer Christian Wolff confined intuitive knowledge to the direct intuition of rational perfection. This view in its turn was criticized by the heretical Wolffian A.G. Baumgarten, who argued for the intuitive knowledge of rational perfection by way of sensible perception, a form of knowledge he christened 'aesthetic'.

Kant's doctrine of intuition must be situated within the agenda established by Aristotle. He remained consistent with the Aristotelian tradition in respect of the direct, unmediated character of intuition, but established his own variant of it which refused the opposition of direct knowledge between the rationalists' *noeta* or the empiricists' *aistheta*. While Kant situates intuition at the level of sensibility or *aisthesis* in the 'Transcendental Aesthetic' of CPR (that is, below the understanding and the reason), he also accords it an a priori formal character, managing in this way to stress the immediate, sensible element in knowledge without being Lockean, and the a priori, formal element without being Cartesian. It was essential to establish this balance in order to satisfy one of the major conditions required 'for solution of the general problem of transcendental philosophy: *how are synthetic a priori judgements possible?*' (CPR B 73). Such judgements synthesize concepts with sensible intuitions which, while heterogeneous to them, nevertheless possess an a priori, intelligible character.

Most of the elements of Kant's doctrine of intuition are present in §10 of ID. He begins by claiming that 'There is (for man) no intuition of what belongs to the understanding . . . thinking is only possible for us by means of universal concepts in the abstract, not by means of a singular concept in the concrete'. Here he subscribes to the orthodox distinction between the immediate knowledge of intuition, and the mediated knowledge of the understanding. The human understanding can only function 'discursively by means of general concepts', but for Kant this does not exclude the possibility of other, differently constituted, understandings and intuitions. The ones which he considers in §10 are intellectual and divine intuition, both of which return in CPR. Intellectual intuition consists in a direct, intellectual knowledge of things in themselves rather than as appearances in space and time (CPR B 307) while divine intuition is productive, producing the objects which it thinks rather than being passively affected by given objects in the manner of human intuition (ibid.).

In the second sentence of §10 Kant writes that 'all our intuition is bound to a certain principle of form, and it is only under this form that anything can be *apprehended* by the mind immediately or as *singular*, and not merely conceived discursively by means of general concepts'. With this he converts intuition from an adjectival characteristic of knowledge into

264

a faculty of knowledge. The faculty of intuition possesses a 'certain principle of form' through which the mind may directly apprehend the concrete singularity of things and not subsume them as instances of abstract and general concepts. In this sentence Kant presents the central paradox of his account of intuition: that it directly apprehends objects yet does so by means of formal principles. This quality of intuition recurs repeatedly in CPR where intuition is both the 'immediate relation' (*sic*) to objects and takes place 'only in so far as the object is given to us' (CPR A 20/B 34).

In the third sentence of ID §10 the formal principles of intuition are revealed as space and time, which are further specified as the conditions 'under which something can be an object of our senses'. Although in ID Kant lists the properties space and time possess as pure intuitions – they are 'singular', neither 'innate' nor 'acquired', both the conditions of sensations and excited into action by them – he does not venture a proof of why they are the conditions for the objects of our senses. This he supplies in CPR and P by means of the analytic and synthetic methods. In the 'Transcendental Aesthetic' of CPR Kant analyzes or breaks sensibility down into its elements. He proposes first to '*isolate* sensibility, by taking away from it everything which the understanding thinks through its concepts' (CPR A 22/B 36). This leaves nothing 'save empirical intuition' from which is separated 'everything which belongs to sensation, so that nothing may remain save pure intuition and the mere form of appearances'. These are then found to be 'the forms of sensible intuition' namely space and time. In P Kant argues synthetically from the forms of intuition to sense objects. He argues that intuitions of present things are not possible without a 'ground of relation between my representation and the object' (§9) which '*precedes all the actual impressions through which I am affected by objects*'; without the a priori forms of intuition to relate the I and its objects, there would be no experience of objects (see also CPR B 132).

In CPR Kant offers proofs for why only space and time qualify as forms of intuition. The one he seems to find most compelling holds that while all concepts except space and time presuppose 'something empirical', space and time are pure and a priori: space does not occupy space and time does not suffer alteration in time (CPR A 41/B 58). This argument also validates the transcendental status of space and time, namely that they are conditions of spatio-temporal experience and cannot be abstracted from sensation or the nature of thinking substance. This accords with the view stated in ID §10 that the forms of intuition provide 'the condition of sensitive cognition' and are prior to sensitive cognition and not derived from it. But this claim sits uneasily with the view that intuition is passive, that the 'matter of cognition' is *given* through the senses, and that intuition is 'only possible in so far as it is possible for something to affect our sense' (ibid.). Intuition here seems both to provide the conditions *for* something to affect our sensibility, and to be conditioned *by* something affecting it.

The paradoxical character of intuition as both condition of and conditioned by objects of sense is used in ID to prevent noumena being 'conceived by means of representations drawn from sensations'. It is further employed in CPR to underpin the critique of claims that space and time are more than the forms which structure our intuition. The latter development is already implied in the distinction between representation and sensation mentioned in ID §10, which anticipates the crucial critical distinction between appearance and sensation in CPR. Appearances are divided into sensation, or 'matter of appearance', and the 'form of appearance', or space and time. The latter are in a state of potentiality, or in Kant's words 'lie ready for the sensations *a priori* in the mind' (CPR A 20/B 34), and are activated by sensation. In this way the notion of appearance makes it possible for the forms of intuition to be regarded as potentially prior to (but in actuality posterior to) sensation or the matter of intuition. A further complexity arises here, which is that the matter of intuition which is directly intuited cannot be considered as objects in themselves, but are already constituted as appearances, since it is axiomatic for Kant 'that the things we intuit are not in themselves what we intuit them as being' (CPR A 42/B 59). This is again paradoxical since it requires that we consider intuition both as direct knowledge of objects, namely 'the things we intuit', and as a mediated appearance or 'what we intuit them as being' (ibid.).

When the perspective on intuition shifts from the relationship between intuition and objects of sense to that between intuition and understanding, an analogous set of paradoxes manifest themselves. It is vital for the critical project that the concepts of the understanding and the forms of intuition be generically distinguished. Intuition corresponds to the 'passive' or 'receptive' aspect of human experience and the understanding to the part played in it by the active, spontaneous synthesis of apperception. While the two must be rigorously distinguished from each other, they must also be related in synthetic a priori judgements. Kant noted this in the lapidary sentence 'Thoughts without content are empty, intuitions without concepts are blind' (CPR A 51/B 75), from which he concluded that concepts must be made sensible and intuitions intelligible without either exchanging their proper function and domain.

The results presented in the 'Transcendental Logic' of CPR show how the *aistheta* and the *noeta* of the tradition may be brought into relation without either being subordinated to the other. In this way the critical philosophy both respects the received Aristotelian distinction, while reconfiguring it in accordance with a doctrine of intuition which combines sensible and intelligible aspects.

J

judgement [*krinein, iudicium, Urteil*] *see also* CANON, DETERMINANT JUDGEMENT, FACULTY OF JUDGEMENT, INFERENCE, PRINCIPLES, REFLECTIVE JUDGEMENT, SCHEMATISM, SUBSUMPTION, SYNTHESIS, UNITY

Judgement provides the matrix of Kant's entire philosophy. Each of the three critiques is directed towards the analysis of a particular class of judgement: theoretical judgements in CPR, practical judgements in CPrR, and aesthetic and teleological judgements in CJ. Moreover, within each critique the analyses of judgement are themselves further articulated and subdivided. Some idea of the centrality of judgement to Kant's philosophy may be gathered from a comment from as early as 1762 in FS in which Kant identifies 'the mysterious power' which 'makes judgement possible' and distinguishes humans from the animals as 'nothing other than the faculty of inner sense . . . the faculty of making one's own representations the objects of one's thought' (p. 60, p. 104). Kant adds that this power or capacity to judge is 'fundamental' and 'cannot be derived from some other faculty', a point he reiterated in CPR (A 133/B 172) and CJ (Preface).

The faculty of judgement can only be known through its activity, which, naturally, consists in making judgements. Judgements form the starting points of Kant's analyses of the workings of the faculty of judgement in its theoretical, practical and aesthetic/teleological modes. Each mode of judgement has a particular distinguishing feature: the theoretical judgement 'contains an is or an is not', the practical judgement an 'ought, the necessity of why something happens for some purpose or other' ('Vienna Logic' in L p. 376), while the aesthetic judgement of taste contains a reference to the feeling of pleasure and displeasure. The critical philosophy as a whole is dedicated to determining the limits of legitimate judgements in each of these fields, and does so by means of a dual but complementary strategy. This first supplies the rules of subsumption necessary for legitimate judgement. It offers an organon for judgement, from which may be derived criteria or principles for a canon with which to discriminate true from false judgement. Elements of both strategies may be found in each of the three critiques.

At the core of CPR is the claim that 'all judgements are functions of unity among our representations' (A 69/B 93) and its consequence that 'we can reduce all acts of the understanding to judgements' (A 69/B 94). With this Kant is able to move from regarding concepts as formal functions of unity in judgement to their serving 'as predicates of possible judgments' related to 'some representation of a not *yet* determined object' (ibid.). From the formal judgements grouped in the table of judgements according to their quantity, quality, relation and modality Kant is able to derive the table of categories. The move from formal judgements to categories is extremely significant, implying a shift of focus from the 'logical form of a judgement' determined by analytical unity of the representations making up a judgement to one which introduces 'a transcendental content into its representations, by means of the synthetic unity of the manifold in intuition in general' (A 79/B 105). The latter form of unity is the synthetic a priori judgement on which hangs the success or failure of the critical philosophy. Unlike analytic judgements, which are determined by the principle of contradiction, the synthetic a priori judgement has a number of principles derived from the pure concepts of the understanding. These are described in the section of CPR on the 'Analytic of Principles' which Kant describes as 'a canon solely for *judgement*, instructing it how to apply to appearances the concepts of the understanding, which contain the condition for *a priori* rules' (A 132/B 171).

The 'Transcendental Analytic' of CPR presents the concepts of understanding and establishes the conditions of their proper use. It provides a 'logic of truth' (A 131/B 170) by developing an organon for correct subsumptive use of the concepts of the understanding as well a canon with which to identify false judgements. In the 'logic of illusion' unfolded in the transcendental dialectic, Kant's attention is devoted to establishing a canon against the illusory inferences of reason. An inference involves a relationship between two or more judgements, which lead to fallacies of understanding which take as immediate what is in reality inferred, and those of the reason which draw conclusions which exceed the limits of experience. The transcendental dialectic shows how the illusory inferences of reason may be detected and limited in their scope.

Similar strategies of argument inform the accounts of practical and aesthetic judgement. Practical judgements are given a principle in the shape of the categorical imperative with which to assess the maxims informing practical judgements; it thus serves as a canon for practical judgement. Similarly, in CJ Kant establishes a canon for aesthetic judgements of taste. He weighs the claims for justifying the aesthetic judgement of taste lodged by the theory of taste and aesthetic according to a 'subjective a priori principle' of judgement. They are found insufficient in terms of

268

the quality, quantity, relation and modality of such judgements. In CJ Kant considerably shifts the focus of his account of judgement, moving from an emphasis on completed judgements to one directed towards the working of the faculty of judgement (*Urteilskraft*). From this perspective judgement is viewed less in terms of subsumption than in those of 'thinking the particular as contained under the universal' (CJ §IV). When the universal is given, and the particular subsumed under it by the faculty of judgement, then the judgement is determinant; when only the particular is given and the universal has to be sought by the faculty of judgement, then its judgement is reflective.

judgement, power and faculty of [*Urteilskraft, Beurteilungsvermögen*] *see also* AESTHETIC, BEAUTY, CONCEPT, DETERMINANT JUDGEMENT, HEAUTONOMY, IMAGINATION, INTUITION, PLEASURE, REFLECTIVE JUDGEMENT, REASON, UNDERSTANDING
The faculty of judgement is one of the three 'higher faculties of knowledge' situated between understanding and reason, and forming 'a middle term between understanding and reason' (CJ Preface). But it not only mediates between understanding and reason, it also encompasses them both; in CPR, for example, Kant describes the understanding as '*a faculty of judgement*' (A 69/B 94), and in CJ the 'critique of pure reason' is none other than that of 'our faculty of judging on *a priori* principles' (Preface). Each of the critiques is concerned fundamentally with the faculty of judgement in its theoretical, practical and aesthetic/teleological applications. In CPR the faculty of judgement synthesizes the concepts of the understanding with the manifold in intuition, with the entire 'Analytic of Principles' devoted to a 'doctrine of judgement' providing a 'canon solely for *judgement*, instructing it how to apply to appearances the concepts of the understanding' (A 132/B 171). The CPrR is in turn devoted to developing a canon for moral judgement by means of assessing maxims for their conformity to the categorical imperative. The CJ finally attempts to answer fundamental questions about the faculty of judgement, such as whether it possesses a priori principles; whether such principles function constitutively or regulatively; and the character of the relationship of judgement to pleasure and pain. CJ tackles these problems by means of an analysis of the peculiar properties of aesthetic judgements of taste.

The faculty of judgement has two basic functions which Kant treats as synonymous in CPR: 'judgement [is] the faculty of subsuming under rules; that is, of distinguishing whether something does or does not stand under a given rule' (A 132/B 171). The two aspects of judgement – subsumption and distinction – are combined in CPR. The first is discussed in the second chapter of the 'Analytic of Principles', which explores the synthetic judgements 'which lie *a priori* at the foundation of all other modes of knowledge' or subsumption under a rule. The second is considered in the first chapter on 'Schematism', which examines the sensible conditions of the employment of the pure concepts of understanding, or the discrimination of possible objects for subsumption.

By way of contrast, in his practical philosophy Kant distinguishes the two functions of judgement from each other. The discriminative function is described as the work of *Beurteilungskraft*, which functions in everyday practical reason by discriminating between actions and courses of actions. Such acts of discrimination do not apply the principle of duty abstractly in its universal form, but do always have it actually in view and use it as the standard of judgement (GMM p. 403, p. 15). The faculty of judgement proper (*Urteilskraft*) makes subsumptive judgements according to present and clearly articulated rational principles.

In CJ Kant tries to bring the two functions of judgement together by means of a 'subjective *a priori* principle'. The architecture of the third critique is determined by the search for a principle which would steer between the excessively discriminative account of aesthetic judgement offered by British theorists of taste, and the excessively subsumptive version of the Wolffian school of aesthetics. Kant admits that establishing such a principle – which can make no appeal to concepts – is 'a task involving considerable difficulties' and hopes that the obscurity of his solution will be ameliorated by the accuracy of his 'statement of the principle' (CJ, Preface). The eventual statement of the subjective a priori principle of the faculty of judgement marked a departure in the critical philosophy, encompassing the *sensus communis*, pleasure in intersubjective communication, and the imaginative productions of genius. In it Kant developed the notion of reflective judgement, in which the rule of judgement is derived from reflection on particulars, and that of originality, wherein the rule of judgement may be challenged and transformed by the exception.

In recent years various aspects of Kant's 'subjective *a priori* principle' of judgement have been the subject of debate in the context of postmodernism. Much of the argument within and against postmodernism has been conducted around the issue of judgement, and its relation to pleasure, intersubjectivity, discrimination and difference. This has led to a reconsideration of Kant's account of judgement in CJ by such philosophers as Arendt (1989), Derrida (1978), Habermas (1985) and Lyotard (1983, 1991). This has not only refreshed the exegesis of Kant's text, but also has led to a reconsideration of his place within the 'modern' philosophical tradition.

jurisprudence *see also* INTERPRETATION, JUSTICE, LAW, RIGHT
In CF Kant distinguishes between the interpretation of law as practised by jurists and as undertaken by philosophers. The former are public officials

who are authorities in interpreting the text of the law as it has been 'promulgated and sanctioned by the highest authority' (CF p. 24, p. 37). Jurists – as it were, legal positivists *avant la lettre* – are not permitted opinions on the truth or justice of laws, for the enacted laws themselves 'first determine what is right, and the jurist must straightaway dismiss as nonsense the further question of whether the decrees themselves are right' (CF p. 25, p. 38). The jurists make 'authentic' philological interpretations of the law, while it is for philosophers to make the doctrinal interpretations of the truth and conformity to right of law according to reason.

justice [*Recht*] *see also* MARRIAGE, POSSESSION, PROPERTY, PUNISHMENT, RIGHT, SOCIETY, STATE

Kant's discussions of justice in MM may be divided according to civil and criminal justice: the first refers to relations of men with each other, the second to relations between individuals and the public criminal law. He presents three forms of civil justice, namely protective, commutative and distributive, regarding the first two as comprising private right, the third, public right. He also paired commutative and distributive justice under natural right, or the non-statutory right known a priori to everyone's reason; as such, natural right includes 'not only the *justice* that holds of persons with one another (*iustitia commutativa*) but also distributive justice (*iustitia distributiva*)' (MM p. 297, p. 113). The first two forms of justice are present in the state of nature, but the third is only possible in 'the *civil* condition' with the existence of a court to administer distributive justice.

The distinction between commutative and distributive justice is nicely illustrated by Kant's example of buying a horse. A right is established 'on the formalities of the act of exchange (*commutatio*) between the possessor of the thing and the one acquiring it' (MM p. 301, p. 116). But this is only a right between persons (*ius ad personam*), not a right to a thing (*ius ad rem*). Consequently it is possible for owners with prior personal rights under commutative justice to come forward and declare an interest. This leads to the situation in which 'no trade in external things, no matter how well it may agree with the formal conditions of this kind of justice (*iustitia commutativa*), can guarantee a secure acquisition' (MM p. 302, p. 117). While acquisition cannot be secured in a state of nature, leading to possible injustice, within the civil state it may be secured before a court by means of distributive justice. This is achieved by the court converting a personal into a real right: 'what is *in itself* a right against a person, *when brought before a court*, holds as a right to a thing' (MM p. 303, p. 118). In this way distributive justice is used to secure the claims of commutative justice to property and exchange.

Kant's view of criminal justice is unswervingly retributive, resting on the

271

ius talionis or an a priori 'principle of equality' through which the court applies a punishment to the offender which is equal to their crime. The thief, for example, may be punished by temporary or permanent state-slavery; murderers and their accomplices must suffer the punishment of death, in express repudiation of the ideas of Cesare Beccaria (1738–94) (see Beccaria, 1764); and Kant suggests that rapists and pederasts should be castrated. Nor does he flinch from this retributive logic in cases such as the maternal infanticide of an illegitimate child: being born outside of marriage places the child 'outside the protection of the law' and thus the law will 'ignore' the 'annihilation' of such a child' (MM p. 337, p. 145). The 'innate personality' of human beings which requires that they should not be treated as 'things' only entails that punishment be inflicted for a crime, and not as a means to some other end (e.g., discouraging others, or rehabilitation). It does not qualify the state's right to punish, but ensures that punishment is predictable and dispassionate. Although Kant's retributive argument was developed by Hegel (1821), it has until very recently been eclipsed by what might be described as 'heteronomous' accounts which stress the deterrent and rehabilitative ends served by punishment. However, since the 1980s there has been renewed interest in retributive philosophies of punishment, with Kant's version achieving fresh prominence.

Kant ends MM with some meditations on divine justice. He argues that divine justice should not be understood through analogies to human civil or punitive justice. Divine justice does not recognize rights and obligations, nor is it punitive; such relations can only be applied to relations between human beings, and not to divinity. This marks an interesting application of the general critical ban on extending relations founded in human finitude to absolute objects.

K

kingdom of ends [*Reich der Zwecke*] *see also* ANALOGY, AS-IF, CATEGORICAL IM-
PERATIVE, END, FREEDOM, INTELLIGIBLE WORLD, MAXIM
The kingdom of ends is introduced in GMM as a consequence of the
concept 'of every rational being as one who must regard himself as legislating universal law by all his will's maxims' (GMM p. 433, p. 39). By
'kingdom' is understood 'a systematic union of different rational beings
through common laws', each of which determines ends according to 'universal validity' (ibid.). To be a member of such a kingdom requires of
rational beings 'that they legislate in it universal laws while also being
themselves subject to such laws', or if they are its sovereign, that they
legislate without being thus subject (GMM p. 233, p. 40). The kingdom of
ends is an 'ideal' or 'intelligible world' which can only be used regulatively,
as an as-if principle for testing practical maxims. Morality, Kant says, consists in the 'relation of all action to that legislation whereby alone a kingdom of ends is possible', or the principle to act only on maxims that can
also be universal laws of which the will can regard itself as legislator (GMM
p. 434, p. 40). This is described later as the rational being acting 'as if they
were through their maxim always a legislating member in the universal
kingdom of ends' (p. 438, p. 43). In CJ the kingdom of ends serves as an
important link in the ethico-theological proof of the existence of God.
God is the 'sovereign head legislating in a moral kingdom of ends' (CJ
§86) and from this may be derived such transcendental qualities as omnis-
cience, omnipotence, eternity and omnipresence.

kingdom of God *see* CHURCH

knowledge [*Wissen*] *see also* COGNITION, FAITH, HOLDING-TO-BE-TRUE, OPINION,
THOUGHT
Knowledge, faith and opinion together make up the three grades of holding a judgement to be true. The holding-to-be-true of faith is insufficient
objectively but sufficient subjectively, and gives rise to conviction; that of
opinion is insufficient in both respects, while knowledge is both objectively

273

and subjectively sufficient, and gives rise to both conviction and certainty (CPR A 822/B 850). Each degree of holding-to-be-true has its own appropriate object and modality of judgement. The object of knowledge 'answers to conceptions whose objective reality can be proved' and are 'matters of fact' or *scibile* (CJ §91). They include the 'mathematical properties of geometrical magnitudes' and the practical idea of freedom; in other words 'things or qualities of things which are capable of being verified by experience' (ibid.). The modality of judgements of knowledge is apodeictic, that is 'universally and objectively necessary (holding for all)' (L p. 571).

knowledge, faculties of [*Erkenntnisvermögen*] *see* COGNITION

L

law [*Gesetz*] *see also* CATEGORY, COMMAND, JUSTICE, MAXIM, NATURE, OBLIGATION, RIGHT, RULE

The general concept of law which spans both theoretical and practical philosophy is characterized by objective universality and necessity. This distinguishes theoretical laws from rules, and practical laws from rules and counsels. A theoretical rule of relation, such as that 'if the sun shines long enough upon a body it grows warm', is converted into a law if it is phrased in terms of causality, as in 'the sun is by its light the cause of heat' (P §29). The 'rule of relation' derived from a judgement of experience is in this way accorded the universal and necessary validity of a law (see CPR A 126). A law of practical philosophy is similarly described as one which carries an 'absolute necessity' (GMM p. 389, p. 2) which distinguishes it from both rules of skill and counsels of prudence; the latter, like the theoretical rule of relation, can only offer hypothetical and not absolute or categorical necessity.

Beyond the similarity between theoretical and practical concepts of law are some extremely significant differences. Theoretical knowledge is concerned with 'what is' according to the causality of natural laws, while practical knowledge is concerned with what ought to be according to the causality of the laws of freedom. Kant's account of theoretical laws explores the character and sources of the universality and necessity of 'what is', or nature in its formal and material aspects, while his account of practical laws inquires into the character and sources informing obligation or 'what ought to be'.

The account of theoretical laws emphasizes the relationship between the empirical laws of nature discovered by the sciences (physics, chemistry and biology) and the pure laws of the understanding. In CPR Kant is concerned mostly with the character and sources of physical laws; in CJ he turns his attention to biology. In CPR he describes all empirical laws as 'special determinations of the pure laws of understanding' which is described as the 'lawgiver of nature' (A 127). Empirical laws apply 'higher principles of understanding' to 'special cases of appearance' and derive

275

their necessity from 'grounds which are valid *a priori* and antecedently to all experience' (A 159/B 198). This follows from Kant's axiom that the conditions of the possibility of experience are the conditions of the possibility of objects of experience, or, the same thought put differently, that 'categories are concepts which prescribe laws *a priori* to appearances, and therefore to nature, the sum of all appearances' (B 163). Thus laws are both prescribed to nature by the subject and are universally and necessarily valid and may, in the case of physics, be gathered into a systematic whole.

In the case of the laws of biology discussed in the second part of CJ Kant is not so confident of the universality and necessity of mechanical laws. He considers it 'quite certain that we can never get a sufficient knowledge of organized beings and their inner possibility, much less get an explanation of them, by looking merely to mechanical principles of nature' (CJ §75). It is absurd even to hope that 'maybe another Newton may some day arise, to make intelligible to us even the genesis of but a blade from natural laws that no design has ordered'. Here the insufficiency of mechanical laws to explain living phenomena is aligned with an argument for the possibility of the existence of an 'author of the world' who has designed natural laws whose intelligibility exceeds the restrictions of our reason.

The discussion of the laws of freedom in the practical philosophy is based on the premise of the capacity of pure reason to be practical. This consists in the 'subjection of the maxim of every action to the condition of its qualifying as universal law' (MM p. 214, p. 42). Since human maxims do not automatically conform to the conditions for being universal laws, the law is prescribed as an imperative or command. Such laws may be distinguished according to whether they are directed towards 'external actions', in which case they are juridical, or towards the 'determining grounds of actions', in which case they are ethical (p. 214, p. 42). Conformity of actions to the former kind constitutes legality, while conformity to the latter kind constitutes morality. Juridical laws which 'can be recognised as obligatory a priori by reason even without external law giving' are natural laws, while those which require 'actual external lawgiving' are positive laws. The fundamental law of morality and source of moral obligation is unique, and is stated in the autonomously founded principle of the categorical imperative: 'So act that the maxim of your will could always hold at the same time as a principle establishing universal law' (CPrR p. 31, p. 30).

law, conformity to [*Gesetzmässigkeit*] *see also* CATEGORICAL IMPERATIVE, END, FINALITY, HETERONOMY, IMPERATIVE, LAW, PRACTICAL PHILOSOPHY
In Kant's practical philosophy, particular laws or ends cannot serve as principles for determining the will since they introduce heteronomous

elements into moral judgement. The only suitable principle is 'universal conformity to law' or 'conformity to law as such (without having as its basis any law determining particular actions)' which is expressed in the formula 'I should never act except in such a way that I can also will that my maxim should become a universal law' (GMM p. 402, p. 14). Without this principle of the will duty is but a 'vain delusion' and 'chimerical concept' (ibid.). In theoretical philosophy the 'conformity to law of all the objects of experience' defines the 'formal aspect of nature' which complements its material aspect as the '*totality of all objects of experience*' (P §16). This 'conformity to law' is 'conferred' upon nature by the understanding, making possible both experience and the objects of experience (CPR A 126). In CJ the apparent contradiction of the imagination being free and conforming to law is resolved by the 'subjective harmonising of the imagination and the understanding without an objective end'. This state describes the 'subjective a priori principle' of the judgement of taste otherwise known as 'finality apart from an end' (CJ §22, see also §35).

legislation [*Gesetzgebung*] *see also* LAW, RIGHT, RULE, STATE
Kant uses the model of legislation in both his theoretical and his practical philosophy. In CPR the understanding is described as the 'legislator of nature', with Kant claiming that nature is only possible by means of the prescribed 'synthetic unity of the manifold of appearances according to rules' (A 127). He refers later to the ideal philosopher as a 'legislator of human reason' (A 839/B 867) and in the context of a discussion of Plato's *Republic* describes the ideal of the perfect state as the harmony of legislation and government within a constitution which makes the freedom of each consistent with that of all others. Intimations of this ideal state are written into one of the formulations of the categorical imperative in GMM, wherein 'all maxims are rejected which are not consistent with the will's own legislation of universal law' (p. 431, p. 38). Such a formulation of the categorical imperative conforms to the criteria of ethical legislation presented in MM: there is a universal law, and an incentive in duty; legislation with an 'incentive other than the idea of duty itself' is, by contrast, juridical (p. 219, p. 46).

lies (*Lüge*) *see also* CATEGORICAL IMPERATIVE, COMMUNICATION, ILLUSION, MAXIM, TRUTH
In the 'Announcement of ... a Treaty ...' (1796) and MM (1797) Kant describes the lie as the 'foul spot on human nature' ('Announcement ...' p. 422, p. 93, MM p. 430, p. 227), and distinguishes it from error in terms of the intent to deceive. The lie breaches the 'duty of honesty' derived in GMM from the categorical imperative. A lie cannot be willed as a universal maxim, it can only be willed to achieve a particular end; only 'the concept

of the action' of truthfulness itself can be made a universal maxim. Kant considers lies as 'directly opposed to the natural purposiveness of the speaker's capacity to communicate his thoughts' and to result in no less than 'the renunciation by the speaker of his personality' and the status of a human being (MM p. 430, p. 226). It is not surprising that Kant did not consider lies to be justified under any circumstances, even in the circumstance cited in the title of an essay of 1797: 'On a Presumed Right to Lie from Love of Mankind'. The duty to be honest 'is a holy, unconditionally commanding decree of reason, which cannot be limited by any conventions' while lies strike at the basis not only of what it is to be human, but also at the entire legal order.

Kant classifies lies according to, first, whether they are 'internal' or 'external', and then according to the consciousness which attends them. An internal lie such as dissembling a belief is contrasted with an external lie, such as deliberately deceiving another person. Both species of lie are further distinguished according to whether the lie presents as truth what the liar is conscious of being an untruth, or whether the liar represents as certain what they are consciously uncertain of ('Announcement . . .', 1796, p. 421, p. 93). While Kant condemns lies made on the basis of 'frivolity or even good nature' and even those made as a means to a worthy end (MM p. 430, p. 226), most of his examples concern breach of promise. The two main cases of lying discussed in GMM involve making false promises. In the first, a false promise justified on the grounds of prudence is condemned because it cannot be made a universal maxim of the will (GMM p. 402, p. 15); in the second the false promise is condemned on the ground that it would entail the promisor using the promisee as a means to an end, and not as an end in themselves (p. 430, p. 37).

life [*Leben*] *see also* BODY, GEMÜT, PLEASURE
Kant's thoughts on life may be divided into three groups, all of which are to be found in CJ. The first group is concerned with what might be described as the 'worth of life' and is exemplified by the footnote to CJ §83. The 'worth of life' measured in terms of enjoyment or happiness is 'less than nothing'; it only receives worth when lived in accordance with reason or 'with a view to an end so independent of nature that the very existence of nature itself can only be an end subject to the condition so imposed'. Alongside this view of the value of life Kant holds another, opposed but internally consistent position. This is summed up by the sentence from §29 that 'of itself alone, the *Gemüt* is all life (the life principle itself), and its hindrance or furtherance has to be sought outside it, and yet in the human beings themselves, and consequently in connection with their bodies'. In this view, life is a complex relationship between the body, the

outside world and the *Gemüt*. This may be related to §1 of CJ where Kant relates the feeling of life possessed by a subject with the 'feeling of pleasure or displeasure', thus bringing together life, the mind or *Gemüt*, and pleasure and pain. In the light of this concept of life, many of Kant's unremarked comments on 'life' in the first part of CJ take on considerable significance. In the third group, Kant considers life in terms of the 'organised products' of nature; it is in this context that he made the celebrated claim concerning the absurdity of the hope 'that maybe another Newton may some day arise, to make intelligible to us even the genesis of but a blade of grass from natural laws that no design has ordered' (§75).

limit [*Schranke*] *see also* END, FINITUDE, KNOWLEDGE, METAPHYSICS, SPACE, TRANSCENDENT

In P Kant introduces a distinction between limits (*Schranken*) and boundaries (*Grenzen*), with the former being 'mere negations which affect a quantity so far as it is not absolutely complete' while the latter 'always presuppose a space existing outside of a certain definite place and enclosing it' (P §57). Kant uses both terms as analogies for the extent of legitimate knowledge. The analogy of limit is derived from the category of limitation, the third of the categories of quality which is defined as 'reality combined with negation' (CPR B 111), while that of the boundary is drawn from the properties of spatial intuition which regard a boundary as marking the enclosure of internal and external spaces. Kant uses this analogy to illustrate the distinction between the limits to mathematics and natural scientific knowledge and the boundaries of metaphysics: knowledge of the former is limited in that it is never complete, while that of the latter is on the boundary between the knowable and unknowable. The former is confined to experience and pursues completeness 'from the conditioned to some other equally conditioned thing' (P §59) but without determining its boundary. Reason and metaphysics attempt to think the boundary between what can and cannot be known, and accordingly must limit itself 'as befits the knowledge of a boundary, to the relation between what lies beyond it and what is contained within it' (P §59).

The distinction between limit and boundary was criticized by Hegel (1812) for being abstract and indeterminate. The positing of a boundary between what is known and what is unknown simply creates an absolute opposition which allows the limit to be experienced unreflectively as mere rather than as determinate negation, or as a 'mediation through which something and other each as well *is*, as *is not*' (Hegel, 1812, p. 127). For Hegel, Kant makes finite thought into an absolute, so banishing the infinite absolute to the realm of the unknowable. By questioning this distinction Hegel would make the first steps toward the comprehension of the absolute.

limitation *see* LIMIT

logic, general/transcendental *see also* ANALYTIC, APPERCEPTION, CANON, CATEGO-
RIES, CONCEPT, DIALECTIC, ELEMENTS, FORM, INFERENCE, JUDGEMENT, METHODOLOGY,
TABLE OF CATEGORIES

Although Kant's entire *oeuvre* may be regarded as an extended meditation
on logic, he is responsible for only two works explicitly dedicated to the
subject. One of these, FS, was a short, early contribution to the reform
of some of the baroque excesses of the Aristotelian tradition. The other,
L, was compiled by Gottlob Benjamin Jäsche from Kant's heavily anno-
tated copy of George Friedrich Meier's textbook on logic *Auszug aus der
Vernunftlehre* (1752). Kant used the latter as the text for the lectures on
logic which he gave over four decades from the outset of his academic
career in 1755–6 to its end in 1796. Transcripts of these lectures have
survived from the early 1770s (the 'Blomberg Logic'), the early 1780s
('Vienna' and 'Heschel' Logics), and the early 1790s ('Dohna-Wundlacken
Logic'), all of which have been translated in volume 9 of the Guyer and
Wood edition (i.e., L). From these sources it is possible to reconstruct the
technical background to Kant's ambitious attempt to redefine the scope
of logic in the critical philosophy.

The contents of each of the three critiques are organized in terms of
an early modern Aristotelian treatise on logic, divided into a 'doctrine of
the elements' (comprising an 'analytic' and a 'dialectic') and a 'doctrine
of method'. Embedded within this structure, and notably in CPR, is another, distinct organization of the contents of logic derived from the anti-
Aristotelian Cartesian tradition exemplified by Arnauld's *Art of Thinking* or
'Port-Royal Logic' (1662). In this tradition, logic is concerned not so much
with the forms of inference which so fascinated the Aristotelian tradition,
but with training the judgement to distinguish between true and false,
thus providing an exercise in 'self-discipline' (see the 'First Discourse'). To
this end, the *Art of Thinking* is organized according to 'conception', 'judgement', 'reasoning' and 'ordering'. This division informs Kant's critical
analysis of theoretical, practical and aesthetic judgement, and is most
evident in CPR, which superimposes the Aristotelian and Cartesian para-
digms in an attempt to produce a 'Transcendental Logic'. The 'Transcendental Aesthetic' serves the function of providing the materials of thought
carried out by 'conception'; the 'Transcendental Analytic' provides the
initial ordering of thought analyzed in 'judgement'; the 'Transcendental
Dialectic' generates the (illusory) syllogistic inferences analysed in 'reasoning'; and the methodology leads to the systematic articulation of
knowledge discussed in 'ordering'.

Kant's sensitivity to the differences between the 'Aristotelian' and 'modern' traditions of logic is evident throughout his writings and lectures on logic. At the most general level, FS may be read as the attempt to replace the traditional emphasis on the subtleties of the syllogistic figures with a new focus on self-consciousness and judgement. The struggle and accommodation between the two traditions of logic announced in this text may be followed throughout Kant's writings. It is most evident in the Preface to the second edition of CPR, where Kant observes that logic since Aristotle 'has not been able to advance a single step, and is thus to all appearance a closed and completed body of doctrine' (B viii). He does not consider the attempts by 'moderns' to enlarge logic by means of material drawn from psychology, metaphysics and anthropology to have contributed much. Kant argued that the 'sole concern [of logic] is to give an exhaustive exposition of the formal rules of all thought, whether it be *a priori* or empirical, whatever be its origin or its object' (CPR B ix). He adds that logic leaves 'the understanding nothing to deal with save itself and its form' (B ix), and regards any attempt to supplement it as simply compromising the integrity of the discipline.

In spite of limiting logic to the exposition of the form of the understanding and renouncing its psychological, metaphysical and anthropological supplements, Kant's commitment to the modern project of extending logic was never in question. His proposed extension is far more ambitious than simply adding 'chapters' from discrete sciences, and entails recasting the 'general logic' of the tradition into a modern 'transcendental logic'. Pure general logic 'deals with nothing but the pure form of thought' (CPR A 54/B 78) and is entirely a priori; it is distinguished from applied general logic which is 'directed to the rules of the employment of understanding under the subjective empirical conditions dealt with by psychology' (A 53/B 77). Both are distinguished from the transcendental logic presented in CPR which 'concerns itself with the laws of understanding and of reason solely in so far as they relate *a priori* to objects' (A 57/B 82).

With the development of a modern, transcendental logic Kant does not intend to reject the achievements of the logical tradition. Instead he takes the analyses of judgement drawn from the tradition and uses them as a clue for discovering the operations of the understanding in transcendental logic. The concepts he uses to make the transition from traditional logic to modern logic are 'unity' and 'synthesis'. The judgements of general logic, abstracted from all content, are 'functions of unity' (CPR A 69/B 94); when translated into transcendental logic they signify the syntheses of a spontaneous, apperceptive subject confronted by a 'manifold of *a priori* sensibility' (A 77/B 102). The transcendental syntheses derived from the logical functions of general logic form the table of the categories or 'the list of all original pure concepts of synthesis that the understanding contains within itself *a priori*' (A 80/B 106). With these syntheses Kant would accommodate both the traditional logic based on forms of judgement and inference and the modern logic stemming from the Cartesian *cogito* and based on self-consciousness and apperception.

A further historical tradition of logic is also manifest in Kant's work: the Epicurean definition of logic as a canon or 'science of the cautious and correct use of the understanding' (L p. 257). This is distinguished from the Aristotelian 'organon for the art of disputation' which offers rules for correct or convincing inferences. Kant professedly follows the Epicurean tradition in his emphasis upon the role of logic as a science of distinguishing between judgements, with CPR providing a canon for distinguishing between true and false judgements and inferences, CPrR between good and bad maxims of action, and CJ between judgements of the beautiful and those of the agreeable and the good. In each of the critiques, both the critical analytic and dialectic are canons in this sense: analytic is a 'canon for adjudication (of the formal correctness of our cognition)' (L p. 531) while dialectic contains 'the marks and rules in accordance with which we could recognise that something does not agree with the formal criteria of truth, although it seems to agree with them' (L p. 532).

Kant's attempt in his transcendental logic to bring together traditional and modern logic was radicalized by successors such as Fichte and Hegel. They did not consider it necessary to reconcile the traditional table of judgements with the syntheses of self-consciousness, but argued directly from the synthetic activity of self-consciousness to both the form and content of judgement. The perceived excesses of this development of Kant's logic eventually provoked a reaction against the project of transcendental logic. This took a variety of influential forms, ranging from psychological and sociological accounts of forms of reasoning to a logic of validity which focused on the formal justification of propositions irrespective of their content or relation to the world.

love [*eros/agape, amor, Liebe*] *see also* FAITH, HOPE, MARRIAGE, RESPECT, SEX
As the third and greatest of the medieval 'theological virtues' (see Aquinas, 1952, II, I, 62), the concept of love followed a long and complex history which combined elements of Greek philosophical *eros*, or desire for the other based on want, with Christian *agape* or love of the neighbour and even of the enemy (see Nygren, 1982). While Kant was not directly interested in the concept of love, and discussed it only tangentially, the framework of his analysis nevertheless combines both erotic and agapic aspects.

When discussing love as a feeling, his discussion is usually couched in an erotic vein, and concerns the disciplining of the sexual instinct. In

CBH the deferral of sexual intercourse is one of the four steps by which 'reason' distinguished humans from animals: '*Refusal* was the device which invested purely sensuous stimuli with an ideal quality, and which gradually showed the way from purely animal desire to love' (CBH p. 113, p. 224). The key feature in this transition is the investing of sensuous desire with the rational qualities of respect. This pairing of love and respect also informs the more agapic account of love of the neighbour in MM, where love 'attracts' human beings to each other, and respect distances them: carrying out the duty of love puts another 'under obligation' to me, while that of respect puts me under an obligation to 'keep myself within my own bounds so as not to detract anything from the worth that the other, as a human being, is authorised to put upon themselves' (MM p. 450, p. 244).

Kant's discussion of love is characteristically Protestant in its emphasis upon intention over works – the three 'duties of love' ('benevolence, gratitude and sympathy') are accordingly states of mind and not works. This emphasis also informs his commentary upon Jesus' two command-ments to 'love God' and to 'love your neighbour as yourself' (Matthew 22: 38–9). The first love is translated into terms of motivation of action: 'Per-form your duty for no motive other than unconditional esteem for duty itself, *i.e.*, love God.' So too is the second: 'further [your neighbour's] welfare from good-will that is immediate and not derived from motives of self-advantage' (RL pp. 160–1, p. 148).

As with so many of Kant's concepts, his comments on love stimulated a great deal of thought, much of it in opposition to his ideas. The immedi-ate post-Kantian generation of German philosophers were deeply con-cerned with the philosophy of love. Hegel, in his *Early Theological Writings*, strove to unify love and respect in the notion of 'mutual recognition'. Novalis and Hölderlin attempted to fuse erotic and agapic love, while Friedrich Schlegel explored aspects of erotic love in his novel *Lucinde*. Nevertheless, in these and in subsequent philosophies of love, Kant's in-fluence was minimal and indirect.

M

manifold *see also* APPERCEPTION, COMBINATION, IDENTITY, INTUITION, RECEPTIVITY, SENSIBILITY, SPONTANEITY, SYNTHESIS, UNITY

Kant described the 'manifold of *a priori* sensibility' as the 'material for the concepts of pure understanding', without which the latter would be 'without any content' (CPR A 77). For knowledge arises from the synthesis of a manifold, which requires that the manifold 'be gone through in a certain way, taken up, and connected' (ibid.) by the spontaneity of thought. Manifolds may be either empirical manifolds of sensibility, or a priori manifolds of space and time, but in both cases they issue from the receptive capacity of the mind, the 'conditions under which alone it can receive representations of objects' (ibid.). Yet this poses the problem of how the synthesis of two heterogeneous capacities – the spontaneous unity and the receptive manifold – may be accomplished. What is required is a 'special act of synthesis of the manifold' (CPR B 139), one which would combine the manifold with the modes of transcendental unity represented by the categories. The exploration of this synthesis forms the core of the critical philosophy, and in particular the discussion of the principles, and foremost among them, of the axioms of intuition (see CPR A 162/B 203 for magnitude as the 'homogeneous manifold').

In the A deduction of the first edition of CPR Kant also describes the specific synthesis of the manifold in terms of the syntheses of apprehension, reproduction and recognition. All involve making the manifold compatible with the unity of the understanding, with the synthesis of apprehension being the most significant. This synthesis 'runs through' the manifold and 'holds it together' (CPR A 99); the synthetically apprehended manifold is then gathered into an image by the reproductive synthesis (A 121), which is then unified in a preliminary way by the synthesis of recognition in a concept.

marriage *see also* CONTRACT, EXTRA-TERRESTRIAL LIFE, JUSTICE, RIGHT, SEX, WOMAN

In MM Kant presents a rigorously secular and contractual account of the Christian sacrament of marriage, listing it among the 'rights to persons akin to rights to things' (MM p. 276, p. 95). This class of private law rights entails 'possession of an external object *as a thing* and use of it *as a person*' (ibid.) and is exercised by men acquiring wives, couples acquiring children, and families acquiring servants. Yet although Kant speaks of the husband acquiring a wife, he stresses the *equality* of the possession held by both parties to a marriage; both husband and wife are formally and equally obliged to, as well as being the possessions of, each other. Their mutual possession both as persons and as things is expressed in sexual intercourse; indeed, Kant defines marriage dispassionately as 'the union of two persons of different sexes for lifelong possession of each other's sexual attributes' (p. 278, p. 96). Apparently, while having intercourse each partner enjoys the other by acquiring, and being acquired by them, as if they were things. But in order to respect the partner's humanity as an 'end in themselves' it is necessary for the act of acquisition to be supplemented contractually by commitment for life.

The peculiar character of marriage as a personal right to possess another human being as if they were the object of a right to a thing has interesting consequences for acquiring a husband or a wife. Kant says nothing about the free consent of partners to a marriage contract, but argues that the contract requires both legal title and real possession. Thus it can take place neither *'facto* (by intercourse) without a contract preceding it nor *pacto* (by a mere marriage contract without intercourse following it) but only *lege'* (MM p. 280, p. 98); that is, through a legal contract followed by possession in sexual intercourse. The absence of any major role for consent in the marriage contract leads to the omission of any discussion of divorce (although see, exceptionally, LE p. 169). Indeed, the possession of the person of the partner requires a life-long, legally enforceable commitment, of which Kant says 'if one of the partners in a marriage has left or given itself into someone else's possession, the other partner is justified, always and without question, in bringing its partner back under its control, just as it is justified in retrieving a thing' (MM p. 278, p. 97).

While the begetting of children is not requisite for marriage – 'otherwise marriage would be dissolved when procreation ceases' (MM p. 277, p. 96) – with procreation the parents incur an obligation to bring up the child. Part of this obligation entails a limitation on the parents' freedom to destroy their child 'as if it were something they had *made*', because the child is a 'being endowed with freedom' (MM p. 281, p. 99). However, at another place in MM, Kant describes a child born outside of marriage as 'outside of the protection of the law' and 'contraband merchandise' which can indeed be destroyed by the mother as if it were a thing (see MM p. 336, p. 144). Here it seems as if the 'endowment of freedom' only holds

285

if the child is born within the law. This view of citizenship as dependent on being born within marriage suggests that an aspect of public law has been smuggled into the private law definition of the marriage contract.

When Kant directs his attention away from the formal aspects of the marriage contract to the real relations between husband and wife that make up the 'domestic society' of family and household, his position becomes distinctly illiberal. In his earlier comments on marriage in OBS he describes the role of the wife as that of providing 'merry conversation' while being 'governed by the understanding of the man' (OBS p. 95). In MM he is more explicit, seeing no conflict between the formal equality of the marriage contract and 'the natural superiority of the husband to the wife in his capacity to promote the common interest of the household' (MM p. 279, p. 98). After the marriage contract, the husband will direct the affairs of the family and household by virtue of his superior understanding, while the wife will provide merry conversation, sex and children.

The comic perversity of Kant's attempt to cast marriage in terms of the categories of contractual law has been the source of a great deal of amusement. A fine example is Brecht's poem 'On Kant's Definition of Marriage in the Metaphysics of Morals', where he imagines partners calling in the bailiffs to reclaim erring sexual organs. More seriously, it can be read as a contradictory attempt to translate the characteristics of sacramental marriage – fidelity, irreversible life-long commitment and legitimate offspring – into contractual terms, while at the same time understating the consensual elements which define personal contracts. The consensual element in a personal contract undermines the very sacramental aspects of marriage which Kant sought to buttress with his ingenious description of marriage as a combination of both personal and real rights.

mathematics *see also* APODEICTIC, AXIOM, CONSTRUCTION, EVIDENCE, INTUITION
In the Preface to the second edition of CPR Kant imagines the origins of mathematics to lie in a '*revolution* brought about by the happy thought of a single man' (B xi). He locates this revolution in Greek geometry, whose method, he claims, consisted in the geometer bringing out 'what was necessarily implied in the concepts that he himself had formed *a priori* and had put into the figure in the construction by which he presented it to himself' (B xii). With this Kant announces his controversial claim that mathematics is concerned 'with objects and with knowledge solely in so far as they allow of being exhibited in intuition' and in particular with a priori intuition (A 4/B 8). This entails the further claim that mathematical knowledge is not analytic, and thereby founded on the principle of contradiction, but synthetic a priori: '*all mathematical judgements, without exception, are synthetic*' (B 14). In CPR Kant strives to justify this claim with

reference to arithmetic, geometry and algebra. He does so in order ostensibly to explicate the problem of why mathematical knowledge may be applied to nature, but also to distinguish between the proofs and procedures of mathematics and philosophy.

Kant's arithmetical example is the proposition $7 + 5 = 12$, which he insists is not an analytical proposition. The sum 12, he argues, is derived from 'the concept of the sum of 7 and 5' which contains 'nothing save the union of the two numbers into one, and in this no thought is being taken as to what that single number may be' (CPR B 15). In order to discover the specific number 12, Kant claims it is necessary to 'call in the aid' of intuition and to construct the number 12 out of the addition of five to seven units (in this case the fingers of his hand). Later in the 'Anticipations of Perception' Kant specifies the synthetic operation carried out in arithmetic as a 'synthesis of the homogeneous (of units)' or a 'numerical formula' which 'produces' a unique sum through the general use of numbers (CPR A 165/B 205). He distinguishes the synthetic production of an arithmetical sum from that involved in the intuitive exhibition of geometrical axioms. These too are synthetic, as Kant shows with the examples of 'the straight line between two points is the shortest', a = a, and (a + b) > a, which can only be admitted because they may be exhibited in intuition (B 17). These axioms are derived from properties of pure intuition which may be manipulated by the productive imagination to construct geometrical figures with which to demonstrate geometrical proofs. Unlike an arithmetical operation such as addition, whose synthesis produces a unique sum, the axioms of intuition can be deployed to construct every possible angle. Algebra, finally, also proceeds by means of exhibiting 'in intuition, in accordance with certain universal rules, all the various operations through which the magnitudes are produced and modified' (CPR A 717/B 745). The presentation of the magnitudes and the algebraic symbols are analogous for Kant to the construction of a geometrical figure, taking the form of a 'symbolic construction' which parallels the 'ostensive construction' of geometry.

Kant's attempt to restrict mathematical constructions to the forms of human intuition contradicts some of his own earlier positions, which entertained the possibility of geometries not confined to the limits of three dimensional space. By generalizing the notion of construction in an early text such as LF (§9) he was able to intimate the possibility of geometries based on axioms quite different from those of Euclid. He was also concerned in PE to distinguish mathematical from philosophical proof and certainty. This was motivated by the desire to distance his philosophy from that of the Wolffian school, which borrowed the authority of mathematical proof for philosophical demonstrations. Kant rested his distinction between philosophy and mathematics on the generic difference between the discursive, acroamatic character of the former, and the intuitive, axiomatic character of the latter. In the words of CPR, philosophical knowledge 'is gained by reason from concepts' while mathematical knowledge 'is gained by reason from the *construction* of concepts' (A 713/B 741); the former 'considers the particular only in the universal', the latter 'the universal in the particular' (A 714/B 742). It is not implausible to suggest that it was Kant's attempt to sustain the distinction between mathematical and philosophical argument which led him to emphasize the intuitive, synthetic character of mathematics, even in the face of some of his own earlier insights to the contrary.

mathematical categories, principles and ideas *see* CATEGORIES, DYNAMIC CATEGORIES, PRINCIPLES, IDEAS

matter [*Materie*] *see also* ACCIDENT, BODY, CONCEPTS OF REFLECTION, DYNAMICS, FORM, MECHANICS, MOTION, PHENOMENOLOGY, PHORONOMY, SUBSTANCE
In the critical philosophy Kant accords a comparatively limited role to the concept of matter. It is defined adjectivally as the 'matter of appearance' and as the 'matter of knowledge', with the former being 'the appearance [which] corresponds to sensation' (CPR A 20/B 34) and the latter that which is 'obtained from the senses' (A 86/B 118). It is always contrasted with form, and in conjunction with it comprises one of the four pairs of concepts of reflection. It signifies 'the determinable in general' as opposed to form, which is determination in general (A 267/B 323). As with all the concepts of reflection, matter and form are not anything in themselves but denote ways in which the understanding orients itself with regard to experience. Hence matter simply designates that in experience which is determined by the forms of intuition and the understanding; it is thus a term of reflection for 'the things themselves which appear' (A 268/B 324), and is not an appearance or a thing in itself.

In CPR matter is distinguished from substance, or the permanent in experience, since it 'does not mean a kind of substance quite distinct and heterogeneous from the object of inner sense (the soul), but only the distinctive nature of those appearances of objects – in themselves quite unknown to us – the representations of which we call outer' (CPR A 385). Indeed, what is called matter is no more than the effects in outer sense of 'changes of place' while the forces informing matter are no more than 'mere tendencies which issue in spatial relations as their effects' (A 386). Nor is matter a thing in itself; as a concept of reflection it is 'not among the objects of pure understanding' and even if we were to consider it as such, 'the transcendental object which may be the ground of this appearance that we call matter is a mere something of which we should not understand what it is, even if someone were in a position to tell us' (A 277/B 333). The critical concept of matter has indeed been stripped of all the dignities which were accorded to the concept in the history of philosophy, being neither the 'matter in itself' (*hyle*) nor even the material substance underlying accidents.

Nevertheless, with MF Kant devotes an entire text to matter, or rather to the 'principles of the construction of concepts that belong to the possibility of matter' (MF p. 472, p. 9), namely those which precede any attempt to apply mathematics to 'the doctrine of body' or natural science. Following the headings of the table of categories, Kant presents 'all determinations of the universal concept of matter in general and, therefore, everything that can be thought a priori respecting it' (MF p. 476, p. 12). He describes his procedure as one of running 'the concept of matter through all four of the functions of the concepts of the understanding' (p. 476, p. 13). The fundamental determination of matter for our sensibility is motion, and thus 'all predicates which pertain to the nature of matter' may be traced back 'to motion' (p. 477, p. 14). Thus matter is analyzed in terms of motion: first, by phoronomy, as a pure quantum of motion, then by dynamics, as the quality of motion as the expression of a force, then again by mechanics, in terms of the relation of moving parts of matter to each other, and finally, by phenomenology, as 'matter's motion or rest determined merely with reference to the mode of representation, or modality, i.e., as an appearance of the external senses' (p. 477, p. 15).

maxim *see also* CATEGORICAL IMPERATIVE, COMMAND, FREEDOM, IMPERATIVE, WILL
A maxim is defined as a 'subjective principle of volition' and is distinguished from the objective principle or 'practical law' (GMM p. 400, p. 13). While the latter is valid for every rational being and is a 'principle according to which they ought to act' a maxim 'contains the practical rule which reason determines in accordance with the conditions of the subject (often their ignorance or inclinations) and is thus the principle according to which the subject does act' (GMM p. 421, p. 30). In GMM Kant lists the conditions for a maxim in terms of the quantitative categories of unity, plurality and totality. A maxim must possess unity in the *form* of universality arising from the unity of the will; plurality in its matter or 'ends'; and totality in the 'complete determination' of 'all maxims by the formula that all maxims proceeding from his own legislation ought to harmonise with a possible kingdom of ends as a kingdom of nature' (p. 436, pp. 41–2). In Kant's view, moral action consists largely in the testing of maxims by the various formulations of the categorical imperative. Such testing of maxims is the way in which the objective law of reason relates to a will

subject to other influences and inclinations. The categorical imperative serves as a canon for estimating maxims of action; moral action requires us to 'Act as if the maxim of your action were to become through your will a universal law of nature' (p. 421, p. 30). Thus the prudential maxim of action that 'when I am in distress I may make a lying promise' fails the test of the categorical imperative, because, Kant maintains, 'I can indeed will the lie but cannot at all will a universal law to lie' (p. 403, p. 15).

mechanics *see also* DYNAMICS, LAW, MATTER, PHENOMENOLOGY, TABLE OF CATEGORIES
Mechanics is one of the four divisions of the system of matter presented in MF. Each of these corresponds to matter considered in terms of one of the headings of the table of categories: phoronomy corresponds to quantity and is the science of the quantity of the motion of matter; dynamics corresponds to quality and is the science of the qualities of matter, namely its attractive and repulsive force; phenomenology corresponds to modality and is the science of the appearance of the motion of matter to perception, while mechanics corresponds to relation, and is the science of the relation of the parts of matter to each other (see MF pp. 536–53, pp. 95–117).

In Part II of CJ Kant doubts the ability of a mechanical explanation (i.e., one which believes that everything may be explained in terms of the relation of the parts of matter to each other) to explain living beings. He resolves the antinomy of the 'Critique of Teleological Judgement', which opposes the thesis that nature be estimated 'as possible on mere mechanical laws', with the antithesis that it cannot be so estimated, by arguing that reason can prove neither, and so judgement should be used in a reflective and not a determinant mode (§70). Similarly, the laws of freedom which inform human moral action also exceed mechanical notions of causation, and obey their own, non-mechanical causality, a position explored at length in the 'Third Antinomy' of CPR (see CPR A 444/B 472ff).

memory *see also* HOPE, IDENTITY, IMAGINATION, SYNTHESIS, TIME
Memory is defined as the 'faculty of visualising the past intentionally' which, along with the 'faculty of visualising something as future', serves to associate 'ideas of the past and future condition of the subject with the present' (A §34). Together, both memory and prevision are important for 'linking together perceptions in time' and connecting 'in a coherent experience what is no more with what does not yet exist, by means of what is present' (ibid.). It can thus be seen to play a significant role in the problem of identity, and more particularly, in the character of synthesis. Memory is implied in two of the three syntheses of the 'transcendental faculty of imagination' presented in the deduction of CPR: in the 'synthesis of apprehension' where it informs the consistency of appearances, and in

the 'synthesis of recognition' where it is implied in the continuity of the consciousness of appearances.

metaphysical deduction *see* DEDUCTION

metaphysics *see also* COSMOLOGY, ONTOLOGY, PSYCHOLOGY, THEOLOGY, TRANSCENDENTAL

Metaphysics was the name given in the first century AD to the corpus of Aristotelian writings which came 'after the physics'. By the time of Aquinas this catalogue title had been converted into the name of the highest science, comprising objects such as God and Angels who 'do not depend upon matter for their being', and of concepts such as 'substance, quality, being, potency, act, one and many and the like' (Aquinas, 1986, p. 14). It is called metaphysics or 'first philosophy' because it is *'beyond physics'* in as much as 'all the other sciences receiving their principles from it, come after it' (ibid., p. 15). In the period immediately prior to Kant the content of metaphysics had settled into four sections: the first was general metaphysics or ontology, which was concerned, in the words of Wolff's metaphysics, with 'The First Grounds of our Knowledge and of Things in General'; the remaining three were the objects and sciences of 'special metaphysics', namely (a) the soul and psychology, (b) the world and cosmology, and (c) God and theology. Kant closely followed this schema in CPR, with the 'Transcendental Analytic' critically treating of ontology, and the three sections of the 'Transcendental Dialectic' considering the three parts of special metaphysics.

Kant's adherence to this schema shows that the pure reason he was subjecting to critique was no other than the metaphysics of the Wolffian school. He was familiar with this tradition through his annual lectures on metaphysics which began in winter 1755–6. These lectures were based on A.G. Baumgarten's *Metaphysica* of 1739, a substantially Wolffian text in form and content. In PE (1764) Kant professes great dissatisfaction with Wolffian metaphysics and its reliance upon the principle of contradiction, as well as expressing sympathetic disagreement with Crusius's pietist critique of Wolff. In DS, Kant describes both Wolff's and Crusius's metaphysics as 'castles in the sky' (p. 342, p. 329), but in a remarkable apostrophe he declares he has nevertheless 'fallen in love' with metaphysics. He sees two advantages promised by the science: the first and least promising is that 'it can solve the problems thrown up by the enquiring mind, when it uses reason to spy after the more hidden properties of things', and the second, most important yet least appreciated is that it can serve as a 'science of the *limits of human reason*' (p. 368, p. 354). With the admission that he has as yet 'not precisely determined this limit' Kant points to the project of establishing the limits of human reason which was to occupy him for the next 15 years and issued in CPR.

The preface to the first edition of CPR begins by evoking a 'species of knowledge' which reason cannot ignore, but which transcends its powers and throws it into a perplexity of darkness and contradiction. This knowledge is metaphysics, the Hecuba of the sciences, once queen but now scorned. Kant proposes a critique of reason in respect of knowledge 'after which it may strive *independently of all experience*' and through which it will become possible to decide on the 'possibility and impossibility of metaphysics in general, and determine its sources, its extent, and its limits' (CPR A xii). For Kant metaphysics is composed of 'a priori *synthetic knowledge*' which 'adds to the given concept something that was not contained in it' and which may extend knowledge beyond the limits of experience (B 18). Thus the critical propaedeutic to metaphysics will examine the proper limits of such judgements in order to establish whether they may be extended to knowledge of such metaphysical objects as God, the world and the soul. Kant will conclude that they cannot, but this does not lead him to abandon metaphysics, but rather to undertake a redefinition of its purpose and scope.

In the penultimate section of CPR on 'The Architectonic of Pure Reason' Kant describes metaphysics as the 'criticism of the faculty of reason in respect of all its pure *a priori* knowledge' and the 'systematic connection [of] the whole body (true as well as illusory) of philosophical knowledge arising out of pure reason' (A 841/B 869). The latter may be divided according to the speculative and practical employments of reason, yielding the metaphysics of nature and the metaphysics of morals (see also GMM p. 388, pp. 1–2). The former contains the 'principles of pure reason that are derived from mere concepts ... employed in the *theoretical* knowledge of all things', the latter 'the principles which in *a priori* fashion determine and make necessary *all our actions*' (CPR A 841/B 869), presented in their true employments in the analytics, in their illusory employments in the dialectics. All three taken together constitute metaphysics, which Kant goes on to suggest is synonymous with philosophy or the love of wisdom as well as the 'full and complete development of human reason' (A 850/B 878).

Metaphysical Foundations of Natural Science Published in 1786, Kant described this work as an 'application' of the 'Metaphysics of Nature' which he planned to write on critical principles in the mid 1780s. It is cast as an attempt to provide 'the metaphysical foundations of the theory of body' (PC p. 119), one which, in the words of the book's preface, presents the conditions which make possible the 'application of mathematics to the doctrine of body' (MF p. 472, p. 9). This requires a 'complete analysis of the concept of matter in general', which is presented in four chapters corresponding to the four headings of the table of categories. In these Kant carries 'the concept of matter through all four of the functions of the understanding' (MF p. 476, p. 13), considering it in terms of motion, since 'all predicates which pertain to the nature of matter' may be traced back 'to motion' (p. 477 p. 14). The first chapter, on the 'Metaphysical Foundations of Phoronomy', considers the quantitative aspects of matter, looking at matter in terms of a pure quantum of motion. The second chapter, on the 'Metaphysical Foundations of Dynamics', considers the qualitative aspects of matter with respect to its being the expression of attractive and repulsive forces. The third chapter, on the 'Metaphysical Foundations of Mechanics', considers the relational aspects of matter, namely the relation of the moving parts of matter to each other. The fourth and final chapter, on the 'Metaphysical Foundations of Phenomenology', corresponds to the modal group of categories, and considers 'matter's motion or rest determined merely with reference to the mode of representation, or modality, i.e., as an appearance of the external senses' (p. 417, p. 15).

Metaphysics of Morals MM is the third of Kant's critical texts in moral philosophy. The first, GMM, published in 1785, analyzed the 'supreme principle of morality'. The second, CPrR, published in 1788, justified morality synthetically. MM, however, published in 1797, derived from the principle of morality a 'metaphysics of morals'. As with MF, MM does not present the entire metaphysical system of morals but only the 'first principles'; in MF these basic principles were those associated with the concept of matter, in MM they concern the concepts of right and virtue. The work is accordingly divided into metaphysical first principles of the 'Doctrine of Right' and of the 'Doctrine of Virtue'. Both sets of principles are derived from the freedom of the will and its correlate of duty, with those of right dedicated to 'duties that can be given by external laws, and the system of the *doctrine of virtue* (*Ethica*), which treats of duties that cannot be so given' (MM p. 379, p. 185). The 'Doctrine of Right' considers the laws of private and public right, moving in the former from the concept of possession to acquisition, and regarding the latter in the light of the rights of property, contract and 'Domestic Right'. In the discussion of public right, Kant moves from the internal rights of states to the 'rights of nations', of their external relations, and to a brief section on cosmopolitan right. The elements of the 'Doctrine of Virtue' which follow are divided according to duties to self and duties to others, while the 'method of ethics' treats of how virtue may be acquired and taught.

293

method *see also* ANALYSIS, ANALYTIC, CRITIQUE, HISTORY OF PHILOSOPHY, LOGIC, SYNTHESIS

Method is generically defined as 'a procedure in accordance with principles' and is subdivided into several different species of method. In CPR Kant distinguishes between 'naturalist' and 'scientific' methods: the former proceeds according to common sense and is dismissed by him as 'mere misology', while the latter comprises dogmatic, sceptical and critical methods. The dogmatic method represented by Wolff follows a systematic procedure borrowed from mathematics, but one which is based on unexamined axioms. The sceptical method represented by Hume systematically questions all the claims of reason to establish necessary connections between events, but without inquiring into possible sources of necessity. Finally, the critical method consists in the systematic self-examination of reason in order to determine the sources and scope of its a priori concepts, and to act as a canon against their improper extension beyond the limits of possible experience.

methodology *see also* ANALYTIC, DIALECTIC, ELEMENTS, LOGIC

Kant followed the early modern division of logic into doctrines of elements and method or methodology. The former comprises an inventory of the essential functions of thought (concepts, judgements, inferences), while the latter presents their practical application in terms of the principles of scientific exposition. Each of the three critiques is organized according to the division of elements and method, with the CPR's doctrine of method being the most fully developed. The latter determines the 'formal conditions of a complete system of pure reason' (A 708/B 736) subdivided according to a 'discipline', a 'canon', an 'architectonic' and a 'history' of pure reason.

mind *see* COGNITION, GEMÜT, I, 'I THINK', KNOWLEDGE, PARALOGISMS, SUBJECT, THINKING

modality *see* APODEICTIC, CATEGORIES, EXISTENCE, JUDGEMENT, NECESSITY, POSSIBILITY, PROBLEMATIC, TABLE OF CATEGORIES

monad *see also* BODY, DIVISIBILITY, DIFFERENCE, MATTER, MOTION, SUBSTANCE

Leibniz defined a monad in the *Monadology* (written 1714, published 1720) as a 'simple substance that enters into composites' (§1), one which is capable of 'perception' (§15) and 'appetition' (§16). In the pre-critical PM (1756) Kant saw body as composed of 'simple substances' or 'monads' (p. 477, p. 53) which occupied space not by virtue of extension, but by exercising an active force (p. 481, p. 57). At this early stage of his career Kant was extremely influenced by Leibniz's dynamics, which was based on the forces exercised by simple substances, although by the time of PE (1764) he has become extremely sceptical of the monad, using it to exemplify an 'invented' philosophical concept (p. 227, p. 249). In the section of CPR entitled 'Amphiboly of the Concepts of Reflection' Kant sharpens this scepticism into a full critique which questions the simplicity of the monads, their power of representation, and the problems raised by the attempt to relate simple substances to each other (see CPR A 267/B 323 and A 274/B 330). However, in his later reply to the Leibnizian Eberhard in OD (1790), where Kant calls CPR 'the genuine apology for Leibniz' (OD p. 251, p. 160), his critical position is more nuanced. He defends Leibniz against his disciples, claiming in the case of the monad that it should not be confused with a physical being, but is an 'unknown substrate', an 'idea of reason' in which 'we must certainly represent to ourselves everything which we think as a composite substance as composed of simple substances' (p. 248, p. 158). Kant here presents CPR as the development of Leibnizian themes, and above all that of the monad.

monogram *see* SCHEMA

morals *see* CATEGORICAL IMPERATIVE, COMMAND, IMPERATIVE, MAXIMS, PERSON

mortality *see* FINITUDE, IMMORTALITY

motion *see also* BODY, DYNAMICS, EXTENSION, FORCE, MATTER, MECHANICS, PHENOM-ENOLOGY, PHORONOMY, SPACE, SUCCESSION, TIME
The concept of motion was extremely significant to Kant at all stages of his authorship, and was often used to exemplify larger, metaphysical arguments. In his first work, LF, he used the concept of motion to criticize the Cartesian view of the body as extended substance; there he followed Leibniz in opting for a dynamical explanation of motion in terms of force or *vis activa* which is prior to extension (§1). Motion played an important role in the cosmology of UNH (1755), where Kant supposes the matter of the universe as scattered, but forming itself through motion and the forces of attraction and repulsion into an orderly, law-governed whole. Here, as eight years later in OPA, Kant argued that mechanical laws of motion indicate an original divine design which does not require the constant intervention of God in the running of the universe. Kant also uses the concept of motion as a part of his critique of the then hegemonic Wolffian philosophy, and in particular its use of the principle of contradiction. The beginnings of this argument are evident in NT (1758), where Kant shows the relativity of the concepts of motion and rest, a point he uses in NM (1763) to distinguish between logical contradiction and real opposition (see pp. 171 and 178, pp. 211 and 217).

In CPR Kant again uses the concept of motion to criticize the principle of contradiction. He maintains that arguing analytically from concepts alone cannot 'render comprehensible the possibility of an alteration, that is, of a combination of contradictorily opposed predicates in one and the same object . . . only in time can two contradictorily opposed predicates meet in one and the same object, namely, *one after the other*' (CPR A 32/ B 49). Thus the experience of motion requires the intuition of time and space, but does not lie at their foundation. The concept of motion requires an 'empirical datum' that is experienced in terms of time and space; it 'presupposes the perception of something existing and of the succession of its determinations; that is to say, it presupposes experience' (A 41/B 58). This point is subsequently spelt out when Kant describes motion 'as an act of the subject (not as a determination of an object)' which is accomplished by 'the synthesis of the manifold in space' (B 154). Kant regards the claim that motion is a 'property of outer things' to mistake 'what merely exists in thought' as a 'real object existing, in the same character, outside the thinking subject' (A 384). Thus extension is regarded not as an appearance but as a property of outer things and from this it is inferred that 'motion is due to these things and really occurs in and by itself, apart from our senses' (A 385). Contrary to this, Kant regards motion as one of three relations that can take place within appearances: extension as 'location in an intuition'; motion as 'change of location' within intuition; and motive force as the 'laws according to which this change is determined' (B 67). The knowing subject can only have knowledge of these relations, and must not consider either them or their objects as things in themselves.

In his presentation of the principles of matter presupposed by a mathematical natural science in MF, Kant proceeds from motion, claiming that 'all predicates which pertain to the nature of matter' (p. 477, p. 14) may be traced back to it. He then develops the fundamental concepts of matter by analyzing motion in terms of the four headings of the table of categories. Its quantity or character as a pure quantum is analyzed in the chapter on phoronomy; its quality as the expression of the basic forces of attraction and repulsion in dynamics; the relation of the parts of matter to each in terms of motion is analyzed in mechanics; and the mode of representation of motion to our consciousness is analyzed in phenomenology. Once again Kant uses the concept of motion as a means to the end of presenting a broader argument concerning both the nature and the character of our knowledge of matter.

motive *see* INCENTIVE, MAXIM, PATHOLOGY, RESPECT

N

natural right *see* ACQUISITION, FREEDOM, JURISPRUDENCE, JUSTICE, LAW, PROPERTY, RIGHT

Kant's legal and political writings contributed to the modern tradition of natural rights theory which succeeded the Aristotelian medieval tradition of natural law. In natural rights theory, the basic element is not an objective, divinely founded justice or proportionality, but an individual in possession of certain rights with respect to things, other individuals, and the state. Kant defines natural right as 'nonstatutory Right, hence simply right that can be known a priori by everyone's reason' (MM p. 297, p. 113); that is, natural rights rest on 'a priori principles' as opposed to positive or statutory right 'which proceeds from the will of a legislator' (MM p. 237, p. 63). Natural right includes the commutative justice that 'holds among persons in their exchanges with one another' and distributive justice in so far as its decisions may be known a priori according to the principle of distributive justice. By emphasising the a priori and principled character of natural right, Kant aligns himself with the German, rationalistic wing of the tradition developed by Pufendorf and Wolff, as opposed to the more affective, Grotian tradition developed by Hutcheson and Smith (see Caygill, 1989, Part One). However, with the exception of a few elements, his work is firmly within the rights tradition, and vulnerable to the criticisms of Hegel and others that it illegitimately extends the real and personal rights characteristic of private law into the realm of public law.

natural science *see* DYNAMICS, MATTER, MOTION, PHENOMENOLOGY, PHILOSOPHY

nature *see also* BEAUTY, FINALITY, FREEDOM, MATTER, SPACE, WORLD

In P Kant describes the question 'how is nature itself possible?' as 'the highest point that transcendental philosophy can ever reach, and to which, as its boundary and completion, it must proceed' (§36). He breaks the question down into two sub-questions: how is nature possible in the material, and how is it possible in the formal sense? With regard to the first question, concerning the possibility of nature in its material sense as the 'totality of appearances', Kant answers that it is possible by means of 'constitution of our sensibility'. With regard to the second question, concerning the possibility of nature in the formal sense as the 'totality of rules under which all appearances must come in order to be thought as connected in an experience', this is only possible by means of the 'constitution of our understanding'.

The distinction between nature in its material and formal senses is developed in the critical philosophy into the two definitions of nature proposed in CPR: one stresses its material aspect as the 'aggregate of appearances' (A 114), the other its formal aspect in 'the order and regularity in the appearances' (A 125). However, in a footnote to the second edition of CPR, Kant regards both the material and the formal definitions of nature to be dynamical: taken formally, nature 'signifies the connection of the determinations of a thing according to an inner principle of causality'; taken materially it is the 'sum of appearances in so far as they stand, in virtue of an inner principle of causality, in thoroughgoing interconnection' (B 446). In addition to these distinctions internal to the concept of nature, Kant also makes two important external distinctions in CPR. The first consists in the distinction between the concepts of nature and world: the world 'signifies the mathematical sum total of all appearances and the totality of their synthesis' while nature is the same world 'viewed as a dynamical whole' (A 418/B 446). The second distinction is between the laws of nature and those of freedom articulated in the third antinomy.

The distinction between nature and freedom informs that between the metaphysics of nature in the first critique (CPR) and that of freedom in the second critique (CPrR). In the latter the freedom of the will is consistently opposed to the necessity of nature, and the fundamental problem of practical philosophy is posed as one of reconciling natural and free causality. In an interesting deviation from this approach in GMM, Kant uses the formal aspect of nature, or 'the existence of things as determined by universal law', to enunciate the categorical imperative as 'Act as if the maxim of your action were to become through your will a universal law of nature' (p. 421, p. 30).

The concept of nature is ubiquitous in CJ, where it features in Part I as the object of natural beauty and the sublime, as well as offering intimations of a supersensible harmony of freedom and necessity. In Part II, the discussion is directed towards a repudiation of exclusively mechanical explanations of nature, with the view that the 'organisation of nature has nothing analogous to any causality known to us' (CJ §65). Here nature is defined as a 'formative power' whose products are those '*in which every part is reciprocally both end and means*' (§66). The products of this formative power cannot be understood through mechanical principles nor 'ascribed to a blind mechanism of nature' (see §70). With this Kant extends the dynamical aspect of nature, described in CPR in terms of forces and laws of motion, to encompass a view of nature as a dynamical or formative, productive power. It was a short step for Schelling to replace the knowing subject of CPR with formative nature, and thus to transform Kant's philosophy of the subject into the philosophy of nature.

necessity [*Notwendigkeit*] *see also* APODEICTIC, CATEGORIES, CAUSALITY, DEDUCTION, POSTULATES OF EMPIRICAL THOUGHT, TABLE OF CATEGORIES, VALIDITY
Necessity is the third category of modality, derived from the third modal or apodeictic judgement, which corresponds to the third postulate of empirical thought. Kant ascribes to the modal judgements 'a quite peculiar function', which is to determine the 'value of the copula' in a proposition with respect 'to thought in general' (CPR A 74/B 100). A proposition such as 'A is the cause of B' may be understood problematically as 'it may be the case that A is the cause of B', or assertorically as 'it is the case A is the cause of B', or apodcictically as 'it must be the case that A is the cause of B'. The 'peculiar function' of the modal judgements has considerable implications for the categories derived from them, in particular for the category of necessity. In the table of categories the modal groups do not determine an object – this can only be achieved in respect of its quantity, quality and relation – but they do determine the way in which objects are categorically determined, whether in terms of possibility, existence or necessity. The category of necessity is thus particularly significant because it, along with universality, determines the character of a priori knowledge.

The category of necessity is particularly problematic with respect to the second category of relation, namely the relation of cause and effect. In P Kant referred to the challenge posed by Hume's having shown 'irrefutably' that reason could not prove the necessary connection of cause and effect (preface). He responded to it by proving that the category of cause and effect was not derived from experience, but was an a priori condition of experience. This was indicated by the two 'criteria' of a priori knowledge, namely 'necessity and strict universality' (CPR B 4); accordingly, the category of cause and effect had to be shown to be universally and necessarily valid in order for experience to be deemed possible. These criteria were extended to the other categories, as well as to any pure a priori judgement, including moral and aesthetic judgement. Yet as a category, necessity must itself be shown to be necessary, and this may be achieved, Kant claims, by showing that 'all necessity, without exception, is grounded in a transcendental condition' (CPR A 106). This condition is 'transcendental apperception' or the unified, 'pure original unchangeable consciousness'

(A 107) which underwrites the organization of experience in terms of categories.

Problems with the relationship between necessity and causality are already manifest in the third antinomy of CPR which opposes the causalities of nature and freedom. The necessity of natural causality seems to imply a denial of freedom, or free causality, which has serious implications for Kant's practical philosophy. His resolution of the antinomy consists in distinguishing between the necessity of natural and of free causality. The causality of freedom has its own necessity which becomes evident in a comparison of the practical imperatives. The hypothetical imperatives which issue in the rules of skill and the counsels of prudence possess a necessity which concerns the means necessary to achieve certain ends. The categorical imperative, on the other hand, has an absolute necessity which follows from the unconditional character of the moral law.

needs [*Bedürfnisse*] *see also* INCLINATIONS, INTEREST, WILL
In GMM Kant relates needs to inclinations, seeing both as arising from the 'dependence of the faculty of desire on sensations' (p. 413, p. 24). On this occasion he regards inclination as 'indicating' a need, while on another he sees needs as 'founded on' inclination (p. 428, p. 35). There is probably little at stake in any debate about which is to be given priority.

negation *see also* DETERMINATION, LIMITATION, NOTHING
In NM Kant distinguishes between two senses of negation, namely, privation and lack. The former is the consequence of a 'real opposition' in which a 'ground of positing' is opposed and cancelled by another ground, while the latter is the consequence of the lack of a positive ground (p. 178, p. 217). The privative view of negation arises from a real opposition of two grounds which cancel each other out. The view of negation as lack arises from logical negation according to the principle of contradiction, in which opposed predicates cannot be present in the same subject. In CPR the view of logical negation as signalling lack remains intact, while privative negation is given a far broader field of application. Kant argues that concepts of negation are derived from reality, and moves from this to claiming that they are 'nothing but limitations' of reality. From this he infers that limitation must be 'based on the unlimited' or the ideal of an *ens realissimum* (CPR A 575/B 603), by which he means that the determination of limited objects can only be accomplished by means of the negation of an unlimited, but also unknowable reality.

nothing *see also* BEING, DETERMINATION, EXISTENCE, LIMITATION, NEGATION
In NM Kant distinguishes between the nothing issuing from logical negation according to the principle of contradiction and that produced by real

opposition. The first arises when contradictory predicates are affirmed of the same subject, such as a body 'both in motion and also, in the very same sense, not in motion'. The first nothing is described as a 'negative nothing which cannot be represented' (NM p. 171, p. 211). In the second nothing, the two predicates, such as 'the motive force of a body in one direction and an equal tendency of the same body in an opposite direction' (p. 172, p. 211) do not logically contradict each other, but cancel each other out and issue in a representable nothing or the state of 'rest'. Kant illustrates the latter form of nothing as the sum of positive and negative numbers in which the cancellation of opposed predicates produces the sum '= 0'. This notion of nothing and the model of real negation which underlies it later emerged in CPR in the view of negation as determination.

In CPR Kant includes the two concepts of nothing in his typology of nothing at the end of the 'Amphiboly of the Concepts of Reflection'. The concepts of reflection are basic distinctions necessary for the orientation of categorical judgement, and by way of an apparent afterthought Kant looks at the most fundamental distinction which consists in whether the object in general of judgement is 'something or nothing'. He follows the distinction between something and nothing through the table of the categories, showing that the contrary of the object of the quantitative categories of all, many and one is 'none', an *ens rationis* or 'empty concept without an object' (CPR A 290/B 347). The contrary to the object in general of the categories of *quality* is 'nothing' – *nihil privatum* – or 'a concept of the absence of an object'. The contrary of the object in general of the categories of *relation* is absence of substance or 'the merely formal condition of an object (as appearance)' namely pure space and time abstracted from the objects in them as '*ens imaginarium*'. Finally, the contrary of the object in general of the categories of modality is a logically self-contradictory object, or the *nihil negativum* – the logical nothing discussed in NM. Kant observes that the *ens rationis* of quantity is not possible since it is only an, albeit logically consistent, fiction; the *nihil negativum* of modality is not possible since its concept cancels itself. This leaves the *nihil privatum* of quality and the *ens imaginarium* of quality as determinate negations which, while themselves not real, are necessary for determination of the real.

notion *see* CATEGORIES, REPRESENTATION

noumenon *see also* APPEARANCE, ARCHETYPE, INTELLIGIBLE WORLD, PHENOMENON, SENSE, SENSIBILITY, THING IN ITSELF

In ID (§§3, 7) and P (§32) Kant refers to the distinction between phenomena and noumena as one of the oldest and noblest achievements of ancient philosophy. In P it is clear that he is referring to Plato's distinction between the apparent world of sensible phenomena and the 'real' intelligible world of ideas. In ID Kant criticizes the 'illustrious Wolff' for abolishing this distinction by proposing a continuum between the clear ideas of the intellect and the confused ideas of sensibility. This has been to the great detriment of philosophy, and Kant accordingly re-states the distinction; but his re-statement is very far from the classical distinction between the real world of ideas and the phenomenal world of sensibility.

The most salient feature of noumena is that they are not objects of intuition but problems 'unavoidably bound up with the limitation of our sensibility', namely 'whether there may not be objects' for a 'quite different intuition and a quite different understanding from ours' (CPR A 287/B 344). This question, and its corollary of whether there can be a sum total of noumena or an intelligible world, is declared by Kant a problem incapable of solution, whether by proof or disproof. In the light of this Kant outlines illegitimate and legitimate uses of the noumena.

The fundamental illegitimate use of noumena is to attribute objectivity to them, to move from 'a mode of determining the object by thought alone – a merely logical form without content' to what 'seems to us to be a mode in which the object exists in itself (*noumenon*) without regard to intuition' (CPR A 289/B 345). Kant identifies two forms of illegitimate objectification or 'positive use' of the noumena in theoretical reason. The first is the transcendent use of the pure concepts of the understanding such as substance, power, action, reality, causality, as if they were either noumena themselves (P §45) or at least applicable to noumena (P §33). The second form arises from reason representing 'objects of experience in a series so extended that no experience can grasp it' and thus seeking 'beyond experience *noumena* to which it can attach that chain' (P §45). These are the transcendental ideas of God, the world and the soul analyzed in the 'Transcendental Dialectic' of CPR.

In theoretical reason noumena may be permitted a negative use in which they are accorded the title 'of an unknown something' (CPR A 256/B 311) or used to 'mark the limits of our sensible knowledge and to leave open a space which we can fill neither through possible experience nor through pure understanding' (A 289/B 345). Their main negative use consists in reminding us of the limits to the categories, that they are not appropriately applied to non-sensible objects (A 287/B 343), while yet ensuring that 'a place remains open for other and different objects; and consequently that these latter must not be absolutely denied' (A 288/B 344). The latter proviso leaves open the option of conceiving of noumenal objects or extensions of the concepts of understanding beyond intuition, an option Kant takes up in the notion of the noumenal cause employed in the solution of the antinomies. There is causality in its 'empirical character' restricted to appearances, and causality in its intelligible character – *causa noumenon* – of freedom: the same subject can be determined in one aspect, but free in the other (see WP p. 291, pp. 118–19). This noumenal application of the category of causality and the noumenal object of freedom marks a point of transition between Kant's theoretical and practical philosophy. In CPrR Kant reiterates that while positive knowledge of noumena was denied theoretical reason, he had nevertheless shown 'the possibility – indeed, the necessity – of thinking of them' with particular respect to freedom. He adds that, for practical reason, the 'moral law' is inexplicable in theoretical terms but points to 'a pure intelligible world' and furthermore 'defines it positively and enables us to know something of it, namely, a law' (CPrR p. 43, p. 44).

number *see* MATHEMATICS

O

object [*Ding, Objekt, Gegenstand*] *see also* APPEARANCE, BEING, EXISTENCE, NOTHING, THING-IN-ITSELF, TRANSCENDENTAL OBJECT

Kant's concept of an object is extremely subtle, although its nuances are often lost in the indiscriminate and unsystematic translation of his terms *Ding, Gegenstand,* and *Objekt.* At the most general level in his practical philosophy, Kant follows the distinction in Roman law between persons and things (see Justinian's *Institutes,* books 1 and 2). A person 'is a subject whose actions can be *imputed* to him' while a thing is that 'to which nothing can be imputed'; the former is specified as a subject in possession of freedom and spontaneity, able to act according to principles, while the latter is without freedom and spontaneity. A human being acting in response to inclinations is a thing, as is one used simply as a means to another's ends.

The thing is distinguished from the person in terms of its passivity and lack of autonomous, free agency, and these are features which broadly determine the character of the thing or object in theoretical philosophy. Yet while the thing is largely passive in Kant's account of experience, he is careful to distinguish between various ways in which things and objects stand against the spontaneous syntheses of the human understanding. These different modes of thinghood may be identified by the different German words Kant uses for them – *Ding, Gegenstand, Objekt* – and the contexts in which they appear.

Ding is the term Kant uses least frequently in the critical philosophy, a fact which may be explained by his attempt to distinguish the critical philosophy from the dogmatic metaphysics of the Wolffian school. The term *Ding* was used by Wolff and his school to determine metaphysical thinghood; it designates everything which is possible, even if it is not actual. The Wolffians rarely if ever used the terms *Objekt* and *Gegenstand* which Kant preferred. In CPR accordingly, *Ding* appears in contexts concerned with metaphysical thinghood, as in the discussion of transcendental affirmation and negation (A 574/B 603). Here Kant argues first that transcendental affirmation establishes reality, and that only through it can

304

objects be considered to possess thinghood, or that '*Gegenstände etwas (Dinge) sind*'. Transcendental affirmation also establishes the possibility of negation, since 'All concepts of negations are derivative' (A 575/B 603), and, what is more, the possibility of all limitation, since Kant regards limitation as a form of negation. Thus he argues that we require a general sense or 'ideal' of thinghood in general, or *omnitudo realitas*, in order to perceive determinate, limited objects. He gives the concept of this undetermined thinghood the name 'thing-in-itself', using the term *Ding an sich*, as opposed to *Gegenstand* or *Objekt an sich*.

Kant underlines the distinction between *Ding* and *Gegenstand* in the postulates of empirical thought. There he distinguishes between the knowledge of a determined existence (*Dasein*) which can only be known as an appearance or 'the existence of effects from given causes in accordance with laws of causality' (CPR A 227/B 279), from the undetermined 'existence of things (substances) [*Dasein der Dinge (Substanzen)*]' (A 227/B 279) which cannot be known. Once again, *Ding* is synonymous with metaphysical substance, and is distinguished from the 'condition [of things] . . . which we can only know from other conditions given in perception, in accordance with empirical laws of causality' (A 227/B 280). With the latter Kant's focus on the concept of the thing or object shifts from *Ding* to *Gegenstand* and *Objekt*.

Kant's distinction between *Gegenstand* and *Objekt* is crucial to his transcendental philosophy, although never explicitly thematized and wholly obliterated in Kemp Smith's translation of CPR. It involves the axiomatic claim that 'the conditions for the *possibility of experience* in general are likewise conditions of the *possibility of objects* [*Gegenstände*] *of experience*' (CPR A 158/B 197), and the complex relationship which this entails between concept and intuition. *Gegenstände* are objects of experience or appearances which conform to the limits of the understanding and intuition; they may be appearances in intuition without 'being related to the functions of the understanding' (A 89/B 122), or 'objects of consciousness' which 'are not in any way distinct from their apprehension' (A 190/B 235). When objects [*Gegenstände*] *of* experience are made into objects *for* knowledge, they become *Objekte*. The knowledge of the understanding 'consists in the determinate relation of given representations to an object [*Objekt*]' with *Objekt* described as 'that in the concept of which the manifold of a given intuition is *united*' (B 137). The 'given intuition' or *Gegenstand* is thus made into an *Objekt* under the condition of the unity of apperception.

Kant's various accounts of the object may, at risk of underestimating their internal differences, be organized in terms of a consistent account of the object. A specific *Objekt* of knowledge knowable through the concepts of the understanding requires an object of experience or *Gegenstand*.

305

For there to be such objects requires that there be something rather than nothing; this latter something or thinghood – *Ding* – is unknowable, but discussed in terms of the metaphysical *Ding an sich* or substance. This reading of the Kantian object stresses the affinity of CPR with the onto-logical tradition which Kant hinted at in CPR A 247/B 303. As Kant noted in MM, 'teachers of ontology' begin with concepts of '*something* and *nothing*' but forget that this distinction is already a division of the concept of 'object in general' (p. 218, p. 46). He thus begins with object in general or *Ding* which is divided into something and nothing by transcendental affirmation and negation. The *Ding* is then further specified as an object of experience – *Gegenstand* – and then finally as an object for knowledge – *Objekt* – thus producing a critically revised version of traditional ontology.

objective *see* SUBJECTIVE

obligation [*Verbindlichkeit*] *see also* CATEGORICAL IMPERATIVE, COMMAND, DUTY, IMPERATIVE, JURISPRUDENCE, LAW, OUGHT
In GMM Kant defines obligation as the 'dependence of a will which is not absolutely good upon the principle of autonomy' and specifies 'the objective necessity of an action from obligation' as duty (p. 439, p. 44). Here obligation denotes the dependent condition of the will while duty refers to the necessity of acting according to obligation. This is confirmed by CPrR where obligation is defined as the general dependence of the human will upon the moral law, and duty as the 'constraint to an action' which follows from it (p. 32, p. 32). In MM Kant maintains this general view of obligation and duty alongside an extension of the concept of obligation to include rights. With respect to the broader definition, obligation stands as the general 'necessity of a free action under a categorical imperative' while duty is 'that action to which someone is bound'. Kant concludes from this that, while there is only one duty to perform an action, there are several possible forms of obligation (MM p. 222, p. 49) but that duty and obligation cannot conflict, since both are necessary (p. 224, p. 50). Obligation informs not only duty but also rights, since the latter will be explicated by Kant in terms of 'the capacity for putting others under obligation' (p. 239, p. 64).

Kant's discussion of the relationship between obligation and rights is couched overwhelmingly in terms of private right, or obligations of individuals to each other, and rarely extends to political obligation. He mentions the latter in MM when discussing the obligation of the head of state to the laws of the sovereign body, but this is largely an aside (p. 317, p. 128). The reason for this emphasis on private rather than political obligation may be gathered from Kant's review of the Wolffian Hufeland's

Grundsatz der Naturrechts ('Basis of Natural Rights') of 1786. Kant criticizes Hufeland for preferring, in Wolffian fashion, the principle of perfecting human beings, if necessary through force, over that of respecting the rights and obligations derived from the form of free will. Kant then wished to base political obligation in the rights of individuals against each other, and by extension, against the state, and to derive these rights from a fundamental obligation to obey the moral law. With this argument he undermined the Wolffian position, which derived individual rights and obligations from the state's fundamental obligation to promote the general welfare.

ontological proof of the existence of God *see* GOD, THEOLOGY

ontology A neologism coined in the seventeenth century, ontology was originally used to describe the 'general metaphysics' which preceded the 'special metaphysics' of cosmology, psychology and theology. It was concerned, in the words of Wolff (1719), with the 'First Principles of Knowledge and of Things in General' and prepared the ground for the knowledge of such particular things as the world, the soul and God. For Baumgarten, in his influential Wolffian *Metaphysica* (1739), ontology was the 'science of the predicates of things in general' (§4). For most of his professional life Kant lectured on metaphysics according to Baumgarten's text, although for didactic purposes he did not follow Baumgarten's order of exposition by beginning with ontology (overwhelmingly the largest part of Baumgarten's metaphysics). As he explained in his *Announcement of the Organisation of his Lectures . . .* for 1765–6, his lectures on metaphysics begin with empirical psychology, proceed to cosmology and only then arrive at ontology and, after it, rational psychology and theology (p. 309, p. 295).

The concern with ontology in the lectures on metaphysics ensured that ontological concerns ranked high on Kant's critical agenda. Indeed, the architecture of CPR critically shadows that of Wolffian metaphysics, with the three sections of special metaphysics considered in the 'Transcendental Dialectic' and ontology in the 'Transcendental Analytic'. Kant explicitly refers to the 'mere analytic of the understanding' taking the place of 'the proud name of an Ontology that presumptuously claims to supply, in systematic doctrinal form, synthetic *a priori* knowledge of things in general' (CPR A 247/B 303). By this he means that the principles of transcendental analytic are 'merely rules for the exposition of appearances', and is concerned not with things in general, but only with objects of experience. In subsequent writings Kant simply referred to the transcendental analytic as ontology; thus in WP ontology is described as 'the science that comprises a system of all concepts and principles of the understanding, but only insofar as these extend to objects given by the senses and can, therefore, be justified by experience' (WP p. 260, p. 53) or as containing 'the elements of a priori human cognition, both concepts and fundamental principles' (p. 315, p. 161).

The ontological hinterground to the 'Transcendental Analytic' of CPR was rediscovered in the twentieth century by German scholars such as Heimsoeth (1956) and Heidegger (1929). Their work recovered aspects of Kant's thought which had been lost under the epistemological interpretations of late-nineteenth-century neo-Kantians. One example is the manifold ways in which Kant spoke of the 'thing' or object. His distinctions between *Ding, Objekt* and *Gegenstand* were lost in the epistemological readings of the neo-Kantians, and are almost imperceptible in a neo-Kantian translation such as Kemp Smith's. They could be recognized and given their proper significance in readings sensitive to the ontological background to the critical philosophy. The ontological readings of Kant have enhanced the appreciation of Kant's place in the history of philosophy, as well as deepened our understanding of the relationship between the various parts of his philosophy.

opinion [*doxa, opinio, Meinung*] *see also* FAITH, HOLDING-TO-BE-TRUE, ILLUSION, KNOWLEDGE, TRUTH
Classically, opinion is opposed to truth, and is situated within a further series of oppositions such as becoming–being, knowledge–sensation. In Parmenides, opinion (*doxa*) is confined to the sensation (*aisthesis*) of the realm of becoming, while knowing (*noesis*) concerns itself with the knowledge of the unchangeable realm of being. In the *Republic* Plato develops a more internally articulated division which situates opinion between the knowing of the true idea and the ignorance of the unreal (Plato, 1961, Rep. 478). While opinion remains confined to sensible things, it is also said to include common knowledge. Later in the *Republic* Plato further divides opinion into 'belief' and 'picture thinking', underlining the relationship between opinion, illusion and common knowledge.

On many occasions Kant maintains the opposition between opinion and truth, as in the Preface to CPR where he distinguishes between opinion and certainty. Most consistently, however, in CPR (A 822/B 850ff), CJ (§91) and L (pp. 570–6) he implicitly follows Plato's tripartite schema by contrasting opinion with truth and belief as one of the three forms in which a judgement may be 'held to be true' (*Fürwahrhalten*). The three forms are distinguished according to degree of conviction, which is in turn divided in terms of 'subjective sufficiency' or '*conviction* (for myself)' and 'objective sufficiency' or '*certainty* (for everyone)' (CPR A 822/B 850). Knowledge, or holding a judgement to be true, is sufficient both subjectively and objectively; a judgement of belief is held to be subjectively sufficient, but objectively insufficient; while holding a judgement of opinion is insufficient both objectively and subjectively.

In CJ the tripartite distinction is extended to the three objects of judgement: matters of fact, belief and opinion. Matters of fact 'answer to conceptions whose objective reality can be proved', matters of belief to those which may be 'thought a priori' but 'whose objective reality cannot be proven in any way' such as the existence of God or the *summum bonum* (highest good), while matters of opinion are those 'objects belonging to the world of sense, but objects of which an empirical knowledge is impossible *for us* because the degree of empirical knowledge we possess is as it is' (CJ §91). Kant's examples of opinionable objects are 'ether' and 'extraterrestrial life'; and they point to a crucial difference between his and the classical understanding of opinion. For Kant opinion, while confined to sensible experience, is not therefore illusory; it is, on the contrary, probable, but as knowledge it is yet insufficiently convincing or certain (CPR A 775/B 803). The provisional status of judgements of opinion is confirmed in L, where Kant distinguishes the three forms of holding-to-be-true in terms of the modality proper to their judgements: certain judgements of fact are apodeictic, convincing judgements of belief are assertoric, while judgements of opinion are problematic. Opinion is a 'preliminary judging', 'a vague awareness of truth' with which we cannot dispense when making judgements; it is 'that [which] I hold in the consciousness of my judgement to be problematic' (L 570–6).

opposition *see* CONCEPTS OF REFLECTION

optimism *see* HISTORY, HOPE, THEODICY

Opus postumum This title was given to the surviving manuscripts of an incomplete work-in-progress dating from the 1790s. In letters to Christian Garve and J.G.C.C. Kiesewetter of 21 September and 19 October 1798 respectively, Kant describes his efforts to produce a work which will settle 'the unpaid bill of my uncompleted philosophy' by filling the 'gap' which 'remains in the critical philosophy' (PC pp. 251, 252). He gives this project the working title 'Transition from the metaphysical foundations of natural science to physics' but the state of his concentration and health in the final years of his life prevented him from seeing the work to the press. After a vexed editorial history an imperfect version of the manuscript was first published in 1882, with the first (incomplete) English translation appearing in 1993, almost two centuries after it was written.

The contents of OP challenge many received ideas about the critical philosophy, above all the claim that it was completed with the publication of the third critique (CJ). The work also challenges the conventional wisdom concerning the break between critical and pre-critical phases in Kant's authorship, since in it many pre-critical themes, notably that of positing, return to prominence. Broadly speaking, the content of OP moves from a number of reflections on the problems of attractive and repulsive force to a redefinition of the self-positing subject and finally to a re-statement of the system of transcendental philosophy itself.

The first series of problems discussed in OP concern the transition from the science of nature considered systematically as 'the moveable in space (matter) under laws of motion, according to concepts a priori' (OP p. 524, p. 36) in MF to 'physics' or nature considered according to 'empirical principles'. The transition from the metaphysical foundations of natural science to physics requires a number of 'intermediate concepts' (p. 476, p. 40) which empirically specify the operation of the forces of attraction and repulsion. However the search for these concepts forced Kant to reconsider such basic themes as space, time, motion and free-will, and following these, to reconsider the nature of the thinking and willing subject. The renewed discussion of the subject led Kant to re-introduce the pre-critical themes of positing and self-affection, and to move from these to a reconsideration of the place of humanity between God and world. Thus from a concern with identifying the 'intermediate concepts' of a transition from MF to physics, the mansucript moves to a re-appraisal of the extent and the meaning of transcendental philosophy. Kant accordingly notes that the transitions at stake are not only those from MF to physics, but also from 'physics to transcendental philosophy' and from 'transcendental philosophy to the system of nature and freedom'; these transitions are concluded in 'the universal connection of the living forces of all things in reciprocal relation: God and the world' (p. 18, p. 224).

When read from the standpoint of OP, the development and the outcome of Kant's philosophizing is cast in an unfamiliar and, for some, disturbing light. Perhaps for this reason the late manuscripts have been regarded as the product of Kant's dotage rather than a legitimate development and deepening of the critical philosophy. There are certainly very few readings of Kant's word which depart from OP (with the exception of Lehmann, 1969), which is unfortunate since the text may potentially clarify many of the breaks and points of continuity not only between the critical and pre-critical philosophy but also between the critical philosophy and its successors.

organon *see* CANON

orientation *see also* CANON, COMMON SENSE, CONCEPTS OF REFLECTION, INCONGRU-
ENT COUNTERPARTS, JUDGEMENT

Kant's writings are replete with metaphors of orientation drawn from
navigation and cartography, but the concept signifies for him far more
than a convenient figure of speech. If the critical philosophy is read as an
Epicurean canon for distinguishing between correct and incorrect theoretical, moral and aesthetic judgements, then Kant's entire philosophy
may be read as an exercise in the orientation of judgement. The notion
of orientation is used in theoretical philosophy to pass judgement on the
speculative use of reason with respect to the supersensible. In L, orientation
is described as the use of the *sensus communis* as a 'touchstone for discovering the mistakes of the artificial use of the understanding' (L p. 563).
In the essay 'What is Orientation in Thinking?' (1786), Kant draws an
analogy between orientation in space by means of the felt difference
between left and right and orientation in the supersensible realm by the
'feeling of a need which is inherent in reason itself' (WO p. 136, p. 240).
It is possible to be oriented in thought by the need of reason by recognizing the 'subjective ground for presupposing and accepting something which
reason cannot presume to know on objective grounds' (p. 137, pp. 240–
1). This orientation recognizes the value of the ideas of reason as regulative principles, while denying that they correspond to objects. Although
Kant focuses in this essay on the relationship between the needs of reason
and the concepts of the understanding, the notion of orientation is also
central to the relationship between sensibility and the understanding determined by the 'transcendental topic' discussed in CPR's 'Concepts of
Reflection'. It is also evident in the account of testing maxims for their
suitability as principles of moral action in the practical philosophy.

origin [*Ursprung*] *see also* ACQUISITION, APPERCEPTION, EVIL, GENIUS, 'I THINK',
PURE, SPONTANEITY

Kant defines origin in RL as 'the derivation of an effect from a first cause'
and distinguishes between origin in *reason* and origin in *time*. The former
is concerned with the mere existence of an effect, the latter with its occurrence 'as an event [related] to its first cause in time' (RL p. 39, p. 35). On
the basis of this distinction Kant separates the rational origin of evil in
human freedom from the temporal origin of evil acts. In CPR Kant uses
the notion of rational origin to distinguish the 'original' (*ursprunglich*) or
its synonym 'pure apperception' from 'empirical apperception'. The
'original synthetic unity of apperception' is produced in an act of spontaneity or 'I think' which, while it 'must be capable of accompanying all
other representations ... cannot itself be accompanied by any further
representation' (CPR B 132). The 'I think' is a 'rational origin' or an

effect which accompanies all experience, but one whose cause cannot be located in terms of experience. Origin thus serves as an important link between the emphasis on spontaneity informing the account of experience in theoretical philosophy, and the emphasis on freedom and autonomy in the practical philosophy. It was as such that it became prominent in Marburg neo-Kantianism towards the end of the nineteenth century, particularly in Hermann Cohen's influential interpretations of Kant (1871, 1902).

original sin *see* EVIL, FREEDOM, GOD, THEOLOGY

originality *see* GENIUS, IMAGINATION, IMITATION

ought [*Sollen*] *see* COMMAND, IMPERATIVE, OBLIGATION, ROUSSEAU

outer *see* CONCEPTS OF REFLECTION, INNER/OUTER

outer sense *see* APPERCEPTION, INNER SENSE, INTUITION, SENSE, SENSIBILITY, SPACE

P

pain *see* PLEASURE

paralogism *see also* GEMÜT, I, 'I THINK', IDENTITY, INFERENCE, PERSON, PSYCHOLOGY, SUBJECT
In the *Poetics* Aristotle defined paralogism as falsely inferring the truth of an antecedent from the truth of a consequent premise: 'Whenever, if A is or happens, a consequent B is or happens, men's notion is that if the B is, the A also is – but that is a false conclusion' (Aristotle, 1941, 1460a, 21). Extending this, Kant defines a *logical* paralogism as 'a syllogism which is fallacious in form, be its content what it may' and a *transcendental* paralogism as 'one in which there is a transcendental ground, constraining us to draw a formally invalid conclusion' (CPR A 341/B 399). The psychological paralogisms of the transcendental dialectic exemplify the latter. In them Kant shows how the transcendental ground of thought, the 'I think' (Aristotle's 'consequent B') is the basis for inferences concerning the substantiality, simplicity, identity and relations of the soul or thinking substance ('antecedent A'). Kant argues that the inference from the formal condition of thought to a substance of thought is paralogistic and gives rise to the dialectical ideas of rational psychology.

part *see* ANTINOMY, CONTINUITY, DIVISIBILITY, MONAD, SIMPLICITY

passion [*Leidenschaft*] *see also* AFFECT, EVIL, FREEDOM, INCLINATION, SEX
Kant describes the passions as the incurable 'cancerous sores for pure practical reason' which 'presuppose a maxim of the subject, namely, to act according to a purpose prescribed . . . by the inclination' (A §181). In RL and A he presents a genealogy of the affects which describes how the passions come into existence. He begins with the propensity (*Hang*) for a particular delight driven by instinct (RL p. 28, p. 24) which 'precedes the representation of its object' (A §80); when the propensity has been indulged it 'arouses in the subject an *inclination* to it' (RL p. 28, p. 24). Passion follows the development of an inclination as the renunciation of

313

'mastery over oneself' (ibid.) and the elevation of the object of inclination to the status of the object of a maxim of the will. Passions are thus distinguished from affects, which are quickly aroused and spent, since they are 'lasting inclinations' on which the mind has formed principles. When the object of a passion is contrary to the law, the adoption of it into a maxim for the will is evil, and results in vice. Kant further distinguishes in A between innate passions of 'natural inclination' and acquired passions 'arising from the culture of mankind'. The first variety includes the 'burning passions' for freedom and sex, while the second includes such 'cold passions' as ambition, lust for power and avarice (A §81).

peace [*Friede*] *see also* FEDERATION OF STATES, POLITICAL WRITINGS, WAR
In MM Kant described perpetual peace as the 'highest political good' and an idea of practical reason towards which 'we must act as if it is something real, though perhaps it is not' (MM p. 354, p. 160). It is defined in both MM and PP as an 'end to hostilities', whether between human beings in the state of nature, or between states in a state of war. Although it is to be achieved 'by gradual reform in accordance with firm principles' (MM p. 355, p. 161) it is also, in the words of PP, '*guaranteed* by no less an authority than the great artist *Nature* herself' (PP p. 360, p. 108) which is revealed in the purposive plan, whether of fate or providence, 'of producing concord among men, even against their will and indeed by means of their very discord' (ibid.). In PP Kant presents the 'firm principles' he has in mind in the form of a treaty with two sections and an appendix. In the first section he presents the 'preliminary articles' of a perpetual peace between states in the guise of prohibitive laws. These comprise the exclusion of secret reservations in treaties between states for future war, the forbidding of the acquisition by any means of one state by another, the gradual abolition of standing armies, the forbidding of raising national debt for the purposes of external affairs, non-interference, and the respect for the laws of war. In the second section of definitive articles, Kant stipulates that every state shall be republican, that the right of nations shall be based on a federation of free states, and that cosmopolitan right shall be limited to the conditions of universal hospitality.

perception [*Wahrnehmung*] *see also* ANTICIPATIONS OF PERCEPTION, COGNITION, INTUITION, JUDGEMENT, THOUGHT
Perceptions are variously described in CPR as appearances 'combined with consciousness' (A 120), 'representations accompanied by sensation' (B 147) and sensations 'of which we are conscious' (A 225/B 272). They are described as 'empirical intuitions' or 'that which is immediately represented, through sensation, as actual in space and time' (B 147) as well

314

as 'empirical consciousness' or a 'consciousness in which sensation is to be found' (A 166/B 207). Thus perceptions partake of both sensation and consciousness, an ambiguity which assures the possibility of experience by allowing the distinction between consciousness and sensibility to be both observed and suspended. For if perceptions were exclusively sensible, then they could not be ordered by the categories; but if they were exclusively generated by consciousness, then they could have no relationship to objects of sense. As a consequence perception also stands in a complex relation to the forms of intuition, space and time. These 'dwell in us as forms of our sensible intuition, before any real object, determining our sense through sensation, has enabled us to represent the object under those sensible relations'; but in order for them to represent this object they must themselves 'presuppose perception' (A 373). In this case, even though they are prior to an object, the forms of intuition nevertheless presuppose perception or 'the reality of something in space' (A 373).

perfection [*Vollkommenheit*] This concept was central to the Wolffian philosophy against which Kant defined many of his characteristic positions. In his metaphysics (1719), Wolff defined perfection as the 'harmony of a manifold' (§152) which may be traced to a common ground (§§153–6). The entire Wolffian system was organized around the principle of promoting perfection, whether perfection of knowledge, self-perfection or social perfection. From an early stage in his career Kant criticized this principle, and in the three critiques unequivocally rejects it as a principle of judgement. In CPR he argues against the perfection of knowledge on the basis of the inherent limitations of human knowledge to appearances in space and time; in GMM and CPrR he rejects moral perfection as a heteronomous principle of practical judgement; while in CJ he opposes perfection and the agreeable as equally unsuitable principles for the aesthetic judgement of taste. In his late political writings Kant also rejects perfection as a principle of political judgement, mainly because it puts citizens under the tutelage of the state, giving it the power to decide for its citizens what for it will best promote their welfare or perfection.

permanence *see* ANALOGIES OF EXPERIENCE, IMMORTALITY, SUBSTANCE

person *see also* HUMANITY, IDENTITY, PARALOGISM, PSYCHOLOGY, SUBJECT
In the third paralogism of personality in CPR Kant defines a person as 'that which is conscious of the numerical identity of itself at different times' (A 361). He argues that it is fallacious to infer from the unity of the thinking subject to the existence of a personality which endures through time. Within the limits of theoretical philosophy only 'psychological

personality' can legitimately be an object of knowledge, namely 'the capacity for being conscious of one's identity in different conditions of one's existence' (MM p. 223, p. 50). Nevertheless the concept of the person 'is necessary for practical employment' (CPR A 365). There, personality is the third and highest of the 'elements in the fixed character and destiny of man', following animality and humanity. It is a predisposition to being 'a rational and at the same time an *accountable* being' (RL p. 26, p. 21). A being with reason, argues Kant, would not necessarily determine its will by merely representing to itself the fitness of its maxims to be moral laws. Yet an accountable and rational being possesses 'respect for the moral law as *in itself a sufficient incentive of the will*' (RL p. 27, p. 23). From the premise of accountability flow two practical consequences: the first is the practical postulate of the immortality of the soul (CPrR p. 123, p. 127), the second that 'a person is subject to no other laws than those he gives to himself' (MM p. 223, p. 50). Thus in order for a person to be properly accountable they must be postulated as being both immortal and autonomous.

phenomenology *see also* DYNAMICS, MECHANICS, MODALITY, MOTION, PHORONOMY
'Phenomenology' is the subject of the fourth chapter of Kant's treatment of natural science in MF. Each of the four chapters considers motion (for Kant the subject matter of natural science) from the standpoint of one of the four groups of the table of categories. 'Phoronomy' considers the quantitative, 'Dynamics' the qualitative, 'Mechanics' the relational, and 'Phenomenology' the modal aspects of motion. In phenomenology 'matter's motion or rest is determined merely with reference to the mode of representation, or modality, i.e., as an appearance of the external senses' (MF p. 477, p. 15). The chapter presents three propositions which determine the modality of motion for the previous three chapters. The first maintains that rectilinear motion of matter, as opposed to the opposite motion of the relative space in which it is situated, is a 'merely possible predicate' and that as a consequence neither the necessity nor actuality of phoronomy can be established. The second proposition presents circular motion of matter in appearance as merely possible (i.e., either it or its space can be in motion), but holds it, in accordance with the 'complex of all appearances', to be actually in motion. Kant argues that such motion 'cannot take place without the influence of a continuously acting external moving force' (MF p. 557, p. 123) which proves the actuality of the forces of attraction and repulsion, and thus the object of dynamics. The third proposition maintains that the motion of a body in relation to another requires the opposite and equal motion of the latter, a requirement which 'follows immediately and inevitably from the concept of the relation of the moved in space to every other thing thereby moveable' (MF p. 558,

p. 124) and which entails that the modality of motion in mechanics is necessary.

Kant took the term phenomenology from J.H. Lambert's *Neues Organon* (1764) (see Lambert 1988) where it forms one of four sections of an epistemology dedicated to distinguishing between truth, error and illusion. The phenomenology considers the forms of appearance and illusion. However, in a letter to Lambert dated September 2, accompanying a copy of ID, Kant reveals a far broader view of the potential of phenomenology, describing it in terms which anticipate those he used later to describe the project of CPR. It is a 'quite special, though purely negative science', one 'presupposed by metaphysics' in which 'the principles of sensibility, their validity and their limitations, would be determined, so that these principles could not be confusedly applied to objects of pure reason, as has heretofore almost always happened.' (PC p. 59) This wide view of phenomenology as a propaedeutic to metaphysics persists ostensibly in MF if not in CPR. It was taken up by Hegel who described his *Phenomenology of Spirit* on the title page as the 'First Part' of the 'System of Science'. The term was revived by Edmund Husserl at the turn of the twentieth century to describe a new beginning for philosophy in the analysis of phenomena (see Husserl, 1913, 1950).

phenomenon *see also* APPEARANCE, ARCHETYPE, INTELLIGIBLE WORLD, INTUITION, NOUMENON, SENSIBILITY

Phenomena are distinguished from both noumena and appearances, but the terms in which Kant couched the distinction changed radically during his career. In his first work, LF (1747), Kant conventionally employs phenomenon in the sense of an external manifestation of an invisible force, as in the proposition 'motion is only the external phenomenon of the state of the body' (LF §3). While elements of this view persist even into the critical philosophy, by ID (1770) the terms of the distinction have shifted from phenomena being the external manifestation of invisible forces or objects, to them being simply 'objects of sensibility' as opposed to noumena or intelligible objects which can only be 'cognised through the intelligence' (ID §3). Kant also intimates a distinction between phenomena and appearances, with the term appearance being used to signify 'that which precedes the logical use of the understanding' and phenomena the 'objects of experience' which result from the comparison of appearances by the understanding (§5). In this view the 'laws of phenomena' comprise 'the laws both of experience and generally of all sensitive cognition' (§5). These distinction are carried over into CPR, with phenomena distinguished from noumena in terms of sensible and intelligible worlds (A 249) and in terms of sensible and intelligible objects (B 306). Similarly, phenomena are distinguished from appearances in so far as they combine the laws of sensible and intellectual cognition or, to use the language of CPR, they are 'Appearances, so far as they are thought as objects according to the unity of the categories' (A 248).

philosophy *see also* HISTORY OF PHILOSOPHY, METAPHYSICS, SYSTEM
Kant offers several characterizations of philosophy, the most extended being in CPR, GMM and L. Although his definitions of philosophy are on the whole formal – concerned with its concept, objects, types, contents and questions – they are usually accompanied by a reference either to contemporary or to ancient Greek philosophy. The definitions of philosophy developed in CPR at A 838/B 866 are polemically addressed against the Wolffian concept of philosophy; the definition proposed in GMM refers to the 'ancient Greek division' of philosophy into physics, ethics and logic; while that in L is situated according to a general history of philosophy ranging from the Greeks to the 'age of critique'. Indeed, the concept of philosophy was intrinsically historical for Kant. For him it rested on a distinction between (a) philosophy as 'a mere idea of a possible science, which nowhere exists *in concreto*', which no one possesses and which cannot be learnt or even recognized; and (b) philosophizing, or exercising 'the talent of reason, in accordance with its universal principles, on certain actually existing attempts at philosophy' (CPR A 838/B 866).

With respect to the *concept* of philosophy, Kant distinguishes in CPR between the scholastic and the cosmic concepts. The former, which Kant says has 'hitherto prevailed' and by which he means the dominant Wolffian conception of philosophy, regards it as 'a system of knowledge which is sought solely in its character as a science ... [and is] consequently no more than the *logical* perfection of knowledge' (CPR A 838/B 866). The cosmic concept of philosophy is wider and has 'always formed the real basis of the term "philosophy", especially when it has been as it were personified and its archetype represented in the ideal *philosopher*' (A 838/B 866). It involves the 'science of the relation of all knowledge to the essential ends of human reason' (A 839/B 867) or 'that in which everyone necessarily has an interest'. In the latter concept of philosophy, the philosopher is a 'lawgiver of human reason' and his legislation, or 'philosophy' has, Kant continues, the two objects of nature and freedom, or 'what is' and what 'ought to be' (A 840/B 868).

The division of the *objects* of philosophy into nature and freedom corresponds to the division of philosophy into physics and ethics which prefaces GMM, except there they are joined by a third division of logic. Echoes of this division are discernible in CPR's classification of philosophy in terms of propaedeutic or 'criticism' 'which investigates the faculty of reason in respect of all its pure *a priori* knowledge' and 'metaphysics' or the system of pure reason divided into metaphysics of nature and metaphysics of morals (A 841/B 869). The metaphysics of nature and morals correspond to the 'speculative' and 'practical' employments of pure reason, with the former comprising the principles of pure reason 'employed in the *theoretical* knowledge of all things', the latter the a priori principles which 'determine and make necessary *all our actions*' (A 841/B 869). Intersecting with this distinction is yet another system of classification couched in terms of empirical and pure philosophy, the one comprising knowledge derived from empirical principles, the other knowledge derived from pure reason; only the latter is philosophy proper. In CPR Kant makes a further, internal distinction within the metaphysics of nature; he describes this as metaphysics in a narrow sense, which consists of (a) 'transcendental philosophy' which treats of understanding and reason and corresponds to ontology, and (b) 'physiology of pure reason', which corresponds to nature. Immediately after making this distinction, Kant describes the system of metaphysics in traditional terms as comprising ontology, physiology, cosmology and theology, with the second including rational physics and rational psychology.

A further definition of philosophy is developed in FI, where philosophy is distinguished as 'the system of rational knowledge by means of concepts' from a critique of pure reason which 'demarcates and examines the very idea of the system' (FI p. 195, p. 3). Here the philosophical system is divided into formal and material domains, with the former (logic) embracing the 'form of thought in a system of rules' and the latter the 'possibility of rational, conceptual knowledge of thinkable objects' (FI p. 195, p. 3). The latter or 'real' system of philosophy is divided according to theoretical and practical objects, with theoretical philosophy concerned with propositions about 'the possibility of things and their determinations' (FI p. 196, p. 3) and practical philosophy with propositions which 'give freedom its law' (p. 197, p. 4).

The myriad definitions of philosophy given in the critiques are further complicated by the definitions of philosophy to be found in L and in the late essays 'On a Newly Arisen Superior Tone in Philosophy' and the 'Announcement of the Near Conclusion of a Treaty for External Peace in Philosophy' (both 1796). The latter continue the project inaugurated in DS of fencing off philosophy in general, and metaphysics in particular, from mysticism and sentimental religiosity. Philosophy is prone to the attentions of the latter because of what is described in CPR as its 'cosmic concept' or the relation of knowledge to the essential ends of humanity. The scope of the latter or the 'field of philosophy' is determined in L in terms of the four questions: (a) what can I know? (b) what ought I to do?

319

(c) what may I hope? (d) what is man? The first three questions recur in CPR as those of the 'interests of reason', but in L they together form the field of philosophy covered by metaphysics, morals, religion and anthropology respectively.

Kant's definition of philosophy is undogmatic and shifting. This is due to his historical view of philosophy as the outcome of philosophizing. Since philosophizing cannot come to end, even in the critical philosophy, the definition of philosophy remains open and subject to current and future philosophizing. The questions which determine the field of philosophy are inseparable from the interests of human reason, and cannot ever be given a dogmatic answer. For this reason, it is impossible to give a definition of the philosophy which would answer these questions: such a philosophy would mark the end of philosophizing and the death of philosophy itself.

phoronomy *see also* DYNAMICS, MATTER, MECHANICS, MOTION, PHENOMENOLOGY
In MF Kant classifies the science of matter and motion according to the four headings of the table of categories. Dynamics, mechanics and phenomenology correspond respectively to quality, relation and modality, while phoronomy corresponds to quantity. As such it concerns only the quantitative aspects of the motion of matter, and is discussed in MF (pp. 480–95, pp. 18–39).

pleasure *see also* AESTHETICS, BEAUTY, BODY, DELIGHT, FEELING, LIFE, SEX
As early as NM Kant claimed that pleasure and displeasure (pain) were complementary: both were expressions of the same 'feeling of pleasure and pain'. In A he describes them as 'opposed to each other, not like gain and deficiency (+ or 0), but like gain and loss (= and –), that is, one is not contrasted with the other merely as an opposite (*contradictorie, sive logice oppositum*), but rather as a counterpart (*contrarie sive realiter oppositum*)' (A §60). Kant maintains that beyond claiming that pleasure and displeasure are counterparts of the same subjective feeling, they 'cannot be explained more clearly in themselves; instead, one can only specify what results they have in certain circumstances' (MM p. 212, p. 41). One of these results follows from whether the feeling incites the subject to abandon or maintain a particular state; another consists in the tendency of pleasure to enhance the feeling of life, and of displeasure or pain to hinder it (A §60). Both however are necessary to each other: without the check of displeasure, the steady advancement of vitality accompanying pleasure would result in a 'quick death'.

In A Kant distinguishes between sensuous and intellectual pleasure and displeasure, subdividing the former according to whether the pleasure/ displeasure is caused by sensation or imagination, and the latter according to whether or not its cause lies in representable concepts or ideas. The pleasures/displeasures of sensation include food, sex and drugs (tobacco and alcohol); those of imagination the partly intellectual pleasures of taste and beauty. The intellectual pleasures/displeasures are discussed more fully in MM. There the distinction is framed in terms of whether the pleasure/displeasure precedes or succeeds a determination of desire. If it precedes desire and involves an object, then it is sensuous or a 'pleasure of inclination'; if it precedes desire but does not involve an object, it is a contemplative pleasure of taste; if it is preceded by a determination of desire, it is an intellectual pleasure occasioned by an 'interest of reason' (MM p. 212, p. 41)

Kant follows an analogous schema in CJ, his great treatise on pleasure. Here the pleasures of taste, which seemed an afterthought in the above taxonomies, are called, in association with judgement, to mediate between the theoretical and the practical faculties. The feeling of pleasure/displeasure which 'denotes nothing in the object, but is a feeling which the subject has of itself and of the manner in which it is affected by the representation' (CJ §1) quickly expands to underlie both the theoretical and practical faculties. A manifestation of this extended definition of pleasure is the new distinction between pleasure/displeasure and delight. The schema of sensuous, imaginative and intellectual pleasures is now translated into the delights of the agreeable, the good and the beautiful. Delight is a sensation of pleasure, its manifestation at the level of the judgement of taste, with analogues in practical and theoretical judgement. Pleasure accompanies practical judgement insofar as 'The attainment of every aim is coupled with a feeling of pleasure', and theoretical judgement, 'by reason of the most ordinary experience being impossible without it [pleasure]'; he adds that it 'has become gradually fused with simple cognition and no longer arrests particular attention' (CJ §VI). Pleasure/ displeasure is well on its way to becoming identified with vital force – or the feeling of life – and even the mind as such, 'For, of itself alone, the mind [Gemüt] is all life (the life principle itself), and hindrance or furtherance has to be sought outside it, and yet within human beings themselves, consequently in connection with their body' (CJ §29). The extremely broad implications of Kant's philosophy of pleasure/displeasure went largely unremarked until the twentieth century, when, under the impulse of critiques of Kantian formalism in ethics and aesthetics, a more sensitive interpretation of his later thought began slowly to emerge.

polemic see DISPUTE

political writings *see also* CONSTITUTION, COSMOPOLITANISM, CULTURE, FEDERAL-
ISM, HISTORY, SOCIABILITY, STATE
Kant made many steps towards a political philosophy in the course of his
lectures on geography and anthropology, but it is only with his articles for
the pro-Enlightenment *Berlinische Monatsschrift* from the mid 1780s that he
began to develop an explicit, public political philosophy. The first texts
which may be included under this heading are IUH and WE of 1784. The
former saw the attainment of a 'civil society which can administer justice
universally', that is, to combine 'freedom under external laws' with 'irresistible force' (p. 22, p. 45) as the most difficult and last problem to be
solved by the human race. It announces what was to become the main
theme of Kant's political philosophy, namely the relationship between a
just civil constitution and international peace. In WE Kant calls for the
widest possible arena of political debate, contributing to the articulation
of a civil public sphere for the discussion of political matters.

The pattern established in these pre-revolutionary texts persists in those
written after the French Revolution (1789), which refer with critical enthusiasm to events in France. The first of these is CJ, regarded by commentators such as Arendt (1989) and Lyotard (1991) as containing in its
account of reflective judgement the core of Kant's political philosophy. CJ
also contains interesting comments in Part II on the constitution of state
and civil society (§83), as well as reflections on the French Revolution
(§65). Further contributions to an explicit political philosophy are also
made in TP (1793), and above all in PP (1795). The latter is Kant's most
considered statement of the republican nature of a just civil constitution,
and its contribution to world peace; if read alongside the political sections
of MM (1797) it offers a good insight into the liberal but anti-democratic
character of Kant's political philosophy.

The sources for Kant's political philosophy should not, however, be
restricted to his political essays. Political insights inform not only GMM
and CPrR but also CPR; they are also evident in Kant's interventions into
institutional politics, such as those of the university in CF and those of the
church in RL. The implications of the ostensibly political texts for the
interpretation of Kant in general have been drawn out in recent work,
which focuses on what Lyotard has described as the 'fourth critique' of
historico-political reason. This gives a fresh slant not only to Kant's moral
and theoretical philosophy, but also to the politics of critique in general.

possession [*possessio, Besitz*] *see also* ACQUISITION, CONTRACT, MARRIAGE, PROP-
ERTY, RIGHT
Possession is defined in MM as the 'subjective condition of any possible
use' (p. 245, p. 68) and is divided into 'sensible' and 'intelligible' possession

or *possessio phaenomenon* and *possessio noumenon*. The former is possession by means of holding an external object in space and time, while the latter is 'rightful possession' which is not restricted to the physical holding of an object. The latter is justified, or given a deduction, according to a postulate of practical reason that 'it is a duty of Right to act towards others so that what is external (usable) could also become someone's' (a maxim in accord with the categorical imperative), thus showing that the concept of external possession presupposes intelligible possession (MM p. 252, p. 74). Possession is thus treated as a synthetic a priori judgement which combines the physical holding of an object with intelligible justification of thus holding it. Furthermore, by distinguishing between sensible and intelligible possession, Kant is able to resolve the antinomy of possession. This holds as follows: thesis, it is possible to have something external as mine, without possessing it; antithesis, it is not possible to have something without being in possession of it. Kant's resolution of the antinomy consists in exposing the equivocal senses in which possession is used in the thesis and antithesis.

Kant's account of possession in MM is important for illuminating the metaphor of the possession of concepts in CPR. He refers to this in MM when he describes how an a priori intuition was held to underlie a given concept, in order to make a synthetic judgement and thus supplement the sensible possession of an object in intuition. Possession of concepts is faced by both the question of fact (*quid facti*) with reference to sensible possession, and that of right (*quid juris*) with reference to intelligible possession (CPR A 84/B 116). The justification of the latter requires a deduction both in MM and CPR in order to establish their legal title.

possibility *see* CATEGORIES

possible experience *see* EXPERIENCE

postulate [*hypothesis, Postulat*] *see also* AXIOMS, DEFINITION, FREEDOM, GOD, IMMORTALITY, PRINCIPLE
In the *Posterior Analytics* (1941, 76a, 31–77a, 5) Aristotle introduces postulates along with axioms and definitions as the indemonstrable principles of demonstrative knowledge. Axioms are indemonstrable principles common to all sciences; definitions state the characteristics peculiar to particular sciences; while postulates are statements of fact 'on the being of which depends the being of the fact inferred' (1941, 76b, 39). The three principles of knowledge may be illustrated by Euclid's *Elements of Geometry*, whose first axiom states the generic truth that 'Things which are equal to the same thing are also equal to one another', whose first definition defines the characteristic of the geometrical point as 'that which has no part', and

323

which postulates that for geometrical objects to exist it must be granted possible 'to draw a straight line from any point to any point' (see Euclid, 1956).

Kant's use of the postulate remains within Aristotelian orthodoxy, seeing it as a procedural specification necessary for demonstrative knowledge of the 'inferred fact'. In L he defines it as 'a practical, immediately certain proposition or a fundamental proposition which determines a possible action of which it is presupposed that the manner of executing it is immediately certain' (L p. 607). The term is used in theoretical philosophy to describe the modal principles of the 'postulates of empirical thought' – the procedural specification of the relation between the understanding and the synthesis of appearances. Its main application, however, is in the practical philosophy.

In L Kant refers to 'theoretical postulates for the purpose of practical reason' and lists them as the existence of God, freedom and the existence of another world (p. 608). These reappear in CPrR, with 'another world' replaced by 'immortality', as the three 'postulates of pure practical reason'. They are the 'necessary conditions for obedience' of a finite being to the moral law which determines its will. They must be postulated in order to establish reverence for the moral law, and the possibility of its being realized. Immortality must be postulated in order to satisfy 'the practically necessary condition of a duration adequate to the perfect fulfilment of the moral law'; freedom for the condition of 'independence from the world of sense and of the capacity of determining man's will by the law of an intelligible world'; and God for the presupposition of 'the highest independent good' (CPrR p. 131, p. 136).

Kant also follows Aristotle in regarding the postulates as indemonstrable. In this way he sustains his critique of attempts to *know* such beings as God, the world and the soul in the 'Transcendental Dialectic' of CPR, while justifying them in CPrR as conditions 'of the possibility of the object of a will determined by that law' (p. 133, p. 138). In a phrasing parallel to Aristotle's definition of the postulates cited above, Kant claims that they are 'postulated through the moral law and for its sake' (p. 131, p. 133). They are statements on which the existence of the moral law depends, but which themselves derive their own validity from its existence.

Kant's successors, first Hegel and subsequently Nietzsche, could not accept the postulates. For them they were, in Aristotle's terms 'illegitimate hypotheses', with Nietzsche even seeing them as Kant's punishment for conceiving of the categorical imperative which 'led him astray – back to "God," "soul," "freedom," and "immortality," like a fox who loses his way and goes astray back into his cage. Yet it had been his strength and cleverness that had broken open the cage!' (Nietzsche, 1882, §335).

324

postulates of empirical knowledge [*Die Postulaten des empirischen Denkens*]
see also CATEGORIES, MODALITY, PHENOMENOLOGY, PRINCIPLES

The postulates of empirical knowledge are the group of principles serving as rules for the employment of the categories of modality. Along with the 'axioms of intuition', 'anticipations of perception' and the 'analogies of experience', they comprise the 'system of principles of pure understanding' in CPR and are also described in P as the 'physiological principles'. Although classed with the analogies as 'dynamic' as opposed to 'mathematical' principles, the postulates differ from the other three sets of principles. The latter are responses to the problem of the ways in which appearances must be related to each other, and find that they are related quantitatively, qualitatively and relationally. These relations are neither directly categorical nor empirical, but form the 'conditions of experience' which are also the 'conditions for the objects of experience' of a finite being with sensible intuition.

The postulates, however, do not govern the relations of discrete appearances to each other, but the relation of appearances to the 'faculty of knowledge'. They ask how appearances are related to a finite being, and accordingly transform the modal categories of possibility, actuality and necessity into spatio-temporal principles. The postulates are neither merely logically significant, 'analytically expressing the form of thought' (CPR A 219/B 266), nor are they ontological predicates of beings such as God (a 'necessary being'). They express the mode or way in which a discrete experience relates to the conditions of possible experience. Furthermore, as postulates, they possess the formal characteristic of all Kant's postulates, which is that they both depend on the 'being' of the conditions of possible experience, as well as forming a condition for the 'being' of experience.

Kant transforms the category of possibility into the 'possible', or 'That which agrees with the formal conditions of experience, that is, with the conditions of intuition and concepts' (CPR A 218/B 266). A possible concept is one that does not contravene the formal conditions of experience, although this makes no claim that an object corresponding to the concept actually exists. The category of actuality is in its turn transformed into the principle of the actual; an actual concept must indeed observe the formal conditions of experience (that is, it must be possible), but it must in addition be 'bound up with the material conditions of experience, that is, with sensation' (A 218/B 266). This does not mean that its object must be perceived, but that it must accord 'with the analogies of experience, which define all real connection in an experience in general' (A 225/B 272). That is, possible experiences cannot be considered actual unless they obey the rules of relating appearances in terms of the permanence of substance, the nexus of cause and effect, and reciprocal action.

Finally, the category of necessity becomes the 'necessary', or 'That which in its connection with the actual is determined in accordance with universal conditions of experience' (A 218/B 266). In this case the actual experience is deemed to conform fully with both the formal and material conditions of experience (A 227/B 279).

Since the postulates determine the relation of the subject of experience to its experiences, they are clearly of great significance for debates around idealism and realism. Indeed, in the second edition of CPR the discussion of the postulates is interrupted by a digression on the 'Refutation of Idealism'. This is to be found between the discussions of the second and third postulates, and develops into a critique of the 'problematic idealism' of Descartes and the 'dogmatic idealism' of Berkeley. Unfortunately more interpretative energy has been expended on the polemical digression than on the systematic account of the postulates which underlies it.

power [*potentia, Gewalt, Macht*] *see also* DRIVE, FORCE, POSSESSION
Power is the term used to translate the German words *Macht* and *Gewalt* and the Latin *potentia*. The three terms, however, have different meanings and are used in different contexts. *Macht* is defined in the 'Analytic of the Sublime' in CJ as a 'power superior to great hindrances' as possessed by nature considered in an aesthetic judgement (§28). Nature has might over us, but no dominion (*Gewalt*), for dominion is a power 'which is superior to that which itself possesses might' (§28). When Kant discusses legitimate political power he inevitably refers to *Gewalt*, as in CJ §83 when he refers to a lawful authority as a '*gesetzmässige Gewalt*'; however, if the context is that of rebellion against the state, the power of the state is its *Macht*, as in TP, where it is used to refer to the 'legislative power' ('*gesetzgebende Macht*') which cannot be resisted by rebellious subjects, or in MM, where in the same paragraph legitimate supreme power is *Gewalt* which, when resisted, becomes absolute power – '*Machtvollkommenheit*' (MM p. 372, p. 177). *Potentia* is yet another sense of power, this time referring to the physical capacity to use an object; as such it forms the basis of physical possession or *possessio phaenomenon*.

practical philosophy/reason *see* AUTONOMY, CATEGORICAL IMPERATIVE, CRITIQUE OF PRACTICAL REASON, GOOD, HETERONOMY, IMPERATIVE, MAXIM, METAPHYSICS OF MORALS, PHILOSOPHY, REASON

pre-critical writings In a letter to J.H. Tieftrunk dated 13 October 1797, Kant agreed to a proposal to 'publish a collection of my minor writings' but with the proviso that 'I would not want you to start the collection with anything before 1770, that is, my dissertation on the sensible world and the intelligible world' (PC p. 239). With this he effectively disowned all the writings of the 'pre-critical period' with the exception of the last, the ID. His judgement of his writings between 1746 and 1770, which amount to 25 published items, has on the whole been tacitly accepted by Kant scholarship. With a few signal exceptions, these texts have been relatively neglected, especially in comparison with the interpretative industry surrounding the critical texts; many of the pre-critical writings remain untranslated and *terra incognita* even for many Kant scholars.

Those interpretations of Kant which have referred to the pre-critical writings have themselves tended to be selective, scouring the texts for themes which are later developed in the critical writings, such as 'transcendental deduction', 'causality' or 'judgement'. This use of the texts carries with it the danger of restricting their exegesis to the illustration of a particular interpretative hobby-horse. With the best will in the world, though, it is difficult to find a framework of classification which would encompass the diversity of the pre-critical writings. However, there is a set of recurrent themes, which may be gathered under the general problem of the condition and possible futures for metaphysics.

For the pre-critical, as indeed for the critical Kant, metaphysics meant specifically the Wolffian metaphysics in which he had been trained, and which he spent his entire professional life teaching. Wolff's influential system of philosophy, in its German and Latin versions, commenced with a logical propaedeutic, and was followed by a metaphysics and thereafter an ethics and a politics. The contents of the metaphysics were organized in terms of a general metaphysics or 'ontology' and a 'special metaphysics' comprising theology, cosmology and psychology. The object of ontology was 'being in general', while the objects of theology, cosmology and psychology were the being of God, the world and the soul. These divisions provided the fronts on which Kant pursued his critique of metaphysics, and inform even his most apparently specific and narrowly defined precritical texts.

The concern with the state and future of metaphysics is already evident in Kant's first published work, *Thoughts on the True Estimation of Living Forces* (1747). This academic meditation upon contemporary disputes concerning the nature of force is informed by a metaphysical agenda. In §19 Kant concludes the first section on 'The Force of Bodies in General' by musing that 'Our metaphysics is like many other sciences, in fact, only on the threshold of properly, well-grounded knowledge; God knows when it will cross that threshold'. This happens because everyone wants knowledge, but is reluctant to make the effort of ensuring that it is well-founded. Throughout this text Kant alludes to the tension between natural science and metaphysics, hinting that metaphysics does not come out well from it.

327

The stage for Kant's engagement with metaphysics is already set in terms of the concepts of matter, space and time.

It has been argued that, following LF, Kant did not return to explicit philosophical themes until 1762, and that the writings between 1747 and the latter date are largely of interest to the history of science. These texts, including reflections on the earth such as 'The Question Whether the Earth is Aging considered from a Physicalist Point of View' (1754, see also texts from 1754 and 1756), on meteorology (1756, 1757), and on cosmology (UNH), nevertheless represent meditations on such metaphysical issues as God's role in natural events and the nature of the universe and creation. They are, furthermore, punctuated by an explicit reflection on metaphysics, namely the *New Elucidation of the First Principles of Metaphysical Cognition* (1755). This text criticizes Wolffian metaphysics, and in particular the centrality of the principle of contradiction to its account of being and truth. The argument, prosecuted in three sections, begins with a critique of the principle of contradiction; proceeds through a discussion of the theoretical and practical issues of a principle of 'determining ground'; and arrives at two new principles of metaphysical cognition, namely the principles of succession and co-existence. While these are couched in the idiom of a metaphysics of substance, they clearly point to Kant's focusing his renewal of metaphysics upon the issues of time and space, with their associated problems of motion and causality. These themes were taken up again in the *New Theory of Motion and Rest . . .* (1758) where Kant inveighs against the 'Wolffian treadmill' and argues for the relativity of judgements of motion and rest.

From 1762 Kant's writings become more explicitly focused upon philosophical issues, but with the concerns about the conditions and prospects for metaphysics remaining uppermost. In the *False Subtlety of the Four Syllogistic Figures* (1762) Kant focuses on the act of judgement, which he discerns to lie at the heart of the syllogistic figures. Among the various interesting matters tackled in this remarkably short text are the relationships between judgement and concepts and between judgement and reflection; the existence of a number of indemonstrable judgements in human knowledge, and the distinction between logical and physical differentiation. The last, which marked a decisive critique of Wolff's principle of contradiction, was developed further in NM and PE, being extended in the latter into a distinction between the synthetic mathematical method of philosophy used by Wolff and an analytic method recommended by Kant. The previous concerns of FS in their turn announce a series of more general themes and problems which Kant continued to work on into the critical period.

Another important departure in FS is the view that the traditional preoccupation with the forms of the syllogism lies at the root of the 'fate of human understanding' to 'brood over deep matters and fall into bizarre ideas, or audaciously [to] chase after objects too great for its grasp and build castles in the air' (p. 57, p. 100). It is precisely this characteristic of the syllogistic inferences of reason which Kant will identify in CPR as the root of the dialectical inferences of special metaphysics. He made a start at criticizing these in OPA where he refused to treat existence as a predicate which could legitimately be predicated of God. The critique of the syllogism is extended into a general critique of prevailing metaphysics in DS, where Kant criticizes 'those who build castles in the sky' naming Wolff and Crusius as such 'dreamers of reason' (p. 342, p. 329). In spite of the metaphysical enormities perpetrated by Swedenborg which Kant satirizes in this text, he ends with a profession of love for metaphysics. He claims that its attraction follows from its two main features, one of which is 'to spy after the more hidden properties of things' which offers only disappointment, and the other of which is 'knowing the limits of human reason' (DS p. 268, p. 354). The latter view, metaphysics as self-knowledge, leads the metaphysician 'back to the humble ground of experience and common sense' (DS p. 368, p. 355).

The programmatic character of Kant's profession of love for metaphysics is unmistakable even in the midst of the relentless satire in DS. As self-knowledge, or the knowledge of the limits of reason, metaphysics becomes closely allied with anthropology. This current of Kant's work surfaces in OBS which uses the distinction of the beautiful and the sublime as a framework through which to pursue a number of anthropological reflections far removed from the 'empty space whither the butterfly wings of metaphysics have raised us' (OBS p. 368, p. 355). A similar tendency is discernible in DRS which, while ostensibly making a case for Newtonian absolute space against the relative version of the Wolffians, discovers a third position which consists in examining the corporeal origins of spatial differentiation. Kant's description of absolute space as a 'fundamental concept' which 'makes possible all outer sensation' marks a point of transition between (a) an objective and (b) a subjective but not relational understanding of space.

The metaphysical reflections of the pre-critical writings are gathered together in the last text of this period, the ID. This begins with some cosmological reflections on the concept of the world, but now described in terms of synthesis, intuition and the understanding. Kant quickly moves to make the point that the limits of the human mind are often mistakenly taken to be those of things themselves. The text then proceeds to establish these limits by reflecting on the distinction between sensible and intelligible things, as well as on sensitive and intellectual cognition. Kant repeatedly criticizes Wolffian metaphysics for confusing these realms, to the detriment of metaphysics, and redefines the latter as the 'first principles of the use of pure understanding' (§8) which encompass the principles of sensitive and intellectual cognition. The former are, above all, the 'principles of the form of the sensible world' (§13), namely time and space. These are presented as subjective forms which are presupposed by the senses. The presentation of them is followed by a brief and relatively underdeveloped section on the 'principle of the form of the intelligible world' followed by a section on 'method in metaphysics' which lists the 'subreptic axioms' which arise when the distinction of sensitive and intellectual cognition is not observed.

With ID much of the general plan of CPR is in place, even though the detailed work required to 'cross the threshold' and make metaphysics into a properly grounded science would require a further decade of work, Kant's so-called 'silent decade'. In spite of the differences in style between the writings either side of the 'silent decade', there is a continuity between the pre-critical and critical periods, one which may be summed up as the diagnosis of the ailing condition of metaphysics, and the prescription of an austere regime of self-knowledge in order to ensure its survival.

predicables *see also* CATEGORIES, PREDICAMENT, TABLE OF CATEGORIES
In the Aristotelian tradition, the predicables are the five, sometimes six, predicates which may be affirmed or denied of the subject in a logical proposition. They are definition, genus, difference, property, accident and species. Kant's use of the term diverges considerably from the received sense, since for him they refer to the 'pure but derivative concepts of the understanding' (CPR A 82/B 108). From the table of judgements Kant derives the set of pure functions of the understanding, and by relating these to 'objects in general' generates the 'pure concepts of the understanding'. From these are derived a 'complete list' of predicables arising from the combination of the categories with each other and with the forms of intuition, space and time (see P §39). In CPR Kant refrains from giving the 'complete inventory' of predicables, but gives some helpful examples. From the category of causality are derived the predicables of force, action and passion; from that of community the predicables of presence and resistance; from modality, those of coming to be, ceasing to be and change (CPR A 82/B 108).

predicament *see also* CATEGORIES, PREDICABLES
Predicament is used in CPR A 81/B 107 as a synonym for the categories; indeed, in WP Kant historically specifies the term as the medieval scholastic equivalent of Aristotle's categories (WP pp. 271–2, pp. 75–7). For him they are the 'primary concepts of the pure understanding' from which are derived the 'post-predicaments' or predicables of pure understanding.

predicate *see also* JUDGEMENT, LOGIC, SUBJECT

Kant regards judgement as the relation in thought of a subject to a predicate, and claims that this relation can take two possible forms. In the first, the 'predicate B belongs to the subject A, as something which is (covertly) contained in this concept A', while in the second, predicate B 'lies outside the concept A, although it does indeed stand in connection with it' (CPR A 6/B 10). The first form of judgement is analytic, the second synthetic. The proof of the possibility of synthetic a priori judgements is the task of CPR, and consists in showing that a predicate can be synthesized with a subject in a judgement. Kant was extremely concerned to ensure that the logical combination of subject and predicate, restricted only by the principle of contradiction, was not extended to real or synthetic combinations. In order to do so he distinguished between logical and real predicates, claiming that 'anything we please can be made to serve as a logical predicate' (CPR A 598/B 626) while real predicates must be confined within the limits of possible experience. He was particularly concerned after OPA to disqualify the use of 'being' as a real predicate. The copula 'is' in a judgement is 'not a concept of something which could be added to the concept of a thing'. It is logically permitted to say 'God is omnipotent' since this proposition is not self-contradictory; but the copula cannot be taken as a real predicate since 'it adds no new predicate, but only serves to posit the predicate *in its relation* to the subject' (CPR A 599/B 627). It is noteworthy that Kant nowhere discusses the predicate as such, but always considers it in relation to the modes of predication; the basic subject–predicate schema of categorical logic is extended by the notion of synthetic a priori judgements, but it is not fundamentally challenged.

prejudice [*Vorurteil*] *see also* ENLIGHTENMENT, PUBLICITY

In CJ §40, on 'Taste as a *sensus communis*', Kant introduces three maxims of 'common human understanding': (a) to think for oneself; (b) to think from the standpoint of everyone else; (c) always to think consistently. All three are opposed to prejudicial thinking, and call for active, enlarged and consistent thought; but the first is explicitly dedicated against prejudice. To think for oneself is the mark of a 'never-*passive* reason' while 'to be given to such passivity, consequently to heteronomy of reason, is called prejudice' (CJ §40). Here Kant particularly targets the prejudice of superstition, and describes enlightenment as freedom from superstition in particular, but also as 'emancipation from prejudices generally'. The broader view of enlightenment is developed in WE, with its claim for freedom of thought against the prejudices of both tradition and revolutionary modernity. Kant shows in that essay how prejudice is promoted by such 'guardians' as priests, soldiers, doctors and other intellectuals who

331

disable the public and lead them to the comfortable, passive and self-incurred tutelage of prejudice. Release from prejudice has to be gradual, and accomplished in full publicity; revolutionary change, says Kant, 'may well put an end to autocratic despotism and to rapacious, power-seeking oppression, but it will never produce a true reform in ways of thinking. Instead, new prejudices, like the ones they replaced, will serve as a leash to control the great unthinking mass' (WE p. 36, p. 55). One of the interesting features of this account of prejudice is that it is not opposed by reason *per se* but by 'freedom to make *public use* of one's freedom in all matters' (p. 36, p. 55); that is, to engage in active rather than passive reasoning. This is sensitive to the danger that reason may itself become a prejudice if its validity is assumed and its criteria passively applied.

presentation [*Darstellung*] *see also* ANALOGY, CONSTRUCTION, HYPOTYPOSIS, JUDGEMENT, REPRESENTATION, SCHEMATISM, SYNTHESIS
Presentation is a specific function of determinant judgement which consists in presentation (*exhibitio*) of an intuition which corresponds to a given concept (see CJ §VIII). The nature of presentation is further specified in FI, where it is situated with respect to the 'three acts of the spontaneous faculty of cognition'. The first act is the '*apprehension (apprehensio)* of the manifold of intuition' which requires imagination; the second is synthesis or 'the synthetic unity of consciousness of this manifold in the concept of an object'; while the third is '*presentation (exhibitio)* in intuition of the object corresponding to this concept' (p. 220, p. 24). It is one of a cluster of terms Kant uses to describe the extremely complex relationship between concept and intuition, and which enables their synthesis to take place.

principle [*arche, principium, Grundsatz*] *see also* PRINCIPLES OF PRACTICAL REASON, PRINCIPLES OF PURE UNDERSTANDING
A principle is a beginning or a starting point classically possessing both ontological and logical characteristics. For Kant, the main point of modern philosophy is to 'supply' adequate principles for the classical Greek divisions of philosophy – physics, ethics and logic (GMM p. 388, p. 1).

In his discussion of the 'Pre-Socratic' and Platonic accounts of *arche* in the *Metaphysics* (1941, 983b–988b) Aristotle describes a development from the single material principle of Thales – who says the principle is water – to the plural material principles of Empedocles. This is succeeded in Aristotle's account by Plato's proposal that the 'ideas' are principles and then followed by Aristotle's own decision to organize the principles around causality – the material, the efficient, the formal and the final causes. These principles are both the ultimate ontological ground for everything that is, as well as the ultimate source of knowledge. The equivocation between the two senses became manifest in the two terms used to translate *arche*: the ontological 'ground' and the epistemological 'reason'.

For the Wolffian tradition, *Grund* and *ratio* were synonymous (see Wolff, 1719, and Meissner, 1737), since for rationalists the reason for existence was at the same time the ground for existing. Thus the science of principles – in Wolff's words 'Of Our Knowledge and of Things in General' – is ontology. For Wolffians the two fundamental principles common to both being and knowing were actually fundamental propositions (*Grundsätze*). The most basic was the principle of contradiction – something cannot simultaneously be and not be – followed by the principle of sufficient-reason, which held that everything that exists has a reason or ground for doing so.

In the pre-critical writings Kant criticizes the Wolffian elision of the reason for knowing with the ground of being. This critique developed into the later distinction in the CPR between formal and transcendental logic, composed respectively of analytic and synthetic a priori judgements. Each of these logics and their judgements has a supreme *Grundsatz* or principle; for the analytical judgement it is the principle of contradiction, while for the synthetic a priori judgement it is that the 'conditions of the *possibility of experience* in general are likewise conditions of the *possibility of the objects of experience*' (CPR A 158/B 197). This means that the conditions for a coherent experience also determine the objects of such experience – marking a philosophically sophisticated attempt to align being and logic which is characteristic of the entire critical philosophy. Heidegger remarked: 'Whoever understands this principle understands Kant's *Critique of Pure Reason*' (1935, p. 183). The immediate generation of post-Kantian philosophers, such as Reinhold and Fichte, tended to emphasize the rational, deductive origin of the principles over the empirical; neo-Kantians later in the nineteenth century emphasized their empirical sources in the practice of the natural and human sciences.

Kant also discusses principles in L where he describes them as 'immediately certain judgements a priori' from which 'other judgements are proved . . . but they themselves cannot be subordinated to any other' (p. 606). He further divides them into two classes: intuitive principles, or axioms, and discursive principles or acroamata, regarding all philosophical principles as belonging to the latter. This distinction was first developed in the anti-Wolffian PE in order to distinguish between the methods of mathematical and philosophical proof. A further, but distinct, discussion of principles is to be found in the practical philosophy where they serve as the source of maxims for determining the will.

principles of pure understanding *see also* ANALOGIES OF EXPERIENCE, ANTICIPATIONS OF PERCEPTION, AXIOMS OF INTUITION, POSTULATES OF EMPIRICAL THOUGHT

The 'Principles of Pure Understanding' are discussed in the second chapter of the 'Transcendental Doctrine of Judgement' (or 'Analytic of Principles') in CPR. Kant introduces the principles as containing in themselves the grounds of other judgements, while not being themselves derived from a higher principle (CPR A 149/B 188). A principle is difficult to prove because it has 'the peculiar character that it makes possible the very experience which is its own ground of proof, and that in this experience it must always itself be presupposed' (A 737/B 765). The proof of a principle then, which is 'indeed, indispensable', has to be established on the basis of the experience that it makes possible, in this case 'the knowledge of an object in general' (A 149/B 188).

Kant distinguishes between the principles which relate to the categories and those which relate to intuition, the latter including principles such as 'space and time are the conditions of the possibility of all things as appearances' (CPR A 149/B 188). He then distinguishes between the principles of analytic and synthetic judgements, discovering two distinct fundamental principles for each class of judgement. The principle of analytic judgements is the same principle of contradiction which served as the fundamental principle of Wolffian logic/ontology; for Kant 'it belongs only to logic' and is a 'universal, though merely negative criterion of all truth' (CPR A 151/B 190). It is of only limited use in the synthetic judgements of transcendental logic, which also possess an ontological character. In order to justify synthetic a priori judgements it is necessary to discover a *Grundsatz* or a number of *Grundsätze*, or fundamental principles, capable of giving an object to a concept, or, in a general sense, of combining logic and ontology.

Kant finds this logico-ontological principle in the statement that 'the conditions of the *possibility of experience* in general are likewise conditions of the *possibility of the objects of experience*' (CPR A 158/B 197). In other words, the same conditions that make experience possible also make possible objects of experience. Kant details these conditions as those of the (a) 'formal conditions of *a priori* intuition', (b) 'the synthesis of imagination' and (c) 'the necessary unity of this synthesis in a transcendental apperception' (ibid.). The first condition, (a), refers to the human experience of space and time; the second, (b), to the presentation of objects of intuition to the understanding; and the third, (c), to the categories of the understanding. Basically the principle states that the combination of the three conditions necessary to constitute a coherent experience also constitutes the objects of experience, or appearances in space and time.

Since there is more than one category, there is also more than one principle – indeed, there is a group of principles corresponding to each group of categories. To the categories of quantity correspond the 'Axioms of Intuition'; to those of quality the 'Anticipations of Perception'; to those of relation the 'Analogies of Experience'; and to those of modality the 'Postulates of Empirical Thought'. Our experience is not merely intuitive, nor directly categorial, but combines intuition, imaginative presentation and the categories. The principles in general determine how things appear in time, or how the categorial quantity, quality, relation and modality are adapted to the limited spatio-temporal experience of a finite being.

The system of the principles was the result of Kant's re-working of the scholastic ontological heritage as transmitted by Wolff into a 'transcendental analytic'. The labours of the 'silent decade' of the 1770s were dedicated to the problem of converting the traditional ontological predicates into the temporal principles of the new 'Transcendental Analytic'. In place of such quantitative ontological predicates as unity and plurality Kant proposed the principle of magnitude; in place of the qualitative ontological predicates of being and nothingness he proposed the principle of intensive degree. Equally, he replaced such eternally valid ontological relations as substance and accident, cause and effect, and community with temporally specific principles of relation in the 'Analogies of Experience', as he did also the modal predicates of possibility, actuality and necessity.

Kant's development of the principles is one of his finest achievements and the place where his philosophical radicalism is most pronounced and evident. Unfortunately, with the exception of the ontological readings of Kant initiated by Heidegger (1929) and Heimsoeth (1956), the beautiful display of philosophical argument in the principles has been eclipsed by discussion of the less scintillating deduction of the categories.

principles of practical reason *see also* CATEGORICAL IMPERATIVE, FREEDOM, GOOD, IMPERATIVE, MAXIM, WILL

The principles of practical reason are propositions expressing a general determination of the will. They are subjective maxims when valid only for a human will, but objective practical laws when valid for every rational being (CPrR, p. 19, p. 17). Kant's analysis of the practical principles takes two directions: a problematic analysis of candidates for the principles of practical reason in the pre-critical writings and GMM, and a synthetic presentation of the principles determining a pure will in CPrR and MM.

The problematic analysis distinguishes between two candidates for possible principles of practical action. The first is the Wolffian principle of perfection, stated by Kant as 'abstain from doing that which will hinder the realisation of the greatest possible perfection' (PE p. 299, p. 273).

Kant regards this candidate for a practical principle as being, like Wolff's principle of contradiction in theoretical philosophy, empty and incapable of serving as the source of a definite obligation. With discrete, material principles such as pleasure, happiness and the moral sense, however, the principle is 'blind', unable to deliver the universality and necessity required from a practical principle. A similar impasse is reached in the GMM, where both the 'rational' principle of 'perfection' and the 'empirical' principle of the 'moral sense' are found not to suffice as a 'supreme principle of morality'.

The only adequate practical principle admitted in GMM is the 'autonomy of the will' – that the will be a law to itself. Such a principle will be experienced as imperative by human beings, and may be enunciated in the categorical imperative 'Always choose in such a way that in the same volition the maxims of the choice are at the same time present as universal law' (GMM p. 440, p. 44; cf. CPrR p. 30, p. 30). Kant then strives to prove, above all in CPrR, that this principle avoids the heteronomy of the rejected formal and material principles. His conclusions have intrigued many readers, but have convinced few. They were further developed in the more detailed 'Metaphysical Principles' of the doctrines of 'Right' and 'Virtue' which comprise MM.

problematic *see* ACTUALITY, APODEICTIC, CATEGORIES, HOLDING-TO-BE-TRUE, HYPOTHETICAL

productive imagination *see* IMAGINATION

Prolegomena to Any Future Metaphysics that will be able to come forward as Science Published soon after CPR in 1783, P was intended by Kant 'not for the use of pupils but of future teachers'. It forms, along with OD, Kant's reply to the first wave of criticism of the critical philosophy, and like OD consists in an explication of the critical philosophy's basic themes. He regarded it as a sequel to CPR, a sketch of the science which would enable readers to grasp the whole. Unlike CPR, which is presented in a synthetic style proceeding from principles, P is 'sketched out after an analytical method' (p. 263, p. 8) which proceeds from the questions of how the given sciences of pure mathematics, pure natural science, metaphysics in general, and metaphysics as a science are possible to establishing the conditions of their possibility. The result is an overview of the contents of the 'Transcendental Doctrine of Elements' of CPR, prefaced by comments on synthetic a priori judgements, and succeeded by reflections on 'the determination of the bounds of pure reason'. The first part, on the conditions of the possibility of pure mathematics, reviews the 'Transcendental

Aesthetic' of CPR; the second, on the conditions of the possibility of pure natural science, reviews the 'Transcendental Analytic'; while the third, on the conditions of possibility of metaphysics in general, reviews the 'Transcendental Dialectic'. Apart from the useful function of producing a sketch of CPR, P is significant not only for bringing out the metaphysical motivations informing CPR, but also for Kant's reflections on the events which provoked him to awake from his 'dogmatic slumbers' and to produce the critical philosophy.

promise *see* CONTRACT, LIES

proofs of the existence of God *see* THEOLOGY

property *see also* ACQUISITION, CONTRACT, JUSTICE, OBLIGATION, POSSESSION
In TP, PP and MM Kant determines the civil state by the three a priori principles of freedom, equality and independence. Within this schema property plays an extremely significant role. In TP, for example, Kant moves from the freedom of every member of the commonwealth as a human being, to their equality before the law. The latter, however, is for him 'perfectly consistent with the utmost inequality of the mass in the degree of its possessions' dubiously defining possessions as 'physical or mental superiority over others', 'fortuitous external property' and 'particular rights (of which there are many) against others' (TP p. 75). By identifying property with other fortuitous endowments, Kant is able to proceed, in his discussion of 'independence', severely to restrict the number of citizens 'entitled to vote on matters of legislation' to property owners (TP p. 78). This restriction is qualified by his extending the definition of property to include not only landowners (possessors of 'permanent property') but also those adult males – 'naturally, not a child, nor a woman' (p. 78) – who possess property in the shape of a skill, a trade, fine art or science. Clearly, a great deal is at stake in the way in which property is acquired and allocated.

Kant disqualifies two conventional justifications for property, the feudal justification in terms of military seizure (TP p. 78) and the labour theory of property (MM p. 268, p. 89). Instead, Kant directs his account of the right to property away from the object possessed and focuses instead on the claims against others that property embodies. He abstracts from sensible possession or the 'sensible conditions of possession, as a relation of a person to *objects*' and focuses instead on possession as a 'relation of a person to persons' (MM p. 268, p. 88). An individual's right to property is one which everyone else is bound to respect; this right is respected because the '*will* of the first person . . . conforms with the axiom of outer

337

freedom, with the *postulate* of his capacity to use external objects of choice, and with the *lawgiving* of the will of all thought as united a priori' (MM p. 268, p. 88). Kant hopes with this analysis to provide a justification of 'intelligible possession', although it is difficult in this case to separate the intelligible from the sensible and the historical. This is particularly the case if those legislators of a commonwealth who unite to found an order of property are themselves already defined as property owners.

proportion *see* ANALOGY

Protestantism *see* CHURCH, GOD, THEOLOGY

prudence *see* IMPERATIVE

psychology *see also* COSMOLOGY, DIALECTIC, 'I THINK', IDENTITY, INFERENCE ONTOLOGY, PARALOGISM, SUBJECT, THEOLOGY

Along with cosmology and theology, psychology comprised one of the branches of 'Special Metaphysics' which, along with ontology, made up the influential system of metaphysics presented by Wolff in his *Rational Thoughts on God, the World, the Human Soul, and on things in General* (1719). For Wolff, each branch of metaphysics had its own object: for ontology it was being-in-general; for theology, God; for cosmology, the world; and for psychology, the soul. Kant mirrored the structure of Wolff's metaphysics in CPR – indeed, the 'Pure Reason' of the latter's title was none other than Wolff's rationalist metaphysics. Accordingly, ontology is replaced by transcendental analytic, and the branches of special metaphysics by the transcendental dialectic. In the critique of special metaphysics, the objects God or 'idea of a complete complex of that which is possible', the world or 'idea of the complete series of conditions', and the soul or 'idea of the absolute subject' are revealed to be dialectical. They are, moreover, sciences ridden with dialectical inferences – theology with transcendental ideas, cosmology with antinomy, and psychology with paralogism.

Already in Wolff's system, however, the position of psychology was anomalous. It was discussed twice, first in chapter 3 from the standpoint of the empirical powers of the human soul (perception, etc.), and then in chapter 5 from the standpoint of the essence of the rational soul as the non-empirical subject of consciousness. The distinction may be traced back to that between naturalistic accounts of the soul, such as Aristotle's in *De anima* ('On the Soul'), and theological versions which stress the soul's separation from the body. Aquinas, in his commentary on Aristotle's text, emphasized that such a distinction was already manifest between Plato and the other Greek 'natural philosophers' (Aquinas, 1951, pp. 48–9). By the time of Descartes the distinction had blurred into an equivocation. He insists on several occasions that the soul is entirely independent of the body, while seeing it on others as residing in the brain. Sometimes he insists that the 'vegetative and sensitive or motor' forces of the body are distinct from the rational soul or the 'thing which thinks', while on others he concedes that the two cannot be separated. By systematically separating the two notions of the soul, Wolff paved the way for Kant's rigorous distinction between empirical and rational psychology and his critique of both sciences.

From at least as early as 1765 Kant was working with the distinction between empirical and rational psychology. The object of the former was the workings of the inner sense, and Kant was convinced that such an inquiry would remain 'a natural description of the soul, but not a science of the soul, nor even a psychological experimental doctrine' (MF p. 471, p. 8). This is because the observation of the soul 'itself alters and distorts the state of the object observed'. For this reason, and because empirical psychology presumes to replace a priori philosophizing, Kant in CPR declares empirical psychology 'banished from the domain of metaphysics' (A 848/B 876). He nevertheless defers sentence 'until it is in a position to set up an establishment of its own in a complete anthropology, the pendant to the empirical doctrine of nature' (A 849/B 877). In spite of these comments, Kant showed an abiding interest in empirical psychology, evident in A as well as in several writings on mental illness (see DS, and 'Essay on the Illnesses of the Mind', 1764).

While Kant maintained a place for empirical psychology within anthropology, the position of rational psychology was more ambiguous. In CJ he described his critical scrutiny of the dialectical idea of 'the thinking subject' in the paralogisms as consigning it to the same fate as that which befell theology: 'It supplies no more than a negative conception of our thinking being' (CJ §89). Kant shows that the search for thinking substance or 'the absolute subject' of 'I think' – 'the sole text of rational psychology' (CPR A 343/B 401) – is bound to be disappointed. It assumes that the subject of 'I think' may be an object of knowledge, and consequently extends the categories beyond their legitimate limits. Thus the soul is treated as if were a substance, as if it were simple, numerically identical and (in the A edition of CPR) capable of standing in a relation to all possible objects in space. Although there are differences between the 1781 (A) and 1787 (B) editions, the basic argument is not materially altered: both maintain that the substantiality, identity and simplicity of the soul rests on a paralogism, or a formally fallacious syllogism.

The first statement of rational psychology criticized in CPR infers from the premises that the absolute subject is substance and that I, as thinking

339

being, 'am the absolute subject of all my possible judgements' (CPR A 348/B 406) the conclusion that 'Therefore I, as thinking being (soul) am *substance*' (ibid.). The paralogism here lies in assuming that the 'I' which accompanies thought is substance; Kant claims, on the contrary, that 'beyond this logical meaning of the "I", we have no knowledge of the subject in itself, which as substratum underlies this "I", as it does all thoughts' (CPR A 350). The second claim of rational psychology, that the thinking I is simple, is criticized for illegitimately transforming the 'formal proposition of apperception' into a thinking subject: 'through the "I", I always entertain the thought of an absolute, but logical, unity of the subject (simplicity). It does not, however, follow that I thereby know the actual simplicity of my subject' (CPR A 356). With the third paralogism of personality, the identity of the soul is once again 'only a formal condition of my thoughts and their coherence, and in no way proves the numerical identity of my subject' (CPR A 363). To infer thus an identical subject is illegitimately to convert the premise of the formal condition of thought into a substantive. Finally, the claim that the soul is in necessary relation to objects in space once again confuses the 'I think' as a condition of thinking with the operation of a thinking substance.

Kant's destruction of rational psychology sealed the distinction between rational and empirical psychology. It was succeeded in the following century by the development of an experimental psychology which increasingly encroached upon what were perceived to be traditional philosophical problems of consciousness and knowledge. These were met at the end of the nineteenth century by a vigorous critique of 'psychologism', first by neo-Kantians and then most influentially by Husserl. Many of these critiques seemed to point to a restoration of the transcendental subject. Another series of developments at the end of the century prepared a different philosophical direction. Nietzsche's (1886) attack on the notion of the subject in the spirit of the paralogisms and Freud's (1915) extension of the bounds of the subject to include the unconscious suggested a way beyond the paralogisms which did not follow the path of empirical psychology. This entailed a reconsideration of problems of knowledge and action without the postulate of a subject, a development which led, after the Second World War, to the emergence in philosophy of new 'anti-humanist' topologies of thought and action. These debates have departed not only from the works of Freud and Nietzsche, but also significantly from the work of Heidegger (1927). (For a representative selection of texts from this tradition, see Cadava et al., 1991.)

providence *see* CHURCH, FAITH, GOD, HISTORY, HOPE, LOVE, OPTIMISM, THEODICY, THEOLOGY

public/publicity *see also* ENLIGHTENMENT, PEACE, PREJUDICE

In PP Kant abstracts from the material aspects of political and international public rights the '*formal attribute of publicness* [*Publizität*] (PP p. 381, p. 125) which may be expressed, in the negative 'transcendental formula', as 'All actions affecting the rights of other human beings are wrong if their maxim is not compatible with their being made public' (PP p. 381, p. 126). Since 'happiness' is the 'universal aim of the public', the maxims of politics directed to this end must be in harmony not only with the negative but also with the positive 'transcendental formula' which is 'All maxims which *require* publicity if they are not to fail in their purpose can be reconciled both with right and with politics' (PP p. 386, p. 130). In WE the 'freedom to make *public use* of one's reason in all matters' is the presupposition of enlightenment. It consists in putting prejudice openly to the test of reason, whether this is an old established conservative, or a newly founded, revolutionary prejudice. Common to both forms of prejudice is the inducement of passivity through a usurped authority. The 'guardians' criticized in WE derive their authority by usurping the right to think for others, whether as clergy, medical doctors, politicians, military officers or intellectuals. Their authority is not subject to the public test of reason, but instead disables the public's judgement by rendering the public passive and incapable of freely using its reason.

The association between reason, communication and enlightenment opened in WE and developed in CJ has been a considerable stimulus to the development of political theory in the twentieth century. Arendt explored the implications of Kant's notion of publicity most fully in her *Origins of Totalitarianism* (1951) and *The Human Condition* (1958), while the relationship between publicity and communicative reason has been extensively studied by Habermas (1981).

punishment *see* JUSTICE

pure [*rein*] *see also* EMPIRICAL, FORM, ORIGIN

In Kant's philosophy pure is inevitably opposed to empirical, and both are aligned with a matrix of oppositions which include form–matter, spontaneity–receptivity, autonomy–heteronomy, original–derived, condition–conditioned, prior–posterior, and a priori–a posteriori. Schmitt in the *Sachregister* to his edition of CPR lists its adjectival uses as extending to concepts such as apperception (B 132), concepts (B 91), consciousness (B 208), thought (B 79), empiricism (B 494), cognition (B 1), form (B 34), principles (B 198), categories (B 304), space and time (B 374), synthesis (B 103) and representation (B 34). Although it was widely used by Kant, the concept itself is rarely thematized. Pure knowledge, for example, is defined in CPR as that which is 'not mixed with anything extraneous' (A 11/B 24), although what it is in itself is harder to determine. To give another example of the negative definition of purity, a representation is pure 'when there is no mingling of sensation' with it (A 50/B 74); in other words, its pure state is largely a reflex of its being mingled with sensation.

Pure is often used synonymously with terms such as a priori, form, condition, autonomy and original, but it is also used to qualify these same terms as in 'pure a priori' (CPR A 85/B 117). On some occasions a priori concepts and intuitions are pure because they are a priori; on others they are a priori because they are pure. One of the few points at which Kant approaches a self-sufficent definition of purity is in his equation of the pure and the original. Pure apperception is distinguished from empirical apperception by virtue of its spontaneity; it is 'original' in being a 'self-consciousness which, while generating the representation "*I think*" . . . cannot itself be accompanied by any further representation' (CPR B 132). By thus locating the source of the purity of theoretical reason in spontaneity, Kant uncovers a link between it and practical purity. Pure practical reason discovers its principle not in the heteronomous grounds of the pursuit of ends such as happiness, but in the autonomously generated pure form of the categorical imperative.

pure reason *see also* CRITIQUE OF PURE REASON
Pure reason was a term used by Wolffians to describe their philosophy. Meissner, in his Wolffian *Philosophisches Lexicon* (1737) defines pure reason as 'a completely distinct cognition in which the understanding is separated from the senses and imagination'. Thus when Kant criticizes 'pure reason' he intends both this form of knowledge and the dominant philosophical viewpoint which laid claim to it. This is evident above all in the structure of CPR, which critically shadows the structure of the Wolffian metaphysics system with its distinction of general metaphysics (ontology–transcendental analytic) and special metaphysics (cosmology, psychology and theology).

purpose/purposiveness *see* END, FINALITY

Q

quaestio quid facti/quid juris *see* DEDUCTION

quality *see* AESTHETICS, CATEGORIES, JUDGEMENT, TABLE OF CATEGORIES

quantity *see* AESTHETICS, CATEGORIES, JUDGEMENT, TABLE OF CATEGORIES

questions of reason *see* ENLIGHTENMENT, INTEREST, PHILOSOPHY, REASON

R

rationalism *see also* CRITICAL PHILOSOPHY, DOGMATISM, EMPIRICISM, SCEPTICISM
Kant's use of this term should not be confused with the 'rationalist' tradition in the history of philosophy (Spinoza, Leibniz, Wolff, etc.), nor identified with dogmatism. On only one occasion does Kant relate the rationalist to the dogmatist (CPR B 417); he does, however, consistently oppose rationalism to empiricism. He concludes the typic of CPrR with the contrast between rationalism and dogmatism, claiming that 'only rationalism of judgements is suitable to the use of moral laws, for rationalism takes no more from sensuous nature than that which pure reason can also think for itself' (CPrR p. 71, p. 73) The rationalist notion of 'lawfulness' in general *guards* and *protests* against the empiricism of practical reason, which 'uproots the morality of intentions' (p. 71, p. 74). Similarly, in the third critique aesthetic judgements resting on an a priori ground evince the rationalism of the aesthetic judgement of taste, while those which rest on empirical grounds evince its empiricism. Beauty in the case of the former would be indistinguishable from the good, while in the case of the latter it would be indistinguishable from the agreeable. As in CPR, the critical position is established by means of a contrast between otherwise opposed positions; here between rationalism and empiricism, there between dogmatism and scepticism. This setting of the scene for critique is put in question by Kant's own account of the first critique in WP; in this version, rationalism features as the privileged term in opposition to empiricism: the claim that all cognition should be derived from experience alone 'would introduce an empiricism of transcendental philosophy and a denial of its rationalism' (WP p. 275, p. 83).

realism *see also* IDEALISM, SPACE, TIME
In CPR Kant exploits the received equivocation between ontological and epistemological senses of realism to establish a dialectical opposition of transcendental realism–empirical idealism and transcendental idealism–empirical realism. In its ontological sense, realism denotes the Platonic primacy of the forms or ideas over particular things. In its epistemological

344

sense it entails a direct and accurate knowledge of the external world. Kant accordingly characterizes transcendental realism in CPR as the belief that 'time and space [are] something given in themselves, independently of our sensibility' and that outer appearances are 'things-in-themselves' (A 369, see also A 491/B 519). Kant then shows that such a belief in the transcendental reality of objects of the senses makes it difficult 'to establish their reality' in particular cases. As a result transcendental realism provokes empirical idealism. This is by contrast with transcendental idealism which maintains that appearances are constituted by subjective structures of experience, but that within these structures reality 'is immediately perceived' (A 371), which thus gives rise to empirical realism.

reality [*Realität*] *see also* ACTUALITY, CATEGORIES, NEGATION, ONTOLOGY, PERCEPTION, SENSATION, TABLE OF CATEGORIES
Reality is the first of the categories of quality which corresponds to the affirmative function of judgement. Along with the remaining categories of quality – negation and limitation – it yields the principles that make up the anticipations of perception. As a category or 'pure concept of the understanding' reality is defined as 'that which corresponds to a sensation in general' or that 'the concept of which points to being (in time)' (CPR A 143/B 182). It is opposed by the second category of quality, namely negation, which represents 'not-being (in time)' (ibid.). Since Descartes, philosophers had conceived of reality as possessing degree, as in the view that substance possessed more reality than its accidents. Kant used this quality of reality to underwrite the claim for the existence of a continuum between reality and negation, one 'which makes every reality representable as a quantum' (CPR A 143/B 183). This quality is then extended to sensation or the representation of objects in intuition.

The correspondence of the category of reality with sensation is accomplished by means of perception. Kant writes at one point that 'the material or real element, the something which is to be intuited in space, necessarily presupposes perception' (CPR A 373). But this perception is not to be understood as pre-categorical, but as a principle or 'anticipation of perception'. Kant's use of the Epicurean term *prolepsis* or 'anticipation' allows him to situate the anticipations of perception between sense and 'formal a priori consciousness': perception is not prior to the category of reality, underwriting it in some way, but requires that the category be given in order to take place. The 'real' intuited in space may indeed presuppose perception, but perception itself is only possible when anticipated by the principle that 'the real that is an object of sensation has intensive magnitude, that is, a degree' (CPR B 207). Kant admits that this must 'appear somewhat strange' and points to the source of the strangeness as the question of 'how the understanding can thus in *a priori* fashion pronounce synthetically upon appearances' (CPR B 217).

The reason for the complex machinery which relates the category of reality to sensation in general is the need to prove that the 'absence of reality from a sensible intuition can never itself be perceived' and that consequently an empty space or time 'can never be derived from experience' (CPR B 214). This proof is desirable as a prop in the argument against the absolute reality of space and time. The reality of the forms of intuition cannot be separated from the reality of the objects of experience; they do not, Kant insists, belong 'to things absolutely, as their condition or property, independent of any reference to the form of our sensible intuition' (CPR A 36/B 52). The category of reality can thus only be applied as empirical reality in space and time, and never absolutely to space and time themselves.

Another critical dimension of the category of reality is revealed in the 'Transcendental Dialectic' where Kant argues against the elision of reality and existence. The word 'reality' 'which in the concept of the thing sounds other than the word "existence" in the concept of the predicate' (CPR A 597/B 625) cannot in fact be applied to something which is not a possible object of experience, such as God. If it was so applied, it would be illegitimately extended beyond the bounds of its proper jurisdiction, which are set by the limits of possible experience.

Although Kant on the whole rigorously confines reality to the limits of possible experience, he does at one point in CPR hint at an extra-categorial dimension to the concept. This is in the context of the discussion of transcendental affirmation and negation, when he identifies the former with 'reality' 'because through it alone, and so far only as it reaches, are objects something (things)' (CPR A 574/B 602). In this context reality is an idea of reason, a 'transcendental substrate' of 'the reality of everything (*omnitudo realitatas*)' (A 575/B 604). With this view of reality, Kant extends the concept far beyond its categorical bounds, while yet keeping it, as an idea of reason, within the wider critical project.

reason [*logos/nous, ratio, Vernunft*] *see also* ABSOLUTE, INTUITION, PRINCIPLE, UNCONDITIONED, UNDERSTANDING, UNITY

The nature of reason is one of the central themes of philosophy, and has provoked continuous controversy for almost two and a half millennia. There are, however, some fixed points in this controversy which help situate Kant's contribution. The first, which is clearly evident in Aristotle, is a tendency to move from the act of reasoning to a power or property of the soul which reasons. This distinction between reasoning and reason appears throughout the history of philosophy, apparent in Aquinas's distinction between the power or faculty which is reason and reason as argumentation, as well as in Descartes' descriptions of reason in the *Discourse on Method* as both 'the power to judge correctly . . . naturally equal in all men' (1637, p. 4) and as a general 'reasoning about affairs' (p. 9). A further abiding characteristic of reason is its elevated character and association with sight and light. Aristotle described it by means of the analogy 'as sight is in the eye, so is reason in the soul' (1941, 108a, 10). Descartes habitually describes it in terms of the 'natural light' of the soul. Possession of reason is also universally taken as the defining characteristic of a human being and the main specific difference between it and animals, or, in Descartes' words, 'it is the only thing which makes us men, and distinguishes us from the beasts' (p. 4).

Kant's use of reason may be broadly situated within these parameters of debate, although he makes some significant departures from the tradition. In the pre-critical FS it is reason which distinguishes human beings from animals, and consists in a fundamental faculty of judgement. The faculty of judgement is 'reason' in a broad sense, but within this definition Kant follows the Wolffian distinction between understanding and 'reason' in a narrow sense. He observes that 'both consist in the capacity to judge' but describes understanding as the faculty of distinct cognition and mediate judgement, and reason in the narrow sense as 'the faculty of syllogistic reasoning' by which 'one draws an inference' (FS p. 59, p. 103). These distinctions between reason in the broad and narrow senses and between reason and understanding are carried over into CPR, as is the view that reason defines what is proper to human beings.

Although Kant maintains many features of the Wolffian distinction between FS and CPR, he strikingly extends the range and significance of reason. This is largely the outcome of his systematic exploration of the relationship between human reason and human freedom. The alignment of reason and freedom had been proposed by Renaissance humanists such as Pico della Mirandola and Pomponazzi (see Cassirer et al., 1948), but it was Kant who revealed that reason and freedom could as easily undermine as support each other. This insight informed his distinction between the theoretical and practical applications of reason. From the standpoint of reason, human beings are free of the determining influence of the world of sense; this allows them to act according to principles which are independent of nature; but it also encourages them to make inferences about the world which exceed the limits of the understanding. Reason allied with freedom is excessive, pursuing the unconditioned, breaking all limits, for 'it is in the power of freedom to pass beyond any and every specified limit' (CPR A 317/B 374). The implications of this power for theoretical reason are discussed in CPR under the title of the 'Transcendental Dialectic', while the quite distinct practical and aesthetic implications are considered in CPrR and the 'Analytic of the Sublime' in CJ.

In CPR Kant proposes two taxonomies of the faculties of knowledge that make up reason in the broad sense. The first is the division of 'higher faculties of knowledge' which places reason after understanding and judgement, and restricts its activity to making 'inferences' (CPR A 131/B 169). In the second taxonomy, reason is placed after sense and understanding, and serves to unify thought; it is this taxonomy which Kant relies upon throughout the 'Transcendental Dialectic' (the former becomes prominent in the introductions to CJ). On the basis of the latter Kant proposes two trajectories of knowledge. The first, from bottom up, 'starts with the senses, proceeds thence to understanding, and ends with reason' (A 298/B 355). The second, from top down, departs from the distinction between the spontaneity of reason and the understanding and the receptivity of sensibility; it begins by viewing 'its objects exclusively in the light of ideas, and in accordance with them determines the understanding, which then proceeds to make an empirical use of its own similarly pure concepts' (A 547/B 575). In both cases reason serves to unify knowledge, but the way in which it does so differs from the unification of the manifold of intuition accomplished by the understanding.

The understanding secures 'the unity of appearances by means of rules' while reason 'secures the unity of the rules of understanding under principles' (CPR A 302/B 359). Each faculty unifies distinct objects in distinct ways, the understanding applying itself to unifying the manifold in intuition, and reason applying itself 'to understanding, in order to give to the manifold knowledge of the latter an *a priori* unity by means of concepts, a unity which may be called the unity of reason, and which is quite different in kind from any unity that can be accomplished by the understanding' (CPR A 302/B 359). Although the respective unities of reason and the understanding are quite different, Kant pursues a strategy for deducing the variously titled 'concepts', 'principles' and 'ideas' of the reason analogous to that employed on the concepts of the understanding or categories. That is, he moves from the logical employment of the judgement to the 'functions of unity' which inform them: in the case of the understanding he moves from the table of judgements to the table of categories; in the case of reason he follows an analogous path from the form of inferences or syllogisms to the ideas (CPR A 321/B 378). Applying the analogy of the deduction to reason leads to the search for 'an *unconditioned*, first, of the *categorical* synthesis in a subject; secondly, of the *hypothetical* synthesis of the members of a *series*; thirdly, of the *disjunctive* synthesis of the parts in a system' (CPR A 323/B 379). From the logical functions of reason in the forms of the syllogism, Kant derives such

348

transcendental or absolute, unconditioned ideas of reason as an absolute 'subject' or 'soul', an absolute 'object' or 'world', and an absolute 'ideal' or God. Each of these ideas of reason has their corresponding scientific presentation in psychology, cosmology and theology.

Reason, unlike the understanding, is not tied to the conditions of a possible experience but is 'directed always solely towards absolute totality in the synthesis of conditions, and never terminates save in what is absolutely, that is, in all relations, unconditioned' (CPR A 326/B 382). Reason's drive for totality is always in practice 'limited and defective' precisely because it is never 'confined within determinable boundaries' (A 328/B 385). In freeing itself from the limitations of experience, it is driven to regard objects such as the soul, the world as a whole, and God as if they were objects of a possible experience. This leads reason in a tangle of paralogism, antinomy and constitutive ideals. Kant's proposal to ameliorate this situation has two broad aspects: the first is to recognize that the ideas of reason are only regulative and not constitutive principles (A 509/B 537); the second is to recognize that the limits faced by the speculative use of reason when confronted by 'what is' do not hold for the practical use of reason when it determines what 'ought to be' (A 547/B 575).

In the 'Transcendental Dialectic' of CPR and throughout CPrR, Kant argues that however much 'natural grounds', 'sensuous impulses' and 'inclinations' may sway the will to act, 'they can never give rise to an ought' (CPR A 548/B 576). The latter must be absolute and unconditioned, and can only be given by the reason. Furthermore, only if it is thus given can action be free and autonomous, determined not by heteronomous principles but by the laws laid down by reason. Kant insists that reason does not 'follow the order of things as they present themselves in appearance, but frames for itself with perfect spontaneity an order of its own according to ideas, to which it adapts the empirical conditions, and according to which it declares actions to be necessary, even though they have never taken place, and perhaps never will take place' (CPR A 548/B 576). The inseparability of reason and freedom is argued on almost every page of CPrR, and enables Kant to translate the three theoretically unjustifiable ideas of reason into the practically justified 'postulates of pure practical reason' of immortality, freedom and the existence of God.

The feeling of reason introduced by Kant as reverence for the law is the same as that which underlines the experience of the sublime discussed in CJ. There reverence is defined as 'the feeling of our incapacity to attain to an idea *that is a law for us*', in this case 'an idea imposed upon us by a law of reason' (CJ §27). The feeling of the 'sublime in nature is respect for our own vocation, which we attribute to an object of nature by a certain subreption' (ibid.). It is this feeling which informs Kant's panegyric to freedom and reason at the end of CPrR in the form of 'the starry heavens above me and the moral law within me' (p. 162, p. 166), one which could have been written three centuries earlier in Florence, and in which recur all the themes present in the humanist equation of reason and freedom.

receptivity *see also* AFFECT, INTUITION, OBJECT, SENSIBILITY, SPONTANEITY
Receptivity involves the 'capacity [of the subject] to be affected by objects' and precedes all discrete intuitions of objects (CPR A 26/B 42). It forms one of the two sources of knowledge identified at the beginning of the transcendental logic, namely the 'capacity for receiving representations (receptivity for impressions)', which is accompanied by the 'spontaneity of concepts' (A 50/B 74). By itself receptivity yields only 'the manifold of representations [which] can be given in an intuition which is purely sensible' according to the form of intuition or 'the mode in which the subject is affected' (CPR B 130). However, in combination with spontaneity it enables the generation of knowledge. Describing the character of this combination is the basic philosophical challenge faced in CPR, particularly since Kant refused the option of subordinating either receptivity or spontaneity each to the other, whether in an empiricism which would abstract concepts from intuitions, or a rationalism which would regard intuitions as confusedly perceived concepts. However, in the course of analysis the distinction between receptivity and spontaneity repeatedly collapses, notably in the antinomies. There Kant finds that he cannot describe receptivity without assuming both the results of the spontaneity of the understanding and the postulate of a transcendental object. He first of all describes 'the faculty of sensible intuition' as 'strictly only a receptivity, a capacity of being affected in a certain manner with representations' and then goes on to point first to these representations being related to each other in terms of the forms of intuition, and then as determinable 'according to the unity of experience' (CPR A 494/B 522). Only having got this far can these representations be entitled objects, and the cause of the representation of these objects through the sensibility be identified as an unknowable correlate of receptivity – in other words, the 'transcendental object' or the 'something corresponding to sensibility viewed as a receptivity' (ibid.).

reciprocity *see* ANALOGIES OF EXPERIENCE, COMMUNITY, DISJUNCTION

recognition *see* APPREHENSION, PRESENTATION, SYNTHESIS

reflection [*Überlegung*] *see also* ABSTRACTION, APPREHENSION, COMPARISON, CONCEPTS OF REFLECTION, REFLECTIVE JUDGEMENT

Kant discusses reflection in the three distinct contexts of epistemology, concept-formation and judgement. The three discussions are clearly linked, although Kant never thematized their connection. The discussion of perception in A follows Leibniz in distinguishing between perception and reflection, with the latter described by Leibniz as awareness of perception or 'apperception' (Leibniz, 1765, p. 134). Kant refines Leibniz's account by dividing self-consciousness or apperception into apprehension and reflection, with the former denoting consciousness of the receptivity of a perception and the latter consciousness of the spontaneity of conception. Apprehension is described as 'empirical' apperception characterized by consciousness of the 'inner sense', while reflection is 'pure' apperception and is characterized by consciousness of the understanding (A §5). While on this account reflection is consciousness of the spontaneity of conception, the version in L is closer to Leibniz in placing reflection in the act of perception itself.

In the discussion of the formation of concepts in L, reflection joins comparison and abstraction as one of the logical acts through which the understanding generates concepts. In converting a representation into a concept, the understanding first compares it with others 'in relation to the unity of consciousness'. Then it reflects or 'goes over' several representations in order to discover 'how they can be comprehended in one consciousness', and finally it abstracts ('removes') 'everything else by which given presentations differ' (L p. 592). Kant gives an example of the formation of the concept of tree. First, representations of several trees are compared in order to mark their differences; these are then reflected upon for what they have in common, in the course of which insignificant differences such as size and shape are removed from consideration.

In CPR Kant divides reflection into logical and transcendental versions. Logical reflection here corresponds to the act of 'comparison' discussed in L. Thus the concepts of reflection (identity and difference, agreement and opposition, inner and outer, and matter and form) can be used comparatively in an act of logical reflection to compare concepts in order to discover their agreement, difference, etc. They can, however, also be used in an act of transcendental reflection which looks to whether or not they are being referred to the understanding or intuition; that is, whether the identity, difference, etc. is formal or whether 'things are themselves identical or different...' (CPR A 262/B 318). Every act of judgement 'requires' transcendental reflection, or the assignment of a representation to its proper cognitive faculty. This is a form of judgement prior to judgement, one which does not consist in referring a concept to an intuition, but in establishing where the given representation belongs with respect to the two faculties and the fundamental orientations of judgement expressed in the concepts of reflection. These are the basic modes of judgement which situate the representations of both sensibility and the understanding.

The appearance of reflection in each of these contexts suggests that it may be of fundamental significance in Kant's philosophy. This was certainly believed to be the case by those of Kant's contemporaries such as his lexicographer G.S.A. Mellin (1797), who saw the entire critical philosophy as an account of the origin of human knowledge in the act of reflection. Reflection is a fundamental act of the human soul, one which was the condition of judgement. Support for this view can be found in Kant's early account of the power of judgement in terms in FS of reflection (see FS p. 60, p. 104) and in the claim made in CJ that the act of reflective judgement was in some sense prior to determinate judgement (§IV). Evidence against, however, may be provided by Kant's consistently oblique discussion of the concept.

Reflection was central to the German idealist development and critique of Kant. Fichte bases the entire *Science of Knowledge* (1794) on the act of reflection, and the exposition of the illusions and inversions of reflection forms the core of Hegel's logic of essence in the *Science of Logic* (1812). In twentieth-century European philosophy, the critique of reflection has been part of a deep-seated suspicion of philosophies based on the self-consciousness of a unified subject. Whether in their psychoanalytic, deconstructive or postmodern forms, these critiques appear to hold only for Fichte's development of the concept. In Kant, the relation between reflection and the subject of reflection is, on the contrary, extremely nuanced – it is by no means clear whether reflection is an act of a subject or whether the subject is nothing but a mode of reflection – while Hegel's entire logic precisely thematizes the tortuous relation between reflection and its subject.

reflective judgement *see also* DETERMINANT JUDGEMENT, JUDGEMENT, REFLECTION
In the first and second introductions to CJ Kant distinguishes between determinant and reflective forms of judgement. Judgement in general is described as 'the faculty of thinking the particular as contained under the universal', and if the universal is already given 'then the judgement which subsumes the particular under it *is determinant*' (CJ §IV). If, on the other hand, 'only the particular is given and the universal has to be found for it, then the judgement is simply *reflective*' (ibid.). The reflective judgement 'is compelled to ascend from the particular in nature to the universal' and is, Kant says, 'in need of a principle'. This principle cannot be a universal, since this would make the judgement determinant, but is located by Kant in judgement proposing to itself the reflective principle of the 'finality of nature'.

In the FI §V – 'Of Reflective Judgement' – Kant is rather more specific. He suggests that judgement be regarded either as a capacity for reflecting on a given representation according to a principle, or as a capacity for making concepts determinate by means of an empirical representation. The former 'compare[s] and combine[s] given representations either with other representations, or with one's cognitive powers . . .', while the latter schematizes given concepts. In the former case, where no appropriate concept is given the judgement proceeds reflectively, *either* by means of comparing and combining concepts with each other according to the 'universal but at the same time undefined principle of a purposive, systematic ordering of nature' – the 'technic of nature' – *or* by comparison and combination with the harmonious play of the cognitive powers (§V). The former yields reflective teleological judgement the latter reflective aesthetic judgements. The analytic and dialectic of these judgements form the two major sections of CJ.

Kant hints on occasion in CJ that reflective judgements are in some sense prior to determinant judgement. It is they which form a bridge between the realms of theoretical and practical reason and their judgements. This suggestion proved immensely fertile, with writers such as Schelling (1800) and Nietzsche (1901) attempting to develop further Kant's allusive hints of a potential post-critical metaphysics based on reflective judgement. The theme has returned to prominence in the work of Arendt (1989) – who conceives of political judgement on the basis of reflective judgement – and also with Lyotard (1983), who has used the reflective judgement as a means of questioning the dogmatic, determinant structures of judgement prevalent in modern societies. Both thinkers are struck by the potential enhancement of freedom implied in making judgements in the absence of a given law.

reform *see* CONSTITUTION, ENLIGHTENMENT, POLITICAL WRITINGS, REVOLUTION, STATE

regulative principles and ideas *see* CONSTITUTIVE PRINCIPLES

relation *see* CATEGORIES

religion *see* CHURCH, GOD, THEOLOGY, *RELIGION WITHIN THE LIMITS OF REASON ALONE*, THEODICY

Religion within the Limits of Reason Alone Kant's text on philosophical theology may be read as a supplement to CPrR. In it he considers religion according to 'pure reason' or 'unassisted principles a priori', a sphere of inquiry which he represents as a smaller concentric circle within the wider circles of faith and the historical and scriptural experience of revelation. He chooses as his point of departure morality and its notion of a free human being who gives themself the law. Morality does not require a supreme being in order to be valid, but it does 'lead ineluctably to religion' in that it 'extends itself to the idea of a powerful moral lawgiver, outside of mankind, for whose will that is the final end (of creation) which at the same time can and ought to be man's final end' (RL p. 6, pp. 5–6). The text explores the religious implications of this conception of the highest good by means of an analysis of the relationship between the good and evil principles in human nature. The first book accordingly discusses 'radical evil' or the relationship between human freedom and evil. This leads to the contents of the second book, which presents the conflict of good and evil principles. Here Kant distinguishes his position from that of the Stoics, who saw the 'moral struggle' as one between duty and inclinations, pointing instead to the struggle taking place between the freely adopted maxims which determine the will. The third book considers the theologico-political implications of this view of the struggle between good and evil, and distinguishes between the 'juridico-civil state' and the 'ethico-civil state' which is only conceivable in the shape of a church. Kant describes the requirements of such a church in a particularly inspired application of the four headings of the table of categories: in terms of quantity it must be 'universal'; quality, pure; relation, freedom by analogy to a republic; modality, the 'unchangeableness of its constitution' (RL pp. 100–1, p. 93). The fourth and final book distinguishes between the church based on the 'pure religion of reason' and historical churches based on statutes and authoritative interpretations of scripture.

In spite of its show of diffidence, RL marked a significant challenge not only to organized religion, but also to theological faculties in the University. In the atmosphere of the clerical regime of Frederick William II, dedicated to stamping out the Enlightenment fostered by Frederick 'the Great' (who died in 1786), RL met with a frosty reception from the censor. Kant's initial plan was to publish the work in instalments in the *Berlinische Monatsschrift*. The first section received the *imprimatur* of the censor of philosophy and was published in April 1792. For the subsequent sections, however, the theology censor was consulted. He refused the *imprimatur* and his decision was confirmed on appeal by the Censorship Commission and the King with the result that remaining sections could not be published in the *Berlinische Monatsschrift*. Kant's response was to submit the entire text to a theology faculty (probably at Königsberg) in order to establish whether it encroached on the field of theology. Having received the favourable verdict that it did not, he forwarded it to the philosophy faculty at the University of Jena where it received the *imprimatur*. The work as a whole was then cleared for publication in 1793. The episode is indicative of the political conditions under which Kant was working during the 1790s, and the ways in which they affected the development of his thinking. One happy outcome of this episode was the book CF, which was conceived as a response to these events.

representation [*repraesentatio, Vorstellung*] *see also* CATEGORY, COGNITION, CONCEPT, INTUITION, IDEA, PERCEPTION, PRESENTATION, SENSATION
In CPR Kant defines representations as 'inner determinations of our mind in this or that relation of time' (A 197/B 242). This ostensibly modest definition belies the central importance of the concept of representation in the critical philosophy. A better idea of its scope may be gathered from the classification of representations which appears later in CPR. The genus 'representation in general' is divided into representations with or without consciousness. While in the more Leibnizian pre-critical writings Kant often discusses unconscious representations (NM p. 191, pp. 228–9), in CPR he is only interested in the former, and proposes a division of conscious representations which includes all the elements of his account of knowledge and experience. Representations with consciousness are entitled perceptions, and these are divided into sensations, or those 'which relate solely to the subject as the modification of its state' and 'objective perceptions' or cognitions (CPR A 320/B 376). Kant had earlier criticized the Leibnizian view that sensibility was the 'confused representation of things' and argued instead that sensibility and its sensations were 'the appearance of something, and the mode in which we are affected by that something' (A 44/B 51). Such subjective perception is '*toto coelo* different' from objective perception.

Objective perception is further divided into intuition and concept, the former relating 'immediately to the object and is single [while] the latter refers to it mediately by means of a feature which several things may have in common' (CPR A 320/B 377). Both are produced in an 'act of *spontaneity*' with intuition being 'given prior to all thought' (B 132); but while the intuition provides a field within which the manifold of intuition may appear as a representation, it is the concept which synthesizes these representations into experience and knowledge. The application of a concept to an intuition in judgement is nothing other than the 'representation of a representation' of an object (A 68/B 93). What is more, the 'I think' which enables such judgement to take place is itself described as 'a representation which must be capable of accompanying all other representations' (B 132). Concepts themselves are further distinguished according to whether they are empirical or pure, with pure concepts, or 'notions' as Kant calls them here, categories in other places, being described as having their 'origin in the understanding alone' (A 320/B 377). In addition to these special representations there is the further class of ideas or 'concepts of reason' which are 'notions' which transcend the possibility of experience.

Although representation is crucial to Kant's account of knowledge and experience, there is little explicit discussion of what is being represented, by whom (or what), and in what way. Kant seems to suggest in CPR that the *Gemüt* possesses a 'representative power' which is disposed passively in the 'capacity of receiving representations' and actively in the 'spontaneity [in the production] of concepts' (CPR A 50/B 74). The nature of this power of representation is further complicated in CJ where Kant states that 'all representations within us, no matter whether they are objectively merely sensible or wholly intellectual, are still subjectively associable with gratification or pain, however imperceptible these may be' (CJ §29). They have this effect because of their 'influence on the feeling of life' and their contribution to either 'promoting or inhibiting the vital forces [*Lebenskräfte*]' (ibid.). With this the entire theory of representation proposed in CPR is situated within the account of pleasure and the Epicurean philosophy of life which is developed between the lines of CJ. The association between representation and corporeal pleasure which Kant hints at in CJ may go some way to explaining why the nature of representation itself, rather than merely its taxonomy, remained relatively unexplored in CPR.

reproduction *see* SYNTHESIS

reproductive imagination *see* IMAGINATION

respect/reverence [*Achtung*] *see also* EXAMPLE, INCENTIVE, KINGDOM OF ENDS, LAW, PERSON, PRACTICAL PHILOSOPHY, SUBLIME
Kant defines *Achtung* in CJ as the 'feeling of our incapacity to attain to an idea that is a law for us' (§27), although he uses the term in several distinct ways. In CJ, for example, the feeling for the sublime in nature 'is respect [*Achtung*] for our own vocation which we attribute to an object of nature by a certain subreption' (ibid.). In this case, *Achtung* should be translated, following Kant's suggestion in CPrR (p. 77, p. 79) as the feeling of admiration or the affect of astonishment. In CPrR the 'moral feeling' of *Achtung* is produced solely by reason, and has nothing pathological in it; it serves only as an incentive to make the moral law our maxim of action. However, even here it is important to distinguish between *Achtung* proper and *Achtung* attributed to persons by 'a certain subreption'. The *Achtung* for our own vocation, which was attributed to nature and made the source of the admiration and astonishment that

constitutes the feeling of the sublime, can also be attributed to persons. In this case *Achtung* may be translated as respect for persons as ends in themselves, a respect 'which always applies to persons only, never to things' (p. 77, p. 79). Yet this too, like the sublime, is also only a subreption of the *Achtung* or reverence for the law: the respect which we have for a person is 'really [reverence] for the law, which his example holds before us' (p. 78, p. 81).

rest *see* MOTION

retribution *see* JUSTICE

reverence *see* RESPECT

revolution *see also* CONSTITUTION, ENLIGHTENMENT, POLITICAL WRITINGS, STATE
Although in WE Kant saw revolution as potentially putting 'an end to autocratic despotism and rapacious or power-seeking oppression' (p. 36, p. 55), he also regarded it as a potential source for new prejudices which 'like the ones they replaced, will serve as a leash to control the great unthinking mass' (ibid.). He puts his faith for social change and the extension of enlightened thought not in institutional change, but in the development of an enlightened public and a 'true reform in thinking'. This reformist position is urged even more strongly in MM where Kant refuses to countenance a 'right to resistance' (p. 320, p. 131). If constitutional change is necessary, it should be carried out 'only through *reform* by the sovereign itself, and not by the people, and therefore not by *revolution*' (p. 322, p. 133).

Yet Kant's response to the revolutions of his time was far more equivocal than might be expected from his theoretical comments. He was an ardent supporter of the American Revolution, and his response to the French Revolution was extremely mixed. In CJ §65 his comments on the 'complete transformation, recently undertaken, of a great people into a state' is entirely supportive of the American Revolution; in CF he speaks of a 'sympathy bordering on enthusiasm' grasping onlookers of the French Revolution which involved the 'moral disposition within the human race' (p. 85, p. 182). The 'moral cause' at work here has two aspects: the first is the '*right* of every people to give itself a civil constitution', and the second, the contribution of a republican constitution to peace. Yet in a footnote Kant insists that these comments do not attribute to people living under monarchic constitutions the right to change them. In MM, Kant's position is even more strongly stated, with the 'moral feeling' of spectators of the revolution turning to horror at the spectacle of the execution of the

357

monarch in which, he says, 'it is as if the state commits suicide' (MM p. 321, p. 132). It may be possible to read a consistency into these comments either by attributing the differences to Kant's reactions to different phases of the revolution, or even to regard him as a Jacobin concerned to cover his traces. What seems most likely, however, is that he allowed his positions to be tested, and altered, in response to historical events.

right/rights [*ius, Recht, Rechte*] *see also* ACQUISITION, CONSTITUTION, CONTRACT, FREEDOM, JURISPRUDENCE, JUSTICE, LAW, NATURAL RIGHT, POLITICAL WRITINGS, STATE
In TP Kant defines right in general as the 'restriction of each individual's freedom so that it harmonises with the freedom of everyone else' (p. 73), and in MM he distinguishes between the various kinds of rights which follow from the general definition. Kant's primary distinction is between (a) natural rights resting on a priori grounds and (b) positive (statutory) rights which 'proceed from the will of a legislator' (MM p. 237, p. 63). This 'doctrinal' distinction is followed by one couched in terms of moral capacities between (a) 'innate' rights belonging to everyone by nature, and (b) acquired rights which require an act for their establishment. Yet these distinctions are subordinate to the juristic distinction between private and public rights, or those rights established between individuals and those between the individual and the state. Kant describes the former as proper to a 'state of nature' and the latter to the civil state. The first part of MM on the 'Metaphysical First Principles of the Doctrine of Right' is accordingly divided into sections on private and public right. Under private right Kant discusses, first of all, the notion of a right to something external, and then the modes of acquiring such rights, whether by original acquisition or by contract. Although the detail of his argument is often obscure and apparently contradictory, he seems broadly to suggest that rights to things (*in re*) are a species of rights between persons (*in personam*). He reverses this emphasis when discussing the rights involved in marriage, parentage and being 'head of the household'; for these he develops 'rights to persons akin to rights to things'. Under public right Kant considers the internal right of a state, the right of nations and cosmopolitan right, all within the context of his broader political argument for a 'republican' state and constitution.

rule [*Regel*] *see also* CONCEPT, IDEA, IMPERATIVE, JUDGEMENT, LAW, REASON, UNDERSTANDING, UNITY
A rule is defined in P as a judgement 'considered merely as the condition of the unification of given representations in a consciousness' (§22), and features as both condition of unity and as procedure for unification. The rule which unifies given representations is given by the understanding to

appearances in the 'order and regularity in the appearances . . . which we ourselves introduce' (CPR A 125) and yet is also discovered by it through the process of cognition. The understanding is characterized by Kant as 'the *faculty of rules*' (A 126). It not only applies rules in unifying the manifold in intuition, but is also 'itself the source of principles according to which everything that can be presented to us as an object must conform to rules' (A 158/B 197). In the first case the understanding is following a procedural rule for unifying the manifold, in the second it is providing the conditions for unification. The role of the understanding as the 'faculty which secures the unity of appearances by means of rules' is complemented by that of reason which 'secures the unity of the rules of understanding under principles' (A 302/B 359). Yet in each case the rule of unification functions differently: for the understanding the rule is constitutive, establishing the conditions of both experience and objects of experience; while for reason the rule is problematic, 'prescribing a regress in the series of the conditions of given appearances, and forbidding it to bring the regress to a close' (A 509/B 537).

In his practical philosophy Kant separates the two senses of rule as condition and procedure. A 'practical rule' is discussed in one context as the condition of what we ought to do – it 'is always a product of reason, because it prescribes action as a means to an effect which is its purpose' (CPrR p. 20, p. 18) – and in another as what is applied in a 'rule of skill' in order to attain a particular end (GMM p. 416, p. 26). The distinction between the kinds of rule is also evident in CJ in the discussion of originality and genius. The original productivity of genius 'gives the rule to art' by producing works 'for which no definite rule can be given' (CJ §46). The rule here provides the condition for works of art; it cannot be made into a procedure or rule of skill, since it 'cannot be one set down in a formula and serving as a precept' (§47). To make the rule prescriptive would stifle originality and turn the products of genius into objects of slavish imitation. Rather, the rule discerned in these works should stimulate more works, 'the rule must be gathered from the performance, i.e., from the product, which others may use to put their talent to the test' (§47). This view of the rule as something both productive and canonical which serves as a condition for further works and discoveries, as well providing a formative experience for the subject, is contrasted with the view which sees the rule as a mere procedure for producing identical effects. The distinction developed in CJ between the original and the imitative rule may indeed be profitably read back into the discussion of rules in the first two critiques, where it makes sense of the distinction between the rule as a condition for unity and the rule as a procedure for unification.

S

scepticism *see* CRITICAL PHILOSOPHY, DOGMATISM, EMPIRICISM, HISTORY OF PHILO-SOPHY, METHOD, RATIONALISM

schema(tism) *see also* ANALOGY, HYPOTYPOSIS, JUDGEMENT, PRINCIPLES, SYMBOL
The schematism of judgement 'schematises concepts a priori and applies these schemata, without which no experiential judgement would be possible, to each empirical synthesis' (FI §V). It is a procedure of the judgement which adapts otherwise heterogeneous concepts to the spatial and temporal conditions of intuition. As such it is a species of the genus hypotyposis or 'rendering in terms of sense' (CJ §59). Hypotyposis involves the presentation of concepts to intuitions, and it does so in two ways: directly by means of schemas, indirectly by means of symbols. A direct, schematic presentation takes place in those cases (namely, determinant judgements) 'where the intuition corresponding to a concept comprehended by the understanding is given a priori' (CJ §59). It is also described as a mechanical presentation, in which the judgement operates 'like a tool controlled by the understanding' (FI §V). The schemas of direct presentation are contrasted with the symbols of indirect presentation. The latter presentations have recourse to analogy or a doubling of judgement, in which the concept is first applied to an object of sensible intuition and then its rule of reflection is applied 'to quite another object, of which the former is but the symbol' (CJ §59). The symbolic use of judgement is distinguished from the schematic as being 'artistic' (FI §V) although in WP Kant describes both forms of judgement as schematisms: direct presentation is a 'real schematism (transcendental)' while indirect presentation is 'schematism by analogy (symbolic)' (WP p. 332, p. 195).

Schemas and schematism play an important but disputed role in the architecture of CPR. They are discussed in the first chapter of the 'Transcendental Doctrine of Judgement' where they are held to be the 'third thing' (CPR A 138/B 177) which mediates between the otherwise heterogeneous concept and intuition. They play a necessary part in the doctrine of judgement by enabling categories to be applied to appearances. But in order to do so they must be homogeneous with both concept and intuition, as much intellectual as sensible, and yet void of the defining characteristics of both (spontaneity and receptivity). If the schemas are peculiar, then how much more so the work of schematism itself, which is described as 'an art concealed in the depths of the human soul, whose real modes of activity nature is hardly likely ever to allow us to discover, and to have open to our gaze' (CPR A 141/B 181). Schematism works in two directions: it prepares the intuition for being determined by the concept, but also adapts the concept for application to intuition. In both cases it enables judgement to take place by offering 'rules of synthesis of the imagination' (CPR A 141/B 180). Kant is further concerned to distinguish the schema from the image; the schema should not be thought exclusively in terms of the analogy of the visual image, although he does occasionally resort to it.

The schemas of the categories or 'pure concepts of the understanding' are laid out in terms of the table of categories. The schema of the quantitative categories is number, while those of the categories of quality are being in time (reality), not being in time (negation), and the same time both filled and empty (limitation) (CPR A 143/B 182). The schemas of relation are 'permanence of the real in time' (substance), 'the real upon which, whenever posited, something else always follows' (causality), and the 'co-existence, according to a universal rule, of the determinations of the one substance with those of the other' (community) (CPR A 144/B 183). The schemas of modality are 'the determination of the representation of a thing at some time or other' (possibility), 'existence in some determinate time' (actuality), and 'existence of an object at all times (necessity). What all these have in common is that they make a category 'capable of representation only as a determination of time' (CPR A 145/B 184). Schematism and the schemas thus have the property of 'realising' the categories at the same time as restricting their scope to appearances. They play a pivotal role in bringing together the otherwise empty 'thoughts without content' and blind 'intuitions without concepts' (CPR A 51/B 75). It is through schematism and the schemas that concepts, which are 'merely functions of the understanding', are given meaning in relation to sensibility 'which realises the understanding in the very process of restricting it' (CPR A 147/B 187).

The character of the schema is illustrated in a quite different context by the discussion of systematicity in the section of CPR on the 'Architectonic of Pure Reason'. There Kant refers to the schema as a way of realizing the idea of a systematic unity of reason. He defines it as a 'constituent manifold and an order of its parts, both of which must be determined *a priori* from the principle defined by its end' (CPR A 833/B 861). Here the schema features as both a manifold and an ordering of a manifold, thus participating materially and formally in producing a unified whole. A schema which unifies empirically according to 'purposes that are contingently occasioned' is technical, while a schema derived from an idea of reason is architectonic. The latter provides an anticipatory outline or *monogramma* of the entire system, a reference which clarifies Kant's earlier description of the schema as 'a monogram, of pure *a priori* imagination, through which, and in accordance with which, images themselves first become possible' (CPR A 141/B 181).

self *see* APPERCEPTION, I, 'I THINK', IDENTITY, PARALOGISM, PSYCHOLOGY, SUBJECT

self-consciousness *see* APPERCEPTION, CONSCIOUSNESS, SPONTANEITY, SYNTHESIS

sensation [*Empfindung*] *see also* AFFECT, GEMÜT, PERCEPTION, REPRESENTATION
A sensation arises out of the faculty of representation being affected by the presence of an object (CPR A 19/B 34). It is described as the 'matter' of appearance and distinguished from perception which is sensation accompanied by consciousness, although it too is occasionally described as the 'matter' of perception. It is also described (in ID §4) as the matter of sensibility, which is complemented by its form or 'co-ordination'.

sense [*Sinn*] *see also* AFFECT, IMAGINATION, SENSIBILITY
In A Kant divides sensibility into sense and imagination, with sense denoting 'the faculty of intuition in the presence of an object', imagination the same without the presence of the object (A §15). He further distinguishes between inner and outer sense, with the latter denoting the affection of the human body by physical things, the former the affection of the body by the *Gemüt* itself. The external senses correspond to the five physical senses discussed in §§17–20, and are divided into the 'objective' senses of touch, sight and hearing, and the 'subjective' senses of taste and smell. The internal sense in turn corresponds to a 'consciousness of what humans experience, as far as they are affected by their own play of thought' (A §24). In CPR the inner sense is far more significant, denoting the determination of our existence in time.

sensible intuition *see* INTUITION, SENSIBILITY, SPACE AND TIME

sensibility [*Sinnlichkeit*] *see also* AESTHETIC, AMPHIBOLY, IMPRESSION, INTUITION, RECEPTIVITY, SPACE AND TIME, UNDERSTANDING
Kant's doctrine of sensibility, which plays a crucial role in the critical philosophy, is an uneasy amalgam of several mutually incompatible forms

of argument. The remote historical precedents for Kant's position were the arguments of Plato and Epicurus (Aristotle is surprisingly absent in this context), with Plato representing the 'intellectualist' relegation of sensibility to the realms of passivity and illusion, and Epicurus the sensualist school who 'maintained that reality is to be found solely in the objects of the senses' (CPR A 853/B 881). The proximate sources of Kant's discussions were what he saw as the latter day representatives of the intellectualist and sensualist schools, namely Leibniz and Locke. Kant argued that both tendencies elided the distinction between sensibility and the understanding, the one by subordinating sensibility to understanding, the other understanding to sensibility. Kant tries to avoid the choice by specifying the relationship between the two in a way which does not collapse either into the other, but which nevertheless allows them to be conjoined in experience.

Such a specification of sensibility leads to some extremely complex and occasionally baffling argumentation concerning its character. Sensibility must be distinguished from the understanding, but nevertheless possesses a formal element; this formal element, however, does not subsume the objects of sensibility in the same way as a concept. Similarly, sensibility is receptive, as opposed to the spontaneity of the understanding, but this does not mean that it is a passive *tabula rasa* merely registering impressions. For sensibility possesses an a priori element, although unlike the a priori categories this not derived from the original unity of apperception. Thus sensibility is neither the confused perception of a rational perfection maintained by the Leibnizian school, nor the immediate receptivity to impressions of Locke, but seems to partake of aspects of both positions, while being fully committed to neither.

Kant's balancing act is evident in ID, both in the proliferation of terms used to denote sensibility and sensitive/sensible (see the translator's note to ID, pp. 487–8) and in the argument of section two 'On the distinction between sensible things and intelligible things in general'. In ID §3 he defines sensibility as 'the *receptivity* of a subject in virtue of which it is possible for the subject's own representative state to be affected in a definite way by the presence of some object'. The character of this receptivity, or the ways in which a subject may possibly be affected by the presence of an object, is not left undefined; Kant proceeds in §4 to distinguish between the matter and form of a 'representation of sense'. The matter or 'sensation' of a 'sensible representation' is not immediately sensed by a subject, but is dependent for its 'quality' on the way in which the nature of the subject 'is capable of modification by the object in question'. The complementary character of the relation between subject and object is even more pronounced in the case of the form of sensibility. In §2 of ID Kant is above all concerned to distinguish the form of sensibility from the

363

form of reason, and describes it as arising from the 'co-ordination' of objects which affect the senses 'by a certain natural law of the mind'. He uses the term 'co-ordination' in order to distinguish the form of sensibility from the 'outline or any kind of schema of the object' which may be given by reason; the form which co-ordinates the objects of sense is described as an 'aspect' which cloaks or clothes the matter of sensibility according to 'stable and innate laws'.

While the discussion of sensibility in §2 of ID emphasizes the ways in which it differs from the rationalist account of sensibility as a confused perception (see §7), in §3 'On the principles of the form of the sensible world' Kant distinguishes it sharply from empiricist arguments. He identifies two principles of the sensible world, space and time. Kant argues that neither principle may be abstracted from the senses, but that both are presupposed by them (§§14–15) and are thus pure and not empirical principles. Furthermore, both are intuitions or subjective conditions 'in virtue of the nature of the human mind, for the co-ordinating of all sensible things in a fixed law' (§14). Their character as pure intuitions distinguishes them both from qualities abstracted from objects of sense, since they presuppose such objects, but also from concepts since objects of sense are conceived of as 'situated *in* time, and not as contained *under* the general concept of time'.

With these arguments the basic outline of the critical view of sensibility is largely in place. In CPR Kant distinguishes between sensibility and the understanding as the 'two stems of human knowledge'; objects are 'given to us' through sensibility and then 'thought' by the understanding (CPR A 15/B 19). Sensibility is receptive (A 19/B 32) but nevertheless contains a priori principles which are discussed in the 'Transcendental Aesthetic' which forms the first part of the doctrine of elements. The matter of sensibility, or 'the appearance which corresponds to sensation', is capable of being 'ordered in certain relations' which constitute the form of sensibility. These are the pure, a priori intuitions of space and time, which are pure and a priori by virtue of their priority to appearances, that is, their not being abstracted from them, and intuitions by virtue of co-ordinating but not subsuming sensations in the manner of concepts. The objects of sense are given to our receptivity, but in a highly organized and articulated way; and although this organization is subjective, it is not a product of our spontaneity in the manner of the pure concepts of the understanding. And while sensibility is rigorously distinguished from the understanding, its intuitions are empty without the contributions of concepts. The intuitions of sensibility and the concepts of the understanding adapt, and are adapted, to each other, the co-ordinated manifolds of the one structuring and being structured by the formal unities of the other.

With this position Kant seems to avoid the idealist Scylla of reducing sense to the 'confused perceptions of reason' (see CPR A 13/B 61 ff) and the empiricist Charybdis of abstracting reason from sense. Both positions for him entail an objectivist view of space and time, the one regarding them as objective conceptual relations confusedly perceived, the other as properties of objects in the world perceived by the senses. Kant attempted to formulate a position which would encompass the virtues of the idealist and empiricist perspectives while not subscribing to the full implications of either position. He does so by maintaining the rational character of the idealist, and the receptive character of the empiricist arguments, by distinguishing the forms of sensibility from concepts, and the matter of sensibility from immediate sensation. However, his solution raises as many questions as it answers, and has proven extremely vulnerable to objections from both the idealist and the empiricist positions which it was meant to supersede.

sensible world *see* INTELLIGIBLE WORLD

sensus communis *see* COMMON SENSE

sex *see also* MARRIAGE, PASSION, WOMAN
Kant's discussion of sex, sexuality and sexual behaviour is surprisingly wide-ranging, and is to be found in MM and LE. He regards sexual difference as a specific difference in the genus humanity, and makes this difference the basis of his account of sexual desire. Central to his view of sex is the morally founded distinction between sexual union according to 'mere animal nature' and that according to 'principle' in marriage. Indeed he explicitly defines marriage as 'sexual union in accordance with principle' (MM p. 277, p. 96) and sees mutual sexual enjoyment as possible only on the basis of marriage, and its corollary of the 'lifelong possession of each other's sexual organs'. Kant did not maintain that sex should be subordinate to the end of procreation, but regarded 'sexual desire' or 'sexuality' as an 'inclination', 'sixth sense' or 'appetite for another human being' (LE p. 163). This appetite is impersonal, it 'is not an inclination which one human being has for another as such, but is an inclination for the sex of another' (LE p. 164) and is said to expose humanity to 'the danger of equality with the beasts'. For this reason Kant restricted the expression of sexuality to the confines of the marriage contract, according to which partners both enjoyed the use of each other's sexual attributes, while recognizing each other as persons or ends in themselves.

Outside of the recognition of a sexual partner's status as an end in themself through marriage, Kant regarded sexuality as leading inevitably to the exploitation of sexual partners as things, or as means to ends. Prostitution and concubinage involve contracts which detract from the partner's humanity and reduce them to the condition of means to another's ends. Kant extends similar reasoning to masturbation, an act by which 'man sets aside his person and degrades himself below the level of animals' by using himself as means to his own 'loathsome' ends (MM p. 425, p. 221). In the case of homosexual behaviour, Kant contradicts himself quite egregiously, regarding it as 'contrary to the ends of humanity', one of which, in respect of sexuality, is now defined as 'to preserve the species without debasing the person' (LE p. 170). However, earlier in LE and in MM Kant explicitly repudiated the link between sexuality and procreation, and sought to order the expression of sexuality by means of the mutual respect of persons as ends in themselves, something which is not incompatible with homosexual desire.

In his discussion of incest Kant saw absolute moral grounds for forbidding sexual relations between parents and children, grounds which he discusses in terms of the 'respect' between parents and children which 'rules out of court any question of equality', and the unequal relation of submission in which children find themselves in relation to their parents. He is, however, equivocal about incestuous sexual relations between siblings, which he considers not to be 'absolutely forbidden by nature' (LE p. 168). He claims that sibling incest is avoided by familiarity and the 'fastidiousness' of sexual desire.

The alleged fastidiousness of sexual desire is severely qualified in Kant's discussion of sexual intercourse with animals of the opposite sex, which he regards as 'contrary to the ends of humanity and against our natural instinct' (LE p. 170). He considers such behaviour as 'the most disgraceful and degrading of which man is capable' (LE p. 170) and in MM regards 'expulsion from civil society' as the appropriate punishment for bestiality (MM p. 363, p. 169). In LE he adds the intriguing caveat that there are even more 'unmentionable', 'abominable' and 'nauseating' vices which are of 'frequent occurrence' but which he cannot mention. He reflects on the dilemma which this raises for the Enlightenment: should these vices be named and thus recognized and avoided by the people, or should they be kept in the dark, so that people would not learn of them and consequently not be led into temptation? Kant opts for the latter option, but not without having considerably extended the limits of discussion.

Kant's discussion of sex is in many respects extremely modern. Like Freud a century later, he regarded sexual desire as an equivocal feature of human life, one capable of stimulating the best and worst in human behaviour. He also, if inconsistently, broke the link between the expression of sexual desire and procreation, choosing to govern sexuality by means of the principle of respect for others as ends in themselves drawn from his moral philosophy. However, the limitations of his position become apparent in the inability to look beyond the institution of heterosexual marriage as the only institution capable of supporting the principle of respect for the other. This led him inexorably to reinstate the link between marriage and procreation, and then procreation and sexuality.

simplicity *see* DIVISIBILITY, MONAD, PARALOGISM

sociability [*Geselligkeit*] *see also* CONSTITUTION, CULTURE, HUMANITY, JUSTICE, PERSONALITY, STATE
Throughout his writings Kant describes human beings as naturally sociable, and in CJ describes sociability 'as a property essential to the requirements of man as a creature intended for society, and one, therefore, that belongs to *humanity*' (§41). However, in IUH he regards this impulse as tempered by a 'continual resistance which constantly threatens to break this society up' (p. 20, p. 44). This leads to the celebrated description of the '*unsocial sociability*' (p. 20, p. 44) of human beings, their 'inclination to live in society' and their tendency 'to live as an individual' with the 'unsocial characteristic of wanting to direct everything in accordance with their own ideas' (p. 21, p. 44). This tension has been ordained by nature in order to bring about the development of innate capacities. It does, however, pose problems for social order, which requires human beings to establish 'a society in which *freedom under external laws* would be combined to the greatest possible extent with irresistible force, in other words of establishing a perfectly *just civil constitution*' (IUH p. 22, pp. 45–6, see also CPR B 373, CJ §83). Kant sees this as the most difficult and the last problem to be solved by the human race, but sees the beginnings of a solution in a republican constitution and a law-governed external relationship with other states.

society *see* COMMUNITY, CULTURE, JUSTICE, SOCIABILITY

soul *see* GEMÜT, I, 'I THINK', IDENTITY, PARALOGISMS, PSYCHOLOGY

space [*kora, spatium, Raum*] *see also* AESTHETIC, FORCE, INCONGRUENT COUNTERPARTS, INTUITION, METAPHYSICS, SPACE AND TIME, TIME
In the *Physics* Aristotle explored some of the 'difficulties that may be raised about the essential nature' of space (1941, 210a, 12), directing his critical comments against Plato's identification of space (or receptacle, *kora*) with matter (*hyle*). The basic difficulty in conceiving of the 'essential nature' of space arises from the inapplicability to it of the distinction of matter and form, a feature which is highlighted by the fact of motion in space, for 'in

367

so far as [space] is separable from the thing, it is not the form: *qua* containing, it is different from the matter' (1941, 209b, 31). Aristotle's suggestion is that space is 'the boundary of the containing body at which it is in contact with the contained' (1941, 212a, 6), thus bringing together the formal and material aspects of space in the notion of the limit. Much subsequent thinking around space remained within the parameters defined by Plato and Aristotle, with positions oscillating between regarding space in Platonic terms as a receptacle or 'vessel' for objects in motion, or in Aristotelian terms as the limits of such a receptacle or vessel. The basic difficulty identified by Aristotle persisted in the philosophical tradition, and consisted in how to specify the nature of space if it was not identified with matter or form.

Descartes' understanding of space inclined towards the Platonic position, with the identification of space with 'extension in length, breadth, and depth' (Descartes, 1644, p. 46). By regarding extension as material substance he was able to regard change of place as accidental, and to maintain the identity of space and extension: 'we attribute a generic unity to the extension of space, so that when the body which fills the space has been changed, the extension of the space itself is not considered to have changed but to remain one and the same' (ibid., p. 44). Descartes' position prompted several fascinating directions of criticism, all of which feature in Kant's account of space.

One direction, taken by Newton, broke with the Cartesian identification of space and extension by distinguishing between absolute and relative space. The former is the space of God, the latter the space of human perception: absolute space is 'without relation to anything external, remains always similar and immovable. Relative space is some movable dimension or measure of the absolute spaces; which our senses determine by its position to bodies; and which is commonly taken for immovable space' (Newton, 1687, p. 8). Another position, developed by Newton's rival Leibniz, counters both Descartes' and Newton's views that space is in some sense substantial; in his 'Correspondence with Clarke' (1715–16) he argued that space is relative, an 'order of things which exist at the same time, considered as existing together' (Leibniz, 1976, p. 682). However, what is ordered by space are not simply existing things, but metaphysical substances or monads, and their order is fully conformable with reason. Locke, also criticizing the Cartesians, regards space as a simple idea which is modified into measures of distance and into figures. For Locke, the sources of the idea of space are the senses of sight and touch, for it is as evident to him that 'men perceive, by their sight, a distance between bodies of different colours, or between the parts of the same body, as that they see colours themselves' (1690, p. 80). By regarding space as a simple

368

idea he is able to avoid the dilemmas raised by regarding space as a substance, whether material or non-material (see 1690, p. 85).

In his pre-critical writings of the 1740s and 1750s Kant's thoughts on space were broadly in the tradition of Leibniz's critique of Descartes. In LF he criticizes Descartes' understanding of substance as extension by arguing, with Leibniz, that a body possesses force prior to extension, and that extension may thus be viewed as an accident of force. From this view of substantial force Kant went on to claim that 'there would be no space and no extension, if substances had no force whereby they can act outside themselves' (LF §9). The character of the laws of substantial force 'determine the character of the union and composition of a multiplicity of them' (§10) which are expressed in extension and three-dimensional space. Kant adds that if God had chosen a different law for the relation of forces, this would have led to an extension and a space 'with other properties and dimensions' than those familiar to us, an observation which raises the possibility of a 'science of all these possible kinds of space [which] would undoubtedly be the highest enterprise which a finite understanding could undertake in the field of geometry' (ibid.). With this Kant effectively situates the validity of Euclidean geometry within the limits of a possible space, but not the only possible space.

Although in LF Kant does go on to analyze the subjective aspects of space, his primary focus here, and in texts such as PM, is upon space as the phenomenon of the relations between substantial forces. In LF he attributes the 'impossibility, which we observe in ourselves, of representing a space of more than three dimensions' to the fact that the soul is constituted in such a way as to be 'affected' or to 'receive impressions from without according to the inverse square of the distances'. In PM the focus is again on the objective relations of substantial force which produce space, and is once more self-consciously directed towards a defence of the Leibnizian metaphysics of force against the Cartesian geometry of extension. The major forces now considered are those of attraction and repulsion, but space remains defined in Leibnizian terms as 'not a substance but a certain appearance of the external relation of substances' (PM p. 481, p. 57). Space, then, is the appearance of substances relating in terms of the forces of attraction and repulsion; it is still defined objectively, and in this text at least, without reference to the subject.

From the mid 1760s Kant's understanding of space seems to have changed considerably, moving away from the Leibnizian definition of space as the objective relation of substances, to a more subjective view. This development emerged from the growing doubts Kant seems to have entertained concerning the Leibniz/Wolff philosophy. Kant's early Leibnizian view of metaphysics which gave insights into the relation of forces denied to Cartesian geometry, which was still evident in PM, is succeeded in DS by a view of metaphysics as the 'science of the *limits of human reason*' (p. 368, p. 354). By considering the hallucinations of the mystics and the philosophers in DS Kant developed an appreciation of the role of subjective perception in the constitution of space. This insight is evident in DRS, where Kant moves from a Leibnizian to a Newtonian position. Ostensibly, the essay is a defence of Newton's absolute space by means of a development of Leibniz's *analysis situs*, his anticipation of topology, against Leibnizian metaphysics. By studying the phenomena of direction and orientation in space, Kant hoped to show that space as an 'ordering' was only defensible with reference to absolute space. He moves from the claim that 'the direction . . . in which this order of parts is orientated, refers to the space outside the thing' to one which claims that the order of things in the universe must be oriented according to 'universal space as a unity, of which every extension must be regarded as a part' (DRS p. 378, pp. 365–6).

Kant's adherence to Newton's doctrine of absolute space was short-lived, but the means by which he sought to establish its validity in terms of 'the intuitive judgements of extension' were destined to have a future in the development of his thought. The three dimensions of space which in LF and PM were derived from the law of the relation between substantial forces are now attributed to the experience of being embodied. Departing from the three intersecting planes which figure three dimensional space, Kant claims that 'the ultimate ground, on the basis of which we form our concepts of directions in space, derives from the relation of these intersecting planes to our bodies' (DRS p. 379, p. 366). The orientations above and below, front and back, left and right are all derived from the spatial experience of a standing body and are described as 'distinct feelings'. These distinctions within spatial experience give rise to the phenomenon of incongruent counterparts, a phenomenon which for Kant decisively refuted Leibniz's conception of space as a rational order, as well as its corollary of the identity of indiscernibles. The phenomenon of incongruent counterparts, founded on fundamental spatial differentiations, suggests that conceptually identical objects differ in terms of spatial orientation.

Throughout DRS Kant consistently relates the differentiations within space back to '*absolute* and *original space*' which, while not an object of outer sensation, is a 'fundamental concept which first of all makes possible all such outer sensation' (p. 383, p. 371). Kant acknowledges that his Newtonian distinction between relative and absolute space 'is not without its difficulties' and that these arise 'when one attempts to philosophise about the ultimate data of our cognition' (p. 383, p. 372). However, postulating an absolute space goes against the grain of his new definition of metaphysics as the science of the limits of human reason. Accordingly, two years later in ID, Kant's position on space has again radically altered, but in a way which builds on the positions he has so far established. His new position rejects the Cartesian identification of matter and space, as well as Leibniz's view of it as a quasi-rational order of substances; the Newtonian moment of DRS has also been left behind, and the Lockean view of space as an abstraction from sensibles consistently rejected. What remains is an understanding of space as: (a) an order of relations between objects of sense, but without the objective ordering of substantial forces underlying them; (b) the co-ordination of objects of sense according to non-conceptual differences; (c) making possible objects of sense without being derived from them; and (d) a phenomenon inseparable from the human experience of possessing a body.

The turn to a more subjective understanding of space coincided with a fresh insistence upon the revised definition of metaphysics. Metaphysics is no longer equated with the science of substantial forces, but is now cast as the science of the limits of human cognition. Geometry in this new definition is no longer opposed to metaphysics, but is recognized as the science of spatial relations. But these too are no longer considered to consist simply of the shapes and quantities assumed by extension, but are now taken to refer to properties of the human intuition of space. In ID space is no longer 'some real and absolutely necessary bond, as it were, linking all possible substances and states' (ID §16) but has become one of the principles of the form of the sensible world. As such, space is an intuition, which means that it is, along with time, part of the mind's passive co-ordination of objects of sense (ID §10) and thus inseparable from the receptive sensibility of a subject. As an intuition, space is not spontaneous and discursive in the manner of a concept, but nevertheless co-ordinates objects of sense; it does not subsume them under general concepts, but *apprehends* them 'immediately or as singular' and in doing so 'clothes them with a certain *aspect*' (ID §4). What is more, space is not derived by abstraction from objects of sense, but is a 'condition under which something can be the object of our senses' (ID §10).

Kant specifies these features in ID §15, where he draws out five signifi-cant features of the definition of the space. The first is that the possibility of 'outer perceptions as such *presupposes* the concept of space; it does not create it', with its corollary that 'things which are in space affect the senses, but space itself cannot be derived from the senses' (§15). The second is that space '*is a singular representation* embracing all things *within itself*; it is not an abstract concept containing them *under itself*' (ibid.). A consequence of this is that space is, thirdly, a 'pure intuition' or singular concept which is 'the fundamental form of all outer sensation'. It cannot be derived, either from sensations or from concepts; in respect to the

371

latter, Kant revives his demonstration of the intrinsic directionality of space and incongruent counterparts to show that there are properties of objects in space which 'cannot be described discursively' (ibid.). Kant does not now use these arguments in support of the existence of absolute space, but rather to argue, fourthly, that *space is not something objective and real*. Explicitly denying the Newtonian and Leibnizian theories of space, Kant says it is not a substance, accident or relation but is 'subjective and ideal', issuing from the 'nature of mind in accordance with a stable law as a scheme, so to speak, for co-ordinating everything which is sensed externally' (ibid.). Fifth and finally, although space is subjective and ideal, it is nevertheless 'the foundation of all truth in outer sensibility'. This is because 'things cannot appear to the senses under any aspect at all except by the mediation of the power of the mind which co-ordinates all sensations according to a law which is stable and which is inherent in the nature of the mind' (ibid.). Things may only be phenomena by virtue of space, and only in accordance with it can nature come before the senses.

With these theses Kant anticipates many of the arguments concerning space presented in CPR where space is discussed along with time in the 'Transcendental Aesthetic'. Both are now described as pure a priori intuitions: they are pure in so far as they cannot be derived from either sensibility or understanding; a priori in that they anticipate, or are presupposed by, sensible perception; and intuitions in that they co-ordinate a manifold without subsuming it in the manner of a concept. Kant justifies the pure, a priori and synthetic character of space by means of a metaphysical and a transcendental exposition. The metaphysical exposition consists in 'the clear, though not necessarily exhaustive, representation of that which belongs to a concept' (CPR A 23/B 38). In this case Kant shows that space cannot be derived from 'outer experience' but is an '*a priori* representation, which necessarily underlies outer appearances' (A 24/B 39); he shows further that space is a pure intuition and thus distinguished from a concept, and that it is an 'infinite *given* magnitude' which, unlike a concept, contains an 'infinite number of representations within itself' (CPR B 40). In the accompanying transcendental exposition, Kant uses geometry as a body of 'a priori synthetic knowledge' which follows from the principle of space.

On the basis of these expositions Kant concludes that space does not represent a property of things themselves or their relations to one another. It is the 'subjective condition of sensibility, under which alone outer intuition is possible for us' (CPR A 26/B 42). This condition consists in the 'receptivity of the subject, its capacity to be affected by objects' and as such precedes actual perceptions. It is the condition for things to be appearances for us, and since there is no other means of access to them but through space it can be said to possess objective validity with respect to 'whatever can be presented to us outwardly as object' (CPR A 28/B 44). Intuitions of objects under the aspect of space are then adapted to, and by, the concepts of the understanding in order to produce experience and knowledge. Claims to knowledge of objects which do not respect the spatial (and of course temporal) limits of human intuition are to be disqualified as invalid.

Although Kant's critical position on space presents a subtle critical synthesis of several philosophical positions on the issue, it in many respects leaves the Aristotelian difficulties concerning the nature of space unresolved. The alignment of space as a form of intuition with passive receptivity leads to problems in conceiving how space can passively co-ordinate objects of sense. Kant does not follow Aristotle's suggestion to focus on space as limit, preferring to emphasize its co-ordinative character, but he clearly shares his difficulty of not being able convincingly to distinguish it from matter and form. By regarding space as an intuition which contains within it an 'infinite number of representations' which it 'clothes' in a certain aspect, Kant may be seen to redescribe the difficulty rather than propose a convincing solution to it.

space and time *see also* AESTHETIC, INCONGRUENT COUNTERPARTS, INTUITION, POSITION, SCHEMA, SENSIBILITY
Space and time are discussed together in section three of ID as the principles of the form of the sensible world. They are the 'schemata and conditions of everything sensitive in human cognition' (§13) and constitute the formal element of sensibility. Kant argues that they are 'pure intuitions' (§14), 'pure' in so far as they are presupposed in the sensation of things and thus cannot 'be abstracted from outer sensations' (§15), and 'intuitions' in that they 'co-ordinate' objects of sense but do not subsume them in the manner of concepts. By so arguing Kant is able to distinguish his account of space and time from the empiricist view that they are abstracted from objects of sense, from the rationalist view that they are confused perceptions of an objective order of things, and from the Newtonian distinction between absolute and relative space and time. Furthermore, although space and time co-ordinate objects of sense, they do so in accordance with 'an internal principle of the mind' governed by 'stable and innate laws' (§4) which is not spontaneously produced by the mind. They are aspects of the receptivity or passivity of the mind as opposed to the active and spontaneous work of the understanding, but they nevertheless organize the matter of sensation.

The discussion of space and time in the 'Transcendental Aesthetic' of CPR further develops the perspective proposed in ID. Space and time are

373

pure a priori forms of intuition which, as outer and inner sense, form the necessary conditions of inner and outer experience as well as the objects of such experience (CPR A 48–9/B 66). They are pure in that they cannot be derived from experience, a priori in that they are 'antecedent to any and every act of thinking' (B 67), formal in that they order 'the manifold of appearance', and intuitions in so far as their manner of ordering the matter of sensibility is distinct from that of a concept (they co-ordinate but do not subsume their manifold). As pure forms of intuition they are able to legitimate bodies of knowledge such as mathematics (in particular geometry), which are concerned with exploring the properties of the formal characteristics of intuition.

The role of space and time within the structure of CPR is to co-ordinate the objects of sensibility prior to their unification in a judgement by the concepts of the understanding. To do so they must be distinguished from the spontaneously produced concepts of the understanding while at the same time organizing the matter of sensibility in a way which is conformable to them. Much of the philosophical action of CPR is dedicated to showing how this may be accomplished, but underlying it is a set of problems generated by Kant's view of space and time. These may be stated in terms of the fundamental difficulty of maintaining that the mind is receptive to the givenness of objects while yet co-ordinating them in definite relations. If sensibility were wholly receptive, there would be no place for any co-ordinating activity; but if this activity is admitted, then it is hard to see how the sensibility can be said to be passive. But if the sensibility is said to be active in co-ordinating objects of sense according to spatio-temporal relations, then the givenness of objects – Kant's bulwark against idealism – begins to look shaky. Yet the importance of establishing space and time as forms of intuition cannot be exaggerated, since it is the basis of not only Kant's critiques of empiricism and idealism, but also of his questioning of whether God, the world and the soul may be legitimate objects of theoretical knowledge, or whether they are simply the illegitimate extension of knowledge beyond the spatio-temporal bounds of human sensibility.

species *see* GENUS

speculative philosophy *see* PHILOSOPHY

spirit *see* DREAMS OF A SPIRIT-SEER, GENIUS, ILLUSION

spontaneity *see also* APPERCEPTION, FREEDOM, GEMÜT, RECEPTIVITY, SYNTHESIS
Spontaneity is the theoretical aspect of freedom, and a close analogue to its practical aspect of autonomy. As in Kant's general discussion of freedom,

spontaneity combines the two properties of freedom *from* external determination and freedom *to* self-legislate. The first aspect is prominent in CPR, where spontaneity is consistently opposed (and yet related) to receptivity. At the beginning of the 'Transcendental Logic' Kant identifies two sources of knowledge in the *Gemüt*: 'the first is the capacity for receiving representations (receptivity for impressions), the second is the power of knowing an object through these representations (spontaneity of concepts)' (CPR A 50/B 74). The former is then described as sensibility, while the latter, or 'the *Gemüt*'s power of producing representations from itself' (A 51/B 75) is the understanding. Only through the combination of both may knowledge arise – 'receptivity can only make knowledge possible when combined with spontaneity' (CPR A 97) – but to understand how this takes place requires that their functions be first rigorously distinguished.

The function of spontaneity is to combine the manifold given by the sensibility or to synthesize it in the production of experience (see CPR B 130). This requires of spontaneity not only that it be purified of all trace of receptivity, but also that it give itself its laws or rules of synthesis. Kant imagines two limit cases of this purification and spontaneous self-legislation: the first, explored in CJ §77, imagines a spontaneous intuition which would not require the supplement of universals in order to generate knowledge; the second, discussed in CPR, imagines reason producing 'laws which are not merely logical rules, but which holding *a priori* also determine our existence – ground for regarding ourselves as *legislating* completely *a priori* . . .' (CPR B 430). The latter, claims Kant, would reveal 'a spontaneity through which our reality would be determinable, independently of the conditions of empirical intuition' (ibid.). However, such spontaneity is both self-legislative and qualified with respect to receptivity and the conditions of intuition.

While the source of spontaneity is recognized by Kant to be freedom – that 'something *a priori*' in 'the consciousness of our existence' – he describes its operation in diverse ways. In a footnote in A, spontaneity is described vaguely as 'the inner action (spontaneity) whereby a concept (a thought) becomes possible', while in CPR it is described first, in the 'A Deduction', as the ground for three-fold synthesis, and second, in the 'B Deduction', as the product of productive imagination. In the first case, Kant develops his claim that both receptivity and spontaneity are required for knowledge into the view that 'spontaneity is the ground of a three-fold synthesis which must necessarily be found in all knowledge; namely, the *apprehension* of representations of the mind in intuition, their *reproduction* in imagination, and their *recognition* in a concept' (CPR A 97). In the second account, the work of synthesis requisite for knowledge is carried out by the 'productive imagination' which 'in so far as imagination is

375

spontaneity' is distinguished from '*reproductive* imagination, whose synthesis is entirely subject to empirical laws' (CPR B 152).

Kant's account of spontaneity was radicalized by Fichte (1794) as part of a deliberate attempt to establish the primacy of practical reason. Taking a direction already considered but rejected by Kant, Fichte proposed an absolute spontaneity, akin to Kant's spontaneity of reason, which would contain within itself the limitations of its own spontaneity (1794, p. 272). This position was further developed by Schelling (1800) but rejected by Hegel, who was wary of any claim to an 'absolute spontaneous subject' which nevertheless was able, and indeed required, to limit itself.

state *see also* CONSTITUTION, FEDERATION OF STATES, HETERONOMY, PEACE, POLITICAL WRITINGS

In his philosophy of the state Kant distinguishes between state and constitution. In CJ §83 he describes the constitution as 'so regulating the mutual relations of men that the abuse of freedom by individuals striving one against another is opposed by a lawful authority centred in a whole', thereby identifying the state as a part of a broader constitution. This allows him in PP to distinguish between a 'republican constitution' and a democratic one. There he lays out two classifications of the state: one in terms of the 'form of sovereignty' which may be autocratic, aristocratic or democratic; the other in terms of 'form of government' which may be either republican or despotic. A republican form of government separates executive from legislative power, and is possible in auto- and aristocratic forms of sovereignty; democracy, however, is for Kant 'necessarily a despotism' (PP p. 352, p. 101). The reason for this is that democracy offers the least potential for republican government of the three forms of sovereignty, and is for Kant the most prone to collapse together the legislature and executive.

Kant's distrust of democracy appears to contradict his three principles of the republican constitution also presented in PP, which are: 'freedom for all members of society'; the 'dependence of everyone upon a single common legislation'; and 'legal equality as citizens' (PP p. 350, p. 99). He presents a similar set of principles in MM to define the citizen and in TP to define the civil, lawful state (p. 290, p. 74). Following a rehearsal of the doctrine of the separation of powers between the sovereign legislator, executive and judicial authorities, he locates sovereignty in 'the united will of the people' (MM p. 313, p. 125). Each citizen is free, equal and independent, although it is quickly apparent that some are more independent than others. Kant goes on to distinguish between passive and active citizens, the former lacking independence, and thus 'civil personality', and who are consequently forbidden to vote. They include apprentices, domestic servants, minors, 'all women', tradesmen, teachers, tenant farmers – basic-ally, 'all the mere underlings of the commonwealth . . . [who] have to be under the direction or protection of other individuals, and so do not pos-sess civil independence' (MM p. 315, p. 126). They are, however, assured freedom and equality; but quite what this is worth in the absence of pol-itical rights is an open question.

subject [*hupokeimenon, subiectum, Subjekt*] *see also* ACCIDENT, I, 'I THINK', PREDI-CATE, SUBSTANCE

In Aristotle the subject, or *hupokeimenon*, designates 'that which lies under' and is used in several senses. It is used logically to speak of the 'subject genus' or that of which things are predicated; it is also used as a way of designating matter, and as a way of designating substance as the 'ultimate subject' or those beings which 'are called substance because they are not predicated of a subject but everything else is predicated of them' (1941, 1017b, 14). With Descartes the ultimate subject was identified with the self-conscious I disclosed by the *cogito ergo sum* ('I think therefore I am'), and this was subsequently regarded as the ground or basis of predication. While Kant accepted that the subject as I was the formal, logical condition of experience, he argued vigorously against the claim that it designated an existing substance.

Kant's account of the logical subject is very close to Aristotelian ortho-doxy. He claims that all judgements (whether synthetic a priori or analyti-cal) are ways of thinking 'the relation of a subject to the predicate' (CPR A 6/B 10). In the analytical judgement 'All bodies are extended' and in the synthetic a priori judgement 'All bodies are heavy' the concept of body is the subject; the concepts of extension and weight are the predi-cates of the judgement. While Kant is willing to concede that the self-conscious I is the ultimate subject of knowing and acting, he is unwilling to grant this subject any substantial existence: the I as absolute subject is a logical function, and not an existing being. Thus while it is possible to represent 'to myself something which can exist only as subject and never as predicate . . . I am ignorant of any conditions under which this logical pre-eminence may belong to anything . . . consequently we do not know whether it signifies anything whatsoever' (CPR A 243/B 301). Thus the I as subject is only 'a mere prefix' or a 'completely empty representation'.

Kant was extremely sensitive to the danger of converting the logical subject and its predicates into the substance and accidents of ontology. The logical subject of knowledge is the I 'which remains after all the accidents (as predicates) are abstracted' (P §45) but the process of ab-straction itself cannot vouch for the existence of the I. To expect it to do so is to commit the fallacy of paralogism, as in the first paralogism which

377

moves falsely from the premises that 'the *absolute subject* of our judgements' is substance, and that 'I, as a thinking being, am the *absolute subject* of all my possible judgements' to the conclusion that 'Therefore I, as thinking being (soul), am *substance*' (CPR A 348). Thus Kant accepts the *cogito* or 'I think' as the proposition of an absolute I or subject, but resists the *ergo sum* or paralogistic inference that this subject is a substantial being.

Kant's theoretical radicalism regarding the subject is qualified in several respects, above all with respect to the practical subject. In the antinomies of CPR and in CPrR Kant assumes that the acting subject is a substance. The acting subject occupies both the intelligible realm of freedom and the realm of natural causality; in its intelligible character this 'subject must be considered to be free from all influence of sensibility' although its acts produce effects in the empirical world (CPR A 541/B 569). The conclusion that the acting subject, like the thinking subject, is also merely a logical function without substantial existence was drawn by Nietzsche (1886) and Freud (1915). Under their inspiration the consequences of Kant's original separation of the *cogito* from the *ergo sum* were drawn by late-twentieth-century writers such as Foucault (1980, 1988), Lacan (1986) and Derrida (1967).

subjective [*subjektiv*] *see also* CONSCIOUSNESS, ILLUSION, REALITY, SELF-CONSCIOUSNESS

With one important exception, this adjective is usually used in qualified opposition to 'objective'. It signifies that a particular claim or judgement is not objectively secured but arises from the peculiar constitution of the empirical human subject. Kant uses this distinction with respect to time and space in ID, which are not 'objective and real' but rather the 'subjective condition[s] which [are] necessary, in virtue of the nature of the human mind, for the co-ordinating of all sensible things in accordance with a fixed law' (ID §14). In CPR Kant distinguishes in a similar way between the 'subjective' and 'objective' unities of self-consciousness, the former being 'a *determination* of *inner sense* – through which the manifold of intuition . . . is empirically given' (CPR B 139) – and between the empirical and transcendental 'I's, one of which forms the empirical, the other the logical condition of thought. Analogously, in GMM, Kant distinguishes between objective ends valid for all rational beings, and subjective ends whose 'subjective ground of desire is the incentive' and which are peculiar to empirical human beings (p. 427, p. 35). However, when in CJ Kant distinguishes between objective and subjective finality, or the 'objective necessity' of a cognitive judgement and the 'subjective necessity' of the aesthetic judgement of taste, he regards the subjective judgement as different but not necessarily inferior to the objective (§VIII and §22). Here the difference hangs on the presence or otherwise of a directly subsumable concept.

The last point indicates an important quality attaching to the notion of objectivity which is opposed to subjectivity. By objectivity Kant does not mean either 'derived from objects' or 'derived from (Platonic) ideas'. An objective ground or judgement is in fact derived from the subject, but the subject understood in transcendental terms. This understanding of objectivity forms the crux of the critical philosophy, and its central difficulty of 'how *subjective conditions of thought* can have *objective validity*, that is, can furnish conditions of the possibility of all knowledge of objects' (CPR A 89/B 122). Kant expressly rules out the possibility of objectivity in either of the above mentioned senses; objectivity is grounded in the 'order and regularity in the appearances' which 'we ourselves introduce'. The 'subjective grounds' for the unity which informs such order and regularity originate in the 'subjective conditions' of the 'cognitive powers of our mind', and are valid by virtue of their constituting 'the grounds of the possibility of knowing any object whatsoever in experience' which are 'at the same time objectively valid' (CPR A 125). Thus Kant's account of objectivity does not exclude subjectivity, but is indeed grounded in it. The nature of this grounding, surveyed in CPR, is most profoundly explored in CJ, where Kant decisively suspends the opposition of subjective and objective in the notion of proportionality.

sublime *see also* AESTHETIC, BEAUTY, MEASURE, PLEASURE, PROPORTION, REASON
In PE the sublime appears in a list of 'partially analysable concepts', including space and time, as well as the feelings of the beautiful and the disgusting (p. 280, p. 252). The reason why feelings such as the sublime and beautiful cannot be analyzed is due to their arising 'not so much [from] the nature of external things that arouse them as upon each person's own disposition to be moved by these to pleasure and pain' (OBS p. 207, p. 45). However, Kant does offer a partial characterization of the feeling of the sublime, mainly by way of contrast to the beautiful: both are pleasant, but while the beautiful charms, the sublime 'moves' the *Gemüt* (OBS p. 209, p. 47); the sublime must be simple, the beautiful adorned and ornamented. In OBS Kant uses the distinction mainly as a means for characterizing objects and human types, but in CJ he has extended the concept to include the feeling aroused by the failure of the imagination to comprehend the 'absolutely great', whether in terms of measure (mathematical sublime) or might (dynamically sublime).

Central to the account of the sublime is the way in which it seems 'to contravene the ends of our power of judgement, and to be ill-adapted to our faculty of presentation, and to be as it were an outrage on the

379

imagination' (CJ §23). However, while the sublime is indeed a check (*Hemmung*) on the vital forces it is 'followed at once by a discharge all the more powerful' (§23). This movement occurs because the check on the power of judgement is followed by a realization of the power and extent of the ideas of reason (§27). The sublime in nature is nothing more than a reflex of the ideas of reason which we read into it by means of subreption, or the 'substitution of respect for the object in place of one by the idea of humanity in our own self' (§27). This unrepresentable aspect of the sublime has made the 'Analytic of the Sublime' extremely significant for the interpretations by Derrida (1978) and Lyotard (1991) which stress the ways in which the critical philosophy is perpetually interrupted by uncontainable moments of excess such as the sublime.

subreption *see also* AMPHIBOLY, CONCEPTS OF REFLECTION, HYPOTYPOSIS, ILLUSION, PREJUDICE

In ID Kant describes subreption as the fallacy of confusing what is sensible with what belongs to the understanding. When a 'sensitive concept' is used as if it were a 'mark deriving from the understanding' a logical 'fallacy of subreption' has been made, whereas if what is sensitive is confused with what belongs to the understanding there has been a 'metaphysical fallacy of subreption' (§24). Subreptic axioms are those which 'pass off what is sensitive as if it necessarily belonged to a concept of the understanding' and may be detected by the 'principle of reduction', which requires that a concept of the understanding predicated of anything in space and time cannot be asserted objectively. Kant proposes three species of subreptic axioms: the first are informed by the 'prejudice' that 'whatever is, is somewhere and somewhen' (§27); the second are those which state that an 'actual multiplicity can be given numerically' and 'whatever is impossible contradicts itself' (§28); the third are those which transfer to objects the 'conditions which are peculiar to subjects' (§29). In each case Kant reveals that a covert spatial or temporal determination has been smuggled into what appear rational determinations of objects by the understanding. His main target in identifying the subreptic axioms is the rational metaphysics of the Wolffian school, which becomes particularly evident in his critique of the temporal assumptions of the 'principle of contradiction' exposed in the discussion of the second species of subreptic axioms. The identification of the fallacy of subreption marked an important stage in the development of the critical philosophy, although the term itself is rarely used in CPR (see exceptionally A 643/B 671). The third species of subreption reappears in CJ, where it describes the attribution to an object of nature of our own moral vocation which gives rise to the feeling of the sublime.

substance *see* ACCIDENT, SUBJECT

subsumption *see also* DETERMINANT JUDGEMENT, SCHEMATISM
In CJ Kant describes determinant judgement as subsumptive insofar as its 'universal (the rule, principle, or law) is given' and 'has no need to devise a law for its own guidance to subordinate the particular in nature to the universal' (CJ §IV). He enters into more detail in the discussion of schematism in CPR. The subsumption of intuitions under pure concepts is the same as the application of a category to appearances. This is only possible if concept and intuition have something in common, 'if the representation of the object [is] *homogeneous* with the concept' (CPR A 137/B 176). Since they are not, 'there must be some third thing, which is homogeneous on the one hand with the category, and on the other with the appearance', which 'must in one respect be *intellectual*' and in another be *sensible* (A 138/B 177). The third thing is the transcendental schema lacking which 'all subsumption becomes impossible [for] nothing is given that could be subsumed under the concept' (A 248/B 304). Most of Kant's discussion of subsumption is thus concerned with the relation between the pure concepts of the understanding and the manifold; however, he also uses the term to describes the inferences of reason which subsume 'the condition of a possible judgement under the condition of a given judgement' (A 330/B 386).

succession *see also* ANALOGIES OF EXPERIENCE, CAUSALITY, IMAGINATION, MOTION, PRINCIPLES, SYNTHESIS, TIME
Succession along with duration and co-existence make up the three modes of time which in turn determine the 'rules of all relations of appearances' which are 'prior to all experience, and indeed make it possible' (CPR B 219). It forms the second of the 'Analogies of Experience' or group of principles corresponding to the·categories of relation, and is the principle for the category of causality and dependence. The second analogy states that 'all alterations take place in conformity with the law of the connection of cause and effect' (CPR B 232) and with it Kant attempts to meet Hume's objections to the necessary connection between cause and effect. Kant argues that causality is not, as Hume believed, derived from the subjective experience of cause and effect, but rather the inverse, that the '*objective succession* of appearances' is the source of the '*subjective succession* of apprehension' (CPR A 193/B 238). He thus argues that 'experience itself' is only possible if 'we subject the succession of appearances, and therefore all alteration, to the law of causality' and that, furthermore, 'the appearances, as objects of experience, are themselves possible only in conformity with the law' (CPR B 234). ·

381

sufficient reason, principle of *see* CONTRADICTION, DETERMINATION

supersensible *see* ARCHETYPE, INTELLIGIBLE, NOUMENON, THING-IN-INSELF, TRANSCENDENTAL OBJECT

syllogism *see* DIALECTIC, INFERENCE, LOGIC

symbol *see* ANALOGY, HYPOTYPOSIS, SCHEMA

synopsis *see* SYNTHESIS

synthesis [*Synthesis, Verbindung*] *see also* APPERCEPTION, COMBINATION, IMAGINATION, SPONTANEITY, UNITY

That knowledge may be referred to an originary act of synthesis is perhaps one of the most fundamental thoughts of Kant's theoretical philosophy. This recognition is mainly a development of the 1770s, and appears throughout CPR (first edition, 1781). Most references to synthesis in the pre-critical writings merely contrast the synthetic, additive method with the analytic, subtractive method, with the former proceeding from simples to complexes, the latter from complexes to simples. However, by the time of the critical philosophy, and consistently thereafter, synthesis is cast as the fundamental activity of the human mind. Thus in the first critique the existence of '*a priori* synthetic modes of knowledge' is shown first by the necessity for 'principles of the understanding which anticipate experience' and then by the derivation of the principles themselves from the act of synthesis.

Synthesis is the basis for transcendental logic, the logic which yields synthetic a priori knowledge through the combination of concepts and intuitions. Indeed, Kant insists that it is to the study of synthesis 'that we must first direct our attention, if we would determine the first origin of our knowledge' (CPR A 78/B 103). Kant defines it as 'the act of putting different representations together, and of grasping what is manifold in them in one [act of] knowledge' (A77/B 103). The synthesis of a manifold, whether this be pure (as the forms of intuition) or empirical 'is what first gives rise to knowledge' (ibid.). What is crucial is that this act of synthesis is excessive: it cannot be derived from the manifold but is always added to it. In Kant's terms, synthesis is transcendental, 'not merely as taking place *a priori*, but also as conditioning the possibility of other *a priori* knowledge' (CPR B 151). For this reason Kant consistently relates synthesis either to 'the power of the imagination, a blind but indispensable function of the soul, without which we should have no knowledge whatsoever, but of which we are scarcely ever conscious' (CPR A 78/B 103), or to 'an act of spontaneity of the faculty of representation' or 'an act of the self-activity of the subject' (B 130). Synthesis, in other words, is a product of the human subject's freedom.

In the first 'subjective' deduction Kant tries to distribute the activity of synthesis between concept and intuition in terms of sense, imagination and apperception. In the deduction of the A edition, synthesis features as both a fundamental form of combination, and as one form of combination alongside synopsis and unity. In order for experience to be possible it is necessary first to combine the manifold of sense through the '*synopsis* of the manifold a priori'. Then follows the '*synthesis* of this manifold through imagination' and then 'the *unity* of this synthesis through original apperception' (CPR A 95, deleted in B). Here synthesis, along with synopsis and unity, presents a particular form of combination. At the same time, however, Kant describes all three forms of combination as the 'threefold synthesis': 'spontaneity is the ground of a threefold synthesis which must necessarily be found in all knowledge; namely, the *apprehension* of representations as modifications of the mind in intuition, their *reproduction* in imagination, and their *recognition* in a concept' (CPR A 97).

In most of the first deduction Kant consistently refers to the three modes of synthesis. The first or 'synthesis of apprehension in intuition', also called the figurative synthesis or *synthesis speciosa*, 'orders, connects, and [brings] into relation' intuitions according to time, or according to their co-presence in a particular moment. The second mode of synthesis, the synthesis of reproduction, ensures continuity at the level of given representations, thus ensuring that the representation is given continuity over time. Since there is nothing in the representation itself to guarantee such continuity, Kant describes this synthesis as the 'transcendental synthesis of imagination'. The third mode of synthesis, the synthesis of recognition or *synthesis intellectualis*, ensures the continuity of the experience of the perceiving subject. It is based on the synthesis of the 'consciousness of identity of the self' with a 'consciousness of an equally necessary unity of the synthesis of all appearances according to concepts' (CPR A 108).

In the second or 'objective' deduction the emphasis on the modes of synthesis and their relationship to time is played down in favour of a treatment of combination in general as the 'representation of the *synthetic* unity of the manifold' (CPR B 130). Thus Kant restricts himself to speaking of the representation of synthesis, and not of the transcendental acts themselves. Yet his stress upon the third synthesis of apperception – the only one of which we can have experience through the certainty of the *cogito* – should not divert attention away from the continuing role of the syntheses of intuition and imagination under the sign of their representation as combination.

The relationship between theoretical synthesis, freedom and spontaneity which informed Kant's exposition in the first critique proved definitive for post-Kantian philosophy. It offered a way to link theoretical and practical philosophy, and was crucial for Fichte's declaration of the primacy of practical reason and his exposition of the *Wissenschaftslehre* (1794). In the twentieth century, outside of exegetical debates within Kantianism, synthesis has played an important role in phenomenology, with Husserl claiming that '*the whole of conscious life is unified synthetically*' (1950, p. 42). It has been seen as a way of describing unity in difference rather than, as in Fichte, serving as an agent of unification. The synthesis of imagination is central to Heidegger's extremely influential reading of Kant (1929), which sees in the modes of synthesis expounded in the first deduction an analysis of the relations between the appearance of being and human finitude.

symbol/symbolization *see* ANALOGY, HYPOTYPOSIS, SCHEMA(TISM)

synthetic a priori judgement *see also* A PRIORI, ANALYTIC JUDGEMENT, JUDGEMENT, PURITY, SYNTHESIS

One of the central themes of the pre-critical writings is the distinction between logical and real grounds of judgement. Kant repeatedly criticized Wolff for reducing all judgements to their logical grounds governed by the principle of contradiction, thus ignoring the fact that some judgements had additional 'real grounds' governed by other principles. This early critical position developed into the critical opposition of analytical and synthetic judgements, with the former governed by the principle of contradiction (see CPR A 150/B 190ff) and the latter by the principle that 'every object stands under the necessary conditions of synthetic unity of the manifold of intuition in a possible experience' (A 158/B 197). An analytic judgement is explicative: it adds nothing to the subject through the predicate of the judgement since the predicate has 'all along been thought in it, although confusedly' (A 7/B 11, see also P §2). A synthetic judgement, on the contrary, is 'ampliative' and adds 'to the concept of the subject a predicate which has not been in any wise thought in it, and which no analysis could possibly extract from it' (A 7/B 11).

In P Kant claims that there are two forms of synthetic judgement, synthetic a posteriori and synthetic a priori, but most of his attention is directed towards the latter. In CPR the 'general problem of transcendental philosophy' is described in the question '*how are synthetic a priori judgments possible?*' (B 73, see also CJ §36). This problem is later described in OD as the 'inevitable stone of offence on which all metaphysical dogmatists must unavoidably founder' (p. 226, p. 139). There are two elements comprising synthetic a priori judgements, namely pure a priori intuitions and pure a priori concepts. Such judgements are only to be deemed possible if it can be shown that the two a priori elements may be synthesized in a judgement. In order to show that such judgements are possible, Kant must establish first that there exist a priori concepts and intuitions, and that these are capable of synthesis. The two tasks comprise much of the analysis in the 'Transcendental Doctrine of Elements'.

The pure a priori forms of intuition, time and space, are 'two sources of knowledge from which bodies of a priori synthetic knowledge can be derived' (CPR A 38/B 55). By themselves they cannot yield the conditions of possibility for synthetic a priori judgements; this can only happen when they are aligned with a priori concepts. Nor may pure a priori concepts or categories by themselves provide the necessary conditions for the possibility of synthetic a priori judgements, since 'no synthetic proposition can be made from mere categories' (CPR B 289). For this reason it is impossible to have 'synthetic a priori knowledge of things in general' as claimed in ontology (A 247/B 303). Synthetic a priori judgements must consequently bring together both intuitive and conceptual elements, with a priori intuitions containing 'that which cannot be discovered in the concept but which is certainly found *a priori* in the intuition corresponding to the concept, and can be connected with it synthetically' (B 73). The way Kant achieves this is by showing not only that such judgements are permitted only 'in relation to objects of possible experience' but that further, they are indeed 'principles of the possibility of this experience' (B 410). What this means is that the conditions of the possibility of synthetic a priori judgements comprise principles which unite conceptual and intuitive elements, and which are presupposed by discrete acts of synthetic a priori judgement. In Kant's own words, 'synthetic *a priori* judgements are thus possible when we relate the formal conditions of *a priori* intuition, the synthesis of imagination and the necessary unity of this synthesis in a transcendental apperception, to a possible empirical knowledge in general' (A 158/B 197). This relation between intuitions, concepts and the presentation of concepts to the intuition though imagination is the answer to the question of how synthetic a priori judgements are possible, one which forms the core of the critical philosophy and which is summed up in the formula 'the conditions of the *possibility of experience* in general are likewise conditions of the *possibility of the objects of experience*' (A 158/B 197).

system/systematic unity *see also* ARCHITECTONIC, PHILOSOPHY, SCHEMA(TISM)
Kant describes systematic unity as 'what first raises ordinary knowledge to the rank of science' or that which 'makes a system out of a mere aggregate of knowledge' (CPR A 832/B 860). The art of constructing such systems

is architectonic, and consists of unifying an aggregate of knowledge by means of an idea. The idea is realized in the system by means of a schema which combines a 'constituent manifold' with an 'order of its parts' (A 833/B 861); a schema derived empirically yields a technical unity of the aggregate, while one derived from the idea itself yields an architectonic unity. Kant focuses his discussion of a system of knowledge on philosophy, whose idea is a *conceptus cosmicus* of philosophy as 'the science of the relation of all knowledge to the essential ends of human reason' (A 839/B 867). The schema of the system of philosophy is best described in FI, where Kant distinguishes the 'system of rational knowledge by means of concepts' which makes up philosophy from a critique of pure reason. The latter provides the schema or monogram of such a system when it 'demarcates and examines the very idea of the system' (FI p. 195, p. 3). According to this, the 'real system of philosophy can be divided into *theoretical* and *practical* philosophy,' a division Kant, not unproblematically, may be said to have followed in MF and MM.

In CPR Kant also develops a set of regulative principles for ensuring the systematic unity of the empirical knowledge gained by the understanding. These are the principles of the '*homogeneity* of the manifold under higher genera', the '*variety* of the homogeneous under lower species' and the '*affinity* of all concepts . . . which prescribes that we proceed from each species to every other by gradual increase of the diversity' (CPR A 657/B 686). Variously titled 'homogeneity', 'variety' and 'affinity'; 'homogeneity', 'specification' and 'continuity'; and 'unity', 'manifoldness' and 'affinity', these three principles are used regulatively to pursue the goal of the unity of the knowledge gained by the understanding. Kant regards the systematic unity of knowledge as a regulative idea; this distinguishes his notion both from the Wolffian system which preceded his work and from the systems of Schelling and Hegel which succeeded it. The former offered only an aggregate of knowledge devoid of any definite principle (A 836/B 864) while the latter converted systematic unity into a constitutive principle, and strove to deliver as the realized system of philosophy what Kant considered to be but the regulative idea of its progressive development.

386

T

table of judgements/categories *see also* CATEGORIES, COMBINATION, JUDGEMENT
SYNTHESIS, UNITY

In CPR Kant described the 'table of judgements' as the 'clue to the discovery of all pure concepts of the understanding'. By this he meant that the 12 categories or pure concepts of the understanding may be derived from the 12 'function[s] of thought in judgement' (CPR A 70/B 95). The concept which links the two tables is that of synthesis, or the unity of a manifold. In a crucial step in his argument Kant claims that 'the same function which gives unity to the various representations *in a judgement* also gives unity to the mere synthesis of various representations *in an intuition*; and this unity, in its most general expression, we entitle the pure concept of the understanding' (CPR A 79/B 104). Thus a pure concept of the understanding corresponds to each of the judgements, as may be seen if the two tables are compared – see tables 1 and 2 in CATEGORIES.

Kant claimed that the categories offered an 'exhaustive inventory' of the powers of the understanding (CPR A 80/B 106), a position which has been consistently disputed since the publication of CPR. Critics ranging from Strawson (1966) to Derrida (1978) have been unanimously critical of the way in which the tables of judgements and categories not only dominated Kant's presentation of his thoughts in CPR, but in also in CPrR and CJ. The second critique (CPrR) presents a 'Table of Categories of Freedom' (p. 66, p. 68) while the third (CJ) expounds the aesthetic judgement of taste in terms of quality, quantity, relation and modality. Opinions are still divided about whether the table of categories is simply an historical and dispensable form of presentation, or whether it is integral to Kant's philosophy.

taste *see* AESTHETIC, BEAUTY, JUDGEMENT, REFLECTIVE JUDGEMENT

technic/technique [*Technik*] *see also* ART, IMPERATIVE, JUDGEMENT, REFLECTIVE
JUDGEMENT, SYSTEM, TELEOLOGY

In FI Kant distinguishes between practical judgements, which are based on freedom, and technical judgements which 'belong to the *art* of realising

387

some desired thing' (FI p. 200, p. 7). He illustrates the distinction by redescribing the imperatives of skill and prudence presented in GMM as 'technical' imperatives. He then extends the concept of technical judgement to include a technical procedure which is followed by the power of judgement, and argues that this procedure is followed when judging natural objects. From this he derives a 'technic of nature' which consists in judging natural objects '*as if* their possibility rested on art' (p. 201, p. 8). The concept of a 'technic of nature' is crucial for Kant's philosophy of nature developed in the second part of CJ and subsequently extended in OP.

In Part II of CJ Kant argues that nature cannot be understood on the basis of mechanical principles alone, but must be supplemented by the principles of teleological judgement. The products of nature may be viewed as ends, and its causality in this respect is described in FI as a '*technic* of nature' (FI p. 219, p. 23). The technic of nature is not a category, and is rigorously distinguished from the 'nomothetic of nature' which consists in bringing nature under the laws of the understanding. The technic of nature arises from the unifying procedures followed by judgement when it brings an empirical intuition under a concept, or the laws of the understanding under common principles. Kant concludes that the 'faculty of judgement is essentially technical; nature is represented as technical only to the extent that it agrees with this procedure and makes it necessary' (FI p. 220, p. 24). The technic of nature thus serves as a principle for reflective judgement, and denotes but 'a relation of things to our power of judging; in the latter alone can be found the idea of that finality which we attribute to nature itself' (p. 221, p. 25).

teleology *see also* END, FINALITY, KINGDOM OF ENDS, TECHNIQUE
A teleological explanation is one couched in terms of final ends. Its origins lie in the Aristotelian distinction between material, formal, efficient and final causes, which he applied to the explanation of physical change. The final cause or '"that for the sake of which" a thing is done' (1941, 195a, 33) was applied both to physical change and to human action. Teleological explanations were applied to both nature and action, until the early modern period when Galileo rejected all the Aristotelian causes, and Descartes banished final causes from the explanation of physical change in favour of efficient causes. Kant, however, argued for a limited role for teleological principles in supplementing mechanical explanations. In the second part of CJ he presented a 'Critique of Teleological Judgement' which, in an analytic, dialectic and methodology, established the limits for the legitimate use of teleological judgement (but see also his 'On the Use of Teleological Principles in Philosophy', 1788). Teleological judgements may supplement determinant judgement as a 'regulative principle' for

reflective judgement, and thus extend 'physical science according to another principle, that, namely, of final causes, yet without interfering with
the principle of the mechanism of physical causality' (CJ §67). Teleological judgements may not be used simply to ascribe human purposes to the
objects of nature, which is simply a form of 'mental jugglery that only
reads the conception of an end into the nature of the things', but may
serve as a means of achieving the systematic completeness of our knowledge. Teleological principles, in other words, have no explanatory significance (CJ introduction to Part II).

Teleology comes into its own in Kant's practical philosophy, although
there it is no longer regarded as teleology proper. What makes practical
judgements teleological for Kant is their reference to an end. The ground
of the self-determination of the will is an 'end' (GMM p. 427, p. 35) and
so technically all moral judgements, since they are determined by an end,
are teleological. However, they are not teleological in the sense of ascribing significance to an accomplished action, but only in so far as these ends
serve as inclinations or motives for the determination of the will. Although
the two forms of teleological judgement seem to be opposed as physical
and ethical teleology (to use the terms of CJ Part II), Kant strove to unite
them in an 'ultimate end' of human freedom culturing itself in the legislation of natural and moral laws. In this respect teleology can be seen to
play a crucial role in the critical philosophy, not only in extending the
realm of knowledge of nature as a regulative principle and acting as a
source for end-directed moral judgements, but above all in integrating the
realms of natural necessity and practical freedom.

theodicy *see also* FAITH, GOD, HISTORY, PROVIDENCE, THEOLOGY
In FPT (1791) Kant returned to the problem of theodicy, which had pre-
occupied him during the mid to late 1750s. He was concerned in the earlier
period with Leibniz's theodicy or 'defence of God's good cause' encapsu-
lated in the proposition that 'this world was the best of all possible worlds'.
Although in *An Attempt at some Reflections on Optimism* (1759) Kant on the
whole defends God's good cause, he had methodological doubts about the
ability of human beings to discern the ways of the Almighty (ibid., p. 35,
p. 76). These were re-stated in FPT on the basis of the critical philosophy's
limitation of legitimate knowledge to the bounds of possible experience.

Defining theodicy as the 'defences of the highest wisdom of the Creator
against the complaints which reason makes by pointing to the existence of
things in the world which contradict the wise purpose' (FPT p. 283), Kant
lays out three areas of complaint: (a) 'the holiness of the creator contrasts
with moral evil in the world'; (b) the goodness of the Creator contrasts
with woes and suffering; (c) the justice of the Creator contrasts with the

impunity of the guilty (FPT p. 285). He argues that in each case 'reason is completely powerless when it comes to determining the *relationship between this world as we know it through experience* and *the supreme wisdom*' (FPT p. 290). In full accord with the results of the critical philosophy, Kant describes this realization of the 'necessary limits of our reflections' as a 'negative wisdom' which by showing the failure of a speculative theodicy, clears the way for a practical one. Through an interpretation of the story of Job, Kant reaches the conclusion that 'theodicy is not a task of science but is a matter of faith' (FPT p. 293).

theology *see also* ANALOGY, CHURCH, COSMOLOGY, GOD, HISTORY, PROVIDENCE, PSYCHOLOGY, THEODICY

Kant's critique of theology engaged with a highly specific object, namely the philosophical theology developed by Christian Wolff which was considered as a branch of 'special metaphysics'. Wolff's theology marked the first stage of the trespass of philosophy – a lower faculty of the eighteenth-century university – into the territory of the higher faculty of theology. This move was vigorously combatted by the theologians who used all means, including court intrigue, to keep philosophy in its place. These struggles led eventually to Wolff's banishment from Prussia and an edict forbidding discussion of his books. Echoes of this struggle between the philosophical and theological faculties still resound in Kant's CF, and determined the character of his critique of theology.

Kant's discussion of theology rarely strays beyond the critique of the Wolffian treatment of God as an object of 'special metaphysics' along with the world (cosmology) and the soul (psychology). His lectures on philosophical theology largely took the form of a critical commentary on the section in Baumgarten's Wolffian *Metaphysica* (1739) on God, and his critique of theology in the 'Transcendental Dialectic' is a feature of the critique's point-by-point demolition of the 'pure reason' of Wolffian metaphysics. Yet in his critique Kant was careful not to surrender philosophical theology to the theologians. Rather he argued that while God could not be an object of speculative knowledge, it could nevertheless be a postulate of practical reason. His denial of knowledge 'to make room for *faith*' (CPR B xxx) was directed at both philosophical theology and the Biblical exegesis of the theology faculty. The discussion of the conflict of philosophy and theology in CF thus concludes with a gesture of solidarity with non-institutional, non-theological religion which takes the form of publishing a letter from Carol Arnold Wilmans on 'separatists and mystics' who claims that although he has never 'found a theologian among them' yet 'if these people were philosophers they would be (pardon the term!) true Kantians' (CF pp. 74–5, pp. 137–8).

Kant's critique of theology is thus an important part of his broader critique of metaphysics, and concentrates almost exclusively upon the proofs for the existence of God. In OPA from 1763 his critique is part of a general movement in his thought against 'false subtlety' (see also FS): 'Providence has not intended that the insights most necessary for human blessedness should rest upon the subtlety of refined inferences' (OPA p. 65, p. 43). But while 'natural common sense' will suffice, it can be 'confused by false artifice' (ibid.) and so it is necessary, as with the logical *False Subtlety of the Four Syllogistic Figures*, written at the same time, to oppose 'false artifice' in reasoning.

In OPA Kant identifies four proofs for the existence of God, and groups them according to whether they are taken 'either from rational concepts of the merely possible, or from empirical concepts of the existent' (p. 155, p. 223). The first group is entitled the 'ontological', the second the 'cosmological' proofs. Of the ontological proofs Kant is critical of the 'so-called Cartesian' proof, which reasons from the perfection of God to its existence. A perfect being would possess all predicates including existence, yet Kant shows that existence is not a predicate but the position of predicates. His own favoured proof does not seek grounds for the existence of God, but instead reasons that God exists because the opposite proposition (God does not exist) is unthinkable (OPA p. 162, p. 237, see also ND p. 392, p. 69); but this quintessentially 'artificial' argument is pursued with all the signs of a bad conscience and palpably decreasing conviction. Kant is, however, equally critical of the first of the cosmological proofs, which reasons through the principle of sufficient reason from perceived effects to a fundamental cause, and which has 'gained much attention through the Wolffian school of philosophy' (OPA p. 158, p. 229). He is less critical of the second cosmological proof, which reasons from the perceived purposive arrangement of the world to a creator, but argues that, while it can never achieve precision, it is to be respected for its power 'to vitalise mankind with elevated sentiments which are productive of noble activity' (OPA p. 161, p. 235). He maintains this position in CJ and LPT where the second cosmological proof was seen as establishing a moral theology on the basis of analogical knowledge of God.

In CPR Kant abandons even the residual and unenthusiastic attempt of OPA to provide a proof for the existence of God. In the third chapter of the 'Transcendental Dialectic', on the 'Ideal of Pure Reason' (which follows the demolitions of rational psychology and cosmology in the paralogisms and antinomies), he declares the three proofs of rational theology – the 'ontological', 'cosmological' and 'physico-theological' – to be unsustainable. An analogous train of argument, with some differences of detail, may be discerned in the first part of LPT on 'Transcendental

Theology'. Both versions of Kant's critique of theology defend the claim that it is impossible for human reason to attain speculative or theoretical knowledge of God.

Kant thinks the ontological proof is impossible because being is not a predicate, and thus cannot be said to belong to the set of predicates which make up the most real being (*ens realissimum*). The predicate being 'only serves to posit the predicate *in its relation* to the subject' (CPR A 599/B 627), and to say 'God is' attaches no new predicate to the concept 'God' but only 'posits [God] as being an *object* that stands in relation to my *concept*' (ibid.). To claim that the most real and perfect being must possess the predicate 'existence' confuses the orders of real and logical predication. For existence is not a concept but the position through which concept and object may be brought into relation. The real position of existence or the 'context of experience as a whole' is rigorously distinguished from the logical concept which simply 'conform[s] to the *universal conditions* of possible empirical knowledge' (CPR A 601/B 629). Any consciousness of existence, whether immediate/perceptive or inferred, can only hold within the field of the 'unity of experience'. Outside of this it makes no sense, and attempting to prove otherwise is 'merely so much labour and effort lost' (CPR A 602/B 630).

Unlike the ontological proof for the existence of God, a wholly a priori argument which moves 'from the highest reality to the necessity of existence' (CPR A 604/B 632), the cosmological proof moves from the major premise 'If anything exists, an absolutely necessary being must also exist' through the minor premise 'I exist' to the conclusion 'an absolutely necessary being exists' (CPR A 604/B 632). Kant claims that this proof contains 'a whole nest of dialectical assumptions', such as the extension of the category of causality – which only possesses meaning within the sensible world – to the supersensible; the inference of a first cause from an infinite series; and the confusion of the logical and transcendental possibilities of an *ens realissimum* (CPR A 610/B 638).

The ontological and cosmological proofs both make the error of converting potentially regulative principles into constitutive ones, thus hypostatizing necessity as a formal principle of thought into a 'material condition of existence' (CPR A 620/B 648). Both proofs move from abstractions such as 'existence in general' to 'concepts of things in general', whereas the physico-theological proof moves from the 'determinate experience' of order in nature to a free 'sublime and wise cause (or more than one)' (CPR A 625/B 653). Yet in order to advance from the experience of this world to its origin, Kant claims that this proof must have recourse to the discredited ontological and cosmological proofs, and must thus fall with them.

By criticizing the three proofs, Kant claims to have undermined speculative theology definitively. In CPR the *ens realissimum* is only permitted as a regulative principle; no speculative inferences from the concept to an object of existence are permissible. In LPT he develops a moral theology, based loosely on Baumgarten which points to a constructive complement to the destruction of the proofs of speculative theology. This proposes the existence of God as a 'necessary postulate for the incontrovertible laws of my own nature' (p. 110) and establishes a determinate concept of God as the necessary condition for morality. In this way, specious knowledge of God is removed in order to make room for practical faith.

theoretical philosophy *see* PHILOSOPHY

thing [*Ding*] *see* APPEARANCE, OBJECT, PERSON

thing-in-itself [*Ding an sich*] *see also* APPEARANCE, ARCHETYPE, IDENTITY, INTELLIGIBLE WORLD, INTUITION, NOUMENON, OBJECT, PHENOMENON, TRANSCENDENTAL OBJECT
Kant uses this term to denote a cluster of meanings which include those properly attributed to noumena and to transcendent ideas. The thing-in-itself shares with these the negative quality of limiting the employment of the understanding and reason to what can be an object of intuition, and the positive quality of denoting a problematic space beyond these limits. Thus the thing-in-itself cannot be known since knowledge is limited to possible experience, but it can be thought, provided that it satisfies the condition of a possible thought which is not to be self-contradictory. In P Kant uses things-in-themselves synonymously with noumena, namely in the application of pure concepts of the understanding 'beyond objects of experience' to 'things in themselves (*noumena*)' (P §29). Similarly in CPR he regards things-in-themselves as potential ideas of reason, and speaks of 'the *unconditioned* which reason, by necessity and by right, demands in things in themselves' (CPR B xx).

What distinguishes the things-in-themselves from the other forms of noumena are their property of being the 'true correlate of sensibility' (CPR A 30/B 45). Kant moves from the premise that 'nothing intuited in space is a thing in itself' to the conclusion that 'the thing in itself is not known, and cannot be known, through these representations [of our sensibility]; and in experience no question is ever asked in regard to it' (CPR A 30/B 45). Yet Kant does not follow his own self-limiting ordinance here, since he assumes that there *must* be a correlate which can be thought, even if not known. On critical principles he can properly say no more than that the thing in itself *may* be a correlate of sensibility. That he does not do so arises from his resistance to the 'absurd conclusion that there can be appearance without anything that appears' (CPR B xxvi).

The residual dogmatism of his position, which rests on the principle of contradiction, was criticized by Hegel and Nietzsche. Neither was convinced of the necessity of there being something beyond appearance which is manifest in it. Hegel's exposition of appearances in the *Phenomenology of Spirit* (1807) is informed by an immanent absolute, not one which is manifest in appearances, while Nietzsche regards the opposition of appearance and thing-in-itself as a Platonic prejudice of the philosophers, one of which, he noted in *The Gay Science* (1882), we know too little to be entitled to use (§355).

thinking [*Denken*] *see also* COGNITION, HOLDING-TO-BE-TRUE, 'I THINK', JUDGEMENT, KNOWLEDGE

Thinking (*Denken*) is distinct from both knowing (*Wissen*) and cognition (*Erkenntnis*), although these distinctions are not observed in translation; nor are they uniformly observed by Kant. Thinking consists in 'uniting representations in a consciousness' and the latter is a description of judgement; 'thinking therefore is the same as judging' (P §22). As such it is an activity proper to the understanding, for 'through mere intuition nothing is thought' (CPR A 253/B 309). The unification of representations accomplished in thinking is based on spontaneous, pure apperception of the 'I think', which is also entitled the '*transcendental* unity of self-consciousness' which indicates 'the possibility of *a priori* knowledge arising from it' (CPR B 132). Although at one point Kant describes thinking as 'cognition by means of concepts' (CPR A 69/B 94), apparently suggesting that thinking is a form of cognition, he otherwise consistently distinguishes between them. In order to cognize an object 'I must be able to prove its possibility, either from its actuality as attested by experience, or *a priori* by means of reason' but 'I can *think* whatever I please, provided only that I do not contradict myself' (CPR B xxvi). Thus it is possible to think things-in-themselves, but not to know them, for as Kant 'reminds' his readers '*for thought* the categories are not limited by the conditions of our sensible intuition, but have an unlimited field' (CPR B 166). It is, of course, also possible for thinking to be consistent with cognition, as in the case of synthetic a priori judgements where 'thinking is the act whereby given intuitions are related to an object' (CPR A 247/B 304). Such thinking must fulfil the conditions for the subsumption of intuitions under concepts, and its objects are accordingly restricted to those of a possible experience.

time *see* AESTHETIC, ANALOGIES OF EXPERIENCE, CONTINUITY, IMMORTALITY, INFINITY, INNER SENSE, INTUITION, SCHEMA(TISM), SPACE, SPACE AND TIME, SUCCESSION

Kant's exploration of the problem of time takes place within the parameters of an ancient tradition of thought whose perplexities inform, at a distance, his critique of the modern theories held by Leibniz, Locke and

Newton. Similarly, his view of the existential and moral significance of time is indebted to Christian speculation, and the crucial roles played in it by the immortality of the soul and the imputation of responsibility for action. It is, of course, impossible to separate the two dimensions of physical and moral time, even though Kant appears to establish a rigorous distinction between the physical time discussed in CPR and the moral time discussed in CPrR.

The distinct positions on the nature of time held by Plato and Aristotle were extremely significant for the subsequent development of the philosophy of time. Less influential upon the tradition, but important for Kant, was the position reported to have been held by Epicurus. The medieval reception of ancient debates was further determined by Augustine's reflection on the moral and spiritual significance of time in his *Confessions* (1960). Put at their crudest, the differences at stake in the various definitions of time involved the relationship between time and eternity, and between time and motion. Plato followed a Pythagorean strain of argument, which distinguished between limited and unlimited, or infinite, time. In his cosmological dialogue *Timaeus* he speaks of time as a 'moving image of eternity', distinguishing between eternal time which 'rests in unity' and the time of 'those states which affect moving and sensible things of which generation is the cause' (Plato, 1961, 37d, e). While Plato begins with eternal time and sees temporal events as oriented towards it, Aristotle begins with the now, and sees time as an accident of motion which emerges from the experience of before and after: 'when we do perceive a "before" and an "after", then we say that there is time. For time is just this – number of motion in respect of "before" and "after"' (1941, 219b, 1–2). Epicurus's position, as reported by Diogenes Laertius (1925, Book X), sees time as an immediate sensation (or in Kant's terms, an 'intuition') which is distinguished from the anticipation or *prolepsis* by not being built up out of successive sensations, but by being presupposed by them.

Plotinus's subtle defence of a Platonic understanding of time in *The Six Enneads* maintains that time is independent of motion, but can be measured in terms of it (see Plotinus, 1971, Third Ennead, VII, 12). Here time is discussed not just in terms of motion, but in terms of an analogy (if it is one) with life, with one term being eternity figured as a 'life changelessly motionless and ever holding the Universal content [time, space and phenomena] in actual presence' (Third Ennead, VII, 3) and the other being the time of before, now, and after as the 'constant progress of novelty . . . contained in the differentiation of life' (Third Ennead, VII, 11). These themes, along with emphasis on the experience of the soul, were taken up by Augustine in Book XI of the *Confessions* on 'Time and Eternity' but reworked into a meditation upon the soul's experience of time and upon the role of the soul in the measure of time. With this, the problem of physical time is inflected in the direction of the problem of the experience of time, and with it the themes of past memory, present despair and future hope.

The difficulties generated by the physical and moral concepts of time persisted into the works of Descartes and such critics as Leibniz, Locke and Newton. Descartes' concept of time distinguished between duration and time, the former described as a 'mode under which we conceive of that thing as long as it continues to exist' (Descartes, 1644, p. 24), with the latter serving as a measure of motion which is 'only in our minds'. Duration is an attribute or mode of the being of things, while time is a subjective mode used as a measure for motion, with duration being held to be prior to time. Locke also emphasizes duration, seeing time and eternity as its simple modes and tracing the origins of duration back to 'one of those sources of all our knowledge, viz., *sensation* and *reflection*' (Locke, 1690, p. 90), in this case the '*reflection* on these appearances of several *ideas* one after the other in our minds'. This reflection gives rise to the idea of succession, and the intervals between the appearance of two successive ideas is duration; since we are aware of our own existence while thinking these successive ideas, we are able to call the continuation of existence of ourselves or of others 'duration'.

The nominalist tendency inherent in the subordination of time to duration was resisted by both Leibniz and Newton. Newton seems to revive a Platonic view of time in his distinction between duration, defined by him as 'Absolute, true, and mathematical time, [which] of itself, and from its own nature, flows equably without relation to anything external' and 'relative, apparent and common time' which is a 'measure of duration by the means of motion' (Newton, 1687, p. 8). Leibniz criticized Locke in the *New Essays* for presupposing a definition of time in his description of succession, claiming against him that 'a train of perceptions arouses the idea of duration in us, but it does not create it' (Leibniz, 1765, p. 152). But he also criticized the view of absolute time maintained by the Newtonians in his correspondence with Clarke. He satisfies both directions of criticism by regarding time as an 'order of successions'; that is, time is 'relative' in so far as it is an 'order' but not a structure, and objective in so far as it is a necessary order. This position was developed by Wolff (1719) into an account of time which regarded it as a confused, sensible perception of a rational order.

The development of Kant's view of time took place within the framework of the debates outlined above. In PE Kant considers time to be a partially analyzable concept, which is not open to a real definition, but only a nominal one. Thus his account remains within the Wolffian view of time which regarded it as a confused concept which could, to a certain extent, be clarified through analysis. However, only a nominal definition was possible – that is, an analysis of the ways in which the word 'time' could be used – and not a real definition, that is, a definition of the nature of time. By the time of writing ID, Kant still maintained that time was incapable of real definition although his justification of this position had changed its character. He no longer considered time to be a confused concept, nor did he consider it to be something real. He developed instead a new concept of time which was critical not only of Locke's derivation of time from sense and reflection, but also of the arguments for the 'objective reality of time' maintained by both the Newtonians and by 'Leibniz and his followers' (ID §14).

He presented his new theory of time in the shape of seven theses which distinguished it from other positions by defining it as an intuition. The first thesis holds that 'time does not arise from but is presupposed by the senses' (ID §14), and implicitly agrees with Leibniz's view that Locke's derivation of time from succession is a *petitio principii*. The second thesis attacks the view held by the Leibnizians that time is a concept: 'you conceive all actual things as situated *in* time, and not as contained under the general concept of time, as under a common characteristic mark' (ibid.). This means, in terms of the third thesis, that time is an intuition, one which, since it is prior to sensation, is a pure intuition. The fourth thesis holds that time is a continuous magnitude, and that moments of time are not parts of time 'but *limits* with time between them'. In the fifth, and most controversial thesis, Kant maintains that 'time is not something objective and real' (ibid.) and is neither a substance, nor an accident, nor a relation. This thesis, directed as much against the Newtonians as the Leibnizians, claims that time is a subjective condition 'necessary, in virtue of the nature of the human mind, for the co-ordinating of all sensible things in accordance with a fixed law' (ibid.). Yet while it is neither real nor objective, it is not simply subjective in the Lockean sense since it is a form of co-ordination prior to the objects of sense that it co-ordinates. Sixth, and following from this, time is not simply imaginary, but supplies the only condition under which objects of the senses can be co-ordinated. It is 'fundamental and originary' and, in the words of the seventh thesis, an 'absolutely first *formal principle of the sensible world*' (ibid.) without which our intuition of objects of sense would not be possible.

In the 'Transcendental Aesthetic' of CPR the insights into the nature of time announced in ID are further developed and refined. As in the case of space, Kant offers a metaphysical and a transcendental exposition of time: the former is a representation of what belongs to the concept of time 'as given *a priori*' (CPR A 23/B 38), the explanation of time as a

397

principle 'from which the possibility of other *a priori* synthetic knowledge can be understood' (B 41). The metaphysical exposition covers five points, with the basic direction of the argument following that of ID. First of all, time is not an empirical concept derived from experience, but is its presupposition: 'Only on the presupposition of time can we represent to ourselves a number of things as existing at one and the same time (simultaneously) or at different times (successively)' (A 30/B 46). It is according to the second point a priori and 'underlies all intuitions' (A 31/B 46). Apodeictic principles concerning relations in time, according to the third point, are grounded in the a priori necessity of time and are not derived from experience. This is a crucial step in the elaboration of the argument for the principles developed in the 'Transcendental Doctrine of Judgement'. The fourth point is that time does not possess the subsumptive properties of a concept, by which objects are collected *under* a general term, but rather those of an intuition which co-ordinates objects *in* a singular intuition. With his fifth point Kant tackles the problem of infinite or unlimited time which had beset philosophers since Plato: he agrees that time is unlimited, and that determinate magnitudes of time are 'possible only through limitations of one single time that underlies it' (A 32/B 48), but he does not locate this unlimited time in the empyrean but in the 'inner sense' which underlies all appearances in determinate times (A 33/B 50).

Although Kant discusses space and time together in the 'Transcendental Aesthetic' he accords time a more fundamental role in the determination of experience. The adaptation of the concepts of the understanding to the appearances given by the forms of intuition is discussed in terms of the 'inner sense' or time. The schemas and the principles may be understood, albeit crudely, as temporally adapted forms of the categories which establish the patterns of intuitive co-ordination and conceptual subsumption which make up experience. The ineluctable temporal dimension of human experience is the basis of Kant's insistence on the subjective nature of time, and thus it brings together theoretical and practical issues. The moral negotiation of human desire is inseparable from the finite character of human life, with its experience composed of an inextricable mesh of memory, hope and fear. In order to underwrite these aspects of temporal experience, Kant postulates 'immortality' in CPrR as the only condition capable of providing 'the practically necessary condition of a duration adequate to the perfect fulfilment of the moral law' (p. 133, p. 137). This move was consistently criticized by nineteenth- and twentieth-century philosophers, notably Nietzsche (1886) and Heidegger (1927), who explored the implications of extending Kant's restriction of theoretical time to the limits of finite human experience to the reflection upon action and responsibility in practical philosophy.

topic, transcendental *see* CONCEPTS OF REFLECTION

totality (third category of quantity) *see* CATEGORIES, JUDGEMENT, TABLE OF CATEGORIES

transcendent [*transzendent*] *see also* ABSOLUTE, REASON, TRANSCENDENTAL
Kant distinguishes between the transcendent and the transcendental. Transcendent is the term used to describe those principles which 'profess to pass beyond' the limits of experience, as opposed to immanent principles 'whose application is confined entirely within the limits of possible experience' (CPR A 296/B 352). Transcendent principles 'which recognise no limits' are to be distinguished from the transcendental employment of immanent principles beyond their proper limits. Such principles include the psychological, cosmological and theological ideas discussed in the 'Transcendental Dialectic'. Kant also described the 'objective employment of the pure concepts of reason' as 'transcendent', confusingly describing them as '*transcendental ideas*' (CPR A 327/B 383). In CJ Kant distinguishes between aesthetic and rational ideas, with the former referred to intuition according to a 'merely subjective principle of the harmony of the cognitive faculties' and the latter referred according to an objective principle which is 'incapable of ever furnishing a cognition of the object' (CJ §57). The latter is transcendent, as opposed to the subjective principle of the aesthetic idea, and the immanent concept of the understanding. As in CPR, the rational ideas are produced by the reason and may be used regulatively in the search for the systematic unity of the understanding, or in a transcendent manner 'once reason advances beyond pursuit of understanding' (CJ §76).

transcendental *see also* TRANSCENDENT
In medieval philosophy the transcendentals denoted the extra-categorical attributes of beings: unity, truth, goodness, beauty (and, in some classifications, thing and something). For Kant, a trace of this usage survives in his use of transcendental as a form of knowledge, not of objects themselves but of the ways in which we are able to know them, namely the conditions of possible experience. Thus he 'entitle[s] *transcendental* all knowledge which is occupied not so much with objects as with the mode of our knowledge of objects in so far as this mode of knowledge is to be possible *a priori*' (CPR A 12). The system of the concepts which constitute a priori knowledge may be described as transcendental philosophy, for which the critique of pure reason is variously described as a propaedeutic, canon or architectonic. The term transcendental is used ubiquitously to qualify nouns such as logic, aesthetic, unity of apperception, faculties,

399

illusion; in each case it signals that the noun it qualifies is being considered in terms of its conditions of possibility.

The precise meaning of the term transcendental shifts throughout CPR, but its semantic parameters may be indicated by showing the ways in which Kant distinguishes it from its contraries. The transcendental is distinguished from the empirical, and aligned with the a priori in so far as the a priori involves a reference to the mode of knowledge; it 'signifies such knowledge as concerns the *a priori* possibility of knowledge, or its *a priori* employment' (CPR A 56/B 86). The distinction of transcendental and empirical thus involves the metacritique of knowledge and its a priori sources. Kant regards the psychological account of knowledge as a branch of the empirical, and thus in turn distinguishes it from transcendental knowledge (A 801/B 829). The transcendental is also distinguished from the metaphysical and the logical. A metaphysical exposition of space, for example, is one which represents what belongs to a concept given a priori (A 23/B 38), while a transcendental exposition explains a concept 'as a principle from which the possibility of other *a priori* synthetic knowledge can be understood' (B 40). A transcendental distinction of the sensible and the intelligible differs from a logical distinction – which involves 'their form as being either clear or confused' – by its concern with 'origin and content' (A 44/B 62). Finally, Kant distinguishes between transcendental and transcendent, contrasting the transcendent principles which 'incite us to tear down all those boundary-fences and seize possession of an entirely new domain which recognises no limits of demarcation' from the transcendental 'misemployment' of the categories, which extends their application beyond the limits of possible experience, and 'which is merely an error of the faculty of judgement' (A 296/B 352).

transcendental aesthetic *see* AESTHETIC, INTUITION, RECEPTIVITY, SENSIBILITY, SPACE, TIME

transcendental analytic *see* ANALYTIC, CATEGORIES, CONCEPTS, JUDGEMENT, LOGIC, ONTOLOGY, PRINCIPLES, TRUTH

transcendental deduction *see* DEDUCTION

transcendental dialectic *see* ANTINOMY, DIALECTIC, IDEAL, ILLUSION, INFERENCE, PARALOGISM

transcendental idea *see* REASON

transcendental illusion *see* DIALECTIC, ILLUSION

transcendental logic *see* ANALYTIC, CATEGORIES, CONCEPTS, INTUITION, LOGIC

transcendental object and subject *see also* I, INTUITION, MANIFOLD, NOUMENON, OBJECT, RECEPTIVITY, SUBJECT, THING-IN-ITSELF, UNITY

The transcendental object was a theoretical consequence of Kant's confining human intuition to the receptivity of appearances and his belief that there can be no 'appearance without anything that appears' (CPR B xxvii). The transcendental object is postulated as that which 'appears' or the correlate to receptivity. When discussing the transcendental object Kant suspends his usual distinctions between *Objekt* and *Gegenstand*, and on occasions even uses 'thing' (*Ding*). This is a consequence of the unknowability of the transcendental object, a property which it shares with the noumenon and thing-in-itself; like them, it can be thought according to the principle of contradiction, but cannot be known as an object of experience. Indeed, on some occasions, mainly in the first edition of CPR, Kant uses the terms noumenon and thing-in-itself as synonyms for transcendental object (A 366, A 358, A 614/B 642). But while all three share the quality of being thinkable but not objects of experience, the transcendental object is specifically the intelligible correlate of sensible appearances. Kant concedes unenthusiastically that we may call 'the purely intelligible cause of appearances in general the transcendental object', with the added qualification 'but merely in order to have something corresponding to sensibility viewed as a receptivity' (A 494/B 522). It is, as he noted earlier in CPR, simply a function of the requirement that appearances as representations must represent something, call it 'the non-empirical, that is, transcendental object = x' (A 109).

On a number of occasions in CPR Kant seems to point beyond the merely functional requirements of the transcendental object as a correlate of appearances. These are the moments at which the transcendental object undergoes metamorphosis into a transcendental subject. The transitional link is the unity informing a manifold of intuition. At A 613/B 641 Kant moves from describing the transcendental object as 'lying at the basis of appearances' and thus 'to us inscrutable' to saying that this is the reason 'why our sensibility is subject to certain supreme conditions rather than others'. This may be placed alongside his earlier comment that the transcendental object 'expresses only the thought of an object in general, according to different modes [of intuition]' (A 247/B 304). By this he does not mean that the transcendental object determines our spatio-temporal mode of intuition, but that it offers 'the unity of the thought of a manifold in general', regardless of the mode of intuition. This unity, however, is subsequently made the property of the 'transcendental subject' or 'a something in general' signified by the expression 'I' which forms the vehicle for every experience. It supplies the most fundamental condition of experience which is that the manifolds of intuition be capable of unity.

transcendental philosophy *see also* METAPHYSICS, ONTOLOGY, PHILOSOPHY, SYNTHETIC A PRIORI, SYSTEM, TRANSCENDENTAL

In CPR (B 73) and CJ (§36) Kant describes the general problem of transcendental philosophy as 'how are synthetic a priori judgements possible?' It is thus concerned with the rules which govern such judgements – given in the pure concept of the understanding – as well as specifying '*a priori* the instance to which the rule is to be applied' (CPR A 135/B 174) or the principles of transcendental judgement. Kant distinguishes transcendental philosophy from the 'critique of pure reason' in that the latter provides an analysis of only 'fundamental concepts' while a full transcendental philosophy would be required to present 'an exhaustive analysis of the whole of *a priori* human knowledge' (A 13/B 27). It is more specific than ontology in that it extends only to the understanding and reason 'in a system of concepts and principles which relate to objects in general but takes no account of objects that *may be given* (*Ontologia*)', but is more general than physiology which for Kant extends only as far as nature or 'the sum of *given* objects' (A 845/B 873). Transcendental philosophy bears with it an obligation to answer questions concerning objects given to pure reason, since the 'very concept which puts us in a position to ask the question must also qualify us to answer it' (A 477/B 505), even if the answer consists in pointing to unjustified assumptions implied in the question.

transcendental reflection *see* CONCEPTS OF REFLECTION

transcendental subject *see* APPERCEPTION, I, SUBJECT, TRANSCENDENTAL OBJECT/SUBJECT

transcendental unity of apperception *see* APPERCEPTION, I, 'I THINK', IDENTITY, JUDGEMENT, SPONTANEITY, SUBJECT, SYNTHESIS, UNITY

treaties *see* FEDERATION OF STATES, PEACE, WAR

truth [*aletheia, veritas, Wahrheit*] *see also* ANALYTIC, APPEARANCE, CERTAINTY, HOLDING-TO-BE-TRUE, ILLUSION

Kant's reply to the question 'what is truth?' is couched in terms of 'the general and sure criterion of the truth of any and every knowledge' (CPR A 58/B 82). After taking as given the nominal definition of truth as 'the agreement of knowledge with its object' (A 58/B 82) he claims that there can be no general criterion 'such as would be valid in each and every instance of knowledge, however their objects may vary' (A 58/B 83). Yet while this holds for the content of knowledge, it is possible to establish a negative, logical criterion of truth in so far as the 'universal and necessary rules of the understanding' (A 59/B 84) expounded by logic are a *conditio sine qua non*. For 'whatever contradicts these rules is false' (ibid.) although agreement with these rules is not in itself a sufficient criterion of truth.

Within the critical framework the notion of the 'agreement of knowledge with its object' takes on a new meaning, particularly in the light of its basic axiom that 'the conditions of the *possibility of experience* in general are likewise conditions of the *possibility of the objects of experience*' (CPR A 158/B 197). This means that the conditions of experience determine the agreement of knowledge and object, or as Kant put it, 'experience supplies the rules and is the source of truth' (A 318/B 375). The conditions of experience comprise appearances given through a priori intuition and synthesized with pure a priori concepts of the understanding. Thus Kant can say that the synthesis of these elements 'as knowledge *a priori*, can possess truth, that is, agreement with the object, only in so far as it contains nothing save what is necessary to synthetic unity of experience in general' (A 158/B 197). This must include, as Kant spells out, the 'formal conditions of *a priori* intuition, the synthesis of imagination and the necessary unity of this synthesis in a transcendental apperception' (A 158/B 197). With this argument Kant rejects any Platonic view of truth as agreement of knowledge with an idea, as well as a Platonic equation of sensibility with illusion. Appearances are no longer considered to be illusions, but are an essential element of experience and consequently of truth.

Alongside this account of truth as 'agreement with an object' Kant also presents one couched in terms of validity. In this version truth is discussed in terms of 'holding-to-be-true' or the subjective and objective validity of judgements. It has three grades: opinion, which is consciously insufficient both subjectively and objectively; faith, which is consciously insufficient objectively but suffices subjectively; and knowledge, which is both subjectively and objectively sufficient and thus certain (CPR A 822/B 850). However, the notion of objective sufficiency may be taken to include within it the definition of 'truth as agreement with an object' (A 58/B 82).

type/typic *see also* ANALOGY, HYPOTYPOSIS, JUDGEMENT, SCHEMA(TISM)
The section of CPrR on the 'Typic of Pure Practical Judgement' addresses the problem of practical judgement, and in particular the problem of presenting the 'ideal' of the morally good *in concreto*. It forms, along with schematism and symbolization, another species of the genre hypotyposis. Kant compares it directly with schematism, noting that the problem

addressed by the schematism of presenting a concept to an intuition in a judgement is further complicated in practical judgement by the supersensible character of the moral law. He does however concede that a 'natural law' may be admitted 'for the purpose of judgement . . . [but] only in its formal aspect, and it may, therefore, be called the *type* of the moral law' (CPrR p. 70, p. 72). The type of the moral law makes it possible to 'compare maxims of action with a universal natural law' without succumbing to 'empiricism of practical reason' which grounds moral judgements in empirical principles, or to a 'mysticism of practical reason'. The latter, Kant observes, 'makes into a schema that which should only serve as a symbol, i.e., proposes to supply real yet non-sensuous intuitions (of an invisible kingdom of God) for the application of the moral law' (p. 71, p. 73). It thus converts what should only be an analogy of a kingdom of ends into a transcendent object.

U

unconditioned *see* ABSOLUTE, ANTINOMY, FREEDOM, IDEA, REASON

understanding [*dianoia, intellectio, Verstand*] *see also* AMPHIBOLY, ANALYTIC, CONCEPTS OF REFLECTION, FACULTY, FINITUDE, INTUITION, LOGIC, REASON, RULES, SENSIBILITY, SPONTANEITY, TABLE OF CATEGORIES/JUDGEMENTS

The history of the understanding has been largely determined by the problems in establishing the relationship between acts of understanding, or thought in general, and the faculty of the mind which is responsible for these acts. The early disputes around the nature of the faculty of understanding motivate one of Aquinas's best known polemics, *On the Unity of the Intellect against the Averroists* (Aquinas, 1968), and persisted throughout medieval philosophy in the guise of the role of divine illumination in acts of understanding and the contribution to knowledge made by the senses and imagination. In the *Meditations* Descartes gave the faculty of understanding a broad role in the creation of knowledge, placing its contribution above that of the imagination and senses. In his reply to objections he clearly distinguished between acts of understanding or 'intellection' and the 'thing which understands' or 'understanding as a faculty' and in so doing clearly identified the complex relationship between the constitution of the faculty and the acts of understanding that it accomplished.

The debate over the nature of the understanding and its relationship to acts of understanding took a fascinating turn in the encounter of Leibniz with Locke's theory of human understanding in the *New Essays on Human Understanding* (1765). In *An Essay Concerning Human Understanding* (1690) Locke described the understanding as 'not much unlike a closet wholly shut from light, with only some little opening left, to let in external visible resemblances, or *ideas* of things without' (p. 76). Leibniz replied that to characterize the work of the understanding fully, it would be necessary for Locke to equip his closet with a screen, and that screen would not be uniform but would be under tension, 'diversified by folds representing items of innate knowledge', and would respond to impressions like the string of a musical instrument (Leibniz, 1765, p. 144). This extremely complex characterization of the operation of the human understanding was not adopted by Leibniz's Wolffian followers, although like both Leibniz and Locke, the Wolffians saw the understanding as the 'capacity to represent possible things' (Meissner, 1737, 'Verstand'); that is, as a power of representation which included sensibility and imagination, and which operated through concepts, judgements and inferences.

Traces of the Wolffian view of the understanding as the general power of representation persist in Kant, although he was concerned to separate the understanding as a faculty from both sensibility and reason. For him it was possible to 'reduce all acts of the understanding to judgements' and thus to represent the understanding as a 'faculty of judgement' (CPR A 69/B 94). By judgement he meant the 'mediate knowledge of an object, that is, the representation of a representation of it' (A 68/B 93), whether this representation be an intuition or a concept. All judgements are accordingly 'functions of unity among our representations', so the understanding may be further characterized as a faculty for unifying representations. Thus from the acts of understanding – judgements – Kant moves to the '*dissection of the faculty of the understanding* itself' in which he 'investigate[s] the possibility of concepts *a priori*' (A 65/B 90). His 'clue' in the search for these basic concepts of the understanding – its basic forms of unification – is the table of judgements comprising the four classes of the quantity, quality, relation and modality of judgements.

In order to characterize how it is possible for the understanding to originate its own pure concepts, Kant has to distinguish it from the other two faculties of sensibility and reason. This leads to what he himself admits are 'various different' definitions of the understanding. It is defined as 'a spontaneity of knowledge (in distinction from the receptivity of sensibility)' (CPR A 126), because its concepts are modes of the transcendental unity of apperception, which is original and spontaneous. It is also described as a 'power of thought', 'a faculty of concepts' in that it comprises the categories through which it gives 'the law of the synthetic unity of all appearances' (A 128), a faculty of judgement, and the 'faculty of rules'. In the guise of the latter, the understanding 'is always occupied in investigating appearances, in order to detect some rule in them' (A 126). These rules, however, 'issue *a priori* from the understanding itself', for it is also characterized as the 'lawgiver of nature' (ibid.). On one of the readings that Kant's description of the understanding seems to invite, the understanding is given the materials of experience by the sensibility, which it then processes by means of subsuming them under a rule. But this does not do justice to the full dignity he accords understanding as the 'lawgiver of nature', for it is able to 'confer upon appearances their conformity to law, and so make experience possible' (A 126).

The relationship Kant establishes between understanding and sensibility is extremely intricate and complex, and consists in bringing together the otherwise heterogeneous intuitions and concepts. Both are representations, but the former originate in the receptivity of human sensibility, the latter in the spontaneity of the understanding. Intuitions and concepts must be adapted to each other in a way which respects their heterogeneity, but which nevertheless permits their synthesis to be accomplished. Kant ventures to describe how this is accomplished in the schematism and in the principles. The understanding's relationship to reason is characterized in a more straightforward way. The understanding secures 'the unity of appearances by means of rules' while reason pursues 'the unity of the rules of understanding under principles' (CPR A 302/B 359). While the understanding is restricted to the range of possible experience, reason is 'directed always towards absolute totality in the synthesis of conditions' (A 326/B 382); this leads it to drive the concepts of the understanding beyond their legitimate limits, and to generate the fallacious inferences scrutinized in the 'Transcendental Dialectic' of CPR.

The understanding has been the site of a great deal of opposition to the critical philosophy. Early 'metacritiques', such as those of Hamann (1967) and Herder (1953), objected to the separation of understanding and sensibility, while later critics such as Fichte (1794) and Hegel (1807, 1812) criticized the separation of understanding and reason. Later generations of critics, above all Nietzsche and the neo-Kantians in the late nineteenth century, resisted Kant's tendency to transform the discussion of acts of understanding into the dissection of the faculty of understanding. This current of criticism, which merged with anti-psychologistic readings of Kant's philosophy, remained extremely influential during the twentieth century, and will be encountered in fairly pure form by readers of Strawson's *The Bounds of Sense* (1966).

unity [*Einheit*] *see also* CATEGORY, CONCEPT, IDENTITY, MANIFOLD, QUANTITY, REASON, RELATION, RULE, UNDERSTANDING
Unity is a ubiquitous concept in Kant's philosophy, and is consequently used in specific and general senses. However, his usage evinces a basic equivocation in the definition of the concept, between (a) the traditional 'transcendental' sense of unity and (b) its critical sense as the first of the categories of quantity. Kant himself reflects on the two senses of unity in CPR when he discusses the scholastic proposition 'being, unity, truth, and the good are convertible' (B 113). Kant recognized that the transcendentals were traditionally regarded as extra-categorical determinations of being, but he audaciously proposed to demote them to being mere categories of quantity: 'These supposedly transcendental predicates of *things* are, in fact,

nothing but logical requirements and criteria of all *knowledge* of things in general, and prescribe for such knowledge the categories of quantity, namely, *unity, plurality,* and *totality*' (B 114). In spite of this claim, the transcendental status of unity returned to haunt Kant in several painful ways.

In OPA Kant followed the traditional transcendental sense of unity, deriving it 'from a ground in the supreme being' (p. 119, p. 160) and seeing it as informing 'natural perfection'. However, by PE unity has become – along with magnitude, plurality and space – one of the fundamental, 'unanalysable' concepts which were subsequently worked through into the table of categories (PE p. 280, p. 252). The two senses of unity co-exist in ID where it features both as the subjective co-ordination of phenomena and as the 'corollary of the dependence of all substances on one being' (ID §20). In CPR the two senses of unity also co-exist, although the extra-categorical sense of the term has lost its theological hue.

Although Kant sought in CPR to reduce unity to a category of quantity, he stresses the distinction between the categorical and extra-categorical senses when he observes that the 'unity, which precedes *a priori* all concepts of combination, is not the category of unity . . . for all categories are grounded in logical functions of judgement, and in these functions combination, and therefore unity of given concepts, is already thought' (CPR B 131). The problem Kant encountered is most clearly stated in P. In seeking to derive the table of categories Kant 'looked about for an act of the understanding which comprises all the rest and is differentiated only by various modifications or moments' (P §39). He found this to consist in the act of judgement which brought the 'manifold of representation under the unity of thinking in general' (P §39). However, the unity in question could not be the category of unity which was supposedly derived from the unity of thinking; the latter then had to be of a different order from the categories; in other words, 'transcendental'.

The resort to an extra-categorical unity posed extremely serious problems for the critical philosophy, but was ineluctable. It was necessary for Kant to postulate a 'pure original unchangeable consciousness' or 'transcendental apperception' whose 'numerical unity' 'is thus the *a priori* ground of all concepts' (CPR A 107). Without it the entire transcendental philosophy would be in danger of becoming an empirical psychology; yet how can he justify the equivocal use of unity as a categorical and extra-categorical synthesis? One avenue Kant explored was to describe the extra-categorical 'unity' of the transcendental subject as an 'identity' which informs categorical 'unity': 'The original and necessary consciousness of the *identity* of the self is thus at the same time a consciousness of an equally necessary *unity* of the synthesis of all appearances according to concepts . . .' (CPR

A 108, my italics). Another avenue was to qualify unity according to whether or not it was intended categorically or transcendentally, as when Kant deliberately entitles the unity of apperception 'the *transcendental* unity of self-consciousness, in order to indicate the possibility of *a priori* knowledge arising from it' (CPR B 132, Kant's italics).

On top of the distinction between categorical and transcendental unity Kant adds the unity of the understanding and the unity of reason. The former is categorical unity while the latter is concerned to 'carry the synthetic unity, which is thought in the category, up to the completely unconditioned' (CPR B 383). The unity of reason differs from transcendental unity in at least one important respect. Transcendental unity enables the act of judgement to take place from which the categories are derived as modes, while the unity of reason is the extension of the already given category of unity beyond the limits of sense to the unconditioned.

universality *see* CATEGORIES, DEDUCTION, INDIVIDUAL, NECESSITY

V

validity [*Geltung/Gültigkeit*] *see also* COMMON SENSE, JUDGEMENT, NECESSITY, PRINCIPLES
In CPR, P and CJ Kant distinguished between the various ways in which judgements can be held to possess validity. Subjectively valid judgements or 'judgements of perception' 'require no pure concept of the understanding, but only the logical connection of perception in a thinking subject' (P §18). Objectively valid judgements, on the contrary, require 'besides the representation of the sensuous intuition, special *concepts originally generated in the understanding*'; they are manifest by the fact that they are universally and necessarily valid, that is, 'if they hold good for us and in the same way for everybody else' (ibid.). In P Kant holds that this shared validity follows from the 'unity of the object to which they all refer and with which they accord' because otherwise 'there would be no reason for the judgements of other men necessarily to agree with mine' (§18). Later, in CJ, he disagreed with his own position, and admitted a *sensus communis* or shared common sense which could lead to universally shared and necessarily valid judgements without a 'unity of the object'. Indeed, he attributed 'exemplary validity' to aesthetic judgements of taste on the basis of common sense as an 'ideal norm', or an idea which is 'subjectively universal' but 'necessary for everyone' (CJ §22). However, the idea of a *sensus communis* cannot be used on a constitutive basis but only on a regulative one; yet this need not necessarily be prejudicial to its validity. This is evident in CPR, where Kant admits into the class of objectively valid judgements those governed by both constitutive and regulative principles. Objective validity is accorded not only to those judgements which possess 'immanent validity' from obeying the formal conditions of a possible experience (CPR A 638/B 666), but also to those asymptotic regulative ideas of reason which possess 'objective but indeterminate validity' (A 663/B 691).

value [*Wert*] *see also* END, MAXIM, PERSON
Kant's philosophy of value is structured around a distinction between absolute and relative value, which in its turn is determined by one between

ends and means. Any thing or action which is a means to an end is valued relative to that end; so, for example, the traditional virtues of courage, resolution and perseverance receive their value only with respect to the ends they serve. If the end is good, then means are good relative to it; if ends are bad, then means are bad. The only things which are good in themselves and thus of absolute worth are a good will and a person. A good will is an end in itself because 'it is good only through its willing, i.e., it is good in itself' (GMM p. 394, p. 7), while persons are ends in themselves, and thus of absolute worth, because 'their nature already marks them out as ends in themselves, i.e., as something which is not to be used merely as means and . . . which are thus objects of respect' (p. 428, p. 36). Persons are so marked out because a rational being cannot will the maxim that another rational being should be used as a means to another's ends should become a universal law. For in willing such a maxim, a rational being wills their own potential subordination as a means to another's ends. In CJ §83 Kant gives this view of value an historical dimension by claiming that the value of life and the final end of creation are determined by the worth we assign to our lives by acting with a view to an absolute end, independent of nature.

variety *see* CONTINUITY, HOMOGENEITY

vice *see* SEX, VIRTUE

virtue [*arete, virtus Tugend*] *see also* JUSTICE, RIGHT, SEX
Although in GMM Kant seems to regard such traditional virtues as moderation and self-control as possessing value only as means relative to the end of a good will, he nevertheless accords the doctrine of virtue a significant part in his metaphysics of morals. The MM is divided into 'the system of the *doctrine of Right* (*ius*), which deals with duties which can be given by external laws, and the system of the *doctrine of virtue* (*Ethica*) which treats of duties which cannot be so given' (p. 379, p. 185). Kant distinguishes between ethical duties which follow from ethical obligation in general and concern only '*what is formal* in the moral determination of the will' and duties of virtue which concern ends which are also duties (MM p. 383, p. 188). The latter form the contents of the doctrine of virtue and are distributed according to the two classes of ends which are also duties, namely those relating to 'one's own perfection' and those relating to 'the happiness of others'. The discussion of these two classes forms the contents of Part I and Part II respectively of the 'Doctrine of Virtue'. Part I discusses duties of virtue to oneself as an animal being, such as not to commit suicide or to defile oneself by lust, or to eat and drink too much; duties

411

to oneself as a moral being such as the avoidance of lying, avarice and servility; the duty of conscience, and the imperfect duty to improve oneself. The second part considers the duties of virtue to others, above all to love and respect them.

Although Kant redefines the content and scope of the traditional, substantive doctrine of virtue in relation to his new, formal definition of moral value and the good, there are traces of the old doctrine throughout his writings. A notable example is provided by the discussions of Platonic and Stoic virtue in CPR as ideals for judging examples of virtue (see A 315/B 372 and A 569/B 597).

void *see* NOTHING

W

war [*Krieg*] *see also* DISPUTE, FEDERATION OF STATES, PEACE, STATE

In MM Kant describes each state as 'living in relation to another state in the condition of natural freedom and therefore in a condition of constant war' (p. 343, p. 150). The rights of states with respect to each other concern their going to war, their actions during wars, and their right after war 'to constrain each other to leave this condition of war and so form a constitution that will establish lasting peace' (p. 343, p. 150; see also PP). For Kant, war is the means by which a state prosecutes its rights with regard to other states through its own force, with grounds for a state going to war including not only such active violations as 'first aggression' or 'a state's taking upon itself to obtain satisfaction for an offence committed against its people by the people of another state' (MM p. 346, p. 153), but also threatened hostility. This includes another state's preparations for hostility, or even the '*menacing* increase in another state's *power*' (ibid.). The rights of a state at war include using any means of defence except those 'which would make its subjects unfit to be citizens', and any means except those which 'would destroy the trust requisite to establishing a lasting peace in the future' such as using its subjects for purposes of espionage, assassination, and the spreading of false reports (p. 347, p. 154). In conducting a war, it is permitted to 'exact supplies and contributions' from an enemy, but not to plunder the people, since for Kant the people and the state are not the same. Kant considered war to be the source of the 'greatest evils which oppress civilised nations' (CBH p. 121, p. 231), and not so much actual warfare as 'the unremitting, indeed ever-increasing *preparation* for war in the future' (ibid.). He noted presciently that all the 'resources of the state, and all the fruits of its culture which might be used to enhance that culture even further, are devoted to this purpose' with the additional unhappy result that 'freedom suffers greatly in numerous areas' (CBH p. 121, p. 232).

will *see also* CATEGORICAL IMPERATIVE, FREEDOM, REASON, SPONTANEITY

Kant's discussion of the will is conducted in terms of a distinction between the will (*Wille*) and the 'capacity for choice' (*Willkür*), with both terms often

413

being translated as 'will'. This is occasionally the case in Kemp Smith's translation of CPR, which has led to claims that Kant developed the distinction of *Wille* and *Willkür* after GMM (1785). Yet it is clearly apparent in CPR (1781), where Kant consistently uses *Willkür* to refer to the capacity of choice. Freedom is defined as the 'independence of the capacity of choice from coercion by sensuous impulses'; and while the human capacity for choice is affected by 'sensuous motives' it is not necessitated by them. This is because, Kant explains, 'there is in man a power of self-determination, independently of any coercion through sensuous impulses' (CPR A 534/B 562). This power of self-determination, manifest in the 'ought', is the will. Kant uses the distinction of *Wille* and *Willkür* when he identifies the will as the source of the ought which determines the capacity for choice, and effects its independence from sensuous impulses. However, even here his distinction shows signs of slippage, with the ought determining the will and the capacity for choice. Yet in spite of this, will is nevertheless consistently associated with freedom, autonomy and spontaneity.

The discussions of the will in GMM and CPrR follow the broad distinction between *Wille* and *Willkür*, although there is some slippage with the 'will' being described as determined by heteronomous principles. On the whole, however, the will is considered to be the source of obligation which directs moral attention away from heteronomous, unworthy maxims of actions, to those consistent with the moral law. In CPrR, while human beings can be supposed to have a pure will, they are nonetheless 'affected by wants and sensuous motives' (p. 32, p. 32); this means that they cannot be said to have a 'holy will' which would be 'incapable of any maxims which conflict with the moral law'. The human will is dependent on the moral, a dependence registered by the term 'obligation' and manifest in the 'constraint to an action' called duty. Obligation originates in the will, and serves to influence a 'pathologically affected capacity of choice [*Willkür*]' by means of the 'constraint of a resistance offered by the practical reason, which may be called an inner, but intellectual compulsion' (CPrR p. 33, p. 33). With this argument Kant can maintain that the will is free and creates an obligation to the moral law, while also claiming that the human capacity of choice (*Willkür* not *Wille*) is pathologically affected by sensuous impulses. Thus Kant can argue that the '*autonomy* of the will [*Autonomie des Willens*] is the sole principle of all moral laws' which is opposed by the '*heteronomy* of the capacity of choice [*Willkür*] . . . opposed to the principle of duty and to the morality of the will' (CPrR p. 33, p. 33).

This direction of Kant's argument is confirmed by RL and MM. When discussing evil in the former, Kant does not see it as a corruption of the will itself (*Wille*) but of the capacity for choice (*Willkür*). The corruption of *Willkür* consists in making 'lower incentives supreme among its maxims' (RL p. 42, p. 38), that is, in choosing ends and actions according to maxims which have a sensible origin. This is a corruption of *Willkür* because it subordinates reason in the shape of maxims to the pursuit of non-rational ends. This tendency is countered by 'the injunction that we *ought* to become better men' (RL p. 45, p. 40), which originates in the 'good will' (*Wille*). The way in which the distinction of *Wille* and *Willkür* works is shown most clearly in MM. *Willkür* is defined as the 'capacity for *doing or refraining from doing as one pleases*' in so far as this capacity is 'joined with one's consciousness of the capacity to bring about its object' (MM p. 213, p. 42). While *Willkür* is concerned with action and the realization of ends, *Wille* is 'the capacity for desire considered not so much in relation to action (as the capacity for choice [*Willkür*] is) but rather in the relation to the ground determining choice to action'. From this Kant infers that in so far as the will 'can determine the capacity for choice, it is indeed practical reason itself' (p. 213, p. 42), and that it does so autonomously, without any 'determining ground', through the form or 'fitness of maxims of choice to be universal law' which is prescribed as an 'imperative that commands or prohibits absolutely' (p. 214, p. 42).

Kant's separation of will and the capacity for choice corrected a tendency to make the will into a faculty, and consequently to conjure up problems concerning the relationship between free will and determinism. By focusing upon maxims to action chosen by *Willkür*, Kant is able to distinguish the freedom and self-legislation of the will from the choices made by the *Willkür*. For his account to be convincing, he has to show the ways in which the will can be the source of an obligation which can discriminate between maxims. The advantages of this position are patent, notably that it avoids the opposition between free will and determinism; its danger, however, lies in it separating the will altogether from the capacity of choice, and hypostatizing it. Schelling took some steps in this direction in *Über das Wesen der menschlichen Freiheit* (1809) (and in later writings) where the will is cast as the 'primordial being [*Wollen ist Ursein*]' (p. 46) which is limited by the understanding and in which both will and being mutually raise and clarify each other in spirit. In the *World as Will and Representation* (1819) Schopenhauer opposed will and representation, making will into an unknowable force. Nietzsche (1887) rejected both the hypostatization of the will and the tendency to treat it as a faculty, and returned to a more Kantian position with his notion of will-to-power as a form of regulative idea with which to test potential courses of action for the presence of reactive elements (*ressentiment*), or what Kant would have described as maxims influenced by 'sensuous impulses'.

415

woman *see also* MARRIAGE, SEX, STATE

Kant's comments on women are, on the whole, the predictably superficial observations of an eighteenth-century *gallant* who is happy to patronize women as long as they keep to their place. In section three of OBS, women are introduced as the 'fair sex' in possession of a 'secret magic' and an 'inborn feeling for all that is beautiful, elegant, and decorated' (p. 229, p. 77). Their 'beautiful understanding' is contrasted with the 'deep understanding' of men; hers is 'not to reason, but to sense' (p. 230, p. 79). As a wife she is to provide children and 'merry talkativeness' and to 'complement her husband's understanding with her taste' (ibid.). In A Kant ventures an explanation for the dependency of women on men: since nature entrusted the future of the species to women's wombs, and was concerned for the preservation of the embryo, it thoughtfully 'implanted fear into the woman's character, a fear of physical injury and a timidity towards similar dangers. On the basis of this weakness, the woman legitimately asks for masculine protection' (A p. 306, p. 219). Not only this, nature also ingeniously provided that the request for protection would also lead to women improving and refining coarse male society. The scope for improvement is limited, however, by the denial of political participation to women. Kant's republicanism is based on the three formal principles of freedom, equality and independence. True, women are deemed to be free by virtue of being human beings, and as equal 'before the law', but they are not independent. And as the only qualification for citizenship, 'apart of course, from not being a child or a woman' (TP p. 295, p. 78) is economic independence, women are consigned by Kant to passive citizenship on grounds both of sex and economic status (see also MM p. 314, p. 126).

Kant seems to raise himself above this dismal catalogue of clichés when he turns to discussing marriage and domestic society in MM. The marriage contract of 'two persons of different sexes for lifelong possession of each other's sexual attributes' (p. 277, p. 96) is a relation between equals. In formal terms both man and woman equally 'possess each other as persons' (p. 278, p. 97), yet in substantive terms, within the domestic society of family and household the wife is subordinate to the husband. Kant sees no essential conflict between the 'equality of partners' and the 'natural superiority of the husband to the wife in his capacity to promote the common interest of the household' (p. 279, p. 98). Indeed, Kant's understanding of women may be summed up in his parenthesis on the relation between the sexes in marriage, namely 'he is the party to direct, she to obey' (ibid.).

world *see also* ANTINOMY, COSMOLOGY, INTELLIGIBLE WORLD, NATURE

In CPR the world is the 'sum total of all appearances' (A 334/B 391 and A 507/B 535) and is the object of cosmology. It is not a 'whole existing in itself' outside of our representations, and therefore cannot itself be an object of legitimate knowledge. The concept of the world is distinguished from that of nature: it is the 'mathematical sum total of all appearances and the totality of their synthesis' while nature is the same world 'viewed as dynamical whole' (A 418/B 446). Kant consistently rejected the Wolffian distinction between sensible and intelligible worlds (A 257/B 312), while admitting one between sensible and intellectual concepts (A 255/B 311); the only admissible 'intelligible world' is the moral world of free causality, determined by the laws of freedom. Kant's most extensive discussion of the concept of world appears in the context of his critique of the 'special metaphysics' of cosmology in the 'Transcendental Dialectic' of CPR. The attempts by cosmologists to treat the world as if it were an object of knowledge, and to inquire into its ultimate spatial and temporal limits (its spatio-temporal beginning and end), its composition (whether ultimately simple or composite), and the nature of its causality (whether free or determined) generate the first three of the four antinomies presented in CPR.

Kant's published writings

NOTE: the following list is arranged in chronological order of publication. For each title it provides information about both the German (or Latin) text and an English translation. It also, wherever possible, gives details of the original printer or book-seller/publisher of the text as well as details of where the German text can be found in the 'Academy Edition' of Kant's writings (*Immanuel Kant's gesammelte Schriften*, 29 volumes, Vols. I–XXII edited by the Prussian Academy of Sciences; Vol. XXIII by the German Academy of Sciences in Berlin; Vols. XXIV–XXIX by the Academy of Sciences in Göttingen). References to the Academy Edition (cited as 'AK') refer to volume and page numbers. Wherever possible the English translation is the text published in the 'Cambridge Edition of the Works of Immanuel Kant' (cited as 'Cambridge Edition' together with the volume number).

1747   *Gedanken von der wahren Schätzung der lebendigen Kräfte und Beurtheilung der Beweise, derer sich Herr von Leibnitz und andere Mechaniker in dieser Streitsache bedienet haben, nebst einigen vorhergehenden Betrachtungen, welche die Kraft der Körper überhaupt betreffen*, Königsberg, gedruckt bey Martin Eberhard Dorn, 1746 (AK I, 1–181).
Thoughts on the True Estimation of Living Forces, and criticism of the proofs propounded by Herr von Leibniz and other mechanists in their treatment of this controversy, along with some preliminary observations concerning the force of bodies in general, in Cambridge Edition VIII, *Natural Science*, ed. H.B. Nisbet, Cambridge University Press, forthcoming.

1754a   'Untersuchung der Frage, ob die Erde in ihrer Umdrehung um die Achse, wodurch sie die Abwechslung des Tages und der Nacht hervorbringt, einige Veränderungen seit den ersten Zeiten ihres Ursprungs erlitten habe und woraus man sich ihrer versichern könne, welche von der Königl. Akademie der Wissenschaften zum Preise für das jetzt laufende Jahr aufgegeben worden', *Wochentliche Königsbergische Frag- und Anzeigungs-Nachrichten*, Nrs, 23 and 24 of 8 and 15 June 1754 (AK I, 183–91).
'Inquiry into the Question whether the Earth in its Rotation around its Axis, by which it produces the Change of Day and Night, has undergone any Alterations since the Time of its Origin', in Cambridge Edition VIII, *Natural Science*, ed. H.B. Nisbet, Cambridge University Press, forthcoming.

1754b   'Die Frage: ob die Erde veralte, physikalisch erwogen', *Wochentliche*

Königsbergische Frag- und Anzeigungs-Nachrichten, Nrs 32–7 of 10 August to 14 September (AK I, 193–213).

'The Question whether the Earth is aging, considered from a physicalist Point of View', in Cambridge Edition VIII, *Natural Science*, ed. H.B. Nisbet, Cambridge University Press, forthcoming.

1755a   *Allgemeine Naturgeschichte und Theorie des Himmels, oder Versuch von der Verfassung und dem mechanischen Ursprunge des ganzen Weltgebäudes nach Newtonischen Grundsätzen abgehandelt*, Königsberg und Leipzig, bey Johann Friedrich Petersen (AK I, 215–368).

Universal Natural History and Theory of the Heavens, or An Essay on the Constitution and Mechanical Origin of the Entire World Edifice treated according to Newtonian Principles, tr. Stanley L. Jaki, Edinburgh, Scottish Academic Press, 1981.

1755b   *Meditationum quarundum de igne succincta delineatio*, manuscript first published in *Kant, Sämtliche Werke*, eds. Karl Friedrich Rosenkranz and Friedrich Wilhelm Schubert, Vol. 5, Leipzig, 1839 (AK I, 369–84).

On Fire, in Cambridge Edition VIII, *Natural Science*, ed. H.B. Nisbet, Cambridge University Press, forthcoming.

1755c   *Principiorum primorum cognitionis metaphysicae nova dilucidatio*, dissertation, Königsberg, J.H. Hartung (AK I, 385–416).

A New Elucidation of the First Principles of Metaphysical Cognition, in Cambridge Edition I, *Theoretical Philosophy 1755–1770*, tr. and ed. David Walford in collaboration with Ralf Meerbote, Cambridge University Press, 1992, pp. 1–45.

1756a   'Von den Ursachen der Erderschütterungen bei Gelegenheit des Unglücks, welches die westlichen Länder von Europa gegen das Ende des vorigen Jahres betroffen hat', *Wochentliche Königsbergische Frag- und Anzeigungs-Nachrichten*, Nrs 4 and 5 of 24 and 31 January (AK I, 417–27).

'Concerning the Causes of the Terrestrial Convulsions on the Occasion of the Disaster which afflicted the Western Countries of Europe towards the End of Last Year', in Cambridge Edition VIII, *Natural Science*, ed. H.B. Nisbet, Cambridge University Press, forthcoming.

1756b   *Geschichte und Naturbeschreibung der merkwürdigsten Vorfälle des Erdbebens, welches an dem Ende des 1755sten Jahres einen grossen Teil der Erde Erschüttert hat*, Königsberg, gedrückt und verlegt von Joh. Heinr. Hartung (AK I, 429–61).

History and Natural Description of the Most Remarkable Occurrences associated with the Earthquake which at the end of 1755 Shook a Large Part of the World, in Cambridge Edition VIII, *Natural Science*, ed. H.B. Nisbet, Cambridge University Press, forthcoming.

1756c   'Fortgesetzte Betrachtung der seit einigen Zeit wahrgenommenen Erderschütterungen', *Wochentliche Königsbergische Frag- und Anzeigungs-Nachrichten*, Nrs 15 and 16 of 10 and 17 April (AK I, 463–72).

'Further Observation on the Terrestrial Convulsions which have been for Some Time Observed', in Cambridge Edition VIII, *Natural Science*, ed. H.B. Nisbet, Cambridge University Press, forthcoming.

1756d *Metaphysicae cum geometria iunctae usus in philosophia naturali, cuius specimen I. continet monadologiam physicam,* dissertation, Königsberg, J.H. Hartung (AK I, 473–87).

The Employment in Natural Philosophy of Metaphysics combined with Geometry, of which Sample I contains the Physical Monadology, in Cambridge Edition I, *Theoretical Philosophy 1755–1770,* tr. and ed. David Walford in collaboration with Ralf Meerbote, Cambridge University Press, 1992, pp. 47–56.

1756e *Neue Anmerkungen zur Erläuterung der Theorie der Winde, wodurch er zugleich zu seinen Vorlesungen einladet,* Königsberg, den 25. April 1756, Gedrückt in der Königl. priviligierten Driestischen Buchdruckerey (AK I, 489–503).

New Notes towards a Discussion of the Theory of Winds, in Cambridge Edition VIII, *Natural Science,* ed. H.B. Nisbet, Cambridge University Press, forthcoming.

1757 *Entwurf und Ankündigung eines Collegii der physischen Geographie nebst dem Anhänge einer Betrachtung über die Frage, ob die Westwinde in unsern Gegenden darum feucht seien, weil sie über ein grosses Meer streichen,* Königsberg, gedruckt bey J.F. Driest, Königl. Preuss. privil. Buchdrucker (AK II, 1–12).

Outline and Announcement of a Course of Lectures on Physical Geography, together with an Appendix of an Inquiry into the Question of Whether the West Winds in our Regions are Humid because they have traversed a Great Sea, in Cambridge Edition VIII, *Natural Science,* ed. H.B. Nisbet, Cambridge University Press, forthcoming.

1758 *Neuer Lehrbegriff der Bewegung und Ruhe und der damit verknüpften Folgerungen in den ersten Gründen der Naturwissenschaft, wodurch zugleich seine Vorlesungen in diesem halben Jahre angekündigt werden,* Den 1sten April 1758 Königsberg, gedruckt bey Johann Friedrich Driest (AK II, 13–25).

New Conception of Motion and Rest and its Consequences for the Primary Grounds of Natural Science, through which at the same time his Lectures for this Semester are Announced, in Cambridge Edition VIII, *Natural Science,* ed. H.B. Nisbet, Cambridge University Press, forthcoming.

1759 *Versuch einiger Betrachtungen über den Optimismus von M. Immanuel Kant, wodurch er zugleich seine Vorlesungen auf das bevorstehende halbe Jahr ankündigt,* den 7. October 1759, Königsberg, gedruckt bey Johann Friedrich Driest (AK II, 27–35).

An Attempt at some Reflections on Optimism by M. Immanuel Kant, also containing an Announcement of his Lectures for the coming Semester 7 October 1759, in Cambridge Edition I, *Theoretical Philosophy 1755–1770,* tr. and ed. David Walford in collaboration with Ralf Meerbote, Cambridge University Press, 1992, pp. 67–76.

1760 *Gedanken bei dem frühzeitigen Ableben des Herrn Johann Friedrich von Funk, in einer Sendschreiben an seine Mutter,* Königsberg, gedruckt bey Johann Friedrich Driest (AK II, 37–44).

Thoughts on the Premature Demise of Herr Johann Friedrich von Funk, in an Epistle to his Mother, untranslated.

1762 *Die falsche Spitzfindigkeit der vier syllogistischen Figuren erwiesen von M. Immanuel Kant,* Königsberg, bey Johann Jacob Kanter (AK II, 45–61).

The False Subtlety of the Four Syllogistic Figures demonstrated by M. Immanuel Kant, in Cambridge Edition I,*Theoretical Philosophy 1755–1770*, tr. and ed. David Walford in collaboration with Ralf Meerbote, Cambridge University Press, 1992, pp. 85–105.

1763a   *Der einzig mögliche Beweisgrund zu einer Demonstration des Daseins Gottes*, Königsberg, bey Johann Jacob Kanter (AK II, 63–163).

The Only Possible Argument in Support of a Demonstration of the Existence of God, by M. Immanuel Kant, in Cambridge Edition I, *Theoretical Philosophy 1755–1770*, tr. and ed. David Walford in collaboration with Ralf Meerbote, Cambridge University Press, 1992, pp. 107–201.

1763b   *Versuch, den Begriff der negativen Grössen in die Weltweisheit einzuführen*, Königsberg, bey Johann Jacob Kanter (AK II, 165–204).

Attempt to Introduce the Concept of Negative Magnitudes into Philosophy, in Cambridge Edition I, *Theoretical Philosophy 1755–1770*, tr. and ed. David Walford in collaboration with Ralf Meerbote, Cambridge University Press, 1992, pp. 203–10.

1764a   *Beobachtungen über das Gefühl des Schönen und Erhabenen*, Königsberg, bey Johann Jacob Kanter (AK II, 205–56).

Observations on the Feeling of the Beautiful and the Sublime, tr. John T. Goldthwaite, Los Angeles, University of California Press, 1973.

1764b   'Versuch über die Krankheiten des Kopfes', *Königsbergsche Gelehrte und Politische Zeitungen*, 13–27 February 1764 (AK II, 257–71).

'An Essay on the Maladies of the Mind', in Cambridge Edition VII, *Anthropology, Philosophy of History and Education*, ed. Guenter Zoeller, Cambridge University Press, forthcoming.

1764c   *Untersuchungen über die Deutlichkeit der Grundsätze der natürlichen Theologie und der Moral. Zur Beantwortung der Frage, welche die Königl Akad. d. Wiss. zu Berlin auf das Jahr 1763 aufgegeben hat*, Berlin (AK II, 273–301).

Inquiry Concerning the Distinctness of the Principles of Natural Theology and Morality. In Answer to the Question which the Berlin Royal Academy of Sciences set for the Year 1763 (published together with Moses Mendelssohn's winning contribution to the same competition), in Cambridge Edition I, *Theoretical Philosophy 1755–1770*, tr. and ed. David Walford in collaboration with Ralf Meerbote, Cambridge University Press, 1992, pp. 243–86.

1764d   'Rezension von Silberschlags Erklärung der vor einigen Jahren erschienenen Feuerkugel', *Königsbersche Gelehrte und Politische Zeitungen*, 23 March.

'Review of Silberschlag's Essay on the Fireball of 1762', in Cambridge Edition VIII, *Natural Science*, ed. H.B. Nisbet, Cambridge University Press, forthcoming.

1765   *Nachricht von der Einrichtung seiner Vorlesungen in der Winterhalbenjahre von 1765–1766*, Königsberg, bey Johann Jacob Kanter (AK II, 303–13).

M. Immanuel Kant's Announcement of the Organisation of his Lectures in the Winter Semester 1765–1766, in Cambridge Edition I, *Theoretical Philosophy 1755–1770*, tr. and ed. David Walford in collaboration with Ralf Meerbote, Cambridge University Press, 1992, pp. 287–300.

1766   *Träume eines Geistersehers, erläutert durch Träume der Metaphysik*, Königsberg, bey Johann Jacob Kanter (AK II, 315–73).
Dreams of a Spirit-Seer elucidated by Dreams of Metaphysics, in Cambridge Edition I, *Theoretical Philosophy 1755–1770*, tr. and ed. David Walford in collaboration with Ralf Meerbote, Cambridge University Press, 1992, pp. 301–59.

1768   'Von dem ersten Grunde der Unterschiedes der Gegenden im Raume', in *Wochentliche Königsbergische Frag- und Anzeigungs-Nachrichten*, Parts 6–8 (AK II, 375–83).
Concerning the ultimate Ground of the Differentiation of Regions in Space, in Cambridge Edition I, *Theoretical Philosophy 1755–1770*, tr. and ed. David Walford in collaboration with Ralf Meerbote, Cambridge University Press, 1992, pp. 361–72.

1770   *De mundi sensibilis atque intelligibilis forma et principiis*, dissertation, Königsberg, Regiomonti, Stanno regiae aulicae et academicae typographae (AK II, 385–419).
On the Form and Principles of the Sensible and Intelligible World ['Inaugural Dissertation'], in Cambridge Edition I, *Theoretical Philosophy 1755–1770*, tr. and ed. David Walford in collaboration with Ralf Meerbote, Cambridge University Press, 1992, pp. 373–416.

1771   'Rezension von Moscatis Schrift: Von dem körperlichen wesentlichen Unterschiede zwischen der Structur der Thiere und Menschen', published anonymously in *Königsbergsche Gelehrte und Politische Zeitungen*, No. 67, 23 August 1771, pp. 265–6 (AK II, 421–5).
'Review of Moscati's Book: On the Essential Physical Differences between the Structures of Animals and Humans', in Cambridge Edition VII, *Anthropology, Philosophy of History and Education*, ed. Guenter Zoeller, Cambridge University Press, forthcoming.

1775   *Von den verschiedenen Racen der Menschen, zur Ankündigung der Vorlesungen der physischen Geographie im Sommerhalbjahre 1775*, Königsberg, gedruckt bey E.L. Hartung, Konigl. Hof- und Academ. Buchdrucker (2nd edition, *Der Philosoph für die Welt*, hsg. von J.J. Engel. Zweiter Theil, Leipzig 1777) (AK II, 427–43).
On the Different Human Races, by way of Announcing the Lectures on Physical Geography for the Summer Semester 1775, in Cambridge Edition VII, *Anthropology, Philosophy of History and Education*, ed. Guenter Zoeller, Cambridge University Press, forthcoming.

1776–7 'Uber das Dessauer Philanthropin', *Königsbergische Gelehrte und Politische Zeitungen*, 28. März 1776 und 27. März 1777 (AK II, 445–52).
'On the Dessau Philanthropin Academy', in Cambridge Edition VII, *Anthropology, Philosophy of History and Education*, ed. Guenter Zoeller, Cambridge University Press, forthcoming.

1777   *Concerning Sensory Illusion and Poetic Fiction* (A Latin address in response to Johann Gottlieb Kreutzfeld's *Dissertatio philologica-poetica de principiis fictionum generalioribus*), in *Kant's Latin Writings: Translations, Commentaries and Notes*, ed. Lewis White Beck, New York, 1986.

1781   *Kritik der reinen Vernunft*, Riga, verlegts Johann Friedrich Hartknoch (AK IV, 1–252); see 1787 below for details of second edition.
Critique of Pure Reason, tr. Norman Kemp Smith, London, Macmillan, 1978.

1782   'Nachricht an Artze', *Königsbergsche Gelehrte und Politische Zeitungen*, 31. Stück, 18 April (AK VIII, 5–8).
'Report to Physicians' in Cambridge Edition VII, *Anthropology, Philosophy of History and Education*, ed. Guenter Zoeller, Cambridge University Press, forthcoming.

1783a   *Prolegomena zu einer jeden künftigen Metaphysik, die als Wissenschaft wird auftreten können*, bey Johann Friedrich Hartknoch (AK IV, 253–83).
Prolegomena to Any Future Metaphysics that will be able to come forward as Science, in *Immanuel Kant: Philosophy of Material Nature*, tr. James W. Ellington, Indianapolis, Hackett Publishing Company, 1985.

1783b   'Recension von Schulz's *Versuch einer Anleitung zur Sittenlehre*', in *Raisonierendes Verzeichnis neuer Bücher*, No. 8, April 1783 (AK VIII, 9–14).
'Review of Schulz's *Attempt at an Introduction to Moral Theory*', in Cambridge Edition IV, *Practical Philosophy*, ed. Mary J. Gregor, Cambridge University Press, forthcoming.

1784a   'Idee zu einer allgemeinen Geschichte in weltbürgerlichen Absicht', in *Berlinische Monatsschrift*, Vol. IV (11 November), pp. 385–411 (AK VIII, 15–31).
'Idea for a Universal History with a Cosmopolitan Purpose', in *Kant: Political Writings*, tr. H.B. Nisbet, ed. Hans Reiss, Cambridge University Press, 1991, 41–53.

1784b   'Beantwortung der Frage: Was ist Aufklärung?', in *Berlinische Monatsschrift*, Vol. IV (12 December), pp. 481–94 (AK VIII, 33–42).
'An Answer to the Question: "What is Enlightenment?"' in *Kant: Political Writings*, tr. H.B. Nisbet, ed. Hans Reiss, Cambridge University Press, 1991, 54–60.

1785a   'Rezensionen von Johann Gottfried Herders *Ideen zur Philosophie der Geschichte der Menschheit*', in *Allgemeine Literatur Zeitung* (Jena und Leipzig, No. 4, 6 January 1785), pp. 17–20, Supplement (*Beilage*) to No. 4, pp. 21–2, and issue No. 271, 15 November, pp. 153–6 (AK VIII, 43–66).
'Reviews of Johann Gottfried Herder's *Ideas on the Philosophy of the History of Mankind*', in *Kant: Political Writings*, tr. H.B. Nisbet, ed. Hans Reiss, Cambridge University Press, 1991, pp. 201–20.

1785b   'Uber die Vulkane im Monde', in *Berlinische Monatsschrift*, Vol. 5, pp. 199–213 (AK VIII, 67–76).
The Volcanoes on the Moon, in Cambridge Edition VIII, *Natural Science*, ed. H.B. Nisbet, Cambridge University Press, forthcoming.

1785c   'Von der Unrechtmässigkeit des Büchernachdrucks', *Berlinische Monatsschrift*, Vol. 5, pp. 403–17 (AK VIII, 77–87).
'On the Unjust Printing of Books', in Cambridge Edition IV, *Practical Philosophy*, ed. Mary J. Gregor, Cambridge University Press, forthcoming.

1785d   'Bestimmung des Begriffs einer Menschenrasse', in *Berlinische Monatsschrift*, Vol. 6, November, pp. 390–417 (AK VIII, 89–106).

'On the Different Human Races', in Cambridge Edition VII, *Anthropology, Philosophy of History and Education*, ed. Guenter Zoeller, Cambridge University Press, forthcoming.

1785e *Grundlegung zur Metaphysik der Sitten*, Riga, bey Johann Friedrich Hartknoch (AK IV, 385–463).

Grounding for the Metaphysics of Morals, tr. James W. Ellington, Indianapolis, Hackett Publishing Company, 1981.

1786a *Metaphysiche Anfangsgründe der Naturwissenschaft*, Riga, bey Johann Friedrich Hartknoch (AK IV, 465–565).

Metaphysical Foundations of Natural Science, tr. James W. Ellington, *Immanuel Kant: Philosophy of Material Nature*, Indianapolis, Hackett Publishing Company, 1985.

1786b 'Mutmasslicher Anfang der Menschengeschichte', in *Berlinische Monatsschrift*, Vol. 7, January 1786, 1–27 (AK VIII, 107–23).

'Conjectures on the Beginning of Human History', in *Kant: Political Writings*, tr. H.B. Nisbet, ed. Hans Reiss, Cambridge University Press, 1991, 221–34.

1786c 'Was heisst: Sich im Denken orientieren?', in *Berlinische Monatsschrift*, Vol. 8, October 1986, pp. 304–30 (AK VIII, 131–47).

'What is Orientation in Thinking?', in *Kant: Political Writings*, tr. H.B. Nisbet, ed. Hans Reiss, Cambridge University Press, 1991, pp. 237–49.

1786d 'Recension von Gottlieb Hufelands *Versuch über den Grundsatz der Naturrechts*', in *Allgemeine Literatur Zeitung*, No. 92, 18 April (AK VIII, 125–30).

'Review of Gottfried Hufeland's *Attempt at a Principle of Natural Right*', in Cambridge Edition IV, *Practical Philosophy*, ed. Mary J. Gregor, Cambridge University Press, forthcoming.

1786e *De medicina corporis, quae philosophorum est*, Rectoral Address (AK XV, 939–53).

On the Philosophers' Medicine of the Body, tr. Mary J. Gregor, in *Kant's Latin Writings: Translations, Commentaries and Notes*, ed. Lewis White Beck, New York, 1986.

1787 *Kritik der reinen Vernunft Zweite hin und wieder verbesserte Auflage*, Riga bei Johann Friedrich Hartknoch.

Critique of Pure Reason, tr. Norman Kemp Smith, London, Macmillan, 1978.

1788a 'Uber den Gebrauch teleologischer Principien in der Philosophie', in *Der Teutsche Merkur*, Weimar, 1st Quarter, No. 1, pp. 36–52, No. 2, pp. 107–36, (AK VIII, 157–84).

'On the Use of Teleological Principles in Philosophy', Cambridge Edition V, *Aesthetics and Teleology*, eds. Eric Matthews and Eva Schaper, Cambridge University Press, forthcoming.

1788b *Kritik der praktischen Vernunft*, Riga, Johann Friedrich Hartknoch (AK V, 1–163).

Critique of Practical Reason, tr. Lewis White Beck, Indianapolis, Bobbs-Merrill, 1976.

1790a   *Kritik der Urtheilskraft*, Berlin und Libau, bey Lagarde und Friederich (AK V, 165–485).
Critique of Judgement, tr. James Creed Meredith, Oxford University Press, 1973.

1790b   'Erste Einleitung in die Kritik der Urteilskraft', hsg. O. Buek in *Kant's Werke*, Vol. V, hsg. E. Cassirer, 1922 (AK XX, 193–252).
First Introduction to the Critique of Judgement, tr. James Haden, Indianapolis, Bobbs-Merrill, 1965.

1790c   *Uber eine Entdeckung, nach der alle neue Kritik der reinen Vernunft durch eine ältere entbehrlich gemacht werden soll*, Königsberg bey Friedrich Nicolovius (AK VIII, 185–241).
On a Discovery according to which any New Critique of Pure Reason has been made Superfluous by an Earlier One, tr. Henry E. Allison, Baltimore and London, Johns Hopkins University Press, 1973.

1791a   'Uber das Misslingen aller philosophischen Versuche in der Theodizee', *Berlinische Monatsschrift*, Vol. 18, September, pp. 194–225 (AK VIII, 253–71).
'On the Failure of all Philosophical Attempts at Theodicy', in Cambridge Edition VI, *Religion and Rational Theology*, ed. George di Giovanni and Allen W. Wood, Cambridge University Press, forthcoming.

1791b   *Uber die von der Königl Akademie der Wissenschaften zu Berlin für das Jahr 1791 ausgesetzte Preisfrage: Welches sind die wirklichen Fortschritte, die die Metaphysik seit Leibnizens und Wolf's Zeiten in Deutschland gemacht hat?*, ed. F.D. Rink, Königsberg, 1804, bey Goebbels und Unzer (AK XX, 253–351).
Concerning the prize question posed by the Royal Academy of Sciences in Berlin for the year 1791: What Real Progress has Metaphysics made in Germany since the Time of Leibniz and Wolff?, tr. Ted Humphrey, New York, Arabis Books Inc., 1983.

1793a   *Die Religion innerhalb der Grenzen der blossen Vernunft*, Königsberg, Friedrich Nicolovius (2nd edition 1794) (AK VI, 1–202).
Religion within the Limits of Reason Alone, trs. Theodore M. Greene and Hoyt H. Hudson, San Francisco, Harper Torchbooks, 1960.

1793b   'Uber den Gemeinspruch: Das Mag in der Theorie richtig sein, taugt aber nicht für die Praxis', *Berlinische Monatsschrift*, Vol. 22, pp. 201–84 (AK VIII, 273–313).
'On the Common Saying: "This may be true in theory, but it does not apply in practice"', in *Kant: Political Writings*, tr. H.B. Nisbet, ed. Hans Reiss, Cambridge University Press, 1991, pp. 61–92.

1794a   'Etwas über den Einfluss des Mondes auf die Witterung', *Berlinische Monatsschrift*, Vol. 23 (AK VIII, 315–24).
'Something on the Moon's Influence over the Weather', in Cambridge Edition VIII, *Natural Science*, ed. H.B. Nisbet, Cambridge University Press, forthcoming.

1794b   'Das Ende aller Dinge', *Berlinische Monatsschrift*, Vol. 23, pp. 495–522 (AK VIII, 327–39).

'The End of all Things', tr. Robert E. Anchor in *Kant: On History*, ed. Lewis White Beck, Indianapolis, Bobbs-Merrill, 1980, pp. 69–84.

1795   *Zum ewigen Frieden: Ein philosophischer Entwurf*, Königsberg bey Friedrich Nicolovius (2nd edition 1796) (AK VIII, 341–86).

Perpetual Peace: A Philosophical Sketch, in *Kant: Political Writings*, tr. H.B. Nisbet, ed. Hans Reiss, Cambridge University Press, 1991, pp. 93–130.

1796a   'Von einem neuerdings erhobenen vornehmen Tone in der Philosophie', in *Berlinische Monatsschrift*, Vol. 27, pp. 387–426 (AK VIII, 389–406).

'On a Newly Arisen Superior Tone in Philosophy', ed. and tr. Peter Fenves, Baltimore and London, Johns Hopkins University Press, 1993, pp. 51–72.

1796b   'Verkündigung des nahen Abschlusses eines Traktes zum ewigen Frieden in der Philosophie', in *Berlinische Monatsschrift*, Vol. 28, pp. 485–504 (AK VIII, 413–22).

'Announcement of the Near Conclusion of a Treaty for Eternal Peace in Philosophy', in *Raising the Tone of Philosophy*, ed. and tr. Peter Fenves, Baltimore and London, Johns Hopkins University Press, 1993, pp. 83–93.

1796c   *Zu Sömmering über das Organ der Seele*, Königsberg, Friedrich Nicolovius.

To Sömmering, Concerning the Organ of the Soul, in Cambridge Edition VII, *Anthropology, Philosophy of History and Education*, ed. Guenter Zoeller, Cambridge University Press, forthcoming.

1797a   *Metaphysik der Sitten: 1. Metaphysische Anfangsgründe der Rechtslehre, 2. Metaphysische Anfangsgründe der Tugendlehre*, Königsberg, Friedrich Nicolovius (AK VI, 203–493).

The Metaphysics of Morals: 1. Metaphysical First Principles of the Doctrine of Right, 2. Metaphysical First Principles of the Doctrine of Virtue, tr. Mary J. Gregor, Cambridge University Press, 1991.

1797b   'Uber ein vermeintliches Recht, aus Menschenliebe zu lügen', *Berlinische Blätter*, No. 10 (AK VIII, 423–30).

'On a Presumed Right to Lie from Love of Mankind', in Cambridge Edition IV, *Practical Philosophy*, ed. Mary J. Gregor, Cambridge University Press, forthcoming.

1798a   *Der Streit der Fakultäten*, Königsberg, Friedrich Nicolovius (AK VII, 1–116).

The Conflict of the Faculties, tr. Mary J. Gregor, New York, Arabis Books Inc., 1979.

1798b   *Anthropologie in pragmatischer Hinsicht*, Königsberg, bey Friedrich Nicolovius (AK VII, 117–333).

Anthropology from a Pragmatic Point of View, tr. Victor Lyle Dowdell, Carbondale and Edwardsville, Southern Illinois University Press, 1978.

1800a   *Logik. Ein Handbuch zu Vorlesungen*, hrsg. von G.B. Jäsche, Königsberg, Friedrich Nicolovius (AK IX, 1–150).

The Jäsche Logic, in Cambridge Edition IX, *Lectures on Logic*, tr. and ed. J. Michael Young, Cambridge University Press, 1992, pp. 517–640.

1800b *Nachschrift eines Freundes zu Heilsbergs Vorrede zu Mielkes Litauischem Wörterbuch* (AK VIII, 443–5).

Postscript to Mielkes' Lithuanian–German and German–Lithuanian Dictionary, in Cambridge Edition VII, *Anthropology, Philosophy of History and Education*, ed. Guenter Zoeller, Cambridge University Press, forthcoming.

1802 *Physische Geographie*, hrsg. von F.T. von Rink, Königsberg, bey Göbbels und Unzer (AK IX, 151–436).

Physical Geography, in Cambridge Edition VIII, *Natural Science*, ed. H.B. Nisbet, Cambridge University Press, forthcoming.

1803 *Kant über Pädagogik*, hsg. F.T. von Rink, Königsberg, bey Friedrich Nicolovius (AK IX, 437–99).

Education, tr. Annette Churton, Ann Arbor, University of Michigan Press, 1966.

1817 *Kants Vorlesungen über die philosophische Religionslehre*, hrsg. K.H.L. Pölitz (AK XXVIII, 525–610).

Lectures on Philosophical Theology, tr. Allen W. Wood and Gertrude M. Clark, Ithaca and London, Cornell University Press, 1978.

1821 *Kants Vorlesungen über die Metaphysik*, hrsg., K.H.L. Pölitz, Erfurt (AK XXVIII).

Lectures on Metaphysics, in Cambridge Edition X, *Lectures on Metaphysics*, ed. Karl Ameriks, Cambridge University Press, forthcoming.

1924 *Eine Vorlesung Kants über Ethik*, ed. P. Menzer (AK XXVII).

Lectures on Ethics, tr. Louis Infield, New York and Evanston, Harper and Row, 1963.

1925–34 *Reflexionen* (*Reflections*; AK XIV–XIX).

1936–8 *Opus postumum*, hsg. Artur Buchenan and Gerhard Lehmann (AK XXI–II).

Opus Postumum, Cambridge Edition XII, ed. and tr. Eckhart Förster and Michael Rosen, Cambridge University Press, 1993.

1967 *Kant: Philosophical Correspondence 1759–99*, ed. and tr. Arnulf Zweig, Chicago, University of Chicago Press.

The editorial organization of the Academy Edition
(*Immanuel Kants gesammelte Schriften*)

Section I   *Werke* (*Works*) (Vols I–IX)
Section II   *Briefwechsel* (*Correspondence*) (Vols X–XIII)
Section III *Handschriftlicher Nachlass* (*Handwritten Remains*) (Vols XIV–XXIII)
Section IV   *Vorlesungen* (*Lectures*) (Vols XXIV–XXIX)

Works referred to in the text

Adorno, Theodor [1966], *Negative Dialectics*, tr. E.B. Ashton, New York, The Seabury Press, 1973
—— [1970], *Aesthetic Theory*, tr. C. Lenhardt, London, Routledge and Kegan Paul, 1984
Adorno, Theodor and Horkheimer, Max [1944], *Dialectic of Enlightenment*, tr. John Cumming, London, Verso, 1979
Aquinas, Thomas [1951], *Aristotle's De anima*, tr. Kenelm Foster et al., London, Routledge and Kegan Paul
—— [1952], *The Summa theologica*, tr. Fathers of the English Dominican Province, Chicago, William Benton
—— [1968], *On the Unity of the Intellect against the Averroists*, tr. Beatrice H. Zedler, Milwaukee, Marquette University Press
—— [1975], *Summa contra gentiles*, tr. Anton C. Pegis, Notre Dame, University Press of Notre Dame
—— [1986], *The Division and Methods of the Sciences*, tr. Armand Maurer, Toronto, Pontifical Institute of Medieval Studies
Arendt, Hannah [1951], *The Origins of Totalitarianism*, New York, Harcourt Brace Jovanovich
—— [1958], *The Human Condition*, Chicago, Chicago University Press
—— [1964], *Eichmann in Jerusalem: A Report on the Banality of Evil*, New York, Viking Press
—— [1989], *Lectures on Kant's Political Philosophy*, ed. Ronald Beiner, Chicago, Chicago University Press
Aristotle [1941], *The Basic Works of Aristotle*, ed. Richard McKeon, New York, Random House
Arnauld, Antoine [1662], *The Art of Thinking*, trs. J. Dickoff and P. James, Indianapolis, Bobbs-Merrill, 1964
Arndt, Johann [1605], *True Christianity*, tr. Peter Erb, London, SPCK, 1979
Arnold, Emil [1894], *Kritische Exkurse im Gebiet der Kantforschung*, in *Gesammelte Schriften*, Vols. IV–V, Berlin, Bruno Cassirer, 1908–9
Augustine, St [1960], *The Confessions of St Augustine*, tr. John K. Ryan, New York, Image Books
—— [1972], *City of God*, tr. Henry Bettenson, Harmondsworth, Penguin
Barnes, Jonathan [1987], *Early Greek Philosophy*, Harmondsworth, Penguin Books
Bataille, Georges [1985], *Visions of Excess: Selected Writings 1927–1939*, tr. Allan Stoekl, Manchester, Manchester University Press
Baumgarten, Alexander Gottlieb [1735], *Reflections on Poetry: A.G. Baumgarten's Meditationes philosophicae de nonnullis ad poema pertinentibus*, tr. K. Aschenbrenner and W.B. Holther, Berkeley, University of Los Angeles Press, 1954

—— [1739], *Metaphysica*, reprint of 7th edition (1779), Hildesheim, Georg Olms, 1963

—— [1740], *Ethica philosophica*, Halle

—— [1750–8], *Aesthetica* (2 vols.), reprinted Hildesheim, Georg Olms, 1961

Beccaria, Cesare [1764], *On Crimes and Punishments*, tr. Henry Paolucci, Indianapolis, Bobbs-Merrill, 1963

Benjamin, Walter [1973], *Illuminations*, tr. Harry Zohn, London, Fontana/Collins

Bloch, Ernst [1959], *Das Prinzip Hoffnung*, Frankfurt-am-Main, Suhrkamp Verlag

—— [1968], *Christian Thomasius, ein deutscher Gelehrter ohne Misere*, Frankfurt-am-Main, Suhrkamp Verlag

Booth, Edward [1983], *Aristotelian Aporetic Ontology in Islamic and Christian Thinkers*, Cambridge, Cambridge University Press

Borowski, L.E., Jachman, R.B. and Wasianski, A.Ch. [1912], *Immanuel Kant: Sein Leben in Darstellungen von Zeitgenossen*, Berlin, Deutsche Bibliothek

Cadava, Peter et al. [1991], *Who Comes After the Subject?*, London, Routledge

Calvin, John [1962], *Institutes of the Christian Religion*, Vols. I and II, tr. Henry Beveridge, London, James Clarke & Co.

Cassirer, Ernst [1918], *Kant's Life and Thought*, tr. James Haden, New Haven and London, Yale University Press, 1981

Cassirer, Ernst et al. [1948], *The Renaissance Philosophy of Man*, Chicago, Chicago University Press

Castoriadis, Cornelius [1987], *The Imaginary Institution of Society*, tr. Kathleen Blumey, Oxford, Polity Press

Caygill, Howard [1989], *Art of Judgement*, Oxford, Basil Blackwell

Cohen, Hermann [1871], *Kants Theorie der Erfahrung*, Berlin

—— [1902], *System der Philosophie I: Logic der reinen Erkenntnis*, Berlin, Bruno Cassirer

de Vries, Joseph [1983], *Grundbegriffe der Scholastik*, Darmstadt, Wissentschaftliche Buchgesellschaft

Deleuze, Gilles [1968], *Difference and Repetition*, tr. Paul Patton, London, Athlone Press, 1993

—— [1988], *Spinoza: Practical Philosophy*, tr. Robert Hurley, San Francisco, City Lights Books

Deleuze, Gilles and Guattari, Felix [1972], *Anti-Oedipus: Capitalism and Schizophrenia*, tr. Robert Hurley et al., London, Athlone Press, 1984

Derrida, Jacques [1962], *Edmund Husserl's Origin of Geometry: An Introduction*, tr. John P. Leavey, Jr, Stony Brook, Nicolas Hays, 1978

—— [1967], *Writing and Difference*, tr. Alan Bass, Chicago, Chicago University Press, 1978

—— [1972], *Margins of Philosophy*, tr. Alan Bass, Chicago, Chicago University Press, 1982

—— [1974], *Glas*, trs. John Leavey and Richard Rand, Lincoln, University of Nebraska Press, 1986

—— [1978], *The Truth in Painting*, trs. Geoff Bennington and Ian McLeod, Chicago, Chicago University Press, 1987

—— [1987], *Of Spirit: Heidegger and the Question*, trs. Geoffrey Bennington and Rachel Bowlby, Chicago, Chicago University Press, 1989

Descartes, René [1637], *Discourse on Method, Optics, Geometry, and Meteorology*, tr. Paul J. Olscamp, Indianapolis, Bobbs-Merrill, 1965

—— [1644], *Principles of Philosophy*, trs. V.R. Miller and R.P. Miller, Dordrecht, D. Riedel

Descartes, René [1968], *The Philosophical Works of Descartes*, trs. Elizabeth Haldane and G.R.T. Ross, Cambridge, Cambridge University Press
——— [1976], *Descartes' Conversation with Burman*, tr. John Cottingham, Oxford, Oxford University Press
——— [1981], *Philosophical Letters*, tr. and ed. Anthony Kenny, Oxford, Basil Blackwell
Diogenes Laertius [1925], *Lives of Eminent Philosophers* (2 vols), tr. R.D. Hicks, Cambridge, Mass., Harvard University Press
Eisler, Rudolf [1930], *Kant Lexicon*, Hildesheim, Georg Olms, 1984
Euclid [1956], *The Thirteen Books of The Elements* (3 vols), tr. Thomas L. Heath, New York, Dover Publications
Evans, Richard J. [1987], *Death in Hamburg: Society and Politics in the Cholera Years*, Harmondsworth, Penguin
Feuerbach, Ludwig [1830], *Thoughts on Death and Immortality*, tr. James A. Massey, Berkeley, University of California Press, 1980
Fichte, J.G. [1794], *The Science of Knowledge*, trs. Peter Heath and John Lachs, Cambridge, Cambridge University Press, 1982
Foucault, Michel [1976], *The History of Sexuality*, Vols 1–3, tr. Robert Hurley, Harmondsworth, Penguin
——— [1980], *Power/Knowledge: Selected Interviews and other Writings*, ed. Colin Gordon, New York, Pantheon Books
——— [1984], *The Foucault Reader*, ed. Paul Rabinow, New York, Pantheon Books
——— [1988], *Politics, Philosophy, Culture*, ed. Lawrence D. Kritzman, London, Routledge
Frege, Gottlob [1950], *The Foundations of Arithmetic*, tr. J.L. Austin, Oxford, Basil Blackwell, 1980
Freud, Sigmund [1915], 'The Unconscious', in *On Metapsychology: The Theory of Psychoanalysis*, tr. James Strachey, Harmondsworth, Penguin, 1984
Gadamer, Hans-Georg [1960], *Truth and Method*, tr. Joel Weinsheimer, London, Sheed and Ward, 1975
Gilson, E. [1949], *Being and some Philosophers*, Toronto, second edition 1952
——— [1955], *History of Christian Philosophy in the Middle Ages*, New York, Random House
Gulyga, Arsenij [1985], *Immanuel Kant: His Life and Thought*, tr. Marijan Despalatovic, Boston, Birkhäuser Inc., 1987
——— [1990], *Die klassische deutsche Philosophie: Ein Abriss*, trs. Wladislaw Hedeler, Leipzig, Reclam-Verlag
Habermas, Jürgen [1981], *Theorie des kommunikativen Handelns*, Frankfurt-am-Main, Suhrkamp Verlag
——— [1985], *Der philosophische diskurs der Moderne*, Frankfurt-am-Main, Suhrkamp Verlag
Hamann, J.G. [1967], *Schriften zur Sprache*, Frankfurt-am-Main
Hegel, G.W.F. [1802], *Faith and Knowledge*, tr. W. Cerf and H.S. Harris, New York, State University of New York Press, 1977
——— [1807], *Phenomenology of Spirit*, tr. A.V. Miller, Oxford, Oxford University Press, 1978
——— [1812], *Science of Logic*, tr. A.V. Miller, London, George Allen and Unwin, 1969
——— [1817], *Encyclopaedia of the Philosophical Sciences in Outline*, ed. Ernst Behler, Continuum Publishing Company, New York, 1990

———— [1821], *Elements of the Philosophy of Right*, ed. Allen W. Wood, tr. H.B. Nisbet, Cambridge, Cambridge University Press, 1991

———— [1830], *The Logic Of Hegel* ('Encyclopaedia Logic'), tr. W. Wallace, Oxford, Oxford University Press, 1977

———— [1835], *Hegel's Aesthetics: Lectures on Fine Art*, tr. T.M. Knox, Oxford, Oxford University Press, 1975

———— [1948], *Early Theological Writings*, tr. T.M. Knox, Philadelphia, University of Pennsylvania Press, 1979

Heidegger, Martin [1927], *Being and Time*, tr. J. Macquarrie and E. Robinson, Oxford, Basil Blackwell, 1978

———— [1928], *The Metaphysical Foundations of Logic*, tr. Michael Heim, Indianapolis, Indiana University Press, 1984

———— [1929], *Kant and the Problem of Metaphysics*, tr. Richard Taft, Bloomington and Indianapolis, Indiana University Press, 1990

———— [1930], *Hegel's Phenomenology of Spirit*, trs. Parvis Emad and Kenneth Maly, Bloomington and Indianapolis, Indiana University Press, 1988

———— [1935], *What is a Thing?*, tr. W.B. Barton and V. Deutsch, South Bend, Regnery/Gateway, 1967

———— [1936], *Schelling's Treatise on Human Freedom (1809)*, tr. Joan Stambaugh, Athens, Ohio University Press, 1985

———— [1947], 'Letter on Humanism', in *Martin Heidegger: Basic Writings*, tr. and ed. David Farrell Krell, London, Routledge and Kegan Paul, 1978

Heimsoeth, Heinz [1956], *Studien zur Philosophie Immanuel Kants: metaphysische Ursprünge und ontologische Grundlagen*, Köln, Kantstudien Ergänzungsheft, 71

Heine, Heinrich [1965], *It Will Be A Lovely Day: Prose Selections*, tr. Frederick Ewen, East Berlin, Seven Seas Publishers

Hellmuth, Eckhart [1990], *The Transformation of Political Culture: England and Germany, the late eighteenth century*, Oxford, Oxford University Press

Herder, J.G. [1953], *Werke in zwei Bänden*, München, Carl Hanser Verlag

Hume, David [1739], *A Treatise of Human Nature*, Oxford, Oxford University Press, 1981

Husserl, Edmund [1913], *Ideas: General Introduction to Pure Phenomenology*, tr. W.R. Boyce Gibson, New York, Collier Books, 1962

———— [1948], *Experience and Judgement*, trs. James S. Churchill and Karl Ameriks, London, Routledge and Kegan Paul, 1973

———— [1950], *Cartesian Meditations: An Introduction to Phenomenology*, tr. Dorion Cairns, Dordrecht, Martinus Nijhoff, 1988

———— [1954], *The Crisis of European Sciences and Transcendental Phenomenology*, tr. David Carr, Evanston, Northwestern University Press

Hyman, Arthur and Walsh James J., eds. [1984], *Philosophy in the Middle Ages*, 2nd ed., Indianapolis, Hackett

Irigaray, Luce [1974], *Speculum of the Other Woman*, tr. Gillian C. Gill, Ithaca, Cornell University Press, 1985

———— [1984], *An Ethics of Sexual Difference*, tr. Carolyn Burke and Gillian C. Gill, London, Athlone Press, 1993

Jacobi, Friedrich Heinrich [1787], *David Hume über den Glauben, oder Idealismus und Realismus: ein Gespräch*, Breslau

Kierkegaard, Soren [1843], *Fear and Trembling*, tr. Howard V. Hong and Edna H. Hong, Princeton, Princeton University Press, 1983

Kierkegaard, Soren [1844], *The Concept of Anxiety*, tr. Reidar Thomte, Princeton, Princeton University Press, 1980

Koyre, Alexandre [1968], *Newtonian Studies*, Chicago, Chicago University Press

Kristeva, Julia [1974], *Revolution in Poetic Language*, tr. M. Waller, Chicago, University of Chicago Press

Lacan, Jacques [1986], *The Ethics of Psychoanalysis 1959–1960*, tr. Dennis Porter, London, Routledge, 1992

Lambert, Johann Heinrich [1988], *Texte zur Systematologie und zur Theorie der wissenschaftlichen Erkenntnis*, hsg. G. Siegwart, Hamburg, Felix Meiner Verlag

Laplanche, J. and Pontalis, J.B. [1973], *The Language of Psychoanalysis*, tr. Donald Nicholson-Smith, London, Institute of Psychoanalysis/Karnac Books, 1988

Lehmann, Gerhard [1969], *Beiträge zur Geschichte und Interpretation der Philosophie Kants*, Berlin, Walter de Gruyter

Leibniz, G.W. [1720], *G.W. Leibniz's Monadology*, tr. Nicholas Rescher, London, Routledge, 1991

—— [1765], *New Essays on Human Understanding*, trs. Peter Remnant and Jonathan Bennett, Cambridge, Cambridge University Press, 1981

—— [1966], *Logical Papers*, tr. G.H.R. Parkinson, Oxford, Oxford University Press

—— [1976], *Philosophical Papers and Letters*, tr. Leroy E. Loemker, Dordrecht-Holland, D. Reidel

Lenin, V.I. [1902], *What is to be Done?*, Peking, Foreign Languages Press, 1975

Levinas, Emmanuel [1961], *Totality and Infinity*, tr. Alphonso Lingis, Pittsburgh, Duquesne University Press

Locke, John [1690], *An Essay Concerning Human Understanding*, ed. John W. Yolton, London, Dent, 1976

Long, A.A. [1986], *Hellenistic Philosophy: Stoics, Epicureans, Sceptics*, 2nd ed., London, Duckworth

Long, A.A. and Sedley, D.N. [1987], *The Hellenistic Philosophers, Vol. 1: Translations of the Principal Sources, with Philosophical Commentary*, Cambridge, Cambridge University Press

Lukács, Georg [1922], *History and Class Consciousness*, tr. Rodney Livingstone, London, Merlin Press, 1971

Luther, Martin [1961], *Martin Luther: Selections from his Writings*, ed. John Dillenberger, New York, Anchor Books

Lyotard, Jean-François [1971], *Discours, Figure*, Paris, Editions Klincksieck

—— [1974], *Libidinal Economy*, tr. Iain Hamilton Grant, London, Athlone Press, 1993

—— [1983], *The Differend: Phrases in Dispute*, tr. Georges Van Den Abbeele, Manchester, Manchester University Press, 1988

—— [1986], *L'enthousiasme. La critique kantienne de l'histoire*, Paris, Editions Galilée

—— [1988], 'Sensus Communis', tr. G. Bennington and M. Hobson, *Paragraph*

—— [1990], *The Lyotard Reader*, ed. Andrew Benjamin, Oxford, Basil Blackwell

—— [1991], *Leçons sur l'Analytique du sublime*, Paris, Editions Galilée

McClelland, Charles E. [1980], *State, Society and University in Germany 1700–1914*, Cambridge, Cambridge University Press

Machiavelli, Niccolò [1531], *The Discourses*, tr. Leslie J. Walker, Harmondsworth, Penguin, 1978

Maimon, Solomon [1790], *Versuch über die Transcendentalphilosophie mit einem Anhang über die symbolische Erkenntnis*, Hildesheim, Georg Olms, 1965

432

Malebranche, Nicolas [1992], *Philosophical Selections*, tr. T.M. Lennon and P.J. Olscamp, Indianapolis, Hackett

Malter, Rudolf [1990], *Immanuel Kant in Rede und Gespräch*, Hamburg, Felix Meiner Verlag

Marx, Karl [1843], *Critique of Hegel's 'Philosophy of Right'* tr. A. Jolin and J. O'Malley, Cambridge, Cambridge University Press, 1977

——— [1848], *The Manifesto of the Communist Party*, Moscow, Progress Publishers

——— [1859], *A Contribution to the Critique of Political Economy*, tr. S.W. Ryazanskaya, Moscow, Progress Publishers, 1977

Meissner, Heinrich Adam [1737], *Philosophisches Lexicon aus Christian Wolffs sämtlichen deutschen Schriften*, Düsseldorf, Stern Verlag Jannsen and Co., 1970

Mellin, G.S.A. [1797], *Encyclopädisches Wörterbuch der kritischen Philosophie*, Aalen, Georg Olms, 1970

Merleau-Ponty, M. [1962], *Phenomenology of Perception*, tr. Colin Smith, London, Routledge and Kegan Paul

Milbank, John [1990], *Theology and Social Theory: Beyond Secular Reason*, Oxford, Basil Blackwell

Moore, A.W. [1990], *The Infinite*, London, Routledge

Newton, Isaac [1687], *Mathematical Principles of Natural Philosophy*, tr. Andrew Motte, revised by Florian Cajori, Chicago, William Benton, 1952

Nietzsche, Friedrich [1872], *The Birth of Tragedy*, tr. Walter Kaufmann, New York, Vintage Books

——— [1882], *The Gay Science*, tr. Walter Kaufmann, New York, Vintage Books, 1974

——— [1886], *Beyond Good and Evil*, tr. R.J. Hollingdale, Harmondsworth, Penguin, 1978

——— [1887], *On the Genealogy of Morals*, tr. Walter Kaufmann, New York, Vintage Books, 1967

——— [1901], *The Will to Power*, tr. Walter Kaufmann and R.J. Hollingdale, Vintage Books, New York, 1968

Nygren, A. [1982], *Agape and Eros*, tr. Philip S. Watson, London, SPCK

O'Neill, Onora [1989], *Constructions of Reason: Explorations of Kant's Practical Philosophy*, Cambridge, Cambridge University Press

Ong, Walter [1983], *Ramus: Method and the Decay of Dialogue*, Cambridge, Mass., Harvard University Press

Peters, F.E. [1967], *Greek Philosophical Terms: A Historical Lexicon*, New York, New York University Press

Plato [1961], *The Collected Dialogues of Plato*, eds Edith Hamilton and Huntington Cairns, Princeton, Princeton University Press

Plotinus [1971], *The Six Enneads*, trs. Stephen MacKenna and B.S. Page, Chicago, William Benton

Polonoff, Irving I. [1973], *Force, Cosmos, Monads and other Themes of Kant's Early Thought*, Bonn, Kantstudien Ergänzungsheft, 107

Proclus [1970], *A Commentary on the First Book of Euclid's Elements*, tr. Glenn R. Morrow, Princeton, Princeton University Press

——— [1992], *The Elements of Theology*, tr. E.R. Dodds, Oxford, Oxford University Press

Pufendorf, Samuel [1672], *De jure naturae et gentium libri octo*, trs. C.H. and W.A. Oldfather, New York and London, 1964

Quintilian [92–5], *The Institutio oratoria of Quintilian with an English Translation* (4 vols), tr. H.E. Butler, Cambridge, Mass., Harvard University Press, 1921

Ramus, Peter [1549], *Arguments in Rhetoric against Quintilian*, tr. Carole Newlands, Dekalb, Illinois, Northern Illinois University Press, 1986

Reinhold, Karl Leonhard [1790–2], *Briefe über die Kantische Philosophie*, Leipzig

Ricken, Friedo [1984], *Lexicon der Erkenntnistheorie und Metaphysik*, München, C.H. Beck

Riedel, Manfred [1975], *Metaphysik und Metapolitik*, Frankfurt-am-Main, Suhrkamp Verlag

Rose, G. [1981], *Hegel Contra Sociology*, London, Athlone Press

—— [1984], *Dialectic of Nihilism*, Oxford, Basil Blackwell

—— [1992], *The Broken Middle: Out of Our Ancient Society*, Oxford, Basil Blackwell

Rosenkranz, Karl [1840], *Geschichte der Kant'schen Philosophie*, Berlin, Akademie-Verlag, 1987

Rousseau, Jean-Jacques [1762], *The Social Contract and Discourses*, London, Dent

—— [1762], *Emile or On Education*, tr. Allan Bloom, New York, Basic Books

Russell, D.A. and Winterbottom, M. [1978], *Ancient Literary Criticism: The Principle Texts in New Translations*, Oxford, Oxford University Press

Sartre, Jean-Paul [1960], *Search for a Method*, tr. Hazel E. Barnes, New York, Vintage Books, 1968

Scheler, Max [1973], *Formalism in Ethics and Non-Formal Ethics of Values*, trs. M.S. Frings and R. Funk, Evanston, Northwestern University Press

Schelling, F.W.J. [1800], *System des transzendentalen Idealismus*, Hamburg, Felix Meiner Verlag, 1957

—— [1809], *Uber das Wesen der menschlichen Freiheit*, Frankfurt-am-Main, Suhrkamp Verlag, 1975

—— [1856], *On the History of Modern Philosophy*, tr. Andrew Bowie, Cambridge, Cambridge University Press, 1994

Schiller, Friedrich [1793], *On the Aesthetic Education of Man*, tr. E. Wilkinson and L.A. Willoughby, Oxford, Oxford University Press, 1967

Schmid, Carl Christian Erhard [1798], *Wörterbuch zum leichtern Gebrauch der Kantischen Schriften*, hsg. Norbert Hinske, Darmstadt, Wissenschaftliche Buchgesellschaft, 1976

Schneiders, Werner, hsg. [1983], *Christian Wolff 1674–1754: Studien zum Achtzehnten Jahrhundert, Band 4*, Hamburg, Felix Meiner Verlag

Schopenhauer, Arthur [1813], *The Fourfold Root of the Principle of Sufficient Reason*, tr. E.F.K. Payne, La Salle, Open Court Publishing Company, 1974

—— [1819], *The World as Will and Representation*, tr. E.F.J. Payne, New York, Dover Publications, 1969

—— [1841], *On the Basis of Morality*, tr. E.F.J. Payne, Indianapolis, Bobbs-Merrill, 1965

Shaftesbury (Anthony Ashley Cooper) [1711], *Characteristics of Men, Manners, Opinions, Times*, New York, 1964

Spinoza, Benedict [1985], *The Collected Works of Spinoza*, Vol. 1, tr. and ed. Edwin Curley, Princeton, Princeton University Press

Stavenhagen, Kurt [1949], *Kant und Königsberg*, Göttingen, Deuerliche Verlagsbuchhandlung

Strawson, P.F. [1966], *The Bounds of Sense: An Essay on Kant's Critique of Pure Reason*, London, Methuen

Suarez, Francisco [1976], *Über die Individualität und das Individuationsprinzip*, tr. Rainer Specht, Hamburg, Felix Meiner Verlag

Taylor, Charles [1975], *Hegel,* Cambridge, Cambridge University Press

Tonelli, Giorgio [1964], 'Das Wiederaufleben der deutsch-aristotelischen Terminologie bei Kant während der Entstehung der "Kritik der reinen Vernunft"', *Archiv für Begriffsgeschichte,* Vol. IX, pp. 233–42

Urmson, J.O. [1990], *The Greek Philosophical Vocabulary,* London, Duckworth

Vaihinger, H. [1911], *The Philosophy of 'As-If': A Philosophy of the Theoretical, Practical, and Religious Fictions of Mankind,* tr. C.K. Ogden, London, 1925

Vorländer, Karl [1911], *Immanuel Kants Leben,* Leipzig, Felix Meiner Verlag

Walker, Mack [1971], *German Home Towns: Community, State, and General Estate 1648–1871,* Ithaca and London, Cornell University Press

Warda, Arthur [1922], *Immanuel Kants Bücher,* Berlin

Weber, Max [1904–5], *The Protestant Ethic and the Spirit of Capitalism,* tr. Talcott Parsons, London, Allen and Unwin

Weber, Peter [1985], *Berlinische Monatsschrift 1783–1796,* Leipzig, Verlag Phillip Reclam

Welsch, Wolfgang [1987], *Aisthesis. Grundzüge und Perspektiven des Aristotelischen Sinneslehre,* Stuttgart

—— [1990], *Asthetisches Denken,* Stuttgart, Philip Reclam Jun.

Wittgenstein, Ludwig [1922], *Tractatus Logico-Philosophicus,* tr. C.K. Ogden, London, Routledge and Kegan Paul, 1983

—— [1953], *Philosophical Investigations,* tr. G.E.M. Anscombe, Oxford, Basil Blackwell, 1973

Wolff, Christian [1719], *Vernünftige Gedanken von Gott, der Welt und der Seele der Menschen, auch alle Dingen überhaupt,* Halle

—— [1720], *Vernünftige Gedanken von der Menschen Thun und Lassen zu Beförderung ihrer Glückseligkeit,* Halle

—— [1721], *Vernünftige Gedanken von dem gesellschaftlichen Leben der Menschen und insonderheit dem gemeinen Wesen zu Beförderung der Glückseligkeit des menschlichen Geschlechts,* Halle

—— [1728], *Preliminary Discourse on Philosophy in General,* tr. Richard J. Blackwell, Indianapolis, Bobbs-Merrill, 1963

Wolfson, Harry Austryn [1962], *The Philosophy of Spinoza* (2 vols), Cambridge, Mass., Harvard University Press

Recommended further reading

GENERAL GERMAN HISTORY

Behrens, C.B.A. [1985], *Society, Government, and the Enlightenment: the Experiences of Eighteenth Century France and Prussia*, London, Thames and Hudson

Dorwart, Reinhold August [1971], *The Prussian Welfare State before 1740*, Cambridge, Mass., Harvard University Press

Hinrichs, Carl [1971], *Preussentum und Pietismus. Der Pietismus in Brandenburg-Preussen als religiös-soziale Reformbewegung*, Göttingen, Vandenhoeck und Ruprecht

Kirby, David [1990], *Northern Europe in the Early Modern Period: The Baltic World 1492–1772*, London and New York, Longman Group

Oestreich, Gerhard [1982], *Neo-Stoicism and the Early Modern State*, tr. David McLintock, Cambridge, Cambridge University Press

Raeff, Marc [1985], *The Well-Ordered Police State – Social and Institutional Change through Law in the Germanies and Russia, 1600–1800*, New Haven, Yale University Press

Rosenberg, Hans [1966], *Bureaucracy, Aristocracy and Autocracy: The Prussian Experience 1660–1815*, Cambridge, Mass., Harvard University Press

Vierhaus, Rudolf [1978], *Deutschland im Zeitalter des Absolutismus*, Göttingen, Vandenhoeck und Ruprecht

Walker, Mack [1971], *German Home Towns: Community, State, and General Estate 1648–1871*, Ithaca and London, Cornell University Press

GERMAN INTELLECTUAL HISTORY

Beck, Lewis White [1969], *Early German Philosophy: Kant and his Predecessors*, Cambridge, Mass., Harvard University Press

Blackall, E.A. [1959], *The Development of German as a Literary Language*, Cambridge, Cambridge University Press

Brunschwig, Henri [1974], *Enlightenment and Romanticism in Eighteenth Century Prussia*, tr. Frank Jellinek, Chicago, Chicago University Press

Cassirer, Ernst [1951], *The Philosophy of the Enlightenment*, Princeton, University of Princeton Press

Erdmann, Benno [1876], *Martin Knutzen und seine Zeit*, Leipzig

Krieger, Leonard [1957], *The German Idea of Freedom*, Boston, Beacon Press

Petersen, Peter [1921], *Geschichte der Aristotelischen Philosophie in Protestantischen Deutschland*, Leipzig

Reill, Peter Hans [1975], *The German Enlightenment and the Rise of Historicism*, Los Angeles, University of California Press

Wolff, Hans M. [1963], *Die Weltanschauung der deutschen Aufklärung in geschichtlicher Entwicklung*, Bern und München, Francke Verlag
Wundt, Max [1939], *Die deutsche Schulmetaphysik des 17. Jahrhunderts*, Tübingen, Verlag von J.C.B. Mohr
────── [1945], *Die deutsche Schulmetaphysik im Zeitalter der Aufklärung*, Hildesheim, Georg Olms, 1964

KANT: SELECTED SECONDARY WORKS

Allison, Henry E. [1990], *Kant's Theory of Freedom*, Cambridge, Cambridge University Press
Bartuschat, Wolfgang [1972], *Zum systematischen Ort von Kants Kritik der Urteilskraft*, Frankfurt-am-Main, Vittorio Klostermann
Batscha, Zwi [1976], *Materialien zu Kants Rechtsphilosophie*, Frankfurt-am-Main, Suhrkamp Verlag
Bäumler, Alfred [1967], *Das Irrationalitätsproblem in der Ästhetik und Logik des 18. Jahrhunderts bis zur Kritik der Urteilskraft*, Tübingen, Max Niemeyer
Beck, Lewis White [1960], *A Commentary on Kant's Critique of Practical Reason*, Chicago, Chicago University Press
Bennett, Jonathan [1966], *Kant's Analytic*, Cambridge, Cambridge University Press
────── [1974], *Kant's Dialectic*, Cambridge, Cambridge University Press
Böckerstette, Heinrich [1982], *Aporien der Freiheit und ihre Auflösung durch Kant*, Stuttgart-Bad Cannstatt, Frohmann-Holzboog
Booth, William James [1986], *Interpreting the World: Kant's Philosophy of History and Politics*, Toronto, University of Toronto Press
Buroker, Jill Vance [1981], *Space and Incongruence*, Dordrecht, D. Reidel
Cohen, Ted, and Guyer, Paul, eds. [1982], *Essays in Kant's Aesthetics*, Chicago, Chicago University Press
Coleman, Francis X.J. [1974], *The Harmony of Reason: A Study in Kant's Aesthetic*, Pittsburgh, University of Pittsburgh Press
de Man, Paul [1986], *The Resistance to Theory*, Manchester, Manchester University Press
de Vleeschauwer, Hermann-J. [1962], *The Development of Kantian Thought: The History of a Doctrine*, tr. A.R.C. Duncan, London, Thomas Nelson and Sons
Deleuze, Gilles [1984], *Kant's Critical Philosophy, The Doctrine of the Faculties*, tr. Hugh Tomlinson and Barbara Habberjam, Athlone Press, London, 1984
Despland, Michel [1973], *Kant on History and Religion*, Montreal and London, McGill-Queens University Press
Findlay, J.N. [1981], *Kant and the Transcendental Object: A Hermeneutic Study*, Oxford, Oxford University Press
Gram, Moltke S. [1967], *Kant: Disputed Questions*, Chicago, Quadrangle Books
Gregor, Mary J. [1963], *Laws of Freedom: A Study of Kant's Method of Applying the Categorical Imperative in the Metaphysik der Sitten*, Oxford, Basil Blackwell
Guyer, Paul [1979], *Kant and the Claims of Taste*, Cambridge, Mass., Harvard University Press
────── [1987], *Kant and the Claims of Knowledge*, Cambridge, Cambridge University Press
────── ed. [1992], *The Cambridge Companion to Kant*, Cambridge, Cambridge University Press
Heimsoeth, Heinz [1966–71], *Transzendentale Dialektik: Ein Kommentar zu Kants 'Kritik der reinen Vernunft'. Erster Teil: Ideenlehre und Paralogism, Zweiter Teil: Vierfache*

Vernunftantinomie, Dritter Teil: Das Ideal der reinen Vernunft, Vierter Teil: Die Methodenlehre, Berlin, de Gruyter

Hinske, Norbert [1970], *Kants Weg zur Tranzendentalphilosophie: der dreissigjährige Kant*, Stuttgart, Kohlhammer

—— [1974], 'Kants neue Terminologie und ihre alten Quellen', in *Kant-Studien, Sonderheft*, Vol. 65

Kersting, Wolfgang [1984], *Wohlgeordnete Freiheit: Immanuel Kants Rechts und Staatsphilosophie*, Berlin and New York, Walter de Gruyter

Koehnke, Klaus Christian [1991], *The Rise of Neo-Kantianism: German Academic Philosophy between Idealism and Positivism*, tr. R.J. Hollingdale, Cambridge, Cambridge University Press.

Körner, Stephan [1955], *Kant*, Harmondsworth, Penguin

Kudielka, Robert [1977], *Urteil und Eros: Erörterungen zu Kants Kritik der Urteilskraft*, Tübingen, dissertation

Kulenkampff, Jens [1974], *Materialien zu Kants 'Kritik der Urteilskraft'*, Frankfurt am Main, Suhrkamp Verlag

—— [1978], *Kants Logik des ästhetischen Urteils*, Frankfurt-am-Main, Vittorio Klostermann

Lehmann, Gerhard [1969], *Beiträge zur Geschichte und Interpretation der Philosophie Kants*, Berlin, Walter de Gruyter

—— [1980], *Kants Tugenden: Neue Beiträge zur Geschichte und Interpretation der Philosophie Kants*, Berlin, Walter de Gruyter

McFarland, J.D. [1970], *Kant's Concept of Teleology*, Edinburgh, Edinburgh University Press

Marc-Wogau, Konrad [1938], *Vier Studien zu Kants Kritik der Urteilskraft*, Uppsala, Lundequistka Bokhandeln

Martin, Gottfried [1955], *Kant's Metaphysics and the Theory of Science*, Manchester, Manchester University Press

May, J.A. [1970], *Kant's Concept of Geography and its Relation to Recent Geographical Thought*, Toronto, University of Toronto Press

Magazine littéraire, special issue, *Kant et la modernité*, No. 309, April 1993

Müller-Lauter, Wolfgang [1964], 'Kants Widerlegung des Materialen Idealismus', in *Archiv für Geschichte der Philosophie*, 46/1, pp. 60–82

Ollig, Hans-Ludwig [1982], *Neukantianismus*, Stuttgart, Phillip Reclam Jun.

Paton, H.J. [1936], *Kant's Metaphysics of Experience*, London, George Allen and Unwin

—— [1965], *The Categorical Imperative: A Study in Kant's Moral Philosophy*, London, Hutchinson

Pippin, Robert B. [1982], *Kant's Theory of Form: An Essay on the Critique of Pure Reason*, New Haven, Yale University Press

Pohlmann, Rosemarie [1973], *Neuzeitliche Natur und bürgerliche Freiheit: eine sozialgeschichtlich angeleitete Untersuchung zur Philosophie Immanuel Kants*, Münster, dissertation

Riedel, Manfred [1989], *Urteilskraft und Vernunft: Kants ursprüngliche Fragestellung*, Frankfurt-am-Main, Suhrkamp Verlag

Riley, Patrick [1983], *Kant's Political Philosophy*, Totowa, Rowman and Littlefield

Rotenstreich, Nathan [1984], 'Legislation and Exposition: Critical Analyses of Differences between the Philosophy of Kant and Hegel', Bonn, *Hegel-Studien Beiheft* no. 29

Saner, Hans [1973], *Kant's Political Thought: Its Origins and Development*, tr. E.B. Ashton, Chicago, Chicago University Press

Schaper, Eva [1979], *Studies in Kant's Aesthetics*, Edinburgh, Edinburgh University Press

Schlipp, Paul Arthur [1938], *Kant's Pre-Critical Essays*, Evanston and Chicago, Northwestern University Press

Shell, Susan Meld [1980], *The Rights of Reason: A Study of Kant's Philosophy and Politics*, Toronto, University of Toronto Press

Tonelli, Giorgio [1962], 'Der historische Ursprung der kantischen terminii "Analytik" und "Dialektik"', *Archiv für Begriffsgeschichte*, Vol. 7, pp. 120–39

—— [1975] 'Conditions in Königsberg and the Making of Kant's Philosophy', in Alexis J. Bacher, hsg., *Bewusst sein: Gerhard Funk zu eigen*, Bonn, 1975, pp. 126–44

—— [1976] 'Analysis and Synthesis in XVIIIth Century Philosophy prior to Kant', *Archiv für Begriffsgeschichte*, Vol. 20, pp. 176–213

van de Pitte, Frederick [1971], *Kant as Philosophical Anthropologist*, The Hague, Martinus Nijhoff

Verneaux, Roger [1967], *Le Vocabulaire de Kant*, Paris, Editions Montaigne

Wald, Samuel Gottlieb [1804], *Gedächtnissrede auf Kant*, hsg. Rudolf Reicke, Königsberg, 1860

Walsh, W.H. [1975], *Kant's Criticism of Metaphysics*, Edinburgh, Edinburgh University Press

Weber, Ludwig [1976], *Das Distinktionsverfahren im mittelalterlichen Denken und Kants skeptische Methode*, Meisenheim am Glan, *Monographien zur philosophische Forschung*

Werkmeister, W.H. [1979], *Kant's Silent Decade: A Decade of Philosophical Development*, Tallahassee, University Presses of Florida

Williams, Howard [1983], *Kant's Political Philosophy*, Oxford, Basil Blackwell

Wolff, Robert Paul, ed. [1968], *Kant: A Collection of Critical Essays*, New York, Doubleday Anchor

Wood, Allen W. [1978], *Kant's Rational Theology*, Ithaca, Cornell University Press

Yovel, Yirmiahu [1980], *Kant and the Philosophy of History*, Princeton, Princeton University Press

Index of philosophers

Adorno, Theodor W. 1903–69: aesthetic; antinomies; determination; enlightenment; formalism; freedom.

Aquinas, Thomas, Saint 1225?–74: abstraction; accident; action; actuality; analysis; art; beauty; categories; essence; evil; genius; happiness; idea; metaphysics; reason; understanding.

Arendt, Hannah 1906–75: action; aesthetic; common sense; communicability; estimation; evil; faculty of judgement; political writings; public/publicity; reflective judgement.

Aristotle 384–321 BC: absolute; accident; action; actuality; affect; analogy; analysis; analytic; art; association; beauty; being; body; canon; categories; common sense; concept; consciousness; dialectic; empirical; end; essence; evil; existence; experience; faculty; faith; form; friendship; genus; happiness; history of philosophy; idea; infinity; intuition; logic; metaphysics; natural right; paralogism; postulates; predicables; predicaments; principle; psychology; reason; space; subject; teleology.

Arnauld, Antoine 1611–94: a priori/a posteriori; categories; logic.

Augustine, Saint 354–430: affect; evil; time.

Baumgarten, Alexander Gottlieb 1714–62: aesthetic; a priori/a posteriori; appearance; beauty; clarity; concept; dispute; duty; empirical; essence; finality; imagination; intuition; metaphysics; ontology; theology.

Boethius, Anicius Manlius Severinus 480–524: analytic; categories; dialectic

Burke, Edmund 1729–97: aesthetic; dispute; empirical.

Cohen, Hermann 1842–1918: a priori/a posteriori; experience; faith; origin.

Deleuze, Gilles 1925–: absolute; action; amphiboly; I think.

Derrida, Jacques 1930–: accident; action; aesthetic; amphiboly; analogy; construction; enlightenment; faculty of judgement; *Gemüt*; 'I think'; subject; sublime; table of categories.

Descartes, René 1596–1650: accident; affect; analysis; a priori/a posteriori; apperception; being; body; categories; causality; certainty; consciousness; deduction; end; essence; experience; extension; force; *Gemüt*; history of philosophy; 'I think'; idea; idealism; impenetrability; inner sense; intuition; motion; psychology; reality; reason; space; subject; teleology; theology; time; understanding.

Diogenes Laertius *c.* 3rd century AD: analysis; impression; time.

Eberhard, Johann Augustus 1739–1809: analytic judgement; clarity; ground; history of philosophy; innate ideas.

Empedocles *c.*490–430 BC: faculty; friendship; principle.

Epicurus 341–270 BC: anticipations of perception; canon; concept; dispute; empirical; evil; finitude; history of philosophy; logic; orientation; reality; representation; sensibility; time.

Euclid *c.*400 BC: analogy; analysis; consciousness; elements; mathematics; postulate; space.

Fichte, Johann Gottlieb 1762–1814: absolute; abstraction; accident; action; actuality; anticipations of perceptions; a priori/a posteriori; appearance; apperception; architectonic; categories; concept; consciousness; dispute; freedom; I; idealism; infinity; logic; principle; reflection; spontaneity; synthesis; understanding.

Foucault, Michel 1926–84: body; enlightenment; 'I think'; subject.

Freud, Sigmund 1856–1939: action; affect; analysis; consciousness; drive; I; 'I think'; psychology; sex; subject.

Galileo 1564–1642: causality; end; teleology.

Habermas, Jürgen 1929–: communication; enlightenment; faculty of judgement; public/publicity.

Hamann, Johann Georg 1730–88: critical philosophy; dispute; faith; formalism; God; understanding.

Hegel, Georg Wilhelm Friedrich 1770–1831: absolute; abstraction; action; actuality; aesthetic; antinomies; appearance; architectonic; art; autonomy; being; categorical imperative; categories; causality; concept; consciousness; cosmology; critical philosophy; culture; determination; dialectic; duty; evil; faith; force; formalism; freedom; I; infinity; justice; limit; logic; love; natural right; phenomenology; postulate; reflection; spontaneity; system; thing-in-itself; understanding.

Heidegger, Martin 1889–1976: acroam/atic; action; actuality; analogies of experience; anticipations of perception; being; existence; finitude; freedom; *Gemüt*; ground; hope; 'I think'; imagination; ontology; principle; principles of pure understanding; psychology; synthesis; time.

Index of concepts

NOTE: Page numbers in **bold** refer to main entries.